Lecture Notes in Computer Science 11482

Commenced Publication in 1973
Founding and Former Series Editors:
Gerhard Goos, Juris Hartmanis, and Jan van Leeuwen

More information about this series at http://www.springer.com/series/7412

Michael Felsberg · Per-Erik Forssén ·
Ida-Maria Sintorn · Jonas Unger (Eds.)

Image Analysis

21st Scandinavian Conference, SCIA 2019
Norrköping, Sweden, June 11–13, 2019
Proceedings

Editors
Michael Felsberg 🆔
Linköping University
Linköping, Sweden

Per-Erik Forssén 🆔
Linköping University
Linköping, Sweden

Ida-Maria Sintorn 🆔
Uppsala University
Uppsala, Sweden

Jonas Unger 🆔
Linköping University
Linköping, Sweden

ISSN 0302-9743   ISSN 1611-3349   (electronic)
Lecture Notes in Computer Science
ISBN 978-3-030-20204-0   ISBN 978-3-030-20205-7   (eBook)
https://doi.org/10.1007/978-3-030-20205-7

LNCS Sublibrary: SL6 – Image Processing, Computer Vision, Pattern Recognition, and Graphics

This Springer imprint is published by the registered company Springer Nature Switzerland AG
The registered company address is: Gewerbestrasse 11, 6330 Cham, Switzerland

Preface

This book constitutes the refereed proceedings of the 21st Scandinavian Conference on Image Analysis, SCIA 2019, held in Norrköping, Sweden, in June 2019. The 40 papers presented herein were reviewed, selected, and thereafter revised, from 63 initial submissions, yielding an acceptance rate of 63%. The Microsoft CMT3 system was used to manage the reviewing process, by distributing each submitted paper to at least three reviewers. In total, 174 reviews were delivered by 39 reviewers, and a minimum of two assessments for each submission was ensured by assigning a number of emergency reviews.

The reviewing process for SCIA 2019 was double-blind, meaning that both the authors and the reviewers remained anonymous throughout the process. For submissions where there was significant disagreement between the reviewers, time was provided for the reviewers to consider the reasoning by the other reviewers in case some detail had been overlooked. Reviewers of such papers were also encouraged to discuss the paper in the CMT forum, and were allowed to update their reviews. The Program Chairs made the final assessments based on the reviews and discussions before the decisions were sent to the authors.

Paper topics include motion analysis and 3D vision, pattern detection and recognition, machine learning, image processing and applications, medical and biomedical image analysis, feature extraction and segmentation, as well as face-, gesture-, and multi-spectral analysis. From the submission statistics it is evident that SCIA is an international conference with a regional focus. We received submissions from Europe, North and South America, Africa, and Asia. Roughly 50% of the submissions were from the Scandinavian countries.

The scientific program consists of the accepted papers and three invited talks. From the 40 accepted contributions, 17 were carefully selected for oral presentation, arranged in four oral sessions, with the option of an accompanying poster. The remaining 23 contributions were arranged in three poster sessions, with the option of a spotlight presentation. The scientific program was complemented with invited presentations by Laura Leal-Taixé (Technical University of Munich), Lourdes Agapito (University College London), and Fred Hamprecht (Heidelberg University). We hope that this high-quality scientific program will influence many researchers from the field and will lead to many fruitful discussions on scientific topics.

We appreciate the support by all companies that sponsored SCIA 2019, as well as Linköping University, the Swedish Society for Automated Image Analysis (SSBA), Springer *Lecture Notes in Computer Science* (LNCS), and the International Association for Pattern Recognition (IAPR).

April 2019

Michael Felsberg
Per-Erik Forssén
Ida-Maria Sintorn
Jonas Unger

Organization

General Chair

Jonas Unger   Linköping University, Sweden

Program Chairs

Michael Felsberg   Linköping University, Sweden
Per-Erik Forssén   Linköping University, Sweden
Ida-Maria Sintorn   Uppsala University, Sweden

Web and Sponsors Chairs

Gabriel Eilertsen   Linköping University, Sweden
Daniel Jönsson   Linköping University, Sweden

International Program Committee

Adrien Bartoli   Université Clermont Auvergne, France
Anders Bjorholm Dahl   Technical University of Denmark, Denmark
Anders Heyden   Lund University, Sweden
Atsuto Maki   Royal Institute of Technology, Sweden
Carl-Fredrik Westin   Harvard University, USA
Cristina Soguero Ruiz   Rey Juan Carlos University, Spain
Domenico Bloisi   University of Basilicata, Italy
Einar Heiberg   Lund University, Sweden
Erkki Oja   Aalto University, Finland
Ewert Bengtsson   Uppsala University, Sweden
Fahad Shahbaz Khan   Linköping University, Sweden
Filip Malmberg   Uppsala University, Sweden
Francesco Ciompi   Radboud University Medical Center, The Netherlands
Fredrik Kahl   Chalmers University of Technology, Sweden
Gunilla Borgefors   Uppsala University, Sweden
Gustau Camps-Valls   University of Valencia, Spain
Heikki Kälviäinen   Lappeenranta University of Technology, Finland
Helene Schulerud   SINTEF, Norway
Hugues Talbot   Université Paris Est, France
Ingela Nyström   Uppsala University, Sweden
Janne Heikkilä   University of Oulu, Finland
Jens T. Thielemann   SINTEF, Norway
Joel Kronander   Linköping University, Sweden
Joni-Kristian Kämäräinen   Tampere University, Finland

Kalle Åström	Lund University, Sweden
Kim Pedersen	University of Copenhagen, Denmark
Kjersti Engan	University of Stavanger, Norway
Lasse Østergaard	Aalborg University, Denmark
Lorenzo Livi	University of Manitoba, Canada
Mads Nielsen	University of Copenhagen, Denmark
Maria Magnusson	Linköping University, Sweden
Marius Pedersen	Norwegian University of Science and Technology, Norway
Nataša Sladoje	Uppsala University, Sweden
Robert Jenssen	UiT - The Arctic University of Norway, Norway
Robin Strand	Uppsala University, Sweden
Simone Scardapane	Sapienza University, Italy
Thomas Moeslund	Aalborg University, Denmark
Volker Krueger	Lund University, Sweden
Walter Kropatsch	TU Wien, Austria

Additional Reviewers

Alex Jørgensen	Aalborg University, Denmark
Anastasios Roussos	University of Exeter, UK
Anderson Tavares	Linköping University, Sweden
Andrea Pennisi	Sapienza University, Italy
Apostolia Tsirikoglou	Linköping University, Sweden
Arto Kaarna	Lappeenranta University of Technology, Finland
Asbjørn Berge	SINTEF, Norway
Camilla Trinderup	Technical University of Denmark, Denmark
Carl Toft	Chalmers University of Technology, Sweden
Claus Madsen	Aalborg University, Denmark
David Malmgren-Hansen	Technical University of Denmark, Denmark
Elisabeth Wetzer	Uppsala University, Sweden
Eva Breznik	Uppsala University, Sweden
Gabriel Eilertsen	Linköping University, Sweden
Gustav Häger	Linköping University, Sweden
Jennifer Alvén	Chalmers University of Technology, Sweden
Jiří Hladůvka	TU Wien, Austria
Joakim Lindblad	Uppsala University, Sweden
Johan Öfverstedt	Uppsala University, Sweden
Jonathan Dyssel Stets	Technical University of Denmark, Denmark
Lasse Lensu	Lappeenranta University of Technology, Finland
Maciej Plocharski	Aalborg University, Denmark
Måns Larsson	Chalmers University of Technology, Sweden
Mohammad Haque	Aalborg University, Denmark
Petter Risholm	SINTEF, Norway
Sahar Zafari	Lappeenranta University of Technology, Finland
Shrinivasan Sankar	Metai Labs Ltd, UK

Simone Gasparini	University of Toulouse, France
Tanaboon Tongbuasirilai	Linköping University, Sweden
Teo Asplund	Uppsala University, Sweden
Tuomas Eerola	Lappeenranta University of Technology, Finland
Vedrana Andersen Dahl	Technical University of Denmark, Denmark
Yamid Espinel	Université Clermont Auvergne, France
Yvain Queau	CNRS, France

Contents

Deep Convolutional Neural Networks

Deep Multi-class Adversarial Specularity Removal 3
John Lin, Mohamed El Amine Seddik, Mohamed Tamaazousti,
Youssef Tamaazousti, and Adrien Bartoli

Predicting Novel Views Using Generative Adversarial Query Network 16
Phong Nguyen-Ha, Lam Huynh, Esa Rahtu, and Janne Heikkilä

CubiCasa5K: A Dataset and an Improved Multi-task Model
for Floorplan Image Analysis 28
Ahti Kalervo, Juha Ylioinas, Markus Häikiö, Antti Karhu,
and Juho Kannala

An Efficient Solution for Semantic Segmentation: ShuffleNet V2
with Atrous Separable Convolutions 41
Sercan Türkmen and Janne Heikkilä

Unstructured Multi-view Depth Estimation Using Mask-Based
Multiplane Representation 54
Yuxin Hou, Arno Solin, and Juho Kannala

Fine-Grained Wood Species Identification Using Convolutional
Neural Networks... 67
Dmitrii Shustrov, Tuomas Eerola, Lasse Lensu, Heikki Kälviäinen,
and Heikki Haario

Spectral-Spatial Hyperspectral Image Classification Using Cascaded
Convolutional Neural Networks 78
Gurbandurdy Dovletov, Tobias Hegemann, and Josef Pauli

Assessing Capsule Networks with Biased Data..................... 90
Bruno Ferrarini, Shoaib Ehsan, Adrien Bartoli, Aleš Leonardis,
and Klaus D. McDonald-Maier

Facial Emotion Recognition with Varying Poses and/or Partial
Occlusion Using Multi-stage Progressive Transfer Learning 101
Sherin F. Aly and A. Lynn Abbott

Feature Extraction and Image Analysis

Compressed Imaging at Long Range in SWIR   115
Andreas Brorsson, Carl Brännlund, David Bergström,
and David Gustafsson

Zonohedral Approximation of Spherical Structuring Element
for Volumetric Morphology   128
Patrick M. Jensen, Camilla H. Trinderup, Anders B. Dahl,
and Vedrana A. Dahl

Image Invariants to Anisotropic Gaussian Blur   140
Jitka Kostková, Jan Flusser, Matěj Lébl, and Matteo Pedone

Material-Based Segmentation of Objects   152
Jonathan Dyssel Stets, Rasmus Ahrenkiel Lyngby, Jeppe Revall Frisvad,
and Anders Bjorholm Dahl

Filtering Specular Reflections by Merging Stereo Images   164
Michael Plattner and Gerald Ostermayer

Near Lossless JPEG Compression Based on Masking Effect
of Non-predictable Energy of Image Regions   173
Mykola Ponomarenko and Karen Egiazarian

Using a Robotic Arm for Measuring BRDFs   184
Rasmus Ahrenkiel Lyngby, Jannik Boll Matthiassen,
Jeppe Revall Frisvad, Anders Bjorholm Dahl, and Henrik Aanæs

Unsupervised Feature Extraction – A CNN-Based Approach   197
Daniel J. Trosten and Puneet Sharma

Automatic Detection of Cervical Vertebral Landmarks
for Fluoroscopic Joint Motion Analysis   209
Ida Marie Groth Jakobsen and Maciej Plocharski

Weight Estimation of Broilers in Images Using 3D Prior Knowledge   221
Anders Jørgensen, Jacob V. Dueholm, Jens Fagertun,
and Thomas B. Moeslund

Salient Object Detection with CNNs and Multi-scale CRFs   233
Yingyue Xu, Xiaopeng Hong, and Guoying Zhao

Dimensionality Reduction for Visualization of Time Series
and Trajectories   246
Pattreeya Tanisaro and Gunther Heidemann

Matching, Tracking and Geometry

Combining Depth Fusion and Photometric Stereo for Fine-Detailed
3D Models.   261
  Erik Bylow, Robert Maier, Fredrik Kahl, and Carl Olsson

Camera Localization by Single View Query Using One Circular Target.   275
  Damien Mariyanayagam, Pierre Gurdjos, Sylvie Chambon,
  and Vincent Charvillat

Global Trifocal Adjustment   287
  Patrik Persson and Kalle Åström

A Robust Human Activity Recognition Approach Using OpenPose,
Motion Features, and Deep Recurrent Neural Network.   299
  Farzan Majeed Noori, Benedikte Wallace, Md. Zia Uddin,
  and Jim Torresen

Video Frame Interpolation via Cyclic Fine-Tuning and Asymmetric
Reverse Flow   311
  Morten Hannemose, Janus Nørtoft Jensen, Gudmundur Einarsson,
  Jakob Wilm, Anders Bjorholm Dahl, and Jeppe Revall Frisvad

Iris Identification in 3D   324
  Fernand Cohen, Sowrirajan Sowmithran, and Chenxi Li

Parametric Model-Based 3D Human Shape and Pose Estimation
from Multiple Views.   336
  Zhongguo Li, Anders Heyden, and Magnus Oskarsson

Efficient Merging of Maps and Detection of Changes   348
  Gabrielle Flood, David Gillsjö, Anders Heyden, and Kalle Åström

Alignment of Building Footprints Using Quasi-Nadir Aerial Photography . . .   361
  Dimitri Bulatov

Evaluation of Feature Detectors, Descriptors and Match Filtering
Approaches for Historic Repeat Photography   374
  Ann-Katrin Becker and Oliver Vornberger

An RNN-Based IMM Filter Surrogate   387
  Stefan Becker, Ronny Hug, Wolfgang Hübner, and Michael Arens

Real-Time Tracking-by-Detection in Broadcast Sports Videos.   399
  Sigurdur Sverrisson, Volodya Grancharov, and Harald Pobloth

Medical and Biomedical Image Analysis

Fast Cross Correlation for Limited Angle Tomographic Data   415
   Ricardo M. Sánchez, Rudolf Mester, and Mikhail Kudryashev

Sulcal and Cortical Features for Classification of Alzheimer's Disease
and Mild Cognitive Impairment   427
   Maciej Plocharski, Lasse Riis Østergaard, and the Alzheimer's Disease
   Neuroimaging Initiative

On the Effectiveness of Generative Adversarial Networks as HEp-2
Image Augmentation Tool   439
   Tomáš Majtner, Buda Bajić, Joakim Lindblad, Nataša Sladoje,
   Victoria Blanes-Vidal, and Esmaeil S. Nadimi

Parameter Selection for Regularized Electron Tomography
Without a Reference Image   452
   Yan Guo and Bernd Rieger

Can SPHARM-Based Features from Automated or Manually Segmented
Hippocampi Distinguish Between MCI and TLE?   465
   Michael Liedlgruber, Kevin Butz, Yvonne Höller, Georgi Kuchukhidze,
   Alexandra Taylor, Aljoscha Thomschevski, Ottavio Tomasi,
   Eugen Trinka, and Andreas Uhl

Color Normalization of Blood Cell Images.   477
   Emmy Sjöstrand, Jesper Jönsson, Adam Morell, and Kent Stråhlén

Generating Diffusion MRI Scalar Maps from T1 Weighted Images
Using Generative Adversarial Networks.   489
   Xuan Gu, Hans Knutsson, Markus Nilsson, and Anders Eklund

Correction to: Iris Identification in 3D C1
   Fernand Cohen, Sowrirajan Sowmithran, and Chenxi Li

Author Index   499

Deep Convolutional Neural Networks

Deep Multi-class Adversarial Specularity Removal

John Lin[1,2(✉)], Mohamed El Amine Seddik[1], Mohamed Tamaazousti[1], Youssef Tamaazousti[1], and Adrien Bartoli[2]

[1] CEA, LIST, Point Courrier 184, 91191 Gif-sur-Yvette, France
{john.lin,mohamedelamine.seddik,mohamed.tamaazousti}@cea.fr,
youssef.tamaazousti@gmail.com
[2] Institut Pascal - UMR 6602 - CNRS/UCA/CHU, Clermont-Ferrand, France
adrien.bartoli@gmail.com

Abstract. We propose a novel learning approach, in the form of a fully-convolutional neural network (CNN), which automatically and consistently removes specular highlights from a single image by generating its diffuse component. To train the generative network, we define an adversarial loss on a discriminative network as in the GAN framework and combined it with a content loss. In contrast to existing GAN approaches, we implemented the discriminator to be a multi-class classifier instead of a binary one, to find more constraining features. This helps the network pinpoint the diffuse manifold by providing two more gradient terms. We also rendered a synthetic dataset designed to help the network generalize well. We show that our model performs well across various synthetic and real images and outperforms the state-of-the-art in consistency.

Keywords: Deep learning · GAN · Dichromatic reflection separation · Specular and diffuse components

1 Introduction

The appearance of an object depends on the way it reflects light. The materials constituting most objects have a dichromatic behaviour: they produce two types of reflection, namely diffuse and specular reflections. Shafer's dichromatic model [21] linearly combines these two terms for the image formation model. The fundamental difference between them is that the diffuse reflection does not change with the viewing direction, while the specular one does. The specular reflection is thus largely responsible for the tremendous difficulty of solving for the parameters of an image formation model. It is then appealing to assume the object's surface to be perfectly diffuse and rule out the specular reflection. This has been extensively used in various computer vision problems, including SLAM, image segmentation and object detection, to name but a few. The price to pay however is failure of the methods when the real object's reflection departs, sometimes even slightly, from diffusion.

© Springer Nature Switzerland AG 2019
M. Felsberg et al. (Eds.): SCIA 2019, LNCS 11482, pp. 3–15, 2019.
https://doi.org/10.1007/978-3-030-20205-7_1

Quite naturally, many approaches have been proposed to solve the problem of specular and diffuse separation, and to be applied as a preprocessing to many algorithms. The separation is also relevant in computer graphics since the specular component conveys precious information about the surface material and illumination [6,14]. We can group model-based methods in two categories: multi-image and single-image approaches. Multi-image methods ingeniously use specular reflections' physical properties to find and remove specularities from an image, such as their polarization properties [18,28] or their dependance to the viewpoint to find matching specular and diffuse pixels from several images [9,15,16]. While obtaining good results, these methods are impractical to use because of the need for multiple images, special equipment (polarizer) or known object geometry. Single-image methods mostly rely on the Dichromatic Reflection Model and the fact that specularities retain the illumination's color to do the separation [2,11,21,22,26]. However, the separation problem with a single image being ill-posed because of the ambiguity of the image formation process [1], they make strong assumptions about the scene such as a single illumination of known color, no saturated pixels and no nonlinearity of the capture device. This obviously hinders the generic applicability of the methods. Therefore, this is still a challenging and open problem.

In this paper, we propose a deep learning approach to overcome the limitations in applicability. The idea is that the network will work out the intricate relationships between an image and its diffuse part. Recently, a handful of learning-based methods have been proposed to solve the diffuse and specular separation problem [4,17,24]. Such data-driven approaches reduce the need to find hand-crafted features and priors, which might not even be relevant for the wide diversity of possible scenes [27]. An immediate challenge is to find a large scale real dataset, since it is extremely time-consuming to produce one. Therefore, we train our network on synthetic data. We specifically rendered the data to overcome some limitations known to the problem of separation, by including known causes of failure cases in hand-crafted methods. Another challenge of learning approaches is to generalize, all the more difficult when training with synthetic data. To overcome this limitation, we build our work on the fairly recent framework of Generative Adversarial Networks (GAN) [5], which we adapt to the separation problem. Just as in GANs, we have a generator network, which we call Specularity Removal Network, trained to generate the diffuse image, while the discriminator network is used only for training by determining whether specularities are well removed. The main difference with a classical GAN resides in the discriminator network, which is not a binary classifier but a categorical classifier. By increasing the number of classes, we help the discriminator pinpoint the desired manifold. This allows it to find more discriminative features for the task at hand. It also prevents an unwanted behaviour of the GAN on synthetic data *i.e.* to generate data that look synthetic. Our method takes a single RGB image as input and does not make any assumption about the scene. We show in the results Sect. 3 that our framework is more stable than existing methods [23,25,26] for a wide range of images, outperforming them qualitatively and quantitatively.

In summary, our work addresses the aforementioned challenges and makes the following contributions:

- A new method of Single-image Specular-Diffuse Separation (SSDS), free from priors on the scene and capable of performing on a wide range of images.
- A new multi-class adversarial loss for the problem of SSDS.
- A new synthetic dataset, designed for the task of specular highlights removal.

2   Deep Specularity Removal

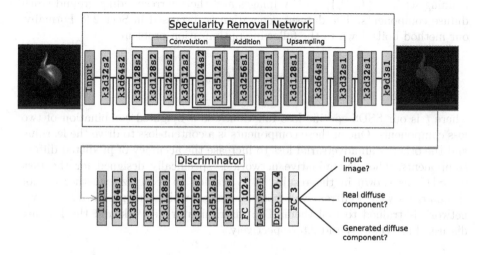

Fig. 1. Overview of our architecture. The Specularity Removal Network takes a single image as input and outputs its diffuse component. The discriminator network is used only for training. It takes the entire image as input and is trained to classify an image into three categories: the input image (I), the diffuse component (D) and the generated diffuse component ($\hat{D}$); while the generator is trained to fool the discriminator to classify $\hat{D}$ as D.

Following the dichromatic model [21], when light hits an object, it is divided in two parts at the surface, at a ratio depending on the material's refraction index. One part, called the specular reflection, is reflected at the surface, in the manner of a mirror reflection. The other part, called the diffuse reflection, penetrates the object and scatters before coming out and being reflected. These two bounced off parts of light then add up, and after integrating all lights coming from the upper hemisphere of the object surface, the image is formed. Integration being a linear operation, we can describe an image I as:

$$I = S + D, \tag{1}$$

where S is the specular image and D the diffuse image. The problem of Single image Specular and Diffuse Separation (SSDS) consists in estimating the specular S and/or the diffuse D component of a given image I, since a consistent estimation of one component suffices to retrieve the other by subtracting from I. Thus, we consider the problem of predicting the diffuse component D for which we have more visual cues since there are often purely diffuse pixels in images.

2.1 Overview

To solve the ill-posed problem of SSDS, we propose a generator $\mathcal{G}_{\theta_g}$, parametrized by its weights θ_g. $\mathcal{G}_{\theta_g}$ is a feed-forward CNN, which takes I as input and generates D. To train $\mathcal{G}_{\theta_g}$, we carefully rendered a realistic and diverse synthetic training set $\mathbb{T} = \{I_i, D_i\}_{i=1}^N$ of N images and their corresponding ground truth diffuse components. The dataset generation is discussed in Sect. 2.2. Formally, our method boils down to the following optimization problem:

$$\hat{\theta}_g = \arg\min_{\theta_g} \frac{1}{N} \sum_{i=1}^N \ell\left(\mathcal{G}_{\theta_g}(I_i), D_i\right), \tag{2}$$

where ℓ is our SSDS-specific loss function. ℓ is a weighted combination of two loss components. One of these components is a content-loss to drive the learning and the other is an adversarial loss to increase the accuracy of predicted diffuse components. The discriminative network is specifically designed for the task of SSDS, as shown in the results. It is trained to recognize whether or not specularities were well removed from an image, while the specularity removal network is trained to fool them. The discriminator network and the loss are discussed in Sects. 2.4 and 2.5 respectively.

2.2 Synthetic Training Dataset

Our training set $\mathbb{T} = \{I_i, D_i\}_{i=1}^N$ consists of $N = 20000$ realistically rendered pairs of images. The generation is automated with a script using Blender and the Cycles engine. Each of the N training frames shows a single object from a set of 8 synthetic 3D models, rendered at the center of the image in a random orientation. We excluded 5 shapes of the training set to also create a test set of 1000 images used in the quantitative evaluation. The diffuse part is rendered with the Lambertian model [12] and the specular part with the Beckmann distribution of a microfacet model (Glossy BSDF in Blender). The specular roughness is randomly chosen in the range $[0.2, 0.5]$. We set a lower bound to this roughness so that the material does not become highly specular, almost mirror-like. To handle mirror-like surfaces, we would need a different dataset and maybe a different network all-together. Among these N frames, we have four sets of data, each one rendered to overcome a learning limitation.

Random Texture Objects. This first set has 10000 images rendered with four area lights, directed towards the object. The position of the lights as well as their intensity are randomized, to increase the diversity of the scenes. With the same intent, we set a random colored texture to each object. This simulates real life objects which do not always show uniform reflectance and also compels the network to render images of high quality by focusing on details. The lights' color is fixed to near white (two are slightly blue and the others yellow to imitate real lights).

White Objects. With only the first set, the generative network simply learns to remove white pixels from the image as it suffices for the training set. Therefore we add this second set with 4000 images of white objects, otherwise rendered in the same manner as the first set, to help the network grasp the difference between white objects and specularities.

Colored Lights. This third set contains 2000 images rendered as the first set but with a random color assigned to each light. This allows us to take into account the real life cases where the lights are not white, although it is not very common (which is why we render only 2000 images for this set). Having different light colors in the scene also ensures that our network does not overfit our dataset by only analyzing white pixels and their intensity.

Environment Maps. Finally, this last set was added to the corpus because in real life specular highlights sometimes spread over a large portion of the object instead of being small and localized. This is due to the inter-reflections that occur in real scenes, whereas our synthesized data only contain one object. To simulate this effect, we render this set with an environment map E_i, randomly sampled from a set of 6 High Dynamic Range (HDR) maps.

2.3   Specularity Removal Network

The specularity removal network is a CNN with skip connections, inspired by U-Net [19]. It takes in a single RGB image, decreases its resolution with strided convolutions before further processing and upsampling it to generate its diffuse counterpart. Figure 1 (top) depicts the architecture of our generator network, where k, d and s respectively mean the kernel size, the depth and stride of the convolutions. We use the ReLU activation function at each convolutional layer. The network was trained with images of size 256×256, but can then be applied to images of any size as it is fully convolutional.

2.4   Discriminator Network

In classical GANs, the discriminator network is a binary classifier, trained to recognize real images from fake ones. Then, the generator is trained to fool it, which results in high perceptual quality image generation, close to the data's distribution. In our case, this framework does not fit for two reasons: (1) we do not want our generator to fit our synthetic data's distribution (*e.g.* a single object in the center of the image), which still lacks diversity compared to real data in spite of our efforts; (2) visual quality is not the sole concern of our problem, the main one being to accurately remove specularities. Therefore we propose a new framework following the GAN paradigm of Goodfellow et al. [5], but differing in the discriminator network's role.

Multi-class Adversarial Optimization. The discriminator network's objective is to classify generated diffuse images from real ones but also from input images I, which show specularities. Instead of returning a single scalar value, it ouputs a tensor of three values, standing for the probabilities of the image belonging to either one of the three classes and which add up to 1. For that we replaced the usual sigmoid activation function at the last layer by a softmax activation. We call $\mathcal{D}_{\theta_d}$ our discriminator network and $\hat{D} = \mathcal{G}_{\theta_g}(I)$ a diffuse image generated by $\mathcal{G}_{\theta_g}$. The discriminator network is then optimized in an alternating manner with $\mathcal{G}_{\theta_g}$ to solve the adversarial min-max problem:

$$\min_{\theta_g} \max_{\theta_d} \sum_{i=1}^{3} \mathbb{E}_{x_i \sim p_{x_i}} \left\{ \log \mathcal{D}_{\theta_d}^{(i)}(x_i) \right\} + \sum_{i=1,j=1,i\neq j}^{3} \mathbb{E}_{x_j \sim p_{x_j}} \left\{ \log \left[1 - \mathcal{D}_{\theta_d}^{(i)}(x_j) \right] \right\},$$

(3)

where:

- $\mathcal{D}_{\theta_d}^{(i)}$ denotes the ith output of $\mathcal{D}_{\theta_d}$ and represents the probability of the image belonging to the class C_i.
- x_i is an image drawn from the distribution p_{x_i} which corresponds to C_i.
- $C_i \in \{C_1, C_2, C_3\} = \{C_I, C_D, C_{\hat{D}}\}$ is one of the three classes.

Note that Eq. (3) depends on θ_g when $j = 3$ and $x_j = \hat{D} = \mathcal{G}_{\theta_g}(I)$. The idea behind this multi-class discriminator is that recognizing D from $\hat{D}$ will ensure visual quality as in a classical GAN, while the classification between I and $\hat{D}$ will compel the discriminator to find features related to the sole difference between them *i.e.* specular highlights, thus ensuring accurate specularity removal.

Architecture. An overview of the discriminator's architecture can be seen in Fig. 1 (bottom). It takes as input the image of size 256×256 and decreases its resolution every other layer with convolutions of stride 2, going from 256×256 to 16×16, while the number of kernel filters increases every other layer, going from 64 to 512. Every convolutional layer is followed by a LeakyReLU activation and a batch normalization except at the last layer. We then apply a Flatten layer before a Dense layer to form the 3-dimensional vector.

2.5 Loss Function

To stabilize the learning and at the same time train an efficient and accurate network, we define our loss to be a combination of a content loss and our SSDS-specific adversarial loss:

$$\ell\left(\mathcal{G}_{\theta_g}(I), D\right) = \ell_{content} + \lambda \times \ell_{SSDS}, \tag{4}$$

where λ is a regularization parameter to scale the two losses.

We use the Mean Square Error (MSE) as our content loss:

$$\ell_{content}\left(\mathcal{G}_{\theta_g}(I), D\right) = \frac{1}{WH} \sum_{x=1}^{W} \sum_{y=1}^{H} \left(D_{x,y} - \mathcal{G}_{\theta_g}(I_{x,y})\right)^2, \tag{5}$$

with W and H are respectively the width and the height of the input image. We explored other options, such as measuring the error on low layer feature maps of a discriminator network in order to extract relevant representations [13,20], but it did not bring improvements on our rather simple data.

The discriminative part of the loss is defined on the probabilities of the discriminator and updates the weights of the generator via the gradient of:

$$\ell_{SSDS} = \log\left\{D_{\theta_d}^{(3)}(\mathcal{G}_{\theta_g}(I))\right\} - \log\left\{D_{\theta_d}^{(1)}(\mathcal{G}_{\theta_g}(I))\right\} - \log\left\{D_{\theta_d}^{(2)}(\mathcal{G}_{\theta_g}(I))\right\}, \tag{6}$$

where, as a reminder, 3, 2 and 1 correspond to $\hat{D}$, D and I respectively. Compared to the adversarial loss of the GAN as formulated by Goodfellow et al. [5], our multi-class adversarial loss has two more terms, which translate into more gradients for the back-propagation.

2.6 Training Details

We trained our networks from scratch simultaneously on an NVIDIA GeoForce GTX using the dataset described in Sect. 2.2. We trained the generator and the discriminator in an alternating manner with batches of size 16. We scaled the range of the input images to $[0, 1]$. Our final model was trained for $30,000$ iterations at a learning rate of $2 \cdot 10^{-4}$ and a decay of 0 using the ADAM optimizer [10]. The generator and the discriminator were updated at each iteration to solve the adversarial min-max (3). In addition, the generator was updated to solve the optimization problem (2) via the gradient of the loss (4), with a regularization parameter set to $\lambda = 10^{-3}$. We implemented our models in Keras [3].

3 Experiments

In this section, we evaluate our Specularity Removal Network quantitatively on synthetic data, for which we have ground-truth, and qualitatively on real data. We compare the performance of our method with three states-of-the-art separation methods: Tan et al. [26] and Shen et al. [23], which are model-based methods, and Shi et al. [24] which is learning-based. The code for the hand-crafted methods are available on the authors' webpages and we downloaded the model of [24] on the author's GitHub[1]. We also show the contribution of the multi-class adversarial loss in Sect. 3.3 and discuss the limits in Sect. 3.4.

Table 1. (Left) Results of the **diffuse** component estimation task of the different methods on five synthetic test images. Best view in PDF. (Right) Quantitative results of the diffuse component estimation task in terms of the different metrics. The values represent the mean distance between the generated diffuse component and ground-truth over 1000 randomly sampled synthetic test images. Baseline (AE) is a simple autoencoder without GAN training and Baseline refers to our method with binary classification (classical GAN framework).

Methods	L2	DSSIM	NET	LIN-NET
Tan et al. [26]	0.020	0.052	0.408	0.054
Shen et al. [23]	0.016	0.048	0.380	0.052
Shi et al. [24]	0.222	0.410	2.363	0.313
Baseline (AE)	0.033	0.046	0.336	0.044
Baseline (GAN)	0.017	0.059	0.474	0.064
Ours	**0.014**	**0.035**	**0.271**	**0.034**

3.1 Evaluation on Synthetic Data

We provide qualitative and quantitative results regarding the estimation of the diffuse component of synthetic images in Table 1. Table 1 (left) shows the results of the diffuse component recovery with the different baseline methods and our method, on five images out of our test set of 1000 images. As can be noticed, our method's outcome is the perceptually closest to the sought diffuse components. Note that, the learning-based approach of Shi et al. [24] shows reconstruction artifacts on the edges of the image. Their method actually has to work with a mask to segment the foreground object, which is limited as the mask is not provided in most scenarios.

Table 1 (right) provides quantitative results of the different methods and two Baseline methods (AE for autoencoder and GAN for classical GAN) averaged on the test set. We use two standard metrics, namely L2 and DSSIM [7], and also consider recently developed perceptual metrics based on computing the similarity of two images in the feature space of a neural network. Indeed, Zhang et al. [29] showed that these metrics provide an embedding of images which agrees surprisingly well with human judgment. In particular, we consider the

---

[1] https://github.com/shi-jian/shapenet-intrinsics.

metric corresponding to the Squeeze network [8] (denoted NET) and its linear version as proposed by [29] (denoted LIN-NET). This quantitative comparison agrees with the perceptual analysis as our method outperforms all the methods by a large margin on all the metrics. Specifically, it outperforms the Baseline method which consists in considering a binary classification for the discriminator rather than the proposed multi-class classification.

3.2 Evaluation on Real Data

Our network being trained on synthetic images, the fact that it outperforms the other methods on synthetic data can seem natural. However, in this section we evaluate our method on real images and show that it performs consistently. The results can be seen in Fig. 2. Our network performs well on a wide range of images, from images resembling our training data with a black background to complex scenes such as the wooden objects and the earth balloon. This attests of a better generalization from our Specularity Removal Network, while artifacts on the edges and on the object are still visible in the results of Shi et al. [24]. Our discriminative network constrains the generator to understand the distribution of specularities and help it remove them from the image by training themselves to differentiate I from D. Visually, our method consistenly outperforms [24].

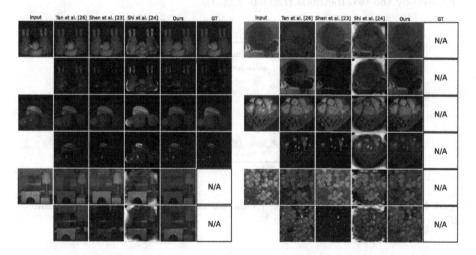

Fig. 2. Results and comparison of our method on real images. The input image is on the left and for each image, the top row is the diffuse component and the bottom row is the specular component. Ground-truths are provided on the right when available. Our baselines include Tan et al. [26], Shen et al. [23] and Shi et al. [24]. Our specular component is obtained by subtracting our estimated diffuse component to the input image. Best view in PDF.

In visual comparison to hand-crafted methods, we perform slightly worse than Shen et al. [23] on the first and the second images (animals and fruits) and slightly worse than Tan et al. [26] on the first and third examples (animals and wooden objects). This can be explained by the fact that these images were taken in laboratory conditions and fit perfectly the hypothesis of the Dichromatic Reflection Model [21], on which hand-crafted models are built. However, albeit subjective since there is no metric to evaluate specularity removal, our method performs best on the other examples, showing its consistency. On the fifth image (the fruit basket), we can clearly see that purely specular (saturated) pixels lose too much energy with hand-crafted methods because they don't show any diffuse color underneath, while our method consistently begins to inpaint them. The same goes for the last image (beans) where our method does not leave holes like the others. In summary, our method separates the reflection components with the best consistency compared to the state-of-the-art.

3.3   Contribution of Our Multi-class GAN

Figure 3 shows learning curves for our method and for a classical binary GAN with the exact same parameters. The amplitudes of the oscillations of both curves easily tell us that the multi-class adversarial loss allows for a more stable learning, while instability is common to adversarial frameworks. It also shows that convergence comes faster and is more accurate, which is visible in the images generated by the two methods (right of Fig. 3).

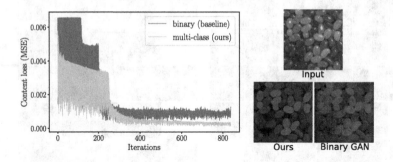

Fig. 3. Learning curves of a classical GAN and our multi-class GAN. (Right) Generated diffuse components.

3.4   Limits

Our network is of course not perfect and can have failure cases in a real life application. First, as mentioned before it does not handle mirror surfaces, which would require a completely different definition of the problem (different data and priors). Furthermore, despite our efforts (white objects and multi-class discriminators), the network still tends to darken the images. This is visible in the earth balloon example of Fig. 2 and shows our network still misses a step of generalization. This can be explained by the simplicity of our data, especially the lack of a background which would normally provide context to work on. Not any random background however, which would have been easy to add, but a true background containing illumination information. We tried to add a white background to help the network discern white material from white specular highlights but did not see any noticeable improvement. We also tried the patchGAN formulation of the GAN framework without noticeable changes.

4   Conclusion

We have proposed a new method to separate diffuse and specular reflections based on a learning approach, which can better infer the complex relations between the object, the lighting condition and the image than existing approaches. Our method takes advantage of synthetic data generation which allows us to easily obtain a large amount of labeled data. We generated our own training set and augmented our data in such a way to account for difficult cases encountered in real scenarios, in order to help the network better generalize to these situations. We also trained our model in a GAN framework adapted to reflection component separation. For that, we defined a new multi-class adversarial loss, which helps the training process by providing more gradients and more precise features. This results in a model that removes specularity from a single image, without any assumption made about the scene. We evaluated our model on both synthetic and real data. Our method outperforms the state-of-the-art in consistency across various scenes.

In future work, we would like to investigate the temporal coherence for live applications in a continuous video stream. Our Specularity Removal Network is not perfect and might not be entirely consistent from one frame to the next. Our network would also greatly benefit from data with more complex scenes in the training set.

References

1. Adelson, E.H., Pentland, A.P.: The perception of shading and reflectance. In: Perception as Bayesian Inference, pp. 409–423 (1996)
2. An, D., Suo, J., Ji, X., Wang, H., Dai, Q.: Fast and high quality highlight removal from a single image. arXiv preprint arXiv:1512.00237 (2015)
3. Chollet, F., et al.: Keras (2015)
4. Funke, I., Bodenstedt, S., Riediger, C., Weitz, J., Speidel, S.: Generative adversarial networks for specular highlight removal in endoscopic images. In: Medical Imaging 2018: Image-Guided Procedures, Robotic Interventions, and Modeling, vol. 10576, p. 1057604. International Society for Optics and Photonics (2018)
5. Goodfellow, I.: NIPS 2016 tutorial: generative adversarial networks. arXiv preprint arXiv:1701.00160 (2016)
6. Hara, K., Nishino, K., Ikeuchi, K.: Determining reflectance and light position from a single image without distant illumination assumption, p. 560. IEEE (2003)
7. Hore, A., Ziou, D.: Image quality metrics: PSNR vs. SSIM. In: 2010 20th International Conference on Pattern Recognition (ICPR), pp. 2366–2369. IEEE (2010)

8. Iandola, F.N., Han, S., Moskewicz, M.W., Ashraf, K., Dally, W.J., Keutzer, K.: SqueezeNet: AlexNet-level accuracy with 50x fewer parameters and <0.5 MB model size. arXiv preprint arXiv:1602.07360 (2016)

9. Jachnik, J., Newcombe, R.A., Davison, A.J.: Real-time surface light-field capture for augmentation of planar specular surfaces. In: 2012 IEEE International Symposium on Mixed and Augmented Reality (ISMAR), pp. 91–97. IEEE (2012)

10. Kingma, D.P., Ba, J.: Adam: a method for stochastic optimization. arXiv preprint arXiv:1412.6980 (2014)

11. Klinker, G.J., Shafer, S.A., Kanade, T.: The measurement of highlights in color images. Int. J. Comput. Vis. **2**(1), 7–32 (1988)

12. Lambert, J.H.: Photometria sive de mensura et gradibus luminis, colorum et umbrae. Klett (1760)

13. Ledig, C., et al.: Photo-realistic single image super-resolution using a generative adversarial network. arXiv preprint (2016)

14. Lin, S., Lee, S.W.: Estimation of diffuse and specular appearance. In: The Proceedings of the Seventh IEEE International Conference on Computer Vision, vol. 2, pp. 855–860. IEEE (1999)

15. Lin, S., Li, Y., Kang, S.B., Tong, X., Shum, H.-Y.: Diffuse-specular separation and depth recovery from image sequences. In: Heyden, A., Sparr, G., Nielsen, M., Johansen, P. (eds.) ECCV 2002. LNCS, vol. 2352, pp. 210–224. Springer, Heidelberg (2002). https://doi.org/10.1007/3-540-47977-5_14

16. Lin, S., Shum, H.Y.: Separation of diffuse and specular reflection in color images. In: Proceedings of the 2001 IEEE Computer Society Conference on Computer Vision and Pattern Recognition, CVPR 2001, vol. 1, p. I. IEEE (2001)

17. Meka, A., Maximov, M., Zollhoefer, M., Chatterjee, A., Richardt, C., Theobalt, C.: Live intrinsic material estimation. arXiv preprint arXiv:1801.01075 (2018)

18. Nayar, S.K., Fang, X.S., Boult, T.: Separation of reflection components using color and polarization. Int. J. Comput. Vis. **21**(3), 163–186 (1997)

19. Ronneberger, O., Fischer, P., Brox, T.: U-Net: convolutional networks for biomedical image segmentation. In: Navab, N., Hornegger, J., Wells, W.M., Frangi, A.F. (eds.) MICCAI 2015. LNCS, vol. 9351, pp. 234–241. Springer, Cham (2015). https://doi.org/10.1007/978-3-319-24574-4_28

20. Seddik, M.E.A., Tamaazousti, M., Lin, J.: Generative collaborative networks for single image super-resolution. arXiv:1902.10467 (2019)

21. Shafer, S.A.: Using color to separate reflection components. Color Res. Appl. **10**(4), 210–218 (1985)

22. Shen, H.L., Cai, Q.Y.: Simple and efficient method for specularity removal in an image. Appl. Opt. **48**(14), 2711–2719 (2009)

23. Shen, H.L., Zhang, H.G., Shao, S.J., Xin, J.H.: Chromaticity-based separation of reflection components in a single image. Pattern Recogn. **41**(8), 2461–2469 (2008)

24. Shi, J., Dong, Y., Su, H., Stella, X.Y.: Learning non-Lambertian object intrinsics across ShapeNet categories. In: 2017 IEEE Conference on Computer Vision and Pattern Recognition (CVPR), pp. 5844–5853. IEEE (2017)

25. Shi, W., et al.: Real-time single image and video super-resolution using an efficient sub-pixel convolutional neural network. In: Proceedings of the IEEE Conference on Computer Vision and Pattern Recognition, pp. 1874–1883 (2016)

26. Tan, R.T., Ikeuchi, K.: Separating reflection components of textured surfaces using a single image. IEEE Trans. Pattern Anal. Mach. Intell. **27**(2), 178–193 (2005)

27. Weiss, Y.: Deriving intrinsic images from image sequences. In: 2001 Proceedings of the Eighth IEEE International Conference on Computer Vision, ICCV 2001, vol. 2, pp. 68–75. IEEE (2001)
28. Wolff, L.B., Boult, T.E.: Constraining object features using a polarization reflectance model. IEEE Trans. Pattern Anal. Mach. Intell. **13**(7), 635–657 (1991)
29. Zhang, R., Isola, P., Efros, A.A., Shechtman, E., Wang, O.: The unreasonable effectiveness of deep features as a perceptual metric. arXiv preprint (2018)

Predicting Novel Views Using Generative Adversarial Query Network

Phong Nguyen-Ha[1]([✉]), Lam Huynh[1], Esa Rahtu[2], and Janne Heikkilä[1]

[1] Center for Machine Vision and Signal Analysis, University of Oulu,
Oulu, Finland
phong.nguyen@oulu.fi
[2] Tampere University, Tampere, Finland

Abstract. The problem of predicting a novel view of the scene using an arbitrary number of observations is a challenging problem for computers as well as for humans. This paper introduces the Generative Adversarial Query Network (GAQN), a general learning framework for novel view synthesis that combines Generative Query Network (GQN) and Generative Adversarial Networks (GANs). The conventional GQN encodes input views into a latent representation that is used to generate a new view through a recurrent variational decoder. The proposed GAQN builds on this work by adding two novel aspects: First, we extend the current GQN architecture with an adversarial loss function for improving the visual quality and convergence speed. Second, we introduce a feature-matching loss function for stabilizing the training procedure. The experiments demonstrate that GAQN is able to produce high-quality results and faster convergence compared to the conventional approach

Keywords: Novel view synthesis ·
Generative Adversarial Query Network ·
Mean feature matching loss

1 Introduction

Humans are easily able to build a mental understanding of the 3D scene based on just 2D images. With such ability, we can effortlessly imagine unseen views of 3D scenes and objects which is currently extremely challenging for computer based systems. Instead of reconstructing the scene as an explicit 3D model, humans can approximate new views by combining images obtained from nearby poses. Such task of predicting an image from a novel view point, given a limited set of other images from the same scene, is referred as a novel view synthesis in computer vision literature.

Novel view synthesis can be considered as a fundamental problem in computer vision and it is still being studied actively by the community. Despite of the tremendous progress obtained during the years, the problem is still far from being solved. There are several reasons making novel view synthesis extremely

© Springer Nature Switzerland AG 2019
M. Felsberg et al. (Eds.): SCIA 2019, LNCS 11482, pp. 16–27, 2019.
https://doi.org/10.1007/978-3-030-20205-7_2

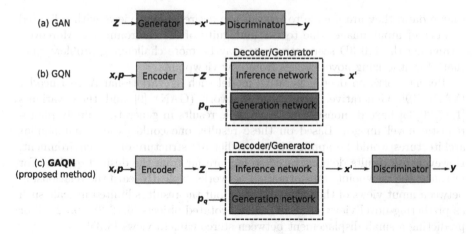

Fig. 1. Illustration of the structure of GAN [9], GQN [7] and our proposed **GAQN** where x, p and p_q are input images, camera poses and queried poses, respectively. z is the latent representation, y is labelled output as real/fake and finally, x' is the generated image.

challenging. First, a perfect solution would require knowledge of the full light field of all visible objects which is usually not possible to obtain due to occlusions and limited number of samples. Second, due to short distance to the scene geometry, even small changes in the viewpoint may lead to substantial changes in the image appearance. Finally, large parts of the scenes are texture-less and textured areas are typically small. Accurate rendering of novel views can be a useful component for many machine vision applications such as robotics and augmented reality.

The outline of this paper is as follows. In Sect. 2, we present works related to novel view synthesis methods. A brief background of two previous works that inspired our method is presented in Sect. 3. In Sects. 4.1 and 4.2, we introduce our Generative Adversarial Query Network with feature matching loss. In Sect. 5, we show our experimental results and discuss the effectiveness of adversarial training and feature matching loss to the previously proposed methods. Finally, we conclude our research in Sect. 6.

2   Related Work

In this paper, we propose a solution to the task of novel view synthesis when multiple source images are given. Early works on this domain manage to cope with small viewing angle changes by interpolation [5], warping [27] or stereo reconstruction [26]. When the input cameras are further separated from each others, these methods do not perform well due to the sparsity of sampled plenoptic function. Traditional structure-from-motion, structure-from-depth and multi-view geometry methods [4,16,31,34] predict novel views through the estimated 3D structure (point clouds, mesh clouds or a collection of predefined primitives) of the environment. Although, these methods show good results on abundant source data, they are unable to recover the desired target views with a limited number of input images due to the ambiguity of 3D environments. Moreover, estimating the full 3D scene structure may be more challenging problem than that of synthesizing novel images from new viewpoints.

Recent works on deep generative model such as Variational Auto Encoder (VAE) [19], Generative Adversarial Network (GAN) [9] and their variants [1,17,20,33] have demonstrated remarkable results in generating highly photo-realistic novel images. Based on these results, one could expect that similar architectures would be applicable to predict 3D structure of the environment. However, the results demonstrated so far, are far from the desired quality. For instance, the viewpoint transformation networks explicitly learn the relationship between input views of the same 3D scene, but the result is limited in scale such as predicting novel views of an individual rotated objects [6,12,28,29,32,36] or predicting a small displacement between stereo camera views [8,35].

A recent generative model that has shown promises in learning representation for 3D scenes structure is Generative Query Network (GQN) [7]. GQN makes use of an iterative latent variable density model [10] to generate images of the 3D scene. Using multiple source images as input, GQN presents an end-to-end learning framework that generates the novel view from the queried pose by leveraging learned knowledge of the 3D scene representation. However, GQN is known for large memory consumption and the predicted novel views are sometimes blurry.

3 Background

In this section, we provide the reader with a brief background of Generative Adversarial Networks (GANs) [9] and Generative Query Network (GQN) [7]. Figure 1 shows the overall structure of our method and compares it to the previously proposed GANs and GQN.

3.1 Generative Adversarial Networks (GANs)

Generative Adversarial Networks (GANs) [9] consist of two competing architectures referred as a generator (G) and a discriminator (D) (see Fig. 1(a)). The generator G maps a given latent representation z (possibly a vector with random values) into a novel image $x' = G(z)$ that is then passed to the discriminator network D. The discriminator aims to determine if the given sample is produced by the generator, or if it is a real image taken from the training set. Denoting the real training samples as x, the conventional generator loss $\mathcal{L}_G^{GAN}$ and discriminator loss $\mathcal{L}_D^{GAN}$ are defined as:

$$\mathcal{L}_G^{GAN} = -\mathbb{E}_{z \sim P_z}[\log D(G(z))] \tag{1}$$

$$\mathcal{L}_D^{GAN} = -\mathbb{E}_{x \sim P_x}[\log D(x)] - \mathbb{E}_{z \sim P_z}[\log(1 - D(G(z)))] \tag{2}$$

Both networks are trained simultaneously in an alternating fashion. In the ideal case, the procedure guides the generator to produce images that are indistinguishable from the training image distribution. However, in practice the training procedure is challenging due to various problems such as mode collapses [21].

3.2 Generative Query Network (GQN)

Generative Query Network (GQN) [7] is a deep generative model that learns the scene representation to perform novel view synthesis. Using an arbitrary number of observations, GQN can be trained to generate new views from the same environment. A GQN network includes a scene encoder(Enc) and a decoder(Dec) as can be seen in Fig. 1(b).

First, the Enc network tries to compress all of the 3D scene information into a latent representation z from multiple pairs of input views x and their camera poses p. The Enc network processes each pair of input views and camera poses by using a feed-forward deep convolutional neural network. Each camera pose p is represented by a 7 dimensional vector of x_t, y_t, z_t, $sin(yaw)$, $cos(yaw)$, $sin(pitch)$ and $cos(pitch)$ where x_t, y_t, z_t are 3D translation, and yaw and $pitch$ are parameters of the 3D rotation matrix. The latent scene information z is the summation of all output pairs from the Enc network.

The goal of the GQN is to predict novel views by using the queried pose p_q. Therefore, p_q and z are input to the Dec network to generate the new view x'. The Dec network is a conditional latent variable model DRAW [11] which includes M pairs of Inference and Generation recurrent sub network [10]. In the language of GANs, the term of decoder Dec and generator G have many similarities since they both synthesize data from the latent vector z (could be also random vector). Both Enc and Dec are trained jointly to minimize the evidence lower bound (ELBO) loss $\mathcal{L}_{GQN}$:

$$\mathcal{L}_{GQN} = -\mathbb{E}_{(x,p),z}\left[-\ln \mathcal{N}(x_{gt}|x') + \sum_{n=1}^{M}\left[\mathcal{N}(q_m, \pi_m)\right]\right] \tag{3}$$

The GQN training loss $\mathcal{L}_{GQN}$ is the expected value over the negative log-likelihood of the target image x_{gt} given the target distribution regularized by the cumulative Kullback Leibler divergence between obtained posterior q_m and prior π_m distributions from m^{th} generation step.

4 Generative Adversarial Query Network

The proposed Generative Adversarial Query Network (GAQN) builds on the GQN architecture by introducing two novel contributions. We will explain both of these in the following subsections. The corresponding experimental results are presented in Sect. 5. Figure 1(c) shows the overall architecture of our method.

4.1 Adversarial Loss

As illustrated in Fig. 1(c), the proposed GAQN consists of three components: an encoder network Enc, a decoder network Dec, and a discriminator network D. The GAQN utilities the same Enc and Dec architecture as standard GQN to generate a novel view $x' = Dec(Enc(x,p), p_q)$. However, inspired by the recent advancement of GANs, we include an additional discriminator network D to distinguish between the generated fake images from the GQN and the ground truth view in the training data. In this way, the discriminator acts as a learn-able loss function that boosts the learning process of GQN.

Numerous works [1,21,24,25] have shown that the training of the GAN may be unstable due to the vanishing gradients problem caused by the binary cross entropy loss as defined in Eqs. (1) and (2). In this paper, we avoid the above problem by adopting the least-square loss function from the previously proposed Least Squares Generative Adversarial Networks (LSGANs) [20]. The idea of LSGANs has been proved to be effective since it tries to pull the fake samples closer to the decision boundary of the least-square loss function. Based on the distance between the sampled data and the decision boundary, LSGANs manages to generate better gradients to update its generator. Furthermore, LSGANs also proves to exhibit less mode-seeking behaviour [3] which also stabilize the training process. Equations (4) and (5) provide the generator and discriminator loss of LSGANs that we use to train the GQN decoder and our proposed discriminator, respectively.

$$\mathcal{L}_G^{LSGAN} = \mathbb{E}_{z \sim P_z}\left[(D(G(z)) - 1)^2\right] \tag{4}$$

$$\mathcal{L}_D^{LSGAN} = \mathbb{E}_{z \sim P_z}\left[(D(G(z)))^2\right] + \mathbb{E}_{x \sim P_x}\left[(D(x') - 1)^2\right] \tag{5}$$

Inspired by recent works [22,33] on GANs, our proposed Discriminator D network adopts the residual blocks architecture [13]. Instead of directly classifying the generated image as real or fake, we follow the patch-based discriminator [15] to restrict the attention to the structure in the local patches. Table 1 shows the design of our discriminator network.

The original GQN includes per-pixel variance annealing technique [7] that is aimed to focus the learning for the scene environment (wall, floor and sky), location and color of objects at the early stage of the training and enhance the low level details later. Even though the annealing strategy was shown to work, we argue that the adversarial loss is able to further speed up the learning and to generate sharper object details at the early stages of the training. Therefore, our GAQN can achieve better visualized novel view earlier than GQN.

Figure 2 illustrates the predicted novel view using the plain GQN architecture and the proposed GAQN architecture. Although the obtained GQN model successfully predicts the correct location and color of three objects in the 3D scene, their edges are blurry. Meanwhile our proposed method manages to produce sharper object edges, especially, to the middle green icosahedron. Further results and implementation details are provided in Sect. 5.

4.2   Feature-Matching Loss

Inspired by the recent works [2,25,30] on improving the stability of the GAN training, we add an extra feature matching loss to train the generator network.

| View 1 | View 2 | View 3 | View 4 | Ground-truth novel view | GQN | GAQN (ours) |

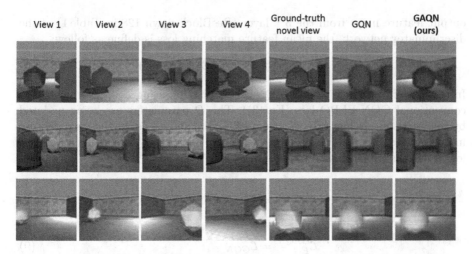

Fig. 2. Comparison between generated novel view using the GQN and the proposed GAQN architectures. The first four columns depict the training views of the scene and the fifth column shows the ground truth image for the novel view. The last two columns illustrate the results obtained using GQN architecture and the proposed approach, respectively. Our method is able to obtain clearly sharper images compared to the plain GQN architecture.

Table 1. Architecture of our discriminator D network using 3 residual blocks [13].

Layers	Input size	Output size
conv2 $\times$ 2, stride $= 2$, channels $= 32$, ReLU	$64 \times 64 \times 3$	$32 \times 32 \times 32$
ResBlock down 64	$32 \times 32 \times 32$	$16 \times 16 \times 64$
ResBlock down 128	$16 \times 16 \times 64$	$8 \times 8 \times 128$
ResBlock down 256	$8 \times 8 \times 128$	$4 \times 4 \times 256$
ResBlock down 512	$4 \times 4 \times 256$	$2 \times 2 \times 512$
conv1 $\times$ 1, stride $= 1$, channels $= 1024$, ReLU	$2 \times 2 \times 512$	$2 \times 2 \times 1024$

The main idea of this feature matching loss is to use the discriminator network as a feature extractor and guide the generator to generate data that matches the feature statistics of the real data. There are several approaches on exploiting the feature matching loss in training the generator.

Specifically, the common GAN generator loss as shown in Eq. (1) is being replaced by a mean feature matching loss. It has been argued that this mean feature matching loss helps preventing the gradient vanishing problem during the training. In our research, we have already adopted the least square loss to address the above problem (Sect. 4.1) but there is no guarantee that the problem is completely solved. Therefore, we train our GAQN generator network using a unified loss function $\mathcal{L}_G^{GAQN}$ as the combination of LSGANs generator loss $\mathcal{L}_G^{LSGAN}$ and mean feature matching loss $\mathcal{L}_{FM}$. Let $f_D()$ be the mean of the output feature maps from the 3rd layer (ResBlock down 128 in Table 1) of the discriminator network, the mean feature matching loss is define as follow:

$$\mathcal{L}_{FM} = ||\mathbb{E}_{x \sim P_x} f_D(x_{gt}) - \mathbb{E}_{z \sim P_z} f_D(x')||_2^2 \qquad (6)$$

In this paper, we jointly train GAQN *Enc* and G by using $\mathcal{L}_{EG}^{GAQN}$ which is the conventional GQN ELBO loss (Eq. (3)). The D parameters are being updated by the least squares loss (Eq. (5)) from LSGANs, and we adopt the mean feature matching loss (Eq. (6)) to update G. Finally, Eqs. (7), (8) and (9) show all the loss functions we have used to train our GAQN model.

$$\mathcal{L}_G^{GAQN} = \mathcal{L}_G^{LSGAN} + \mathcal{L}_{FM} \qquad (7)$$

$$\mathcal{L}_D^{GAQN} = \mathcal{L}_D^{LSGAN} \qquad (8)$$

$$\mathcal{L}_{EG}^{GAQN} = \mathcal{L}_{GQN} \qquad (9)$$

5   Experiments

5.1   Experimental Settings

We evaluate our method using the *rooms ring camera* dataset that was provided and used by Eslami et al. in [7]. The dataset contains various rendered 3D square rooms that contain random objects of various shapes, colors and locations. Moreover, the scene textures, walls and lights are also randomly generated. Therefore, the task of predicting the novel views on this data-set is a relatively challenging problem.

The original GQN construction proposed in [7] consumes a large amount of computing and memory resources. Due to computational restrictions, we demonstrate the advantages of the proposed architectural changes using a smaller version of the basic GQN network and a subset of the training data. Originally, training a 12 generative-layers GQN model with batch size of 36 requires 4 NVIDIA K80 GPUs as shown in [7]. In this paper, we use a single NVIDIA Tesla P100 GPU to train our GAQN model which has 8 generative layers and batch size is 20. As far as we experimented, this change would not affect the quality of results. Despite of the smaller network size, our method is able to produce results (see Figs. 2 and 4) that are very close to those presented in the original work [7] that uses clearly larger network and training set. This further, emphasized the benefits of the proposed architectural modifications. Moreover, we only use the first halve of the original GQN's training and testing data for faster training procedure.

We implement our model on PyTorch [23] and our GAQN model is trained end-to-end using ADAM optimization [18] with hyper-parameter $\beta_1 = 0.9$ and $\beta_2 = 0.999$. The generator network is trained using the learning rate of 10^{-4} and the discriminator is trained using a learning rate of 4×10^{-4}. Recent work by Heusel et al. [14] shows that if we update the generator slower than the discriminator then it helps to reach the convergence easier.

5.2   Results

Table 2. Comparison of training, testing loss, KL testing loss and SSIM testing score between our GAQN model (GQN + LSGANs + FM), original GQN and a variant (training GQN with LSGANs loss).

	GQN	GQN + LSGANs	GAQN (ours)
Training loss	7012	6988	**6951**
Testing loss	7003	6974	**6957**
KL testing loss	17.59	19.36	**22.91**
SSIM	0.742	0.815	**0.865**

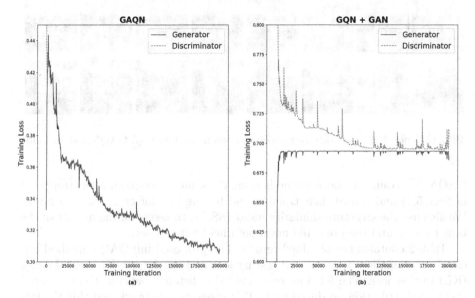

Fig. 3. Comparison of generator and discriminator training loss between our proposed GAQN (a) and GQN + GAN (b). Both generator and discriminator of GQN+GAN are suffering from mode collapsing and vanishing gradients. Using the least-square loss and the mean feature loss, our GAQN achieves a stable learning process.

Our approach relies on two new components, namely, an adversarial training pipeline using the least-square GANs loss and the discriminator feature matching loss functions to enhance the previously proposed GQN model. In this section, we will experimentally investigate the impact of the both components. The results corresponding to only GQN and adversarial loss are denoted as (GQN + LSGANs), whereas the results with the proposed full model are denoted as

View 1	View 2	View 3	View 4	GQN	GQN + GAN	GAQN (ours)	Ground-truth novel view

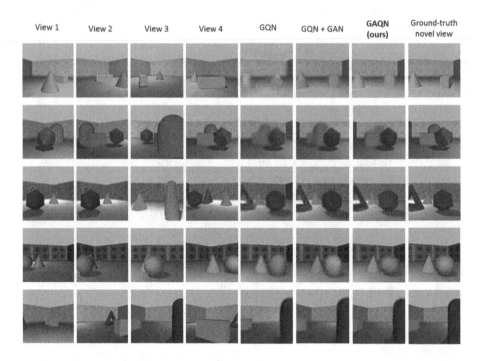

Fig. 4. Generated novel view comparison between our proposed GAQN and variants

GAQN. We train the above methods using the same hyper-parameters (reported in Sect. 5.1) and record their training and testing loss for evaluation purposes. We also use the structure similarity index (SSIM) to assess on the quality of the target image and the predicted novel on a held-out test set.

Table 2 contains the obtained results. The proposed full GAQN method has clearly the smallest training and testing loss and the largest Kullback–Leibler (KL) testing loss. The KL loss represents the distance between the estimated and true distribution produced by GQN's generation network and this KL loss is the second term in the ELBO loss (Eq. (3)). If the model manages to produce high KL loss then the predicted novel view tends to be close to the ground-truth data. It is also evident that the adversarial loss is able to improve the results compared to the plain GQN architecture. However, the largest gain is obtained by combining both of the proposed contributions.

In Fig. 4, we show qualitative examples of the generated novel views produced by different versions of the proposed GAQN method and the baseline. Although the baseline manages to correctly generate the colors and positions of objects in most cases, theirs edges are blurry. Based on the SSIM, our GAQN model achieves highest score and produce sharper edges on predicted images.

Finally, we illustrate how the least squares loss of LSGANs and discriminator feature matching loss affect the training procedure of the method. In this experiment, we compare the generator and discriminator training loss of our proposed

GAQN and GQN + GAN. As can be seen in Fig. 3(b), the training procedure of GQN + GAN is highly unstable due to mode collapsing and diminishing gradients. Our GAQN model eliminates both problems by using the least-squares loss and the discriminator mean feature loss as shown in Fig. 3(a).

6   Conclusion

We have introduced an novel adversarial training pipeline to improve the previously proposed GQN network architecture. Our experimental results demonstrate that training an additional discriminator network encourages the GQN model to predict more accurate novel views. Moreover, using the combination of least square loss and the feature matching loss helps stabilizing both generator and discriminator training process. In our future work, we will explore how to generate novel views in the bigger scale of indoor scenes where there are more objects and different lighting conditions.

References

1. Arjovsky, M., Chintala, S., Bottou, L.: Wasserstein generative adversarial networks. In: Proceedings of the 34th International Conference on Machine Learning, ICML 2017, 6–11 August 2017, Sydney, NSW, Australia, pp. 214–223 (2017). http://proceedings.mlr.press/v70/arjovsky17a.html
2. Bao, J., Chen, D., Wen, F., Li, H., Hua, G.: CVAE-GAN: fine-grained image generation through asymmetric training. In: IEEE International Conference on Computer Vision, ICCV 2017, 22–29 October 2017, Venice, Italy, pp. 2764–2773. IEEE Computer Society (2017). https://doi.org/10.1109/ICCV.2017.299
3. Bishop, C.M.: Pattern Recognition and Machine Learning (Information Science and Statistics). Springer, Heidelberg (2006)
4. Chaurasia, G., Duchene, S., Sorkine-Hornung, O., Drettakis, G.: Depth synthesis and local warps for plausible image-based navigation. ACM Trans. Graph. **32**(3), 30:1–30:12 (2013). https://doi.org/10.1145/2487228.2487238
5. Chen, S.E., Williams, L.: View interpolation for image synthesis. In: Proceedings of the 20th Annual Conference on Computer Graphics and Interactive Techniques, SIGGRAPH 1993, pp. 279–288. ACM, New York (1993). https://doi.org/10.1145/166117.166153
6. Dosovitskiy, A., Springenberg, J.T., Brox, T.: Learning to generate chairs with convolutional neural networks. In: 2015 IEEE Conference on Computer Vision and Pattern Recognition (CVPR), pp. 1538–1546, June 2015. https://doi.org/10.1109/CVPR.2015.7298761
7. Eslami, S.M.A., et al.: Neural scene representation and rendering. Science **360**(6394), 1204–1210 (2018). https://doi.org/10.1126/science.aar6170. http://science.sciencemag.org/content/360/6394/1204
8. Flynn, J., Neulander, I., Philbin, J., Snavely, N.: Deepstereo: learning to predict new views from the world's imagery. In: The IEEE Conference on Computer Vision and Pattern Recognition (CVPR) (2016)

9. Goodfellow, I.J., et al.: Generative adversarial nets. In: Proceedings of the 27th International Conference on Neural Information Processing Systems - Volume 2, NIPS 2014, pp. 2672–2680. MIT Press, Cambridge (2014). http://dl.acm.org/citation.cfm?id=2969033.2969125

10. Gregor, K., Besse, F., Jimenez Rezende, D., Danihelka, I., Wierstra, D.: Towards conceptual compression. In: Lee, D.D., Sugiyama, M., Luxburg, U.V., Guyon, I., Garnett, R. (eds.) Advances in Neural Information Processing Systems 29, pp. 3549–3557. Curran Associates, Inc. (2016). http://papers.nips.cc/paper/6542-towards-conceptual-compression.pdf

11. Gregor, K., Danihelka, I., Graves, A., Rezende, D., Wierstra, D.: Draw: a recurrent neural network for image generation. In: Bach, F., Blei, D. (eds.) Proceedings of the 32nd International Conference on Machine Learning, Proceedings of Machine Learning Research, PMLR, 07–09 July 2015, Lille, France, vol. 37, pp. 1462–1471. http://proceedings.mlr.press/v37/gregor15.html

12. Habtegebrial, T., Varanasi, K., Bailer, C., Stricker, D.: Fast view synthesis with deep stereo vision. arXiv preprint arXiv:1804.09690 (2018)

13. He, K., Zhang, X., Ren, S., Sun, J.: Deep residual learning for image recognition. In: 2016 IEEE Conference on Computer Vision and Pattern Recognition, CVPR 2016, 27–30 June 2016, Las Vegas, NV, USA, pp. 770–778. IEEE Computer Society (2016). https://doi.org/10.1109/CVPR.2016.90

14. Heusel, M., Ramsauer, H., Unterthiner, T., Nessler, B., Hochreiter, S.: GANs trained by a two time-scale update rule converge to a local Nash equilibrium. In: Guyon, I., et al. (eds.) Advances in Neural Information Processing Systems 30, pp. 6626–6637. Curran Associates, Inc. (2017). http://papers.nips.cc/paper/7240-gans-trained-by-a-two-time-scale-update-rule-converge-to-a-local-nash-equilibrium.pdf

15. Isola, P., Zhu, J.Y., Zhou, T., Efros, A.A.: Image-to-image translation with conditional adversarial networks. In: IEEE Conference on Computer Vision and Pattern Recognition (2017)

16. Jimenez Rezende, D., Eslami, S.M.A., Mohamed, S., Battaglia, P., Jaderberg, M., Heess, N.: Unsupervised learning of 3D structure from images. In: Lee, D.D., Sugiyama, M., Luxburg, U.V., Guyon, I., Garnett, R. (eds.) Advances in Neural Information Processing Systems 29, pp. 4996–5004. Curran Associates, Inc. (2016)

17. Karras, T., Aila, T., Laine, S., Lehtinen, J.: Progressive growing of GANs for improved quality, stability, and variation. In: International Conference on Learning Representations (2018). https://openreview.net/forum?id=Hk99zCeAb

18. Kingma, D.P., Ba, J.: Adam: a method for stochastic optimization. arXiv preprint arXiv:1412.6980 (2014)

19. Kingma, D.P., Welling, M.: Auto-encoding variational bayes. arXiv preprint arXiv:1312.6114 (2013)

20. Mao, X., Li, Q., Xie, H., Lau, R.Y.K., Wang, Z., Smolley, S.P.: On the effectiveness of least squares generative adversarial networks. IEEE Trans. Pattern Anal. Mach. Intell. (2018)

21. Metz, L., Poole, B., Pfau, D., Sohl-Dickstein, J.: Unrolled generative adversarial networks. arXiv preprint arXiv:1611.02163 (2016)

22. Miyato, T., Kataoka, T., Koyama, M., Yoshida, Y.: Spectral normalization for generative adversarial networks. In: International Conference on Learning Representations (2018). https://openreview.net/forum?id=B1QRgziT-

23. Paszke, A., et al.: Automatic differentiation in PyTorch. In: NIPS-W (2017)

24. Qi, G.J.: Loss-sensitive generative adversarial networks on Lipschitz densities. arXiv preprint arXiv:1701.06264 (2017)

25. Salimans, T., Goodfellow, I., Zaremba, W., Cheung, V., Radford, A., Chen, X.: Improved techniques for training gans. In: Advances in Neural Information Processing Systems, pp. 2234–2242 (2016)
26. Scharstein, D.: View Synthesis Using Stereo Vision. LNCS, vol. 1583. Springer, Heidelberg (1999). https://doi.org/10.1007/3-540-48725-5
27. Seitz, S.M., Dyer, C.R.: Physically-valid view synthesis by image interpolation. In: Proceedings IEEE Workshop on Representation of Visual Scenes (In Conjunction with ICCV 1995), pp. 18–25, June 1995. https://doi.org/10.1109/WVRS.1995.476848
28. Sun, S.H., Huh, M., Liao, Y.H., Zhang, N., Lim, J.J.: Multi-view to novel view: synthesizing novel views with self-learned confidence. In: The European Conference on Computer Vision (ECCV), September 2018
29. Tatarchenko, M., Dosovitskiy, A., Brox, T.: Multi-view 3D models from single images with a convolutional network. In: Leibe, B., Matas, J., Sebe, N., Welling, M. (eds.) ECCV 2016. LNCS, vol. 9911, pp. 322–337. Springer, Cham (2016). https://doi.org/10.1007/978-3-319-46478-7_20
30. Warde-Farley, D., Bengio, Y.: Improving generative adversarial networks with denoising feature matching. In: International Conference on Learning Representations 2017 (Conference Track) (2017). https://openreview.net/forum?id=S1X7nhsxl
31. Wu, J., Zhang, C., Xue, T., Freeman, B., Tenenbaum, J.: Learning a probabilistic latent space of object shapes via 3D generative-adversarial modeling. In: Lee, D.D., Sugiyama, M., Luxburg, U.V., Guyon, I., Garnett, R. (eds.) Advances in Neural Information Processing Systems 29, pp. 82–90. Curran Associates, Inc. (2016)
32. Yan, X., Yang, J., Yumer, E., Guo, Y., Lee, H.: Perspective transformer nets: Learning single-view 3D object reconstruction without 3D supervision. In: Lee, D.D., Sugiyama, M., Luxburg, U.V., Guyon, I., Garnett, R. (eds.) Advances in Neural Information Processing Systems 29, pp. 1696–1704. Curran Associates, Inc. (2016). http://papers.nips.cc/paper/6206-perspective-transformer-nets-learning-single-view-3d-object-reconstruction-without-3d-supervision.pdf
33. Zhang, H., Goodfellow, I., Metaxas, D., Odena, A.: Self-attention generative adversarial networks. arXiv preprint arXiv:1805.08318 (2018)
34. Zhang, Y., Xu, W., Tong, Y., Zhou, K.: Online structure analysis for real-time indoor scene reconstruction. ACM Trans. Graph. 34(5), 159:1–159:13 (2015). https://doi.org/10.1145/2768821
35. Zhou, T., Tucker, R., Flynn, J., Fyffe, G., Snavely, N.: Stereo magnification: learning view synthesis using multiplane images. In: SIGGRAPH (2018)
36. Zhou, T., Tulsiani, S., Sun, W., Malik, J., Efros, A.A.: View synthesis by appearance flow. In: Leibe, B., Matas, J., Sebe, N., Welling, M. (eds.) ECCV 2016. LNCS, vol. 9908, pp. 286–301. Springer, Cham (2016). https://doi.org/10.1007/978-3-319-46493-0_18

CubiCasa5K: A Dataset and an Improved Multi-task Model for Floorplan Image Analysis

Ahti Kalervo[1]([✉]), Juha Ylioinas[1], Markus Häikiö[2], Antti Karhu[2], and Juho Kannala[1]

[1] Department of Computer Science, Aalto University, Espoo, Finland
{ahti.kalervo,juha.ylioinas,Juho.kannala}@aalto.fi
[2] CubiCasa Inc., Oulu, Finland
{markus.haikio,antti.karhu}@cubicasa.com

Abstract. Better understanding and modelling of building interiors and the emergence of more impressive AR/VR technology has brought up the need for automatic parsing of floorplan images. However, there is a clear lack of representative datasets to investigate the problem further. To address this shortcoming, this paper presents a novel image dataset called CubiCasa5K, a large-scale floorplan image dataset containing 5000 samples annotated into over 80 floorplan object categories. The dataset annotations are performed in a dense and versatile manner by using polygons for separating the different objects. Diverging from the classical approaches based on strong heuristics and low-level pixel operations, we present a method relying on an improved multi-task convolutional neural network. By releasing the novel dataset and our implementations, this study significantly boosts the research on automatic floorplan image analysis as it provides a richer set of tools for investigating the problem in a more comprehensive manner. **Data and code at:** https://github.com/CubiCasa/CubiCasa5k.

Keywords: Floorplan images · Dataset · Convolutional neural networks · Multi-task learning

1 Introduction

Floorplan image analysis or understanding has long been a research topic in automatic document analysis, a branch of computer vision. Floorplans are drawings to scale, they show the structure of a building or an apartment seen from above, and their purpose is to convey this structural information and related semantics to the viewer. Usual key elements in a floorplan are rooms, walls, doors, windows and fixed furniture, but they can cover more technical information as well, such as building materials, electrical wiring or plumbing lines.

While floorplans are often initially drawn using a CAD software resulting in a vector-graphics format, for the usual use case that is in real estate economics,

© Springer Nature Switzerland AG 2019
M. Felsberg et al. (Eds.): SCIA 2019, LNCS 11482, pp. 28–40, 2019.
https://doi.org/10.1007/978-3-030-20205-7_3

Fig. 1. An example result using our dataset and pipeline. The images from left to right are original floorplan image, the SVG label, and the automatic prediction.

they are often rasterized before printing or publication in a digital media for marketing purposes, e.g. selling or renting. However, for the present day applications, such as 3D real estate virtual tours or floorplan-based 3D model creation, this process is fatal as it discards all the structured geometric and semantic information, rendering effortless further utilization of these floorplan drawings troublesome.

Recovering the lost information from a rasterized floorplan image is not trivial. Current state of the art models in automatic floorplan image analysis are based on deep convolutional neural networks (CNNs). A promising training scheme is based on using only one network backbone together with several multi-task heads trained to recover the lost objects, structure and semantics. While the results are already promising [13] the utilized datasets for training and benchmarking are still quite small (less than 1000 [13]) compared to those datasets commonly applied in other mainstream computer vision domains, such as image classification (millions of images [9, 18, 19]) or image segmentation (tens of thousands images [15, 20]). It is well known that deep learning models require large amounts of data to be effective and most likely increasing dataset sizes would always yield better results [15, 19].

In this paper we propose a novel floorplan image dataset comprising out of 5000 images with dense and rich ground-truth annotations encoded all as polygons. The dataset covers three different floorplan image categories, namely high quality, high quality architecture and colorful. The annotations, generated by human experts, cover over 80 different floorplan element classes. The proposed dataset is over five times larger compared with the previously largest dataset [13] and the annotation is more accurate as it includes precise shape and direction of objects. It also exhibits a larger variability in terms of the apartment type and in the style of the drawing. For a strong baseline, we present a fully automatic multi-task learning scheme inspired by the recent efforts reported in the literature. In detail, we use the recent 'multi-task uncertainty loss' capable of deriving the weights for the losses of the network automatically. Our preliminary results indicate the method's great value in practice as it saves time from hyperparameter tuning in cases where the range of weights are totally unknown. We combine this loss with an encoder-decoder convolutional architecture and demonstrate state-of-the-art results in a previous floorplan analysis benchmark dataset. We release the proposed novel benchmarking dataset and our codes with trained models for easily reproducing the results of this paper.

2 Related Work

As in many visual recognition problems, the research focus in 2D floorplan analysis has shifted from careful feature engineering to methods relying on learning from data. This shift is due to the ability to train larger and more powerful deep neural networks within a reasonable time [11]. In our context, the breakthrough is [13], which proposed an automatic floorplan parsing approach relying on CNNs. Instead of applying a bunch of low level image processing and consequent heuristics, a regular fully convolutional network was trained to label objects (rooms, icons, and openings) and to localise wall joints. The extracted low-level information was then fed in a post-processor to recover the original floorplan object items as 2D polygons. In [13], the model was jointly optimized with respect to segmentation and localization tasks. The major finding was that deep neural networks can act as an effective precursor to the final post-processing heuristics to restore the floorplan elements, including their geometry and semantics. The method significantly improved the state of the art and has inspired recent research in the field.

Parallel to [13], a CNN-based method for parsing floorplan images using segmentation, object detection, and character recognition was proposed in [6]. The main difference to [13] is that the given tasks are all performed using isolated networks. The experiments performed in [6] on wall segmentation clearly demonstrated the superiority of a CNN-based approach compared with some traditional patch-based models utilizing standard shallow classifiers like support vector machines. In summary, the era of deep neural networks has given rise to significantly better methods for 2D floorplan analysis. According to [6,13], especially fully convolutional CNNs have a huge potential in extracting accurate pixel-level geometric and semantic information that can be further utilized in later post-processing steps to construct more effective heuristics to restore the lost floorplan elements.

The problem of constructing better CNNs for floorplan parsing boils down to two design choices that are related to the network architecture and the objective. The breakthrough in semantic segmentation research happened with the introduction of fully convolutional networks (FCNs) [14]. A refined architecture for general purpose dense pixel-wise prediction is the U-net architecture with skip-connections [17]. As showed in [13], the capacity can be further boosted by changing the plain convolutional layers in the top-down path to residual blocks [7]. This model, also known as the hourglass architecture [3], has proven effective in such dense problems as semantic segmentation [16] and human pose estimation via heatmap regression [3]. The final task is to choose the training objective. For a plain segmentation problem this is often a single cross-entropy loss or in heatmap regression a single euclidean loss layer. However, many problems in practice (like ours) can benefit from several objectives that are active during training, better known as multi-task learning [4]. The success of using this approach is highly dependent on the additional hyperparameters which is the relative weighting between each task's loss. Kendall et al. [10] proposed a simple solution to train this weighting in a multi-task setting composed of segmentation, depth estimation, and instance segmentation. In contrast to [13], we apply the method of [10] (revised in [12]) to automatically tune the weighting between the tasks reducing the need for extensive hyperparameter tuning. Our results yield significant performance gains compared with the results reported in [13].

To conclude, the current research on automatic floorplan conversion continues to lack representative large-scale datasets. At the moment, the largest annotated dataset publicly available contains less than 1K. The diversity of objects (e.g. different room and icon types) and consistency and accuracy in their annotation (e.g. thickness of walls) are both limited. This in turn implies that there are room for further studies to investigate the benefits of using larger datasets richer in their content for the training of deep CNNs. In this paper, we propose a dataset with 5K samples, to our knowledge the largest annotated floorplan dataset available.

3   CubiCasa5K: A Novel Floorplan Dataset

The CubiCasa5K dataset is a byproduct of an online, partially manual, floor plan vectorization pipeline[1], mainly operating on real estate marketing material conversions from Finland region. Its main mission is to provide means for the research community to develop more accurate and automated models for real estate and other use cases.

The dataset consists of 5000 floorplans (with man-made annotations) that were collected and reviewed from a larger set of 15 000 mostly Finnish floorplan images. These are divided into three sub categories: high quality architectural, high quality and colorful, each containing 3732, 992 and 276 floorplans, respectively. To train powerful machine learning models, the dataset is randomly splitted into training, validation and test sets so that there are 4200, 400, and 400 floorplan in each of these, respectively. The annotations are in per-image SVG vector graphics format, and each of them contain the semantic and geometric annotations for all the elements appearing in the corresponding floorplan.

---

[1] http://cubitool.cubi.casa.s3-website-us-west-2.amazonaws.com/?
config=customize&rl=2&loc=na&id=8000&color=000000.

Annotations and Their Consistency. All samples of the proposed dataset have gone through an annotation pipeline resulting in a vectorized floorplan image with rich annotations. A sample input is always a raster scan (usually a scanned copy) generated from the original floor plan drawing. The annotation was done manually by human annotators who were educated to this task. Single image annotation took from 5 to 120 min, depending on the complexity and clearness of the source and amount of floors.

Each floorplan has been annotated following an annotation protocol which describes the order for annotating the elements. That is to utilize all available information from the previously annotated elements (e.g. walls are boundaries to rooms) for a given floorplan. The annotation has been done using a special CAD tool tailored for drawing floorplans. To ensure annotation consistency, there is a QA process which has two stages. This process is applied to each annotated sample image. In detail, the applied QA process targets to control placement accuracy of the annotations as well as the correct label. The first round of the process is done by the annotator, who checks the annotated floor plan and reviews all the annotations, and finally corrects all possible errors. The second round is done by a different QA person who does the same checking procedure as the initial annotator and corrects errors slipped through the first round if any.

Dataset Statistics. Figures 2, 3 and 4 provide statistical information about the CubiCasa5K dataset highlighting the aspects on the distribution of classes and complexity of the floorplan samples in relation to the dataset of [13]. Figure 3 shows the distribution of ranked room and icon classes, respectively. In Fig. 4, we compare the frequency of images with a fixed number of annotated icons, walls, and rooms in the CubiCasa5K dataset and in the dataset of [13]. In Fig. 2 we report the distribution of the image resolution across the dataset. Finally, in Table 1, we further compare some key statistics to all existing annotated floorplan datasets. In the light of all this information, it can be conluded that the CubiCasa5K is currently the largest and the most versatile floorplan dataset publicly available.

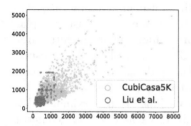

Fig. 2. Source image resolutions of CubiCasa5K and Liu et al. [13].

Table 1. Metrics between available datasets.

	R-FP-500 [6]	CVC-FP [8]	Liu et al. [13]	CubiCasa5K
Images	500	122	815	5000
Res	56–1427	905–7383	96–1920	50–8000
Object	N/A	50	27	83
Room	N/A	1320	7466	68877
Icon	N/A	2345[a]	15040	136676
Wall	N/A	6089	16139	147024

[a]Dataset included more icons labels, but without location or the polygon. We ignored these icons.

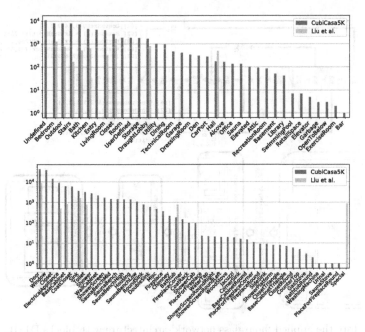

Fig. 3. Number of room (top) and icon (bottom) instances in our dataset. We made our best to match our labels with those in [13]. For example, the 'Entrance' room type in [13] is considered as the 'Draught Lobby' room type in CubiCasa5K, and the 'PS' icon type in [13] is considered as the 'Electrical Appliance' in CubiCasa5K.

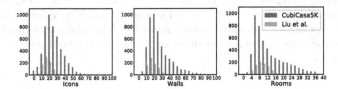

Fig. 4. The frequency of floorplans containing certain number of annotated instances (from left to right) for icons, walls, and rooms.

4   Our Multi-task Model

Our task is to parse all common elements in an input 2D floorplan image. Following [13], we rely on a network with outputs for two segmentation maps (one for different room types and one for different icon types) and a set of heatmaps to pinpoint wall junctions, icon corners, and opening endpoints (from now on, these three are referred to as interest points). Using the localized interest points, a set of heuristics is then applied to infer the geometry, i.e. location and dimensions, of all elements possibly appearing. Finally, the two segmentation maps are used to acquire the semantics, i.e. the types of rooms and icons. Our main contribution is in the latter step of the pipeline where we apply a trainable module [10] for tuning the relative weighting between the multi-task loss terms.

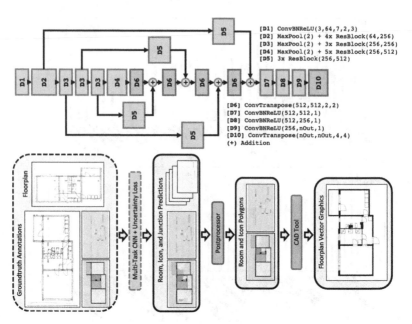

Fig. 5. On top, the applied 'hourglass network' architecture with blocks D1–10, where x and y of Resblock (x, y) denote the number of channels in the very first and the number of outputs in the very latest block in the given '$n\times$ Resblock' sequence, respectively. ConvBNReLU (x, y, k, s, p) follows the standard notation for a sequence of convolution, batch normalization and ReLU, where the arguments k, s, p stand for the kernel size, stride and padding, respectively. ConvTranspose (x, y, k, s) denotes transposed convolution with arguments k and s for the kernel size and stride, respectively. On bottom, the proposed pipeline for automatic floorplan parsing. The components outlined with a dashed line highlight our main contributions, i.e. a novel dataset and an improved multi-task model.

Network Architecture. We utilize the network architecture used in [13], which is based on ResNet-152 [7] pretrained with ImageNet [5]. The organization of the layers is depicted on top in Fig. 5 giving the details of each layer operation therein. Following [13], the bulk of the network layers depicted in Fig. 5 are initialized via training first on ImageNet [18] and then on the MPII Human Pose Dataset [2]. To have it tailored for the problem studied in this paper, some changes had to be made. Specifically, D1 was changed with respect to input channels (from 19 to 3), and the last two layers, namely D9 and D10, were both replaced to implement the required number of output channels for the two segmentation maps and 21 heatmaps. As a result, the three given layers (D1, D9, and D10) had to be randomly initialized.

Training Objective. In [13], the approach relies on a shared representation for densely predicting semantic labels for pixels and regressing the locations for interest points. This means that there is a multi-task loss applied in the end of the network shown in Fig. 5. In detail, there are altogether 21 output maps for different interest points (wall junctions, icon corners, and opening endpoints). What is learned is a pixel-accurate location for all the interest points by means of separate heatmap regression tasks which all are based on a mean squared error (MSE) as the training objective. Besides this, the network outputs two segmentation maps. The first one is for segmenting background, rooms, and walls; and the second for segmenting the different icons and openings (windows and doors). The two segmentation tasks are both trained by applying a standard cross-entropy loss. In [13], all these tasks were used to train the given shared representation in a multi-task fashion using a relative weighting fixed by hand.

A recent study by Kendall et al. [10] shows that the relative weighting between the multi-task losses can be learnt automatically. This releases the developer from the difficult, time-consuming, and very expensive step of tuning the weights by hand. In specific, the weights are implicitly learnt via so called homoscedastic uncertainty terms that are predicted as an extra output for each task. The details can be found from [10] and we proceed here directly to the final loss that is in our case given as $\mathcal{L}_{tot} = \mathcal{L}_{\mathcal{H}} + \mathcal{L}_{\mathcal{S}}$ where:

$$\mathcal{L}_{\mathcal{H}} = \sum_i \left[\frac{1}{2\sigma_i^2} \left\| y_i - f_i^{\mathbf{W}}(x) \right\| + \log(1 + \sigma_i) \right], \tag{1}$$

and

$$\mathcal{L}_{\mathcal{S}} = - \sum_{k \in \{rooms, icons\}} \frac{1}{\sigma_k} y_k \cdot \log \operatorname{softmax}(f_k^{\mathbf{W}}(x)) + \log \sigma_k. \tag{2}$$

$\mathcal{L}_{\mathcal{H}}$ is for training the heatmap regressors and it is composed of a bunch of terms (as many as there are specific interest points to locate) minimized based a re-weighted MSE. The weighting is inversely proportional to a so called uncertainty parameter σ_i that is learnt during training. The terms $\log(1+\sigma_i)$ [12] act as a regularizer to avoid the trivial solution. Furthermore, by summing one before taking logs, we enforce it to be always positive [12]. $\mathcal{L}_{\mathcal{S}}$, in turn, is for the segmentation part and it is composed of two cross-entropy terms, in this case for room and icon segmentation tasks, to be minimized. The weighting in this case appears without squaring [10]. Based on our experimental findings, the regularizer $\log \sigma_k$ stays positive whole the time during training.

Post-processing. To generate the final vector graphics equivalent representation of the input rasterized floorplan, the outputs of the multi-task CNN are dispatched to a post-processor which consists of four steps. The target is to extract all floorplan elements (walls, rooms, icons, and openings) present in the given input in a format precisely encoding their location, dimensions, and the category label.

The post-processor starts with inferring wall polygons. In detail, the procedure starts with the same step as in [13]: the junctions are pair-wisely connected based on their joints' orientation, i.e. if there are two junctions vertically/horizontally aligned (with a possible few pixel misalignment) in a manner where both have a joint facing each other. The procedure results in a wall skeleton which is next pruned based on the wall segmentation. Finally, the width of the wall is inferred by sampling along the wall lines and inspecting the intensity profile of the wall segmentation map.

The location and dimensions of rooms are partly inferred based on the wall junctions. In detail, we search for all junction triplets that span a rectangular area that does not contain any junctions. This results in a cell gridding of the floorplan interiors. The resulting cells are then labeled according to a voting mechanism based on the room segmentation map. Finally, all neighboring cells are merged if an only if there is no fully separating walls between them and they share the same room label. The procedure for restoring icons is very similar to rooms extraction, but instead of the wall junction heatmaps, we utilize the triplets from the maps responsible for the icon corner heatmap prediction.

Finally, doors and windows are inferred. This is done by connecting the two vertically/horizontally aligning opening endpoints using the predictions from the corresponding heatmaps. The label is again derived based on the segmentation maps. The width of the opening is the same as the wall polygon. All such opening endpoints that do not fall inside the wall segmentation are rejected.

5 Results

In this section we introduce the evaluation metrics and the obtained results. Prior to presenting the baseline results for our novel CubiCasa5K dataset, we validate our method on the same dataset used in [13].

Preliminary Experiments. Following [13], the network was initialized with the weights of the human pose network of [3] (trained on ImageNet and MPII). Those layers that had to be replaced (see Sect. 4) were initialized randomly. We trained the network with uncertainty driven task weighting for 400 epochs with a batch size of 20. The data augmentations were $90°$ rotations, color jitter, and randomly selecting between crop and scaling to 256×256 with zero padding. We used the Adam optimizer with an initial learning rate of 1×10^{-3}, $\epsilon = 1 \times 10^{-8}$ and β values of 0.9 and 0.999. We used a scheduler that reduced the learning rate with a factor of 0.1 if no improvement were noticed during the previous 20 epochs based on the validation loss. After dropping, the training was then continued from the phase that had yielded the best validation loss up to that point. Finally, the best model was selected based on the validation loss. Based on our experiments, the learning rate had to be dropped only once and the training seemed to converge just before the epoch number 300. The training took three hours on a Nvidia GeForce GTX TitanX GPU card.

For evaluating our model we used the same evaluation setup as in [13]. As can be seen in Table 2 we significantly improve the results presented in [13]. We further applied a test-time augmentation (TTA) scheme in which the final predictions were based on feeding the same image four times to the same network, each time rotating it 90 degrees. The final prediction was based on the mean of the four predictions. As it can be seen, the augmentation seems to be beneficial in both cases, with and without integer programming (IP).

Table 2. Evaluation results on the dataset proposed in [13].

Method	Junction		Opening		Icon		Room	
	Acc	Recall	Acc	Recall	Acc	Recall	Acc	Recall
[13]	70.7	**95.1**	67.9	91.4	22.3	77.4	80.9	78.5
[13] + IP	94.7	91.7	91.9	90.2	84.0	74.6	84.5	88.4
[13] (our eval)	75.5	90.0	74.6	91.8	25.3	79.9	84.6	83.5
[13] + IP (our eval)	92.9	86.6	92.3	90.6	86.8	78.5	89.9	88.3
Best reproduced from [13]	75.6	88.4	72.5	89.3	23.1	73.2	85.9	83.3
Best reproduced from [13] + IP	93.1	84.5	91.4	88.1	80.7	72.1	89.1	87.1
Ours	82.4	92.0	82.3	93.3	34.6	**88.3**	90.0	87.6
Ours (TTA)	90.2	91.9	89.6	**93.9**	46.1	88.0	91.5	88.0
Ours + IP	94.1	89.6	93.2	92.6	92.9	87.7	91.7	**90.8**
Ours (TTA) + IP	**95.0**	89.7	**94.5**	92.9	**93.6**	87.3	**92.2**	90.2

We noticed an error in the original annotations[2] of the dataset proposed in [13]. After re-evaluating the model of [13] using our fixes, we noticed that the performance of [13] (see 'our eval') is actually better than originally reported in [13]. We further trained the model ('best reproduced from [13]') by following the details reported in the original paper, and the results were more or less similar. Finally, we compared our best model ('Ours') without test-time augmentations to the 'our eval' version of [13], and as it can be seen, our model is clearly better.

CubiCasa5K Experiments. In the present experiment utilizing the Cubi-Casa5K dataset, some original room types and icon types are coupled so that our targets cover altogether 12 room and 11 icon classes (see the chosen classes in Table 4 and further details from the project website). As for other details, the network contains the same heatmap regression layers and is trained using the same objective as in the previous experiment. However, the following adjustments to the training scheme were done: We started the training with the pre-trained weights as a result of the previous experiment using ImageNet, MPII, and Liu et al. [13] datasets. We trained the first 100 epochs with the same augmentations given in Sect. 5.1. After that, we continued training with the best weights up to that point (according to the losses on the validation set) by first initializing optimizer parameters to their starting values and then dropping the augmentation that resizes the image to 256×256. We then trained the network for 400 epochs which resulted in convergence.

---

[2] Please see the target labels corrected by us on our project webpage.

Table 3. Evaluation results of the CubiCasa5K dataset.

	Overall acc		Mean acc		Mean IoU	
	Val	Test	Val	Test	Val	Test
Rooms	84.5	82.7	72.3	69.8	61.0	57.5
Room$_P$	79.0	77.3	64.2	61.6	52.4	49.3
Icons	97.8	97.6	62.8	61.5	56.5	55.7
Icons$_P$	97.0	96.7	94.8	45.3	43.7	41.6

Table 4. Class-specific results on the CubiCasa5K dataset.

		Background	Outdoor	Wall	Kitchen	Living Room	Bedroom	Bath	Hallway	Railing	Storage	Garage	Other rooms	Empty	Window	Door	Closet	Electr. Appl.	Toilet	Sink	Sauna bench	Fire Place	Bathtub	Chimney
IoU	val	88.3	62.6	74.0	71.6	68.2	80.0	66.5	63.0	29.0	51.6	32.2	45.2	97.8	67.3	56.7	69.8	67.4	65.3	55.5	72.7	38.4	16.7	13.8
	test	87.3	64.4	73.0	65.0	66.6	74.2	60.6	55.6	23.6	44.8	33.7	41.4	97.6	66.8	53.6	69.2	66.0	62.8	55.7	67.3	36.2	26.7	11.2
IoU$_P$	val	80.3	44.9	50.8	66.3	63.5	74.6	62.3	60.4	7.8	46.6	28.7	42.4	96.9	47.7	46.8	62.5	60.6	60.8	43.4	52.1	4.7	0.0	5.7
	test	79.2	48.5	47.9	58.3	62.2	68.7	56.6	53.5	5.8	40.8	30.0	39.8	96.7	40.9	41.2	63.3	59.8	56.2	45.5	48.0	3.1	0.0	2.9
Acc	val	95.3	71.4	86.5	86.3	82.2	91.7	81.7	75.8	34.6	60.7	42.1	59.5	99.3	75.2	63.3	77.7	76.6	72.5	67.4	80.4	45.2	19.1	14.4
	test	93.6	77.7	85.8	79.9	82.6	86.2	73.4	71.2	28.7	53.9	47.2	57.1	99.3	73.7	59.8	77.6	75.7	68.4	66.1	74.2	40.4	30.1	11.7
Acc$_P$	val	93.5	56.9	55.8	82.9	80.4	89.4	79.1	72.8	8.2	57.0	37.1	57.3	99.4	52.3	53.5	67.5	68.3	67.5	52.0	54.8	4.8	0.0	5.7
	test	92.9	60.6	52.8	74.2	81.3	83.6	69.9	68.3	6.1	49.4	43.8	55.8	99.4	44.8	47.4	69.1	67.6	60.8	52.9	49.7	3.1	0.0	2.9

Following the common practice in the art of semantic segmentation [14, 20], we report the results using three evaluating metrics, namely the *overall accuracy* indicating the proportion of correctly classified pixels, and the *mean accuracy* for the proportion of correctly classified pixels averaged over all the classes. Finally, we report the *mean intersection over union* (IoU) which indicates the area of the overlap between the predicted and ground truth pixels, averaged over all the classes. We further report the results with respect to the raw segmentations and polygonized (P) instances, i.e. after the post-processing step. We take a different approach to [13] for model evaluation as we believe the problem of floorplan parsing is very close to the problem of semantic segmentation.

We report the performance with respect to described metrics in Table 3. According to the results, the raw segmentation test scores are clearly better than the ones based on polygonized segmentation instances. The main reason is that if wall or icon junctions are missed or are not correctly located the polygons can not be created regardless the quality of the segmentation. In Table 4, we further report the class-specific IoUs and accuracies with respect to all room and icon classes used in this study. Figure 1 illustrates an example result from our pipeline.

6   Conclusions

In this paper, we have proposed a novel floorplan image dataset called Cubi-Casa5K. Compared to other existing annotated floorplan datasets, our dataset is over 5× larger and more varied in its annotations which cover over 80 floorplan object categories. Together with the novel dataset, we provided baseline results using an improved multi-task convolutional neural network yielding state-of-the-art performance.

For future directions, we plan to integrate the object detector used in [6] as one of the tasks into our pipeline. It would be also of interest to try the method of [1] to directly infer floorplan elements as polygons.

References

1. Acuna, D., Ling, H., Kar, A., Fidler, S.: Efficient interactive annotation of segmentation datasets with polygon-RNN++. In: Proceedings of CVPR (2018)
2. Andriluka, M., Pishchulin, L., Gehler, P., Schiele, B.: 2D human pose estimation: New benchmark and state of the art analysis. Proc. CVPR pp. 3686–3693 (2014)
3. Bulat, A., Tzimiropoulos, G.: Human pose estimation via convolutional part heatmap regression. In: Leibe, B., Matas, J., Sebe, N., Welling, M. (eds.) ECCV 2016. LNCS, vol. 9911, pp. 717–732. Springer, Cham (2016). https://doi.org/10.1007/978-3-319-46478-7_44
4. Caruana, R.: Multitask learning. Mach. Learn. **28**(1), 41–75 (1997)
5. Deng, J., Dong, W., Socher, R., Li, L., Li, K., Fei-Fei, L.: ImageNet: a large-scale hierarchical image database. In: Proceedings of CVPR, pp. 248–255 (2009)
6. Dodge, S., Xu, J., Stenger, B.: Parsing floor plan images. In: MVA, pp. 358–361 (2017)
7. He, K., Zhang, X., Ren, S., Sun, J.: Deep learning for image recognition. In: Proceedings of CVPR, pp. 770–778 (2016)
8. de las Heras, L.P., Terrades, O., Robles, S., Sánchez, G.: CVC-FP and SGT: a new database for structural floor plan analysis and its groundtruthing tool. IJDAR **18**, 15–30 (2015)
9. Hinton, G., Vinyals, O., Dean, J.: Distilling the knowledge in a neural network. In: NIPS (2015)
10. Kendall, A., Gal, Y., Cipolla, R.: Multi-task learning using uncertainty to weigh losses for scene geometry and semantics. In: Proceedings of CVPR (2018)
11. Lecun, Y., Bengio, Y., Hinton, G.: Deep learning. Nature **521**(7553), 436–444 (2015)
12. Liebel, L., Körner, M.: Auxiliary tasks in multi-task learning. CoRR abs/1805.06334 (2018)
13. Liu, C., Wu, J., Kohli, P., Furukawa, Y.: Raster-to-vector: revisiting floorplan transformation. In: The IEEE International Conference on Computer Vision (ICCV) (2017)
14. Long, J., Shelhamer, E., Darrell, T.: Fully convolutional networks for semantic segmentation. In: Proceedings of CVPR (2015)
15. Neuhold, G., Ollmann, T., Rota Bulo, S., Kontschieder, P.: The mapillary vistas dataset for semantic understanding of street scenes. In: Proceedings of ICCV (2017)
16. Pohlen, T., Hermans, A., Mathias, M., Leibe, B.: Full-resolution residual networks for semantic segmentation in street scenes. In: Proceedings of CVPR (2017)

17. Ronneberger, O., Fischer, P., Brox, T.: U-net: convolutional networks for biomedical image segmentation. In: Navab, N., Hornegger, J., Wells, W.M., Frangi, A.F. (eds.) Proceedings of MICCAI, pp. 234–241 (2015)
18. Russakovsky, O., et al.: Imagenet large scale visual recognition challenge. IJCV **115**(3), 211–252 (2015)
19. Sun, C., Shrivastava, A., Singh, S., Gupta, A.: Revisiting unreasonable effectiveness of data in deep learning era. In: Proceedings of ICCV (2017)
20. Zhou, B., Zhao, H., Puig, X., Fidler, S., Barriuso, A., Torralba, A.: Scene parsing through ADE20K dataset. In: Proceedings of CVPR (2017)

An Efficient Solution for Semantic Segmentation: ShuffleNet V2 with Atrous Separable Convolutions

Sercan Türkmen[✉] and Janne Heikkilä

Center for Machine Vision Research, University of Oulu, Oulu, Finland
sercanturkmen@outlook.com, janne.heikkila@oulu.fi

Abstract. Assigning a label to each pixel in an image, namely semantic segmentation, has been an important task in computer vision, and has applications in autonomous driving, robotic navigation, localization, and scene understanding. Fully convolutional neural networks have proved to be a successful solution for the task over the years but most of the work being done focuses primarily on accuracy. In this paper, we present a computationally efficient approach to semantic segmentation, while achieving a high mean intersection over union (mIOU), 70.33% on Cityscapes challenge. The network proposed is capable of running real-time on mobile devices. In addition, we make our code and model weights publicly available.

Keywords: Semantic image segmentation · Real-time · Efficient · Fast · Lightweight · Mobile

1 Introduction

Semantic segmentation is a major challenge in computer vision that aims to assign a label to every pixel in an image. [6,16] Fully convolutional networks are shown to be the state-of-art approach in semantic segmentation tasks over the recent years and offer simplicity and speed during learning and inference [17]. Such networks have a broad range of applications such as autonomous driving, robotic navigation, localization, and scene understanding.

These architectures are trained by supervised learning over numerous images and detailed annotations for each pixel. Data sets that offer semantic segmentation annotations on a rich variety of objects and stuff categories have emerged such as COCO [16], ADE20K [25], Cityscapes [8], PASCAL VOC [10], thus opening new windows in the field.

Computationally efficient convolutional networks have been gaining momentum over the recent years but the segmentation task is still an open problem. Proposed networks for the semantic segmentation task are deep and resource hungry because of their purpose of achieving the highest accuracy such as [4,6,20,24]. These approaches have high complexity and may contain custom operations

© Springer Nature Switzerland AG 2019
M. Felsberg et al. (Eds.): SCIA 2019, LNCS 11482, pp. 41–53, 2019.
https://doi.org/10.1007/978-3-030-20205-7_4

which are not suitable to be run on current implementations of neural network interpreters offered for mobile devices. Such devices lack the computation power of specialised GPUs, resulting in very poor inference speed. Mobile capable approaches in the feature extraction task such as Mobilenet V2 [21], ShuffleNet V2 [18] have motivated us to explore the performance of such architectures to be used in this context.

In this paper, we explore ShuffleNet V2 [18], as the feature extractor with simplified DeepLabV3+ [6] heads and recently proposed DPC [4] architecture, and report our findings of both model on scene understanding using Cityscapes [8] data set. Furthermore, we present the number of floating point operations(FLOPs) and on-device inference performance of each approach. Our contributions to the field can be listed in three points:

1. We achieve state-of-art computation efficiency in the semantic segmentation task while achieving 70.33% mean intersection over union (mIOU) on Cityscapes test set using ShuffleNet V2 along with DPC [4] encoder and a naive decoder module.
2. Our proposed model and implementation is fully compatible with TensorFlow Lite and runs real-time on Android and iOS-based mobile phones.
3. We make our Tensorflow implementation of the network, and trained models publicly available at https://github.com/sercant/mobile-segmentation[1].

2   Related Work

In this section, we talk about the current state-of-art in the task of semantic segmentation, especially mobile capable approaches and performance metrics to measure the efficiency of networks.

CNNs have shown to be the state-of-art method for the task of semantic segmentation over the recent years. Especially fully convolutional neural networks (FCNNs) have demonstrated great performance on feature generation task and end-to-end training and hence is widely used in semantic segmentation as encoders. Moreover, memory friendly and computationally light designs such as [13,18,21,23], have shown to perform well in speed-accuracy trade-off by taking advantage of approaches such as depthwise separable convolution, bottleneck design and batch normalization [14]. These efficient designs are promising for usage on mobile CPUs and GPUs, hence motivated us to use such networks as encoders for the challenging task of semantic segmentation.

FCNN models for semantic segmentation proposed in the field have been the top-performing approach in many benchmarks such as [8,10,16,25]. But these approaches use deep feature generators and complex reconstruction methods for the task, thus making them unsuitable for mobile use, especially for the application of autonomous cars where resources are scarce and computation delays are undesired [22].

---

[1] DOI: https://doi.org/10.5281/zenodo.2620377.

In this sense, one of the recent proposals in feature generation, ShuffleNet V2 [18], demonstrates significant efficiency boost over the others while performing accurately. According to [18], there are four main guidelines to follow for achieving a highly efficient network design.

1. When the channel widths are not equal, there is an increase in the memory access cost (MAC) and thus, channel widths should be kept equal.
2. Excessive use of group convolutions should be avoided as they raise the MAC.
3. Fragmentation in the network should be avoided to keep the degree of parallelism high.
4. Element-wise operations such as ReLU, Add, AddBias are non-negligible and should be reduced.

To achieve such accuracy at low computation latency, they point out two main reasons. First, their guidelines for efficiency allow each building block to use more feature channels and have a bigger network capacity. Second, they achieve a kind of "feature reuse" by their approach of keeping half of the feature channels pass through the block to join the next block.

Another important issue is the metric of performance for convolutional neural networks. The efficiency of CNNs is commonly reported by the total number of floating point operations (FLOPs). It is pointed out in [18] that, despite their similar number of FLOPs, networks may have different inference speeds, emphasizing that this metric alone can be misleading and may lead to poor designs. They argue that discrepancy can be due to memory access cost (MAC), parallelism capability of the design and platform dependent optimizations on specific operations such as cuDNN's 3×3 Conv. Furthermore, they offer to use a direct metric (e.g., speed) instead of an indirect metric such as FLOPs.

Next, we shall examine the state-of-art on the semantic image segmentation task by focusing on the computationally efficient approaches.

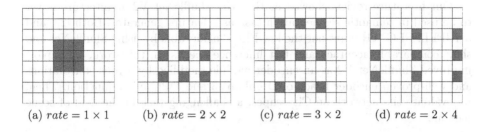

(a) $rate = 1 \times 1$ (b) $rate = 2 \times 2$ (c) $rate = 3 \times 2$ (d) $rate = 2 \times 4$

Fig. 1. Atrous convolutions, also known as dilated convolutions, with a kernel size of 3×3 at different dilation rates.

Atrous convolutions, or dilated convolutions, are shown to be a powerful tool in the semantic segmentation task [5]. By using atrous convolutions it is possible to use pretrained ImageNet networks such as [18,21] to extract denser feature maps by replacing downscaling at the last layers with atrous rates, thus allowing us to control the dimensions of the features. Furthermore, they can be used to enlarge the field of view of the filters to embody multi-scale context. Examples of atrous convolutions at different rates are shown in Fig. 1.

DeepLabV3+ DPC [4] achieves state-of-art accuracy when it is combined with their modified version of Xception [7] backbone. In their work, Mobilenet V2 has shown to have a correlation of accuracy with Xception [7] while having a shorter training time, and thus it is used in the random search [2] of a dense prediction cell (DPC). Our work is inspired by the accuracy that they have achieved with the Mobilenet V2 backbone on Cityscapes set in [4], and their approach of combining atrous separable convolutions with spatial pyramid pooling in [5]. To be more specific, we use lightweight prediction cell (denoted as basic) and DPC which were used on the Mobilenet V2 features, and the atrous separable convolutions on the bottom layers of feature extractor in order to keep higher resolution features.

Semantic segmentation as a real-time task has gained momentum on popularity recently. ENet [19] is an efficient and lightweight network offering low number of FLOPs in the design and ability to run real-time on NVIDIA TX1 by taking advantage of bottleneck module. Recently, ENet was further fine-tuned by [3], increasing the Cityscapes mean intersection over union from 58.29% to 63.06% by using a new loss function called Lovasz-Softmax [3]. Furthermore, SHUFFLESEG [11], demonstrates different decoders that can be used for Shufflenet, prior work to ShuffleNet V2, comparing their efficiency mainly with ENet [19] and SegNet [1] by FLOPs and mIOU metrics but they do not mention any direct speed metric that is suggested by ShuffleNet V2 [18]. The most comprehensive work on the search for an efficient real-time network was done in [22] and they report that SkipNet-Shufflenet combination runs 15 frames per second (fps) with an image resolution of 640×360 on Jetson TX2. This work again, like SHUFFLESEG [11], is based on the prior design of the channel shuffle based approach.

Our literature review showed us that the ShuffleNet V2 architecture is yet to be used in semantic segmentation task as a feature generator. Both [22] and SHUFFLESEG [11] point out the low FLOP achievable by using ShuffleNet and show comparable accuracy and fast inference speeds. In this work, we exploit improved ShuffleNet V2 as an encoder module modified by atrous convolutions and well-proven encoder heads of DeepLabV3 and DPC in conjunction. Then, we evaluate the network on Cityscapes, a challenging task in the field of scene parsing.

3   Methodology

This section describes our network architecture, and the training procedures, and evaluation methods. The network architecture is based upon the state-of-art efficient encoder, ShuffleNet V2 [18], and DeepLabV3 [5] and DPC [4] heads built on top to perform segmentation. Training procedure includes restoring from an Imagenet [9] checkpoint, pre-training on MS COCO 2017 [16] and Cityscapes [8] coarse annotations, and fine-tuning on fine annotations of Cityscapes [8]. We then evaluate the trained network on Cityscapes validation set according to their evaluation procedure in [8].

3.1   Network Architecture

In this section, we will give a detailed explanation of each step of the proposed network. Figure 2 shows the different stages of the network and how the data flows from the start to the end. We start with Shufflenet V2 feature extractor, then add the encoder head (DPC or basic DeepLabV3), and finally use resize bilinear as a naive decoder to produce the segmentation mask. The final downsampling factor of the feature extractor is denoted as *output_stride*.

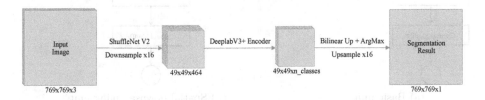

Fig. 2. General view of the network at 769×769 with *output_stride* = 16.

For the task of feature extraction, we choose Shufflenet V2 because of its success for speed versus accuracy trade-off. Our selection for the *depth_multiplier* of ShuffleNet V2 is ×1 as it can be seen in the output channels column of Table 1. Our decision was purely made by accuracy and speed results of this variation on the ImageNet data set and we have not run experiments on different variations of the *depth_multiplier*. Although, one might choose lower values for this hyperparameter to achieve faster inference time by compromising on accuracy and conversely higher values might result in a gain of accuracy in favour of inference speed.

Figure 3 shows the building blocks of the feature extractor architecture in detail. Each stage consists of one spatial downsampling unit and several basic units. In the original implementation of Shufflenet V2 [18], *output_stride* goes as low as 32. In our approach, entry flow, *Stage2* and *Stage3* of the proposed feature extractor is implemented as in [18]. In the case of *output_stride* = 16, the last stage, namely *Stage4*, has been modified by setting *stride* = 1 instead of 2 on the downsampling layer and the atrous rate of the preceding depth-wise convolutions are set to *network_stride* divided by *output_stride* as described in [5] to adjust the final downsampling factor of the feature extractor. However, in the case of *output_stride* = 8, stride and atrous rate modification starts from *Stage3*. We choose to focus on *output_stride* = 16 due to its faster computation speed.

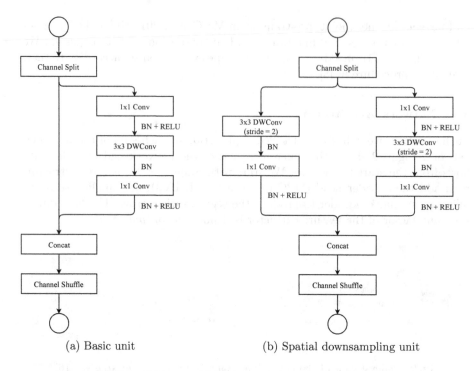

Fig. 3. Shufflenet V2 units (**DWConv** means depthwise convolution).

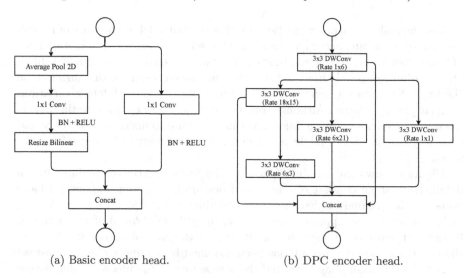

Fig. 4. Encoder head variants.

After ShuffleNet V2 features are extracted we employ the DPC encoder. Figure 4 shows the design of the basic encoder head [5] and the DPC head [4].

Fig. 5. Exit flow.

The basic encoder head does not contain any atrous convolutions in its design for lower complexity. On the other hand, DPC is using five different depthwise convolutions at different rates to understand features better. After the encoder heads, as seen in Fig. 5, features are reduced down to $depth = 256$, then to the number of classes. Afterwards, a drop out layer with 0.9 probability of keeping is applied.

For decoding, we are using the same naive approach as [5], where a simple bilinear resizing is applied to upscale back to the original image dimensions. In the case of $output\_stride = 16$, the upscaling factor is 16. In their later work, DeepLabV3+[6], they propose an approach where features from earlier stages (e.g. $decoder\_stride$ of 4) are concatenated with the upsampled features of the last layer where the upscaling factor is $output\_stride$ divided by $decoder\_stride$ to preserve the finer details in the segmentation result. We have not included this part as it adds more complexity and slowing down the inference time.

Table 1. Proposed network architecture at $output\_stride = 16$. **DLV3** denotes DeepLabV3+.

	Layer	Output size	Kernel	Stride	Rate	Repeat	Output channels
	Image	769 × 769					3
ShuffleNet V2	Conv2D	385 × 385	3 × 3	2		1	24
	MaxPool	193 × 193	3 × 3	2			
	Stage 2	97 × 97		2	1	1	116
		97 × 97		1	1	3	
	Stage 3	49 × 49		2	1	1	232
		49 × 49		1	1	7	
	Stage 4	49 × 49		1	1	1	464
		49 × 49		1	2	3	
DLV3	DPC	49 × 49		1	1	1	512
	Conv2D	49 × 49	1 × 1	1			256
	Conv2D	49 × 49	1 × 1	1			$n\_classes$
	Bilinear up	769 × 769					$n\_classes$
	ArgMax	769 × 769					1

3.2 Training

Proposed feature extractor weights are initially restored from an ImageNet [9] checkpoint. After that, we pre-train the network end-to-end on MS COCO [16]. Further pre-training was done on Cityscapes coarse annotations before we finalize our training on Cityscapes fine annotations. During the training at each step data augmentation was performed on the images by randomly scaling between 0.5 and 2.0 with steps of 0.25, randomly cropping by 769×769 and randomly flipping left and right.

Preprocessing. For preprocessing the input images, we standardize each pixel to $[-1, 1]$ range according to Eq. 1.

$$inputs \times \frac{2}{255} - 1 \tag{1}$$

MS COCO 2017. We pre-train the network on MS COCO as suggested in [4–6]. Only the relevant classes to the Cityscapes task, which are person, car, truck, bus, train, motorcycle, bicycle, stop sign and parking meter, were chosen and other classes were marked as background. Also, we further filter the samples by criteria of having a non-background class area of over 1000 pixels. This yields us 69795 training and 2956 validation samples. Training was done end-to-end by using a batch size of 16, *output_stride* of 16, weight decay set to $4e-5$ to prevent over-fitting, and a "poly" learning rate policy as shown in Eq. 2 where $lr^{(k)}$ is the learning rate at step k, $lr_{initial}$ set to 0.001 and *power* set to 0.9 [5] for 60K steps using Adam optimizer [15]($beta1 = 0.9$, $a2 = 0.999$, $epsilon = 10^{-8}$).

$$lr^{(k)} = lr_{initial} \left(1 - \frac{k}{max\_iter} \right)^{power} \tag{2}$$

Cityscapes. First, we pre-train the network further using 20K coarsely annotated samples for 60K steps, following the same parameters that we used in MS COCO training. Then, as the final step, we fine-tune the network for 120K steps on finely annotated set (2975 train, 500 validation samples) with an initial learning rate of 0.0001, a slow start at learning rate $1e-5$ for the first 186 steps. We found out that lowering the learning rate at the fine-tuning stage is crucial to achieving good accuracy. Other parameters are kept the same as the previous steps.

4   Experimental Results on Cityscapes

Cityscapes [8] is a well-studied data set in the field of scene parsing task. It contains roughly 20K coarsely annotated samples, and 5000 finely annotated samples which are split into 2975, 500 and 1525 for training, validation, and testing respectively.

Our approach of combining ShuffleNet V2 with DeepLabV3 basic and DPC head achieves both state-of-art mIOU and inference speed with the respective GFLOPs counts. Table 2 shows the comparison of GFLOPs to mIOU performance on the validation set. ShuffleNet V2 with basic DeepLabV3 encoder head, having 2.18 GFLOPs, surpasses the SkipNet-ShuffleNet [22] which has similar floating operations count by 12.2% gain on mIOU. On the other hand, DPC variation performs +0.6% more accurate than the Mobilenet V2 with basic heads, which has 1.54 times more GFLOPs.

Table 2. Cityscapes **validation** set performance. GFLOPs is measured on image resolution of $640 \times 360 \times 3$.

Method	GFLOPs	mIOU(%)
SkipNet-ShuffleNet [22]	2.0	55.5
ENet [22]	3.83	n/a
MobileNet V2 + basic	4.69	70.7
MobileNet V2 + DPC	5.56	n/a
ShuffleNet V2 + basic (ours)	2.18	67.7
ShuffleNet V2 + DPC (ours)	3.05	71.3

ShuffleNet V2 with DPC heads outperforms state-of-art efficient networks on the Cityscapes test set. Table 3 shows that we make a gain of 7.27% mIOU over the best performing ENet architecture. Furthermore, on each of the classes highlighted here, ShuffleNet V2+DPC shows a great improvement. Also, as seen in the Table 4, our approach outperforms the previous methods on the category mIOU and instance level metrics.

We visualize the segmentation masks generated both by the basic and DPC approach in Fig. 6. From the visuals, we can see that the DPC head variant is able to segment thinner objects such as poles better than the basic encoder head. The figure is best viewed in colour.

Table 3. Comparison of class and category level accuracy on the test set.

Method	mIOU	Building	Sky	Car	Sign	Road	Person	Fence	Pole	Sidewalk	Bicycle
SkipNet-MobileNet	61.52	86.19	92.89	89.88	54.34	95.82	69.25	39.40	44.53	73.93	58.15
Enet Lovasz	63.06	87.22	92.74	91.01	58.06	97.27	71.35	38.99	48.53	77.20	59.80
ShuffleNet V2+DPC (ours)	70.33	90.7	93.86	93.95	66.93	98.11	78.47	50.93	51.47	82.46	67.48

4.1   Inference Speed on Mobile Phone

In this section, we provide inference speed results and our procedure for the measurements. As discussed in ShuffleNet V2 [18], we believe that the computational efficiency of the network should be measured on the target devices rather than purely comparing by the FLOPs. Thus, we convert the competing networks to Tensorflow Lite, a binary model representation for inferencing on mobile phones, for the speed evaluation. Tensorflow Lite has a limited number

Table 4. Comparison of class level accuracies efficient architectures on Cityscapes **test** set.

Method	Class IOU	Class iIOU	Cat. IOU	Cat. iIOU
SegNet [1]	56.1	34.2	79.8	66.4
ShuffleSeg [11]	58.3	32.4	80.2	62.6
SkipNet-MobileNet [22]	61.52	35.16	82.00	63.03
Enet Lovasz [3]	63.06	34.06	83.58	61.05
ShuffleNet V2+DPC (ours)	70.33	43.58	86.48	69.92

of available operations in its current implementation, thus complex architectures such as [12] cannot be converted without implementing the missing operations on the Tensorflow Lite. But, both Mobilenet V2 and ShuffleNet V2 are compatible and require no additional custom operations.

The measurements were done on OnePlus A6003, Snapdragon 845 CPU, 6 GB RAM, 16 + 20 MP Dual Camera, Android version 9, OxygenOS version 9.0.3. The device is stabilized in place, put to airplane mode, background services are disabled, the battery is fully charged and kept plugged to the power cable. The rear camera output image is scaled so that the smaller dimension is 224, then the middle of the image is cropped to get an input image of 224 × 224. The downscaling and cropping is not included in the inference time shown in Table 5 however the preprocessing of the input image, according to Eq. 1, and the final ArgMax is included in the inference time. Inference speed measurements, presented in Table 5, are averaged over 300 frames after 30 s of an initial warm-up period.

Table 5 shows that our approach of using ShuffleNet V2 as a backbone is capable of performing real-time, close to 20 Hz, semantic segmentation on a mobile phone. Even with the complex DPC architecture, ShuffleNet V2 backbone ends up with 1.54 times fewer GFLOPs over the Mobilenet V2 with basic encoder head. Furthermore, model size is significantly lower which is desired for embedded devices that might have limited memory or storage size. One surprising finding is that the Mobilenet V2 variants show much higher variance in the inference time compared to the ShuffleNet V2 backbone, thus our approach provides a more stable fps.

Table 5. Inference performance on OnePlus A6 with an input size of 224 × 224.

Backbone	Encoder	GFLOPs	Inference (ms)	Var (ms)	FPS	Size (MB)
ShuffleNet V2	Basic	0.47	50.89	0.57	19.65	4.6
	DPC	0.65	64.89	3.53	15.41	6
MobileNet V2	Basic	1.00	101.46	25.04	9.86	8.4
	DPC	1.18	116.16	44.01	8.61	9.9

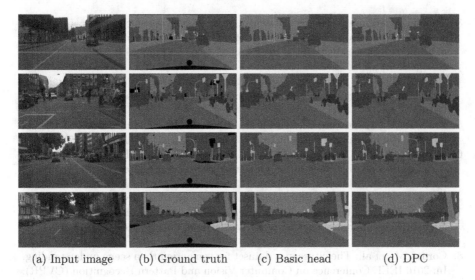

(a) Input image   (b) Ground truth   (c) Basic head   (d) DPC

Fig. 6. Segmentation visualisations on the validation set. Best viewed in colour. (Black coloured regions on ground truth are ignored)

5 Conclusion

In this paper, we have described an efficient solution for semantic segmentation by achieving state-of-art inference speed without compromising on the accuracy. Our approach shows that ShuffleNet V2 is a powerful and efficient backbone for the task of semantic segmentation. It achieves 70.33% mIOU when combined with the DPC head, and 67.7% mIOU[2] combined with the basic encoder head on Cityscapes challenge. Furthermore, we showed that our network is capable of running real-time, the DPC head at 15.41 fps and the basic encoder head at 19.65 fps, on a mobile phone with an input image size of 224×224. Future work is to implement an efficient decoder architecture to get more refined edges along the borders of the objects on the segmentation mask.

References

1. Badrinarayanan, V., Kendall, A., Cipolla, R.: SegNet: a deep convolutional encoder-decoder architecture for image segmentation. IEEE Trans. Pattern Anal. Mach. Intell. **39**(12), 2481–2495 (2017)
2. Bergstra, J., Bengio, Y.: Random search for hyper-parameter optimization. J. Mach. Learn. Res. **13**, 281–305 (2012)

---

[2] The validation set result.

3. Berman, M., Rannen Triki, A., Blaschko, M.B.: The lovász-softmax loss: a tractable surrogate for the optimization of the intersection-over-union measure in neural networks. In: Proceedings of the IEEE Conference on Computer Vision and Pattern Recognition, pp. 4413–4421 (2018)
4. Chen, L.C., et al.: Searching for efficient multi-scale architectures for dense image prediction. In: Advances in Neural Information Processing Systems, pp. 8713–8724 (2018)
5. Chen, L.C., Papandreou, G., Schroff, F., Adam, H.: Rethinking atrous convolution for semantic image segmentation. arXiv preprint arXiv:1706.05587 (2017)
6. Chen, L.-C., Zhu, Y., Papandreou, G., Schroff, F., Adam, H.: Encoder-decoder with atrous separable convolution for semantic image segmentation. In: Ferrari, V., Hebert, M., Sminchisescu, C., Weiss, Y. (eds.) ECCV 2018. LNCS, vol. 11211, pp. 833–851. Springer, Cham (2018). https://doi.org/10.1007/978-3-030-01234-2_49
7. Chollet, F.: Xception: Deep learning with depthwise separable convolutions. In: 2017 IEEE Conference on Computer Vision and Pattern Recognition (CVPR), July 2017
8. Cordts, M., et al.: The cityscapes dataset for semantic urban scene understanding. In: 2016 IEEE Conference on Computer Vision and Pattern Recognition (CVPR), June 2016
9. Deng, J., Dong, W., Socher, R., Li, L.J., Li, K., Fei-Fei, L.: ImageNet: a large-scale hierarchical image database. In: CVPR 2009 (2009)
10. Everingham, M., Eslami, S.M.A., Van Gool, L., Williams, C.K.I., Winn, J., Zisserman, A.: The pascal visual object classes challenge: a retrospective. Int. J. Comput. Vis. **111**(1), 98–136 (2015)
11. Gamal, M., Siam, M., Abdel-Razek, M.: ShuffleSeg: real-time semantic segmentation network. arXiv preprint arXiv:1803.03816 (2018)
12. He, K., Gkioxari, G., Dollar, P., Girshick, R.: Mask R-CNN. In: 2017 IEEE International Conference on Computer Vision (ICCV), October 2017
13. Howard, A.G., et al.: MobileNets: efficient convolutional neural networks for mobile vision applications. arXiv preprint arXiv:1704.04861 (2017)
14. Ioffe, S., Szegedy, C.: Batch normalization: accelerating deep network training by reducing internal covariate shift. In: Proceedings of the 32nd International Conference on International Conference on Machine Learning, ICML 2015, vol. 37, pp. 448–456. JMLR.org (2015)
15. Kingma, D.P., Ba, J.: Adam: a method for stochastic optimization. arXiv preprint arXiv:1412.6980 (2014)
16. Lin, T.-Y., et al.: Microsoft COCO: common objects in context. In: Fleet, D., Pajdla, T., Schiele, B., Tuytelaars, T. (eds.) ECCV 2014. LNCS, vol. 8693, pp. 740–755. Springer, Cham (2014). https://doi.org/10.1007/978-3-319-10602-1_48
17. Long, J., Shelhamer, E., Darrell, T.: Fully convolutional networks for semantic segmentation. In: Proceedings of the IEEE Conference on Computer Vision and Pattern Recognition, pp. 3431–3440 (2015)
18. Ma, N., Zhang, X., Zheng, H.-T., Sun, J.: ShuffleNet V2: practical guidelines for efficient CNN architecture design. In: Ferrari, V., Hebert, M., Sminchisescu, C., Weiss, Y. (eds.) Computer Vision – ECCV 2018. LNCS, vol. 11218, pp. 122–138. Springer, Cham (2018). https://doi.org/10.1007/978-3-030-01264-9_8
19. Paszke, A., Chaurasia, A., Kim, S., Culurciello, E.: ENet: a deep neural network architecture for real-time semantic segmentation. arXiv preprint arXiv:1606.02147 (2016)

20. Ronneberger, O., Fischer, P., Brox, T.: U-Net: convolutional networks for biomedical image segmentation. In: Navab, N., Hornegger, J., Wells, W.M., Frangi, A.F. (eds.) MICCAI 2015. LNCS, vol. 9351, pp. 234–241. Springer, Cham (2015). https://doi.org/10.1007/978-3-319-24574-4_28

21. Sandler, M., Howard, A., Zhu, M., Zhmoginov, A., Chen, L.C.: MobileNetV2: inverted residuals and linear bottlenecks. In: 2018 IEEE/CVF Conference on Computer Vision and Pattern Recognition, June 2018

22. Siam, M., Gamal, M., Abdel-Razek, M., Yogamani, S., Jagersand, M., Zhang, H.: A comparative study of real-time semantic segmentation for autonomous driving. In: 2018 IEEE/CVF Conference on Computer Vision and Pattern Recognition Workshops (CVPRW), pp. 700–70010. IEEE (2018)

23. Zhang, X., Zhou, X., Lin, M., Sun, J.: ShuffleNet: an extremely efficient convolutional neural network for mobile devices. In: 2018 IEEE/CVF Conference on Computer Vision and Pattern Recognition, June 2018

24. Zhao, H., Shi, J., Qi, X., Wang, X., Jia, J.: Pyramid scene parsing network. In: 2017 IEEE Conference on Computer Vision and Pattern Recognition (CVPR), July 2017

25. Zhou, B., Zhao, H., Puig, X., Fidler, S., Barriuso, A., Torralba, A.: Scene parsing through ADE20K dataset. In: Proceedings of the IEEE Conference on Computer Vision and Pattern Recognition (2017)

Unstructured Multi-view Depth Estimation Using Mask-Based Multiplane Representation

Yuxin Hou$^{(\boxtimes)}$![ORCID], Arno Solin ![ORCID], and Juho Kannala ![ORCID]

Department of Computer Science, Aalto University, Espoo, Finland
{yuxin.hou,arno.solin,juho.kannala}@aalto.fi

Abstract. This paper presents a novel method, MaskMVS, to solve depth estimation for unstructured multi-view image-pose pairs. In the plane-sweep procedure, the depth planes are sampled by histogram matching that ensures covering the depth range of interest. Unlike other plane-sweep methods, we do not rely on a cost metric to explicitly build the cost volume, but instead infer a multiplane mask representation which regularizes the learning. Compared to many previous approaches, we show that our method is lightweight and generalizes well without requiring excessive training. We outperform the current state-of-the-art and show results on the SUN3D, SCENES11, MVS, and RGBD test data sets.

Keywords: Computer vision · Depth estimation · Multi-view stereo

1 Introduction

Multi-view stereo (MVS) aims at reconstructing depth (or disparity) maps from a collection of overlapping images, which is a fundamental problem in computer vision. Any progress in the field will have a direct impact on applications like augmented reality and self-driving cars. Conventional methods often use hand-crafted features and compute similarity between patches. However, these approaches may suffer from limitations of the features, especially regarding poorly textured or reflective regions. As deep convolutional neural networks (CNNs) have shown great success in many vision tasks such as image classification, it has triggered the interest to overcome the weakness of traditional methods and improve 3D reconstruction using deep models.

There are already several works that approach two-view stereo using deep models with successful results (*e.g.*, [10,13]). However, rigid two-view stereo is a simpler problem than unstructured multi-view stereo, where camera motion can be arbitrary and varying. Yet, unstructured multi-view stereo is a highly relevant problem that appears in the context of depth estimation from moving monocular cameras. In fact, there are already robust and accurate approaches for real-time tracking of motion (*e.g.*, commercially deployed solutions such as

© Springer Nature Switzerland AG 2019
M. Felsberg et al. (Eds.): SCIA 2019, LNCS 11482, pp. 54–66, 2019.
https://doi.org/10.1007/978-3-030-20205-7_5

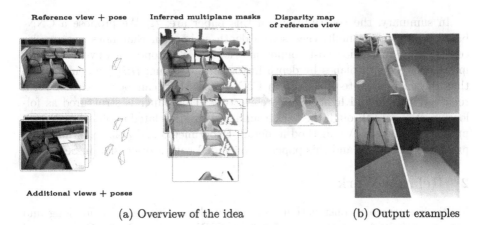

Reference view + pose   **Inferred multiplane masks**   **Disparity map of reference view**

Additional views + poses

(a) Overview of the idea   (b) Output examples

Fig. 1. (a) Overall idea of our method: To estimate a depth map with an arbitrary number of images and known camera poses, we back-project images onto a set of planes to generate the multiplane masks representation via a convolutional neural network. The inferred masks are then passed through a second network to reconstruct the final disparity map. (b) Our method performs well in textureless and varying depth cases.

ARCore by Google and ARKit by Apple) but depth estimation remains a challenge. For example, some smartphones nowadays contain stereo cameras but the small baseline due to the size restriction of the device is a limitation for long-range depth estimation. Thus, multi-view depth estimation is helpful also in such cases since the additional baseline arising from motion can alleviate some of the problems.

Recently, various deep learning based multi-view depth estimation methods have been proposed, e.g. [6,17,21]. They typically discretize the depth space and utilize a plane-sweep approach to compute a matching cost volume from which the disparity map is inferred via CNNs. The benefit is that the cost volume based approach force the network to learn disparity estimation via matching instead of just learning the single-view cues, which is beneficial for generalization. However, these methods have also problems: the depth range must be approximately known in advance and discretization poses an inherent trade-off between depth resolution and computational complexity. In addition, manually specified features and metrics are often used in the construction of the cost volume [17,21] or the used networks are large and complex hampering computation speed [6].

In this paper, we propose our own plane-sweep based approach, which aims at avoiding some of the shortcomings of the previous methods. In particular, our method does not use manually specified features or cost metrics but instead infers a set of masking planes to regularize the learning of features (Fig. 1). In addition, we propose selecting intermediate depth planes by depth histogram matching if the depth range of interest is approximately known *a priori*. In comparison to recent approaches like [6], our architecture is relatively simple, lightweight, and more accurate.

In summary, the contributions of this paper are: *(i)* We propose a CNN-based approach for multi-view stereo depth estimation that does not require constructing an explicit cost-volume metric; *(ii)* We propose a way of selecting intermediate depth-planes by depth histogram matching; *(iii)* We demonstrate that the current state-of-the-art in CNN-based MVS can be matched with a relatively simple and lightweight architecture. This paper is structured as follows. Sect. 2 goes through the background and covers related approaches. Sect. 3 presents our MaskMVS method in detail. Experiments and ablation studies are presented in Sect. 4, and this paper is concluded with a discussion in Sect. 5.

2   Related Work

Multi-view stereo reconstruction has been under active research for long and only recently it has gotten a boost from CNN-based methods. Conventional MVS algorithms typically seek to design photometric error measures and solve an optimization task subject to penalizing visual inconsistency (see review in [3]). The most prominent traditional method is COLMAP [14] which jointly estimates depths and surface normals by leveraging photometric and geometric priors. While conventional MVS methods deliver impressive results in the best case, they fail in poorly textured regions where the photometric consistency is not reliable. They also cannot use visual cues for depth such as shadows or lighting, and typically require many frames as input.

The success of convolutional neural networks in computer vision has spawned a number of methods that leverage the capability of CNNs to learn visual cues. The extreme case is purely monocular depth estimation [1,12], while left–right stereo reconstruction [10,13] relies on the 1D correlation layer along the disparity line. Other approaches use nearby images as the supervision by warping and computing image reconstruction error [4,20,22], but the CNN-based prediction still only utilize single view information.

Unlike left–right two-view stereo, images collected from monocular videos are more unstructured and they also suffer from dynamic moving objects, which makes the task more challenging. DeMoN [16] can learn depth and motion for unconstrained image pairs, but it cannot handle multiple images as input. Current attempts on learned MVS mainly employ plane-sweeping approaches and regard the depth estimation problem as a multi-class classification problem [6,19,21]. In practice, these methods employ classical plane-sweep stereo approaches with a defined cost metric to build a cost volume, and the CNN is used to infer depth from the cost volume and refine the depth map. For example, DeepTAM [21] computes the sum of absolute difference (SAD) of 3×3 patches between warped image pairs. To increase the density of sampled planes, an adaptive narrow band strategy is used. DeepMVS [6] proposed a patch matching network to extract features that can aid in the comparison of patches. To do the feature aggregation, it considers both an intra-volume feature aggregation network and inter-volume aggregation network. Semantic features from pre-trained VGG-19 on ImageNet also aids in intra-volume feature aggregation. The Dense-CRF is used to refine the final depth map. MVDepthNet [17] computes the

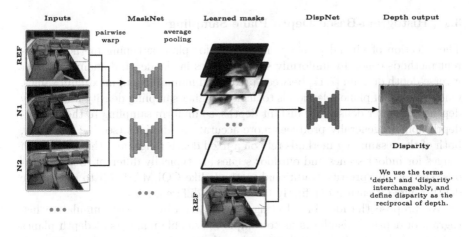

Fig. 2. Overview of our MaskMVS architecture. The MaskNet (left, green) will generate multi-plane mask maps to represent the probability of real surfaces being hit by a ray before each plane. Given the mask-based representation and the reference image, the DispNet (right, red) will learn to predict the disparity map for the reference image. (Color figure online)

absolute difference directly without a supporting window to generate the cost volume, as the pixel-wise cost matching enable the volume to preserve detail information. MVSNet [19] proposes a variance-based cost metric and employ four-scale 3D CNN to obtain smooth cost volume automatically. DPSNet [7] concatenate warped image features firstly and use a series of 3D convolutions to learn the cost volume generation.

Attempts on learned MVS without cost metrics have shown promise in reconstructing 3D objects. [5] propose a CNN to learn multi-patch similarity directly, but it still matches patches explicitly. SurfaceNet [8], and LSM [9] use 3D grid to fuse information. However, due to the volumetric structure, SurfaceNet and LSM are limited to small-scale reconstructions (see discussion in [19]).

3 Methods

The overall architecture of MaskMVS is shown in Fig. 2. The estimation scheme consists of two parts, MaskNet and DispNet. Given (an arbitrary number of) image pairs and known camera poses, we back-project images onto virtual planes to construct the warped volume to feed the MaskNet. The MaskNet will generate multi-plane mask maps to represent the probability of a surface being hit by each ray before each plane. Given the mask-based representation and the reference image, the DispNet learns to predict the disparity map for the reference image. Our methods will be introduced as follows. Sect. 3.1 presents our novel idea of depth plane sampling. Sects. 3.2 and 3.3 explain the details of MaskNet and DispNet, respectively.

3.1   Histogram-Based Depth Plane Sampling

The selection of virtual planes is important for plane-sweeping methods. Current methods generally uniformly sample planes in the depth domain [19,21] or inverse-depth domain [7,17] between predefined minimum and maximum values. One principle of plane selection is to achieve higher sampling density for close by depths and lower density for distant depths, so uniform sampling in the inverse-depth domain generally produces more accurate predictions (see [7]). However, both of these sampling methods rely on a fixed depth range, and the ideal depth ranges for indoor scenes and outdoor scenes are typically different. Some methods, such as [6], pre-run traditional methods like COLMAP [14] to obtain the depth range for each input firstly to deal with different scenes.

We propose the idea of selecting planes according to the cumulative histogram of depth. This allows us to sample reasonable numbers of depth planes in both nearby and far away depths when the training set is a mixed data set. There will be more pixels covering areas closer to the camera in general, so the histogram of depth distribution is naturally in accordance with the selection principle mentioned above. We define the depth density and cumulative depth density functions as

$$p(d_i) = \frac{n_i}{N} \quad \text{and} \quad P(d_i) = \sum_{j=1}^{i} p(d_i), \tag{1}$$

where n_i is the frequency of the depth value d_i, and N is the total number of pixels in the training data set. These discrete density functions, $p : [0, d_{\max}] \rightarrow [0, 1]$ and $P : [0, d_{\max}] \rightarrow [0, 1]$, can be seen as the normalized histogram and normalized cumulative histograms of the depths (we use a binning of 200 points in the experiments). Based on the cumulative density function, we can choose a set of depths covering the entire range by considering the inverse cumulative density function $P^{-1} : [0, 1] \rightarrow [0, d_{\max}]$. By choosing to cover the quantiles $\theta_1, \theta_2, \ldots, \theta_D$ of P uniformly, we find a set of depths $\{d_i\}_{i=1}^{D}$ such that $d_i = P^{-1}(\theta_i)$, where D is the number of planes.

3.2   MaskNet: Mask-Based Multiplane Representation

Similar to traditional plane-sweep stereo, we firstly construct a warped volume from each image pair by warping the neighbour image via the fronto-parallel planes at fixed depths to the reference frame using the planar homography:

$$\mathbf{H} = \mathbf{K}\left(\mathbf{R} + \mathbf{t}\left(0\ 0\ \tfrac{1}{d_i}\right)\right)\mathbf{K}^{-1}, \tag{2}$$

where $\mathbf{K}$ is the known intrinsics matrix and the relative pose $(\mathbf{R}, \mathbf{t})$ is given in terms of a rotation matrix and translation vector with respect to the neighbour frame. d_i denotes the depth value of the ith virtual plane. The input of the MaskNet has size $3(1 + D) \times H \times W$ consisting of the reference image and concatenated warped neighbour images from D planes ($D+1$ RGB images with height H and width W). The output of the MaskNet is a set of mask maps of size $D \times H \times W$.

Traditional plane-sweep based methods need to design a cost metric based on photo-consistency of warped images to select an optimal depth plane for each pixel. In that case, the predicted depth maps will be noisy and the accuracy will be limited by the density of the chosen planes. Instead of using a distance metric, we propose a novel mask-based multiplane representation to roughly encode the near–far relationship. In our method, the intuition is that given a reference image and warped neighbour image on two successive planes, if the relative position of a warped pixel flips, it tells that the surface will be hit by the ray between the two planes. To enable the network to learn this, we assign a supervised binary classification task to the MaskNet, where the ground truth for masks can be obtained from ground truth depth maps directly. The MaskNet will predict whether the ray will hit a surface in front of the plane (including on the plane) or behind the plane for each pixel.

For this purpose, the MaskNet consists of an encoder–decoder architecture that shares a similar architecture with [17]. The encoder includes five convolutional layers, and convolutional filter sizes decrease towards deeper layers: 7×7 for the first layer, 5×5 for the second layer, and 3×3 for the following three layers. There are four skip connections between the encoder and the decoder, and mask maps are predicted in four scales. All layers are followed by batch normalization and ReLU except for the mask prediction layers that are followed by a sigmoid function. Each pixel on each plane has a value in range $[0, 1]$, representing the predicted probability that the true surface is located in front of the sampled plane. To support arbitrary length of sequence, we deal with neighbour images separately and then use average pooling for predicted masks with the finest resolution to fuse information from different neighbours. We compute the pixel-wise cross-entropy between the averaged mask map and the ground truth mask map as loss function to train the MaskNet.

3.3 DispNet: Continuous-Disparity Prediction

To regress continuous depth values, given prediction results from MaskNet and the reference image, we concatenate them into an input of size $(3 + D) \times H \times W$ to feed the DispNet. The encoder–decoder architecture of our DispNet is similar to the DispNet in [13]. There are six convolutional layers for the encoder (3×3 filters except for the first two layers, which have a 7×7 filter and a 5×5 filter, respectively) to extract features, and the decoder will gradually upsample the feature maps, considering also features from the encoder with six skip connections. All convolutional layers are followed by batch normalization and LeakyReLU, and all deconvolution layers are followed by LeakyReLU. Unlike [17,22] that use scale and sigmoid functions to constrain the range of the output, our inverse depth prediction layer consists of a convolutional layer and a ReLU layer to only ensure that predicted inverse depth maps have values larger than zero for all pixels. The DispNet will generate depth maps in six resolutions and

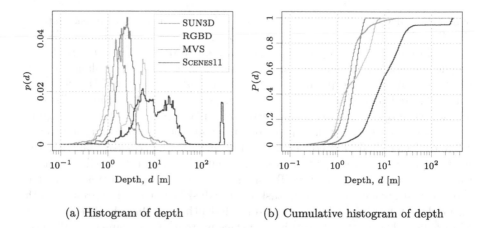

(a) Histogram of depth   (b) Cumulative histogram of depth

Fig. 3. Depth distributions (log-scale) for the four data sets used in training and evaluation. The typical depths in the data are highly dependent on the type of environments covered (*e.g.*, SUN3D covering mostly indoor scenes and SCENES11 having high variability in the type of scenes covered.)

the finest resolution is the same as in the reference image. During training, the loss function is defined as the sum of the average L1 loss at different resolutions:

$$L = \sum_{s=0}^{6} w_s \frac{1}{n_s} \sum_i |\hat{d}_{s,i} - d_{s,i}|, \qquad (3)$$

where $\hat{d}_{s,i}$ is the estimated inverse depth at scale s and $d_{s,i}$ is the corresponding ground truth inverse depth. n_s is the number of valid pixels and w_s is the loss weight for scale s. We assign the highest weight for the loss with the finest resolution as 0.5 and others 0.1.

4   Experiments

Similar to DeepMVS [6], we train our networks with the same data sets as used in DeMoN [16]. The training data set includes short sequences from real-world data sets SUN3D [18], RGBD [15], MVS (includes CITYWALL and ACHTECK-TURM [2]), and a synthesized data set SCENES11 [16]. SUN3D consists of a variety of indoors scenes, RGBD provides scenes of an office and an industrial hall. MVS data sets include both indoor and outdoor scenes, and the ground truth depth maps of outdoor scenes are often sparse. SCENES11 provides perfect ground truth but lack realism. Combined, there are 92,558 training samples and each training sample consists of a sequence of three frames, the ground truth depth map for the reference frame, and provided ground truth camera poses. The resolution of the input images is 320 × 240.

Our training procedure consists of two stages as we pre-train the MaskNet first and then employed the pre-trained parameters of MaskNet to predict masks to train the DispNet. For both networks we use the Adam solver [11] with $\beta_1 = 0.9$ and $\beta_2 = 0.999$. The learning rate for MaskNet and DispNet is $2 \cdot 10^{-4}$ and 10^{-4}, respectively. Our framework is trained using only $D = 16$ sampled depth planes as sparse sampling can present the effect of plane selection more clearly and provide speed-up. The whole framework is implemented on PyTorch for 500k iterations with a mini-batch size of four.

Error Metrics. In our evaluations, we use three common measures: (i) L1-rel, (ii) L1-inv, and (iii) sc-inv (see, e.g., [1]). The two L1 metrics are the mean absolute relative difference and mean absolute difference in inverse depth, respectively. They are given in terms of

$$\text{L1-rel} = \frac{1}{n} \sum_i \frac{|d_i - \hat{d}_i|}{\hat{d}_i} \quad \text{and} \quad \text{L1-inv} = \frac{1}{n} \sum_i \left| \frac{1}{d_i} - \frac{1}{\hat{d}_i} \right|, \quad (4)$$

where d_i [meters] is the predicted depth value, $\hat{d}_i$ [meters] is the ground truth value, n is the number of pixels for which the depth is available. The third, scale-invariant metric, is given as:

$$\text{sc-inv} = \sqrt{\frac{1}{n} \sum_i z_i^2 - \frac{1}{n^2} \left(\sum_i z_i \right)^2} \quad (5)$$

where $z_i = \log d_i - \log \hat{d}_i$. The L1-rel metric normalizes the error, L1-inv metric gives more importance to close depth values and sc-inv is a scale-invariant metric.

4.1 Ablation Study: The Effect of Plane Selection

As the training set is a mixed data set that consists of both indoor scenes, outdoor scenes, and synthesized scenes, the depth ranges of image samples vary with type of data set. Figure 3 shows the distribution of depth for different sets separately. To examine the effects of plane selections, we conducted an ablation study for our method. We compare two options for plane selection: uniform sampling in the inverse-depth space and uniform sampling in the distribution space. Namely, to uniformly sample $D = 16$ planes in the inverse-depth space from $d_{\min} = 0.5$ m to $d_{\max} = 50$ m, the ith depth plane is given by:

$$\frac{1}{d_i} = \left(\frac{1}{d_{\min}} - \frac{1}{d_{\max}} \right) \frac{i}{D-1} + \frac{1}{d_{\max}}. \quad (6)$$

To uniformly sample planes in the distribution space of the whole data set, we set $\theta_{\min} = 0.1$ and $\theta_{\max} = 1$, then the ith depth plane is given by:

$$\theta_i = \theta_{\min} + (\theta_{\max} - \theta_{\min}) \frac{i}{D}, \quad \text{such that} \quad d_i = P^{-1}(\theta_i), \quad (7)$$

where $i \in \{0, 1, ..., D-1\}$. Figure 4a shows the two sampling schemes. The curve is the cumulative histogram of depth of the whole mixed data set and the

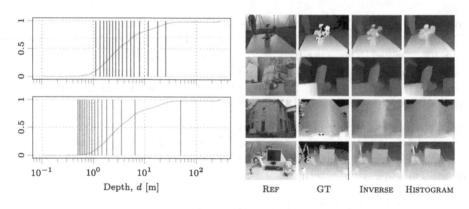

(a) Two ways of depth plane sampling   (b) Comparison of disparity maps

Fig. 4. Setup and results for the ablation study. In (a), the upper figure shows the chosen depth plane depths for the histogram-based sampling and the bottom shows the depths for inverse depth based sampling. In (b), we show qualitative comparison between the two depth plane selection methods used in combination with our MaskMVS.

vertical lines present sampled depths. The higher slope of the curve corresponds to denser distribution of objects. It shows that using histogram-based sampling successfully gives planes within the range with higher slope, and the density is also higher in the closer areas than distant areas.

The evaluation results in Table 1 shows that selecting histogram-based planes perform much better in outdoor and synthesized scenes as it has more planes put in for distant depths. The performance of indoor scenes remains comparable with using inverse-depth sampled planes as it still samples densely-enough in close by depths. Figure 4b shows comparison of the disparity maps from the two sampling approaches. Generally, using histogram-based sampling can provide good quality of prediction in both small-scale and large-scale depth scenes even with sparse depth planes. The last row in the figure shows that our methods with both sampling strategies give good predictions, but using histogram-based sampling failed to capture small objects like cans on the table in the close areas. It is mainly because our sampled planes started from the value farther than 1 m, while the office scenes in RGBD contain many objects within 1 m (see the first bump of RGBD in Fig. 3a); conversely, inverse-space sampled planes are very dense within the range, so its prediction captures these details well.

4.2   Comparisons

We provide both qualitative and quantitative comparisons to the state-of-the-art by evaluating using unstructured view pairs from the test sets in MVS, SUN3D, RGBD, and SCENES11. We compare our methods with two CNN-based multi-view stereo methods (DeepMVS [6] and MVDepthNet [17]) and one traditional

Table 1. Comparison results between MVDepthNet, DeepMVS, COLMAP, and our method. We outperform other methods in most of the data sets and error metrics (smaller better).

	MVDepth-16	DeepMVS	COLMAP	Ours (hist)	Ours (inv.)
scenes11					
L1-rel	0.2352	0.3755	0.7205	**0.1475**	0.2144
L1-inv	0.0292	0.0495	0.0936	**0.0231**	0.0308
sc-inv	0.3207	0.5810	0.7814	**0.2483**	0.2985
MVS					
L1-rel	0.3835	0.8217	0.9921	**0.2669**	0.4030
L1-inv	0.1384	**0.1065**	0.1812	0.1377	0.1600
sc-inv	0.3427	0.5325	0.6892	**0.3001**	0.3100
sun3d					
L1-rel	0.1840	0.8604	1.8499	0.1797	**0.1611**
L1-inv	0.0865	0.1317	0.4511	**0.0818**	0.0808
sc-inv	0.2013	0.4992	1.1219	0.1916	**0.1769**
RGBD					
L1-rel	0.1628	0.5066	2.2992	0.1748	**0.1572**
L1-inv	**0.0789**	0.1717	0.5593	0.0846	0.0802
sc-inv	0.2360	0.5238	1.2970	0.2304	**0.2062**

multiview stereo method (COLMAP [14]). The original MVDepthNet is trained with 64 planes and a larger data set (covering also the standard test samples in the sets). In order to make a fair comparison, we retrained the MVDepthNet with our training data set and 16 planes. The results are reported in Table 1. Our predictions have significantly lower errors in SCENES11 and MVS, and comparable performance in SUN3D and RGBD. The improvement of the outdoor scenes and synthesized scenes can be explained by the consideration of far depth planes. As mentioned in Sect. 4.1, almost half of the scenes of RGBD include objects closer than 1 m that is below our histogram-based sampling range, so the performance is slightly worse. We also evaluated the inference time for CNN-based models on a desktop workstation (NVIDIA GTX 1080 Ti, i7-7820X CPU and 63 GB memory; average over 100 predictions): DeepMVS 5.81 s, MVDepth-16 0.063 s, ours 0.089 s. The running time of our model is comparable to MVdepth-16 but our accuracy is better. Both models are significantly faster than DeepMVS.

Figure 5 shows qualitative comparisons between MVDepthNet, DeepMVS, COLMAP, and our MaskMVS approach. It should be noted that our method is the only method that can capture the small objects in the top left of the third row and the bottom left of the last row. Moreover, our method provide more accurate prediction for close areas (see the brightest parts of ground truths) in the first row and the fourth row.

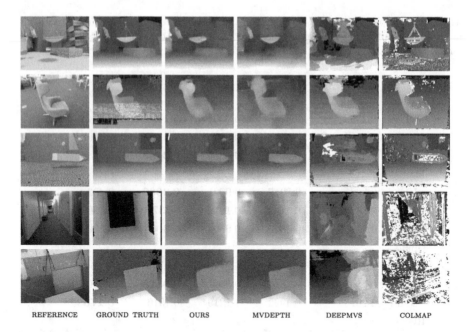

REFERENCE   GROUND TRUTH   OURS   MVDEPTH   DEEPMVS   COLMAP

Fig. 5. Qualitative comparisons between different algorithms on the MVS, SCENES11, SUN3D, and RGBD test sets. The traditional COLMAP method fails in low-texture environments. Our methods successfully captures small objects in close areas and provides better shape estimates for objects in far areas at the same time. Missing values in ground truth are shown in black.

5   Discussion and Conclusions

We have proposed a novel CNN-based architecture for multi-view stereo depth estimation that is inspired by traditional plane-sweep algorithms without the need of constructing an explicit cost-volume metric. Instead, we designed a binary classification task for our MaskNet and used the mask-based multiplane representations to aggregate information from multiple views and exploit geometric relationships. Moreover, we discussed the effect of depth selection and proposed a novel way of sampling depth planes based on histogram matching. Our ablation study showed that uniformly sampling in the distribution domain can deal with both small depths such as indoor scenes and large depths such as in outdoor scenes, even with sparsely sampled planes. As the running time will drop when reducing the number of planes, our proposed sampling method can be beneficial for real-time systems that have restrictions on computation time and memory. Moreover, compared to traditional multi-view stereo methods, our approach can handle low-texture inputs and does not need iterative refinement; compared to other CNN-based methods that also employ a plane-sweep scheme, our method do not need to compute any distance metrics, which makes our method time-efficient.

As ideal plane selection can lead to better prediction, one direction to improve our architecture might be adjusting depth planes according to inputs automatically. It should be noted that using predicted mask maps from our MaskNet, the depth distribution can be roughly estimated. Then it is possible to obtain uniform samples in distribution domain by just 1D linear interpolation. This might offer the possibility for varying sampled depth planes with different scenes in the future. Codes are available at https://github.com/AaltoVision/MaskMVS.

Acknowledgements. We acknowledge computing resources by Aalto Science-IT and CSC, and funding from the Academy of Finland (308640 and 277685).

References

1. Eigen, D., Puhrsch, C., Fergus, R.: Depth map prediction from a single image using a multi-scale deep network. In: NIPS (2014)
2. Fuhrmann, S., Langguth, F., Goesele, M.: MVE - a multi-view reconstruction environment. In: GCH (2014)
3. Furukawa, Y., Hernández, C.: Multi-view stereo: a tutorial. Found. Trends® Comput. Graph. Vis. **9**(1–2), 1–148 (2015)
4. Godard, C., Mac Aodha, O., Brostow, G.J.: Unsupervised monocular depth estimation with left-right consistency. In: CVPR (2017)
5. Hartmann, W., Galliani, S., Havlena, M., Van Gool, L., Schindler, K.: Learned multi-patch similarity. In: ICCV, pp. 1595–1603 (2017)
6. Huang, P.H., Matzen, K., Kopf, J., Ahuja, N., Huang, J.B.: DeepMVS: learning multi-view stereopsis. In: CVPR (2018)
7. Im, S., Jeon, H.G., Lin, S., Kweon, I.S.: DPSNet: end-to-end deep plane sweep stereo. In: ICLR (2019)
8. Ji, M., Gall, J., Zheng, H., Liu, Y., Fang, L.: SurfaceNet: an end-to-end 3D neural network for multiview stereopsis. In: ICCV (2017)
9. Kar, A., Häne, C., Malik, J.: Learning a multi-view stereo machine. In: NIPS (2017)
10. Kendall, A., et al.: End-to-end learning of geometry and context for deep stereo regression. In: CVPR (2017)
11. Kingma, D.P., Ba, J.: Adam: a method for stochastic optimization. arXiv preprint arXiv:1412.6980 (2014)
12. Liu, F., Shen, C., Lin, G., Reid, I.D.: Learning depth from single monocular images using deep convolutional neural fields. IEEE Trans. Pattern Anal. Mach. Intell. **38**(10), 2024–2039 (2016)
13. Mayer, N., et al.: A large dataset to train convolutional networks for disparity, optical flow, and scene flow estimation. In: CVPR (2016)
14. Schönberger, J.L., Zheng, E., Frahm, J.-M., Pollefeys, M.: Pixelwise view selection for unstructured multi-view stereo. In: Leibe, B., Matas, J., Sebe, N., Welling, M. (eds.) ECCV 2016. LNCS, vol. 9907, pp. 501–518. Springer, Cham (2016). https://doi.org/10.1007/978-3-319-46487-9_31
15. Sturm, J., Engelhard, N., Endres, F., Burgard, W., Cremers, D.: A benchmark for the evaluation of RGB-D SLAM systems. In: IROS (2012)
16. Ummenhofer, B., et al.: DeMoN: depth and motion network for learning monocular stereo. In: CVPR (2017)
17. Wang, K., Shen, S.: MVDepthNet: real-time multiview depth estimation neural network. In: International Conference on 3D Vision (3DV) (2018)

18. Xiao, J., Owens, A., Torralba, A.: SUN3D: a database of big spaces reconstructed using SFM and object labels. In: ICCV (2013)
19. Yao, Y., Luo, Z., Li, S., Fang, T., Quan, L.: MVSNet: depth inference for unstructured multi-view stereo. In: ECCV (2018)
20. Yin, Z., Shi, J.: GeoNet: unsupervised learning of dense depth, optical flow and camera pose. In: CVPR (2018)
21. Zhou, H., Ummenhofer, B., Brox, T.: DeepTAM: deep tracking and mapping. In: ECCV (2018)
22. Zhou, T., Brown, M., Snavely, N., Lowe, D.G.: Unsupervised learning of depth and ego-motion from video. In: CVPR (2017)

Fine-Grained Wood Species Identification Using Convolutional Neural Networks

Dmitrii Shustrov[1], Tuomas Eerola[1(✉)] (ID), Lasse Lensu[1] (ID),
Heikki Kälviäinen[1] (ID), and Heikki Haario[2] (ID)

[1] School of Engineering Science, Department of Computational
and Process Engineering, Machine Vision and Pattern Recognition Laboratory,
Lappeenranta-Lahti University of Technology LUT, P.O.Box 20,
53851 Lappeenranta, Finland
{dmitrii.shustrov,tuomas.eerola,lasse.lensu,heikki.kalviainen}@lut.fi
[2] School of Engineering Science, Department of Computational
and Process Engineering, Inverse Problems Research Group, Lappeenranta-Lahti
University of Technology LUT, P.O.Box 20, 53851 Lappeenranta, Finland
heikki.haario@lut.fi

Abstract. This paper considers the wood species identification from images of boards. The identification using only visual features of the surface is a challenging task even for an expert. The task becomes especially difficult when the wood species are from the same family. We propose a CNN based framework for the fine-grained classification of wood species. The framework includes a patch extraction procedure where board images are divided into image patches. Each patch is separately classified using the CNN resulting in multiple classification results per board. Finally, the patch classification results for a single board are combined. We evaluate various CNN architectures using the challenging data, consisting of species from the *Pinaceae* family. In addition, we propose three alternative decision rules for combining the patch classification results. By selecting a suitable amount of image patches, the proposed framework was able to achieve over 99% identification accuracy and real-time performance.

Keywords: Wood species identification ·
Convolutional neural networks · Fine-grained classification ·
Visual inspection · Machine vision application

1 Introduction

In a sawmill, it is important to be able to control that tree species do not get mixed in the sawing and quality grading process. This is due to the fact that proper and accurate wood processing, for example, drying or storage, often directly depends on the wood species. More importantly, supplying boards of incorrect wood species to customers results in reclamations and financial loss

© Springer Nature Switzerland AG 2019
M. Felsberg et al. (Eds.): SCIA 2019, LNCS 11482, pp. 67–77, 2019.
https://doi.org/10.1007/978-3-030-20205-7_6

for the sawmill. In the modern highly automated sawmills with large production capacities, manual verification of every board is impossible. This calls for automated solutions for the tree species identification of wooden boards.

A typical sawmill specializes in a certain type of timber, for example, conifers. Because of this, the sawmill typically processes only species from the same wood family with very similar appearance and the identification method should be able to perform the fine-grained classification between them. Figure 1 shows example board images of three species from the *Pinaceae* family: Pine (*Pinus*), Spruce (*Picea*), and Fir (*Albies*). It can be seen that the intra-species variation, for example, in color is larger than between the species, and designing image features that distinguish the species from each other is very challenging. Convolutional neural networks (CNNs), however, are able to learn the features from data making them an attractive approach for the task.

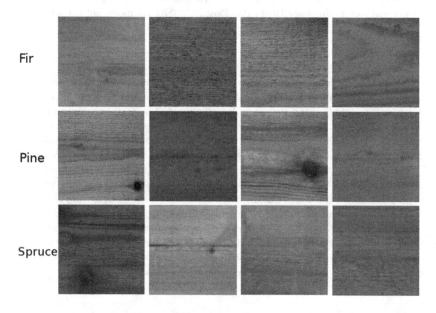

Fig. 1. Example images of the board surface images from the species considered in this study. Each row contains four image patches from one species.

In this paper, a framework for fine-grained classification between wood species is proposed. The framework starts with a patch extraction step where a high resolution image of a wooden board is divided into multiple image patches. Each image patch is fed into CNN which classifies the patch resulting in multiple classification results for each board. Finally, the classification results are combined using a selected decision rule to obtain the final identification result for the whole board. Extensive experiments are performed to select the suitable CNN architecture and the decision rule for the board identification.

2   Related Work

With the development of visual inspection systems in the sawmill industry, automated systems have been actively used to identify species and defects in wooden material. For example, Tou et al. [10,12] proposed a recognition and classification method for microscopic images. Gray-level co-occurrence matrix (GLCM) based features were used to train a multi-layer perceptron (MLP). As a result, the obtained accuracy for the classification of five wood species ranged from 60 to 72%. In [11], multiple features extraction methods were compared for the task and the best results were obtained using Gabor filter-based covariance matrix features. For the classification, k-NN was used. Khalid et al. [5] presented a classification system capable for recognizing 20 different species of wood. The system uses images of wood samples that were prepared by boiling and cutting them into thin sections using a microtome. For the feature extraction, GLCM was used and the classification was performed using MLP. The obtained recognition accuracy was 95%. Hafemann et al. [2] utilized a shallow CNN to solve wood species identification task. Using the database from [7], the recognition accuracy was 95% with a dataset consisting of macroscopic images of 41 wood species. Slightly higher accuracy was obtained for microscopic images.

The existing methods contain various drawbacks. The methods proposed in [10–12] do not provide accuracy high enough for the industrial environment. Also, the approach is based on microscopic images, so the image acquisition step may need sample preparation and calibration actions. The main drawback of the approach in [5] is the complexity and high cost of preparing the wood samples which makes this work inapplicable for practical applications. The method proposed in [2] obtained rather high accuracy on both macroscopic and microscopic images of the wood. However, it should be noted that the databases used for the experiment contained species that are clearly visually different from each other and the variance inside individual species was low.

3   Proposed Method

The scheme of the proposed method is illustrated in Fig. 2. The images are acquired from the both faces of the board. To cover the whole board with reasonable accuracy, multiple slightly overlapping images are captured. Multiple image patches are extracted from each image. A single image patch represents a square image extracted from the board excluding the background. The subsequent identification of individual image patches is done using a CNN-based classifier. Finally, a decision rule is used to combine the image patch classification results into the final identification of the wood species of the whole board.

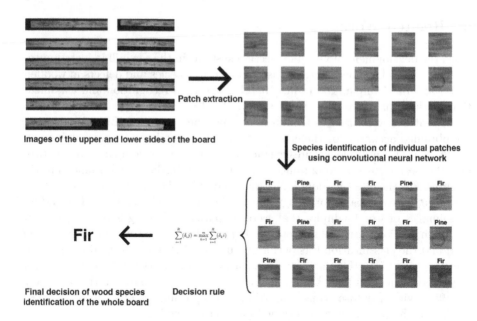

Fig. 2. Proposed method for wood species identification.

3.1 Image Patches Extraction

To extract image patches the board should be separated from the background. To do this, the image is first binarized using thresholding to separate bright board from the dark background. The largest connected component is assumed to correspond to the board. The rotation of the board is computed and compensated by rotating the image, and a bounding box is drawn around the connected component. Finally, overlapping image patches are extracted from the bounding box.

3.2 Decision Rule

The image patches are classified using CNN producing multiple identification results for each board. To be more specific, each patch classifier produces a class probability to each class that need to be combined to obtain the final species identification. For this purpose we utilize decisions rules. The following decision rules are considered: (1) Majority vote rule, (2) Mean probability rule, and (3) Max rule.

Let p_{ij} be the class probability for the wood species i obtained from the jth batch from a board Z. Then *Majority vote rule* is defined as follow. Assign Z to class label (species) $\hat{C}$ as

$$\hat{C} = \arg \max_{i=1}^{K} \sum_{j=1}^{N} c_{ij}, \tag{1}$$

where

$$c_{ij} = \begin{cases} 1 & p_{ij} = \max p_{ij} \\ 0 & otherwise \end{cases},$$ (2)

K is the number of species, and N is the number of image patches. In practice, each patch has one vote and the final classification is made based on the number of votes for each species.

Mean probability rule is defined as follows. Assign Z to class label $\hat{C}$ as

$$\hat{C} = \arg\max_{i=1}^{K} \frac{1}{N} \sum_{j=1}^{N} p_{ij}.$$ (3)

Finally, *Max rule* is defined as follows. Assign Z to class label $\hat{C}$ as

$$\hat{C} = \arg\max_{i=1}^{K}(\max_{j=1}^{N} p_{ij}).$$ (4)

4   Experiments and Results

4.1   Data

The data consist of board images obtained during the sawmill process. The data were collected from several sawmills using the existing camera-based board sorting systems. Imaging systems including illumination varied between sawmills resulting a challenging and realistic dataset. Each board was imaged with multiple cameras from both faces to capture the full surface of the board. Depending on the length of the board, the data contains 3 to 5 images with resolution varying from 2480×280 to 2480×480 per one face of a board. Figure 3 shows an example image of a board.

Fig. 3. Example of a board image.

The image patches were extracted from each image. Figure 4 shows examples of extracted image patches. It should be noted that due to, for example, defects in boards and varying types of the background, some patches were not extracted accurately (see Fig. 5). These patches were included into the dataset to evaluate the robustness of the proposed method.

Table 1 shows the numbers of boards and extracted image patches for each wood species. The total number of all extracted image patches from all boards

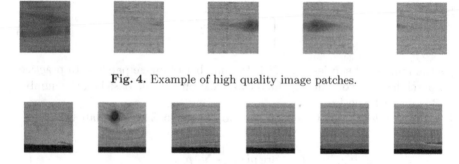

Fig. 4. Example of high quality image patches.

Fig. 5. Example of inaccurately extracted image patches.

Table 1. Number of the boards and extracted image patches for each wood species.

Wood species	Number of boards	Number of image patches
Fir	455	104353
Pine	256	58713
Spruce	404	92656
Total	1115	255724

Table 2. Number of boards for the training, validation, and test sets.

Wood species	Training set	Validation set	Test set
Fir	318	65	72
Pine	178	35	43
Spruce	282	59	62
Total	778	159	177

was 255724 where 242938 patches were extracted accurately. On the average, approximately 250 image patches were extracted from each board. The boards were randomly splitted into the training, validation, and testing sets, i.e., all patches from one board were allocated to one of the three sets. Table 2 shows the number of boards in each sets.

4.2   Experimental Arrangements

The following CNN architectures were selected for the experiments: AlexNet [6], VGG-16 [8], GoogLeNet [9], and ResNet-50 [3]. Transfer learning with ImageNet pretrained models were used for the following convolutional neural networks: VGG-16, GoogLeNet, and ResNet-50. AlexNet was trained from the scratch. The dropout rate was 0.5 for the CNN regularization to avoid the overfitting.

All experiments were performed using the Caffe deep learning framework [4] which utilizes the CUDA 9.0 deep learning library with CUDNN 7.1 [1]. All experiments were performed on the computer with the following computational resources: two NVIDIA GeForce GTX TITAN Black GPU, Intel Xeon CPU E5-2680, and 128 gygabytes of random access memory.

4.3 Results

The following performance measures were used: the classification accuracy (ACC) defined as the percentage of the correctly classified samples, and the F-measure defined as

$$F = \frac{2PPV \cdot TPR}{PPV + TPR} \qquad (5)$$

where PPV is the positive predictive value and TPR is the true positive rate.

Table 3 shows the comparison between the CNN architectures for the task of the species identification from individual patches. Figure 6 shows the corresponding confusion matrices. As it can be seen, the identification performance varies between the architectures. For VGG-16 there is a lot of misclassifications between pine and spruce when the true label is pine. Also fir and spruce are mixed when the true label is fir. Within spruce the wood species is predicted more accurately. ResNet-50 shows the opposite. The misclassifications occurred mainly in the spruce class confusing spruce with pine. AlexNet and GoogleNet show more accurate predictions without strong confusion in any combination of the classes. The shallower architectures appear to outperform the very deep ones. One reason for this could be the fact that high-level knowledge is not needed for the species identification and the method does not have to be invariant, for example, to view-point. Therefore, the task favors the shallower networks with less down-sampling operations that do not destroy the gradient information essential for the identification.

Table 3. Performance comparison of the different architectures in case of the wood species identification based on single patches.

Architecture	ACC	F-measure
AlexNet	0.915	0.915
VGG-16	0.687	0.681
GoogLeNet	0.947	0.940
ResNet-50	0.715	0.685

Table 4 compares the performance of the wood species identification for the whole boards using the selected decision rules. Figure 7 represents the confusion matrices for the board identification when the best decision rule is used for each CNN architecture.

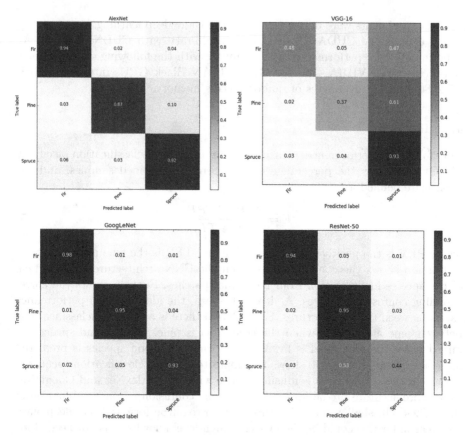

Fig. 6. Confusion matrices of the classification models in case of the wood species identification based on single patches.

Table 4. Identification accuracies for the different architectures and decision rules in case of board species identification. The rows in bold are the architectures with the best performance.

Architecture	Majority vote	Mean probability	Max rule
AlexNet	**0.989**	**0.989**	**0.989**
VGG-16	0.721	0.721	0.721
GoogLeNet	**0.994**	**0.994**	**0.994**
ResNet-50	0.783	0.764	0.764

When all the patches (on the average 250) extracted from the board are used for the identification the computation time is too long for the industrial environment even with architectures with smaller number of parameters. To address this issue, an additional experiment was carried out to determine how

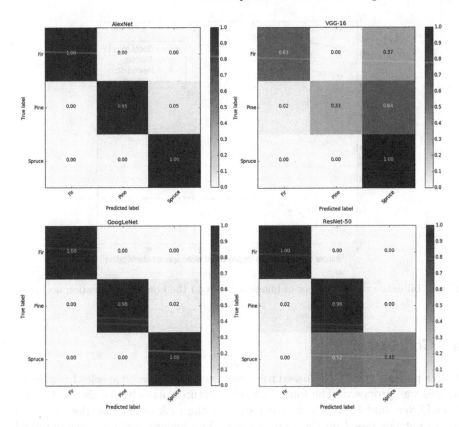

Fig. 7. Confusion matrices of the classification models in case of board identification.

Table 5. The accuracy and the inference time when only 25 image patches are used per board.

Architecture	ACC	τ_B, seconds
AlexNet	0.986	0.26
VGG-16	0.721	0.72
GoogLeNet	0.994	0.47
ResNet-50	0.780	0.95

the number of patches affects the accuracy of the identification. Figure 8 shows the mean accuracy with respect to the number of image patches. For each number of patches the experiment was repeated 100 times and the means of the obtained accuracies were computed. As it can be seen, the accuracy close to the maximum can be obtained with only 25 image patches per board. Table 5 represents the accuracies and the inference times τ_B of the board identification when 25 image patches per board are used.

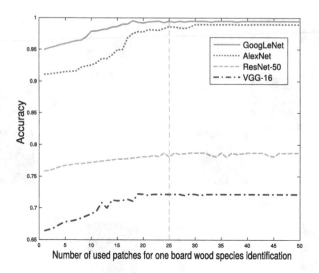

Fig. 8. Influence of the number of image patches on the board identification accuracy.

5 Conclusion

In this paper a novel CNN-based framework to identify wood species from board images was proposed. The four CNN architectures, namely, AlexNet, VGG-16, GoogLeNet, and ResNet were compared on the task of classification of board image patches based on the wood species. The highest accuracy was obtained with the GoogLeNet architecture that correctly classified 94.7% of the patches. Furthermore, three decision rules were proposed to be used to make the final species identification for the board based on multiple patch classification results. No significant difference on performance were found between the proposed decision rules. Using any of the rules and GoogLeNet, close to perfect accuracy of 99.4% was obtained. Finally, the effect of the number of image patches used for the identification was studied and it was shown that over 99% identification accuracy can be achieved by using only 25 patches per board, providing inference time of 0.47 s. These results indicate that it seems to be possible to sort the boards in real-time in the sawmill environment.

Acknowledgements. The research was carried out in the DigiSaw project (No. 2894/31/2017) funded by Business Finland. The authors would like to thank FinScan Oy for providing the data for the experiments.

References

1. Chetlur, S., et al.: cuDNN: efficient primitives for deep learning. arXiv preprint arXiv:1410.0759 (2014)
2. Hafemann, L.G., Oliveira, L.S., Cavalin, P.: Forest species recognition using deep convolutional neural networks. In: Proceedings of the 22nd International Conference on Pattern Recognition (ICPR), pp. 1103–1107 (2014)
3. He, K., Zhang, X., Ren, S., Sun, J.: Deep residual learning for image recognition. In: Proceedings of the IEEE Conference on Computer Vision and Pattern Recognition (CVPR), pp. 770–778 (2016)
4. Jia, Y., el al.: Caffe: convolutional architecture for fast feature embedding. In: Proceedings of the 22nd ACM International Conference on Multimedia, pp. 675–678 (2014)
5. Khalid, M., Lee, E.L.Y., Yusof, R., Nadaraj, M.: Design of an intelligent wood species recognition system. Int. J. Simul. Syst. Sci. Technol. **9**(3), 9–19 (2008)
6. Krizhevsky, A., Sutskever, I., Hinton, G.E.: ImageNet classification with deep convolutional neural networks. In: Advances in Neural Information Processing Systems, pp. 1097–1105 (2012)
7. Martins, J., Oliveira, L.S., Nisgoski, S., Sabourin, R.: A database for automatic classification of forest species. Mach. Vis. Appl. **24**(3), 567–578 (2013)
8. Simonyan, K., Zisserman, A.: Very deep convolutional networks for large-scale image recognition. arXiv preprint arXiv:1409.1556 (2014)
9. Szegedy, C., et al.: Going deeper with convolutions. In: Proceedings of the IEEE Conference on Computer Vision and Pattern Recognition (CVPR) (2015)
10. Tou, J.Y., Tay, Y.H., Lau, P.Y.: One-dimensional grey-level co-occurrence matrices for texture classification. In: Proceedings of International Symposium on Information Technology (2008)
11. Tou, J.Y., Tay, Y.H., Lau, P.Y.: A comparative study for texture classification techniques on wood species recognition problem. In: Proceedings of the Fifth International Conference on Natural Computation (2009)
12. Tou, J.Y., Lau, P.Y., Tay, Y.H.: Computer vision-based wood recognition system. In: Proceedings of International Workshop on Advanced Image Technology (2007)

Spectral-Spatial Hyperspectral Image Classification Using Cascaded Convolutional Neural Networks

Gurbandurdy Dovletov[(✉)] [iD], Tobias Hegemann, and Josef Pauli

Intelligent Systems, Faculty of Engineering, University of Duisburg-Essen,
Duisburg, Germany
gurbandurdy.dovletov@uni-due.de

Abstract. In this paper, we present a framework for classifying hyperspectral images using convolutional neural networks. In order to compare the importance of spectral and spatial information as well as the effect of dimension reduction prior to classification, we propose different architectures utilizing 2D and 3D convolutions. We introduce a novel coarse-to-fine two-stage fusion architecture employing a cascade of consecutive neural networks to deal with the problem of separating classes which are very similar to each other. Using this approach, we can boost the classification accuracies significantly with little additional effort. The results of the proposed framework indicate that further research regarding cascaded architectures could help in distinguishing similar classes in hyperspectral images.

Keywords: Machine leaning · Classification · Hyperspectral imagery ·
PCA · Convolutional neural network

1 Introduction

In the context of remote sensing, hyperspectral imagery (HSI) has long been used to take advantage of the rich spectral information in order to distinguish between different surface areas on the ground [18]. Common applications include urban mapping [3], mineral detection [17], environmental monitoring [8] and crop analysis [22]. The challenge of classifying different materials in a hyperspectral image remains due to the high intraclass variability and sometimes low interclass variability [9], even though recent years have seen a lot of improvement in this area, mainly due to deep learning approaches [4,14,21,25]. Instead of using handcrafted features to differentiate between substances, deep features can be learned using convolutional neural networks (CNNs). This not only reduces the manual work of creating different features for each particular scene [24], but also helps in surpassing previous state of the art classification accuracies and setting a new standard for hyperspectral image classification.

In this paper, we use the benchmark datasets *Salinas scene*, *Pavia University* and *Pavia Center* to demonstrate the effects of using principle component

© Springer Nature Switzerland AG 2019
M. Felsberg et al. (Eds.): SCIA 2019, LNCS 11482, pp. 78–89, 2019.
https://doi.org/10.1007/978-3-030-20205-7_7

analysis (PCA) prior to CNN classification as opposed to having the CNN learn the low-dimensional data structure itself. We introduce a novel two-stage architecture in order to effectively deal with problems of low interclass variability between problematic classes. In a feasibility analysis, we show that this novel architecture is able to significantly enhance the classification model's ability to differentiate between materials and that further research in this direction would aid the classification process significantly, especially in the presence of low interclass variability.

2   Related Work

Initially, CNNs for hyperspectral image classification only used spectral information without considering the importance of spatial context [14]. As a consequence, obtained predictions suffered from the "salt and paper" appearance problem. Soon it became clear that spectral information alone is not sufficient when classifying remote sensing images. Shadows, which significantly alter the spectral response of materials, thus increasing the intraclass variability can result in misclassifications. Additionally, mixed pixels caused by low spatial resolution and a low interclass variability, which is due to very similar classes in the images, make HSI classification a challenging problem.

When introducing the spatial context into the CNN, it is possible to improve classification accuracies significantly. To this effect, different techniques of combining spatial context and spectral information have been introduced [10,13,27]. Yue et al. [26] utilized combination of CNN, logistic regressions and principle component analysis for HSI classification. Li et al. [20] proposed an alternative way of learning spectral features without previously applying dimension reduction techniques.

In the field of hyperspectral imaging there is a high probability that several classes will have very low interclass variability, and thus, their spectral signatures would look very similar. One such example is classes 8 and 15 of agricultural Salinas scene (detailed information in Subsect. 4.1) representing 'Grapes_untrained' and 'Vinyard_untrained'. Several proposed convolutional neural networks trying to classify Salinas hyperspectral data [12,14,27] struggle to differentiate between these problem classes.

In this paper, we address this problem of distinguishing between similar classes in order to improve overall classification results. To this end, we devise a cascaded CNN architecture which is explained in the following.

3   Proposed Approach

We propose a novel coarse-to-fine two-stage fusion architecture employing consecutive convolutional neural networks to deal with the problem of separating two classes which are very similar to each other. To our knowledge this is the first time a cascaded architecture is used for hyperspectral image classification.

Cascaded architectures have shown their capability in a variety of applications. Christ *et al.* [6] used cascaded CNNs in the medical area for better liver and lesion segmentations in CT images. Cheng *et al.* [5] utilized a cascaded convolutional neural network to simultaneously cope with road detection and centerline extraction tasks.

The motivation behind the cascaded approach for hyperspectral image classification is the following. If the network separates almost everything correctly, it is better to train a second network trying to eliminate the few misclassifications of the first network, rather than to train a single deeper architecture. Given the fact that HSI images are only partially labeled and taking into consideration their high spectral resolution, deeper networks could aggravate the overfitting problem extremely.

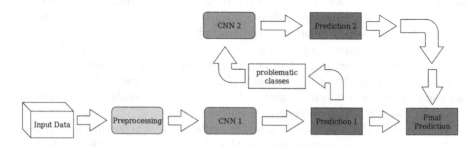

Fig. 1. Proposed two-stage cascaded pipeline.

Figure 1 illustrates the pipeline for the proposed approach. The first step of the framework is an optional preprocessing step, in which dimension reduction (DR) is applied to the input data. This is done in order to compress spectral information into few bands, and thus, decrease the number of trainable parameters in the subsequent classifier. Principle component analysis (PCA), which projects data into a lower-dimensional space, is the most used DR technique for hyperspectral images since the number of available training samples is limited compared to the number of spectral bands, making HSI classification susceptible to the curse of dimensionality [11,13].

After the preprocessing step, hierarchical features from the entire available input dataset are learned by the framework and the prediction is made. Based on the obtained confusion matrix, problematic classes are identified dynamically by choosing the pair of classes with the maximal number of misclassifications.

After that, the framework starts propagating inputs, which correspond to previously identified challenging classes, through the second CNN. Final prediction can be obtained by fusing the results from both networks.

The advantage of such a two-stage process is a potentially higher overall classification accuracy. This is due to the fact that the second network's weights are trained only to differentiate between two confusing classes, which can be expected to produce better results. Moreover, the framework implementation does not require far more effort, since the second CNN has the same architecture as the first network, except of the number of outputs in the last layer, so the architecture of the first network can be reused. Weights of the second network are initialized randomly.

4 Experiments

The proposed approach is trained and evaluated on publicly available datasets. We also consider the combination of several CNN architectures utilizing both spectral and spatial information simultaneously. A detailed description about the used hyperspectral images and the experimental set-ups is provided in the following subsections.

4.1 Datasets

Three hyperspectral benchmark datasets are used in this paper. The first hyperspectral image was captured by the Airborne Visible/Infrared Imaging Spectrometer (AVIRIS) sensor over the agricultural Salinas Valley in California, United States. Two other scenes were acquired by the Reflective Optics System Imaging Spectrometer-03 (ROSIS-03) sensor during the flight over Pavia city and university in northern Italy.

The Salinas scene covers an area of about 1900 × 800 meters in a 512 × 217 pixel image with a spectral resolution of 224 bands (400–2500 nm). We use the corrected Salinas dataset, in which the water absorption bands have been discarded, resulting in 204 spectral bands. The dataset is partially labeled and includes vegetables, bare soils and vineyard fields which are grouped into 16 classes and can be seen in Fig. 2.

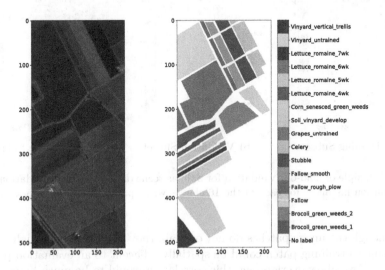

Fig. 2. Salinas dataset with its corresponding ground truth.

The Pavia University dataset comprises 640×340 pixels and covers the Engineering School at the University of Pavia. It consists of different classes including trees, asphalt, bitumen, gravel, metal sheets, shadow, brick, meadows, and soil. The Pavia Center dataset was captured over the city-center and was originally 1096×1096 pixels, however a 381-pixel-wide stripe in the left part of image was removed, leading to 1096×715 pixels. The ROSIS-03 sensor has a spatial resolution of 1.3 m and has 115 data channels with a spectral coverage ranging from 430 to 860 nm [2]. We use corrected Pavia University and Pavia Center datasets, where 12 and 13 channels respectively have been removed due to noise.

We split the data into three disjoint subsets for training, validation and evaluation. It is particularly important to ensure that no part of the evaluation set is included in the training sets, or else we cannot assert the generalization ability of our classifier. When using spatial information in order to classify a pixel, i.e. an image patch surrounding this pixel, it is essential that no pixel in a validation and evaluation patch is also part of a training patch.

Thus, for Salinas scene and Pavia University we randomly select 30 non-overlapping patches (15 for validation and 15 for evaluation) of size 5×5 per class. Since the Pavia Center dataset has a higher spatial resolution, the number of validation and evaluation samples per class is increased up to 30. An example of data split for Salinas scene is shown in Fig. 3.

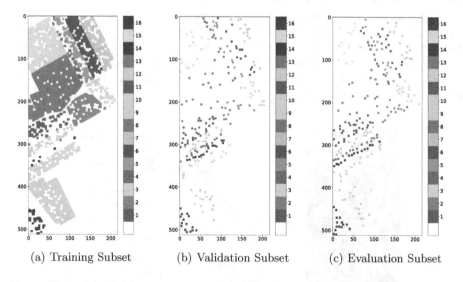

(a) Training Subset   (b) Validation Subset   (c) Evaluation Subset

Fig. 3. Example of hold-out validation for Salinas scene dataset with 15 validation and 15 evaluation instances for each of the 16 classes with spatial resolution of 5×5.

Although the image patches do not overlap, they still could have high correlation since a training patch could be spatially adjacent to an evaluation patch. However, if we allow overlapping, this correlation would to be much higher.

4.2 Experimental Set-Ups

Convolutional neural networks [19] are state of the art approaches in many image processing tasks nowadays, similarly so in hyperspectral image classification. In order to evaluate the proposed approach three different CNN architectures utilizing both spectral and spatial information simultaneously are used as our baseline. For all experimental set-ups a spatial context of 5×5 pixels is utilized.

The first experimental set-up is a 2D CNN in which the kernels applied in spatial dimensions. This is the typical type of convolution seen in many CNNs for image classification [16, 23]. The detailed architecture of 2D CNN is given in Table 1, where n_λ and n_{cl} represent the spectral resolution of the dataset and the number of output classes respectively.

Table 1. Detailed architecture of 2D CNN.

Layer	Kernel size	# Kernel	Output size	# Features
Input			$5 \times 5 \times n_\lambda$	1
Conv1	$3 \times 3 \times n_\lambda$	64	$3 \times 3 \times 64$	64
Conv2	$3 \times 3 \times 1$	128	$1 \times 1 \times 128$	128
FC3	-	-	$1 \times 1 \times 1$	200
FC4	-	-	$1 \times 1 \times 1$	84
FC5	-	-	$1 \times 1 \times 1$	n_{cl}

The second experimental set-up has the same architecture as previously, with the only difference that dimension reduction with PCA is utilized prior.

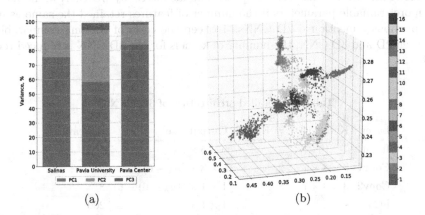

(a)   (b)

Fig. 4. The explained variance for the first three principle components for three datasets is presented in (a). In (b), the 3D plot of Salinas data after transformation with the first three principal components is displayed.

When deciding how many principal components (PCs) to retain, it is reasonable to investigate how much information is discarded when keeping only a certain number of principal components. We use the explained variance for this and demonstrate in Fig. 4(a) that it is reasonable to retain three principal components for all three dataset since less than 1% of the variance is lost. Figure 4(b) shows the transformed Salinas data when using three principal components.

After PCA, the spectral information of datasets has thus been compressed into three bands. We utilize these bands together with a spatial context of 5×5 pixels, as an input to the network. Detailed architecture of 2D CNN PC3 is presented in Table 2.

Table 2. Detailed architecture of 2D CNN PC3.

Layer	Kernel size	# Kernel	Output size	# Features
Input			$5 \times 5 \times 3$	1
Conv1	$3 \times 3 \times 3$	64	$3 \times 3 \times 64$	64
Conv2	$3 \times 3 \times 1$	128	$1 \times 1 \times 128$	128
FC3	-	-	$1 \times 1 \times 1$	200
FC4	-	-	$1 \times 1 \times 1$	84
FC5	-	-	$1 \times 1 \times 1$	n_{cl}

For the third experimental set-up we use a 3D CNN, in which the kernel is moved over the input in three directions. For hyperspectral data, the kernel thus slides over the two spatial and the spectral directions. We do not utilize a dimension reduction step to compress the spectral information, rather let the network find correlations between spectral bands internally. 3D CNN would have far more trainable parameters if the number of features retained the same as in the previously mentioned 2D CNNs. To keep the costs of training comparable between 2D and 3D CNN, the number of kernels for the 3D CNN is reduced (cf. Table 3).

Table 3. Detailed architecture of 3D CNN.

Layer	Kernel size	# Kernel	Output size	# Features
Input			$5 \times 5 \times n_\lambda$	1
Conv1	$3 \times 3 \times 7$	2	$3 \times 3 \times (n_\lambda - 6)$	2
Conv2	$3 \times 3 \times 7$	8	$1 \times 1 \times ((n_\lambda - 6) - 6)$	8
FC3	-	-	$1 \times 1 \times 1$	200
FC4	-	-	$1 \times 1 \times 1$	84
FC5	-	-	$1 \times 1 \times 1$	n_{cl}

For all described architectures, the Rectified Linear Unit (ReLU), which is the recommended activation function for image classification networks [16], is used. As an optimizer, we chose the stochastic gradient-based Adam optimizer [15] with a learning rate of 0.005. While training the networks, the batch size is set to 512 and each training is performed for 10 epochs. For experiments with the proposed cascaded approach the learning rate for the second stage is set to 0.0005 and each training of the second stage is performed for 50 epochs. The threshold for choosing a pair of problematic classes is set to be the maximum number of misclassified instances from the first stage. Especially for multi-stage architectures, the threshold could be set so that all classes with unsatisfactory classification rates are chosen for subsequent fine training. All input datasets are standardized before splitting into train, validation and evaluation subsets.

5   Evaluation

For better generalization each architecture is tested 10 times with random split of data into training, validation and evaluation datasets. Overall accuracies (OA) and standard deviations (std) on evaluation subsets are presented here, together with the number of trainable parameter (first stage + second stage). All implementations are done using the TensorFlow framework [1] on the NVIDIA GeForce GTX 1080ti with 11 GB graphic memory.

From the results presented in Table 4 it can be seen that the proposed 2D CNN architecture in combination with dimension reduction (PCA) performs worst, while the 2D CNN achieves decent results and the 3D model significantly outperforms the other two approaches for all three datasets. We can therefore state that the dimension reduction with PCA prior to 2D CNN weakens the networks capability to correctly classify the samples, even though more than 99% of variance was explained by the used principal components (cf. Fig. 4(a)). Thus, we can verify that spectral as well as spatial features are important for classifying hyperspectral images, but that it is the combination of both that aids the network in achieving the best classification results.

As expected, for all 10 evaluation rounds of Salinas scene, the learning framework identified classes 8 ('Grapes_untrained') and 15 ('Vinyard_untrained') as the most challenging classes, and thus, they are the main factors contributing to a lower overall accuracy. When using an exclusive 3D CNN for these two classes only, the classification accuracy of classes 8 and 15 improves from 75% and 81%, assuming a single CNN, to 89% and 94% with cascaded CNN, respectively, on the evaluation subset. For the Pavia Center and Pavia University datasets, different challenging classes were identified for the 10 evaluation rounds. In case of Pavia University, the average accuracy increased by around 1%, while for Pavia Center the improvement is very small (around 0.1%).

Notably, 3D CNNs evaluated on Pavia Center and Pavia University datasets have outperformed their corresponding 2D CNNs even with smaller number of parameters. Thus, implicit supervised dimension reduction within the 3D CNN yields better results than explicit unsupervised dimension reduction using PCA.

Table 4. Evaluation results. Overall accuracy (OA) with standard deviation (std) in % and the number of trainable parameters (first stage + seconds stage) for all experiments.

Dataset	Architecture	Num. train. param	OA ± std (single CNN)	OA ± std (cascaded CNN)
Salinas	2D CNN	235,553 + 234,278	93.417 ± 2.107	94.333 ± 1.884
	2D CNN PC3	119,777 + 118,502	90.333 ± 3.348	90.917 ± 3.348
	3D CNN	326,873 + 325,598	94.083 ± 1.871	**96.083 ± 0.898**
Pavia U.	2D CNN	176,782 + 176,102	94.519 ± 2.911	96.222 ± 1.944
	2D CNN PC3	119,182 + 118,502	89.852 ± 2.672	91.333 ± 2.458
	3D CNN	164,678 + 163,998	96.741 ± 2.929	**97.704 ± 1.828**
Pavia C.	2D CNN	176,206 + 175,526	97.296 ± 3.134	98.593 ± 0.841
	2D CNN PC3	119,182 + 118,502	96.778 ± 0.923	97.407 ± 0.663
	3D CNN	163,078 + 162,398	98.963 ± 0.519	**99.074 ± 0.556**

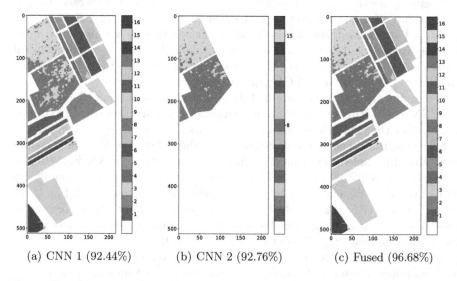

(a) CNN 1 (92.44%)   (b) CNN 2 (92.76%)   (c) Fused (96.68%)

Fig. 5. Classification results with corresponding overall accuracy ratings for the entire image: first 3D CNN (a); second 3D CNN (b); cascaded 3D CNN with fusion (c).

In Fig. 5 the overall performance of the 3D CNN with and without fusion is shown for one of ten rounds. The presented accuracies in the figure indicate the overall accuracy on all image patches, not just the evaluation data, for which the results are given in Table 4. Only inputs that are predicted to be of class 8 or 15 by the first CNN are additionally classified by the cascaded second-stage CNN. Thus, all other classes in the fused prediction remain the same.

From Fig. 5, it is obvious that the misclassifications between classes 8 and 15, seen in (a), are significantly reduced when employing the proposed cascaded CNN architecture, as shown in the (b) and (c).

6   Conclusion and Future Work

In this paper, we have presented different 2D and 3D CNN architectures for classifying hyperspectral images. We have shown the power of spectral information in combination with spatial context using convolutional neural networks. The introduced cascaded approach has shown its potential in achieving better classification accuracies on the benchmark HSI datasets.

We proposed an automated approach of first identifying problematic classes after an initial CNN training and prediction process. In this way, we can find which classes the network had trouble classifying correctly and which classes were confused most often. Based on a chosen threshold (maximal misclassification) specifying a confusion score, classes can be selected for further analysis automatically. We proposed to use the same architecture to keep the process of dynamically adding new CNNs to the training pipeline as simple as possible, since automatically choosing hyperparameters for convolutional neural networks is very challenging [7].

Since a significant improvement has been made by utilizing cascaded two-stage classification process for the task of distinguishing between classes with low interclass variability, it is appropriate to examine further improvements to the approach more closely, especially concerning an automation procedure for finding the problem classes.

We were not able to directly compare our results with existing state-of-art contributions, since in HSI classification field many researchers allow overlapping of training and evaluation patches. Therefore, for fair comparison we have to implement existing architectures ourselves. We are planning to do that in our future works.

The proposed pipeline for an automated two-stage training process is presented in Fig. 1. One potential improvement would be automatically adapting the number of additional CNN stages according to the challenge of the dataset. Thus, more sophisticated analyzing algorithms could be integrated.

Even though reconstructed data after PCA with three principal components retains over 99% of the original variance, the classification accuracies of both single and cascaded CNNs suffered when using PCA as a preprocessing tool. Potentially, the unsupervised nature of PCA results in information being discarded, that is still important for subsequent supervised classification. It might be a reasonable idea, therefore, to investigate the potential of supervised dimension reduction techniques such as linear discriminant analysis (LDA), as this approach is able to transform data such that the distance between classes is maximized while the distance within a class is minimized. Also more advanced techniques, like balanced local discriminant embedding (BLDE) [27], could further improve the enhancing effect of the additional neural networks.

This paper shows that further research in the area of multi-stage, coarse-to-fine CNN architectures is advisable when trying to classify challenging hyperspectral images. This does not only apply to the datasets evaluated in this paper, but also for other hyperspectral data, where different classes are similar. This is especially true for datasets with a low interclass variability, such as Salinas, where the classification accuracies can be significantly improved by a cascaded architecture.

References

1. Abadi, M., et al.: TensorFlow: a system for large-scale machine learning (2016)
2. Benediktsson, J.A., Ghamisi, P.: Spectral-Spatial Classification of Hyperspectral Remote Sensing Images. Artech House, Norwood (2015)
3. Benediktsson, J.A., Palmason, J.A., Sveinsson, J.R.: Classification of hyperspectral data from urban areas based on extended morphological profiles. IEEE Trans. Geosci. Remote Sens. **43**(3), 480–491 (2005)
4. Chen, Y., Lin, Z., Zhao, X., Wang, G., Gu, Y.: Deep learning-based classification of hyperspectral data. IEEE J. Sel. Top. Appl. Earth Obs. Remote Sens. **7**(6), 2094–2107 (2014)
5. Cheng, G., Wang, Y., Xu, S., Wang, H., Xiang, S., Pan, C.: Automatic road detection and centerline extraction via cascaded end-to-end convolutional neural network. IEEE Trans. Geosci. Remote Sens. **55**(6), 3322–3337 (2017)
6. Christ, P.F., et al.: Automatic liver and lesion segmentation in CT using cascaded fully convolutional neural networks and 3D conditional random fields. In: Ourselin, S., Joskowicz, L., Sabuncu, M.R., Unal, G., Wells, W. (eds.) MICCAI 2016. LNCS, vol. 9901, pp. 415–423. Springer, Cham (2016). https://doi.org/10.1007/978-3-319-46723-8_48
7. Domhan, T., Springenberg, J.T., Hutter, F.: Speeding up automatic hyperparameter optimization of deep neural networks by extrapolation of learning curves. In: IJCAI, vol. 15, 3460–3468 (2015)
8. Ellis, R.J., Scott, P.W.: Evaluation of hyperspectral remote sensing as a means of environmental monitoring in the St. austell china clay (kaolin) region, Cornwall, UK. Remote Sens. Environ. **93**(1–2), 118–130 (2004)
9. Fauvel, M., Chanussot, J., Benediktsson, J.A.: A spatial-spectral kernel-based approach for the classification of remote-sensing images. Pattern Recogn. **45**(1), 381–392 (2012)
10. Fauvel, M., Tarabalka, Y., Benediktsson, J.A., Chanussot, J., Tilton, J.C.: Advances in spectral-spatial classification of hyperspectral images. Proc. IEEE **101**(3), 652–675 (2013)
11. Feng, F., Li, W., Du, Q., Zhang, B.: Dimensionality reduction of hyperspectral image with graph-based discriminant analysis considering spectral similarity. Remote Sens. **9**(4), 323 (2017)
12. Gao, Q., Lim, S., Jia, X.: Hyperspectral image classification using convolutional neural networks and multiple feature learning. Remote Sens. **10**(2), 299 (2018)
13. Ghamisi, P., et al.: New frontiers in spectral-spatial hyperspectral image classification: the latest advances based on mathematical morphology, markov random fields, segmentation, sparse representation, and deep learning. IEEE Geosci. Remote Sens. Mag. **6**(3), 10–43 (2018)

14. Hu, W., Huang, Y., Wei, L., Zhang, F., Li, H.: Deep convolutional neural networks for hyperspectral image classification. J. Sens. **2015**, Article ID 258619, 12 p. (2015). https://doi.org/10.1155/2015/258619
15. Kingma, D.P., Ba, J.: Adam: a method for stochastic optimization. arXiv preprint arXiv:1412.6980 (2014)
16. Krizhevsky, A., Sutskever, I., Hinton, G.E.: ImageNet classification with deep convolutional neural networks. In: Advances in Neural Information Processing Systems, pp. 1097–1105 (2012)
17. Kruse, F.A., Boardman, J.W., Huntington, J.F.: Comparison of airborne hyperspectral data and EO-1 hyperion for mineral mapping. IEEE Trans. Geosci. Remote Sens. **41**(6), 1388–1400 (2003)
18. Landgrebe, D.: Hyperspectral image data analysis. IEEE Signal Process. Mag. **19**(1), 17–28 (2002)
19. LeCun, Y., et al.: LeNet-5, convolutional neural networks, p. 20 (2015). http://yann.lecun.com/exdb/lenet
20. Li, Y., Zhang, H., Shen, Q.: Spectral-spatial classification of hyperspectral imagery with 3D convolutional neural network. Remote Sens. **9**(1), 67 (2017)
21. Makantasis, K., Karantzalos, K., Doulamis, A., Doulamis, N.: Deep supervised learning for hyperspectral data classification through convolutional neural networks. In: 2015 IEEE International Geoscience and Remote Sensing Symposium (IGARSS), pp. 4959–4962. IEEE (2015)
22. Muhammed, H.H., Larsolle, A.: Feature vector based analysis of hyperspectral crop reflectance data for discrimination and quantification of fungal disease severity in wheat. Biosyst. Eng. **86**(2), 125–134 (2003)
23. Szegedy, C., et al.: Going deeper with convolutions. In: Proceedings of the IEEE Conference on Computer Vision and Pattern Recognition, pp. 1–9 (2015)
24. Tao, C., Pan, H., Li, Y., Zou, Z.: Unsupervised spectral-spatial feature learning with stacked sparse autoencoder for hyperspectral imagery classification. IEEE Geosci. Remote Sens. Lett. **12**(12), 2438–2442 (2015)
25. Yu, S., Jia, S., Xu, C.: Convolutional neural networks for hyperspectral image classification. Neurocomputing **219**, 88–98 (2017)
26. Yue, J., Zhao, W., Mao, S., Liu, H.: Spectral-spatial classification of hyperspectral images using deep convolutional neural networks. Remote Sens. Lett. **6**(6), 468–477 (2015)
27. Zhao, W., Du, S.: Spectral-spatial feature extraction for hyperspectral image classification: a dimension reduction and deep learning approach. IEEE Trans. Geosci. Remote Sens. **54**(8), 4544–4554 (2016)

Assessing Capsule Networks
with Biased Data

Bruno Ferrarini[1]([⊠])[iD], Shoaib Ehsan[1][iD], Adrien Bartoli[2][iD], Aleš Leonardis[3][iD],
and Klaus D. McDonald-Maier[1][iD]

[1] CSEE, University of Essex, Wivenhoe Park, Colchester CO4 3SQ, UK
{bferra,sehsan,kdm}@essex.ac.uk
[2] Faculté de Médecine, 28 Place Henri Dunant, 63000 Clermont-Ferrand, France
Adrien.Bartoli@gmail.com
[3] School of Computer Science, University of Birmingham, Birmingham B15 2TT, UK
a.leonardis@cs.bham.ac.uk

Abstract. Machine learning based methods achieves impressive results
in object classification and detection. Utilizing representative data of the
visual world during the training phase is crucial to achieve good performance with such data driven approaches. However, it not always possible
to access bias-free datasets thus, robustness to biased data is a desirable
property for a learning system. Capsule Networks have been introduced
recently and their tolerance to biased data has received little attention.
This paper aims to fill this gap and proposes two experimental scenarios to assess the tolerance to imbalanced training data and to determine
the generalization performance of a model with unfamiliar affine transformations of the images. This paper assesses dynamic routing and EM
routing based Capsule Networks and proposes a comparison with Convolutional Neural Networks in the two tested scenarios. The presented
results provide new insights into the behaviour of capsule networks.

Keywords: Capsule Networks · Bias · Comparison · Evaluation

1 Introduction

A robust classification system is expected to give the same prediction for every
image of the same class or for images representing the same element in different poses. Machine learning methods, such as Convolutional Neural Networks (CNN), have been used in many classification, detection and recognition
tasks [3,10,16]. However, in order to achieve good performance with data driven
approaches, well representative data of the visual word are required [11,14,19].
While it is possible to mitigate some bias effects with de-biasing techniques
[12] or with data augmentation [23], it is important to use machine learning
approaches with good generalization performance as it contributes to design
more robust applications to unseen or underrepresented imaging conditions.
This paper focuses on the latter topic and presents a comparison between Convolutional Neural Networks (CNNs) and Capsule Networks (CapsNets) [7,22].

© Springer Nature Switzerland AG 2019
M. Felsberg et al. (Eds.): SCIA 2019, LNCS 11482, pp. 90–100, 2019.
https://doi.org/10.1007/978-3-030-20205-7_8

The neurons in a CapsNet are organized in groups denoted as Capsules [8]. In contrast to a single neuron, a capsule can learn a specific image entity over a range of viewing conditions such as viewpoint and rotation. With the use of a routing algorithm to interconnect the capsules, a CapsNet model would be affine invariant and spatially aware. While the behaviour of CNNs with biased data has been extensively investigated [11,14,15], how bias influences CapsNets' performance has received little attention so far.

This paper aims to fill this gap by proposing two experimental scenarios. The first experiment set evaluates a model's classification accuracy with unfamiliar affine transformations. It introduces a capture bias [26] obtained with training and test data having transformation intensities sampled from different distributions. The second test scenario is to assess the variation of a network's performance when trained with a dataset presenting several overrepresented classes with respect to evenly distributed classes. The results are presented for five network models: three dynamic routing-based CapsNet [22] with one, two and three capsule layers respectively, an EM-Matrix routing CapsNet [7] and for a CNN, which represents a comparison baseline.

The rest of this paper is organized as follows. Section 2 provides an overview of related work; Sect. 3 gives an introduction on capsule networks; Sect. 4 describes the method and criteria used for the performance evaluation. The results obtained are presented and discussed in Sect. 5. Finally, Sect. 6 draws conclusions and proposes possible extensions.

2 Related Work

The impact of bias on data driven methods have been extensively explored in the literature. A review of various types of bias in machine learning datasets is provided in [5]. The problem of bias in popular datasets dissected by cause is presented in [26] and further discussed in [25] where several de-biasing methods are compared. The generalization performance of CNNs is assessed with unfamiliar scale factor in [11] and with unfamiliar yaw pose and lighting conditions in [14], utilizing face recognition tasks. The analysis of imbalanced data is addressed in [19] and [2]. In [19] several imbalanced datasets are built from CIFAR-10 [15] by means of class down and over-sampling and used to assess CNNs. In [2], the importance of choosing the suitable performance evaluation metric in the presence of imbalanced classes is discussed. To the best of our knowledge, the only work addressing the generalization problem for CapsNets is [6], which demonstrates that dynamic routing based CapsNets generalize faster than CNNs when training data is injected with a few examples of an unfamiliar class. Only a few other works analyze this type of CapsNet but without considering bias or generalization performance: [27] and [20] only test CapsNets with more complex data than those utilized in the original paper [22]. Our paper aims to fill these gaps by proposing an analysis of the generalization performance with unfamiliar affine transformations and imbalanced training data for both the available architectures of CapsNets: dynamic routing [22] (denoted as Vector-CapsNet from now on) and EM-Matrix routing based [7] (MatrixEM-CapsNet).

3   Capsule Networks

A capsule is a group of neurons whose activity is a tensor which can learn to detect a specific entity over a domain of limited range of viewing conditions such as viewpoint, rotation and lighting [8]. Two Capsule Networks (CapsNets) are proposed in [22] and [7] which are characterized by the architecture outlined as follows. (1) An input stage including one or more regular convolution layers; (2) a single Primary Capsule Layer consisting of a convolutional stage whose neurons are grouped into capsules; (3) one or more Capsule Layers, with the last one as network output, and consists of a capsule per class. Every pair of capsule layers (this includes the Primary layer) are fully connected by means of a routing stage. Routing allows a CapsNet to learn relationships between entities by directing the output of a capsule to the proper parent capsule located in the next level. For example, a capsule that learned to recognize eyes, will be routed towards the parent capsule for faces but not to a torso capsule.

CapsNets from [22] and [7] have significant differences in their capsule architecture and routing algorithm. The architecture from [22] (Vector-CapsNet) utilizes 1D vector capsules whose length is an hyperparameter. A capsule encodes an entity and its pose like a CNN, deeper capsules encoding higher level entities. The routing stage fully connects two consecutive capsule layers (L and $L + 1$), thus the total input of a capsule (j) in $L + 1$ depends on the output of every capsule in L. Dynamic routing between capsules works as follows. The output (u_i) of a capsule is multiplied by a transformation matrix W_{ij} to obtain the prediction vector ($\hat{u}_{i|j}$). If the prediction vector is similar to the output of the parent capsule j, then the routing algorithm concludes that i and j are highly related and assigns a high value to the related coupling coefficient (c_{ij}). As the contribution to the total input of j provided by the capsule i is computed as $\hat{u}_{i|j}c_{ij}$, the coupling coefficient expresses how likely capsule i will activate capsule j. Furthermore, the capability of learning relationship between entities that characterize CapsNets is due to a transformation matrix W for each capsule pair $i \in L$ and $j \in L + 1$.

The capsules of the network proposed in [7] (MatrixEM-CapsNet) consist of a scalar activation (a) and a 4×4 pose matrix (M). As in Vector-CapsNet, capsule layers are fully connected. Thus, each capsule i in a layer L is connected to each capsule j in the next layer $L+1$ by means of a 4×4 transformation matrix (W_{ij}) which is learned with an iterative routing algorithm based on EM (Expectation Maximization) clustering and denoted as EM Routing. The prediction of the parent capsule's pose matrix V_{ij} (vote) is computed as the product between M_i and W_{ij} and utilized along with a_i by a routing algorithm to assign routes between capsule i in layer L and capsule j in layer $L + 1$ ($\forall i, j$).

The main difference between CapsNet and CNN is how features are routed between layers. CNN utilizes single neurons for representing image features and pooling operations as routing mechanisms. Pooling ensures invariance to small image changes (translation in particular) at the cost of information loss [17] and makes nearly impossible for a CNN to learn relationship between image entities.

4 Experimental Setup

The proposed approach consists of two types of experiment to assess a network's performance with unseen affine transformations and with prominent class imbalance.

4.1 Capture Bias Experiment

Training data and test data are built from the same dataset by applying affine transformations whose intensity is sampled from different distributions. Hence, a model becomes familiar with several image transformations which appear at different intensities in the training and test datasets. For example, if the considered transformation is rotation, the training set would be augmented by a rotation angle sampled in a range, such as $[-20°, +20°]$, while the transformation magnitude for testing would be sampled from a wider range such as $[-90°, +90°]$.
The performance metric utilized for these experiments is classification accuracy, which is the number of correct predictions from all predictions made. Hence, more general models are those achieving higher accuracy on unseen magnitude of a given affine transformation.

In order to provide more comprehensive insights about the influence of unseen imaging conditions, two different criteria for sampling training data are used: uniform and sparse sampling.

Uniform Sampling. Let T be an affine transformation, D_r a training dataset, D_e the relative test dataset, R_r and R_e two magnitude ranges such that $R_r \subset R_e$. A network is trained with D_r whose every sample s, is augmented with $T(s, t_r)$ where t_r is the magnitude uniformly sampled from R_r: $t_r \in R_r$. Our tests consist of running the model along the complete axis of transformation range R_e. Thus, a set of magnitudes are sampled at fixed size steps starting from the lower bound of R_e until the end of the range. For each $t_{e_i} \in R_e$, the complete dataset D_e is transformed with $T(t_{e_i})$ and used to compute a network's accuracy. This process results in a curve showing the relationship between transformation magnitude and a model's accuracy.

Sparse Sampling. Let T be an affine transformation, D_r a training dataset, D_e the relative test dataset, R_r and R_e two magnitude ranges such that $R_r \subset R_e$. A subset of n of values are chosen from R_r to form a set $K = \{t_{r_1}, t_{r_2}, \ldots t_{r_n}\}$. A network is trained with D_r whose sample s is augmented with $T(s, t_r)$ where t_r is the magnitude uniformly sampled from K: $t_r \in R_r$. Our test procedure is the same as in the Uniform Sampling experiment.

4.2 Imbalanced Data

A model trained with imbalanced classes presents a bias towards the overrepresented ones, which results in more frequent prediction of such majority classes

[5]. The performance measure is the Matthew's Correlation Coefficient (MCC) for multiple classes [9] as it is proven to be more insensitive to imbalanced data than accuracy [2]. MCC value can fall in $[-1, +1]$, where $+1$ corresponds to a perfect classification. A network is trained with both balanced and imbalanced data and the resulting MCC values are compared. Better models are expected to have a narrower gap between MCC scores of balanced and imbalanced data.

5   Results

Results are presented for several models as listed in Table 1: cnn-wp is a CNN with three layers and max pooling, vcaps-s, vcaps-d and vcaps-t are Vector-CapsNet with one, two and three layers of capsules respectively and caps-em is a MatrixEM-CapsNet. All the networks are implemented with Tensorflow [1]. In particular, vcaps-s, vcaps-d and vcaps-t are built on top of the source code provided by the authors of Vector-CapsNet [21], while caps-em is derived from the code shared at [28]. The cnn-wp model is implemented from scratch and has similar architecture and hyperparameters as the comparison baseline from [22] used to evaluate Vector-CapsNet on the MNIST dataset [18]. For the notation in Table 1, the following convention is utilized. $C(k, s, o)$ represents a convolutional layer with kernel k, stride s and o filters; $P(k, s)$ indicates a max pool layer with kernel k and stride s; $F(i, h, o)$ is a fully connected network with a single hidden layer of h neurons; $Pr(c, l, r_i)$ indicates a Primary Capsule Layer having c capsules with length l and utilizing r iterations for the routing algorithm; $Cps(c, l, r)$ represents a capsule layer and c, l and r have the same meaning as for $Pr(c, l, r)$. Except for an additional convolutional layer at the start, caps-em has the same architecture as proposed in [7] but uses less capsules per layer. While in [7] the hyperparameters A, B, C, D are all equal to 32, our implementation reduces the complexity of the network by setting B, C and D to 24. This compromise was necessary to run caps-em with at least 2 routing iterations on our 8 GB RAM graphics card. The models have been trained with the Adam [13] optimizer with default parameters ($\beta_1 = 0.9$ and $\beta_2 = 0.999$) and with an initial learning rate of 0.001 for Vector-CapsNet and cnn-wp, and 0.0005 for MatrixEM-CapsNet. The loss function to train vcaps-s, vcaps-d and vcaps-t is Margin Loss [22] with parameters $m^+ = 0.9, m^-, \lambda = 0.5$. The Spread Loss [7] has been used for caps-em with margin m increasing from 0.2 up to 0.95 in around 10 epochs. Regularization has been obtained with a reconstruction stage consisting of a neural network with two hidden layers of 512 and 1024 units respectively.

5.1   Generalization Performance on Unfamiliar Affine Transformations

Generalization performance with uniformly sampled affine transformations (Sect. 4.1) has been assessed utilizing affMNIST [24] as training data and MNIST [18] for tests. AffMNIST is a dataset obtained from MNIST by applying to each

Table 1. Models assessed: cnn-wp is a CNN similar to the comparison baseline from [22], vcaps-s, vcaps-d and vcaps-t are Vector-CapsNet with single, double and triple capsule layers respectively, caps-em is a MatrixEM-CapsNet.

Model	Layers
cnn-wp	$C(5,1,256); P(3,1); 2 \times [C(5,1,256); P(3,2)]; F(328,192,10)$
vcaps-s	$C(9,1,256); C(9,2,256); Pr(1152,8,3); Cps(10,16)$
vcaps-d	$C(9,1,64); C(9,2,64); Pr(288,8,3); Cps(20,10); Cps(10,16)$
vcaps-t	$C(9,1,128); C(9,2,128); Pr(1152,4,3); 2 \times [Cps(32,8)]; Cps(10,16)$
caps-em	$C(6,2,32); A{:}32; B{:}24; C{:}24; D{:}24; E{:}10; K{:}3;$

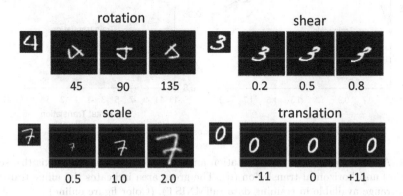

Fig. 1. Several MNIST images as they are transformed and padded for testing a model accuracy.

image several uniformly sampled transformations, namely rotation in $[-20°, 20°]$, scale between 0.8 and 1.2, shear along the x axis in $[-0.2, 0.2]$ and translation. As compared to MNIST, which has 28 pixel images, affMNIST has 40 pixel images in order to fit scaled up digits. Accuracy data is obtained for each transformation using the MNIST test set with the following extended ranges: rotation $[-90°, 90°]$, scale factor $[0.5, 2.0]$, horizontal shear $[-0.8, 0.8]$ and horizontal translation (x axis) $[-13, 13]$. As test required wider range of transformations with respect to those available during training, the models have been fed with 56 pixel images obtained by zero-padding affMNIST images. Padding allowed us to test the models with scale factors up to 2.0 and wider translations than those present in affMNIST without any crop to MNIST digits. Figure 1 shows some samples from MNIST as they are transformed and padded for testing a model accuracy.

The results for uniform sampling experiments are shown in Fig. 2 where the accuracy as a function of an affine transformation is plotted for each model. The most prominent difference among models occurs with unfamiliar scales where vcaps-t outperforms both cnn-wp and the other capsule networks. A closer look at the scale plot (Fig. 2c) allows us to infer a positive relationship between the

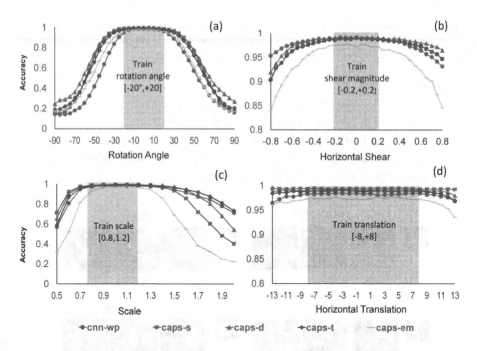

Fig. 2. Accuracy as a function of rotation angle (a), shear along the x axis (b), scale factor (c) and horizontal translation (d). The green area indicates the affine transformation range available in training data (affMNIST). (Color figure online)

number of capsule layers in Vector-CapsNets and generalization performance with unfamiliar scale factors. Indeed, vcaps-t achieves better accuracy at each unfamiliar scale than vcaps-s and vcaps-d for scale factors larger than 1.2, which is the largest scale present in affMNIST. On the contrary, for small test scale this trend is inverted and it appears that Vector-CapsNet has the slowest decay in accuracy among the considered models. Also with rotation, CapsNets generalize better than other types of networks, keeping the accuracy above 90% in the interval $[-35°, 35°]$, which is 15° wider than the sample interval for the rotation used to generate affMNIST.

The same four affine transformations have been considered in sparse sampling experiments. Model training is carried out by augmenting MNIST samples with a single transformation a time whose intensity is sampled in a finite set. Hence, rotation is sampled in $\{-90°, 0, +90°\}$, scale in $\{0.5, 2.0\}$, horizontal shear in $\{-0.5, 0.5\}$ and horizontal translation in $\{-11, 11\}$.

The models do not present significant differences with respect to each other for rotation and horizontal shear (Fig. 3). In particular, the networks show a very good generalization performance to unseen shear magnitudes. In fact, just including two values for shear in the training set, yields an almost flat accuracy plot along all shear test range. Generalization performance with sparse shear sampling is coherent with the results obtained with uniform sampling. Indeed, the models' accuracy has a flat trend along the entire test interval $\{-0.8, 0.8\}$. Similarly to the uniform sampling scenario, the scale results show that deeper Vector-CapsNets generalize better than the other models with unfamiliar scale factors.

The results from sparse translation experiments show that cnn-wp and the three considered Vector-CapsNet have a prominent accuracy drop in the middle of the test interval, while caps-em has stable accuracy on the entire test interval. The reason for the performance gap between caps-em and Vector-CapsNet is probably due to the routing algorithm, which is the main difference between these two types of network (Sect. 3).

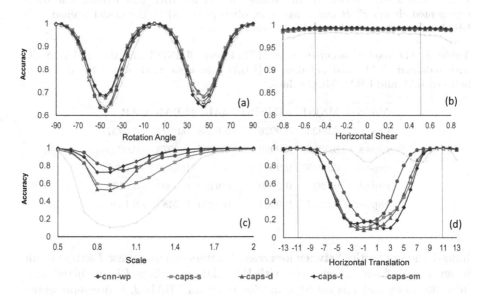

Fig. 3. Effect of sparse sampling of affine transformations in the training data. Accuracy is represented as a function of rotation angle (a), shear along the x axis (b), scale factor (c) and horizontal translation (d).

5.2   Performance Analysis with Imbalanced Data

The datasets utilized for these experiments have been generated from EMNIST-Letters [4], which consists of 26 balanced classes of handwritten letters with 4800 samples each. The balanced dataset (BAL) is a subset of EMNIST including 10 of its classes (D to M) with 2400 samples each, while for the imbalanced dataset (I-BAL) classes have been down-sampled to 600 images, except for E, H and L which have the same 4800 samples from EMNIST-Letters. Figure 4 shows the confusion matrices of vcaps-t for BAL and I-BAL. As expected, the three overrepresented classes, E, H and L, are predicted more often. This is particularly evident for classes that are similar to each other such as L and I.

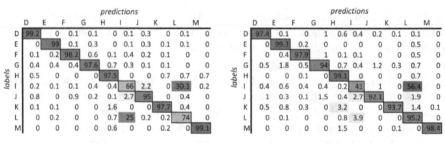

Fig. 4. Confusion matrices of the vcaps-t model for BAL and I-BAL. The over-represented classes E, H and L are more often predicted by the model trained with I-BAL thus, this results in misclassification increase.

Table 2. The models' accuracy with MNIST and affMNIST and the models' MCC with balanced (BAL) and imbalanced (I-BAL) datasets. GAP shows the difference between BAL and I-BAL MCC values.

Model	MNIST	affMNIST	BAL	I-BAL	GAP
cnn-wp	0.9923	0.9926	0.9258	0.9021	−0.0237
caps-s	0.9958	0.9999	0.9202	0.8973	−0.0229
caps-d	0.9935	0.9981	0.9336	0.8929	−0.0407
caps-t	0.9933	0.9999	0.9139	0.9004	−0.0135
caps-em	0.9827	0.9961	0.8899	0.7483	−0.1416

Indeed, the similarities between lowercase L letters and uppercase I letters result in several misclassifications even with BAL datasets where I is predicted as L in 30.3% cases and I is called L in 25% cases. In I-BAL, L is overrepresented as compared to I, which is wrongly classified as L more than half of the time (56.4%). MCC for all the models are summarized in Table 2. The least robust model to imbalanced data is caps-em, with a gap between BAL and I-BAL of 0.1416. cnn-wp and vcaps-s have similar results while vcaps-t capture the best performance with a gap of 0.0135, which is about one half of vcaps-s' gap.

The number of capsule layers alone does not explain the better performance of vcaps-t over vcaps-s. Indeed, vcaps-d outperforms the other networks with BAL (MCC of 0.9306) but it also has the widest gap with unbalanced data among Vector-CapsNet: 0.0407. Several double layer architectures were examined other than vcaps-d, but it was neither possible to find a better model nor to precisely determine the factor that influences the performance the most. For example, replacing the two capsule layers of vcaps-d (Table 1) with $2 \times Cps(128, 4, 3)$ increased the learnable parameters from $5M$ to $8.9M$ however, the performance decreased sightly from 0.938 for BAL to 0.8938 for I-BAL (with a gap of 0.0442) in our experiments.

6   Conclusions

The analysis of capsule networks has received little attention. This paper aimed to provide novel insights into this new type of neural network and proposed several experiments to assess the performance of a network with biased data. Overall, CapsNet outperforms CNNs in most of the cases but not by a large gap. Our results have allowed us to infer that the number of capsule layers (depth) influences generalization performance, this is particularly evident in scale plots (Fig. 2c) where the accuracy at unseen scales improves with a network depth. Apart from this, the influence of a CapsNet's hyperparameters is not totally understood and would deserve a more detailed and specific analysis. On imbalanced data vcaps-t outperforms all the other networks by a consistent gap but the contribution of the triple capsule layer of vcaps-d remains unclear, which is affected by imbalance data more than vcaps-s. Finally, the worst model in any scenario is caps-em with the exception of sparse translation (Fig. 3). However, it is worth mentioning that the caps-em implementation it not from its authors and includes less capsules than the model originally proposed in [7]. Indeed, our Tensorflow implementation is very demanding in terms of RAM and caps-em is the most complex model that can fit in an 8 GB Graphics card. A natural extension of this work would include MatrixEM-CapsNet once an official implementation is available. Furthermore, new insights would be provided from a more specific analysis of the relationship between hyperparameters and generalization performance such as the depth and the distribution of capsules among a CapsNet's layers.

Acknowledgment. This work has been supported by the UK Engineering and Physical Sciences Research Council EPSRC [EP/K004638/1, EP/R02572X/1 and EP/P017487/1].

References

1. Abadi, M., et al.: TensorFlow: large-scale machine learning on heterogeneous systems (2015). https://www.tensorflow.org/
2. Akosa, J.: Predictive accuracy: a misleading performance measure for highly imbalanced data. In: Proceedings of the SAS Global Forum (2017)
3. Arandjelovic, R., Gronat, P., Torii, A., Pajdla, T., Sivic, J.: NetVLAD: CNN architecture for weakly supervised place recognition. In: Proceedings of the IEEE Conference on Computer Vision and Pattern Recognition, pp. 5297–5307 (2016)
4. Cohen, G., Afshar, S., Tapson, J., van Schaik, A.: EMNIST: an extension of MNIST to handwritten letters. arXiv preprint arXiv:1702.05373 (2017)
5. Glauner, P., Valtchev, P., State, R.: Impact of biases in big data. arXiv preprint arXiv:1803.00897 (2018)
6. Gritsevskiy, A., Korablyov, M.: Capsule networks for low-data transfer learning. arXiv preprint arXiv:1804.10172 (2018)
7. Hinton, G., Frosst, N., Sabour, S.: Matrix capsules with EM routing (2018)
8. Hinton, G.E., Krizhevsky, A., Wang, S.D.: Transforming auto-encoders. In: Honkela, T., Duch, W., Girolami, M., Kaski, S. (eds.) ICANN 2011. LNCS, vol. 6791, pp. 44–51. Springer, Heidelberg (2011). https://doi.org/10.1007/978-3-642-21735-7_6

9. Jurman, G., Furlanello, C.: A unifying view for performance measures in multi-class prediction. arXiv preprint arXiv:1008.2908 (2010)
10. Kalliatakis, G., et al.:: Evaluating deep convolutional neural networks for material classification. arXiv preprint arXiv:1703.04101 (2017)
11. Karianakis, N., Dong, J., Soatto, S.: An empirical evaluation of current convolutional architectures' ability to manage nuisance location and scale variability. In: Proceedings of the IEEE Conference on Computer Vision and Pattern Recognition, pp. 4442–4451 (2016)
12. Khosla, A., Zhou, T., Malisiewicz, T., Efros, A.A., Torralba, A.: Undoing the damage of dataset bias. In: Fitzgibbon, A., Lazebnik, S., Perona, P., Sato, Y., Schmid, C. (eds.) ECCV 2012. LNCS, vol. 7572, pp. 158–171. Springer, Heidelberg (2012). https://doi.org/10.1007/978-3-642-33718-5_12
13. Kingma, D., Ba, J.: Adam: a method for stochastic optimization. arXiv preprint arXiv:1412.6980 (2014)
14. Kortylewski, A., Egger, B., Schneider, A., Gerig, T., Morel-Forster, A., Vetter, T.: Empirically analyzing the effect of dataset biases on deep face recognition systems (2017, Preprint)
15. Krizhevsky, A., Hinton, G.: Learning multiple layers of features from tiny images. Technical report, Citeseer (2009)
16. Krizhevsky, A., Sutskever, I., Hinton, G.E.: ImageNet classification with deep convolutional neural networks. In: Advances in Neural Information Processing Systems, pp. 1097–1105 (2012)
17. LeCun, Y., Bengio, Y., Hinton, G.: Deep learning. Nature **521**(7553), 436 (2015)
18. LeCun, Y., Bottou, L., Bengio, Y., Haffner, P.: Gradient-based learning applied to document recognition. Proc. IEEE **86**(11), 2278–2324 (1998)
19. Masko, D., Hensman, P.: The impact of imbalanced training data for convolutional neural networks (2015)
20. Nair, P., Doshi, R., Keselj, S.: Pushing the limits of capsule networks. Technical note (2018)
21. Sabour, S.: Dynamic routing between capsules, source code (2017). https://github.com/Sarasra/models/tree/master/research/capsules. Accessed 05 Feb 2019
22. Sabour, S., Frosst, N., Hinton, G.E.: Dynamic routing between capsules. In: Advances in Neural Information Processing Systems, pp. 3859–3869 (2017)
23. Savinov, N., Seki, A., Ladicky, L., Sattler, T., Pollefeys, M.: Quad-networks: unsupervised learning to rank for interest point detection. In: Proceedings of IEEE Conference on Computer Vision and Pattern Recognition (CVPR) (2017)
24. Tieleman, T.: affMNIST (2013). https://www.cs.toronto.edu/~tijmen/. Accessed 05 Feb 2019
25. Tommasi, T., Patricia, N., Caputo, B., Tuytelaars, T.: A deeper look at dataset bias. In: Csurka, G. (ed.) Domain Adaptation in Computer Vision Applications. ACVPR, pp. 37–55. Springer, Cham (2017). https://doi.org/10.1007/978-3-319-58347-1_2
26. Torralba, A., Efros, A.A.: Unbiased look at dataset bias. In: 2011 IEEE Conference on Computer Vision and Pattern Recognition (CVPR), pp. 1521–1528. IEEE (2011)
27. Xi, E., Bing, S., Jin, Y.: Capsule network performance on complex data. arXiv preprint arXiv:1712.03480 (2017)
28. Zhang, S.: Matrix-capsules-EM-tensorflow, source code (2018). https://github.com/www0wwwjs1/Matrix-Capsules-EM-Tensorflow. Accessed 05 Feb 2019

Facial Emotion Recognition with Varying Poses and/or Partial Occlusion Using Multi-stage Progressive Transfer Learning

Sherin F. Aly[1]([⊠]) [iD] and A. Lynn Abbott[2] [iD]

[1] Information Technology Department, Institute of Graduate Studies and Research,
Alexandria University, Alexandria, Egypt
igsr.sherin@alexu.edu.eg
[2] Bradley Department of Electrical and Computer Engineering, Virginia Tech,
Blacksburg, VA, USA
abbott@vt.edu

Abstract. This paper describes the use of multi-stage Progressive Transfer Learning (MSPTL) to improve the performance of automated Facial Emotion Recognition (FER). Our proposed FER solution is designed to work with 2D images, and is able to classify facial emotions with high accuracy in 6 basic categories (happiness, sadness, fear, anger, surprise, and disgust) for both frontal and (more challenging) non-frontal poses. We perform supervised fine-tuning on an AlexNet deep convolutional neural network in a three-stage process, using three FER datasets in succession. The first two training stages are based on FER datasets containing frontal images only. The final training stage uses a third FER dataset that includes non-frontal poses in images that are relatively low in resolution and/or with partial occlusion. Experimental results demonstrate that our proposed MSPTL approach outperforms typical TL and other PTL systems for FER in both frontal and non-frontal face poses. These results are demonstrated using two different testing datasets (VT-KFER and 300W), which corroborates the generality of the proposed solution and its robustness for handling a wide range of varying poses, occlusion, and expression intensities.

Keywords: Facial Emotion Recognition · Deep learning ·
Transfer learning · Progressive transfer learning

1 Introduction

The automatic detection of emotional cues from the face has many applications in psychology, human-computer interaction, games, and other areas. However, automated analysis of the face is still a challenging problem due to the wide variety of expressions the human face can make and the relatively small size of available datasets. Several researchers have addressed the problem of automated

© Springer Nature Switzerland AG 2019
M. Felsberg et al. (Eds.): SCIA 2019, LNCS 11482, pp. 101–112, 2019.
https://doi.org/10.1007/978-3-030-20205-7_9

Fig. 1. Examples of the six basic facial expressions in our testing datasets. The examples include various poses, expression intensities, and partial occlusion.

Facial Emotion Recognition (FER), typically with emphasis on six common emotions: happiness, sadness, fear, anger, disgust, and surprise. (See examples of these emotions in Fig. 1.) Even though strong progress has been made on FER, and most existing FER systems work well on frontal poses and/or with small variations in head pose [7,8,25,27], increased accuracy and robustness against pose variations is still desired. The latter has proven to be more challenging [9,18] with only a few researchers having explicitly tested their approach on non-frontal data [1,6,11,18,22].

In this paper we introduce a novel method that, by adding new levels to proven transfer learning techniques, successfully achieves higher accuracy in both frontal and non-frontal poses. The next section of this paper contains related work. Section 3 presents the proposed method. Section 4 presents the experimental setup. Section 5 presents the experimental results. Finally, Sect. 6 presents concluding remarks.

2   Related Work

Several researchers have employed deep convolutional neural networks (CNNs) for the task of FER [4,5,12,14,19–21,30] to avoid the traditional feature extraction approaches such as HOG which are relatively complex and time-consuming [1,25,26]. However, training CNN from scratch requires a large amount of labeled training data. To address this problem, it is common to use the weights of a pretrained CNN as the initial state for further training in what is called transfer learning (TL) [19]. TL has provided a reasonable compromise that enhances the accuracy of CNN-based FER systems without requiring very large datasets. However, the "forgetting effect" of TL and the model initialization process, given learned weights from a sequence of related tasks, limit the use of TL [23].

Therefore, a progressive transfer learning (PTL) approach was recently developed to alleviate these limitations [23]. Progressive networks are used to train sequences of tasks by freezing the previously trained tasks and using their intermediate representations as inputs into the new network. PTL therefore prevents the "forgetting effect" of TL by freezing and preserving the source task weights. Our approach extends the use of PTL for FER by adding additional stages that, in turn, increase the accuracy of the overall system.

Regarding the use of CNN for FER, most of the existing approaches have been tested on frontal poses only, non-frontal poses expressions with small datasets, non-varying expression intensity datasets, and/or using 1 or 2 levels of knowledge transfer [19,23,27,29].

Mavani et al. [19] have fine-tuned the AlexNet CNN model [15] using two widely used facial expression datasets (CFEE and RaFD) of the 6 basic expressions plus neutral. Their model yielded test accuracies of 74.79% on CFEE and 95.71% on RaFD. In [23], Ng et al. proposed a PTL scheme for the facial expression recognition of the basic expressions presented by the EmotiW challenge. They also used AlexNet CNN to progressively transfer knowledge to the facial expression task. They first performed fine tuning of AlexNet using the FER28 dataset [10]. Then, a second fine-tuning step on the dataset of interest was performed. Their approach showed significant improvement in accuracy (up to 16%) over the baseline.

This paper proposes a multi-stage progressive transfer learning-based approach of 3 stages of fine-tuning for the recognition of the six basic expressions which goes beyond the TL and PTL approaches described above. We trained and tested our approach on four widely used FER datasets, JAFEE, CK+, VT-KFER and 300W. These datasets include facial expressions with several head poses, intensities and occlusion. We employ the AlexNet CNN, trained initially on the ImageNet database, as our base architecture. We selected AlexNet as the underlying Deep Neural Network (DNN) architecture due to its known reputation and quality for image classification. Moreover, this is an architecture that has been thoroughly studied and its performance is generally well understood in the community. The use of the proposed methodology is, however, not limited to AlexNet. Configuration and use of other DNN architectures is straightforward.

Contributions: There are three main contributions of this work: (1) A novel FER system that is more robust to pose variations; (2) in contrast to existing TL [19] or PTL approaches [23], our approach transfers knowledge progressively using 3 stages with varying content in gender and pose, and has been explicitly tested on non-frontal poses; and, relying only on 2D images, (3) our proposed system outperforms other 2D-based and 3D-based FER systems by more than 10% and some 2D+3D-based systems by more than 17%, when tested on VT-KFER.

3   Proposed Method

Our proposed approach is composed of three main steps: (1) preprocessing the input datasets to extract the face data and prepare the extracted faces for the deep learning step, (2) multi-stage progressive transfer learning and CNN fine tuning, and (3) classification. Each of these steps is described next.

3.1 Preprocessing

We employed 4 FER datasets in our experiments, two for training (JAFEE [17] and CK+ [13,16]) and two for testing (VT-KFER [2] and 300W [24]). A hierarchical face detection (HFD) approach is applied on each image of the datasets. As part of this approach, a group sparse learning method [28] that automatically selects the most salient facial landmarks and thus extracts the face location is applied. If no face is detected, then an approach based on mixtures of trees with a shared pool of parts [31] is applied. This approach models every facial landmark as a part and uses global mixtures to capture topological changes due to viewpoint. Finally, if no face is detected in a particular image, we manually select the face region. (Note that manual processing, if any, is done on the training datasets to ensure that the largest dataset is used; manual processing is not done online.) The Kinect SDK is employed for automatic face detection on the VT-KFER testing datset. Similarly, cropped faces are provided for the 300W testing dataset. All extracted faces are resized to $227 \times 227 \times 3$. Gray scale images are concatenated into 3 channels to be compatible with the input data size of AlexNet.

3.2 Multi-stage Progressive Transfer Learning (MSPTL)

We propose a multi-stage progressive fine-tuning transfer learning FER system of 3 stages based on AlexNet architecture. Our system not only uses the transferred knowledge from training over 1M images of the ImageNet dataset, but also fine tunes this knowledge, progressively, using widely used FER datasets. The progressive fine-tuning here means to adjust the weights of the pretrained network by continuing the backpropagation first on a simple FER dataset, and then repeating the same process on a larger dataset with more variations in gender, pose, and lightening conditions.

In the typical TL paradigm, the transferred knowledge is directly fine-tuned on the dataset of interest (either alone or combined with other datasets in training as is shown in Fig. 2). As opposed to the typical TL paradigm, in MSPTL, the pretrained CNN weights are adjusted using two FER related datasets, JAFEE and CK+, in two separate stages, before being fine-tuned to the dataset of interest in the final stage. With every fine tuning step, the network weights are adjusted with progressive knowledge from the corresponding dataset. In contrast to [23] (shown in Fig. 3), which employs PTL fine-tuning using one large dataset, we employ 3 stages of gradual fine-tuning starting on relatively simple dataset and ending by fine-tuning the model on a dataset with varying poses, varying intensities, and occluded facial expressions. Proposed MSPTL is shown in Fig. 4.

PTL is applied on three stages as follows. First, we transfer the knowledge from AlexNet to a new CNN and fine tune it on a small FER dataset of female-only actors (JAFEE). Then, in stage 2, the resulting CNN model is used to transfer the knowledge gained from AlexNet and JAFEE to a new CNN which is further trained on a larger FER dataset (CK+) that has a larger number of both male and female subjects. Then the resulting model is further fine-tuned and then tested on the datasets of interest.

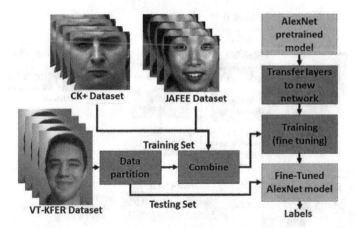

Fig. 2. Transfer learning (TL) approach as proposed in [19], where transferred knowledge is directly obtained from the dataset of interest.

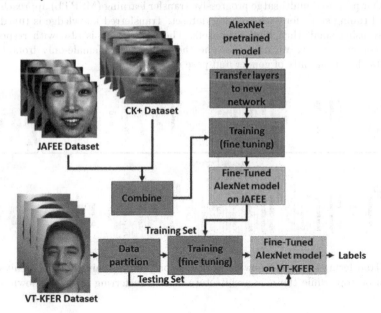

Fig. 3. Progressive transfer learning (PTL) approach as proposed in [23] where transferred knowledge is acquired indirectly using combined and related datasets before the one of interest.

Transfer Layers to a New Network: The first step in MSPTL is to construct a new CNN of N layers where the first $N - i$ layers are transferred from the pretrained model and the last i layers are constructed according to the number of expressions that we want to recognize. In this work, we adopt the AlexNet network as our pretrained CNN. AlexNet comprises 25 layers (illustrated in Fig. 5). There are 8 layers with learnable weights: 5 convolutional layers, and 3 fully connected layers.

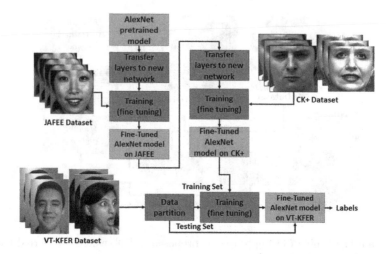

Fig. 4. Our proposed multi-satge progressive transfer learning (MSPTL) approach with separated tuning steps for each training dataset. Transferred knowledge is tuned progressively using small then bigger datasets. The progression is also with respect to dataset contents, where we first fine-tune the model using female-only frontal only FER data then using mix of gender and pose datsets.

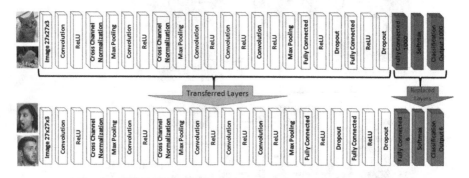

Fig. 5. Transfering layers to a new network. The original pretrained model architecture is shown on top, while the new architecture after transferring layers is shown at the bottom.

We transfer the first 23 layers from AlexNet and replace the last fully-connected layer with a new one that outputs the desired number of classes. Specifically, we replaced the last 3 layers of AlexNet that recognize 1000 classes with three layers for 6 expressions. The three new layers are (1) fully connected that classifies 6 classes, (2) softmax, and (3) classification to adjust the softmax output to a class labels format. The new network is illustrated in the lower part of Fig. 5. We apply this step at each stage in the PTL paradigm. At stage 1 we apply it on AlexNet pretrained network. In stage 2 we apply it on the pretrained network on JAFEE dataset. In stage 3 we apply it on the pretrained network on CK+ dataset.

Deep Learning (Fine Tuning) and Classification: The training is applied in three phases. First, we train the new CNN, composed of transferred layers from AlexNet, on the JAFEE dataset. This training step is for fine tuning the weights of AlexNet to the new classes in JAFEE. For transfer learning, we keep the features from the early layers of the pretrained network (the transferred layer weights) and initialize the weights of the replaced layers randomly. Then we conduct the training by setting a small global learning rate of 10^{-4} to slow down learning in the transferred layers based on the intuition that we may already be close to a good result. We also increased the learning rate for the fully connected layer to speed up learning in the new added layers. This combination of learning rate settings results in fast learning only in the new layers and slower learning in the other layers. We set the number of epochs (i.e., training cycles on the entire dataset) to 4. When performing transfer learning, we do not need to train for as many epochs. During training, the network is validated once per epoch, and automatically stops training if the validation loss stops improving. Stochastic Gradient Descent with Momentum (SGDM) is employed as the optimization algorithm. SGDM updates the weights and biases (parameters) by taking small steps in the direction of the negative gradient of the loss function to minimize the loss. It updates the parameters using a subset of the data every iteration.

At stages 1 and 2 the resulting fine-tuned networks are tested on images randomly selected from JAFEE and CK+, respectively, in order to select the best networks for stages 2 and 3. The final fine-tuned CNN in stage 3 is then used for classifying the six basic expressions in the testing dataset.

4   Experimental Setup

We employed the JAFEE [17] and Cohn-Kanade-plus (CK+) [13,16] datasets for training and VT-KFER [2] and 300W [24] datasets for testing.

JAFEE Dataset: It contains 213 posed images of 7 frontal facial expressions (6 basic facial expressions + neutral) by 10 Japanese female models. All images are in gray scale.

CK+ Dataset: It includes 4,001 posed images in 593 sequences from 123 subjects. Each sequence includes one of the 6 basic expressions in frontal pose only and starts with a neutral face. CK+ includes both gray-scale and RGB images.

VT-KFER Dataset: The dataset includes 11,619 posed images of the 6 basic expressions (plus neutral), in 3 different intensities, captured from 32 subjects by the Kinect 1.0. The data includes expressions performed in frontal, right, and left poses, with 4,732 frontal frames and 5,066 non-frontal. In the testing set, there are 1,005 frontal and 1,062 non-frontal images all in RGB format.

Faces-in-the-Wild (300W): The dataset consists of 300 indoor and 300 outdoor in-the-wild images. It covers a large variation of illumination conditions, poses, occlusion, and face size. For our experiments, we only selected the faces of the six basic expressions, happiness, sadness, surprise, disgust, fear, and anger. A total of 240 images were selected.

To train the first two stages, we used a holdout cross-validation strategy where 90% of the JAFEE and CK+ datasets were randomly selected for training and 10% for testing. To train the third stage on VT-KFER, we used "leave-p-sequence-out" cross-validation, where $100 - p\%$ ($p = 20\%$) sequences of VT-KFER were randomly selected for training the fine-tuned model in stage 3 and the rest for testing. To train the third stage on 300W, we used hold-out cross validation where 80% of 300W were randomly selected for training and 20% for testing.

5   Results and Discussion

We compare our proposed approach to the typical TL paradigm [19] and to the PTL paradigm of [23]. For fairness of comparison, and since we used JAFEE and CK+ for training our model, we combined JAFEE and CK+ datasets with the dataset of interest to train the TL model of [19]. For PTL approach in [23], we used JAFEE and CK+ to fine-tune the model in the first stage while the dataset of interest is used to fine-tune the model in the second stage. To prove the generality of our approach, we tested our approach on two challenging datasets, namely, the VT-KFER and 300W. Experiments were conducted on frontal, non-frontal, and both frontal and non-frontal expressions in VT-KFER to compare the effect of the three tested approaches with respect to the pose.

Our experimental results, illustrated in Fig. 6, show that progressive MSPTL outperforms the typical TL paradigm [19] and the PTL paradigm of [23], especially for non-frontal poses. See Fig. 7 for example frontal and non-frontal expressions from 300W dataset where our MSPTL outperforms both TL and PTL. In the frontal pose, MSPTL approach achieved 84.2% vs. 81.2% for TL and 83% for PTL.

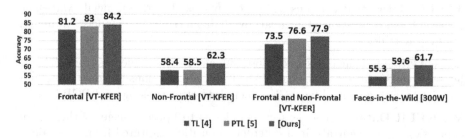

Fig. 6. Accuracy of TL [19] vs. PTL [23] vs. our proposed MSPTL approach tested on VT-KFER and 300W. Columns in groups 1 to 3 shows the testing results on VT-KFER when frontal, non-frontal, and both frontal and non-frontal poses were employed, respectively. The accuracy is based on training on JAFEE, CK+ and VT-KFER and tested using VT-KFER using leave-p-sequence-out cross validation. Columns in group 4 illustrates the testing results on the 300W dataset. The accuracy is based on training on JAFEE, CK+ and 300W and tested using 300W using holdout cross validation.

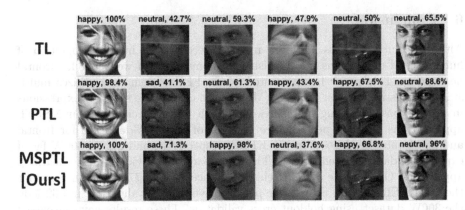

Fig. 7. Sample testing results of TL, PTL, and MSPTL [Ours] approaches on the 300W dataset. The text describes the predicted expression of each image below it with corresponding recognition probability.

MSPTL achieved a 62.3% accuracy on non-frontal poses while TL and PTL have 58.4% and 58.5%, respectively, with increase of around 4% compared to 1% in the frontal pose case. Overall, on VT-KFER, MSPTL showed better performance in all poses data with accuracy of 77.9% compared to 73.5% and 76.6% for TL and PTL, respectively. The results of experiments with 300W dataset show the superior performance of our MSPTL approach as well, with 61.7% accuracy vs. 55.3% obtained with TL, and 59.6% obtained with PTL approach in [23].

Quantitative comparison with the state-of-the-art FER systems tested on all poses data in VT-KFER is given in Table 1. Although MSPTL is based on 2D data only, it shows better performance than all other 2D-based and 3D-based FER systems. It also showed better performance than most of the 2D+3D-based systems with comparative results to the best 2D+3D-based system proposed in [1].

Table 1. Quantitative comparison with state-of-the-art FER systems tested on VT-KFER using leave-p-sequence-out cross validation, where $p = 20\%$. Note that our MSPTL solution outperforms all 2D-only and 3D-only systems. Our approach also achieved competitive results to the state-of-the-art 2D+3D system [1] although it relied only on 2D images.

System	Modality	Leave-p-sequence-out
[3]	3D	49%
[25]	2D	59%
[2]	2D+3D	60%
[26]	2D	67%
[1]	2D+3D	80%
Proposed MSPTL	2D	78%

6   Conclusion

Although much progress has been made in recent years in the recognition of human facial expressions, most existing systems perform well only for frontal head poses. This paper has presented a new FER system that utilizes multi-stage progressive transfer learning (MSPTL) to classify the six basic expressions in varying poses, varying intensities, and with partial occlusion. Our MSPTL approach has led to a performance increase of about 1% and 4% for frontal and non-frontal head poses in VT-KFER, respectively, and 2% on 300W facial expressions dataset taken in the wild, as compared to previous transfer learning approaches. Overall, the system achieved an accuracy of 77.9% on all poses for the VT-KFER dataset, using leave-p-sequence-out cross validation and 62% on the 300W dataset using holdout cross validation. These results have surpassed exiting systems tested on VT-KFER dataset, utilizing 2D or 3D information only. In addition, the system is either better or almost as good as all published 2D+3D systems.

References

1. Aly, S., Abbott, A.L., Torki, M.: A multi-modal feature fusion framework for Kinect-based facial expression recognition using dual kernel discriminant analysis (DKDA). In: IEEE Winter Conference on Applications of Computer Vision (WACV), pp. 71–78 (2016)
2. Aly, S., Trubanova, A., Abbott, L., White, S., Youssef, A.: VT-KFER: a kinect-based RGBD+time dataset for spontaneous and non-spontaneous facial expression recognition. In: IEEE International Conference on Biometrics (ICB), pp. 90–97, May 2015. https://doi.org/10.1109/ICB.2015.7139081
3. Aly, S., Youssef, A., Abbott, L.: Adaptive feature selection and data pruning for 3D facial expression recognition using the Kinect. In: IEEE International Conference on Image Processing (ICIP), pp. 1361–1365 (2014)
4. Bazrafkan, S., Nedelcu, T., Filipczuk, P., Corcoran, P.: Deep learning for facial expression recognition: a step closer to a smartphone that knows your moods. In: International Conference on Consumer Electronics (ICCE), pp. 217–220, January 2017. https://doi.org/10.1109/ICCE.2017.7889290
5. Chen, J., Chen, Z., Chi, Z., Fu, H.: Emotion recognition in the wild with feature fusion and multiple kernel learning. In: International Conference on Multimodal Interaction, ICMI 2014, pp. 508–513. ACM, New York (2014)
6. Eleftheriadis, S., Rudovic, O., Pantic, M.: Discriminative shared gaussian processes for multiview and view-invariant facial expression recognition. IEEE Trans. Image Process. **24**(1), 189–204 (2015). https://doi.org/10.1109/TIP.2014.2375634
7. Fasel, B., Luettin, J.: Automatic facial expression analysis: a survey. Pattern Recognit. **36**(1), 259–275 (2003)
8. Garg, A., Bajaj, R.: Facial expression recognition & classification using hybridization of ICA, GA, and neural network for human-computer interaction. J. Netw. Commun. Emerg. Technol. (JNCET) **2**(1) (2015)
9. Güney, F., Arar, N.M., Fischer, M., Ekenel, H.K.: Cross-pose facial expression recognition. In: IEEE International Conference and Workshops on Automatic Face and Gesture Recognition (FGR), pp. 1–6, April 2013. https://doi.org/10.1109/FG.2013.6553814

10. Goodfellow, I.J., et al.: Challenges in representation learning: a report on three machine learning contests. ArXiv e-prints, July 2013

11. Hu, Y., Zeng, Z., Yin, L., Wei, X., Tu, J., Huang, T.S.: A study of non-frontal-view facial expressions recognition. In: IEEE International Conference on Pattern Recognition (ICPR), pp. 1–4 (2008)

12. Kahou, S.E., et al.: Combining modality specific deep neural networks for emotion recognition in video. In: International Conference on Multimodal Interaction, ICMI 2013, pp. 543–550. ACM, New York (2013). https://doi.org/10.1145/2522848.2531745

13. Kanade, T., Cohn, J.F., Tian, Y.: Comprehensive database for facial expression analysis. In: IEEE International Conference on Automatic Face and Gesture Recognition (Cat. No. PR00580), pp. 46–53 (2000). https://doi.org/10.1109/AFGR.2000.840611

14. Karali, A., Bassiouny, A., El-Saban, M.: Facial expression recognition in the wild using rich deep features. In: International Conference on Image Processing (ICIP), pp. 3442–3446, September 2015. https://doi.org/10.1109/ICIP.2015.7351443

15. Krizhevsky, A., Sutskever, I., Hinton, G.: ImageNet classification with deep convolutional neural networks. In: Pereira, F., Burges, C.J.C., Bottou, L., Weinberger, K.Q. (eds.) Advances in Neural Information Processing Systems, pp. 1097–1105. Curran Associates, Inc. (2012). http://papers.nips.cc/paper/4824-imagenet-classification-with-deep-convolutional-neural-networks.pdf

16. Lucey, P., Cohn, J.F., Kanade, T., Saragih, J., Ambadar, Z., Matthews, I.: The extended Cohn-Kanade dataset (CK+): a complete dataset for action unit and emotion-specified expression. In: IEEE Computer Society Conference on Computer Vision and Pattern Recognition - Workshops, pp. 94–101, June 2010. https://doi.org/10.1109/CVPRW.2010.5543262

17. Lyons, M., Akamatsu, S., Kamachi, M., Gyoba, J.: Coding facial expressions with Gabor wavelets. In: IEEE Inter. Conference on Automatic Face and Gesture Recognition, pp. 200–205, April 1998. https://doi.org/10.1109/AFGR.1998.670949

18. Malawski, F., Kwolek, B., Sako, S.: Using kinect for facial expression recognition under varying poses and illumination. In: Ślęzak, D., Schaefer, G., Vuong, S.T., Kim, Y.-S. (eds.) AMT 2014. LNCS, vol. 8610, pp. 395–406. Springer, Cham (2014). https://doi.org/10.1007/978-3-319-09912-5_33

19. Mavani, V., Raman, S., Miyapuram, K.: Facial expression recognition using visual saliency and deep learning. CoRR abs/1708.08016 (2017). http://arxiv.org/abs/1708.08016

20. Mayya, V., Pai, R., Pai, M.: Automatic facial expression recognition using DCNN. Proc. Comput. Sci. 93(Suppl. C), 453–461 (2016). https://doi.org/10.1016/j.procs.2016.07.233, http://www.sciencedirect.com/science/article/pii/S1877050916314752. International Conference on Advances in Computing and Communications

21. Mollahosseini, A., Chan, D., Mahoor, M.H.: Going deeper in facial expression recognition using deep neural networks. In: IEEE Winter Conference on Applications of Computer Vision (WACV), pp. 1–10, March 2016. https://doi.org/10.1109/WACV.2016.7477450

22. Moore, S., Bowden, R.: Local binary patterns for multi-view facial expression recognition. Comput. Vis. Image Underst. 115(4), 541–558 (2011)

23. Ng, H., Nguyen, V.D., Vonikakis, V., Winkler, S.: Deep learning for emotion recognition on small datasets using transfer learning. In: International Conference on Multimodal Interaction, ICMI 2015, pp. 443–449. ACM, New York (2015). https://doi.org/10.1145/2818346.2830593

24. Sagonas, C., Antonakos, E., Tzimiropoulos, G., Zafeiriou, S., Pantic, M.: 300 faces in-the-wild challenge: database and results. Image Vis. Comput. **47**, 3–18 (2016). https://doi.org/10.1016/j.imavis.2016.01.002
25. Shan, C., Gong, S., McOwan, P.: Facial expression recognition based on local binary patterns: a comprehensive study. Image Vis. Comput. **27**(6), 803–816 (2009)
26. Valstar, M., Jiang, B., Mehu, M., Pantic, M., Scherer, K.: The first facial expression recognition and analysis challenge. In: International IEEE Conference on Automatic Face & Gesture Recognition & Workshops (FG), pp. 921–926 (2011)
27. Xu, M., Cheng, W., Zhao, Q., Ma, L., Xu, F.: Facial expression recognition based on transfer learning from deep convolutional networks. In: International Conference on Natural Computation (ICNC), pp. 702–708, August 2015. https://doi.org/10.1109/ICNC.2015.7378076
28. Yu, X., Huang, J., Zhang, S., Yan, W., Metaxas, D.: Pose-free facial landmark fitting via optimized part mixtures and cascaded deformable shape model. In: International Conference on Computer Vision (ICCV), December 2013
29. Zhang, F., Yu, Y., Mao, Q., Gou, J., Zhan, Y.: Pose-robust feature learning for facial expression recognition. Front. Comput. Sci. **10**(5), 832–844 (2016). https://doi.org/10.1007/s11704-015-5323-3
30. Zhang, T.: Facial expression recognition based on deep learning: a survey. In: Xhafa, F., Patnaik, S., Zomaya, A.Y. (eds.) IISA 2017. AISC, vol. 686, pp. 345–352. Springer, Cham (2018). https://doi.org/10.1007/978-3-319-69096-4_48
31. Zhu, X., Ramanan, D.: Face detection, pose estimation, and landmark localization in the wild. In: IEEE Conference on Computer Vision and Pattern Recognition (CVPR), pp. 2879–2886 (2012)

Feature Extraction and Image Analysis

Compressed Imaging at Long Range in SWIR

Andreas Brorsson[ID], Carl Brännlund[ID], David Bergström[ID],
and David Gustafsson[(✉)][ID]

FOI - Swedish Defence Research Agency, C4ISR, Linköping, Sweden
{andbro,carbra,davber,davgus}@foi.se

Abstract. In this paper, we present a single pixel camera operating in
the Short Wave InfraRed (SWIR) spectral range that reconstructs high
resolution images from an ensemble of compressed measurements. The
SWIR spectrum provides significant benefits in many applications due
to its night vision characteristics and its ability to penetrate smoke and
fog. Walsh-Hadamard matrices are used for generating pseudo-random
measurements which speed up the reconstruction and enables reconstruction of high resolution images. Total variation regularization is used for
finding a sparse solution in the gradient space. The edge response for
the single pixel camera is analysed. A large number of outdoor scenes
with varying illumination has been collected using the single pixel sensor. Visual inspection of the reconstructed SWIR images indicates that
most scenes and objects can be identified after a sample ratio of 3%. The
reconstruction quality improves in general as the sample ratio increases,
but the quality is not improved significantly after the sample ratio has
reached roughly 10%. Dynamic scenes in the form of global illumination
variations can be handled by temporal local average suppression of the
measurements.

Keywords: Compressed sensing · Single pixel imaging · SWIR ·
Total variation

1 Introduction

Conventional infrared camera systems capture the scene by measuring the
radiation incident at each of the thousands of pixels in a focal plane array. In
compressed sensing a relatively small number of measurements from the scene
is combined with sparse reconstruction procedures to recover a full resolution
image. Using Compressive Sensing (CS) an image can be acquired with the content of a high resolution image captured with a high resolution focal plane array
while using smaller, cheaper and lower bandwidth components. A single pixel
camera in Short Wave InfraRed (SWIR), which combines a Digital Micromirror
Device (DMD), an InGaAs photodiode and a compressive sensing reconstruction
procedure is presented. In many applications the SWIR spectrum provides significant benefits over the visual spectrum. For example SWIR enables separation

© Springer Nature Switzerland AG 2019
M. Felsberg et al. (Eds.): SCIA 2019, LNCS 11482, pp. 115–127, 2019.
https://doi.org/10.1007/978-3-030-20205-7_10

between camouflage and vegetation and penetrate fog and smoke to some extent which enable imaging through scattering media. Furthermore, SWIR sensors can be used for passive imaging in moonless condition due to the night-glow of the sky that provides SWIR illumination.

The single pixel camera in SWIR is evaluated on realistic natural scenes with different lighting condition at long distances. Compensation methods for illumination variation in the scene while capturing the scene is proposed, implemented and evaluated.

2   Related Work

"Sparse Modeling" by Rish and Grabarnik [10] and "Sparse and redundant representation" by Elad [5] cover the fundamental principles and constraints that needs to be fulfilled in CS. "An architechture for compressive imaging" [13] and "A New compressive imaging camera architecture using Optical-Domain Compression" [12] by Wakin et al. present the first single pixel camera architecture using CS. "Single-Pixel Imaging via Compressive Sampling" [11] by Duarte et al. contains an introduction to CS, different scanning methodologies and the SPC architecture. "A high resolution SWIR camera via compressed sensing" [8] by McMackin et al., at Inview Technology (which develop and produces compressive sensing cameras), contains a brief review of Compressive Imaging (CI) followed by a presentation of Inview Technology camera architecture.

Chengbo Li:s master's thesis "An Efficient Algorithm For Total Variation Regularization with Applications to the Single Pixel Camera and Compressive Sensing" [9] describes a total variation algorithm that Li constructed which solves the CS problem. The algorithm is faster and produces better results for images than previous popular algorithms.

The articles [3,6] describes why and how to implement Structurally Random Matrices (SRM). In these articles the Hadamard or DCT matrices are proposed to replace the random measurement matrix. With SRM the reconstruction time is reduced by replacing matrix multiplication with fast transforms. In addition to improving the reconstruction time, the new method does not need to store the measurement matrix in memory, which enables reconstruction of high resolution images. "An Improved Hadamard Measurement Matrix Based on Walsh Code For Compressive Sensing" [14] shows that sequency-ordered Walsh-Hadamard matrices give better reconstruction than the Hadamard matrix with the same benefits of using the Hadamard matrix. The resulting reconstructed image has near optimal reconstruction performance.

Deep learning [7] and Generative Adverserial Networks (GAN:s) [1] have also been used for image reconstruction from an ensemble of single pixel measurements. For specific scenes, Deep learning and GAN:s often generate superior image reconstruction. Unfortunately, those machine learning approaches generalise poorly to unseen scenes.

"Single Pixel SWIR Imaging using Compressed Sensing" [2] by Brännlund and Gustafsson, shows the initial results and proof of concept of the proposed SPC architecture in SWIR.

3   Single Pixel Camera (SPC) Architecture

The SPC platform consists of a Digital Micromirror Device (DMD), acting as a Spatial Light Modulator (SLM), a Newtonian telescope and a single pixel detector. This design has a narrow field of view ($22 \times 14 \ \mu rad$), which gives highly detailed scenes from a great distance. The aluminium Newtonian telescope consists of a concave primary mirror (108 mm, F4.1), and a flat secondary mirror, focusing the scene onto the DMD, see Fig. 1. The motivation to use a Newtonian telescope instead of a lens is partly that chromatic aberration is eliminated and partly that a reflective optical system works over a greater range of wavelengths. A visual spectrum reference camera is also mounted viewing the DMD to simplify setup and focusing of the system (the visual image is acquired in real time). The light on the DMD is reflected either onto the single pixel sensor or the reference camera. The lens mounted on the single pixel sensor is a 50 mm fixed focal length lens (f/1.4, 800–2000 nm spectral range). The single pixel sensor is a large area InGaAs photodiode with a built-in amplifier (Thorlabs PDA20C/M, 800–1700 nm spectral range). The DMD (Texas Instruments DLP4500NIR, 912 × 1140, 700–2500 nm spectral range) is a matrix of micro mirrors that can be individually tilted $\pm 12°$. The pseudo-random patterns are streamed as a video with a media player, from a computer through a video port (HDMI) to the control unit (DLPR LightCrafterTM 4500). The software (DLP LightCrafter 4500 Control Software) is setup to divide the received 24-bit color image into 1 bit planes which are displayed in consecutive order. The DLP control unit can be operated at a maximum speed of 2880 Hz (24 bit video signal at 120 Hz), but in the current configuration only 1440 Hz was achieved (24bit @60 Hz). At this rate with a subsampling ratio of 10% (number of measurements divided by number of pixels) with 512×512 pixel patterns, all samples are streamed in 17 s. The reconstructed image from the system will have the same resolution as the DMD patterns.

3.1   Signal Processing

The signal from the detector is greatly oversampled by a data acquisition device (NI USB-6210), such that a single value corresponding to each measurement matrix should be obtained. This is performed in two steps; first we omit samples when the DMD is changing pattern, then the mean is calculated and a signal $\mathbf{y}[m]$ that can be processed by the reconstruction algorithm is finally created, as seen in Fig. 2.

3.2   Dynamics in Scene

In natural outdoor scenes the sun is the primary light source. However, even on a clear day the intensity from the sun is not constant. This will reduce the reconstruction performance, because the mean intensity of the measured signal $\mathbf{y}$ is assumed to be stationary. Therefore the luminance change can be modelled as uniform additative noise.

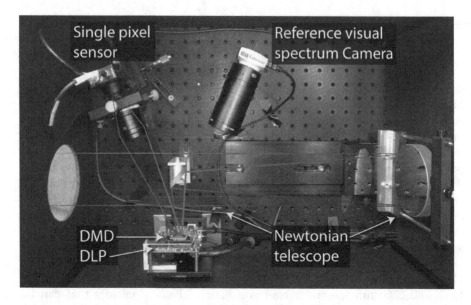

Fig. 1. The single pixel camera architecture used in this work. The optics, DMD, reference camera and the single pixel sensor are shown including red lines showing the light path. (Color figure online)

The measurements y can be decomposed according to

$$y = \Phi x + c, \tag{1}$$

where Φ is the measurement matrix, x is the scene viewed as an vectorized image, and c is the uniform intensity change vector. The goal is to remove the uniform intensity change vector c from signal y. c can be approximated by the moving average computed over k measurements and removed from y.

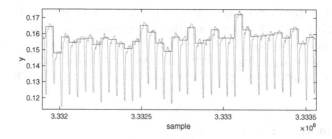

Fig. 2. Calculated mean values (blue) for each measurement matrix with transition measurements (green) omitted. (Color figure online)

4 Sparse Reconstrution Using Compressed Sensing

4.1 Sparse Reconstruction

Compressive Imaging (CI) exploits the fact that natural images are compressible or approximately sparse in some basis and therefore only a few measurements relative to the image pixel resolution needs to be measured in order to reconstruct the image. Two constraints must be fulfilled in order to utilize CS sampling: the image needs to be compressible and the measurement matrix need to be incoherent with the sparse transform. The first constraint is fulfilled because it is known that natural images are compressible using for example JPEG or JPEG2000 (using wavelet transform) and the second constraint is fulfilled using a measurement matrix with a random characteristic.

The single pixel sensor captures a scene by measuring the light intensity focused onto the detector reflected from the DMD pattern. The DMD pattern changes to obtain new measurements. M measurements are sampled to reconstruct an image with N pixels, where $M \ll N$. Each element in the measurement matrix is encoded as one or zero (turning the mirror onto or away from the sensor).

The compressive imaging sampling model is defined as

$$\mathbf{y} = \mathbf{\Phi} \mathbf{x} + \epsilon, \tag{2}$$

where $\mathbf{x}_{N \times 1}$ is the scene considered as an image rearranged as an array with N pixels, $\mathbf{y}_{M \times 1}$ is the sampled signal with M measurements, $\mathbf{\Phi}_{M \times N}$ is the measurements matrix and ϵ is the noise. CS states that M can be relatively small compared to N given how compressible the image is. This is because the image $\mathbf{x}$ can be represented as

$$\mathbf{\Psi} \theta = \mathbf{x}, \tag{3}$$

where $\mathbf{\Psi}_{N \times N}$ is some basis matrix and $\theta_{N \times 1}$ is the coefficients where θ is K-sparse. K-sparse means that the image $\mathbf{x}$ has K non-zero elements in basis $\mathbf{\Psi}$, $\|\theta\|_0 = K$. Given (3), (2) can be expanded to

$$\mathbf{y} = \mathbf{\Phi} \mathbf{x} + \epsilon = \mathbf{\Phi} \mathbf{\Psi} \theta + \epsilon = \mathbf{A} \theta + \epsilon, \tag{4}$$

where, $\mathbf{A}_{M \times N} = \mathbf{\Phi} \mathbf{\Psi}$ is called the reconstruction matrix.

The revelation in (4) is what makes CS powerful. By sampling the scene using the measurement matrix $\mathbf{\Phi}$ (as in (2)), but then in the reconstruction process transforming the measurement matrix $\mathbf{\Phi}$ to the reconstruction matrix $\mathbf{A}$ using some basis $\mathbf{\Psi}$, the optimization algorithm can solve the system for the sparse coefficients θ instead of the dense spatial image coefficients in $\mathbf{x}$ [10].

4.2 Permutated Sequency Ordered Walsh-Hadamard Measurement Matrix

Besides from eliminating the need to store the measuring matrix in computer memory for reconstruction, the Permutated Sequency Ordered Walsh-Hadamard matrix (PSOWHM) can be generated when sent to the DMD and thus eliminating the need to store the matrix. PSOWHM has approximately the same characteristics and properties as an independent and identically distributed (i.i.d.) random matrix but generally has a higher number of measurements for exact reconstruction of the image, $M \sim (KNs)\log^2(N)$, where s is the average number of non-zero indices in the measurement matrix. Research has however shown that there is no significant loss in recovery of the image relative to the i.i.d. random measurement matrix [14]. In order to construct the PSOWHM, the fist step is to define the naturally ordered Hadamard matrix and then follow a few additional steps. The naturally ordered Hadamard matrix of dimension 2^k is constructed by the recursive formula

$$H_0 = 1, \qquad H_1 = \begin{bmatrix} 1 & 1 \\ 1 & -1 \end{bmatrix},$$

and in general,

$$H_k = \begin{bmatrix} H_{k-1} & H_{k-1} \\ H_{k-1} & -H_{k-1} \end{bmatrix} = H_1 \otimes H_{k-1} \tag{5}$$

where $\otimes$ denotes the Kronecker product. The (natural ordered) Walsh-Hadamard matrix is converted to permutated sequency ordered Walsh-Hadamard matrix.

To use the sequency ordered Walsh-Hadamard matrix as a measurement matrix the first row is omitted, permutations to the columns are performed, M rows are choosen at random and the indices with -1 are shifted to 0. The permutations of the matrix is stored and used in the reconstruction [3,9,14].

4.3   Total Variation Regularization

To reconstruct the image $\mathbf{x}$, the most sparse set of coefficients in θ is desired. The optimal approach to find these coefficients would be to use ℓ_0-minimization

$$\hat{\theta} = \arg \min \; ||\theta||_0 \text{ subject to } \mathbf{y} = \mathbf{A}\theta. \tag{6}$$

Unfortunately, minimizing the non-zero indices in θ in the sparsifying basis $\mathbf{\Psi}$ is NP-hard. A better approach is the ℓ_1 minimization, for example Basis Pursuit denoise (BPDN),

$$\hat{\theta} = \arg \min \; ||\theta||_1 \text{ subject to } ||\mathbf{y} - \mathbf{A}\theta||_2 < \epsilon. \tag{7}$$

Donoho [4] proved the ℓ_0/ℓ_1 equivalence holds in the CS case, which implies a ℓ_1-minimizer is guaranteed to find the most spare solution in polynomial time in the noiseless case which can be approximated in the noisy and compressible signal case. The drawback with the ℓ_1-minimizer is that it requires more measurements than the optimal case with ℓ_0, but $M \ll N$ still holds [4,11,12].

The total variation (TV) based TVAL3 (Total Variation Augmented Lagrangian Alternating Direction Algorithm) is used for image reconstruction

[9]. Natural images often contain sharp edges and piecewise smooth areas which the TV regularization algorithm is good at preserving. The main difference between TV and other reconstruction algorithms is that TV considers the gradient of signal to be sparse instead of the signal itself, thus finding the most sparse gradient. The TV optimization problem in TVAL3 is defined as

$$\min_{\mathbf{x}} \Sigma_i ||D_i \mathbf{x}||, \text{ subject to } \mathbf{\Phi x} = y, \mathbf{x} \geq 0, \qquad (8)$$

where $D_i \mathbf{x}$ is the discrete gradient of $\mathbf{x}$ at position i. TVAL3 is an optimization method for solving constrained problems by substituting the original constrained problem with a series of unconstrained subproblems and introducing a penalty term. To solve the new subproblems the alternating direction method is used [9].

The main reason to use the PSOWH matrix is to eliminate the need to store the matrix in computer memory during reconstruction and to speed up the reconstruction. In TVAL3 there are two multiplications between a matrix and a vector that dominates the computation time, $\mathbf{\Phi x}^k$ and $\mathbf{\Phi}^\top (\mathbf{\Phi x} - y)$. The multiplication can be replaced with a fast transform. The sequence ordered Walsh-Hadamard matrix is a transform matrix, which also can be computed with the Fast Walsh-Hadamard Transform (FWHT), $\mathbf{Wx} = \text{FWHT}(\mathbf{x})$, where W is a sequence ordered Walsh Hadamard matrix and $\mathbf{x}$ is the image vector. The Walsh-Hadamard Transform (WHT) is a generalized class of Fourier transforms, which decomposes the input vector into a superposition of Walsh functions.

5   Experiments

The performance of the SPC is analyzed by evaluating a range of methods. All images captured by the SPC of natural scenes were taken at a distance between 200 to 900 m on sunny days with some clouds. Due to the DMD's matrix indexing and diamond shape, the rows of the patterns were repeated before it was sent to the DMD (two mirrors per pixel binned, 1024×512). That indexing made the pattern's ratio on the DMD to correspond to the correct ratio of 1 to 1. In the cases where the resolution was lower than 512×512, the pattern was scaled up so that it filled the maximum area of the DMD.

5.1   Image Reconstruction - Dynamic Scenes

Varying light conditions in the scene during image readout result in poor reconstruction performance, especially during long exposure times. The sensor sums up half the scene's light - 50% of the mirrors are oriented toward the sensor -, which make the intensity change for each sensor readout a global change. In Fig. 3, signals and a reconstructed image (captured in good conditions with strong lighting) with and without the moving mean algorithm are shown. The moving mean is corresponding to light intensity change. The number of neighboring samples to calculate the average was set to $k = 75$, which corresponds to a window of 50 ms. This method increases the image quality significantly for outdoor scenes.

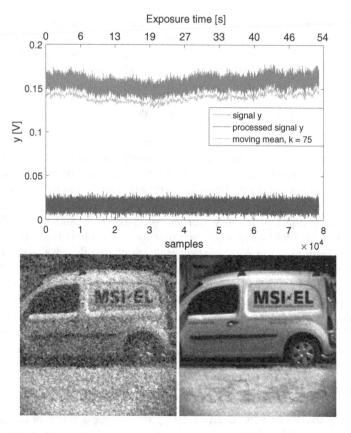

Fig. 3. Top: Sampled signal from SPC with light intensity change distortion and the signal processed by the moving mean algorithm. Bottom: Reconstructed images before (left) and after (right) applying moving mean algorithm on the sampled signal

Fig. 4. Shows images captured with the SPC with a zoomed-in view of a sample edge.

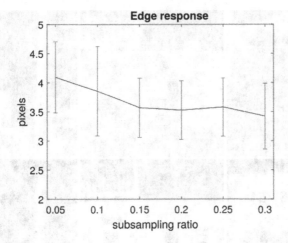

Fig. 5. Edge response, as the distance (pixels) to rise from 10% to 90% in average for an edge.

5.2 Edge Response Anlaysis

The edge response is used to compare and characterize the image quality of camera systems (including lenses) and in this section the edge response for SPC is analysed. Two scenes were captured by the SPC, containing printed sheets of paper with tilted edges lit by a 135 W halogen lamp placed two meters from the sheet.

Fig. 6. Varying minimum subsampling ratios (2%, 3% and 3%) to reconstruct sample images captured by the SPC.

The mean and the standard deviation are estimated for the SPC, for all edges in the images. For the SPC, images reconstructed from 5% to 30% were tested in order to see if the subsampling ratio affected the edge response result. The images are presented in Fig. 4. The edge response is measured as the distance in (pixels) required for an edge to rise from 10% to 90% intensity change. The result from the experiment is presented in Fig. 5.

Fig. 7. Varying subsampling ratios - first row: visual image, second row: 5%, third row: 10% and fourth row 15% - to reconstruct sample images captured by the SPC.

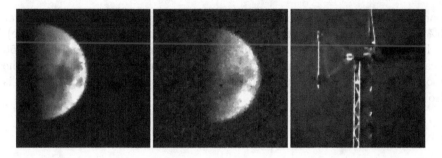

Fig. 8. (left) The moon captured at night at resolution 128 × 128, subsampling ratio 0.3 and sampling time 1 s, (middle) the moon captured at resolution 256 × 256, subsampling ratio 0.2 and sampling time 9 s. The noise is due to the motion of the moon during sampling. (right) A construction crane captured at resolution 128 × 128, subsampling ratio 0.3 and sampling time 1 s.

Some improvement is seen when the subsample ratio is increased, but the standard deviation is almost constant.

5.3   Image Reconstruction

The number of measurements needed to reconstruct an image depends on the sparsity or compressibility of the image. It is hard to give a good estimate of the subsampling ratio needed to obtain a desired quality of the reconstruction. In addition, using an SPC where noise contaminates the signal and the scene may not be completely stationary, the number of measurements needed will increase in proportion to the noise and the change in the scene.

Reconstruction of an image using a minimum of sample results in a noisy image. A subjective investigation of the minimum subsampling ratio was performed on the images captured by the SPC, where the quality of each image was studied in 1% subsample ratio increment. A recognizable image was obtained when the ratio was in the range from 2% to 4%.

In the sample images in Fig. 6, the minimum subsampling ratio varied between 2% to 3%. However, as can be seen in the images the motive is merely recognizable, large structures can be identified but details are lost. In general a subsampling ratio of 5% has always succeeded to reconstruct an identifiable image with some fine details.

In Fig. 7 three scenes are reconstructed using different subsample ratios ranging 5%, 10% and 15%. This result can give a perception of which subsampling ratio is good enough for a given purpose. As can be seen, the increase of the subsampling ratio is not linearly proportional to the increase in perceived image quality.

From the images in Fig. 7, it can be observed that already at 5% subsampling ratio the scene can be properly identified. At 10% the finer details appear, like the gap between the panels in the facade. The outline of the text on the car and door are getting sharper and the structures in the faces start to appear. After 15% the reconstitution quality does not improve much (not shown in the figure).

In Fig. 8 the moon captured at night at resolution 128×128 and 256×256 is captured. The noise in the 256×256 reconstruction is due to motion of the moon during sampling. A construction crane captured at resolution 128×128 is also shown in Fig. 8 .

6   Conclusions

The main attractiveness of compressive imaging, in comparison to conventional imaging using focal plane arrays, lies in the relaxation of the size, weight, power and cost of components for both image collection and transmission. The single pixel camera (SPC) developed and here presented has demonstrated the possibility to capture high quality SWIR images at resolutions up to 512×512 pixels, with about the tenth of the cost a conventional camera with the same resolution. A large number of outdoor scenes with varying illumination and over relatively long distances has been collected. We also capture images of the moon at 128×128 after sunset.

Visual inspection of the reconstructed images show that image quality generally increases up to about 15–20% subsampling ratios, but that often an adequate quality can be achieved already at 5–10% and that the minimum subsampling ratio is about 2–4 % for most of the collected scenes. Reconstruction speed of the SPC and image resolution has been increased by introducing the Walsh-Hadamard pseudo-random matrices presented in the paper, but the collection time for a full resolution 512×512 image at a 10% subsampling ratio still takes about 17 s with the current system setup. Such long collection times naturally introduces sensitivities to scene and light changes, mainly manifested as noise in the reconstructed images, but it has been shown that the latter can be somewhat mitigated by introducing a moving average in the signal processing chain. It is however still a high priority to reduce both collection and reconstruction time, in order to make the system more useful for more dynamic scenes and real-time operation. This will be the focus of future work.

References

1. Bora, A., Jalal, A., Price, E., Dimakis, A.G.: Compressed sensing using generative models. In: International Conference on Machine Learning (ICML) (2017)
2. Brännlund, C., Gustafsson, D.: Single pixel SWIR imaging using compressed sensing. In: Symposium on Image Analysis, 14–15 March 2017, Linköping, Sweden (2017)
3. Do, T.T., Gan, L., Nguyen, N., Tran, T.: Fast and efficient compressive sensing using structurally random matrices. IEEE Trans. Signal Process. **60**(1), 139–154 (2012)
4. Donoho, D.L.: Compressed sensing. IEEE Trans. Inf. Theory **52**(4), 1289–1306 (2006)

5. Elad, M.: Sparse and Redundant Representations. Springer, New York (2010). https://doi.org/10.1007/978-1-4419-7011-4
6. Gan, L., Do, T.T., Tran, T.D.: Fast compressive imaging using scrambled block Hadamard ensemble. In: 16th European Signal Processing Conference (2008)
7. Higham, C.F., Murray-Smith, R., Padgett, M.J., Edgar, M.P.: Deep learning for real-time single-pixel video. Sci. Rep. **8**, 2369 (2018)
8. McMackin, L., Herman, M.A., Chatterjee, B., Weldon, M.: A high-resolution SWIR camera via compressed sensing. In: SPIE, vol. 8353 (2012)
9. Li, C.: An efficient algorithm for total variation regularization with applications to the single pixel camera and compressive sensing. Master's thesis, Rice University (2009)
10. Rish, I., Grabarnik, G.Y.: Sparse Modeling. CRC Press, Boca Raton (2015)
11. Takhar, D., Laska, J.N., Duarte, M.F., Kelly, K.F., Baraniuk, R.G., Davenport, M.A.: Single-pixel imaging via compressive sampling. IEEE Signal Process. Mag. **25**, 83–91 (2008)
12. Takhar, D., et al.: A new compressive imaging camera architecture using optical-domain compression. In: IS&T/SPIE Computational Imaging, vol. 5 (2006)
13. Wakin, M.B., et al.: An architecture for compressive imaging. In: IEEE International Conference on Image Processing (ICIP), 8–11 October 2006, pp. 1273–1276 (2006)
14. Zhuoran, C., Honglin, Z., Min, J., Gang, W., Jingshi, S.: An improved Hadamard measurement matrix based on Walsh code for compressive sensing. In: 9th International Conference on Information, Communications Signal Processing (2013)

Zonohedral Approximation of Spherical Structuring Element for Volumetric Morphology

Patrick M. Jensen[⊠], Camilla H. Trinderup, Anders B. Dahl,
and Vedrana A. Dahl

Department of Applied Mathematics and Computer Science,
Technical University of Denmark, Kgs. Lyngby, Denmark
patmjen@dtu.dk

Abstract. Performing dilation and erosion using large structuring elements can be computationally slow – a problem especially pronounced when processing volumetric data. To reduce the computational complexity of dilation/erosion using spherical structuring elements, we propose a method for approximating a sphere with a zonohedron. Since zonohedra can be created via successive dilations/erosions of line segments, this allows morphological operations to be performed in constant time per voxel. As the complexity of commonly used methods typically scales with the size of the structuring element, our method significantly improves the run time. We use the proposed approximation to detect large spherical objects in volumetric data. Results are compared with other image analysis frameworks demonstrating constant run time and significant performance gains.

Keywords: Morphology · Computational efficiency · Zonohedra

1 Introduction

Morphological operations of dilation and erosion are well-established image processing methods, and significant effort has been put into developing efficient algorithms for gray-scale morphology. An important advance, also for our work, is the van Herk/Gil-Werman algorithm [8,20] which computes 1D dilation and erosion in constant time per pixel – regardless of the length of the structuring element. This opens a possibility for efficient 2D and 3D algorithms, if the structuring element can be decomposed in linear components.

Decompositions and approximations of various 2D structuring elements have been known for decades, while 3D structuring elements have received almost no attention. This also holds true for the 3D sphere, which is a structuring element of large practical importance, as it is invariant to rotation. To our knowledge, approximation of the 3D sphere has not been treated in the context relevant for

© Springer Nature Switzerland AG 2019
M. Felsberg et al. (Eds.): SCIA 2019, LNCS 11482, pp. 128–139, 2019.
https://doi.org/10.1007/978-3-030-20205-7_11

morphological filtering of digital volumes. Furthermore, when investigating how 3D morphology is handled by software commonly used for image processing, we found no evidence of fully utilizing the approximation of the sphere.

Efficient computation is especially important in 3D image processing, where the volume of a spherical structuring element grows cubically with the radius, and datasets are often large. In particular, applications requiring multiple passes of morphological filtering, like granulometry or porosity analysis, might be seriously affected by the lack of efficient algorithms for 3D dilation and erosion.

In this paper we treat the problem of approximating a 3D sphere of an arbitrary radius with linear components. Our main contribution is an algorithm for approximating a 3D sphere using a zonohedron. The resulting linear components can be used for morphological filtering in any image processing framework. When combined with the van Herk/Gil-Werman algorithm, computational complexity of dilation or erosion is independent of the radius of the sphere. Furthermore, based on our sphere approximation, we implemented an efficient GPU-based dilation/erosion which is available at https://github.com/patmjen/Zonohedra. To exemplify the use of our method we apply gray-scale opening to detect spheres in μCT data of cement and stone wool. And lastly, we perform tests showing the benefits of our sphere approximation, and the efficiency of our implementation.

1.1   Related Work

Research in increasing the computational speed in 2D morphology [18] generally falls in two categories. The first seek to exploit simplifying assumptions, for example by only considering binary or integer data [13,19] or by assuming a flat structuring element [17]. The other category attempts to decompose or approximate the structuring element with a series of shapes which can be processed quickly. The flat line segment is particularly attractive thanks to the van Herk/Gil-Werman [8,20] algorithm. They have shown that erosion/dilation with a horizontal, vertical or diagonal structuring element requires only three operations per pixel. This was improved [7] and generalized to operations with discrete lines at arbitrary angles [16].

Many structuring elements cannot be decomposed into line segments and one has to resort to a approximation. As stated by Adams [1], a 2D disk can be approximated via successive dilations/erosions of line segments. This technique was extended to 3D in the context of solid modeling [10]. However, they only deal with the case where all line segments have equal and continuous length, which makes it impractical for digital images defined on a discrete grid. An extensive theoretical study of the approximation of n-dimensional spheres (and other shapes) using dilations of continuous line segments has been performed by Bourgain et al. [3] and Campi et al. [5]. Techniques for exact decomposition have also been explored, e.g. where a structuring element is decomposed into elements of size 3×3 [14,15], or with an explicit focus on spheres [21]. However, these still scale with the size of the structuring element and are therefore still problematic when working with large structures – especially for volumetric data.

2   Method

2.1   Computational Complexity of Mathematical Morphology

Fundamental operations of mathematical morphology are the dilation and erosion. For an image I and a binary (flat) structuring element S, dilation and erosion are given by, respectively,

$$(I \oplus S)(\mathbf{x}) = \max_{\mathbf{y} \in S} \{I(\mathbf{x} + \mathbf{y})\}, \tag{1}$$

and

$$(I \ominus S)(\mathbf{x}) = \min_{\mathbf{y} \in S} \{I(\mathbf{x} + \mathbf{y})\}, \tag{2}$$

where $\mathbf{y} \in S$ refers to the position of non-zero values in S. A direct implementation of dilation/erosion leads to an algorithm requiring s comparisons per image pixel, s being a number of non-zero values in S. In 3D morphology using a spherical structuring element, the direct algorithm scales with the cube of the sphere radius.

An important reduction in computational complexity can be made in the special case where non-zero voxels are arranged on a line. In this case, the van Herk/Gil-Werman algorithm [8, 20] allows dilation/erosion with only three comparisons per image pixel, independent of the structuring element size.

Since dilation is associative [9] we have

$$I \oplus (S_1 \oplus S_2 \oplus ... \oplus S_m) = (...((I \oplus S_1) \oplus S_2) \oplus ....) \oplus S_m, \tag{3}$$

with the dual property valid for erosion

$$I \ominus (S_1 \oplus S_2 \oplus ... \oplus S_m) = (...((I \ominus S_1) \ominus S_2) \ominus ....) \ominus S_m. \tag{4}$$

Thus, if a sphere S can be decomposed such that $S = S_1 \oplus S_2 \oplus ... \oplus S_m$, dilation/erosion with S may be accomplished via successive dilations/erosions with $S_1, S_2, ..., S_m$. When the number of non-zero values in S exceeds the sum of non-zero values in the decomposition, the implementation utilizing decomposition of S will be more efficient. Even better, if m is fixed and decomposition is such that dilations/erosions with $S_1, S_2, ..., S_m$ exploit the constant-time algorithm of van Herk/Gil-Werman, we can achieve an implementation with computational complexity independent of the radius of S. This will reduce the computational work per voxel from $O(r^3)$ to $O(1)$ and allow efficient morphological filtering with large structuring elements.

Our aim is to approximate a 3D spherical structuring element using a series of dilations with line segments. The similar 2D approximation, utilized for 2D image morphology by Adams [1], is illustrated in Fig. 1. Since a series of dilations with line segments corresponds to a Minkowski sum, the resulting shape will, by definition, be a zonohedron [11].

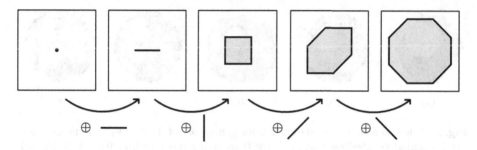

Fig. 1. Successive dilations with line segments. The resulting shape approximates a disk.

2.2   Constructing the Zonohedral Approximation

A zonohedron is a convex polyhedron defined as a Minkowski sum (dilation) of a finite number of line segments [11]. For a zonohedron centered around the origin, line segments are usually represented as vectors $V = \{\mathbf{v}_1, \mathbf{v}_2, ..., \mathbf{v}_n\}$, $\mathbf{v}_i \in \mathbb{R}^3$, called generators. The zonohedron is then given as

$$Z = \left\{ \sum_{i=1}^{n} d_i \mathbf{v}_i \;\middle|\; -1/2 \leq d_i \leq 1/2, \mathbf{v}_i \in V \right\}. \tag{5}$$

For the purpose of volumetric filtering, generators with a simple voxelization are of highest interest. Therefore, we restrict ourselves to three sets of direction vectors

$$
\begin{aligned}
V_1 &= \{(1,0,0), (0,1,0), (0,0,1)\}, \\
V_2 &= \{(1,1,0), (-1,1,0), (0,1,1), (0,-1,1), (1,0,1), (1,0,-1)\}, \\
V_3 &= \{(1,1,1), (-1,1,1), (1,-1,1), (1,1,-1)\}.
\end{aligned}
\tag{6}
$$

On a unit cube, vectors in V_1 connect centers of opposite faces, those in V_2 connect midpoints of opposite edges, and those in V_3 connect opposite corners.

To change the shape and the size of a zonohedron, while keeping it roughly spherical, we scale the direction vectors in each set with $a_j \geq 0, j = 1, 2, 3$, and consider zonohedra defined by the set of 13 generators

$$V = a_1 V_1 \cup a_2 V_2 \cup a_3 V_3, \tag{7}$$

where $a_j V_j = \{a_j \mathbf{v} \mid \mathbf{v} \in V_j\}$. Examples of zonohedra generated by these vectors are shown in Fig. 2, which also shows the most general case, a truncated rhombicuboctahedron. Note that for integer values of a_1, a_2, a_3 the generators will all have integer coordinates, and simple voxelization.

2.3   Minimizing Approximation Error

To find a good approximation, we chose to minimize the directed Hausdorff distance d_h between the surface of Z, denoted ∂Z, and a sphere with radius r,

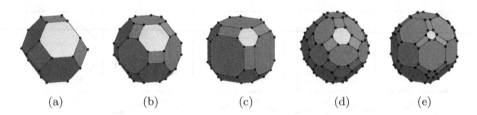

(a)   (b)   (c)   (d)   (e)

Fig. 2. A few zonohedra constructed from generator set $\mathcal{V} = a_1\mathcal{V}_1 \cup a_2\mathcal{V}_2 \cup a_3\mathcal{V}_3$. (a) Truncated octahedron from $\mathcal{V}_2$. (b) Truncated cuboctahedron from $\mathcal{V}_1 \cup \mathcal{V}_2$. (c) Truncated cuboctahedron from $3\mathcal{V}_1 \cup \mathcal{V}_2$. (d) Truncated rhombicuboctahedron from $\mathcal{V}_1 \cup \mathcal{V}_2 \cup \mathcal{V}_3$. (e) Truncated rhombicuboctahedron from $4\mathcal{V}_1 \cup \mathcal{V}_2 \cup 2\mathcal{V}_3$.

denoted ∂B. The directed Hausdorff distance is defined by [12]

$$d_{\mathrm{h}}(\partial Z, \partial B) = \sup_{\mathbf{x} \in \partial Z} \inf_{\mathbf{y} \in \partial B} d(\mathbf{x}, \mathbf{y}), \tag{8}$$

and since ∂B is a sphere this reduces to

$$d_{\mathrm{h}}(\partial Z, \partial B) = \max_{\mathbf{x} \in \partial Z} |\|\mathbf{x}\| - r| \,. \tag{9}$$

The directed Hausdorff distance finds the point in ∂Z which has the greatest distance to ∂B and then reports that distance. The point in question, in our case, will either be the point in ∂Z furthest away from the origin (maximizer of $\|\mathbf{x}\| - r$), or the point closest to the origin (maximizer of $r - \|\mathbf{x}\|$).

The point in ∂Z furthest away from the origin has to be a vertex of Z, and since all vertices of our zonohedron have one of two distances from the origin (see Fig. 3(a)), only two vertices need to be considered when maximizing $\|\mathbf{x}\| - r$.

To find the point in ∂Z closest to the origin, we notice that Z has four different types of faces (see Fig. 3(a)). Three of those (two kinds of octagons and a hexagon) have the point closest to the origin in the center of the face. It can be shown that the last type of face (quadrilateral) never contains a point either furthest or closest to the origin, so these need not be considered. In conclusion, we can reduce (9) to

$$d_{\mathrm{h}}(\partial Z, \partial B) = \max \left\{ \max_{k=1,2} \{\|\mathbf{p}_k\| - r\}, \max_{k=3,4,5} \{r - \|\mathbf{p}_k\|\} \right\}, \tag{10}$$

where $\mathbf{p}_k$ are two vertices of Z and centers of three faces of Z as indicated in Fig. 3(b).

Each of five points $\mathbf{p}_k$ can be expressed as a linear combination of generators from $\mathcal{V}$. Due to our grouping of the generators, we can find five matrices $\mathbf{M}_k$ such that

$$\mathbf{p}_k = \mathbf{M}_k \mathbf{a} \,,$$

where $\mathbf{a} = (a_1, a_2, a_3)^T$. For the points indicated in Fig. 3(b) we identified the five matrices as

$$\mathbf{M}_1 = \begin{bmatrix} \frac{1}{2} & 0 & 1 \\ \frac{1}{2} & 1 & 1 \\ \frac{1}{2} & 2 & 1 \end{bmatrix}, \mathbf{M}_2 = \begin{bmatrix} \frac{1}{2} & 0 & 0 \\ \frac{1}{2} & 1 & 0 \\ \frac{1}{2} & 2 & 2 \end{bmatrix}, \mathbf{M}_3 = \begin{bmatrix} \frac{1}{2} & 2 & 2 \\ 0 & 0 & 0 \\ 0 & 0 & 0 \end{bmatrix}, \mathbf{M}_4 = \begin{bmatrix} \frac{1}{2} & \frac{3}{2} & 1 \\ \frac{1}{2} & \frac{3}{2} & 1 \\ 0 & 0 & 0 \end{bmatrix}, \mathbf{M}_5 = \begin{bmatrix} \frac{1}{2} & 1 & 1 \\ \frac{1}{2} & 1 & 1 \\ \frac{1}{2} & 1 & 1 \end{bmatrix}. \quad (11)$$

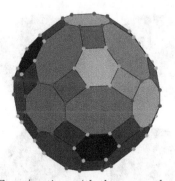
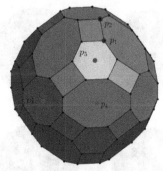

(a) Faces/vertices with the same color are equivalent with respect to the distance from the origin.

(b) Points needed for the directed Hausdorff distance. Blue are vertices, red are face centers.

Fig. 3. The symmetry of the truncated rhombicuboctahedron. (Color figure online)

To find the values of $\mathbf{a} = (a_1, a_2, a_3)^T$ resulting in the best zonohedral approximation, we solve the following optimization problem

$$\min_{\mathbf{a}} \max \left\{ \max_{k=1,2} \{ \|\mathbf{M}_k \mathbf{a}\| - r \}, \max_{k=3,4,5} \{ r - \|\mathbf{M}_k \mathbf{a}\| \} \right\} \quad (12)$$
$$\text{s.t. } 0 \leq a_j.$$

Rewriting this on epigraph form results in a second order cone problem which is convex [4]. Thus, using a branch and bound method [2], we can find integer solutions which are globally optimal but not necessarily unique.

It should be noted that one can additionally constrain the zonohedron so it is either contained within, or contains, the sphere of radius r, without losing convexity. Furthermore, it is useful to add the constraint that $a_1 \geq 1$, otherwise the resulting structuring element is not guaranteed to be solid – instead it will have a checkerboard pattern.

3   Results

We first assess the quality of the zonohedral approximation by comparing it with a sphere. Figure 4 shows the result of dilating a single voxel with a discretized sphere and with a corresponding zonohedral approximation. For small radii the discretized sphere and its zonohedral approximation are equal, but for larger radii the difference is more apparent. This is also illustrated in Fig. 5, which shows that the directed Hausdorff distance increases linearly with the radius. When the zonohedron is constrained to be inside or outside the sphere the distance roughly doubles. The jagged lines are due to constraining the zonohedron to have integer side lengths.

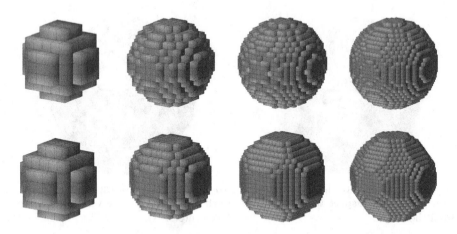

Fig. 4. Discretized spheres (top) and their zonohedral approximations (bottom). The radii are (left to right): 3, 6, 9, and 12 voxels.

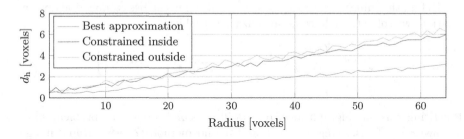

Fig. 5. Directed Hausdorff distances between zonohedral approximation and a sphere at different radii. Distances are shown for the best possible approximation, and two constrained cases.

We now apply the developed method to two 3D X-ray μCT scans containing large spherical structures. The first is a porous cement sample which contains spherical bubbles of varying size. The second is a network of stone wool fibers, that holds a number of spherical impurities. The volumes consist of $2048 \times 2048 \times 2048$ for the cement sample and $958 \times 1011 \times 3642$ voxels for the stone wool sample. A morphological opening was performed on both volumes using a discretized sphere of radius 16 and a zonohedral approximation, with

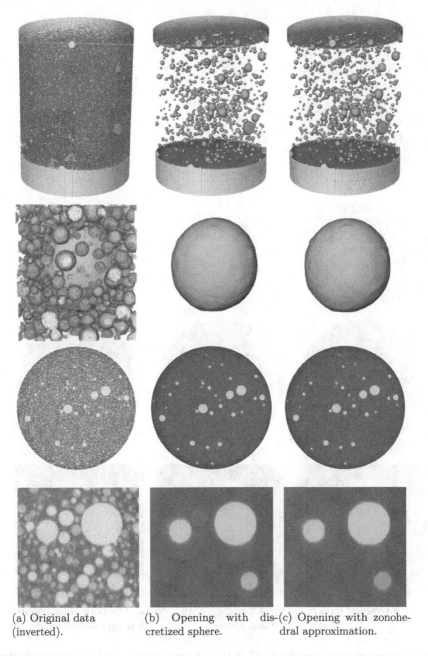

(a) Original data (inverted).

(b) Opening with discretized sphere.

(c) Opening with zonohedral approximation.

Fig. 6. Morphological opening of a 3D X-ray CT scan of cement containing spherical bubbles. Data has been inverted and thresholded to make the structures of interest more visible. The two top rows show a 3D rendering of the full volume and a zoom on a small region. The bottom rows show a horizontal slice of the full and zoomed volume. Results are shown using both a discretized sphere of radius 16 and its zonohedral approximation as the structuring element.

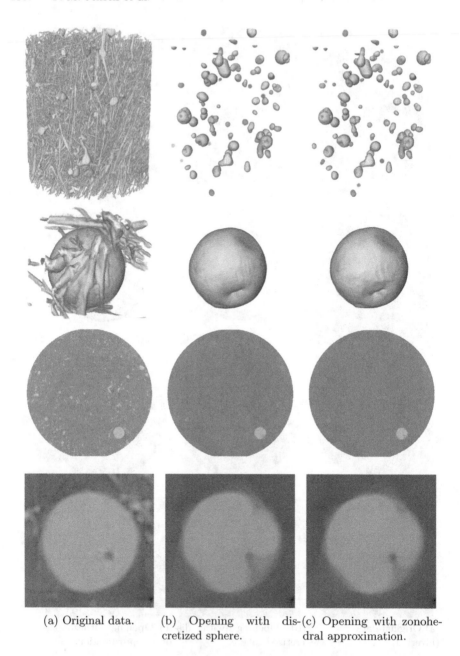

(a) Original data.   (b) Opening with dis-(c) Opening with zonohe-
                       cretized sphere.   dral approximation.

Fig. 7. Morphological opening of a 3D X-ray CT scan of stone wool containing spherical impurities. The data has been thresholded to enhance structures of interest. The two top rows show a 3D rendering of a subset of the full volume and a zoom on a small region. The bottom rows show a horizontal slice of the full and zoomed volume. Results are shown using both a discretized sphere of radius 16 and its zonohedral approximation as the structuring element.

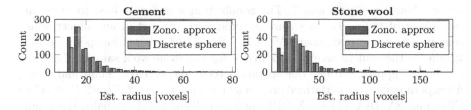

Fig. 8. Radius distributions for the detected objects shown in Figs. 6 and 7.

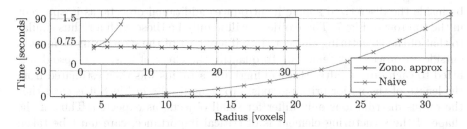

Fig. 9. Run times for dilation with a spherical structuring element using a naive implementation and a zonohedral approximation. Benchmarks were run on a volume of unsigned 8-bit integers with size $500 \times 500 \times 500$.

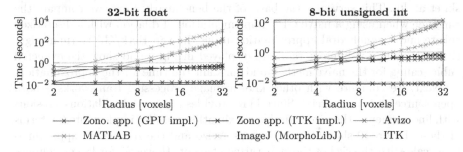

Fig. 10. Comparison of run times for different implementations of dilation with a spherical structuring element shown in a log-log plot. Benchmarks were run on a volume of size $100 \times 100 \times 100$.

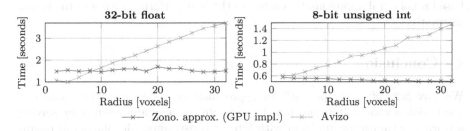

Fig. 11. Comparison of run times for dilation with a spherical structuring element using the zonohedral approximation and the one provided by Avizo. Benchmarks were run on a volume of size $500 \times 500 \times 500$.

results shown in Figs. 6 and 7. The zonohedron was constrained to be within the sphere of radius 16, to ensure it could be contained in any object which contains the discretized sphere. With the discretized sphere, the operation took 40 min for the cement sample and 15 min for the stone wool sample. Using the zonohedral approximation, the operation took, respectively, 2 min and 1 min. All experiments were performed on a machine with an Intel® Xeon® E5-2637 v3 CPU, and NVIDIA TITAN X GPU, and 256 GB of RAM. Visually, the results are quite similar; the main difference lies with small objects as illustrated in the bottom right of Fig. 6(c). Furthermore, since the zonohedron is constrained to be inside the discretized sphere it introduces additional objects, as is apparent in the top row of Fig. 7. These objects will mainly be those with a radius similar to that of the structuring element since if any part of the structuring element is outside an object it is removed. To quantify the effect of this, an ellipsoid was fitted to each object (after thresholding) and a radius was then estimated from the length of the major principal axis. From the results in Fig. 8 it is clear that the radius distributions only differ for small objects, as expected. Thus, if the shape of the structuring element is of critical importance, care must be taken before applying the zonohedral approximation.

Finally, we evaluate the computational performance of our method. In order to make the method viable for large volumes we made a GPU implementation of the van Herk/Gil-Werman algorithm [8,20] based on the description by Domanski et al. [6]. This serves as the basis of the benchmark. First, we compare the run time when using a naive GPU implementation of dilation with a discretized sphere and a zonohedral approximation using the van Herk/Gil-Werman algorithm. Results for different radii are displayed in Fig. 9 and show the expected cubic scaling for the naive method and constant run time for the approximation.

Next, we compare with other known image processing frameworks – both open source and commercial. Since ITK provides a way to do dilations/erosions with line segments, the zonohedral approximation was also implemented in terms of these. Figure 10 shows that all except Avizo and the zonohedral approximation scale with the size of the structuring element. However, for larger volumes Avizo does scale with the radius which is evident from Fig. 11. The reason for ITK's improvement when using integers is that it changes to a moving histogram algorithm, such as the one proposed by Droogenbroeck et al. [19]. Still, the GPU based zonohedral approximation achieves the best performance out of the tested alternatives.

4   Conclusion

We have presented an approach for approximating a spherical structuring element with a zonohedron and how to compute its generator vectors by solving a convex optimization problem with integer constraints. Morphological operations with the zonohedral approximation can easily be implemented in any image processing framework which supports dilation/erosion with line segments. This allows morphological filtering to be run efficiently with significantly reduced computation times compared to other frameworks. Finally, the run times are independent of the size of the structuring element, which further increases the performance benefit for large structures.

References

1. Adams, R.: Radial decomposition of disks and spheres. CVGIP: Graph. Models Image Process. **55**(5), 325–332 (1993)
2. Belotti, P., Kirches, C., Leyffer, S., Linderoth, J., Luedtke, J., Mahajan, A.: Mixed-integer nonlinear optimization. Acta Numerica **22**, 1–131 (2013)
3. Bourgain, J., Lindenstrauss, J., Milman, V.: Approximation of zonoids by zono-topes. Acta mathematica **162**(1), 73–141 (1989)
4. Boyd, S., Vandenberghe, L.: Convex Optimization. Cambridge University Press, Cambridge (2004)
5. Campi, S., Haas, D., Weil, W.: Approximation of zonoids by zonotopes in fixed directions. Discrete Comput. Geometry **11**(4), 419–431 (1994)
6. Domanski, L., Vallotton, P., Wang, D.: Parallel van Herk/Gil-Werman image mor-phology on GPUs using CUDA. In: GPU Technology Conference (2009)
7. Gil, J., Kimmel, R.: Efficient dilation, erosion, opening, and closing algorithms. IEEE Trans. Pattern Anal. Mach. Intell. **24**(12), 1606–1617 (2002)
8. Gil, J., Werman, M.: Computing 2-D min, median, and max filters. IEEE Trans. Pattern Anal. Mach. Intell. **15**(5), 504–507 (1993)
9. Haralick, R.M., Sternberg, S.R., Zhuang, X.: Image analysis using mathematical morphology. IEEE Trans. Pattern Anal. Mach. Intell. **4**, 532–550 (1987)
10. Martinez, J., Hornus, S., Claux, F., Lefebvre, S.: Chained segment offsetting for ray-based solid representations. Comput. Graph. **46**, 36–47 (2015)
11. McMullen, P.: On zonotopes. Trans. Am. Math. Soc. **159**, 91–109 (1971)
12. Munkres, J.: Topology. Featured Titles for Topology Series, 2nd edn. Prentice Hall, Incorporated, Upper Saddle River (2000)
13. Nikopoulos, N., Pitas, I.: A fast implementation of 3-D binary morphological trans-formations. IEEE Trans. Image Process. **9**(2), 283–286 (2000)
14. Park, H., Chin, R.T.: Decomposition of arbitrarily shaped morphological structur-ing elements. IEEE Trans. Pattern Anal. Mach. Intell. **17**(1), 2–15 (1995)
15. Shih, F.Y., Wu, Y.T.: Decomposition of binary morphological structuring elements based on genetic algorithms. Comput. Vis. Image Underst. **99**(2), 291–302 (2005)
16. Soille, P., Breen, E.J., Jones, R.: Recursive implementation of erosions and dilations along discrete lines at arbitrary angles. IEEE Trans. Pattern Anal. Mach. Intell. **18**(5), 562–567 (1996)
17. Urbach, E.R., Wilkinson, M.H.: Efficient 2-D gray-scale dilations and erosions with arbitrary flat structuring elements. In: IEEE International Conference on Image Processing, pp. 1573–1576. IEEE (2006)
18. Van Droogenbroeck, M., Buckley, M.J.: Morphological erosions and openings: fast algorithms based on anchors. J. Math. Imaging Vis. **22**(2–3), 121–142 (2005)
19. Van Droogenbroeck, M., Talbot, H.: Fast computation of morphological opera-tions with arbitrary structuring elements. Pattern Recogn. Lett. **17**(14), 1451–1460 (1996)
20. Van Herk, M.: A fast algorithm for local minimum and maximum filters on rect-angular and octagonal kernels. Pattern Recogn. Lett. **13**(7), 517–521 (1992)
21. Vaz, M.S., Kiraly, A.P., Mersereau, R.M.: Multi-level decomposition of Euclidean spheres. In: International Symposium on Mathematical Morphology, pp. 461–472 (2007)

Image Invariants to Anisotropic Gaussian Blur

Jitka Kostková[1]([✉])([iD]), Jan Flusser[1], Matěj Lébl[1], and Matteo Pedone[2]([iD])

[1] The Czech Academy of Sciences, Institute of Information Theory and Automation,
Pod Vodárenskou věží 4, 182 08 Prague 8, Czech Republic
{kostkova,flusser,lebl}@utia.cas.cz
[2] The Center for Machine Vision Research,
Department of Computer Science and Engineering, University of Oulu,
90014 Oulu, Finland
matped@ee.oulu.fi

Abstract. The paper presents a new theory of invariants to Gaussian blur. Unlike earlier methods, the blur kernel may be arbitrary oriented, scaled and elongated. Such blurring is a semi-group action in the image space, where the orbits are classes of blur-equivalent images. We propose a non-linear projection operator which extracts blur-insensitive component of the image. The invariants are then formally defined as moments of this component but can be computed directly from the blurred image without an explicit construction of the projections. Image description by the new invariants does not require any prior knowledge of the particular blur kernel shape and does not include any deconvolution. Potential applications are in blur-invariant image recognition and in robust template matching.

Keywords: Gaussian blur · Semi-group · Projection operator · Image moments · Moment invariants

1 Introduction

One of the most common degradations in image processing is *blur*. Capturing an ideal scene f by an imaging device with the blurring point-spread function (PSF) h, the observed image g can be modeled as a convolution of both

$$g = f * h. \tag{1}$$

This linear image formation model is a reasonably accurate approximation of many imaging devices and acquisition scenarios. In this paper, we concentrate our attention to the case when the PSF is a general anisotropic Gaussian function with unknown parameters.

This work was supported by the Czech Science Foundation (Grant No. GA18-07247S), by the *Praemium Academiae*, and by the Grant Agency of the Czech Technical University (Grant No. SGS18/188/OHK4/3T/14).

© Springer Nature Switzerland AG 2019
M. Felsberg et al. (Eds.): SCIA 2019, LNCS 11482, pp. 140–151, 2019.
https://doi.org/10.1007/978-3-030-20205-7_12

Gaussian blur appears whenever the image has been acquired through a turbulent medium and the acquisition/exposure time is by far longer than the period of Brownian motion of the particles in the medium. Ground-based astronomical imaging through the atmosphere, taking pictures through a fog, underwater imaging, and fluorescence microscopy are typical examples of such situation (in some cases, the blur may be coupled with a contrast decrease). Gaussian blur is also introduced into the images as the sensor blur which is due to a finite size of the sampling pulse. Gaussian blur may be sometimes applied intentionally, for instance due to an on-chip denoising.

A complete recovering of f from Eq. (1) is an ill-posed inverse problem, whose solution, regardless of the particular method used, is ambiguous, unstable and time consuming [1,2,13,14].

If our goal is an object classification, a complete knowledge of f is not necessary. Highly compressed information about the object, even if it has been extracted from a blurred image without any restoration, could be sufficient provided that the features used for object description are not much affected by blur. This idea was originally proposed by Flusser et al. [4–6,12] who introduced so-called *blur invariants* with respect to non-parametric centrosymmetric and N-fold symmetric h. For Gaussian blur, first heuristically derived blur invariants were proposed by Liu and Zhang [10]. Later on, Zhang et al. [15] proposed a distance measure between two images which is independent of a circular Gaussian blur. Most recently, Flusser et al. [3] introduced a complete set of moment-based Gaussian blur invariants for the case that the Gaussian PSF has a diagonal covariance matrix.

In this paper, we substantially generalize the invariants proposed in [3]. While in [3] the Gaussian kernel must be in the axial position (which is constrained by the diagonal form of its covariance matrix), here we resolve the general case of an anisotropic *arbitrary oriented* Gaussian blurring kernel with a general covariance matrix. This allows to apply the invariants directly without testing the blur kernel orientation (which is in fact not feasible in practice).

2   Group-Theoretic Viewpoint

In this Section, we establish the necessary mathematical background which will be later used for designing the invariants. The new blur invariants are defined by means of *nonlinear projection operators*.

By *image function* (or just image for short) $f(\mathbf{x})$ we understand any function from $L_1(\mathbb{R}^2)$ space the integral of which is nonzero. 2D Gaussian G_Σ is defined as

$$G_\Sigma(\mathbf{x}) = \frac{1}{2\pi\sqrt{|\Sigma|}} \exp\left(-\frac{1}{2}\mathbf{x}^T \Sigma^{-1} \mathbf{x}\right), \tag{2}$$

where $\mathbf{x} \equiv (x, y)^T$ and Σ is a 2×2 regular covariance matrix which determines the shape of the Gaussian (the eigenvectors of Σ define the axes of the Gaussian and the ratio of the eigenvalues determines its elongation).

The set S of all Gaussian blurring kernels is

$$S = \{aG_\Sigma(\mathbf{x}) | a > 0, \Sigma \text{ positive definite}\}. \tag{3}$$

For the sake of generality, we consider unnormalized kernels to be able to model also the change of the image contrast and/or brightness. The basic properties of the set S, among which the *closure properties* play the most important role in deriving invariants, are listed below.

Proposition 1: $S \subset L_1$ since $\int aG_\Sigma = a$. However, S is *not* a linear vector space because the sum of two different Gaussians is not a Gaussian.

Proposition 2: *Convolution closure.* S is closed under convolution as

$$a_1 G_{\Sigma_1} * a_2 G_{\Sigma_2} = aG_\Sigma,$$

where $a = a_1 a_2$ and $\Sigma = \Sigma_1 + \Sigma_2$.

Proposition 3: *Multiplication closure.* S is closed under point-wise multiplication as

$$a_1 G_{\Sigma_1} \cdot a_2 G_{\Sigma_2} = aG_\Sigma,$$

where

$$a = \frac{a_1 a_2}{2\pi\sqrt{|\Sigma_1 + \Sigma_2|}}$$

and $\Sigma = (\Sigma_1^{-1} + \Sigma_2^{-1})^{-1}$.

Proposition 4: *Fourier transform closure.* Fourier transform of a function from S always exists, lies in S and is given by

$$\mathcal{F}(aG_\Sigma) = \frac{a}{2\pi\sqrt{|\Sigma|}} G_{\Sigma_1},$$

where

$$\Sigma_1 = \frac{1}{4\pi^2}\Sigma^{-1}.$$

Proposition 2 says that $(S, *)$ is a commutative *semi-group* (when considering δ-function to be an additional element of S). Hence, convolution with a function from S is a *semi-group action* on L_1.

Orbits of this semi-group action are formed by Gaussian-blur equivalent images. We say that f and g are Gaussian blur equivalent ($f \sim g$), if and only if there exist $h_1, h_2 \in S$ such that $h_1 * f = h_2 * g$. The orbits (i.e. the blur-equivalent classes) can be described by their "origins" – the images, that are not blurred versions of any other images. We are going to show that each orbit contains only one such element. We are going to find these "origins" (we will call them *primordial images*) and describe them by means of properly chosen descriptors – *invariants* of the orbits. For instance, set S itself forms an orbit with δ being its primordial image. The invariants should stay constant within the orbit while should distinguish any two images belonging to different orbits.

Such invariance is in fact the invariance w.r.t. arbitrary Gaussian blur. The main trick, which makes this theory practically applicable, is that the invariants can be calculated from the given blurred image without explicitly constructing the primordial image.

In next Section, we define a *projection operator* that "projects" each image on S. The primordial images and, consequently, Gaussian blur invariants are constructed by means of this projection operator.

3   Projection Operators and Invariants

The main idea is the following one. We try to construct a proper image projection onto the set S, eliminate somehow the Gaussian component of the image and define the invariants in the complement. However, since S is not a vector space, such projection cannot be linear.

Let us define the projection operator P such that it projects image f onto the nearest unnormalized Gaussian, where the term "nearest" means the Gaussian having the same integral and covariance matrix as the image f itself. So, we define

$$Pf = m_{00}G_C,   \tag{4}$$

where

$$C = \frac{1}{m_{00}} \begin{pmatrix} m_{20} & m_{11} \\ m_{11} & m_{02} \end{pmatrix},$$

and m_{pq} is a centralized image moment

$$m_{pq} = \iint (x - c_1)^p (y - c_2)^q f(x, y) \, dx \, dy   \tag{5}$$

with (c_1, c_2) being the image centroid.

Clearly, P is well defined for all images of non-zero integral of regular C. Actually, $Pf \in S$ for any such f. Although P is not linear, it can still be called projection operator, because it is idempotent $P^2 = P$. In particular, $P(aG_\Sigma) = aG_\Sigma$. By means of P, any function f can be uniquely expressed as $f = Pf + f_n$, where Pf is a Gaussian component and f_n can be considered a "non-Gaussian" component of f.

A key property of P, which will be later used for construction of the invariants, is that it commutes with a convolution with a Gaussian kernel. It holds, for any f and G_Σ,

$$P(f * G_\Sigma) = Pf * G_\Sigma.   \tag{6}$$

Now we can formulate the main Theorem of this paper.

Theorem 1. *Let f be an image function. Then*

$$I(f) = \frac{\mathcal{F}(f)}{\mathcal{F}(Pf)}$$

is an invariant to Gaussian blur, i.e. $I(f) = I(f * h)$ for any $h \in S$.

The proof follows immediately from Eq. (6). Note that $I(f)$ is well defined on all frequencies because the denominator is non-zero everywhere.

The following Theorem says that invariant $I(f)$ is *complete*, which means the equality $I(f_1) = I(f_2)$ occurs if and only if f_1 and f_2 belong to the same orbit.

Theorem 2. *Let f_1 and f_2 be two image functions and $I(f)$ be the invariant defined in Theorem 1. Then $I(f_1) = I(f_2)$ if and only if there exist $h_1, h_2 \in S$ such that $h_1 * f_1 = h_2 * f_2$.*

The proof is straightforward by setting $h_1 = Pf_2$ and $h_2 = Pf_1$. The completeness guarantees that $I(f)$ discriminates between the images from different orbits, while stays constant inside an orbit due to the invariance property.

Invariant $I(f)$ is a ratio of two Fourier transforms which may be interpreted as a deconvolution in frequency domain. Having an image f, we seemingly "deconvolve" it by the kernel $P(f)$, which is in fact the Gaussian component of image f. This deconvolution always sends the Gaussian component to δ-function. We call the result of this seeming deconvolution the *primordial image*

$$f_r = \mathcal{F}^{-1}\left(I(f)\right).$$

Hence, $I(f)$ can be viewed as its Fourier transform, although f_r may not exist in L_1 or may even not exist at all. Note that f_r is actually the "maximally possible" deconvolved non-Gaussian component of f plus δ-function and creates the origin of the respective orbit. It can be viewed as a kind of normalization (or canonical form) of f w.r.t. arbitrary Gaussian blurring (see Fig. 1 for illustration).

4   The Invariants in the Image Domain

Although $I(f)$ itself could serve as an image descriptor, its direct usage brings certain difficulties and disadvantages. On high frequencies, we divide by small numbers which may lead to precision loss. This effect is even more severe if f is noisy. This problem could be overcome by suppressing high frequencies by a low-pass filter, but such a procedure would introduce a user-defined parameter (the cut-off frequency) which should be set up with respect to the particular noise level. Another disadvantage is that we would have to actually construct $\mathcal{F}(Pf)$ in order to calculate $I(f)$. That is why we prefer to work directly in the image domain, where moment-based invariants equivalent to $I(f)$ can be constructed and evaluated without an explicit calculation of Pf.

First of all, we recall that geometric moments of an image are Taylor coefficients (up to a constant factor) of its Fourier transform

$$\mathcal{F}(f)(\mathbf{u}) = \sum_{\mathbf{p} \geq 0} \frac{(-2\pi i)^{|\mathbf{p}|}}{\mathbf{p}!} m_{\mathbf{p}}^{(f)} \mathbf{u}^{\mathbf{p}} \tag{7}$$

(we use the multi-index notation). Theorem 1 can be rewritten as

$$\mathcal{F}(Pf)(\mathbf{u}) \cdot I(f)(\mathbf{u}) = \mathcal{F}(f)(\mathbf{u}).$$

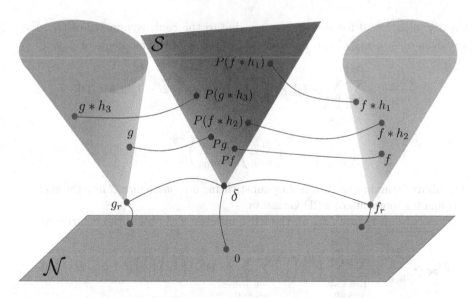

Fig. 1. Projection operator P divides each image into its Gaussian component Pf, which is projected onto S and a non-Gaussian component. The orbits are symbolically depicted as cones with the primordial image in the vertex. The primordial image represents the orbit, its non-Gaussian component provides discriminative description of the orbit.

All these three Fourier transforms can be expanded similarly to (7) into absolutely convergent Taylor series

$$\sum_{\mathbf{p}\geq 0} \frac{(-2\pi i)^{|\mathbf{p}|}}{\mathbf{p}!} m_{\mathbf{p}}^{(Pf)} \mathbf{u}^{\mathbf{p}} \cdot \sum_{\mathbf{p}\geq 0} \frac{(-2\pi i)^{|\mathbf{p}|}}{\mathbf{p}!} M_{\mathbf{p}} \mathbf{u}^{\mathbf{p}} = \sum_{\mathbf{p}\geq 0} \frac{(-2\pi i)^{|\mathbf{p}|}}{\mathbf{p}!} m_{\mathbf{p}}^{(f)} \mathbf{u}^{\mathbf{p}} . \quad (8)$$

Comparing the coefficients of the same powers of $\mathbf{u}$ we obtain, for any $\mathbf{p}$,

$$\sum_{\mathbf{k}\leq \mathbf{p}} \frac{(-2\pi i)^{|\mathbf{k}|}}{\mathbf{k}!} \frac{(-2\pi i)^{|\mathbf{p}-\mathbf{k}|}}{(\mathbf{p}-\mathbf{k})!} m_{\mathbf{k}}^{(Pf)} M_{\mathbf{p}-\mathbf{k}} = \frac{(-2\pi i)^{|\mathbf{p}|}}{\mathbf{p}!} m_{\mathbf{p}}^{(f)} , \quad (9)$$

which can be read as

$$\sum_{\mathbf{k}\leq \mathbf{p}} \binom{\mathbf{p}}{\mathbf{k}} m_{\mathbf{k}}^{(Pf)} M_{\mathbf{p}-\mathbf{k}} = m_{\mathbf{p}}^{(f)} . \quad (10)$$

In 2D, Eq. (10) reads as

$$\sum_{m=0}^{p} \sum_{n=0}^{q} \binom{p}{m} \binom{q}{n} m_{mn}^{(Pf)} M_{p-m,q-n} = m_{pq}^{(f)} . \quad (11)$$

Since $Pf = m_{00}^{(f)} G_C$, where C is given by the second-order moments of f, we can express its moments $m_{mn}^{(Pf)}$ without actually constructing the projection Pf.

Clearly, $m_{mn}^{(Pf)} = 0$ for any odd $m + n$ due to the centrosymmetry of G_C. For any even $m + n$, $m_{mn}^{(Pf)}$ can be expressed in terms of the moments of f as

$$
\frac{m_{mn}^{(Pf)}}{m_{00}} = \sum_{i=0}^{\lfloor \frac{m}{2} \rfloor} \sum_{\substack{j=0 \\ j \geq \frac{m-n}{2}}}^{i} (-1)^{i-j} \binom{m}{2i} \binom{i}{j} (m+n-2i-1)!!(2i-1)!! \cdot
$$

$$
\cdot \left(\frac{m_{11}}{m_{00}} \right)^{m-2j} \left(\frac{m_{20}}{m_{00}} \right)^{j} \left(\frac{m_{02}}{m_{00}} \right)^{\frac{n-m}{2}+j} . \tag{12}
$$

The above formula was obtained by substituting our particular C into the general formula for moments of a 2D Gaussian.

Now we can isolate M_{pq} on the left-hand side and obtain the recurrence

$$
M_{pq} = \frac{m_{pq}^{(f)}}{m_{00}} - \sum_{\substack{l=0 \\ l+k \neq 0, \\ l+k \text{ even}}}^{p} \sum_{k=0}^{q} \binom{p}{l} \binom{q}{k} \sum_{i=0}^{\lfloor \frac{k}{2} \rfloor} \sum_{\substack{j=0 \\ j \geq \frac{k-l}{2}}}^{i} (-1)^{i-j} \binom{k}{2i} \binom{i}{j} (l+k-2i-1)!! \cdot
$$

$$
\cdot (2i-1)!! \left(\frac{m_{11}}{m_{00}} \right)^{k-2j} \left(\frac{m_{20}}{m_{00}} \right)^{\frac{l-k}{2}+j} \left(\frac{m_{02}}{m_{00}} \right)^{j} M_{p-l,q-k} . \tag{13}
$$

This recurrence formula defines Gaussian blur invariants in the image domain. Since $I(f)$ has been proven to be invariant to Gaussian blur, all coefficients M_{pq} must also be blur invariants. The M_{pq}'s can be understood as the moments of the primordial image f_r. The power of Eq. (13) lies in the fact that we can calculate them directly from the moments of f, without constructing the primordial image explicitly either in frequency or in the spatial domain and also without any prior knowledge of the blurring kernel shape and orientation.

Thanks to the uniqueness of Fourier transform, the set of all M_{pq}'s carries the same information about the function f as $I(f)$ itself, so the cumulative discrimination power of all M_{pq}'s equals to that of $I(f)$.

Some of the invariants (13) are always trivial. Regardless of f, we have $M_{00} = 1$, $M_{10} = M_{01} = 0$ because we work in centralized coordinates, and $M_{20} = M_{11} = M_{02} = 0$ since these three moments had been already used for the definition of Pf.

Note that the joint null-space of all M_{pq}'s except M_{00} equals the set S, which is implied by the fact that $P(aG_\Sigma) = aG_\Sigma$ and $f_r = \delta$.

5 Experiments

5.1 Verification on Public Datasets

This basic experiment is a verification of the invariance of functionals M_{pq} from Eq. (13). We used two public-domain image databases, which contain series of Gaussian-blurred images (see Fig. 2 for examples).

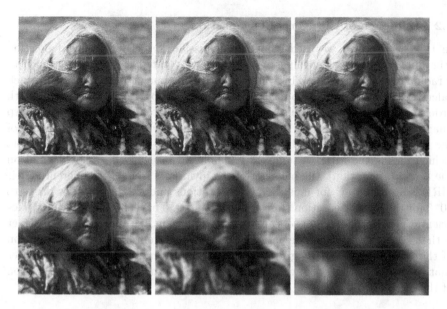

Fig. 2. An example of a Gaussian-blurred image series from the CSIQ database.

We used 30 series (original and five blurred instances of various extent) from the CID:IQ dataset [11] and 23 series from the CSIQ dataset [9]. For each of them, we calculated the invariants up to the 9th order. The relative error of all invariants on each image series was always between 10^{-4} and 10^{-3}, which illustrates a perfect invariance. The fluctuation within a single series is so small that in no way diminishes the ability to discriminate two different originals, as is illustrated in Fig. 3.

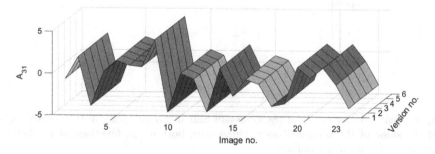

Fig. 3. The values of a single invariant calculated over 23 series (from left to right) consisting of six blurred instances (from front to back). The value is always almost constant on an individual series while significantly different for distinct images.

5.2   Influence of the Kernel Orientation

In this experiment, we used elongated Gaussian kernel in the axial position (the quotient of its eigenvalues was 2) and we rotated it gradually from 0 to π radians by one degree. We blurred standard Lena image by each rotated kernel, calculated the invariants from [3] and those given by Eq. (13) up to the 8th order, compared them to the same invariants calculated from the original sharp image, and plotted their mean relative errors (see Fig. 4). While the MRE of the new invariants only slightly oscillates around 10^{-8} due to sampling errors (which means the MRE is sufficiently small and basically does not depend on the kernel orientation), the behavior of the invariants from [3] is different. Their MRE is around 10^{-3} for most kernel orientations and exhibits narrow drops to 10^{-8} for the axes orientation close to 0, $\pi/2$ and π. This is because for these axes orientations, both invariant sets are exactly equivalent. The most remarkable fact is that even for very small deviations from the "horizontal/vertical" orientation of the Gaussian, the MRE grows up quickly by several orders. This illustrates that the new invariants are actually a significant improvement and generalization of the method from [3].

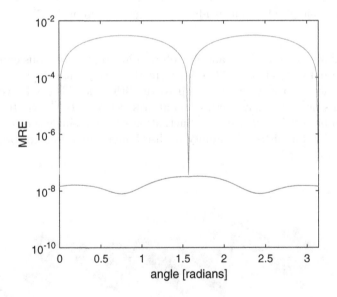

Fig. 4. Mean relative errors of the Gaussian blur invariants from [3] (red curve, top) and the same of the proposed ones (blue curve, bottom) as functions of the kernel orientation. (Color figure online)

5.3   Recognition of Blurred Faces

In the last experiment we show the performance of the proposed invariants in face recognition applied on blurred photographs. We compare our method with the

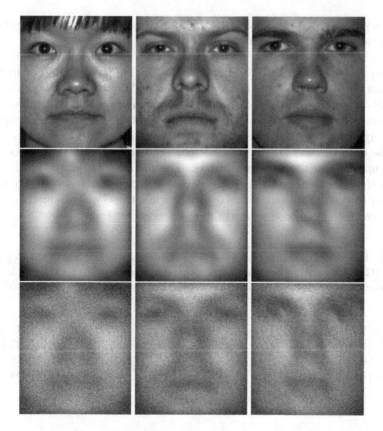

Fig. 5. Sample face images used in the experiments: clear database faces (top row), blurred (middle) and noisy (bottom).

approach proposed by Gopalan et al. [8], which is probably the most relevant competitor. Gopalan et al. derived invariants to image blurring and claimed they are suitable particularly for face recognition. They did not employ any parametric form of the blur kernel when constructing invariants (in that sense, their method is more general than ours which is restricted to Gaussian blur) but assumed the knowledge of its support size.

We used 38 distinct human faces from the Extended Yale Face Database B [7] (the same database was used in [8]). This database contains only sharp faces, so we created the blurred and noisy query images artificially (see Fig. 5 for some examples). In all tests, moment invariants up to the 9th order were used. The results are summarized in Table 1.

First, we tested the recognition rate with respect to the blur size. The blurred query image was always classified against the clear 38-image database. While moment invariants are 100% successful even for relatively large blurs, the Gopalan's method does not reach any comparable results and the success rate drops very rapidly with the increasing blur size, even if we provided the correct blur size as the input parameter of the algorithm.

Then, we tested the noise robustness of both methods. We corrupted the probe images with AWGN of SNR from 50 to 5. The success rate of moment invariants remains 100%, but the Gopalan's method appears to be very vulnerable. This can be explained by the fact that the moments, being integral features, average-out the noise while the Gopalan's invariants do not have this property.

Finally, we compared the speed of both methods, again for various image size. The data in the table are related to a single query, they do not comprise pre-calculations on the database images. The moment method is much faster because the invariants up to the 9th order are a highly-compressed image representation (but still sufficient for recognition) while the Gopalan's method works with a complete pixel-wise representation to construct invariants.

Table 1. The recognition rate [%] of the moment invariants (MI) and of the Gopalan's method (GM) for various blur size (left table) and for various SNR (middle table). The CPU time [s] comparison of both algorithms for various image sizes (right table).

Blur size	MI	GM
7×7	100	65.79
11×11	100	23.68
15×15	100	5.26

SNR	MI	GM
50	100	92.11
20	100	71.05
15	100	57.89
10	100	42.11
5	100	28.95

Image size	MI	GM
32×28	0.00258	7.89
40×35	0.00261	50
196×168	0.00842	n/a

6   Conclusion

We proposed new invariants w.r.t. Gaussian blur. Unlike all earlier works, we do not assume the blurring kernel to be circularly symmetric or in axial position. Still, we found a non-linear projection operator by means of which the invariants are defined in the Fourier domain. Equivalently, the invariants can be calculated directly in the image domain, without an explicit construction of the projections. We proved by experiments superior recognition abilities, stability and robustness, at least on simulated data that follow the assumed degradation model.

References

1. Carasso, A.S.: The APEX method in image sharpening and the use of low exponent Lévy stable laws. SIAM J. Appl. Math. **63**(2), 593–618 (2003)
2. Elder, J.H., Zucker, S.W.: Local scale control for edge detection and blur estimation. IEEE Trans. Pattern Anal. Mach. Intell **20**(7), 699–716 (1998)
3. Flusser, J., Farokhi, S., Höschl IV, C., Suk, T., Zitová, B., Pedone, M.: Recognition of images degraded by Gaussian blur. IEEE Trans. Image Process. **25**(2), 790–806 (2016)

4. Flusser, J., Suk, T.: Degraded image analysis: an invariant approach. IEEE Trans. Pattern Anal. Mach. Intell. **20**(6), 590–603 (1998)
5. Flusser, J., Suk, T., Boldyš, J., Zitová, B.: Projection operators and moment invariants to image blurring. IEEE Trans. Pattern Anal. Mach. Intell. **37**(4), 786–802 (2015)
6. Flusser, J., Suk, T., Saic, S.: Recognition of blurred images by the method of moments. IEEE Trans. Image Process. **5**(3), 533–538 (1996)
7. Georghiades, A., Belhumeur, P., Kriegman, D.: From few to many: illumination cone models for face recognition under variable lighting and pose. IEEE Trans. Pattern Anal. Mach. Intell. **23**(6), 643–660 (2001)
8. Gopalan, R., Turaga, P., Chellappa, R.: A blur-robust descriptor with applications to face recognition. IEEE Trans. Pattern Anal. Mach. Intell. **34**(6), 1220–1226 (2012)
9. Larson, E.C., Chandler, D.M.: Most apparent distortion: full-reference image quality assessment and the role of strategy. J. Electron. Imaging **19**(1), 011006 (2010)
10. Liu, J., Zhang, T.: Recognition of the blurred image by complex moment invariants. Pattern Recognit. Lett. **26**(8), 1128–1138 (2005)
11. Liu, X., Pedersen, M., Hardeberg, J.Y.: CID:IQ – a new image quality database. In: Elmoataz, A., Lezoray, O., Nouboud, F., Mammass, D. (eds.) ICISP 2014. LNCS, vol. 8509, pp. 193–202. Springer, Cham (2014). https://doi.org/10.1007/978-3-319-07998-1_22
12. Pedone, M., Flusser, J., Heikkilä, J.: Blur invariant translational image registration for N-fold symmetric blurs. IEEE Trans. Image Process. **22**(9), 3676–3689 (2013)
13. Xue, F., Blu, T.: A novel SURE-based criterion for parametric PSF estimation. IEEE Trans. Image Process. **24**(2), 595–607 (2015)
14. Zhang, W., Cham, W.K.: Single-image refocusing and defocusing. IEEE Trans. Image Process. **21**(2), 873–882 (2012)
15. Zhang, Z., Klassen, E., Srivastava, A.: Gaussian blurring-invariant comparison of signals and images. IEEE Trans. Image Process. **22**(8), 3145–3157 (2013)

Material-Based Segmentation of Objects

Jonathan Dyssel Stets, Rasmus Ahrenkiel Lyngby$^{(\boxtimes)}$, Jeppe Revall Frisvad,
and Anders Bjorholm Dahl

Technical University of Denmark, 2800 Kgs. Lyngby, Denmark
{stet,raly,jerf,abda}@dtu.dk
http://eco3d.compute.dtu.dk/

Abstract. We present a data-driven proof of concept method for image-based semantic segmentation of objects based on their materials. We target materials with complex radiometric appearances, such as reflective and refractive materials, as their detection is particularly challenging in many modern vision systems. Specifically, we select glass, chrome, plastic, and ceramics as these often appear in real-world settings. A large dataset of synthetic images is generated with the Blender 3D creation suite and the Cycles renderer. We use this data to fine-tune the pre-trained DeepLabv3+ semantic segmentation convolutional neural network. The network performs well on rendered test data and, although trained with rendered images only, the network generalizes so that the four selected materials can be segmented from real photos.

Keywords: Semantic segmentation · Deep learning · Synthetic data

1 Introduction

Semantic image segmentation is the task of labeling the parts of an image that contain specific object categories. Previous research has focused mainly on seg-

Fig. 1. Sample rendering of a scene. Two objects (torus and sphere) with materials assigned are placed on a cobble stone textured ground plane. All light in the scene comes from a spherical HDR image.

© Springer Nature Switzerland AG 2019
M. Felsberg et al. (Eds.): SCIA 2019, LNCS 11482, pp. 152–163, 2019.
https://doi.org/10.1007/978-3-030-20205-7_13

menting objects such as humans, animals, cars, and planes [3,4,6,16,20,22]. In this paper, we present a data-driven method for image-based semantic segmentation of objects based on their material instead of their type. Specifically, we choose to target glass, chrome, plastic, and ceramics because they frequently occur in daily life, have distinct appearances, and exemplify complex radiometric interactions. We generate synthetic images with reference data using the Blender 3D creation suite (Fig. 1) and train an existing Convolutional Neural Network (CNN) architecture, DeepLabv3+ [9], to perform semantic segmentation.

Generally, most vision systems perform best on Lambertian-like surfaces. This performance is because the appearance of an opaque, diffuse, and non-specular object is not dependent on the incident angle of surrounding light sources. Some materials can be hard to automatically detect due to their appearance. Specifically, objects with transparent or glossy materials are problematic as lights from the surroundings can refract or reflect upon interaction. Examples of these can be glass, plastics, ceramics, and metals whose appearances are highly determined by the surrounding illumination. Lightpath artifacts, such as specular highlights or subsurface scattering, can occur, resulting in a drastic change of appearance between viewing angles. These differences complicate the apprehension from a vision system resulting in false negative or inaccurate detections. Consequently, such materials are often avoided in research even though they often occur in real life settings.

With this paper, we show that it is possible to segment materials with complex radiometric properties from standard color images including the visually complex materials glass and chrome. This also means that the appearance difference between refraction (glass) and reflection (chrome) can be learned by a CNN. Finally, we provide a few examples visually indicating that segmentation of synthetic images of the four chosen materials generalize to real photos.

1.1   Related Work

Our study is inspired by researchers reconstructing the shape of glass objects using a dataset of synthetic images [28]. This work was based on an earlier investigation verifying that physically based rendering can produce images that are pixelwise comparable to photographs of specifically glass [27]. Considering this information, we wish to explore the potential of rendering of different materials with complex radiometric properties. In the following, we discuss existing work related to the topics of synthetic training data and material segmentation.

Synthetic Data. A large image set with reference data is required to properly train a CNN [17], but manually annotating the images to obtain reference data is a time-consuming process. Previous work has been successful in training with synthetic images and showing that the learned models generalize well to photographs [12,24]. Some of this work considers semantic segmentation [24], but the focus is labels related to an urban environment rather than materials. The appearance of materials depends on their reflectance properties, and rendering provides fine-tuned control over all parameters related to reflectance properties [21]. Image synthesis enables us to produce large scale, high precision, annotated datasets quickly. Several examples exist of such large scale synthetic datasets [18,26,29]. However, the ones including semantic segmentation reference data [18,26] do not have labels based on materials.

Materials in Data-Driven Models. As humans, we can typically identify a material by observing its visual appearance, but especially materials with complex reflectance properties have turned out to be difficult to segment. Several research projects address materials and their appearance in images. Georgoulis et al. [14] use synthetic images of specular objects as training data to estimate reflectance and illumination, Li et al. [19] recover the SVBRDF of a material also using rendered training data, and Yang et al. [30] use synthetic images containing metal and rubber materials as training data for visual recognition. These authors however do not consider segmentation. Bell et al. [5] target classification and segmentation of a set of specific materials like we do, but while our data is synthesized theirs is based on crowdsourced annotation of photographs.

2   Method

To make a good training set of synthetic images we have aimed at generating images that have a realistic appearance using a physical-based rendering model and realistic object shapes. Furthermore, we have strived at spanning a large variation by choosing largely varying environment maps.

2.1   Rendering Model

We generate a large synthetic dataset that consists of rendered images of a selection of shapes with different materials applied. This is done using the Cycles physically based renderer in Blender[1] v2.79. We construct a scene consisting of a textured ground plane, a number of shapes with applied materials and global illumination provided by a High Dynamic Range (HDR) environment map. To add additional variation, we randomly assign a camera position for each image. A sample rendering of the scene is shown in Fig. 1. The shapes, assigned materials, ground plane texture and environment map are interchangeable and controlled by a script. We describe each of the components in the following.

Shapes. We create a database of 20 shapes with varying geometry, while avoiding shapes that are too similar to the real world objects we later use for performance test. We strive to cover a broad range of shapes to both include convex- and concave-like shapes as well as soft and sharp corners to obtain a good variety of appearances. The shading is selected for each individual shape based on whether the material type maintains a realistic appearance for the given object. Each rendered image is based on one to three shapes being randomly positioned on the ground plane. We use five new shapes when rendering the test set.

---

[1] https://www.blender.org/. Accessed: January 30th 2019.

Fig. 2. Rendered samples of the four materials used in the dataset: glass, chrome, black plastic and white ceramic.

Materials. The following four materials are selected for evaluation: glass, chrome, black plastic, and white ceramic. These materials are targeted as we consider them to be complex in appearance while frequently occurring in real-life settings. We use built-in shaders provided by the Cycles renderer. Figure 2 exemplifies the appearances of the four materials.

Ground Plane. A ground plane is added to the scene and assigned a random texture from a database of 10 textures. The ground plane provides more accurate specular reflection of the nearby surface that real objects would usually stand on and better grounding of the objects due to inclusion of shadows. This adds an extra element of photorealism to the image. If caustics had been supported by the Cycles renderer, these would have appeared on the ground plane as well.

Environment Maps. Spherical HDR environment maps are used as the only illumination source in the scene. We use a total of seven environment maps and one of these is selected before each rendering. Both indoor and outdoor scenes are used to provide a variety in the type of illumination.

Images. The scenes are rendered as 640 × 480 RGB images with 8-bit color depth per channel. The images are rendered with 900 samples per pixel with a maximum of 128 bounces. To produce the reference label images of the scene, we switch off the global illumination and replace the material shaders with shaderless shaders. A color in the HSV-space is assigned for each material respectively by only varying the hue value. The result is an image with zero values for all background pixels and a color for all material pixels respectively as shown in Fig. 3. The label images are rendered with 36 samples per pixel and the images are post processed by thresholding a hue range to obtain a sharp delimiting border between label and background pixels.

Flat shading   Labels

Fig. 3. Labels for **glass**, **chrome**, **plastic** and **ceramic**, respectively. Same image as in Fig. 2, but rendered with flat shading ("shaderless shader" resulting in a single uniform color). To the right, all illumination was removed from the scene. (Color figure online)

Dataset. We used our rendering model to generate a total of $m = 26{,}378$ scene images with accompanying label images. The following hue color values were used as labels for the materials: 0.0 = glass, 0.1 = chrome, 0.2 = black plastic, 0.3 = white ceramic. Each of the material-label colors has a Value, as specified in the HSV color-space, of 1.0 and the background has a Value of 0.0. Each pair of RGB and label images are accompanied by a metadata-file listing the objects and materials present in the respective scene. Based on a finding that $1/\sqrt{2m}$ is the optimal number of samples in the validation set [2], we choose a 99% to 1% training-validation split of the renderings. Additionally, we rendered a test set of 300 images with the same four materials but with four shapes that were neither in the training nor in the validation set. The ground plane textures and environment maps remain the same set across training, test, and validation set.

2.2   Segmentation Model

We decided to use DeepLabv3+ which is a state-of-the-art semantic segmentation network [9]. It is a goal for us to show that it is generally possible to segment materials based on synthetic images, and we therefore decided not to change the network's architecture or specialize it in any way. By doing so, we demonstrate both the broadness of DeepLabv3+'s application domain and the model's ability to learn real things from physically based renderings. We postulate that this ability is transferable to other kinds of networks and applications precisely because we did not design the system specifically to learn from rendered data.

DeepLabv3+ is as an encoder-decoder network. The encoder condenses the semantic information contained in the input image's pixels into a tensor. This information is then decoded, by the decoder, into a segmentation image with a class label assigned to each pixel and of the same size as the input image. The DeepLabv3 [8] network forms the encoder with its last feature map before logits as encoder output. This network is a combination of the Aligned Xception image classification network [10,23], which extracts high-level image features, and an Atrous Spatial Pyramid Pooling network [7], which probes the extracted features at multiple scales. Atrous convolutions are convolutions with a "spread-out" kernel that has holes in between the kernel entries. An image pyramid is constructed by varying the size of these holes. The decoder has several depth-wise separable convolution layers [1], which take in both the encoder output and the feature map from one of the first convolutional layers.

The specific network structure is described in previous work [9]. We therefore only cover it in brief. Figure 4 illustrates the network layout. The encoder begins with extracting image features using a modified version of the Aligned Xception network. This version deepens the model and replaces all max-pooling layers with depthwise separable convolutions which significantly reduces the number of trainable weights compared to the original Xception model. The resulting feature extractor has 69 layers (including residual connection layers [15]). The output feature map has 2048 channels and is used to form the Atrous Spatial Pyramid. Three $3 \times 3 \times 2048$ Atrous Convolutions with three different strides are used together with one $1 \times 1 \times 2048$ convolution filter and one pooling layer. The combined output has five channels, one for each of the filters in the pyramid. The encoder then combines the channels into a one channel encoder output by applying a $1 \times 1 \times 5$ filter. This final output map is eight times smaller than the input image.

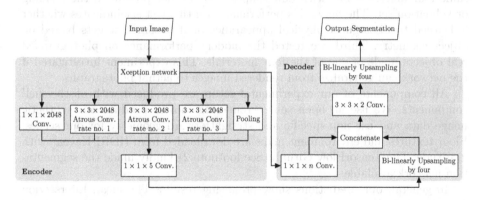

Fig. 4. Illustration of the semantic segmentation network.

The decoder up-samples the encoder output by a factor eight such that its size matches that of the input image. It starts by taking out one of the low-level feature maps from the Xception network, after the input image's size has been reduced four times, and applies a $1 \times 1 \times n$ filter to collapse it into one channel (where n is the number of channels in the feature map). Then the encoder output feature map is bi-linearly up-sampled by a factor of four and concatenated together with

Table 1. DeepLabv3+ settings

Property	Setting
Base learning rate	0.002
Learning rate decay factor	0.05
Train batch size	3
Atrous rate no. 1	6
Atrous rate no. 2	12
Atrous rate no. 3	18
No. of training steps	80,000

the Xception feature map. A 3×3 depthwise separable convolution is applied to the now two channel map which reduces it into one channel, and the result is upsampled four times to match the size of the input image. This result is the predicted semantic segmentation image.

Implementation. We adapted the DeepLabv3+ TensorFlow-based implementation[2] by Chen et al. [9] to train on our dataset. The Xception network is pre-trained on ImageNet [11,25] and the DeepLabv3+ network is pre-trained on the PASCAL VOC 2012 dataset [13]. Table 1 records our model settings.

3   Experiments and Results

We conducted three individual experiments. First, we tested the model on the 264 rendered images in our validation set. These images had never before been "seen" by the segmentation network but contained the same kind of objects as those in the training set. Second, we rendered a test set of 300 images with the same four materials but with new shapes that are not present in the training or validation set. The network's performance on this test set indicates whether it learned to distinguish physical appearance or if it somehow gets biased on object geometry. Third, we tested the model's performance on photographed real objects made of one of the four materials. This experiment investigated if the network can generalize from rendered images to actual photographs.

All components of our experimental setup are produced with off-the-shelf components. We use an open source rendering tool to produce our synthetic image data and use non-specific and straightforward geometry for our scenes. Floor textures and environment maps are downloaded from HDRI Haven[3] with gratitude. The TensorFlow Github (See footnote 2) kindly made the segmentation network available.

In general, our predictions show promising results. The mean Intersection Over Union (mIOU) score is used to indicate the performance on the rendered datasets. The validation set yielded an mIOU score of 95.69%, and the test set yielded 94.90%. The score is not computed for the real images since we did not have the ground truth semantic segmentations for these images. The scores indicate that the network is relatively good at predicting labels and that it seems not to be dependent on the shapes of the objects.

The following paragraphs showcase examples and discuss results from our three studies.

Validation Set. Figure 5 exhibits predicted segmentation masks from images in the validation set. We observe that the prediction is surprisingly good, even

---

[2] https://github.com/tensorflow/models/tree/master/research/deeplab.   Accessed: January 30th 2019.

[3] https://hdrihaven.com/. Accessed: January 30th 2019.

for difficult materials such as glass and chrome. The networks ability to distinguish these kinds of objects is impressive, as the objects are not as such directly visible but instead reveal their presence by distorting light coming from the environment. The segmentation is, however, not perfect. Segmentation labels tend to "bleed" into each other when objects touch. This effect is seen in the middle row of Fig. 5. As seen in the bottom row, some environment maps caused over-saturation of the chrome material at certain view angles which caused the network to identify the material as white ceramic. Small objects and thin structures are difficult to segment and apt to disappear in the predictions.

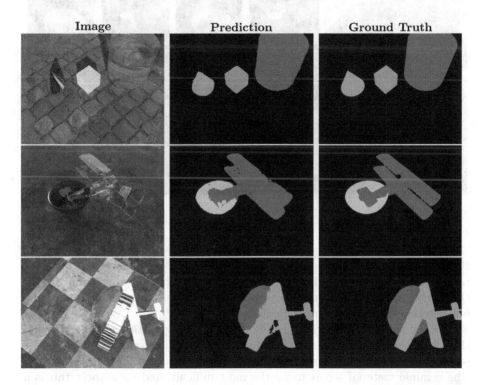

Fig. 5. Examples of segmentation results obtained on the validation set.

Test Set. The network's performance on the test set, with never before seen objects, are shown in Fig. 6. We observe that the performance is on par with that observed on the validation set in Fig. 5. This indicates that the material predictions are independent of object shape.

Real Images. Beyond the rendered test set, we captured three real images to test if the network can generalize to this data. Note that we do not have ground truth for these images, so the evaluation is solely by visual inspection. Results obtained on real images are in Fig. 7. Keeping in mind that we trained

Image   Prediction   Ground Truth

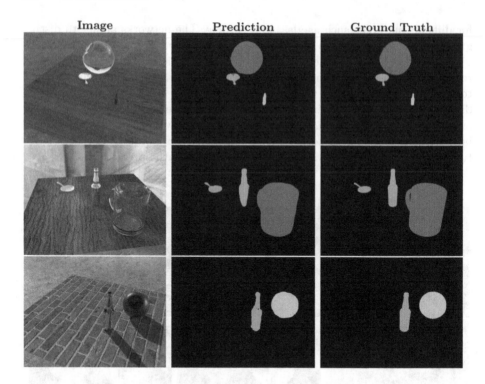

Fig. 6. Examples of segmentation results obtained on the test set.

the network for material segmentation only on rendered images, we find the results to be rather convincing. They are not perfect, but they are promising for the future potential of training networks with synthetic images in general and for material segmentation in particular.

The network found the glass objects with a good segmentation border, despite them being difficult to see with the human eye. Both chrome and plastic were segmented but with a few misclassified pixels as seen in the predicted images. The ceramic material seems to be the most difficult, and we suspect this is a result of our training data. Even though we rendered with a rather large number of samples per pixel, the images seem not to be fully converged and therefore do not reveal all specular highlights. Missing specular highlights is primarily an issue for the appearance of the ceramic material. Through further testing with real images, we also noted that the performance is highly dependent on the background. Non-textured surfaces, such as an office desk, confuse the network, which mistakes them for a specular material, often chrome, plastic, or glass. Additionally, the segmentation fails if the background is white, which we also believe to be an artifact of the too diffuse ceramic material.

The synthetic data could be improved in multiple ways. The materials we render are perhaps too "perfect" in their appearance. Adding random impurities, such as small scratches or bumps, to the materials would give a more realistic

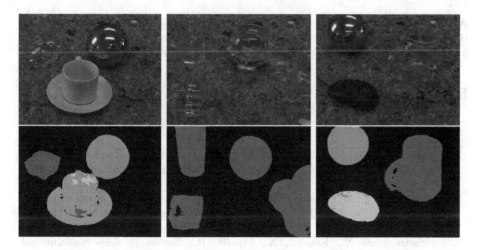

Fig. 7. Examples of segmentation results obtained from real images.

appearance. The environment maps are approximately 1k in resolution, resulting in a blurry background which gives a clear distinction between foreground objects and background. Real images with an in-focus background consequently result in predictions on this background. Thus, we believe higher resolution environment maps can help the network better distinguish between foreground and background in real photos. Finally, it is problematic that our included materials can occur in the environment maps without being labeled, which could hamper the network. This problem could potentially be mitigated either by making sure the environment maps are devoid of the targeted materials or by also generating those synthetically with material labels. Despite these current issues, we believe that the results of our study deliver a solid proof of concept with promising potentials for future work within semantic segmentation of complex materials.

4   Conclusion

We targeted the problem of segmenting materials in images based on their appearance. We presented a data-driven approach utilizing recent deep learning technology and rendering techniques to train a model on synthetic images. The learned model generalizes well to real photographs. The method allows us to detect specific materials in three channel color images without multi-spectral information. We achieved this feat using open source software which is freely available and requires no exceptional hardware components. Thus, the approach is available to anybody with a computer and a modern graphics card. Based on our results, and on the previous work that also uses synthetic training data, we firmly believe that physically based rendering is a vital component in the training of the deep learning models of tomorrow. Synthetic data generation is likely to push the boundaries of what deep learning can achieve even further.

Acknowledgements. The models we use are from turbosquid.com and the Make-Human software. Environment maps used to render our training data are from hdrihaven.com and textures for the ground plane are from texturehaven.com.

References

1. Abadi, M., et al.: TensorFlow: a system for large-scale machine learning. OSDI **16**, 265–283 (2016)
2. Amari, S., Murata, N., Müller, K.R., Finke, M., Yang, H.H.: Asymptotic statistical theory of overtraining and cross-validation. IEEE Trans. Neural Netw. **8**(5), 985–996 (1997)
3. Athanasiadis, T., Mylonas, P., Avrithis, Y., Kollias, S.: Semantic image segmentation and object labeling. IEEE Trans. Circuits Syst. Video Technol. **17**(3), 298–312 (2007)
4. Badrinarayanan, V., Kendall, A., Cipolla, R.: SegNet: a deep convolutional encoder-decoder architecture for image segmentation. IEEE Trans. Pattern Anal. Mach. Intell. **39**(12), 2481–2495 (2017)
5. Bell, S., Upchurch, P., Snavely, N., Bala, K.: Material recognition in the wild with the materials in context database. In: IEEE Conference on Computer Vision and Pattern Recognition (CVPR), pp. 3479–3487 (2015)
6. Chen, L.C., Papandreou, G., Kokkinos, I., Murphy, K., Yuille, A.L.: Semantic image segmentation with deep convolutional nets and fully connected CRFs. arXiv preprint arXiv:1412.7062 (2014)
7. Chen, L.C., Papandreou, G., Kokkinos, I., Murphy, K., Yuille, A.L.: DeepLab: semantic image segmentation with deep convolutional nets, atrous convolution, and fully connected crfs. IEEE Trans. Pattern Anal. Mach. Intell. **40**(4), 834–848 (2018)
8. Chen, L.C., Papandreou, G., Schroff, F., Adam, H.: Rethinking atrous convolution for semantic image segmentation. arXiv preprint arXiv:1706.05587 (2017)
9. Chen, L.-C., Zhu, Y., Papandreou, G., Schroff, F., Adam, H.: Encoder-decoder with atrous separable convolution for semantic image segmentation. In: Ferrari, V., Hebert, M., Sminchisescu, C., Weiss, Y. (eds.) ECCV 2018. LNCS, vol. 11211, pp. 833–851. Springer, Cham (2018). https://doi.org/10.1007/978-3-030-01234-2_49
10. Chollet, F.: Xception: deep learning with depthwise separable convolutions. In: IEEE Conference on Computer Vision and Pattern Recognition (CVPR), pp. 1800–1807 (2017)
11. Deng, J., Dong, W., Socher, R., Li, L.J., Li, K., Fei-Fei, L.: ImageNet: a large-scale hierarchical image database. In: IEEE Conference on Computer Vision and Pattern Recognition (CVPR), pp. 248–255 (2009)
12. Dosovitskiy, A., et al.: FlowNet: learning optical flow with convolutional networks. In: IEEE International Conference on Computer Vision (ICCV), pp. 2758–2766 (2015)
13. Everingham, M., Van Gool, L., Williams, C.K., Winn, J., Zisserman, A.: The PASCAL visual object classes (VOC) challenge. Int. J. Comput. Vis. **88**(2), 303–338 (2010)
14. Georgoulis, S., et al.: Reflectance and natural illumination from single-material specular objects using deep learning. IEEE Trans. Pattern Anal. Mach. Intell. **40**(8), 1932–1947 (2018)

15. He, K., Zhang, X., Ren, S., Sun, J.: Deep residual learning for image recognition. In: IEEE Conference on Computer Vision and Pattern Recognition (CVPR), pp. 770–778 (2016)
16. Kanade, T.: Region segmentation: signal vs semantics. Comput. Graph. Image Process. **13**(4), 279–297 (1980)
17. Krizhevsky, A., Sutskever, I., Hinton, G.E.: Imagenet classification with deep convolutional neural networks. In: Advances in Neural Information Processing Systems, pp. 1097–1105 (2012)
18. Li, W., et al.: InteriorNet: Mega-scale multi-sensor photo-realistic indoor scenes dataset. In: British Machine Vision Conference (BMVC) (2018)
19. Li, Z., Sunkavalli, K., Chandraker, M.: Materials for masses: SVBRDF acquisition with a single mobile phone image. In: Ferrari, V., Hebert, M., Sminchisescu, C., Weiss, Y. (eds.) ECCV 2018. LNCS, vol. 11207, pp. 74–90. Springer, Cham (2018). https://doi.org/10.1007/978-3-030-01219-9_5
20. Liu, Z., Li, X., Luo, P., Loy, C.C., Tang, X.: Semantic image segmentation via deep parsing network. In: IEEE International Conference on Computer Vision (ICCV), pp. 1377–1385 (2015)
21. Nielsen, J.B., Stets, J.D., Lyngby, R.A., Aanæs, H., Dahl, A.B., Frisvad, J.R.: A variational study on BRDF reconstruction in a structured light scanner. In: IEEE International Conference on Computer Vision Workshop (ICCVW), pp. 143–152 (2017)
22. Noh, H., Hong, S., Han, B.: Learning deconvolution network for semantic segmentation. In: IEEE International Conference on Computer Vision (ICCV), pp. 1520–1528 (2015)
23. Qi, H., et al.: Deformable convolutional networks-COCO detection and segmentation challenge 2017 entry. In: ICCV COCO Challenge Workshop, vol. 15 (2017)
24. Ros, G., Sellart, L., Materzynska, J., Vazquez, D., Lopez, A.M.: The SYNTHIA dataset: a large collection of synthetic images for semantic segmentation of urban scenes. In: IEEE Conference on Computer Vision and Pattern Recognition (CVPR), pp. 3234–3243 (2016)
25. Russakovsky, O., et al.: ImageNet large scale visual recognition challenge. Int. J. Comput. Vis. **115**(3), 211–252 (2015)
26. Song, S., Yu, F., Zeng, A., Chang, A.X., Savva, M., Funkhouser, T.: Semantic scene completion from a single depth image. In: IEEE Conference on Computer Vision and Pattern Recognition (CVPR), pp. 190–198 (2017)
27. Stets, J.D., et al.: Scene reassembly after multimodal digitization and pipeline evaluation using photorealistic rendering. Appl. Opt. **56**(27), 7679–7690 (2017)
28. Stets, J.D., Li, Z., Frisvad, J.R., Chandraker, M.: Single-shot analysis of refractive shape using convolutional neural networks. In: IEEE Winter Conference on Applications of Computer Vision (WACV), pp. 995–1003 (2019)
29. Xu, Z., Sunkavalli, K., Hadap, S., Ramamoorthi, R.: Deep image-based relighting from optimal sparse samples. ACM Trans. Graph. (SIGGRAPH) **37**(4), 126 (2018)
30. Yang, J., Lu, J., Lee, S., Batra, D., Parikh, D.: Visual curiosity: learning to ask questions to learn visual recognition. Proc. Mach. Learn. Res. (CoRL) **87**, 63–80 (2018)

Filtering Specular Reflections by Merging Stereo Images

Michael Plattner$^{(\boxtimes)}$ and Gerald Ostermayer

Research Group Networks and Mobility, University of Applied Sciences
Upper Austria, Hagenberg, Austria
{michael.plattner,gerald.ostermayer}@fh-hagenberg.at

Abstract. Due to the horizontal distance between the cameras taking stereo images, the position of specular reflections on objects differ in the two images of a stereo pair. In this paper we propose an algorithm to merge such stereo images in order to filter specular reflections by utilizing different types of disparity maps. Results show that merging stereo images reduces specular reflections by 75% in average.

Keywords: Specular reflections · Stereo images · Merging images

1 Introduction

Specular reflections are interfering with camera-based visual light communication systems. Existing approaches to filter reflections are designed for images without any other uncontrolled light sources, e.g. endoscopic camera images. They can't distinguish between reflections and active light sources. The transmitting light sources would also be removed and therefore the error rate can't be improved. In stereo images the reflections are only visible in one of the images at a certain position, in the other image the same reflection is either present at a different position or not visible at all. In contrast, active light sources and diffuse illumination are identical in both images of a stereo pair. By merging those stereo images according to the disparity map, only the specular reflections in the images are reduced.

2 Related Work

There are different approaches to remove such specular reflections or highlights in images, one was proposed by Yang et al. [14] from the University of Illinois. Their method is based on the key observation that the so called maximum diffuse chromaticity in local patches of color images changes smoothly. A low-pass filter is applied on the maximum fraction of the color components of the original image, to restore the smooth changes and remove specular reflections. This method works fine for illuminated objects. In our case we could potentially also have

© Springer Nature Switzerland AG 2019
M. Felsberg et al. (Eds.): SCIA 2019, LNCS 11482, pp. 164–172, 2019.
https://doi.org/10.1007/978-3-030-20205-7_14

active light sources in the images we want to use. This method will not work as properly, hence the key observation this method is based on, is not correct anymore.

Feris et al. [2] published an approach closely related to ours. They also combine multiple images to reduce specular reflections, by capturing multiple photos with different positions of the flash. The specular reflections caused by the flash are different in all images, hence if they combine the images they can reduce the specular reflections. In our case we mainly want to filter reflections from external light sources that can't be moved, e.g. the sunlight, which is not possible with this approach.

Another way to detect and remove specularity Tchoulack et al. [12] describe, is to analyze a combination of the saturation component S of the HSV plan and the gray-level image. Similar methods are also described by Saint et al. [10] and Gröger et al. [5] from the German Aerospace Center (DLR). The idea is to build a mask that illustrates regions of the image where specular reflections were detected. To reconstruct the image the parts of the image without any reflections stay unchanged, the regions with specularity are removed and inpainted using neighboring pixels. A navier strokes based method described by Bertalmio et al. [1] and the method by Telea [13] for inpainting images is implemented in the OpenCV library.

3 Approach

Similar to the approach of Feris et al. [2] our method also uses multiple images that are combined to reduce specular reflection. Instead of capturing multiple images at the same position and moving the light source our approach uses two images captured at different positions without moving the light sources.

This movement of the camera is realized by using stereo images. The external light sources will be reflected differently in both images of the stereo pair, hence if we merge both images, the reflections are filtered as they appear only in one image at that specific position. To merge images the geometric mean of the correlating pixel values is calculated with

$$\overline{x}_{geom} = \sqrt[n]{\prod_{i=1}^{n} x_i} \tag{1}$$

to weight low values more than high values, as reflections result in brighter spots which have high values in the RGB color space.

Precondition for such a fusion of the stereo image is to know how the positions correlate. This information can be calculated or estimated by various methods and is usually stored in a disparity map. The disparity refers to the distance between two corresponding pixels in the left and the right image when putting both images on top of each other. Such a disparity map also represents the depth map of the stereo image, because objects close to the camera result in a higher disparity than objects further away.

To avoid erroneous merging at positions without specular reflection, we additionally use the specularity mask which is calculated as intermediate step in the approach of Tchoulack et al. [12] to only merge pixels at positions of potential specular reflections, other areas stay untouched.

Figure 1 shows a block diagram to give an overview of the method's steps.

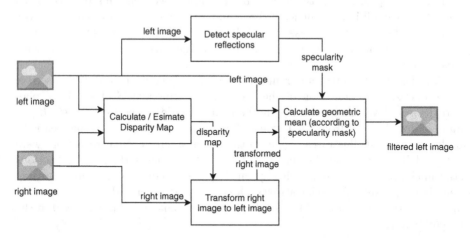

Fig. 1. Block diagram of stereo fusion (left image as base)

3.1   Demonstration Example

Following example uses a simple 12×12 stereo image of a red sphere as depicted in Fig. 2. In both images we see specular reflections that should be removed.

The first step is to calculate or estimate the disparity map of the stereo image. There are many different methods to calculate the disparity map, but the more accurate the disparity map, the better the result of the stereo fusion. In this example a perfect disparity map looks like shown in Fig. 2c, the brighter the pixel, the closer the object. In this depiction the disparity values are also written onto the image for each pixel for clarification.

Now we can transform the right image to match the left image by considering the disparity for each pixel. The transformed right image should then look like depicted in Fig. 2e. As we can see of course the reflection in the right image is also transformed and still visible.

Additionally, we need to detect the pixels in the left image which show a reflection. The result is stored in the binary specularity mask, which is shown in Fig. 2d. If a value in the mask is 0 (depicted black), there was no reflection detected at this position, so we don't need to merge the pixels here. Otherwise, if the value is 1 (depicted white), the corresponding pixels are merged.

The last step is to merge all the corresponding pixels of the left image and the transformed right image. As the two images now match, they just have to be pixel-wise multiplied to then calculate the square root.

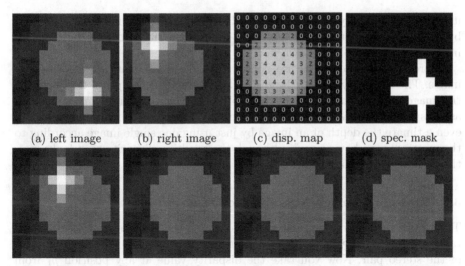

(a) left image   (b) right image   (c) disp. map   (d) spec. mask

(e)   transformed (f) filtered left image (g) filtered left image (h) perfect reference
right image   not using spec. mask using spec. mask   result

Fig. 2. Stereo fusion example of red sphere (Size: 12 × 12) (Color figure online)

The result is then a fusion of the left image and the right image as shown in Fig. 2g, where the left image is the base in this example. For comparison, Fig. 2h shows the original left image without reflection which is the perfect reference result for this example.

3.2 Disparity Map

There are multiple ways to calculate or to estimate the disparity map of stereo images. A very simple approach is to use a rectified stereo image pair, which means both images have the same image plane, and look for the corresponding points in the same row of the image. You just take a defined window of horizontal pixels and compare them with a sliding window in the same row of the other image. The comparison can be done by computing the sum of absolute differences (SAD), sum of squared distances (SSD) or preforming normalized cross-correlation (NCC), where last will be the most accurate. The index of the sliding window with the highest correlation value is then used as the disparity value for the position of the static window in the first image. This has to be repeated for every position in the image. To increase the performance, the minimum and maximum disparity are defined, which sets the range where the window has to slide.

Other approaches are block-matching algorithms which don't just use pixel windows of one row, but blocks of pixels to find the corresponding positions, e.g. the block-matching algorithm by Konolige [8] or the semi global matching algorithm by Hirschmüller [6] that are implemented in OpenCV. Additionally, it is possible to apply post-filtering to the result of such a matching algorithm by combining the left-to-right and right-to-left disparity and considering edges in the original image like shown in [11].

More advanced solutions use neural networks to estimate the depth of an image. The DispFlowNet by Mayer et al. [9] estimates the optical flow between the images of a stereo pair to get the depth of the image, which can also be seen as a disparity map. Godard et al. [3] have shown that a deep neural network can even estimate the depth of an image by just using one single image according to the motto "Learn how to see", although the resulting disparity map looks nice, the accuracy is not sufficient for our use case.

3.3   Transform Image According to Disparity

The transformation of the right image to match the left image or vice versa is rather simple. First you create a new image with the same size as the images of the stereo pair. Now you take the disparity value at any position p_1 from the disparity map and add this value to the horizontal index to get position p_2. Now you set the pixel value of the new image at position p_2 to the value of the original right image at position p_1. This must be repeated for every position in the image. If there are collisions of the transformed position, which will happen if you have different disparity values, the pixel with the highest disparity is used, hence other pixels are occluded by objects closer to the camera. Of course, it will also happen that parts of the transformed image are not set to any value if those areas are occluded. In this case we are not able to merge the images for these areas and instead keep the pixel values of the base image. In our algorithm we achieve that by initializing the transformed image with the values of the base image. Thus, when calculating the geometric mean of two identical values, the result is equal to the values.

3.4   Detect Specular Reflections

Our system uses the algorithm by Tchoulack et al. [12] to detect specular reflections in images. They analyze a combination of the saturation component S of the HSV color space and the gray-scale image to decide if a pixel shows a specular reflection. This information is stored in a binary image which is called specularity mask, where positions with reflections are marked with 1, otherwise they are 0. This mask is then used to only merge pixels where reflections are detected, to prevent errors caused by unnecessary fusion of the images.

3.5   Calculate Geometric Mean

After the right image was transformed, it matches the left image, so we can pixel-wise calculate the geometric mean with formula 1. Reflections are usually bright, and therefore have a high value in the RGB color space, that's why we use the geometric mean. Low values are weighted higher, so reflections are reduced more than when using the arithmetic mean, for example.

4   Evaluation

For evaluation we calculate the color difference for every pixel between the resulting image and a perfect reference result, where we removed all specular reflections by hand. The distance in the RGB color space is not proportional to the perceived color difference, hence we converted the images to CIELab color space to measure differences in the images with the Euclidian distances in CIELab (ΔE) [7].

We tested the system with 40 stereo images of a car exhibition from Golubinsky [4] where many reflections are visible due to the spotlights. All the images were captured with the same stereo camera, therefore the focal length and the distance between the cameras is always the same. Those 40 images are used for the evaluation below.

We evaluate our system using three different methods to calculate the disparity map of the stereo image: line-based window matching with normalized cross-correlation (NCC), semi global blockmatching with post-filtering (SGBM-PF) and DispFlowNet [9]. We use those three setups with and without specularity mask (SpecMask). For comparison we also evaluate the inpaint method by Tchoulack [12].

Additionally, we evaluate the average color difference ΔE_{orig} of the original unfiltered image compared to the perfect reference result. This value we use in

$$reduction[\%] = 100\% - \frac{\Delta E_{result}}{\Delta E_{orig}} \cdot 100\% \qquad (2)$$

to calculate the percentage reduction of reflections in an image. A reduction of 0% represents no filtering, the reference image filtered by hand represents a reduction of 100%. If the average color difference ΔE in the result is even worse than in the original image, this percentage value might be below zero.

In Fig. 3a we see that the inpaint method sometimes works very good and reduces the reflections by approx. 90% compared to the original image, but in total the result is quite unstable with a standard deviation of 32.2% and an average of 75%. For our approach, the NCC disparity map works best, in average the reflections are reduced by approx. 75% with a standard deviation of only 9.9%. With the usage of the specularity mask, some reflections can't be removed that well, because they were not detected as such. Here we achieved an average of 62% with a standard deviation of 16.8%.

Figure 3b shows the error that is introduced to parts of the images that don't contain any reflection. Here of course the original image and the perfect result are identical. We see that the use of the specularity mask in our approach is crucial as the error can be kept 75% lower in average compared to the results when omitting it. What we also see is that the inpaint method also introduced a big and unstable error compared to our method, because it can't distinguish between specular reflections that should be reduced and active light sources or diffuse illumination. Comparing our NCC method with specularity mask to the inpaint method by Tchoulack [12] the error introduced by the inpaint method is in average more than 5 times bigger.

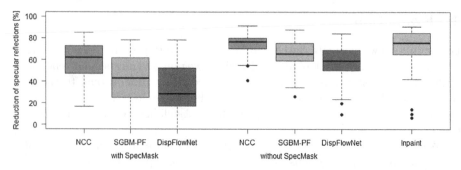

(a) Percentage reduction of reflections by comparing the average color difference ΔE to perfect reference results at areas with reflections

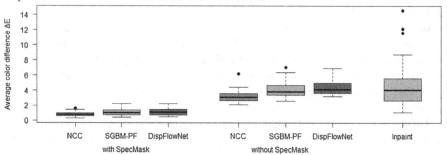

(b) Average color difference ΔE compared to perfect reference result at areas without reflections

Fig. 3. Evaluation charts

5   Results

Overall, our approach using the disparity map from line-based window matching with NCC and using the specularity mask delivered the best results shown in Fig. 4b. Obviously this is the case, because the transformation process also works line-based. Other disparity maps derived from SGBM with post-filtering or DispFlowNet more rely on blocks in the image, which makes the depth map more realistic but introduces more errors when transforming the image accordingly.

Figure 4c shows the problem with the inpaint method, the reflections are removed well, but also the logo in the top right vanished, which is bad. In a visual light communication system where this logo could be the transmitting light source, the communication would be cancelled completely instead of only filtering the misleading reflections. Our method is able to recognize such active light sources or diffuse illuminations, because they are visible in both images of the stereo pair and therefore stay when the images are merged.

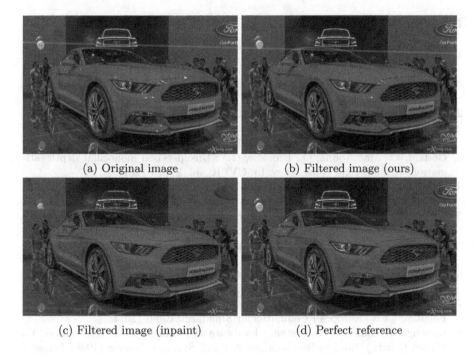

(a) Original image   (b) Filtered image (ours)

(c) Filtered image (inpaint)   (d) Perfect reference

Fig. 4. Filtering on real stereo image [4]

6   Conclusion

With our method, the reduction of specular reflection itself could not be improved compared to other approaches, but our method works much better if there are other light sources and diffuse illuminations apart from reflections, because it is able to recognize them and doesn't remove them. In the future this method can be used to filter reflections in camera-based visual light communication systems using multiple cameras by implementing an optical multiple input multiple output (MIMO) system. The idea is to reduce the false positive rate when detecting the state of a modulated light source in a VLC system, by filtering specular reflections near the sender.

Acknowledgements. This project has been co-financed by the European Union using financial means of the European Regional Development Fund (EFRE). Further information to IWB/EFRE is available at www.efre.gv.at.

 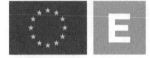

Europäische Union Investitionen in Wachstum & Beschäftigung. Österreich.

References

1. Bertalmio, M., Bertozzi, A.L., Sapiro, G.: Navier-stokes, fluid dynamics, and image and video inpainting. In: Proceedings of the 2001 IEEE Computer Society Conference on Computer Vision and Pattern Recognition 2001, CVPR 2001, vol. 1, pp. I-I. IEEE (2001)
2. Feris, R., Raskar, R., Tan, K.H., Turk, M.: Specular reflection reduction with multi-flash imaging. In: Proceedings 17th Brazilian Symposium on Computer Graphics and Image Processing 2004, pp. 316–321. IEEE (2004)
3. Godard, C., Mac Aodha, O., Brostow, G.J.: Unsupervised monocular depth estimation with left-right consistency. In: CVPR, vol. 2, p. 7 (2017)
4. Golubinsky, Y.: MIAS 2014 in 3D (2015). http://urixblog.com/en/2015/03/01/mias-2014-3d-normal-size-cars-moscow-russia/
5. Gröger, M., Sepp, W., Ortmaier, T., Hirzinger, G.: Reconstruction of image structure in presence of specular reflections. In: Radig, B., Florczyk, S. (eds.) DAGM 2001. LNCS, vol. 2191, pp. 53–60. Springer, Heidelberg (2001). https://doi.org/10.1007/3-540-45404-7_8
6. Hirschmuller, H.: Stereo processing by semiglobal matching and mutual information. IEEE Trans. Pattern Analy. Mach. Intell. **30**(2), 328–341 (2008)
7. I.S. EN ISO 11664-4 Colorimetry - Part 4: CIE 1976 l* a* b* colour space. Brussels, Belgium, CEN (European Committeefor Standardization) (2011)
8. Konolige, K.: Small vision systems: hardware and implementation. In: Shirai, Y., Hirose, S. (eds.) Robotics Research, pp. 203–212. Springer, London (1998). https://doi.org/10.1007/978-1-4471-1580-9_19
9. Mayer, N., et al.: A large dataset to train convolutional networks for disparity, optical flow, and scene flow estimation. In: Proceedings of the IEEE Conference on Computer Vision and Pattern Recognition, pp. 4040–4048 (2016)
10. Saint-Pierre, C.A., Boisvert, J., Grimard, G., Cheriet, F.: Detection and correction of specular reflections for automatic surgical tool segmentation in thoracoscopic images. Mach. Vis. Appl. **22**(1), 171–180 (2011)
11. Samartzidis, T.: Open CV stereo - depth image generation and filtering with python 3+, ximgproc and OpenCV 3+ (2017). http://timosam.com/python_opencv_depthimage
12. Tchoulack, S., Langlois, J.P., Cheriet, F.: A video stream processor for real-time detection and correction of specular reflections in endoscopic images. In: 2008 Joint 6th International IEEE Northeast Workshop on Circuits and Systems and TAISA Conference 2008, NEWCAS-TAISA 2008, pp. 49–52. IEEE (2008)
13. Telea, A.: An image inpainting technique based on the fast marching method. J. Graph. Tools **9**(1), 23–34 (2004)
14. Yang, Q., Wang, S., Ahuja, N.: Real-time specular highlight removal using bilateral filtering. In: Daniilidis, K., Maragos, P., Paragios, N. (eds.) ECCV 2010. LNCS, vol. 6314, pp. 87–100. Springer, Heidelberg (2010). https://doi.org/10.1007/978-3-642-15561-1_7

Near Lossless JPEG Compression Based on Masking Effect of Non-predictable Energy of Image Regions

Mykola Ponomarenko[✉] and Karen Egiazarian

Faculty of Information Technology and Communication Sciences,
Tampere University, Tampere, Finland
{mykola.ponomarenko,karen.egiazarian}@tuni.fi

Abstract. This paper studies near lossless JPEG image compression. A method of estimation of image regions masking ability (maximal level of distortions invisible for human visual system) using non-predictable energy of image regions is described. A novel method of zeroing quantized DCT coefficients of JPEG images to increase their compression ratio without introducing visible distortions is proposed. A numerical analysis of effectiveness of the proposed near lossless compression method using 300 noise free test images of TAM-PERE17 database is carried out. It is shown that the proposed method provides an increase of compression ratio of JPEG images without visible distortions at about 1.35 times in average. Additionally, the proposed method results in decreasing of variability of compression ratio values for different images. It is shown that the proposed method increases minimal compression ratio for highly textured JPEG images from 1.1...1.5 times to 2 times. Carried out experiments demonstrated once again that the traditional PSNR metric does not correspond to human perception for this task.

Keywords: Human visual system · Lossy image compression ·
Near lossless image compression · JPEG · Masking effect

1 Introduction

Although the standard JPEG image coding has been proposed in 1992 [1], it is still the main standard of lossy image compression used in digital cameras and mobile devices as well as in internet applications. At the same time, users prefer near lossless modes of JPEG by choosing maximal visual quality of images. Compression ratio (CR) of such JPEG images compressed in near lossless mode usually does not exceed a ratio 2...3, which, in a combination with constantly increasing pixel resolution of photos, significantly increases the load of data transmission channels to deliver images to cloud based storage services as well as requires larger capacity of memory cards. Therefore, the task of increasing CRs for near lossless JPEG image compression without introducing of visible distortion is still very actual.

One of the most widely used techniques of optimization of JPEG compression is a rate-distortion analysis based optimization [2]. It deals with a quantization around of

© Springer Nature Switzerland AG 2019
M. Felsberg et al. (Eds.): SCIA 2019, LNCS 11482, pp. 173–183, 2019.
https://doi.org/10.1007/978-3-030-20205-7_15

zero level and allows to increase CRs of JPEG images in near lossless mode in average by around 5%.

Another widely used approach in optimization of JPEG compression consists in chroma sub-sampling, using different quantization steps (QS) for different spatial frequencies in image luminance color component, larger QS for color components Cb and Cr [1, 3]. However, contrast sensitivity function (CSF) of human visual system (HVS) strongly depends on the pixels size of a viewing device as well as on a viewing distance. Because of it, distortions invisible on a laptop screen, may be visible on a larger screen of e.g. 75" TV or on a big poster. Moreover, a contrast sensitivity for red-green and blue-yellow components are lower than luminance CSF for high frequencies, but higher for low frequencies [4]. Thus, a use of larger quantization steps for color components is also inappropriate for near lossless compression if a screen size and viewing distance are a priory unknown.

In addition to abovementioned approaches, for estimation of a threshold of visually undistinguished distortions the following features are used: average luminance, local variance, RMS contrast, edge density, entropy, mean saturation, etc. [5].

In the paper, we take into account another important peculiarity of HVS - ability of image regions with low predictability to effectively mask noise-like distortions [6]. We propose to set to zero a part of quantized discrete cosine transform (DCT) coefficients of JPEG image. Number of zeroed coefficients depends on masking ability of the image region. This masking ability is estimated by a proposed algorithm. A place of the proposed method in the conventional JPEG compression scheme is shown in Fig. 1.

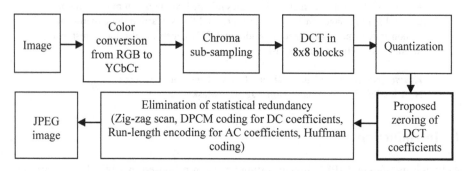

Fig. 1. Place of the proposed method in JPEG compression flow chart

The paper is organized as follows. A difference between masking ability of local variance and non-predictable energy and the algorithm of calculation of masking ability of image pixels are considered in Sect. 2. The proposed method of zeroing quantized DCT coefficients, providing an increase of CR for near lossless JPEG compression, is described in Sect. 3. Finally, Sect. 4 contains the results of numerical analysis of effectiveness of the proposed method.

2   Non-predictable Energy and Local Variance

Figure 2a, shows a noise free reference image which is a combination of two images of TAMPERE17 database [7]. Figure 2b, shows a map of local variance (calculated in 5 × 5 sliding window). Local variance is widely used in practice to estimate masking effect values [5]. At the same time, Fig. 2c, contains a map of non-predictable energy (NPE). Hereinafter, for a visualization we will use square roots of energies (for better visibility of the details).

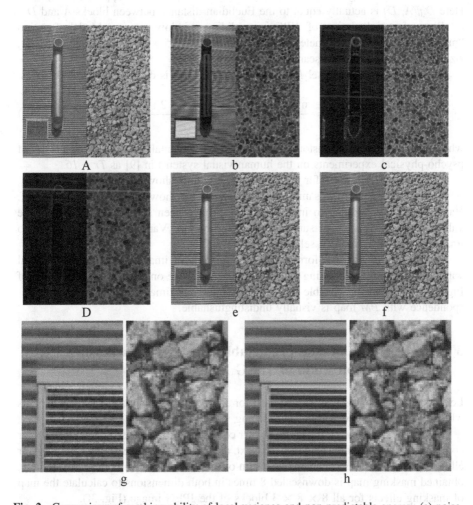

Fig. 2. Comparison of masking ability of local variance and non-predictable energy: (a) noise free reference image; (b) local variance map; (c) map of non-predictable energy; (d) map of masking ability of pixels; (e) image with noise added according to local variance, MSE = 8; (f) image with noise added according to non-predictable energy, MSE = 8; (g) enlarged fragments of the image 2e; (h) enlarged fragments of the image 2f.

NPE for an image block A is calculated according to the following equation:

$$\text{NPE}_A = P(n, k) \min_{D \in U}(\text{Diff}(A, D)), \ \text{Diff}(A, D) = \frac{1}{NM}\sum_{i=1}^{N}\sum_{j=1}^{M}(A_{ij} - D_{ij})^2, \quad (1)$$

where A is a given image block of size $N \times M$ pixels, U is an image area in some neighborhood of A, n denotes the number of patches D in the area U, $k = N \times M$, and $P(n, k)$ is a correcting factor (for a simplicity, in this paper we suppose $P(n, k) = 1$). Here $Diff(A, D)$ is actually equal to the Euclidian distance between blocks A and D.

For a fast calculation of *NPE* in a sliding window we use Matlab function "mapdissim.m" (with parameters: sliding window size 5×5, search zone 21×21, size of area excluded from searching 3×3) [8].

Masking ability of a pixel *PM(i, j)* with indexes *i, j* is calculated in this paper as

$$PM(i, j) = \frac{\min\{\text{NPE}(i - 2 : i + 2, j - 2 : j + 2)\}}{Tr} \quad (2)$$

where Tr is a threshold of distortions visibility, experimentally estimated (as a result of psycho-physical experiments on the human visual system) in [9] as $Tr = 16$.

The map of *PM* values for the image in Fig. 2a, is shown in Fig. 2d.

Noisy images with the same MSE equal to 8 are shown in Fig. 2e, and Fig. 2f. Variances of noise added to image in Fig. 2e, have been selected as 1/64 from the values of local variance of surrounding image region. Variances of noise added to image in Fig. 2f, have been selected as *PM(i, j)*.

As one can clearly see form enlarged fragments of images (Fig. 2g and h) local variance is not always masking a noise. A noise is visible on textures in the left part of Fig. 2g, which are predictable for HVS. At the same time, a noise added in correspondence with *PM* map is visually undistinguishable.

3   Usage of Map of Non-predictable Energy for Increasing of Compression Ratio of JPEG Images

Let us show how a *PM* map can be used for a selection of quantized DCT coefficients which would be zeroed without introducing visible distortions.

At the first step, for an image in YCbCr color space, PM maps for each three color components are calculated (Fig. 3a–d). Next, an aggregated image of masking map, for all color components is calculated as a sum of these three *PM* maps (Fig. 3e). Finally, obtained masking map is downscaled 8 times in both dimensions to calculate the map of masking effects for all $8 \times 8 \times 3$ blocks of the JPEG image (Fig. 3f).

It is reasonable to set to zero primarily DCT coefficients with small absolute values. Such a strategy provides maximum CR increase together with minimum introduced error.

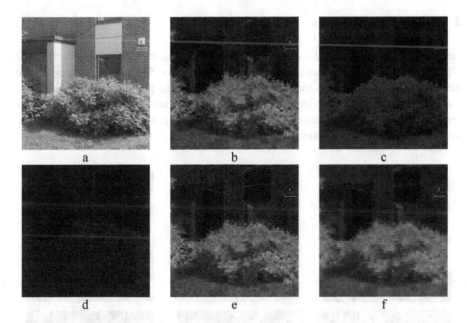

Fig. 3. Calculation of masking effect value for each 8×8 block of JPEG image: (a) JPEG image; (b) PM for Y color component; (c) PM for Cb color component; (d) PM for Cr color component; (e) Sum of three PMs; (f) masking effects of 8×8 blocks of the image (Color figure online)

For each image block $8 \times 8 \times 3$ (3 here corresponds to image color components) the following steps are carried out for the quantized DCT coefficients of all three color components:

1) Quantized DCT coefficients are sorted in ascending order. As a result, an array of C_i is formed, where $i = 1 \ldots 192$.
2) First N coefficients are zeroed, where N is a maximum number of coefficients that fulfils the following criterion: $M \geq \sum_{i=1}^{N} C_i^2$, where M is an aggregated masking effect for this block.
3) All coefficients are returned to their positions in 3D image block $8 \times 8 \times 3$ coefficients.

This procedure can be carried out during JPEG compression right after DCT coefficients quantization, and also can be applied to already compressed JPEG images. In the last case, JPEG image shall be partially decoded to quantized DCT coefficients. After this is done, the proposed calculation of masking map and zeroing of DCT coefficients shall be performed and JPEG image should be recompressed starting from the zig-zag scan.

4 Numerical Analysis

For a numerical analysis in this paper we have used the test image database Tampere 17 [7] containing 300 noise free color test images of 512×512 pixels. Images for the database were obtained with monitoring of noise level (the photo shooting was carried out on calibrated cameras with fixed ISO) and without any interpolation, lossy compression or other spatial processing (denoising, sharpening, etc.). The database contains images of different types (examples are given in Fig. 4).

Fig. 4. Examples of noise free images of TAMPERE17 database

All 300 images have been compressed into JPEG images. To provide a near lossless compression, chroma sub-sampling was not performed and the same $QS = 1$ was used for all DCT coefficients (for luminance and color components).

Then all these JPEG images were recompressed using the proposed algorithm of zeroing of quantized DCT coefficients with the different Tr values.

The curve of dependence between increasing of CR and Tr value is in Fig. 5 for $Tr = \{8, 16, 32\}$.

Further, in our analysis, $Tr = 16$ will be used as recommended in [9]. An average increase of CR for $Tr = 16$ for the proposed method is 1.35 times.

A histogram of an increase of CR for 300 images of TAMPERE17 is shown in Fig. 6. One can see that for the majority of images an increase of CR does not exceed the factor 1.6. At the same time, for some images CR is increased more than twice.

A scatter plot in Fig. 7 helps to understand for which images the proposed method is most effective.

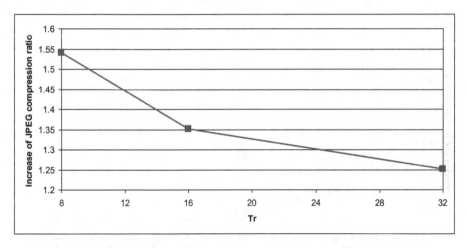

Fig. 5. Dependence of increase of average CR of JPEG images on Tr value

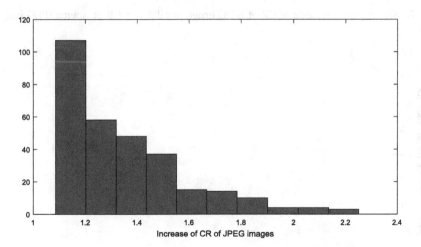

Fig. 6. Histogram of increase of CR of JPEG images for Tr = 16

It is clearly seen that best CR are reached for most complicated images for which a conventional near lossless JPEG provides CRs on the levels 1.1 … 1.5 times higher. The proposed method compresses such images 1.4 … 2 times better.

Figure 8 shows a scatter plot of CR of JPEG images of TAMPERE17 before and after applying of the proposed method.

Analysis of the scatter plot allows to formulate an interesting conclusion. One can see that for the conventional JPEG there are many images with CR ration increase less than 1.5 times. One can see also that after applying the proposed method for 98% CR exceeds 2, which is a very good feature of the proposed method. The proposed compression provides better predictability of the compression ratios of JPEG images.

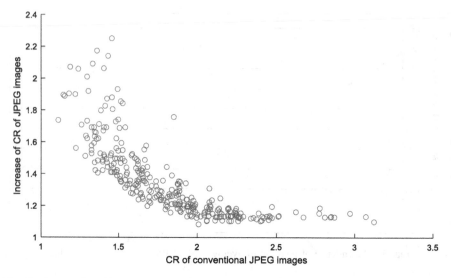

Fig. 7. Scatter plot of increase of CR of JPEG images for different CR of source JPEG images

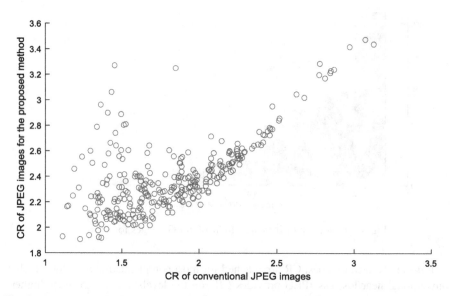

Fig. 8. Scatter plot of CR of JPEG images for the proposed method versus CR of source JPEG images

Figure 9 presents two images from TAMPERE17 database for which the proposed method provides the highest increase of CR. Also values of full-reference metrics PSNR, SSIM [10], PSNR-HMA [11], and CSSIM4 which is a color modification of SSIM taking into accounting *NPE* [12], are shown. Metrics are calculated between the source JPEG image and the image after applying the proposed method (with zeroed part of DCT coefficients).

a   b

Fig. 9. Images with two largest increase of CR by the proposed method: (a) image #282, increase of CR is 2.18 times, PSNR = 35.9 dB, PSNR-HMA = 47.5 dB, SSIM = 0.9997, CSSIM4 = 0.9999; (b) image #192, increase of CR is 2.25 times, PSNR = 37.8 dB, PSNR-HMA = 49.4 dB, SSIM = 0.9998, CSSIM4 = 0.9999

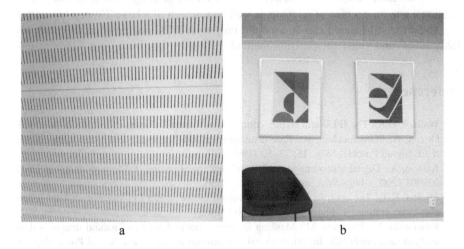

a   b

Fig. 10. Images with two smallest increase of CR by the proposed method: (a) image #251, increase of CR is 1.09 times, PSNR = 54.9 dB, PSNR-HMA = 65.6 dB, SSIM = 1, CSSIM4 = 1; (b) image #274, increase of CR is 1.10 times, PSNR = 54.3 dB, PSNR-HMA = 61.6 dB, SSIM = 0.9998, CSSIM4 = 1.

These images consist mostly from contrast textures complicated for prediction by HVS, and, thereby having high masking ability, that allows to set to zero a large number of DCT coefficients without introducing any visible errors.

Let us also note inoperability of the widely used PSNR metric in this case. Demonstrated values 35.9 dB and 37.8 dB usually correspond to visible distortions.

Figure 10 contains two images of TAMPERE17 database for which the proposed method provides lowest increase of CR. It can be explained by the absence of regions with a good masking ability on these images. The image in Fig. 10a, consists from a texture with high local variance. But the texture is easily predictable for HVS and because of this it is not able to mask big distortions.

In the webpage http://ponomarenko.info/scia2019.html one can compare images before and after applying the proposed method, switch images, enlarge image fragments, and show pixel values. Even after very large upscaling of images, it is very difficult to find a difference between them.

5   Conclusions

In the paper we have proposed a new method of optimization of near lossless JPEG compression based on masking ability of non-predictable energy of image regions. The method allows to increase CR of compressed JPEG images 1.35 times in average without introducing visible distortions.

A serious advantage of this masking approach in comparison with, for example, contrast masking of different spatial frequencies, is its robustness to pixels size and viewing distance. Therefore, a newly compressed JPEG image will look like a conventional one on a screen of a laptop as well on a screen of a large TV or a big poster.

The proposed method can be used not only with JPEG compression, but with any lossy image and video compression methods.

References

1. Wallace, G.K.: The JPEG still picture compression standard. Comm. ACM **34**, 30–44 (1991)
2. Ortega, A., Ramchandran, K.: Rate-distortion methods for image and video compression. IEEE Signal Process. Mag. **15**, 23–50 (1998)
3. Kassim, A.: Digital video image quality and perceptual coding. J. Electron. Imaging **16**(3), 039901 (2007). https://doi.org/10.1117/1.2778686
4. Mullen, K.T.: The contrast sensitivity of human colour vision to red-green an blue-yellow chromatic gratings. J. Physiol. **359**, 381–400 (1985)
5. Kitanovski, V., Pedersen, M.: Masking in chrominance channels of natural images – data, analysis, and prediction. In: International Symposium on Image and Signal Processing and Analysis, pp. 131–136 (2017)
6. Ieremeiev, O.I., Ponomarenko, N.N., Lukin, V.V., Astola, J.T., Egiazarian, K.O.: Masking effect of non-predictable energy of image regions. Telecommun. Radio Eng. **76**(8), 685–708 (2017)

7. Ponomarenko, M., Gapon, N., Voronin, V., Egiazarian, K.: Blind estimation of white Gaussian noise variance in highly textured images. Image Proc. Algorithms Syst. **XVI**, 5 (2018)
8. Egiazarian, K., Ponomarenko, M., Lukin, V., Ieremeiev, O.: Statistical evaluation of visual quality metrics for image denoising. In: International Conference on Acoustics, Speech and Signal Processing (ICASSP), p. 5 (2018)
9. Ponomarenko, M., Ieremeiev, O., Lukin, V., Egiazarian, K.: An expandable image database for evaluation of full-reference image visual quality metrics (2019). Submitted to ICIP
10. Wang, Z., Bovik, A., Sheikh, H., Simoncelli, E.: Image quality assessment: from error visibility to structural similarity. IEEE Trans. Image Process. **13**(4), 600–612 (2004)
11. Ponomarenko, N., Ieremeiev, O., Lukin, V., Egiazarian, K., Carli, M.: Modified image visual quality metrics for contrast change and mean shift accounting. In: Proceedings of CADSM, pp. 305–311 (2011)
12. Ponomarenko, M., Egiazarian, K., Lukin, V., Abramova, V.: Structural similarity index with predictability of image blocks. In: Proceedings of International Conference MMET 2018, p. 4, 2–5 July 2018

Using a Robotic Arm for Measuring BRDFs

Rasmus Ahrenkiel Lyngby, Jannik Boll Matthiassen, Jeppe Revall Frisvad[⊠],
Anders Bjorholm Dahl, and Henrik Aanæs

Technical University of Denmark, Kongens Lyngby, Denmark
jerf@dtu.dk
http://eco3d.compute.dtu.dk/

Abstract. The measurement of a bidirectional reflectance distribution
function (BRDF) requires a purpose-built instrument. We ease this
requirement by presenting a relative method for measuring a BRDF using
a multipurpose robotic arm. Our focus is on the alignment of the system to perform accurate camera positioning and orientation. We use a
six degrees of freedom robotic arm to move a camera on a hemisphere
surrounding a flat material sample. Point-like light sources, fixed on a
quarter circle arc, sequentially illuminate the sample from different directions. The resulting images are used to reconstruct the material BRDF.
We limit ourselves to tristimulus (RGB) isotropic BRDF acquisition.

Keywords: Robot arm · BRDF · Camera pose estimation

1 Introduction

Material appearance is important when using image analysis for quality assurance [12], and one way to represent the appearance of materials is by means of
their reflectance properties. To understand the reflectance properties of materials, we need devices for measuring them. A gonioreflectometer is a device for
measuring reflectance distribution functions [3,6,8]. Such an instrument is usually an expensive, purpose-built machine that does only one job. While gonioreflectometers have important applications in computer graphics and computer
vision, purchasing one is a substantial investment (around €150k). To pursue
scientific discoveries within these areas while limiting the amount of cash tied up
in specialized equipment, we propose to use a multipurpose robot arm (around
€40k) as a gonioreflectometer. Our point is not so much the lower cost of the
robot arm, as other equipment needs to be added to make it useful as a gonioreflectometer. Our point is to describe a setup where the robot arm can be used
for various other research purposes as well.

Many six-axis robots, including the one we use, have a low absolute position
precision. They do, however, have very high repeatability. We exploit this feature
in our BRDF acquisition by measuring the angles between camera and light
directions relative to a 3D artifact using pose estimation. We avoid measuring

M. Felsberg et al. (Eds.): SCIA 2019, LNCS 11482, pp. 184–196, 2019.
https://doi.org/10.1007/978-3-030-20205-7_16

the light source radiant exitance and the absolute camera intensity response, as well as exact distances between camera and surface and between surface and light source. This is done by normalizing observed pixel intensities using Spectralon, which is an almost perfectly diffuse (Lambertian) material.

2   Previous Work

Several precise, robot-based gonioreflectometers exist today [1,4,5,8,15,16]. At Physikalisch-Technische Bundesanstalt (PTB), for example, they have developed a robot-based gonioreflectometer with a five-axis robot holding the sample and a homogeneous sphere radiator mounted on a ring-shaped rotation stage for illumination [4,5]. This system relies on calibrated incident radiance and is generally comprised of more purpose-built components than our setup. Baribeau et al. [1] also use a five-axis robot for holding the sample and others [15,16] use a six-axis robot for the same task. These systems employ a ring-shaped rotation stage for holding either a light source [1,15] or a spectroradiometer [16]. Instead of holding the sample, we let the robot hold a camera, as we can then use the robot in a wider range of applications [18]. The facility at Fraunhofer [8] is similar to ours but more elaborate. They have the robotic arm hanging upside down holding a spectrometer, the sample on a rotation table, and a light source moving on a quarter circle. This enables full 5D (wavelength and two directions) measurement of BRDFs. This is however a one-purpose instrument, and the authors do not discuss how they accurately position and orient the detector.

Techniques for positioning and orientation of a camera mounted on a robot's end effector are available when the camera observes an object with known features [19]. However, feature extraction from the acquired images is oftentimes the main source of error [10]. Feature extraction is typically based on 3D features from a CAD model [19] or features in a 2D calibration object [2,10]. Our samples vary in shape and a 2D calibration grid is not observed well from all the viewing angles that we need. We therefore introduce a 3D artifact and rely on the high repeatability of the robot. We consider our method for ensuring that the robot accurately positions and orients a camera our main contribution. To enable the same robot to be used for multiple purposes, we built a simple light arch that can be moved away from the system when the robot with camera mount is needed for other purposes. Moreover, as stated above, our method is relative and does not rely on calibration of light emission or camera response.

3   Instrumentation

We use a six-axis ABB IRB 1600 10/1.45 industrial robot capable of carrying a payload of 10 kg. It has a repeatability of 50 μm, which means that the sensors are guaranteed to arrive at the same poses within 50 μm. Figure 1 (left) shows the robot in the experimental setup. The camera we use is a Point Grey Grasshopper3 9.1MP RGB camera.

Fig. 1. Left: robotic arm holding a camera in a lightproof enclosure. Right: light arch and camera system measuring the BRDF of an aluminum laptop.

As seen in Fig. 1, the robot is painted black and our setup is completely surrounded by an enclosure also painted black. This shields our setup from any illumination from the surroundings and prevents most internal reflections from disrupting our experiments (a co-bot surrounded by blackout curtains is another option). For lighting, we built an arc-shaped light source covering 90° vertical angle with an array of light sources placed 7.5° apart, see Fig. 1. This setup provides us with control over sensor pose and lighting conditions.

4   BRDF Acquisition

The BRDF characterizes material appearance by describing the change in surface reflectance for varying view and light directions. In terms of geometry, the BRDF is a four-dimensional function. For many materials, this can be reduced to three dimensions by assuming isotropic reflectance. This means that the reflectance does not change with the orientation of the material. We make this assumption and thus exclude materials such as brushed metals and some fabrics.

The BRDF is defined by the ratio of an element of reflected radiance dL_r to an element of irradiance dE [11]:

$$f_r(\theta_i, \phi_i; \theta_o, \phi_o) = \frac{dL_r(\theta_o, \phi_o)}{dE(\theta_i, \phi_i)},$$

where θ_i, ϕ_i denote the direction of incoming light in spherical coordinates, θ_o, ϕ_o denote the direction of outgoing light in spherical coordinates, L_r is the reflected radiance, and E is the irradiance of the sample. The ratio is taken in the limit where only one direction of incidence is considered. The BRDF obeys Helmholtz reciprocity, which means that $f_r(\theta_i, \phi_i; \theta_o, \phi_o) = f_r(\theta_o, \phi_o; \theta_i, \phi_i)$.

In principle, it is easy to measure the BRDF using a gonioreflectometer, by observing a flat homogeneous material sample under all possible view and illumination combinations. Unfortunately, dense sampling of BRDFs requires many samples to accurately capture the appearance of a material, which is a comprehensive task to perform, even with an automated robot.

4.1   Isotropic BRDF Capture

By equipping a robotic arm with a camera and combining this setup with our arc-shaped point-light array, we can semi-densely sample light reflections off of a flat material sample for various configurations of incoming and outgoing light directions. See Fig. 2 for an illustration of the measurement setup.

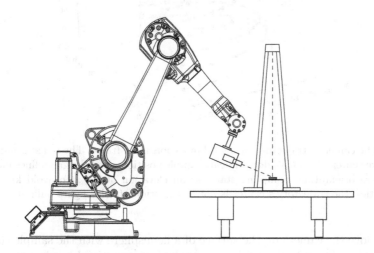

Fig. 2. Our surface reflectance measuring system consisting of robot, light arch, table, sample stand, and sample. The latter is illustrated by the small gray box.

We move the camera around a sample placed under the light arch while imaging the reflectance. As the BRDF obeys Helmholtz reciprocity, one image provides two reciprocal configurations of light and camera. In addition, since we limit ourselves to isotropic BRDFs, consecutive rotation around the surface-normal of both incoming and outgoing rays does not change the BRDF. Thus, we need only move the camera during acquisition.

The spacing between lights in the light array and the spatial resolution of the robotic arm limits how densely we can sample the surface reflectance. The robot has a non-uniform grid of reachable positions, but, in general, the spacing between two reachable locations is sub-millimeter. The light arch has a radius of 1000 mm and has a fixed set of bulbs with a spacing of 7.5°. This configuration provides a compromise between sample rate and measurement time for semi-dense sampling within a reasonable time frame.

Ideally, lights would be point sources and the camera's field of view would be only a fraction of a degree. However, in practice, we have to make compromises. To make the lights more point-like, we keep the sample-to-light distance at around three times the camera-to-sample distance. For the camera, we use the mean value of received light within a broader field of view to estimate reflected radiance as this eases the camera tracking.

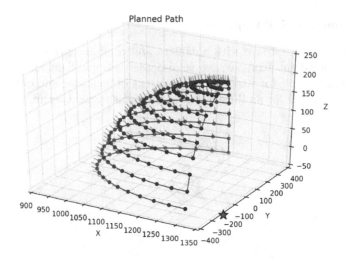

Fig. 3. The camera's trajectory in the robot's coordinate frame. The red star indicates the sphere center, the purple dots indicate sample positions, and the green lines indicate the camera orientation. Sampling starts at an elevation of 7.5°. To avoid kinematic singularities, the trajectory's center is not at the origin. (Color figure online)

We move the camera on the surface of a hemisphere with the sample surface at the center. The robot's arm-length resulted in an optimal hemisphere radius of 350 mm. Due to reciprocity, an isotropic BRDF is mirror symmetric around the vertical plane of the light arc. In other words, the sample's appearance at the right-hand side is identical to its appearance on the left-hand side. Thus, slicing the hemisphere by this plane, we need only sample half of it. The camera path is defined in spherical coordinates with a resolution of 7.5° in both azimuth and elevation. The Cartesian equivalent of a given spherical camera position is then

$$x_{ij} = x_0 + r \left(\sin \theta_i \cos \phi_j, \sin \theta_i \sin \phi_j, \cos \theta_i \right),$$

where θ_i is the inclination angle of sample row i and ϕ_j is the azimuthal angle of sample column j. The position x_0 is the center of the sphere, and r is the radius. The orientation of the camera is then

$$(\beta_{ij}, \gamma_{ij}) = \left(\frac{\pi}{2} + \theta_i, \phi_j \right),$$

where β_{ij} is the camera pitch and γ_{ij} is the camera yaw. For each sample point, we compute the Cartesian coordinates and orientations and store them in a matrix. We feed these to the robot one by one at run time. The camera trajectory with sample positions is illustrated in Fig. 3.

The orientation of the robots coordinate system must be taken into account. In practice, we let points on the robot's x-axis correspond to an azimuth of 0°. In order to operate the robot within its working area, we had to position the light arc along the robot's y-axis. This is illustrated in Fig. 4 (left).

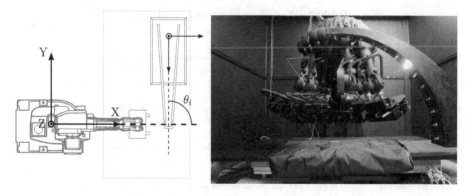

Fig. 4. The position of the light arc in the robot's coordinate system (left). The sample is at the intersection of the two stippled lines, which indicates the center of the spherical robot path. The azimuth of the incoming light is here $\theta_i = 90°$. We merged a sequence of images as the robot sweeps across one row of the path (right) to illustrate the measurement process for a single light source.

To avoid absolute measurements of radiance emitted from light sources and radiance received in camera pixels, we use Spectralon (patented and manufactured by Labsphere). This is a very white material exhibiting $> 99\%$ diffuse reflectance, and the reflection is fairly direction-independent (except at very grazing angles). Thus, with very little loss, Spectralon uniformly spreads incident flux across the hemisphere surrounding the point of incidence. This enables us to measure the BRDF for a given material and pair of incoming and outgoing directions by calculating the ratio of intensities received by the camera when observing material $I^{(M)}$ and Spectralon $I^{(S)}$ from the same direction:

$$f_r(\theta_i, \theta_o, \phi_o) = \frac{I^{(M)}(\theta_i, \theta_o, \phi_o)}{\pi\, I^{(S)}(\theta_i, \theta_o, \phi_o)}. \tag{1}$$

As this is a relative measure, the unit used to measure the intensity is irrelevant. It could be radiant exposure, but it might as well be pixel intensity in $[0, 1]$ or in $[0, 255]$. This concludes the description of the different parts of our BRDF measurement system. The work flow is defined in Table 1 and the process is illustrated in Fig. 4 (right).

The robot is guided in its own coordinate system (Fig. 4, left) by specifying positions of its end effector. However, we would like to directly specify the camera's position and orientation, which requires that we find the spatial transform from end effector to camera. This transformation has to be known rather precisely, as we want the camera to keep pointing as closely as possible toward the same surface point. We deal with this issue in the following section.

5   Hand-Eye Calibration

The position of the robot's end effector is defined for a standard tool. For BRDF measurement, we instead have a camera that we need to position relative to a

Table 1. Work flow to measure a BRDF.

Step		Time	Notes
1	Tool transform	1[h]	Ideally, we would only have to estimate the tool transform once. However, as the tool changes with temperature, humidity, and wear and tear, it is good practice to re-estimate it regularly
2	Aligning spectralon to arch	5[min]	The surface of the Spectralon sample has to be carefully aligned with the center of the semicircle formed by the light arch
3	Spectralon measurement	3[h]	As with the tool transform, this process can be omitted. However, it should be conducted at least once for every new measurement day
4	Aligning material to arch	5[min]	Replace the spectralon sample with the material sample. Make sure the surface of the material align exactly with the surface of the Spectralon
5	Material measurement	3[h]	
6	BRDF calculation	5[min]	Use Eq. 1 to calculate the BRDF of the material
Total		7[h]:15[min]	
Another sample		3[h]:10[min]	

sample. We thus need to accurately determine the six degrees of freedom (DoF) transformations between the robot's standard tool and the camera. Having these transformations, we can determine the position of the camera within the robot's coordinate system by $P_c = P_{rt}T_{ct}$, where T_{ct} is the robot tool to camera transformation, P_{rt} is the six DoF standard tool position, and P_c is the resulting six DoF camera position.

We estimate the transformation T_{ct} using hand-eye calibration, which is based on a set of relative camera and tool motions. Specifically, the solution X to the system $AX = XB$ is found, where A represents the relative motions of the camera, B represents the corresponding relative motions of the tool, and X is the transformation between the camera and the tool. Several algorithms exist to solve this problem. We use the one by Liang and Mao [7]. Using a Kronecker product and singular value decomposition (SVD), we find a closed-form solution to the rotation part of the transformation. This becomes an initial guess in a least-squares optimization used to find the optimal rotation. We then find the translation using a least-squares optimization based on the optimal rotation. This procedure combines the performance of the closed-form solutions with the accuracy and noise invariance of the least-squares solutions, thus providing a good estimate of the transformation in a short amount of time.

To practically solve this transformation, a checkerboard is positioned in the working area. Then, 20 images of the checkerboard are captured from different locations with the camera. For each location, we record two positions: (1) the position of the robot tool with respect to the robot's base and (2) the position of the camera with respect to the checkerboard. The latter is obtained through camera calibration [20]. We manually select the 20 locations by jogging the robot tool so that the locations span the hemisphere over the checkerboard. We vary all six degrees of

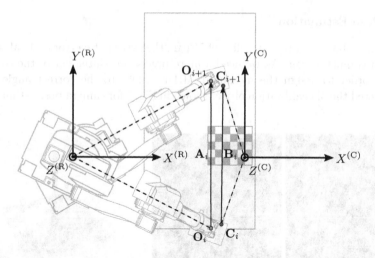

Fig. 5. The hand-eye calibration process for two robot/camera positions. The coordinate systems of robot (R) and checkerboard (C) are marked. The red dots represent the position of the robot tool relative to its coordinate system, and the blue dots represent the camera position relative to the checkerboard. The pair of relative transformations are calculated based on these positions. We use multiple pairs to do the calibration. (Color figure online)

freedom of the robot and ensure that the entire checkerboard is within the field of view of the camera. The saddle points of the checkerboard must be easily identifiable in all images. Thus, the viewing angle of the checkerboard cannot be too steep. The process is illustrated in Fig. 5.

5.1 Photometric Optimization

Although the hand-eye calibration provides a good estimate of the tool transformation of the camera, we wish to further refine it through optimization. We do this to ensure that the uncertainty in camera position is as close as possible to be within the size of a pixel.

From the hand-eye calibration, we get an estimate of the location of the camera's optical axis relative to the end effector. We now capture two images of a checkerboard: before and after rotating the camera 90° around its estimated optical axis. The second image is digitally counter-rotated by 90°. The difference between these two images assesses the correctness of the estimated camera axis. If the difference image is dark with no apparent edges, the optical axis is estimated to within a pixel. Suppose $M_{0°} \in \mathbb{N}^{n \times n}$ is the square-cropped first image and $M_{90°} \in \mathbb{N}^{n \times n}$ is the second image, then the transformation error is $E_{T_{ct}} = \sum \left| M_{0°} - M_{90°}^{T} \right|$. This error depends on T_{ct}. Figure 6 shows examples of difference images. We use the BFGS algorithm [14] to minimize $E_{T_{ct}}$ by optimizing T_{ct}, which has six dimensions in total.

5.2   Pose Estimation

While the robot has a repeatability of 50 μm, the systematic error of its absolute position is much larger. As we need a more precise measurement of the camera pose in order to assign the measured BRDF values to the correct angles, we constructed the 3D calibration object shown in Fig. 7 for camera pose estimation.

Fig. 6. Difference of orthogonal images acquired by the camera before and after a roll of 90°. When taking the difference, the second image is digitally counter-rotated by 90°. We show the result before (left) and after refinement to minimize the error (right). This ensures an accurate tool offset.

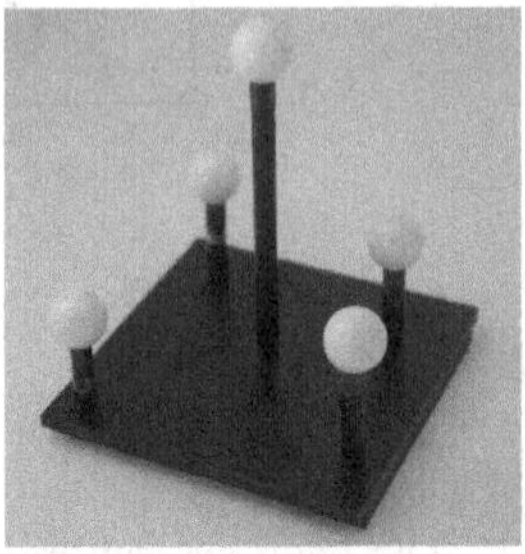

Fig. 7. 3D artifact used for camera pose estimation.

We manually position our artifact underneath the light arch. The robot then traverses the camera trajectory while capturing an image of the artifact at each sample position. Precision of the artifact positioning is unimportant as long as the artifact is visible in all camera views. After pose estimation, all positions and directions will be in the coordinate system of the artifact. The sphere centers of the artifact are annotated manually in the first image. A least-squares optimization then minimizes the error between the back-projection of the spheres onto the image plane and the segmented spheres by adjusting the estimated camera pose. As the relative transformation between two positions on the planned trajectory can be calculated roughly, the estimated sphere centers can be projected into subsequent images and used as an initial guess. Finally, the absolute camera poses for all positions, relative to the pose at the first position, are computed from the poses estimated relative to the artifact.

In a second step, the stereo camera system observes the light bulbs through a mirror at positions from the sample trajectory with now known poses. The pose of each light bulb is then estimated using triangulation.

Pose estimation was found to increase the quality of the BRDF measurements significantly. Better highlights were observed, due to the increased angle precision. Note that the sample itself was not pose estimated. The vertical position of the material surface was mechanically calibrated to precisely align with the base of the calibration artifact.

6 Representation and Sample Interpolation

A common format for storing BRDFs is the MERL binary format [9]. Data is stored in a non-linear voxel-grid using the 3D Rusinkiewicz parametrization $(\theta_h, \theta_d, \phi_d)$ [17], allowing a fine data-resolution around specular highlights. Most BRDF tools and physically based renderers support this format, why it is a convenient way of representing the measured BRDFs.

Fig. 8. Photo of a yellow toy brick made from ABS polymer. A point light source is positioned directly opposite the camera. Two diffuse light sources, positioned above and below the camera, illuminate the brick from the front. The specular highlight due to the point light is clearly visible on the top surface. The image is slightly blurred due to use of a wide aperture. Black tape was added to remove glares from the edges. (Color figure online)

Although our BRDFs consists of hundreds to thousands of samples, they are still somewhat sparse compared to the MERL cubes' $90 \times 90 \times 180 \approx 1.5 \cdot 10^6$ values. To convert the observations to this much finer resolution format, we thus impose two different strategies: an unbiased and a biased approach.

In our unbiased interpolation strategy, all values in the MERL cube are obtained through 1-Nearest-Neighbour (1NN) interpolation. Euclidean distances between neighbours are however not necessarily meaningful in a 4D angular domain. Instead, we perform the 1NN search in a 6D Euclidean space based on the 3D direction vectors toward light and camera. To ensure a meaningful search, we calculate the vectors in the same hemisphere of a Cartesian coordinate system. We keep the light direction vector on the semicircle through the zenith of the hemisphere and place it in the first three dimensions of the 6D space. The camera direction vector is placed in the other three dimensions. From 1NN interpolation in this space, a MERL cube is filled with information by copying the exact measurements to their neighbouring voxels without introducing any new values. The resulting MERL cube accurately reflects the raw measurements, and can thus be used to visualize the data. The cost is that the information is very discrete and does not utilize the full potential of the MERL representation. We therefore only use this interpolation for visualization of the measurements, and not as actual BRDFs. It should also be noted that by applying nearest neighbor interpolation, the property of energy conservation is likely to be violated as $\iint f_r(\theta_i, \theta_o, \phi_o) \cos \theta_o \sin \theta_o d\theta_o \, d\phi_o$ may become greater than 1.

Fig. 9. Visualization of the BRDF measured from the toy brick shown in Fig. 8. We rendered a sphere using the unbiased interpolated BRDF (left) and a sphere and a dragon using the biased interpolated BRDF (middle and right).

In our biased interpolation strategy, we use the principal component based method of Nielsen et al. [13] to reconstruct the missing information in the MERL cube using a prior learned from the MERL dataset [9]. This method creates a smooth and continuous interpolation of the MERL volume with high quality highlights. It is thus a plausible estimate of the missing values, but confined to the data-variation in the MERL database. More info on this biased interpolation method is available in our previous work [18].

7   Results and Discussion

We use the yellow toy in Fig. 8 as a challenging test case. The brick is made of acrylonitrile butadiene styrene (ABS) polymer with a very smooth specular surface. The measured BRDF is illustrated in Fig. 9. The unbiased interpolation (leftmost) visualizes the raw data. The left hemisphere is a reversed mirroring of the right. The dark area originates from an impossible camera position (the camera can not be at the same position as the light source). The measurements look consistent, with no apparent discontinuities other than the dark spot. We rendered a sphere and a dragon using the biased interpolation (middle and right-most). This reconstruction method struggles to correctly represent the specular highlight, as indicated by the small dark spot visible exactly in the middle of the specular highlight of the sphere. This might indicate that the highlight should be sampled more densely [13]. It could also stem from a bias in the MERL dataset. Reconstructions of other materials with less defined highlights were much better: BRDFs of white and gray cardboard and white cloth were measured with our system in our previous work [18]. This work did not present the calibration and unbiased interpolation techniques covered here, but it does provide a larger selection of measured BRDF data delivered by the system and validated to some extent through comparison of rendered images with photographs.

In some tests, we found that the relative intensity method (Eq. 1) can fail for materials that absorb all wavelengths inside either of the red, green or blue color channel. The measured intensity of $I^{(M)}$ in Eq. 1 then drops below the camera's noise floor, which results in a noisy BRDF. Furthermore, Spectralon is nearly but not perfectly diffuse. When observed at grazing angles, $I^{(S)}$ tended to drop below the noise floor, especially for the blue channel. The denominator in Eq. 1 was then mostly noise tending to zero. In a case where $I^{(M)}$ was also mostly noise, the effect of noise divided by noise was seen as a purple tint in the BRDF at grazing angles of observation. The purple color was due to the blue channel being more susceptible to noise, which is most likely due to the quantum efficiency of the blue channel being slightly lower than that of the red and green channels. For most of our tests, this was not a problem. We see it as a limitation that applies to certain types and colors of materials. More powerful light sources or more sensitive cameras may be employed to address this in future work.

References

1. Baribeau, R., Neil, W.S., Côté, É.: Development of a robot-based gonioreflectometer for spectral BRDF measurement. J. Mod. Opt. **56**(13), 1497–1503 (2009)
2. Boby, R.A., Saha, S.K.: Single image based camera calibration and pose estimation of the end-effector of a robot. In: IEEE International Conference on Robotics and Automation, ICRA 2016, pp. 2435–2440 (2016)
3. Erb, W.: Computer-controlled gonioreflectometer for the measurement of spectral reflection characteristics. Appl. Opt. **19**(22), 3789–3794 (1980)
4. Höpe, A., Atamas, T., Hünerhoff, D., Teichert, S., Hauer, K.O.: ARGon³: 3D appearance robot-based gonioreflectometer at PTB. Rev. Sci. Instrum. **83**(4), 045102 (2012)
5. Hünerhoff, D., Grusemann, U., Höpe, A.: New robot-based gonioreflectometer for measuring spectral diffuse reflection. Metrologia **43**(2), S11 (2006)
6. Li, H., Foo, S.C., Torrance, K.E., Westin, S.H.: Automated three-axis gonioreflectometer for computer graphics applications. Opt. Eng. **45**(4), 043605 (2006)
7. Liang, R., Mao, J.: Hand-eye calibration with a new linear decomposition algorithm. J. Zhejiang Univ. Sci. A **9**(10), 1363–1368 (2008)
8. Martínez, M.L., Hartmann, T.: Multispectral gonioreflectometer facility for directional reflectance measurements and its use on materials and paints. In: Target and Background Signatures IV. Proceedings of SPIE, vol. 10794, p. 107940V (2018)
9. Matusik, W., Pfister, H., Brand, M., McMillan, L.: A data-driven reflectance model. ACM Trans. Graph. **22**(3), 759–769 (2003). (SIGGRAPH 2003)
10. Meng, Y., Zhuang, H.: Autonomous robot calibration using vision technology. Robot. Comput. Integr. Manuf. **23**(4), 436–446 (2007)
11. Nicodemus, F.E., Richmond, J.C., Hsia, J.J., Ginsberg, I.W., Limperis, T.: Geometrical considerations and nomenclature for reflectance. Technical report NBS Monograph 160, National Bureau of Standards (US), October 1977
12. Nielsen, J.B., et al.: Quality assurance based on descriptive and parsimonious appearance models. In: Material Appearance Modeling, MAM 2015, pp. 21–24 (2015)
13. Nielsen, J.B., Jensen, H., Ramamoorthi, R.: On optimal, minimal BRDF sampling for reflectance acquisition. ACM Trans. Graph. **34**(6), 186:1–186:11 (2015). (SIGGRAPH Asia 2015)

14. Nocedal, J., Wright, S.J.: Numerical Optimization, 2nd edn. Springer, Heidelberg (2006). https://doi.org/10.1007/978-0-387-40065-5
15. Obein, G., Audenaert, J., Ged, G., Leloup, F.B.: Metrological issues related to BRDF measurements around the specular direction in the particular case of glossy surfaces. In: Measuring, Modeling, and Reproducing Material Appearance 2015. Proceedings of SPIE, vol. 9398, p. 93980D (2015)
16. Rabal, A.M., et al.: Automatic gonio-spectrophotometer for the absolute measurement of the spectral BRDF at in- and out-of-plane and retroreflection geometries. Metrologia **49**(3), 213–223 (2012)
17. Rusinkiewicz, S.: A new change of variables for efficient BRDF representation. In: Drettakis, G., Max, N. (eds.) Rendering Techniques '98 (EGWR 1998), pp. 11–22. Springer, Heidelberg (1998). https://doi.org/10.1007/978-3-7091-6453-2_2
18. Stets, J.D., et al.: Scene reassembly after multimodal digitization and pipeline evaluation using photorealistic rendering. Appl. Opt. **56**(27), 7679–7690 (2017)
19. Wilson, W.J., Hulls, C.C.W., Bell, G.S.: Relative end-effector control using cartesian position based visual servoing. IEEE Trans. Robot. Autom. **12**(5), 684–696 (1996)
20. Zhang, Z.: A flexible new technique for camera calibration. IEEE Trans. Pattern Anal. Mach. Intell. **22**(11), 1330–1334 (2000)

Unsupervised Feature Extraction – A CNN-Based Approach

Daniel J. Trosten[1]([✉]) and Puneet Sharma[2]

[1] UiT Machine Learning Group, Department of Physics and Technology,
UiT The Arctic University of Norway, Tromsø, Norway
`daniel.j.trosten@uit.no`
[2] Department of Engineering and Safety (IIS-IVT),
UiT The Arctic University of Norway, Tromsø, Norway

Abstract. Working with large quantities of digital images can often lead to prohibitive computational challenges due to their massive number of pixels and high dimensionality. The extraction of compressed vectorial representations from images is therefore a task of vital importance in the field of computer vision. In this paper, we propose a new architecture for extracting such features from images in an unsupervised manner, which is based on convolutional neural networks. The model is referred to as the Unsupervised Convolutional Siamese Network (UCSN), and is trained to embed a set of images in a vector space, such that local distance structure in the space of images is approximately preserved. We compare the UCSN to several classical methods by using the extracted features as input to a classification system. Our results indicate that the UCSN produces vectorial representations that are suitable for classification purposes.

1 Introduction

An inherent property of digital images is their large, and often varying dimensionality. A typical image can contain thousands, or even millions of pixels, meaning that the curse of dimensionality [2] can be devastating if not handled properly. This fact has led to the development of a multitude of techniques for computing compressed representations of images, that attempt to retain important information in the representation. Moreover, it is often required that for a database of images, the pairwise similarities between images are approximately preserved through the extraction process. This is vital for the performance of image classification systems, which rely on the quantitative viewpoint provided by a collection of representations. In general, it is easier to design and train a classification system which uses less complex decision functions (e.g. linear), as opposed to systems that rely on more complex decision functions. Hence, a feature extraction technique which is suitable for classification should transform an image database such that the categories one wishes to distinguish form compact and linearly separable "clusters" in the feature space.

Many of the widely used feature extraction techniques are based on the idea of one or more *image descriptors*, that can be computed either over the whole

M. Felsberg et al. (Eds.): SCIA 2019, LNCS 11482, pp. 197–208, 2019.
https://doi.org/10.1007/978-3-030-20205-7_17

image (globally), or from certain subregions of the image (locally). An example of a global descriptor is the *Histogram of Oriented Gradients* (HOG), which has been successfully applied to human recognition and tracking [8]. Examples of local descriptors include the *Scale Invariant Feature Transform* (SIFT) [15], *Speeded Up Robust Features* (SURF) [1], and *Gradient Location and Orientation Histogram* (GLOH) [17].

With these local descriptors, the main idea is to identify points of interest in the input image, and then compute vectorial descriptors based on neighborhoods around these points. The SIFT algorithm identifies keypoints by locating minima or maxima in a scale space, which is constructed by convolving the input image with discretized Laplacian of Gaussians at different scales. The SURF algorithm is based on a similar approach, in which the scale space is constructed using box-filters of varying widths, instead of Gaussians.

Once a set of local descriptors has been computed for an image, these have to be further quantized into a single vector representing the entire image. This can be achieved using the *Bag of Visual-words* (BOV) [7], in which all descriptors from the entire dataset are clustered with k-means, thus creating a vocabulary of visual-words. The feature vector for a given image is then the histogram produced when assigning each of its descriptors to one of the visual-words. Another approach to quantization is the *Improved Fisher Vector* (IFV) [11], which fits a Gaussian mixture model to the complete set of descriptors. Then, for a given image, the feature vector is constructed based on the average gradient of the mixture's log-likelihood, evaluated at each of the descriptors extracted from the image.

Recently, the image processing community has seen a shift in methodology with the introduction of models based on deep learning. The *convolutional neural network* (CNN) [14] has received much attention due to advancements in training strategies and computational capacity [13]. Although a vast majority of the CNN-based models are applied to supervised problems, there are no direct restrictions within the CNN architecture on performing unsupervised tasks. In other words, a modification in the training regime can be adopted to train a CNN-based model for feature extraction in an unsupervised manner.

In an unsupervised feature-extracting CNN, the learned feature vector – and therefore also its quality with respect to the task at hand will depend on the large number of parameters contained in the network. The development of training strategies, and more specifically, loss functions, for training deep learning architectures in an unsupervised manner is a field of research which still is in its early stages. Notable contributions within this field include loss functions designed for joint feature learning and clustering [26, 27], as well as the *Convolutional Autoencoder* (CAE) [16].

The CAE consists of two CNNs, referred to as the encoder and decoder, respectively. The task of the encoder is to embed the input image in a vector space, while the task of the decoder is to reconstruct the input image based only on the embedded representation. These networks are trained together to minimize the mean squared reconstruction error, causing the encoder to learn a mapping which aims to preserve as much information about the input image as possible. When the training process terminates, the decoder is discarded and the encoder can be used as a feature extractor.

In this article, we propose the *Unsupervised Convolutional Siamese Network* (UCSN). It is a new deep learning based feature extractor which consists of a convolutional neural network that is trained end-to-end to learn an adaptive neighborhood embedding in an unsupervised manner, similarly to the weakly supervised *Siamese Networks* [6]. In contrast to the convolutional autoencoder [16], our model does not rely on a decoder network during training.

The rest of the paper is structured as follows: In Sect. 2, we provide an in-depth explanation of the proposed architecture. In Sect. 3, we explain the details of our experiments. In Sects. 4 and 5 we present and discuss our results, respectively. Finally, we provide some concluding remarks in Sect. 6.

2 Method

In this section we introduce the concept of siamese networks, and provide a detailed explanation of our proposed Unsupervised Convolutional Siamese Network.

2.1 Siamese Networks

Feature extraction can be regarded as learning a mapping from some input space X to an output space Y:

$$f_\theta : X \to Y \subseteq \mathbb{R}^D$$

where f denotes the parameterized mapping, and θ is a vector of parameters. D denotes the dimensionality of the extracted features, and depends on the design of the function f. In a *siamese network* [6,10,20], f is parameterized by either a fully-connected neural network or by a convolutional neural network. In both these cases, the final layer is responsible for producing the extracted feature. The chosen network is trained to minimize the contrastive loss function:

$$\mathcal{L}_c = \sum_{i=1}^{n-1} \sum_{j=i+1}^{n} \left(a_{ij} \|\boldsymbol{y}_i - \boldsymbol{y}_j\|^2 + (1 - a_{ij}) \max(0, c - \|\boldsymbol{y}_i - \boldsymbol{y}_j\|)^2 \right), \quad (1)$$

where c is a hyperparameter, $\|\cdot\|$ denotes the Euclidean norm on Y, $\boldsymbol{y}_i = f_\theta(\boldsymbol{x}_i)$ is the feature extracted from the input observation $\boldsymbol{x}_i$, and a_{ij} is an indicator variable defined as

$$a_{ij} = \begin{cases} 1, & (i,j) \text{ is a positive pair} \\ 0, & (i,j) \text{ is a negative pair} \end{cases}.$$

Two observations constitute a positive pair if they belong to the same class or category. Minimizing the contrastive loss function in Eq. (1) causes the network to learn a discriminative embedding by minimizing the distance within embedded positive pairs, while ensuring that the distance within negative pairs is sufficiently large. Thus, the network learns to embed points from the same class close to each other, while ensuring a large distance between points from different classes. The dependency on the a_{ij} in the loss function means that a siamese network requires weakly labeled data in the training process, making it a supervised model.

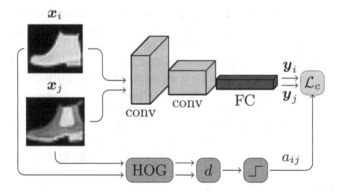

Fig. 1. Outline of the proposed architecture. The loss function considers distance structure in both the input space and the output space, ensuring that similar images are mapped to similar points, and vice versa. For more details on the exact CNN architecture, please see Table 4, Appendix A.

2.2   The Unsupervised Convolutional Siamese Network

To eliminate the need for weakly labeled data, we propose to construct positive and negative pairs based on a distance function in the input space. An overview of the architecture is provided in Fig. 1. The CNN receives as input a set of n images $\boldsymbol{x}_1, \ldots, \boldsymbol{x}_n \in X$, and produces the learned features $\boldsymbol{y}_1, \ldots, \boldsymbol{y}_n \in Y$. The model is trained by minimizing the loss function in Eq. (1), however the a_{ij} are now constructed in an *unsupervised* manner.

More specifically, the a_{ij} are constructed by labeling a pair as positive if the distance between them is less than ε, and negative otherwise:

$$a_{ij} = \begin{cases} 1, & d(\boldsymbol{x}_i, \boldsymbol{x}_j) < \varepsilon \\ 0, & d(\boldsymbol{x}_i, \boldsymbol{x}_j) \geq \varepsilon \end{cases},$$

where d is a suitable symmetric distance function on X, and ε was chosen such that the probability of two random training points being marked as a positive pair was approximately 0.02. This choice resulted in well-separated embeddings.

Note that this modification was previously done in [21], but they only considered the pixel-wise Euclidean distance. To construct a more robust distance function, we compute the Euclidean distance between HOG descriptors extracted from the respective images:

$$d(\boldsymbol{x}_i, \boldsymbol{x}_j) = ||\text{HOG}(\boldsymbol{x}_i) - \text{HOG}(\boldsymbol{x}_j)||.$$

3   Experiment Setup

3.1   Classifier

To quantitatively assess the performance of the extracted features with respect to classification, we train a linear support vector machine (SVM) [3,22] to classify the learned features. The linear SVM was chosen as it is a linear classifier which is fast to train, and has been successfully applied to many classification tasks [23], making it a suitable classification component in the benchmarking process. We use a one-vs-rest SVM from the scikit-learn Python module, with default hyperparameters.

3.2 Models

In our experiments we evaluate two different versions of the UCSN. UCSN-Euc uses the Euclidean distance to determine positive and negative pairs, while UCSN-HOG uses the distance between HOG-features. We compare the proposed models to several state-of-the-art methods for image feature extraction [5]:

- *SIFT-BOV*: SIFT descriptors encoded with the bag of visual words (BOV) encoding, with a vocabulary size of 4096 visual words. The 128 dimensional descriptors were transformed to 80 dimensional vectors using PCA, before running k-means. The dimensionality reduction has been empirically found to improve the classification accuracy in similar models [4]. Each of the transformed descriptors were augmented with the normalized position of their respective keypoints, i.e. $(x/W, y/H)$, where (x, y) is the position of the keypoint in the image, and (W, H) is the width and height of the image, respectively.
- *SIFT-IFV*: SIFT descriptors encoded using the improved Fisher vector (IFV) encoding with 256 mixture components. Similarly to SIFT-BOV, the descriptors were reduced in dimensionality and augmented before fitting the Gaussian mixture model.
- *SURF-BOV*: Same as SIFT-BOV, but with SURF descriptors instead. Note that the 128 dimensional extended SURF descriptor was used. Dimensionality reduction with PCA, and position augmentation was done before running k-means.
- *SURF-IFV*: Same as SIFT-IFV, but with the 128 dimensional extended SURF descriptor. Dimensionality reduction with PCA, and position augmentation was done before fitting the Gaussian mixture model.
- *HOG*: The HOG descriptor.
- *CAE*: A fully convolutional autoencoder as described in [16]. Note that we train the model end-to-end instead of layer-wise, and use standard upsampling layers in the decoder, instead of the pooling scheme suggested in [16]. These modifications were made to reduce the computational complexity associated with training the model.

The dimensionality of the extracted features for the models can be found in Table 1, and the complete list of hyperparameter values for all models can be found in Table 4, Appendix A.

Note that the dimensionality of the extracted features is very large for some of the models and datasets. For the models based on local descriptors, the dimensionality can be adjusted by tuning either the number of clusters in BOV, or the number of mixture components in IFV. However, as pointed out in [4], values lower than 4096 clusters, or 256 mixture components, can lead to a drop performance.

Table 1. Dimensionalities of the extracted features. The last column indicates whether the dimensionality is a hyperparameter in the model.

Model	Dataset			Parameter
	SVHN [18]	Fashion-MNIST [25]	Cats and dogs [9]	
HOG	1764	1296	142884	✗
SIFT-BOV	4094	4096	4096	✔
SIFT-IFV	41984	41984	41984	✔
SURF-BOV	4094	4096	4096	✔
SURF-IFV	41984	41984	41984	✔
CAE	64	64	64	✔
UCSN-Euc/HOG	64	64	64	✔

Table 2. Properties of the different datasets used for evaluation.

	SVHN [18]	Fashion-MNIST [25]	Cats and dogs [9]
Image size	32×32	28×28	256×256
Color	RGB	Grayscale	RGB
# Samples	99289	60000	8192
# Classes	10	10	2
Contents	Natural images of house numbers	Clothing items	Natural images of cats and dogs

3.3 Datasets

The datasets chosen for evaluation are listed in Table 2. These constitute a range of object recognition tasks, without introducing auxiliary challenges, like multiple labels, large amounts of noise, and very high resolutions. Each dataset was randomly split into a training set, validation set, and test-set. 80 % of the images were used for training, 10 % were used for hyperparameter validation, while the last 10 % were used for performance evaluation. Note that the training set was used to train both the feature extractors and the corresponding SVMs.

3.4 Implementation

The experiments were implemented using the Python programming language, with the NumPy and SciPy modules for numerical computations. The HOG, SIFT and SURF descriptors were computed using the OpenCV module, while BOV and IFV were implemented on top of the KMCuda and scikit-learn modules, respectively. The SVM from the scikit-learn module was used, while the UCSN and the CAE were implemented and trained using the TensorFlow framework. Both these models were trained for 200 iterations, using stochastic mini-batches of size 1024 and the Adam optimizer [12].

Table 3. Classification accuracies for the different models and datasets.

Model	Dataset		
	SVHN	Fashion-MNIST	Cats and dogs
HOG	0.77	0.89	0.70
SIFT-BOV	0.50	0.74	0.69
SIFT-IFV	0.60	0.82	0.68
SURF-BOV	0.69	0.75	0.69
SURF-IFV	0.60	0.70	0.71
CAE	0.66	0.86	0.62
UCSN-Euc	0.38	0.80	0.59
UCSN-HOG	0.78	0.86	0.62

4   Results

The classification accuracies obtained from the different models and datasets are shown in Table 3. These indicate that the performance of the UCSN-HOG is comparable to the benchmark models. For the SVHN dataset, we observe that both UCSN-HOG and HOG outperform the rest of the models. This indicates that the HOG descriptors are suitable for discriminating between classes, and that the UCSN-HOG is able to exploit this information when extracting its features. This is not observed with the UCSN-Euc model, which performs significantly worse than all other models.

For the Fashion-MNIST dataset, UCSN-Euc is not as far behind, but still performs worse than UCSN-HOG, HOG, and the CAE. This again implies that these three models are able to extract features with better discriminative properties. On the other hand, the results for the Cats and Dogs dataset show that all deep learning based models perform worse than the other benchmark methods. Interestingly, this is opposite to what is commonly observed for fully supervised models, where CNN-based classifiers regularly outperform the classical approaches [5, 13].

To further evaluate the validity of our results, the Fashion-MNIST features were projected to two dimensions using t-SNE [24] for selected models. Figure 2 shows the transformed features. These plots reveal a large difference in class separability, with the SURF-IFV features being significantly less separable than the other three. The classes are more separated by the CAE's representation, however, the features provided by HOG and UCSN-HOG still show better class separability. There is also a noticeable similarity between the HOG features and the UCSN-HOG features, which is expected since the UCSN-HOG is trained to preserve local HOG distances.

Figure 3 shows image pairs extracted from the SVHN and Cats and Dogs datasets, respectively. The normalized distances in the tables to the right are computed as $d_{norm} = \frac{d}{d_{max}}$ where d is the distance between feature vectors extracted from the two images for the given model, and d_{max} is the maximum observed distance between any two extracted feature in the dataset, for the given model.

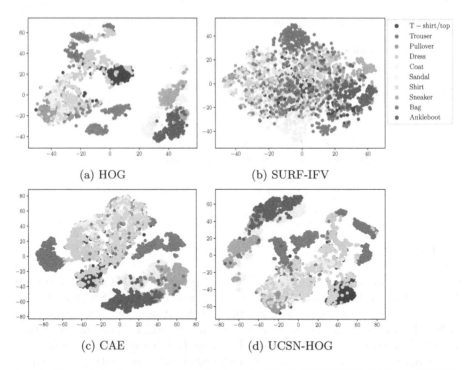

(a) HOG   (b) SURF-IFV

(c) CAE   (d) UCSN-HOG

Fig. 2. Plots of the features extracted using the HOG, SURF-IVF, CAE, and UCSN-HOG feature extractors. Note the large difference in class separability. The features were transformed to two dimensions using *t*-SNE [24].

HOG	SIFT-BOV
0.53	0.40
SIFT-IFV	SURF-BOV
0.69	0.71
SURF-IFV	CAE
0.79	0.48
UCSN-Euc	UCSN-HOG
0.47	0.18

(a)

HOG	SIFT-BOV
0.90	0.86
SIFT-IFV	SURF-BOV
0.85	0.40
SURF-IFV	CAE
0.71	0.62
UCSN-Euc	UCSN-HOG
0.58	0.91

(b)

Fig. 3. Image-pairs and their corresponding normalized distances. The distances are normalized by dividing the distance between extracted features, with the maximum observed distance, for each model and dataset.

The pair in Fig. 3a shows two images that are both labeled as "1". Note that the distance between UCSN-HOG embeddings is small, even though the image backgrounds are quite dissimilar, and the rightmost image contains an additional "4" which acts as a distraction. This indicates that UCSN-HOG has learned to recognize the "1" in the images. However, in Fig. 3b the cats depicted in the images are quite similar, but the distance between UCSN-HOG embeddings is large. This shows that UCSN-HOG is unable to pick up the similarities between these two images. This is also the case for most of the benchmark models, with the exception of UCSN-Euc and SURF-BOV.

5   Discussion

Although the CNN-based models, i.e. CAE and our proposed UCSN, perform well on the SVHN and Fashion-MNIST datasets, this was not observed with the Cats and Dogs dataset, where both these models performed worse than the other benchmark methods. This indicates that, when trained in an unsupervised manner, the filters learned by the CAE and the UCSN do not produce sufficiently discriminative representations in the output space. It is possible that this problem can be alleviated by employing different initialization techniques, for instance, through transfer learning [19], where the CNN is pre-trained as a classifier on a different dataset where ground truth labels are available. After pre-training, the network can be fine-tuned to the task at hand using the loss function in Eq. (1). Another option is to consider different distance functions in the image space, as this governs the local similarity structure of the extracted features. We emphasize that the proposed architecture can work with any symmetric distance function, making it applicable to a diverse set of domains. The exploration of these potential modifications is left as future work.

6   Conclusions

In this article, we outline a new architecture for image feature extraction that is based on convolutional neural networks. The proposed Unsupervised Convolutional Siamese Network (UCSN) is trained to embed a set of images in a vector space such that local distance structure is approximately preserved. We compare the UCSN model to several classical models by using the extracted features as input to a classification system. The overall results obtained from three different datasets indicate that the UCSN produces vectorial representations that are suitable for classification purposes. In the end, we suggest possible techniques that can be used for improving the performance of UCSN for feature extraction applications.

A   Hyperparameters

Table 4. A summary of all the hyperparameters in all the models. Please consult the OpenCV documentation for an explanation of the HOG, SIFT and SURF hyperparameters.

Model	Parameter	Dataset		
		SVHN	Fashion-MNIST	Cats and Dogs
HOG	blockSize	8	8	8
	blockStride	4	4	4
	cellSize	4	4	4
	nbins	9	9	9
SIFT-BOV	nfeatures	64	64	32
	sigma	0.8	0.8	1.6
	nOctaveLayers	3	3	5
	contrastThreshold	0.001	0.001	0.004
	k	4096	4096	4096
SIFT-IFV	nfeatures	64	64	32
	sigma	0.8	0.8	1.6
	nOctaveLayers	3	3	5
	contrastThreshold	0.001	0.001	0.004
	k	256	256	256
SURF-BOV	hessianThreshold	0.0	0.0	200
	nOctaves	5	5	4
	nOctaveLayers	5	5	3
	extended	True	True	True
	k	4096	4096	4096
SURF-IFV	hessianThreshold	0.0	0.0	200
	nOctaves	5	5	4
	nOctaveLayers	5	5	3
	extended	True	True	True
	k	256	256	256
CAE	layers	Conv $5 \times 5 \times 32$ ReLU MaxPool 2×2 Conv $5 \times 5 \times 32$ ReLU MaxPool 2×2 Dense 64	Conv $5 \times 5 \times 32$ ReLU MaxPool 2×2 Conv $5 \times 5 \times 32$ ReLU MaxPool 2×2 Dense 64	MaxPool 2×2 Conv $7 \times 7 \times 16$ ReLU MaxPool 2×2 Conv $5 \times 5 \times 8$ ReLU MaxPool 2×2 Dense 64
UCSN	layers	Conv $5 \times 5 \times 32$ ReLU MaxPool 2×2 Conv $5 \times 5 \times 32$ ReLU MaxPool 2×2 Dense 64	Conv $5 \times 5 \times 32$ ReLU MaxPool 2×2 Conv $5 \times 5 \times 32$ ReLU MaxPool 2×2 Dense 64	MaxPool 2×2 Conv $7 \times 7 \times 16$ ReLU MaxPool 2×2 Conv $5 \times 5 \times 8$ ReLU MaxPool 2×2 Dense 64
	c	1	1	1
	ε (Euc/HOG)	12.41/5.10	5.86/3.39	110.56/48.1

References

1. Bay, H., Tuytelaars, T., Van Gool, L.: SURF: speeded up robust features. In: Leonardis, A., Bischof, H., Pinz, A. (eds.) ECCV 2006. LNCS, vol. 3951, pp. 404–417. Springer, Heidelberg (2006). https://doi.org/10.1007/11744023_32
2. Bellman, R.: Dynamic Programming. Princeton University Press, Princeton (1957)
3. Chang, C.C., Lin, C.J.: LIBSVM: a library for support vector machines. ACM Trans. Intel. Syst. Technol. **2**(3), 1–27 (2011). https://doi.org/10.1145/1961189.1961199
4. Chatfield, K., Lempitsky, V., Vedaldi, A., Zisserman, A.: The devil is in the details: an evaluation of recent feature encoding methods. In: Procedings of the British Machine Vision Conference 2011, pp. 76.1–76.12. British Machine Vision Association, Dundee (2011). https://doi.org/10.5244/C.25.76
5. Chatfield, K., Simonyan, K., Vedaldi, A., Zisserman, A.: Return of the devil in the details: delving deep into convolutional nets. arXiv:1405.3531 [cs], May 2014
6. Chopra, S., Hadsell, R., LeCun, Y.: Learning a similarity metric discriminatively, with application to face verification. In: 2005 IEEE Computer Society Conference on Computer Vision and Pattern Recognition, CVPR 2005, vol. 1, pp. 539–546, June 2005. https://doi.org/10.1109/CVPR.2005.202
7. Csurka, G., Dance, C.R., Fan, L., Willamowski, J., Bray, C.: Visual categorization with bags of keypoints. In: In Workshop on Statistical Learning in Computer Vision, ECCV, pp. 1–22 (2004)
8. Dalal, N., Triggs, B.: Histograms of oriented gradients for human detection. In: 2005 IEEE Computer Society Conference on Computer Vision and Pattern Recognition (CVPR 2005), vol. 1, pp. 886–893. IEEE, San Diego (2005). https://doi.org/10.1109/CVPR.2005.177
9. Elson, J., Douceur, J.J., Howell, J., Saul, J.: Asirra: A CAPTCHA that exploits interest-aligned manual image categorization. In: Proceedings of 14th ACM Conference on Computer and Communications Security (CCS). Association for Computing Machinery, Inc., October 2007
10. Hadsell, R., Chopra, S., LeCun, Y.: Dimensionality reduction by learning an invariant mapping. In: 2006 IEEE Computer Society Conference on Computer Vision and Pattern Recognition - Volume 2 (CVPR 2006), vol. 2, pp. 1735–1742. IEEE, New York (2006). https://doi.org/10.1109/CVPR.2006.100
11. Perronnin, F., Sánchez, J., Mensink, T.: Improving the Fisher Kernel for large-scale image classification. In: Daniilidis, K., Maragos, P., Paragios, N. (eds.) ECCV 2010. LNCS, vol. 6314, pp. 143–156. Springer, Heidelberg (2010). https://doi.org/10.1007/978-3-642-15561-1_11
12. Kingma, D.P., Ba, J.: Adam: a method for stochastic optimization. In: International Conference on Learning Representations (ICLR) (2015)
13. Krizhevsky, A., Sutskever, I., Hinton, G.E.: ImageNet classification with deep convolutional neural networks. Adv. Neural Inf. Process. Syst. **25**, 1097–1105 (2012)
14. Lecun, Y.: Generalization and network design strategies. In: Pfeifer, R., Schreter, Z., Fogelman, F., Steels, L. (eds.) Connectionism in perspective. Elsevier (1989)
15. Lowe, D.G.: Distinctive image features from scale-invariant keypoints. Int. J. Comput. Vis. **60**(2), 91–110 (2004). https://doi.org/10.1023/B:VISI.0000029664.99615.94
16. Masci, J., Meier, U., Cireşan, D., Schmidhuber, J.: Stacked convolutional auto-encoders for hierarchical feature extraction. In: Honkela, T., Duch, W., Girolami, M., Kaski, S. (eds.) ICANN 2011. LNCS, vol. 6791, pp. 52–59. Springer, Heidelberg (2011). https://doi.org/10.1007/978-3-642-21735-7_7

17. Mikolajczyk, K., Schmid, C.: A performance evaluation of local descriptors. IEEE Trans. Pattern Anal. Mach. Intell. **27**(10), 16 (2005)
18. Netzer, Y., Wang, T., Coates, A., Bissacco, A., Wu, B., Ng, A.Y.: Reading digits in natural images with unsupervised feature learning. In: Neural Information Processing Systems (NIPS), p. 9 (2011)
19. Pratt, L.Y., Mostow, J., Kamm, C.A.: Direct transfer of learned information among neural networks. In: Proceedings of the Ninth National Conference on Artificial Intelligence, AAAI 1991, vol. 2, pp. 584–589. AAAI Press, Anaheim (1991)
20. Shaham, U., Lederman, R.R.: Learning by coincidence: Siamese networks and common variable learning. Pattern Recogn. **74**, 52–63 (2018). https://doi.org/10.1016/j.patcog.2017.09.015
21. Shaham, U., Stanton, K., Li, H., Basri, R., Nadler, B., Kluger, Y.: SpectralNet: spectral clustering using deep neural networks. In: International Conference on Learning Representations (2018)
22. Smola, A.J., Schölkopf, B.: A Tutorial on Support Vector Regression (2004)
23. Theodoridis, S., Koutroumbas, K.: Pattern Recognition, 4th edn. Elsevier Academic Press, Amsterdam (2009). oCLC: 550588366
24. van der Maaten, L., Hinton, G.: Visualizing data using t-SNE. J. Mach. Learn. Res. **9**, 2579–2605 (2008)
25. Xiao, H., Rasul, K., Vollgraf, R.: Fashion-MNIST: A Novel Image Dataset for Benchmarking Machine Learning Algorithms, August 2017
26. Xie, J., Girshick, R., Farhadi, A.: Unsupervised deep embedding for clustering analysis. In: Proceedings of the 33rd International Conference on Machine Learning. Proceedings of Machine Learning Research, vol. 48, pp. 478–487, June 2016
27. Yang, J., Parikh, D., Batra, D.: Joint unsupervised learning of deep representations and image clusters. In: 2016 IEEE Conference on Computer Vision and Pattern Recognition (CVPR), pp. 5147–5156, June 2016. https://doi.org/10.1109/CVPR.2016.556

Automatic Detection of Cervical Vertebral Landmarks for Fluoroscopic Joint Motion Analysis

Ida Marie Groth Jakobsen and Maciej Plocharski[✉] iD

Department of Health Science and Technology,
Aalborg University, Aalborg, Denmark
mpl@hst.aau.dk

Abstract. Real-time motion assessment of the cervical spine provides an understanding of its mechanics and reveals abnormalities in its motion patterns. In this paper we propose a vertebral segmentation approach to automatically identify the vertebral landmarks for cervical joint motion analysis using videofluoroscopy. Our method matches a template to the vertebral bodies, identified using two parallel segmentation approaches, and validates the results through comparison to manually annotated landmarks. The algorithm identified the vertebral corners with an average detection error under five pixels in the C3–C6 vertebrae, with the lowest average error of 1.65 pixels in C4. C7 yielded the largest average error of 6.15 pixels. No significant difference was observed between the intervertebral angles computed using the manually annotated and automatically detected landmarks ($p > 0.05$). The proposed method does not require large amounts of data for training, eliminates the necessity for manual annotations, and allows for real-time intervertebral motion analysis of the cervical spine.

Keywords: Cervical spine · Segmentation · Automatic detection ·
Vertebral landmarks · Videofluoroscopy

1 Introduction

Individual motion contributions of the cervical vertebrae provide valuable information about the natural neck movement and reveal abnormalities associated with spinal injuries or medical conditions [1]. Digital videofluoroscopy is an imaging modality which allows a real-time *in vivo* analysis of unrestricted cervical motion, otherwise is not possible when using static radiographic images. Cervical range of motion has been investigated in whiplash-associated disorders [1], in neck pain [1,2], as well as in healthy subjects [1,3,4], and it has been shown to be significantly decreased in whiplash and neck pain [1]. New evidence indicates that the cervical joints contributions to the range of motion, previously thought to be regular and continuous [3], in fact prove to be opposite to the direction of movement [4–6], and that the vertebral motion patterns to and from

© Springer Nature Switzerland AG 2019
M. Felsberg et al. (Eds.): SCIA 2019, LNCS 11482, pp. 209–220, 2019.
https://doi.org/10.1007/978-3-030-20205-7_18

the end ranges of movement are not mirror images of each other [5,7]. Therefore, a rotational and translational cervical motion analysis is of considerable importance.

Motion analysis of the cervical spine requires an annotation of landmarks on vertebral corners [3]. The majority of studies analyzing cervical joint motion employed manual and semi-automated approaches for landmark annotations [3,4,6,8,9,11]. Manual methods have been shown to be highly reliable [4,6,12], but also time-consuming, and thus impractical for large data analysis. Automatic vertebral tracking studies have used template matching [11,13], Active Appearance Models [14–16], or feature tracking algorithms [17]. However, these methods still require manual identification of vertebral landmarks in the first frames of the videos. Fully automatic landmark identification has been successful in the lumbar spine [8,10,18,19], due to the larger size and better visibility of the vertebral bodies, or when using imaging modalities providing higher contrast and spatial resolution, such as Computed Tomography [15,20,21] or X-ray [14,16,22]. Nonetheless, these approaches have not been successful when applied to the cervical vertebrae in fluoroscopic images, due to their smaller size, small field-of-view, lower image quality, and considerable presence of motion blur.

In this paper we propose a procedure for automatic identification and segmentation of cervical vertebrae in videofluoroscopic sequences. It allows an accurate computation of vertebral landmarks necessary for a real-time cervical motion analysis, and eliminates the prerequisite for manual annotation (Fig. 1a) of the C3–C7 vertebrae.

2 Method

2.1 Experimental Procedure

Four young adult subjects were included in this study: two women (age: 23.5 ± 0.71 years; height: 167.5 ± 17.7 cm; weight: 73.8 ± 26.6 kg, and two men (age: 25.0 ± 1.4 years; height: 184.5 ± 6.4 cm; weight: 77.5 ± 6.4 kg. Exclusion criteria were: neck disorders, any neck symptoms up to three months prior to the study, and possible pregnancy. Fluoroscopic video sequences (Fig. 1a) were acquired at 25 frames per second, with a resolution of 576×768 pixels, using the Phillips BV Libra mobile diagnostic fluoroscopic image acquisition and viewing system. For each subject, two average quality fluoroscopic sequences were recorded: one at the onset of flexion, and one at the onset of extension. The average source-to-participant distance (C7 spinous process) was 76 cm, and the average exposure of 45-kV, 208-mA, 6.0-ms X-ray pulses yielded 0.12 mSv per individual motion from upright to end-range (PCXMC software, STUK, Helsinki, Finland). Subjects were asked to sit in the normal upright position and perform movement in the sagittal plane, starting from the neutral position to the end-range of movements. They all wore plastic glasses with two small metal bearings on each side, attached to the glasses by metal wires. The purpose of them was to serve as external markers of the occiput visible under fluoroscopy (Fig. 1a).

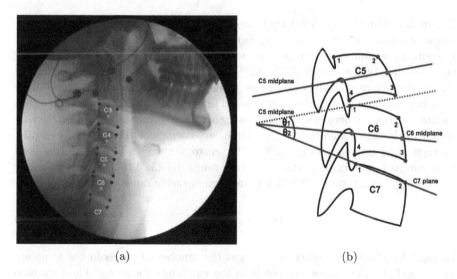

(a)   (b)

Fig. 1. (a) Manually annotated corners on the cervical spine, from C3 to C7, with visible external markers. (b) Marking order for the corners, as well as the posterior and anterior midpoints (red) which form the mid-planes used for joint angle calculations, illustrated on the C5, C6, and C7 vertebrae. (Color figure online)

2.2 Automatic Identification of Vertebral Landmarks

The automatic vertebral landmark identification algorithm consisted of the following steps (Fig. 2): template matching; two parallel segmentation methods, using contrast-limited adaptive histogram equalization and gradient magnitude approaches; registration of the segmented vertebrae to the template; and identification of the vertebral corners as landmarks.

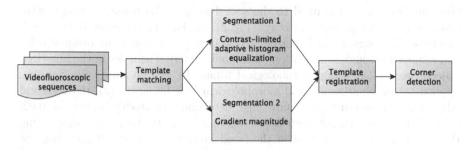

Fig. 2. Procedure workflow for an automatic identification of the cervical vertebral landmarks.

Template Matching: A binary template was created to represent an average shape of the cervical vertebrae (Fig. 5a). Videofluoroscopic sequences of subjects in neutral position were preprocessed with a local range filter. Canny edge detection (sensitivity thresholds [0.02, 0.05]) and a morphological closing (spherical structuring element, radius of 2 pixels) were then performed. Next, the binary template was matched to the preprocessed image at every location, and the candidate locations where the template matched the vertebrae were identified by means of the following criteria: Dice similarity coefficient (DSC) > 0.34 (Eq. 1); average pixel intensity range [100, 150]; entropy threshold > 1.99; gray-level co-occurrence matrix properties: contrast range [0.045, 0.12], correlation range [0.93, 0.98], energy range [0.2, 0.34], and homogeneity range [0.94, 0.98].

$$DSC = \frac{2\,|X \cap Y|}{|X| + |Y|} \tag{1}$$

In Eq. 1 for the Dice coefficient, $|X|$ was the number of pixels in the template image and $|Y|$ the number of pixels in the candidate locations. The identified candidate locations were then edge-, and contrast-enhanced using a power law transformation ($\gamma = 1.1$, $c = 1$). Finally, a quadratic anisotropic diffusion filter was applied. At the end of this step, regions-of-interest (ROIs) around the vertebral bodies were identified for segmentation, using two parallel approaches (Fig. 2), both of which were applied only to these ROIs.

Segmentation 1 - Contrast-Limited Adaptive Histogram Equalization: First, a contrast-limited adaptive histogram equalization (CLAHE) algorithm was applied in order to enhance the contrast in the identified gray-scale candidate ROIs (Fig. 3). The candidate locations were sharpened to enhance the contrast of the edges. Next, adaptive thresholding was applied to 3-by-3 neighborhoods of the vertebral ROIs to filter the noise, while simultaneously preserving the edges. The gray-level co-occurrence matrix was calculated once more and adaptive thresholding was applied to the scaled image. The resulting images were processed in three parallel pathways (Fig. 3). In (1), a fourth order Butterworth bandpass filter was applied (cut-off frequencies: [5, 71]), and the residual noise was removed through binarization (threshold = 0.99). The holes in the binarized objects were filled using morphological filling. In (2), no image filtering was applied before binarization and morphological hole filling. In (3), the vertebral edges were computed using Canny edge detection (sensitivity thresholds [0.02, 0.05]). The three images were fused together, so that the pixels constituting the vertebral edges were kept in the fused images if and only if they had the same value of 1 (white) at the same pixel locations. Finally, this step concluded with morphological opening and then closing. The results of Segmentation 1 are illustrated in Fig. 5b.

Segmentation 2 - Gradient Magnitude: In Segmentation 2 (Fig. 4), a gradient magnitude was applied to the fluoroscopic images, filtered with a

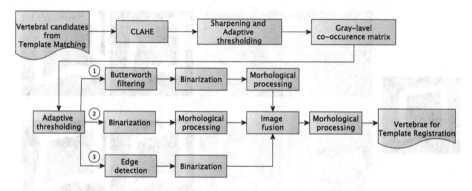

Fig. 3. The workflow of Segmentation 1 procedure using contrast-limited adaptive histogram equalization.

quadratic anisotropic diffusion filter. The images were then filtered using an edge-preserving, local Laplacian filter ($\sigma = 0.9$, $\alpha = 0.1$). The vertebral ROIs were then sharpened to enhance the contrast along the edges (radius $= 3$; sharpening strength $= 2$, minimum contrast threshold $= 0$). Next, adaptive thresholding was applied for binarization, and morphological opening and closing for filling the holes and bridging the edges in the segmented vertebrae. The results of Segmentation 2 are illustrated in Fig. 5c.

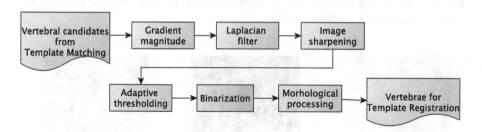

Fig. 4. The workflow of Segmentation 2 procedure using the gradient magnitude.

Template Registration: At the beginning of this step, each vertebral ROI was segmented using the two aforementioned segmentation procedures. In order to quantitatively determine which of them provided the best results, the template image (Fig. 5a) was matched once again with the vertebral boundaries by means of affine registration (Fig. 5d and e). The registration was optimized by means of mean squared error, with a regular step gradient descent configuration, initial step length of 0.01, and 1000 iterations. The segmentation result with the highest DSC (Fig. 6a) was selected.

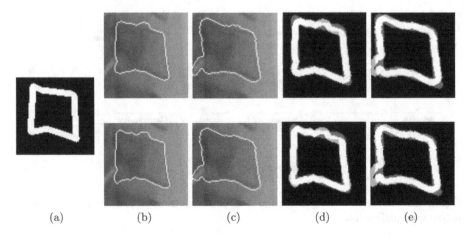

(a)   (b)   (c)   (d)   (e)

Fig. 5. (a) Binary template; (b) representative examples of Segmentation 1 and (c) of Segmentation 2; (d) and (e) results of template registrations to vertebrae segmented in (b) and (c), respectively.

Corner Detection: The corners of the segmented vertebrae (Fig. 6a) were located by determining the largest Euclidean distance between all the points of the vertebral boundary (Fig. 6b). The four corners obtained in this process were then selected as vertebral landmarks (Fig. 6c). The results of the corner detection are shown in red in Fig. 7, superimposed on a fluoroscopic image with manually annotated vertebral corners (blue).

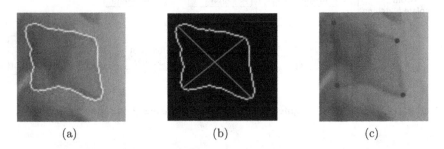

(a)   (b)   (c)

Fig. 6. (a) Segmented vertebral body; (b) two largest Euclidean distances within the vertebral boundary; (c) vertebral corners.

2.3   Manual Annotation of Vertebral Corners

For the purpose of validating the algorithm, vertebral corners were also manually annotated on the fluoroscopic images in C3–C7 (Fig. 1a). Additionally, intervertebral joint angles were computed using the automatically detected and manually annotated vertebral corners. The marking procedure is described in detail in Plocharski et al. [12]. Briefly, four corners were manually marked on the C3–C6 vertebrae at points where lines through soft or cancellous corners intersect with the outer edges of the compact bone. Figure 1b illustrates the placement and the order of the markings. Due to the fact that C7 is often partially obscured in fluoroscopic recordings, it was only marked with two points on the superior cancellous corners under the superior vertebral plate [12]. In order to compute the cervical joint angles, we incorporated the vertebral landmark methodology developed by Frobin et al. [3]. A line connecting the posterior and anterior midpoints, defined as equidistant points between corners 1 and 4, and 2 and 3 respectively (red points in Fig. 1b) formed a mid-plane, which was used for angle computation between two adjacent vertebrae (angles θ_1 and θ_2, Fig. 1b). The C6/C7 angle was computed between the C6 mid-plane and a line going through the two corners of C7. All angles were calculated as four-quadrant inverse tangents of the determinant and dot product of the two direction vectors, measured counterclockwise from the posterior to the anterior midpoints in the range from 0° to 180° [12].

3 Results

Figure 7 illustrates the automatically identified (red), and manually annotated vertebral corners (blue) on C3–C7. For C3–C6 vertebrae, the automatic detection method provided locations in close proximity to the manual annotations. A few inaccurate detections of the first and fourth corners were observed in C3 (Fig. 7a and g), and in the second and fourth corners of C6 (Fig. 7a, d, and d). Corner detection of C7 yielded somewhat inferior results to, especially for the second corner (Fig. 7d, h), likely due to an absence of clear vertebral edges. For each vertebral corner, we compared point coordinates of the automatically identified corners and the corresponding manual annotations. Error was calculated as the average Euclidean distance between the two corresponding corners in ($n = 8$) fluoroscopic images (Eq. 2):

$$Error = \frac{1}{n} \sum_{n=1}^{n} \sqrt{(x_A - x_M)^2 + (y_A - y_M)^2} \tag{2}$$

where (x_A, y_A) was the automatically detected corner, and (x_M, y_M) was the manually annotated one. Table 1 illustrates the mean errors and standard deviations in pixels. Errors smaller than five pixels were deemed acceptable. Additionally, a one-tailed t-test was computed for every automatically identified corner to test the null hypothesis that the average detection error was equal to or smaller than five pixels. The p-values for all tests are shown in Table 1. Statistical analysis was performed in SPSS (IBM Statistics, v.25). All data in Tables 1 and 2 was initially tested for normality using the Shapiro-Wilk test. Normality of the data was confirmed ($p > 0.05$). Statistical analysis indicates that the average corner detection errors were not significantly larger than five pixels. Table 2 illustrates the intervertebral angles, computed using the approach illustrated in Fig. 1b, using both the manually annotated and the automatically detected vertebral

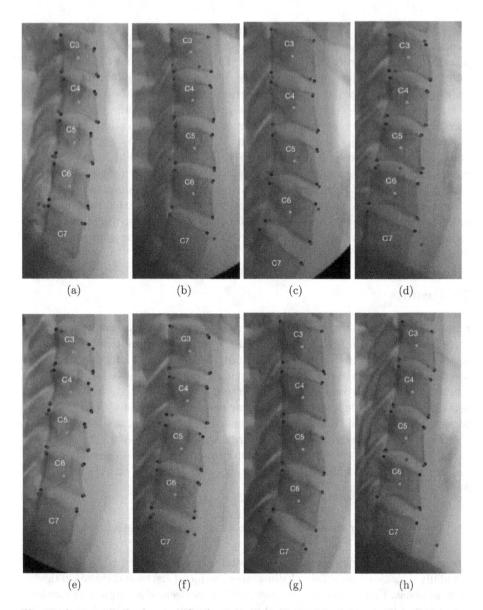

Fig. 7. Automatically located (red) and manually annotated vertebral landmarks (blue) in the four subjects, at the onset of extension ((a), (b), (c), (d)) and flexion ((e), (f), (g), (h)). (Color figure online)

corners. A paired-sample t-test was computed for each joint to determine if the angles obtained using the two approaches differed significantly. No significant difference was found between the two methods ($p > 0.05$ for all cervical joints).

Table 1. Detection errors (pixels) computed for each corner in the C3–C7 vertebrae in the eight fluoroscopic images, as well as in average for every vertebra.

Corner	Vertebra									
	C3		C4		C5		C6		C7	
	Error	p	Error	p	Error	p	Error	p	Error	p
1	4.96 ± 3.04	0.51	2.73 ± 1.92	0.99	3.65 ± 2.93	0.88	2.81 ± 2.07	0.99	6.73 ± 7.41	0.27
2	1.43 ± 1.44	0.99	1.32 ± 0.83	1.00	1.15 ± 1.07	1.00	5.54 ± 7.29	0.42	5.57 ± 4.50	0.37
3	3.25 ± 4.79	0.83	0.79 ± 0.42	1.00	1.27 ± 0.98	1.00	0.66 ± 0.70	1.00	N/A	N/A
4	3.31 ± 4.55	0.84	1.77 ± 2.13	1.00	2.30 ± 2.18	1.00	3.40 ± 2.47	0.95	N/A	N/A
Average	3.24 ± 3.74	0.99	1.65 ± 1.60	1.00	2.09 ± 2.13	1.00	3.10 ± 4.19	0.99	6.15 ± 5.95	0.23

Table 2. Intervertebral joint angles obtained using the manual and automatic methods. All values are presented in degrees.

Motion	Subject	C3/C4		C4/C5		C5/C6		C6/C7	
		Manual	Auto.	Manual	Auto.	Manual	Auto.	Manual	Auto.
Onset of extension	1	2.07	9.90	1.64	−4.72	−3.88	0.99	10.60	7.26
	2	1.17	2.41	2.48	6.94	5.17	−5.80	10.22	11.67
	3	0.06	1.34	2.02	7.64	9.88	7.51	14.31	12.47
	4	3.28	2.24	−0.93	−6.18	2.32	−0.46	4.58	23.08
Onset of flexion	1	−3.41	−1.19	−2.73	−7.51	−0.38	−1.50	12.75	15.78
	2	2.98	4.42	−0.60	−0.46	1.93	2.11	5.62	11.18
	3	−1.49	6.69	6.37	5.41	9.34	5.64	11.08	12.15
	4	3.36	0.15	0.62	6.05	−1.95	−18.46	3.92	26.83
p		0.15		0.88		0.13		0.12	

4 Discussion

Vertebral landmarks are a requirement for range of motion analysis, which is a crucial tool for understanding the spine joint mechanics [1]. The time-consuming process of manual landmark annotations is still a prerequisite of the state-of-the-art automatic vertebral tracking algorithms [11,17,19,20]. In this paper we propose a method to automatically identify and segment the C3–C7 vertebral bodies in videofluoroscopic images, and to detect the vertebral landmarks necessary for cervical joint motion analysis. We compare this automatic detection method with manually annotated vertebral landmarks.

Results from Table 1 showed the average detection error under five pixels in the C3–C6 vertebrae, with the lowest average error of 1.65 ± 1.60 pixels in the C4 vertebra. The one-sample, one-tailed t-test for each of the average detection errors of the four corners in C3–C7 vertebrae revealed that the errors were not significantly greater than five pixels. Given the spatial resolution of 576×768 pixels, five pixels corresponded to respectively 0.9% and 0.7% of the height and width of the images. However, the average errors for C7 vertebrae were larger than the other vertebrae. A possible explanation may be partial occlusion, a lower contrast, and a lack of well-defined edges on the C7. The joint angles results for C3–C7 were also not significantly different from the angles computed with the manually annotated corners ($p > 0.05$). This suggests that the presented method can be suitable for large data analysis of cervical joint motion using automatic tracking algorithms.

Comparison of these results with other work is difficult, since similar vertebral landmark detection methods in the cervical spine using videofluoroscopic sequences were not found in literature. A similar study by Xu et al. [14] used a combination of Haar-like features and Active Appearance Models training algorithms for automatic segmentation of cervical vertebrae in X-ray images. They obtained the lowest average error of 4.79 pixels. Al-Arif et al. reported the lowest average median error of 2.08 mm using Haar-like features in radiographic images [20], and the lowest average error of 0.7688 mm using Active Shape Models with Random Classification Forest in X-ray images [16]. Automatic approaches to detect and label the vertebral landmarks have also been developed using deep learning [23,24]. However, they require large data sets and high quality imaging modalities, such as CT or MRI, and thus are not directly comparable to fluoroscopic sequences of the cervical spine.

The following limitations to this study need to be addressed. First, a larger number of participants would be beneficial. Secondly, the fluoroscopic images were of relatively good quality, and thus we did not evaluate the ability of our approach to automatically identify the cervical corners in images with higher degrees of image blurring. However, the aim of this approach was vertebral detection at the onset of movement, with stationary subjects in a neutral position, and thus motion blur was not expected to occur. Finally, our approach did not aim to detect C1 or C2. C1 does not have the vertebral body and is seldom used in most vertebral analyses, while C2 is often obscured and its corners are often not visible.

5 Conclusion

The proposed method to automatically detect and segment the cervical vertebrae allows a computation of the vertebral landmarks for a real-time intervertebral motion analysis in videofluoroscopy. It also eliminates the necessity for a manual annotation of the C3–C7 vertebrae for automatic landmark tracking. Additionally, our approach does not require large datasets necessary for training the algorithm to be able to detect the vertebrae, as is the case in deep learning approaches.

Acknowledgements. Ethical approval: The study was conducted according to the Declaration of Helsinki and approved by The Scientific Ethical Committee for the Region of North Jutland (N20140004).

Conflicts of Interests. None.

Funding. None.

References

1. Stenneberg, M.S., et al.: To what degree does active cervical range of motion differ between patients with neck pain, patients with whiplash, and those without neck pain? A systematic review and meta-analysis. Arch. Phys. Med. Rehabil. **98**(7), 1407–1434 (2017)
2. Qu, N., Lindstrøm, R., Hirata, R.P., Graven-Nielsen, T.: Origin of neck pain and direction of movement influence dynamic cervical joint motion and pressure pain sensitivity. Clin. Biomech. **61**, 120–128 (2019)
3. Frobin, W., Leivseth, G., Biggemann, M., Brinckmann, P.: Sagittal plane segmental motion of the cervical spine. A new precision measurement protocol and normal motion data of healthy adults. Clin. Biomech. **17**(1), 21–31 (2002)
4. Wang, X., Lindstroem, R., Plocharski, M., Østergaard, L.R., Graven-Nielsen, T.: Cervical flexion and extension includes anti-directional cervical joint motion in healthy adults. Spine J. **18**(1), 147–154 (2018)
5. Wu, S.K., Kuo, L.C., Lan, H.C.H., Tsai, S.W., Su, F.C.: Segmental percentage contributions of cervical spine during different motion ranges of flexion and extension. Clin. Spine Surg. **23**(4), 278–284 (2010)
6. Wang, X., Lindstroem, R., Plocharski, M., Østergaard, L.R., Graven-Nielsen, T.: Repeatability of cervical joint flexion and extension within and between days. J. Manipulative Physiol. Ther. **41**(1), 10–18 (2018)
7. Anderst, W.J., Donaldson, W.F., Lee, J.Y., Kang, J.D.: Cervical spine intervertebral kinematics with respect to the head are different during flexion and extension motions. J. Biomech. **46**(8), 1471–1475 (2013)
8. Breen, A.C., Teyhen, D.S., Mellor, F.E., Breen, A.C., Wong, K.W., Deitz, A.: Measurement of intervertebral motion using quantitative fluoroscopy: report of an international forum and proposal for use in the assessment of degenerative disc disease in the lumbar spine. Advances in Orthopedics (2012)
9. Lecron, F., Benjelloun, M., Mahmoudi, S.: Cervical spine mobility analysis on radiographs: a fully automatic approach. Comput. Med. Imaging Graph. **36**(8), 634–642 (2012)
10. Ahmadi, A., Maroufi, N., Behtash, H., Zekavat, H., Parnianpour, M.: Kinematic analysis of dynamic lumbar motion in patients with lumbar segmental instability using digital videofluoroscopy. Eur. Spine J. **18**(11), 1677–1685 (2009)
11. Nøhr, A.K., et al.: Semi-automatic method for intervertebral kinematics measurement in the cervical spine. In: Sharma, P., Bianchi, F.M. (eds.) SCIA 2017. LNCS, vol. 10270, pp. 302–313. Springer, Cham (2017). https://doi.org/10.1007/978-3-319-59129-2_26
12. Plocharski, M., Lindstroem, R., Lindstroem, C.F., Østergaard, L.R.: Motion analysis of the cervical spine during extension and flexion: reliability of the vertebral marking procedure. Med. Eng. Phys. **61**, 81–86 (2018)
13. Cerciello, T., Romano, M., Bifulco, P., Cesarelli, M., Allen, R.: Advanced template matching method for estimation of intervertebral kinematics of lumbar spine. Med. Eng. Phys. **33**(10), 1293–1302 (2011)
14. Xu, X., Hao, H.W., Yin, X.C., Liu, N., Shafin, S.H.: Automatic segmentation of cervical vertebrae in X-ray images. In: The 2012 International Joint Conference on Neural Networks (IJCNN), pp. 1–8. IEEE, June 2012
15. Klinder, T., Ostermann, J., Ehm, M., Franz, A., Kneser, R., Lorenz, C.: Automated model-based vertebra detection, identification, and segmentation in CT images. Med. Image Anal. **13**(3), 471–482 (2009)

16. Al Arif, S.M.M.R., Gundry, M., Knapp, K., Slabaugh, G.: Improving an active shape model with random classification forest for segmentation of cervical vertebrae. In: Yao, J., Vrtovec, T., Zheng, G., Frangi, A., Glocker, B., Li, S. (eds.) CSI 2016. LNCS, vol. 10182, pp. 3–15. Springer, Cham (2016). https://doi.org/10.1007/978-3-319-55050-3_1

17. Nauman, M., et al.: Automatic tracking of cervical spine using fluoroscopic sequences. In: Intelligent Systems Conference (IntelliSys) 2017, pp. 592–598. IEEE, September 2017

18. Sa, R., Owens, W., Wiegand, R., Chaudhary, V.: Fast scale-invariant lateral lumbar vertebrae detection and segmentation in X-ray images. In: 2016 IEEE 38th Annual International Conference of the Engineering in Medicine and Biology Society (EMBC), pp. 1054–1057. IEEE, August 2016

19. Wang, L., Zhang, Y., Lin, X., Yan, Z.: Study of lumbar spine activity regularity based on Kanade-Lucas-Tomasi algorithm. Biomed. Sig. Process. Control **49**, 465–472 (2019)

20. Al Arif, S.M.R., Asad, M., Knapp, K., Gundry, M., Slabaugh, G.: Cervical vertebral corner detection using Haar-like features and modified hough forest. In: 2015 International Conference on Image Processing Theory, Tools and Applications (IPTA), pp. 417–422. IEEE, November 2015

21. Zhang, G., Shao, Y., Kim, Y., Guo, W.: Vertebrae detection algorithm in CT scout images. In: Tan, T., et al. (eds.) IGTA 2016. CCIS, vol. 634, pp. 230–237. Springer, Singapore (2016). https://doi.org/10.1007/978-981-10-2260-9_26

22. Mahmoudi, S.A., Lecron, F., Manneback, P., Benjelloun, M., Mahmoudi, S.: GPU-based segmentation of cervical vertebra in X-ray images. In: 2010 IEEE International Conference on Cluster Computing Workshops and Posters (CLUSTER WORKSHOPS), pp. 1–8. IEEE, September 2010

23. Yang, D., et al.: Automatic vertebra labeling in large-scale 3D CT using deep image-to-image network with message passing and sparsity regularization. In: Niethammer, M., et al. (eds.) IPMI 2017. LNCS, vol. 10265, pp. 633–644. Springer, Cham (2017). https://doi.org/10.1007/978-3-319-59050-9_50

24. Shi, D., Pan, Y., Liu, C., Wang, Y., Cui, D., Lu, Y.: Automatic localization and segmentation of vertebral bodies in 3D CT volumes with deep learning. In: Proceedings of the 2nd International Symposium on Image Computing and Digital Medicine, pp. 42–46. ACM, October 2018

Weight Estimation of Broilers in Images Using 3D Prior Knowledge

Anders Jørgensen[1,2(✉)], Jacob V. Dueholm[1,2], Jens Fagertun[2],
and Thomas B. Moeslund[1]

[1] Aalborg University, Aalborg, Denmark
[2] IHFood A/S, Copenhagen, Denmark
anders_aau@hotmail.com

Abstract. Cameras are already widely used for inspection and monitoring tasks in poultry slaughter houses. In this paper we evaluate the use of computer vision for broiler carcass weight estimation. We compare the use of 2D image features with 3D features extracted from a statistical shape model fitted to the image. The statistical shape model is built from 45 3D scans captured from broiler carcasses collected at a slaughter house. The use of this 3D prior gave a reduction in mean absolute error compared to 2D features alone and achieved an overall mean average percentage error of 3.47%. The algorithm can run real time and was tested on a dataset containing 136,472 images of broilers, captured at a real production site.

Keywords: Weight estimation · Statistical shape model ·
3D prior knowledge · Model fitting · Broiler

1 Introduction

The produced amount of poultry meat is increasing as the production gets more and more automated. 40.6 billion chickens were slaughtered in 2000 which has increased to 65.8 billion in 2016 [7]. Broilers are slaughtered and cut up almost entirely by robots and automated equipment at speeds up to 13,500 birds per hour for one slaughter line [15]. To keep the production line running smoothly the equipment needs to be adjusted for size and weight.

Broilers are typically weighed with a conveyor scale installed as part of the processing line. Such scales are typically quite large and maybe require the bird to be transferred off and back on the conveyor. Maintenance and replacements require that the line is stopped or that the line bypasses the scale.

The average weight of a flock can be used to adjust the equipment that cuts up the chicken into breast, legs, and wing parts. The individual size and weight are used to direct the broiler to the right cut-up station. By setting the equipment correctly the factory minimises waste and optimises their profits.

Very light or small birds should be removed early, as these are likely sick or underdeveloped. Trying to eviscerate these birds can cause the equipment to damage the intestines, causing faecal contamination on the following birds [9].

© Springer Nature Switzerland AG 2019
M. Felsberg et al. (Eds.): SCIA 2019, LNCS 11482, pp. 221–232, 2019.
https://doi.org/10.1007/978-3-030-20205-7_19

Many slaughter houses already have multiple camera systems installed along the processing line for inspection and monitoring tasks. These are installed in a non-intrusive manner, so they are relatively inexpensive to install and easily replaceable. These cameras can be utilised for weight estimation. A 2D image only shows the size of the bird from a single perspective, but because broilers are bred to be similar there is a high correlation between size and weight [2].

However, some variation may not be explained in a 2D image, e.g. dimensional changes can happen in the direction towards the camera. The contribution of this paper is to investigate whether adding 3D features from a 3D prior will increase the performance of the weight estimation. The prior knowledge consists of 45 3D scans of broilers gathered at a poultry processing plant. A statistical shape model (SSM), generated from the 3D scans, is fitted to the 2D image of the broiler to extract 3D features for the weight estimation.

2   Related Works

Weight estimation from images is especially useful in situations where physical weighing is not feasible. In production of fresh lettuce, where you can't uproot the plants to weigh them, [12] showed that it is possible to estimate the weight from an image using both morphology and pixel-based methods.

A lot of work has been done in the field of estimating the weight of livestock in a non-intrusive fashion. The weight is an important parameter in rearing, but physical weighing requires large scales for animals like cattle and pigs and it can be a cumbersome affair to weigh hundreds of animals. Work by [13] shows that live weight of individual pigs can be estimated with an accuracy of 96.2% using a camera installed over the pig pen. The body area of the pig is found by fitting an ellipse to the pig's back which is used in a transfer function to estimate the weight every minute.

In the fishing industries, [3] showed that good results could be achieved with an RGB sensor and polynomial regressions when estimating the weight of salmon. Early work by [19] demonstrated a structured light setup capable of determining the weight of flatfish as they passed the camera and laser on a conveyor. A similar approach was used by [16], but on herring. The structured light gives a measure of the depth which is useful when estimating volumes, which for similar objects are highly correlated with the weight.

A similar top view approach was used to estimate the live weight of broilers but using the Kinect sensor to acquire the depth. Using a combination of 2D and 3D features, [17] achieved a relative error of 7.8% across all broilers. The system was installed in a commercial production setting and operated fully automatically.

3 Approach

The goal is to estimate the weight of broilers from 2D images captured in-line at a poultry processing plant. 2D cameras are already in use in many slaughter houses for inspection and adding a 3D sensor would increase the complexity and cost of the weight estimation.

The 3D information should therefore come from prior knowledge. In a pre-processing step multiple 3D scans of broilers are combined in an SSM. This step is performed off-line and should only be done once.

The in-line process starts with the image acquisition that captures an RGB 2D image. From this image 2D landmarks are extracted, which are used to fit the SSM to the broiler in the image. From the fitted SSM 3D features are extracted and combined with 2D features which are used to estimate the weight of the broiler. The in-line processing is constrained to a maximum processing time of 266 ms, which corresponds to 13,500 birds per hour.

A flow chart of the system described in this paper is depicted in Fig. 1.

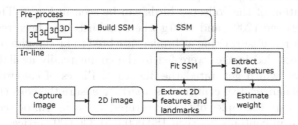

Fig. 1. Flow chart of the weight estimation pipeline described in this paper.

4 Statistical Shape Model Generation

Fitting statistical models to images gained traction with the invention of Active Shape Models (ASM) [6] and Active Appearance Models (AAM) [5]. ASM and AAM have an inbuilt prior from the shapes used to construct the models.

An SSM captures the underlying physical characteristics of the object and this is what we are interested in when modelling broilers. By matching the model to a 2D image, we gain information about the broilers measures in the third dimension. The proportions of the broiler's body parts, like breast and drum, could even lead to a detailed weight estimation of the individual parts.

4.1 Creating 3D Scans of Broilers

45 birds have been collected at a poultry slaughter house and recorded using a Canon EOS 5DS camera over the course of three weeks to ensure diversity. The recording setup consisted of a hanger in the centre of a room and the camera was rotated around the chicken. One full rotation with the camera placed higher than

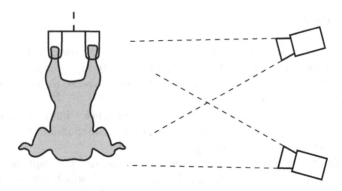

Fig. 2. Sketch of the setup used for capturing images for the 3D scan generation. The camera is approximately 1 m from the bird.

the chicken and one with the camera placed lower than the chicken. Between 90 and 120 images where captured per bird. See Fig. 2 for a sketch of the setup. The weight distribution of the collected birds can be seen in Fig. 3. The histogram shows a gap between 1200 g and 1600 g where no birds have been recorded. This is not ideal, but not unsurprising as broilers are bred to be slaughtered at specific weights. The recorded images were fed to the commercially available software, ContextCapture, which generated the 3D scans. Pieces of coloured tape were attached to the hanger, two centimetres apart, to ensure the correct scale of the bird in the 3D scan. Examples of three captured 3D scans can be seen in Fig. 4a, b and c. Each scan contains between 180,000 and 330,000 vertices.

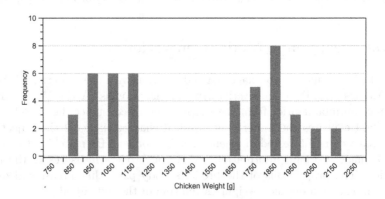

Fig. 3. Distribution of the weight of all birds used in the SSM.

4.2   Registering the 3D Scans

The 3D scans were manually trimmed to remove the wings, the knees and the neck skin as these parts can be very different between birds and therefore difficult to register. It is also assumed that especially the neck skin and the knees have a small or constant impact on the total weight. The scans were then smoothed to remove small bumps on the skin, which would otherwise create very fluctuating surface normals.

One scan was chosen as the template and scaled down to around 25,000 vertices using a surface simplification method [8]. The template was then registered to the other scans with a non-rigid iterative closest point method: N-ICP-A [1]. The algorithm assigns an affine transformation to each vertex and starts with a stiff template to find the global alignment, then gradually reduces the stiffness to allow more localized deformations. The stiffness is used to regularize the deformation and controlled by penalizing the difference between neighbour vertices' transformations.

Each registration produces a few sets of vertices with very skewed faces, especially around the end of the legs due to badly registered vertices. To remove these faulty faces, it was chosen simply to remove a few vertices around the end of both legs. The same vertices must be removed from all registered scans to keep the correspondence between the models. Unconnected vertices are also removed from all scans. As the last step all scans are set to use the faces from the template. The resulting meshes for the three birds in Fig. 4a, b and c, can be seen in Fig. 4d, e and f.

The area around the groin proved difficult to register as there is a large variation between the birds in this area. This can be seen in Fig. 4a and b, where there is a big height difference between the backside of the thigh and the end of the breast bone between the birds. As a result, vertices around the cloaca were removed. The registered and trimmed scans are now used to generate the SSM. All scans are aligned with Procrustes analysis [18] without scaling and flipping. The mean of all scans is then subtracted from the individual scans before Principal Component Analysis (PCA) is used to model the variation in the data. Studying the explained variances show that the first seven components contain more than 95% of the total variation. The mean shape can be seen in Fig. 5. New samples can now be generated using Eq. 1.

$$\underset{3n \times 1}{\mathbf{x}} = \underset{3n \times 1}{\bar{\mathbf{x}}} + \underset{3n \times m}{\mathbf{P}} \cdot \underset{m \times 1}{\mathbf{b}} \tag{1}$$

where $\mathbf{x}$ is a new sample, $\bar{\mathbf{x}}$ is the mean shape, $\mathbf{P}$ is the eigenvectors found with PCA and $\mathbf{b}$ defines a set of parameters that deform the SSM. n is the number of vertices in the model and as the vertex coordinates are stored as $x_1, y_1, z_1, x_2, y_2, z_2, \ldots x_n, y_n, z_n$, the number of rows in $\mathbf{x}$, $\bar{\mathbf{x}}$ and $\mathbf{P}$ becomes $3n$. m is the number of principal components.

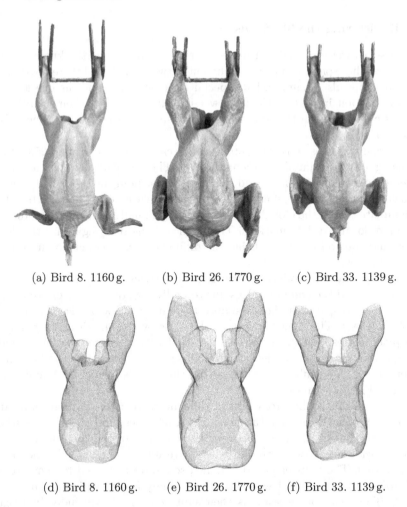

(a) Bird 8. 1160 g.   (b) Bird 26. 1770 g.   (c) Bird 33. 1139 g.

(d) Bird 8. 1160 g.   (e) Bird 26. 1770 g.   (f) Bird 33. 1139 g.

Fig. 4. Three 3D scans created by ContextCapture, top row. Template scan registered to bird above, bottom row.

5   Fitting the SSM to a 2D Image

All birds are presented the same way, hanging in the legs with the breast facing the camera. This allows us to lock the yaw and pitch rotation of the SSM reducing the degrees of freedom in the fitting problem. Due to the way the broilers are transported on the line, some differences in roll must be expected.

The fitting is done with automatically extracted landmarks. If corresponding vertices in the SSM are fitted to these landmarks the rest of the model should match the broiler in the image. Eight landmarks are extracted from the bird in the 2D image using an IHFood ClassifEYE system [10]. These are the left and right wing pit, shoulder, hip and groin. The eight points are depicted in

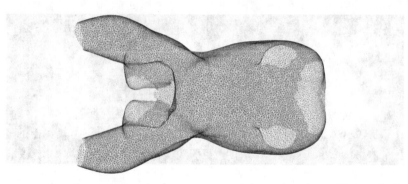

Fig. 5. Mean of the SSM. Rotated for better viewing.

Fig. 7b. These points were chosen as they could be found most consistently. Eight corresponding vertices are selected in the SSM. These vertices are handpicked and only selected once, as they should always correspond to the same landmarks in the images.

When the landmarks are extracted from the image, Procrustes analysis, without scaling, is used to align the landmarks to the selected vertices in the SSM. The SSM and image landmarks are now aligned and ready for the model to be fitted. As the orientation of the SSM is now locked, only the x and y values are used for the fitting which gives a total of 16 values in $\mathbf{x}$. Equation 1 will now have the dimensions showed in Eq. 2. Only the seven first principal components are used.

$$\underset{16 \times 1}{\mathbf{x}} = \underset{16 \times 1}{\bar{\mathbf{x}}} + \underset{16 \times 7}{\mathbf{P}} \cdot \underset{7 \times 1}{\mathbf{b}} \tag{2}$$

$$0 = \mathbf{Pb} - (\mathbf{x} - \bar{\mathbf{x}}) \tag{3}$$

Equation 3 is an over-determined problem and can therefore have multiple solutions. $\mathbf{b}$ is unknown, but we want to constrain its values to ± 3 standard deviations. As PCA is a linear model, going beyond ± 3 standard deviations will in most cases cause the model to diverge greatly from the true population. $\mathbf{b}$ in Eq. 3 will therefore be solved with an optimiser. The minimisation is done with SciPy's [11] minimise method. The algorithm used is L-BFGS-B [4] and each scalar in $\mathbf{b}$ is bound to ± 3 standard deviations. Initial values for $\mathbf{b}$ are all zeros.

Once $\mathbf{b}$ is found, it can be inserted in Eq. 1 to generate the new sample that fits the broiler in the 2D image. $\mathbf{b}$'s size comes from the number of principal components used, so the resulting model will still be in 3D although $\mathbf{b}$ was found using only 2D points.

The resulting fit for three broilers can be seen in Fig. 6.

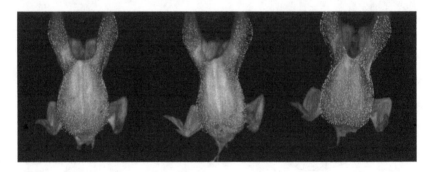

Fig. 6. The SSM fitted to three different images. Red dots are vertices in the model. (Color figure online)

6   Features

The weight can be calculated from the volume of the fitted 3D model, if the density of a chicken is constant across all parts. We cannot just assume this, however, and perhaps more importantly, we know that the chicken's cavity is empty after the evisceration. We will therefore extract multiple 3D and 2D features to estimate the weight.

One 3D feature is indeed the volume, which is calculated as the sum of all tetrahedrons formed by the faces of the SSM and the origin which is placed roughly in the centre of the SSM. The SSM is not a closed surface so the volume will not be what one might expect from a chicken.

The remaining 3D features are areas and distances on the surface of the SSM. Because there is point correspondence between all fitted SSMs, areas can be calculated from the same set of vertices every time, as it is just the location of these vertices that have changed. The surface area is the sum of all faces spanned by these vertices. The area features include the left and right breast, left and right upper thigh and a band around each drum.

The same principle is used for distance features. Pre-specified vertices make a path that is used to calculate the distance between two points on the surface. This path is the shortest in the mean shape, but because the vertices move individually when the SSM is fitted to the 2D image, it is not necessarily the shortest path in the fitted SSM. It is however much faster to calculate the distance of a fixed path than searching for the shortest path between two vertices for every fit. The distance features include the path from the collarbone to the bottom of the breast, the circumference of each drum and the path from each wing pit to the centre of the breast. In total 12 3D features are extracted from the fitted SSM.

2D features are extracted using an IHFood ClassifEYE system outputting a total of 23 features. These features are primarily area features like the area of the chest, but also distances like the distance from wing pit to wing pit.

All features are augmented by finding the square root and squaring each of them. This is done to introduce some non-linearities. With augmentation there are 36 3D features and 69 2D features.

7 Data Acquisition

2D images of broilers are recorded with a Jai BB-141GE RGB camera installed at a slaughter house in Chesterfield, England. The images are recorded after defeathering and evisceration where the broilers are transported sideways hanging in their legs with the breast facing the camera. Their weight is measured with a LINCO 520 Weigh Transfer [14] mechanical weight with an accuracy of ±0.25%. The weight is paired with the images and will function as ground truth. An example of a captured image can be seen in Fig. 7a. All 2D images have been recorded over the course of four days. Images of broilers weighing less than 800 g or more than 2200 g are discarded, to ensure that the 2D images are in the same weight range as the broilers used for the SSM. The remaining 136,472 images are randomised and 102,412 images are used for training and 34,060 images are used for testing.

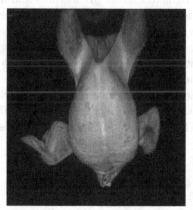 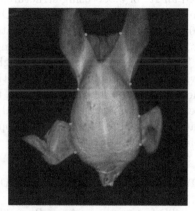

(a) Image recorded with the 2D camera.   (b) Landmarks used to fit the SSM to the image.

Fig. 7. Captured 2D image with and without landmarks.

8 Results

Performance are measured for 2D features only (2D), 3D features only (3D) and for a combination of 2D and 3D features (2D3D). The number of features used to train the regression models are listed in Table 1. All features are normalised by subtracting the mean and dividing by the standard deviation. Both the mean and the standard deviation are calculated using only the training samples.

The regression model chosen for comparison is a linear robust regression. The robust variant means the linear model is fitted iteratively and for each iteration data points are weighted based on their residual value. Outliers will be down weighted and therefore have a smaller effect on the fit. The resulting errors of the regression models are listed in Table 1. The error gets smaller by combining

Table 1. Results for the linear regression models. Mean Absolute Error (MAE) and Mean Absolute Percentage Error (MAPE) are reported.

Model	# Features	MAE	MAPE
2D	23 (69)	47.22 g	3.53%
3D	12 (36)	63.49 g	4.72%
2D3D	35 (105)	**46.37 g**	**3.47%**

2D and 3D features and mean absolute error is reduced by 1.80% compared to 2D alone. The mean absolute error in percent is 3.47. An unpaired t-test was performed on the 2D and 2D3D residuals to investigate whether this reduction is significant, which the resulting p-value of 0.0129 strongly indicates.

As there are no studies done on the same dataset, we will compare our results to related weight estimation papers. Weight estimation of herring by [16] achieved an R^2 of 0.980 using structured light to extract 3D features and had a sample size of 179. They used 2D and 3D features where our method achieved an R^2 of 0.963 using 2D and pseudo 3D features. In work by [13], weight estimation of pigs, they got an R^2 of 0.962 working on multiple frames extracted from a video. They did however track the weight of individual pigs as it grew over 13 days where as we sample and estimate the weight once.

The coefficient of determination, R^2, is also used to investigate the individual features' correlation with the weight and the 3D features generally have a higher correlation than the 2D features. The top five correlated 2D and 3D features can be seen in Table 2.

Table 2. R^2 for the top 5 2D and 3D features with respect to the weight.

2D features	Aug.	R^2	3D features	Aug.	R^2
PitLeft2PitRight	$\sqrt{x}$	0.808	LeftPit2BreastMid	$\sqrt{x}$	0.855
BreastArea	x	0.788	RightPit2BreastMid	$\sqrt{x}$	0.852
SaddleArea	x	0.779	Volume	x	0.845
BreastHeight	$\sqrt{x}$	0.774	LeftBreastArea	$\sqrt{x}$	0.834
SaddleHeight	$\sqrt{x}$	0.755	BreastHeight	$\sqrt{x}$	0.833

8.1 Timing

The system should be able to operate in-line at production speeds up to 13,500 birds per hour. That is 266 ms of available processing time per bird and the existing 2D pipeline already takes an average time of 125 ms. This includes landmark extraction.

In this work we have added the SSM fitting and 3D feature extraction to the existing pipeline. The code is implemented in python 3.6 using NumPy and Numba for speed-up where possible. Timing showed that the average processing time for fitting the SSM and extracting 3D features was just 7 ms per image. This is clearly within the remaining 141 ms, so the 3D features can easily be added to the already existing analysis. The test was performed on an i7-4770K CPU running at 3.7 GHz.

9 Conclusion

The results showed that the mean absolute error is reduced by 1.80% by adding 3D features from the SSM to the existing 2D features extracted directly from the image. A t-test was used to ensure that the results were significant.

Investigating R^2 for the individual features, showed that the 3D features were more correlated with the weight than the 2D features. It is however very likely that there is a high collinearity between the 3D features as the overall weight estimation error were higher when comparing the regression models using either 3D or 2D features.

The SSM was fitted to the 2D image using only 8 landmarks. This meant the SSM could be fitted very quickly, in just a couple of milliseconds, allowing the entire fit and 3D feature extraction to run real time. The soft curves and the bland textures of the broiler made it difficult to extract more than these eight landmarks and especially the landmarks around the wings proved to be volatile. The angle of the wings could deviate a lot on some birds, which have a large impact on the wing pit and shoulder landmarks. Figure 4a is a good example of how different wings can look on some birds. All 3D features depend on the fit, so a bad fit would lead to bad 3D features. For future work it would be interesting to try a more robust way to fit the SSM to the 2D image.

Constructing an SSM is a time-consuming task. Capturing 90–120 images of each broiler is a tedious job and building the 3D scans is computationally expensive and therefore also time consuming. After this comes the manual process of inspecting and trimming the scans before they can be registered to each other, which also is computationally expensive.

Many steps in this process can however be automated which will make it easier to expand the SSM with more broilers and therefore more variance. For this paper we built the statistical model from 45 3D scans of broilers, which we used to estimate the weight of over 100,000 birds. 45 3D scans can clearly not represent the variation of the true population, but the results indicate that the weight estimation error can be reduced by adding prior knowledge and it is our belief that an SSM with more 3D scans can improve the performance further.

References

1. Amberg, B., Romdhani, S., Vetter, T.: Optimal step nonrigid ICP algorithms for surface registration. In: IEEE Conference on Computer Vision and Pattern Recognition, CVPR 2007, pp. 1–8. IEEE (2007)
2. Aviagen: ROSS 308 BROILER: Performance Objectives (2014). http://en.aviagen.com/assets/Tech_Center/Ross_Broiler/Ross-308-Broiler-PO-2014-EN.pdf

3. Balaban, M.O., Ünal Şengör, G.F., Soriano, M.G., Ruiz, E.G.: Using image analysis to predict the weight of Alaskan Salmon of different species. J. Food Sci. **75**(3), E157–E162 (2010). https://doi.org/10.1111/j.1750-3841.2010.01522.x

4. Byrd, R.H., Lu, P., Nocedal, J., Zhu, C.: A limited memory algorithm for bound constrained optimization. SIAM J. Sci. Comput. **16**(5), 1190–1208 (1995). https://doi.org/10.1137/0916069

5. Cootes, T.F., Edwards, G.J., Taylor, C.J.: Active appearance models. In: Burkhardt, H., Neumann, B. (eds.) ECCV 1998. LNCS, vol. 1407, pp. 484–498. Springer, Heidelberg (1998). https://doi.org/10.1007/BFb0054760

6. Cootes, T., Taylor, C., Cooper, D., Graham, J.: Active shape models-their training and application. Comput. Vis. Image Underst. **61**(1), 38–59 (1995). https://doi.org/10.1006/cviu.1995.1004

7. Food and Agriculture Organization of the United Nations: Total poultry production. Online Statistics Database (2017)

8. Garland, M., Heckbert, P.S.: Surface simplification using quadric error metrics. In: Proceedings of the 24th Annual Conference on Computer Graphics and Interactive Techniques - SIGGRAPH 1997, pp. 209–216 (1997). https://doi.org/10.1145/258734.258849

9. Guerrero-Legarreta, I.: Handbook of Poultry Science and Technology: Primary processing, vol. 1. Wiley, Hoboken (2010)

10. IHFood: ClassifEYE Vision System. IHFood, Copenhagen (2019). http://www.ihfood.dk/poultry

11. Jones, E., Oliphant, T., Peterson, P., et al.: SciPy: open source scientific tools for Python (2001). http://www.scipy.org/. Accessed 08 Dec 2017

12. Jung, D.H., Hyun Park, S., Zhe Han, X., Kim, H.J.: Image processing methods for measurement of lettuce fresh weight. J. Biosyst. Eng. **40**(1), 89–93 (2015). https://doi.org/10.5307/JBE.2015.40.1.089

13. Kashiha, M., et al.: Automatic weight estimation of individual pigs using image analysis. Comput. Electron. Agric. **107**, 38–44 (2014). https://doi.org/10.1016/j.compag.2014.06.003

14. Linco Food Systems: Linco 520 Weigh Transfer (2018). http://baader.ca/files/products/poultry/Leaflet_A17_520_Weigh_Transfer_01.pdf

15. Stork, M.: The world of poultry processing. Online Brochure (2016)

16. Mathiassen, J.R., Misimi, E., Toldnes, B., Bondø, M., Østvik, S.O.: High-speed weight estimation of whole herring (clupea harengus) using 3D machine vision. J. Food Sci. **76**(6), 458–464 (2011). https://doi.org/10.1111/j.1750-3841.2011.02226.x

17. Mortensen, A.K., Lisouski, P., Ahrendt, P., Krogh Mortensen, A., Lisouski, P., Ahrendt, P.: Weight prediction of broiler chickens using 3D computer vision. Comput. Electron. Agric. **123**, 319–326 (2016). https://doi.org/10.1016/j.compag.2016.03.011

18. Schönemann, P.H.: On two-sided orthogonal procrustes problems. Psychometrika **33**(1), 19–33 (1968). https://doi.org/10.1007/BF02289673

19. Storbeck, F., Daan, B.: Weight estimation of flatfish by means of structured light and image analysis. Fish. Res. **11**(2), 99–108 (1991). https://doi.org/10.1016/0165-7836(91)90101-K

Salient Object Detection with CNNs and Multi-scale CRFs

Yingyue Xu, Xiaopeng Hong, and Guoying Zhao[(⊠)]

Center for Machine Vision and Signal Analysis, University of Oulu, Oulu, Finland
{yingyue.xu,xiaopeng.hong,guoying.zhao}@oulu.fi

Abstract. Recent CNNs based salient object detection approaches tend to embed a fully connected Conditional Random Field (CRF) layer to refine the saliency maps from CNNs for post processing. Due to the significant performance enhancement by the CRF layer, in this paper, we propose a more flexible CRF refinement framework by embedding the CRF inference to multiple levels of side outputs from CNNs for multi-scale saliency refinement. A fully convolutional neural networks based on the simple yet effective encoder-decoder architecture with only three scales of side output maps is pre-trained. Then, the CRF layers are embedded to each scale of the side output respectively to complement the defects of each side output maps. Finally, the refined side output maps are fused and refined by another CRF inference for the final saliency map. The proposed multi-scale CRFs model (MCRF) is trained with low computational costs and shows competitive performance over four datasets in comparison with the existing state-of-the-art saliency models.

Keywords: Saliency detection · CRF · Multi-scale FCNs

1 Introduction

Salient Object Detection (SOD) refers to the perceptual selective process that highlights the most distinct regions on the scenes by the human vision system. In practice, object-level saliency detection can be broadly applied as a pre-processing technique for various computer vision tasks, such as image and video segmentation [27], video compression [6], image cropping [28], video summarizing [23], image fusion [7], *etc.*

Due to the prevalence of the convolutional neural networks (CNNs), the performance of salient object detection has been largely improved [5,9,13,16–19, 24,32,33]. Further, the integration of fully convolutional neural networks (FCNs) facilitates salient object detection tasks to an end-to-end phase [12,18,30,34, 42]. However, current CNNs based SOD approaches still face ~~with~~ significant challenges due to its network structures. Firstly, as salient object detection is a pixel-level labelling task, the outputs from the convolutional layers with large receptive fields can be rather rough after being restructured back to pixel-level labelled maps [21]. Hence, the output saliency maps from CNNs may result in

© Springer Nature Switzerland AG 2019
M. Felsberg et al. (Eds.): SCIA 2019, LNCS 11482, pp. 233–245, 2019.
https://doi.org/10.1007/978-3-030-20205-7_20

blob-like defects. Secondly, salient object detection emphasizes on recognizing the salient regions in object-level. As the CNNs lacks smoothness constraints for label agreement, the output saliency maps may consist poor object delineation and spurious regions [25]. In summary, the output maps from CNNs are relatively coarse and further refinement is needed to improve object boundary division and saliency density smoothness.

One prevalent approach adopted by recent state-of-the-art saliency models is to introduce a Conditional Random Field (CRF) layer, *i.e.* Dense-CRF [11], fully connected to the FCNs [9,14,17] for coarse saliency map refinement. The fully connected CRF layer does not participate in finetuning the front-end FCNs. Instead, it acts as a post-processing layer to reconcile the spatial and appearance coherence of the coarse saliency maps through cross validations. On one hand, the CRF layer efficiently enhances the accuracy of the saliency maps in practice; on the other hand, it makes the training stage of the front-end deep neural networks compact and efficient.

However, existing saliency models only connect one CRF layer to the end of the pre-trained deep neural networks for refinement. In this paper, we extend the CRF layer as a more flexible integration to any of the side output layers of the FCNs to enhance the quality of the intermediate outputs, and thus to further improve the performance of the whole networks. Therefore, we propose the multi-scale CRFs model (MCRF) based on multi-scale side outputs from FCNs for salient object detection. Specifically, a fully convolutional neural network based on the encoder-decoder architecture with three scales of side output maps is trained with pixel-wise labels. Then, a CRF layer is connected to each side output layer to refine the delineation and smoothness of the side output maps. Finally, the refined side output maps are fused and then refined by another CRF layer for the final saliency map. The contributions of the paper are two folds:

- The proposed MCRF model integrates multiple CRF layers to refine the multi-scale side output maps from FCNs, and thus to complement the defects of each side outputs for a unified and refined saliency map. The multi-scale CRFs refinement structure largely improves the refinement effectiveness than integrating one CRF layer at the end of the network.
- The multi-scale CRFs refinement structure results in highly competitive performance based on the simple encoder-decoder networks with only three scales of side outputs. Hence, the multi-scale CRFs structure is able to avoid the over-fitting issues due to complex deep network architectures with limited training samples.

The rest of the paper is organized as follows. Section 2 summarizes the related works. Section 3 introduces the framework of the proposed multi-scale CRFs saliency model. Section 4 presents the implementation details and the experimental results and Sect. 5 concludes the work.

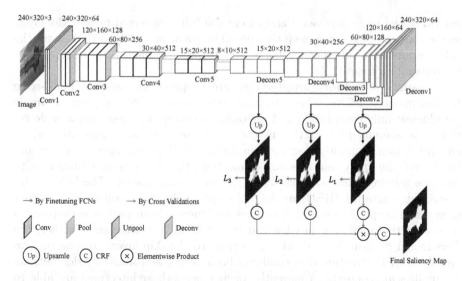

Fig. 1. Framework of the proposed multi-scale CRFs model. Three scales of side output maps are selected from the encoder-decoder networks. The encoder network is based on the VGG-16 net [31]. Then, the decoder network is connected to the "pool5" layer, which gradually unpools the features from the corresponding pooling layers. The decoder convolutional layers are all followed by a BN layer and a ReLU layer. To upsample the three scales of side outputs from "Deconv1", "Deconv2" and "Deconv3", a convolutional layer with 1×1 kernel size is used to compute the one channel feature map and a deconvolutional layer followed with a crop layer is connected to upsample the feature maps to the image size respectively. To finetune the front-end encoder-decoder networks, each side output map is connected with a side loss (L_1, L_2, L_3) for optimization. Then, one CRF layer is connected to each side output map for multi-scale refinement and the refined side output maps are fused by element-wise production. Finally, another CRF layer is connected to refine the fused map for the final saliency map. The CRF layers are tuned by cross validations and all the CRF layers share the same parameter settings.

2 Related Works

This section presents a brief review of representative network architectures of FCNs and previous deep saliency models that adopt fully connected conditional random field (CRF) for saliency refinement.

2.1 Saliency Detection via FCNs

Previous works [41] suggest that the convolutional layers of the CNNs can describe the high-level semantic features at different scales and maintain their spatial information. To put the merits of convolutional layers into full use, Long *et al.* [21] propose the fully convolutional networks (FCNs) for semantic segmentation. The FCNs addresses the advantages of the convolutional layers to get rid of the large parameter costs from the fully connected layers. Moreover, as the convolutional layers keep the spatial information on the output maps, the side outputs from different levels are able to produce multi-scale feature maps for recognition tasks [2, 22].

A variety of network architectures are proposed to compute multi-scale feature maps of FCNs. The encoder-decoder network [40] proposes a simple yet efficient fully convolution and unpooling structure for object contour detection. The seminal FCNs [21] constructs skip connections to generate end-to-end prediction at multiple scales. Similarly, the Hypercolumns FCNs [8] and the U-Net [29] apply multiple skip-connections through concatenations to capture the features from multiple scales for precise localization. The holistically-nested edge detector (HED) model [35] employs skip-layer connections to construct even deeper supervised structures, and fuses side outputs at various scales to resolve the ambiguity in edge and object boundary detection. Further, the DSS model [9] introduces short connections to the skip layers to construct an enhanced HED structure that combines both deeper and shallower side outputs for multi-scale contexts. Apparently, deeper network architectures are able to learn richer semantic features for more accurate predictions. However, complex network architectures may lead to the time consuming training process and may face with over-fitting problems. Thus, constructing a compact yet efficient FCNs structure for targeted tasks is crucial in balancing the accuracy and efficiency.

2.2   CRFs for Saliency Refinement

Prior to the pervasive applications of the CNNs, most of the best performed traditional saliency methods firstly compute a coarse saliency map and then refine it by handcraft features from the input image. Such refinement is based on some common context-aware assumptions and theories from graphical models. As the conditional random fields (CRFs) is a flexible framework for incorporating various features and is capable to accommodate inference functions for graphical models, it has been frequently adopted for labeling refinement tasks. For instance, Qiu *et al.* [26] take advantages of handcraft image features and spatially weighted distance to infer a CRF model to refine coarse saliency maps.

Deeplab [3] firstly implements the dense CRFs framework to deep neural networks to refine the semantic segmentation results based on unary and pairwise potentials proposed by [11]. The proposed dense CRFs is fully connected to CNNs as a post-processing step for end-to-end refinement. Later, several works [36,37,44] unroll the CRF inference by [11] to an end-to-end trainable feed-forward networks.

For efficient computation, existing saliency models tend to integrate the fully connected CRFs on top of the deep neural networks for end-to-end post processing. MDF saliency model [15] involves the CRFs from Deeplab [3] to integrate multiple output saliency maps from CNNs with inputs of different contexts. Later, the DCL model [16] incorporates the dense CRFs [3] to improve spatial coherence and contour localization for the fused result from two streams of

CNNs. The MSRNet [14] model and DSS [9] model both integrates the fully connected dense CRFs [11] to refine the fused output maps from the CNNs. In this work, a more flexible and efficient incorporation of dense CRFs will be explored on top of the pre-trained CNNs.

3 Multi-scale CRFs Model

The Multi-scale CRFs Model is based on a simple yet effective encoder-decoder architecture. Firstly, multi-scales of side output feature maps are computed from the pre-trained encoder-decoder networks. Then, each side output maps are refined by a fully connected CRF layer to enhance the delineation and smoothness. Finally, the enhance feature maps are fused and refined by another CRF layer for the final saliency map.

3.1 The Encoder-Decoder Networks

Given the input image $I = \{I_i, i = 1, \cdots, |I|\}$ with three-dimensional size of $H \times W \times 3$, and the ground truth $G = \{G_i, i = 1, \cdots, |G|\}$, $G_i \in \{0, 1\}$ with the size of $H \times W \times 1$, the encoder-decoder networks $\mathcal{F}$ is adopted to produce $M = \{m = 1, \cdots, M\}$ scales of side output feature maps, denoted as s_m respectively as follow:

$$s_m = \mathcal{F}(W, w_m), \tag{1}$$

where W denotes the generic weights of the encoder-decoder networks and w_m denotes the scale specific weights. In the training phase, the cross-entropy loss is utilized as the side objective function $L_m(W, w_m)$ to train the network weights:

$$
\begin{aligned}
&L_m(W, w_m) \\
&= - \sum_{\mathcal{S}_m^j \in \mathcal{S}_m} [\mathcal{S}_m^j \log P(\mathcal{S}_m^j = 1 | \mathcal{I}; W, w_m) + (1 - \mathcal{S}_m^j) \log P(\mathcal{S}_m^j = 0 | \mathcal{I}; W, w_m)]
\end{aligned}
\tag{2}
$$

where $\mathcal{I} = \{\mathcal{I}^j, j = 1, \cdots, |\mathcal{I}|\}$ denotes all the pixels in the training image set and $\mathcal{S}_m = \{\mathcal{S}_m^j, j = 1, \cdots, |\mathcal{S}_m|\}$ denotes all the saliency values from the side output layer at the m-th scale of the encoder-decoder networks. $P(\mathcal{S}_m^j = 1 | \mathcal{I}; W, w_m)$ represents the probability of the activation value at location j at the m-th scale side output map.

3.2 Multi-scale CRFs Refinement

Through the encoder-decoder networks, M scales of side output maps are computed to primarily locate the salient objects. In order to further improve the prediction accuracy, a fully connected CRF [11] layer is integrated to each side output layer for refinement as follow:

$$\hat{s}_m = \mathcal{C}_m(s_m, I, \Theta_m), \tag{3}$$

where $\mathcal{C}_m(\cdot)$ refers to the CRF layer at the m-th scale, Θ_m refers to all the parameters for the m-th CRF layer, and $\hat{s}_m$ represents the refined side output map at the m-th scale.

To each side output map $\hat{s}_m$, the energy function of the CRF is

$$E(G) = \sum_i \phi_u(s_m^i) + \sum_{i<k} \phi_p(s_m^i, s_m^k). \tag{4}$$

$\phi_u(s_m^i)$ refers to the unary term, where the side output maps are directly regarded as the input. $\phi_p(s_m^i, s_m^k)$ is the pairwise term, which accounts for the coherence of the saliency information and image features between the current pixel and its neighbors. Thus, the pairwise term is defined as:

$$\phi_p(s_m^i, s_m^k) = \mu(s_m^i, s_m^k)[\nu_1 \exp(-\frac{\|p_i - p_k\|^2}{2\sigma_\alpha^2} - \frac{\|I_i - I_k\|^2}{2\sigma_\beta^2}) + \nu_2 \exp(-\frac{\|p_i - p_k\|^2}{2\sigma_\gamma^2})], \tag{5}$$

where $\mu(s_m^i, s_m^k) = 1$ if $s_m^i = s_m^k$ and otherwise 0. I_i represents the RGB image features of the i-th pixel, while p_i is the pixel position. The Gaussian kernel $\exp(-\frac{\|p_i-p_k\|^2}{2\sigma_\alpha^2} - \frac{\|I_i-I_k\|^2}{2\sigma_\beta^2})$ measures the appearance coherence which refines the nearby pixels with similar features with similar saliency scores, while the Gaussian kernel $\exp(-\frac{\|p_i-p_k\|^2}{2\sigma_\gamma^2})$ measures the spatial coherence which reconciles close pixels with similar saliency scores. Parameters ν_1 and ν_2 control the contributions of each Gaussian kernel respectively.

The energy minimization is based on the mean field approximation to the CRF distribution proposed by [11], and high-dimensional filtering can be utilized to speed up the computation.

Then, the refined saliency maps from each scale of the CRF layer are fused by element-wise production:

$$\tilde{s} = \prod_{m=1}^{M} \hat{s}_m. \tag{6}$$

Finally, another CRF layer is connected to further refine the fused map as the final saliency map:

$$\bar{s}_{final} = \mathcal{C}_{final}(\tilde{s}, I, \Theta_{fuse}) \tag{7}$$

4   Experiment

4.1   Implementation

In this work, the fully convolutional encoder-decoder networks is adopted to obtain the multi-scale side output maps. The network architecture is demonstrated in Fig. 1 with detailed layer descriptions. The encoder network is based on the VGG-16 net [31]. The decoder network firstly unpools the features from the corresponding maxpooling layers and properly upsample and crop the side

Table 1. Evaluation results over four datasets, with models including MDF [15], RFCN [34], DHS [18], Amulet [42], UCF [43], DCL [16], MSR [14], DSS [9], RA [4] and the proposed MCRF model. "+" marks the models utilizing dense CRF [11] for post-processing. "−" means that the corresponding dataset is used as the training data. The evaluation on MSRA-B is performed on the testing set. The best performances are in **bold** while the second best results are <u>underlined</u>.

Dataset	Metric	MDF+	RFCN	DHS	Amulet	UCF	DCL+	MSR+	DSS+	RA	MCRF
MSRA-B	F_β	0.862	-	-	-	-	0.898	0.880	**0.917**	0.901	**0.917**
	MAE	0.066	-	-	-	-	0.047	0.053	**0.034**	0.050	<u>0.038</u>
DUT-OMRON	F_β	0.677	0.693	-	0.668	0.630	0.716	0.695	**0.757**	0.719	<u>0.726</u>
	MAE	0.092	0.095	-	0.098	0.120	0.080	0.078	**0.063**	0.076	<u>0.074</u>
HKU-IS	F_β	0.809	0.868	0.863	0.849	0.816	0.851	0.864	**0.904**	0.879	<u>0.894</u>
	MAE	0.076	0.073	0.052	0.050	0.061	<u>0.049</u>	**0.040**	**0.040**	0.057	**0.040**
ECSSD	F_β	0.818	0.871	0.875	0.865	0.835	0.874	0.838	**0.899**	0.876	<u>0.893</u>
	MAE	0.106	0.091	0.059	0.061	0.071	0.068	0.062	**0.055**	0.080	<u>0.058</u>

output maps to the image size. All the decoder convolutional layers are followed by batch normalization and ReLU activation functions. We also add a dropout layer after each ReLU layer in the decoder networks.

The hyper-parameters for the finetuning the encoder-decoder networks are set as: a fixed learning rate (1e−8), weight decay (0.0005), momentum (0.9), loss weight for each side output (1). The batch size is set as 12, and 100 epochs are performed for tuning the encoder decoder network. The sigmoid cross entropy loss layers are used for model optimization.

The fully connected dense CRF layers share the same parameter settings and are tuned via cross validations on the validation set, and ν_1, ν_2, σ_α, σ_β, and σ_γ are set to 3.0, 3.0, 60.0, 5.0, and 3.0, respectively. Only 3 iterations of the meanfield approximation are set to each CRF layer.

All the implementation is based on the public Caffe library [10]. The CRF is based on the PyDenseCRF implementation [11]. The GPU for training acceleration is the Nvidia Tesla P100 with 16 GB memory. Totally 100 epochs are performed to train the encoder-decoder networks, which takes about 16 h. In the testing phase, it takes averagely 1.68 s to compute the final saliency maps.

Table 2. Comparisons of Mean F-measure by implementing multi-scale CRFs versus implementing single-scale CRF respectively. "s_1, s_2, s_3" refer to the three scales of side output maps from the encoder-decoder networks respectively. "$s_{123}+\mathrm{CRF}^1$" fuses the maps "s_1, s_2, s_3" by elementwise production and then connect a single CRF layer with 3 meanfield iterations to compute the saliency maps. "$s_{123}+\mathrm{CRF}^2$" also fuses the side output maps and connect a single CRF layer with 10 meanfield iterations. Note that the parameter settings of CRF layer for "$s_{123}+\mathrm{CRF}^2$" are the same as DSS model. The evaluations are performed on ECSSD dataset.

Maps	s_1	s_2	s_3	$s_{123}+\mathrm{CRF}^1$	$s_{123}+\mathrm{CRF}^2$	MCRF
F_β	0.856	0.849	0.839	0.867	0.868	0.893

4.2   Datasets

We follow the training protocol as in [9,16] by using the MSRA-B dataset [20] as the training data for fair comparisons. The MSRA-B dataset consists of 2,500 training images, 500 validation images and 2000 testing images. The images are resized to 240×320 as the input to the data layer. Horizontal flipping is used for data augmentation such that the number of training samples is twice as large as the original number.

The proposed model is evaluated over four datasets, including: MSRA-B [20], ECSSD [38], DUT-OMRON [39], and HKU-IS [17]. MSRA-B is the training dataset. ECSSD contains a pool of 1000 images with even more complex salient objects on the scenes. DUT-OMRON dataset contains a large number of 5168 more difficult and challenging images. HUK-IS consists of 4447 challenging images and pixel-wise saliency annotation.

4.3   Evaluation Metrics

We employ two types of evaluation metrics to evaluate the performance of the saliency maps: mean F-measure and mean absolute error (MAE). When a given saliency map is slidingly thresholded from 0 to 255, a precision-recall (PR) curve can be computed based on the ground truth. F-measure is computed to count for the saliency maps with both high precision and recall:

$$F = \frac{(1 + \beta^2) \cdot precision \cdot recall}{\beta^2 \cdot precision + recall}, \tag{8}$$

where $\beta^2 = 0.3$ [1] to emphasize the precision. In this paper, the mean F-measure is chosen for evaluation and the saliency maps are thresholded by twice of the mean saliency values.

MAE measures the overall pixel-wise difference between the saliency map sal and the ground truth gt as follow:

$$MAE = \frac{1}{H} \sum_{h=1}^{H} |sal(h) - gt(h)|, \tag{9}$$

where H is the number of pixels on the map.

4.4   Experimental Results

We compare the proposed MCRF model with nine state-of-the-art deep saliency models including MDF [15], RFCN [34], DHS [18], Amulet [42], UCF [43], DCL [16], MSR [14], DSS [9], and RA [4]. All the models are CNN-based approaches. All the implementations are based on public codes and suggested settings by the corresponding authors (Fig. 2).

Table 1 lists the mean F-measure and MAE of the nine saliency models and the proposed MCRF model over four datasets. It is clearly observed that the

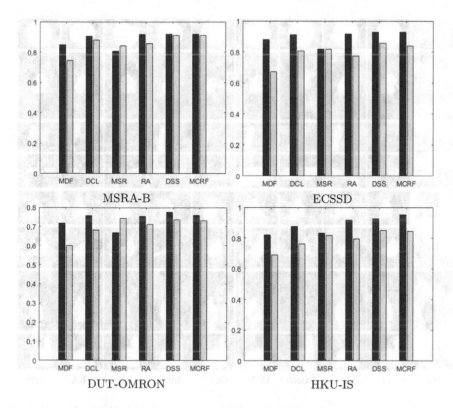

Fig. 2. Comparisons of the mean precision and mean recall on MSRA-B testing set, DUT-OMRON, HKU-IS and ECSSD datasets respectively.

MCRF model surpasses most of the existing saliency models with much better performances. Compared to MDF [15], DCL [16], MSR [14] that apply single CRF [11] layers, the multi-scale CRF model results in superior performances. Moreover, the proposed MCRF model receives comparable performances with the DSS [9] model. Compared to the DSS [9] that uses the enhanced HED architecture with five scales of side outputs (totally 53 convolutional and deconvolutional layers), the proposed MCRF model is based on the simple encoder-decoder architecture and only three scales of side outputs (totally 31 convolutional and deconvolutional layers) are fused for multi-scale integration. Thus, the multi-scale CRF structure is proved to be efficient. We also evaluate the performances of embedding multi-scale CRFs versus single-scale CRFs to the pre-finetuned model as in Table 2. Clearly, multi-scale CRFs model receives the best performances. Figure 3 presents saliency maps from the compared models and the proposed MCRF model.

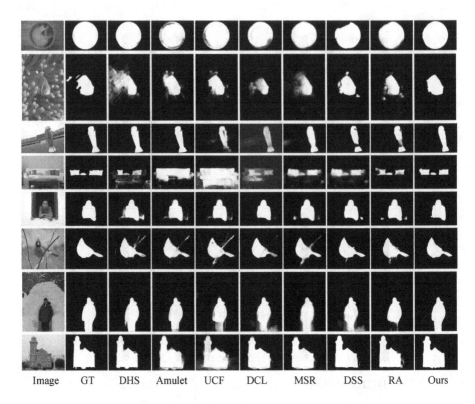

Image   GT   DHS   Amulet   UCF   DCL   MSR   DSS   RA   Ours

Fig. 3. Examples of saliency maps from DHS [18], Amulet [42], UCF [43], DCL [16], MSR [14], DSS [9], RA [4] and the proposed MCRF model.

5   Conclusion

This paper proposes to refine the side outputs efficiently from multiple scales of FCNs by embedding multi-scale CRF layers. Firstly, the front-end FCNs is based on the simple yet efficient encoder-decoder networks which involves much fewer convolutional layers and parameters such that the front-end network is easy to train. Secondly, only three scales of side outputs from the FCNs are integrated but competitive performances are received. In future, the side output refinement based on CRF inference with upper level side output from the FCNs will be further explored for a hierarchical refinement architecture.

References

1. Achanta, R., Hemami, S., Estrada, F., Susstrunk, S.: Frequency-tuned salient region detection. In: Proceedings of the CVPR, pp. 1597–1604. IEEE (2009)
2. Arbeláez, P., Pont-Tuset, J., Barron, J.T., Marques, F., Malik, J.: Multiscale combinatorial grouping. In: Proceedings of the CVPR, pp. 328–335. IEEE (2014)

3. Chen, L.C., Papandreou, G., Kokkinos, I., Murphy, K., Yuille, A.L.: DeepLab: semantic image segmentation with deep convolutional nets, atrous convolution, and fully connected CRFs. TPAMI **40**(4), 834–848 (2018)
4. Chen, S., Tan, X., Wang, B., Hu, X.: Reverse attention for salient object detection. In: Ferrari, V., Hebert, M., Sminchisescu, C., Weiss, Y. (eds.) ECCV 2018. LNCS, vol. 11213, pp. 236–252. Springer, Cham (2018). https://doi.org/10.1007/978-3-030-01240-3_15
5. Dai, J., Li, Y., He, K., Sun, J.: R-FCN: object detection via region-based fully convolutional networks. In: NIPS, pp. 379–387 (2016)
6. Guo, C., Zhang, L.: A novel multiresolution spatiotemporal saliency detection model and its applications in image and video compression. TIP **19**(1), 185–198 (2010)
7. Han, J., Pauwels, E.J., De Zeeuw, P.: Fast saliency-aware multi-modality image fusion. Neurocomputing **111**, 70–80 (2013)
8. Hariharan, B., Arbeláez, P., Girshick, R., Malik, J.: Hypercolumns for object segmentation and fine-grained localization. In: Proceedings of the CVPR, pp. 447–456. IEEE (2015)
9. Hou, Q., Cheng, M.M., Hu, X.W., Borji, A., Tu, Z., Torr, P.: Deeply supervised salient object detection with short connections. TPAMI (2018)
10. Jia, Y., et al.: Caffe: convolutional architecture for fast feature embedding. In: Proceedings of the Multimedia, pp. 675–678. ACM (2014)
11. Krähenbühl, P., Koltun, V.: Efficient inference in fully connected CRFs with Gaussian edge potentials. In: Advances in Neural Information Processing Systems, pp. 109–117 (2011)
12. Kuen, J., Wang, Z., Wang, G.: Recurrent attentional networks for saliency detection. In: Proceedings of the CVPR. IEEE (2016)
13. Lee, G., Tai, Y.W., Kim, J.: Deep saliency with encoded low level distance map and high level features. In: Proceedings of the CVPR, pp. 660–668. IEEE (2016)
14. Li, G., Xie, Y., Lin, L., Yu, Y.: Instance-level salient object segmentation. In: Proceedings of the CVPR, pp. 247–256. IEEE (2017)
15. Li, G., Yu, Y.: Visual saliency based on multiscale deep features. In: Proceedings of the CVPR. IEEE (2015)
16. Li, G., Yu, Y.: Deep contrast learning for salient object detection. In: Proceedings of the CVPR. IEEE (2016)
17. Li, G., Yu, Y.: Visual saliency detection based on multiscale deep CNN features. TIP **25**(11), 5012–5024 (2016)
18. Liu, N., Han, J.: DHSNet: deep hierarchical saliency network for salient object detection. In: Proceedings of the CVPR, pp. 678–686 (2016)
19. Liu, Q., Hong, X., Zou, B., Chen, J., Chen, Z., Zhao, G.: Hierarchical contour closure based holistic salient object detection. TIP (2017)
20. Liu, T., et al.: Learning to detect a salient object. TPAMI **33**(2), 353–367 (2011)
21. Long, J., Shelhamer, E., Darrell, T.: Fully convolutional networks for semantic segmentation. In: Proceedings of the CVPR, pp. 3431–3440. IEEE (2015)
22. Luo, P., Wang, X., Tang, X.: Pedestrian parsing via deep decompositional network. In: Proceedings of the ICCV, pp. 2648–2655. IEEE (2013)
23. Ma, Y.F., Lu, L., Zhang, H.J., Li, M.: A user attention model for video summarization. In: Proceedings of the Multimedia, pp. 533–542. ACM (2002)
24. Mahendran, A., Vedaldi, A.: Salient deconvolutional networks. In: Leibe, B., Matas, J., Sebe, N., Welling, M. (eds.) ECCV 2016. LNCS, vol. 9910, pp. 120–135. Springer, Cham (2016). https://doi.org/10.1007/978-3-319-46466-4_8

25. Mottaghi, R., et al.: The role of context for object detection and semantic segmentation in the wild. In: Proceedings of the CVPR, pp. 891–898 (2014)

26. Qiu, W., Gao, X., Han, B.: A superpixel-based CRF saliency detection approach. Neurocomputing **244**, 19–32 (2017)

27. Rahtu, E., Kannala, J., Salo, M., Heikkilä, J.: Segmenting salient objects from images and videos. In: Daniilidis, K., Maragos, P., Paragios, N. (eds.) ECCV 2010. LNCS, vol. 6315, pp. 366–379. Springer, Heidelberg (2010). https://doi.org/10.1007/978-3-642-15555-0_27

28. Santella, A., Agrawala, M., DeCarlo, D., Salesin, D., Cohen, M.: Gaze-based interaction for semi-automatic photo cropping. In: Proceeding of the CHI, pp. 771–780. ACM (2006)

29. Sermanet, P., Kavukcuoglu, K., Chintala, S., LeCun, Y.: Pedestrian detection with unsupervised multi-stage feature learning. In: Proceedings of the CVPR, pp. 3626–3633. IEEE (2013)

30. Shengfeng, H., Jianbo, J., Zhang, X., Han, G., Rynson, W.: Delving into salient object subitizing and detection. In: Proceedings of the ICCV. IEEE (2017)

31. Simonyan, K., Zisserman, A.: Very deep convolutional networks for large-scale image recognition. ICLR (2015)

32. Tang, Y., Wu, X.: Saliency detection via combining region-level and pixel-level predictions with CNNs. In: Leibe, B., Matas, J., Sebe, N., Welling, M. (eds.) ECCV 2016. LNCS, vol. 9912, pp. 809–825. Springer, Cham (2016). https://doi.org/10.1007/978-3-319-46484-8_49

33. Wang, L., Lu, H., Ruan, X., Yang, M.H.: Deep networks for saliency detection via local estimation and global search. In: Proceeding of the CVPR, pp. 3183–3192. IEEE (2015)

34. Wang, L., Wang, L., Lu, H., Zhang, P., Ruan, X.: Saliency detection with recurrent fully convolutional networks. In: Leibe, B., Matas, J., Sebe, N., Welling, M. (eds.) ECCV 2016. LNCS, vol. 9908, pp. 825–841. Springer, Cham (2016). https://doi.org/10.1007/978-3-319-46493-0_50

35. Xie, S., Tu, Z.: Holistically-nested edge detection. In: Proceedings of the ICCV, pp. 1395–1403. IEEE (2015)

36. Xu, D., Ouyang, W., Alameda-Pineda, X., Ricci, E., Wang, X., Sebe, N.: Learning deep structured multi-scale features using attention-gated CRFs for contour prediction. In: NIPS, pp. 3964–3973 (2017)

37. Xu, D., Ricci, E., Ouyang, W., Wang, X., Sebe, N.: Monocular depth estimation using multi-scale continuous CRFs as sequential deep networks. TPAMI (2018)

38. Yan, Q., Xu, L., Shi, J., Jia, J.: Hierarchical saliency detection. In: Proceedings of the CVPR, pp. 1155–1162. IEEE (2013)

39. Yang, C., Zhang, L., Lu, H., Ruan, X., Yang, M.H.: Saliency detection via graph-based manifold ranking. In: Proceedings of the CVPR, pp. 3166–3173. IEEE (2013)

40. Yang, J., Price, B., Cohen, S., Lee, H., Yang, M.H.: Object contour detection with a fully convolutional encoder-decoder network. In: Proceedings of the CVPR, pp. 193–202 (2016)

41. Zeiler, M.D., Fergus, R.: Visualizing and understanding convolutional networks. In: Fleet, D., Pajdla, T., Schiele, B., Tuytelaars, T. (eds.) ECCV 2014. LNCS, vol. 8689, pp. 818–833. Springer, Cham (2014). https://doi.org/10.1007/978-3-319-10590-1_53

42. Zhang, P., Wang, D., Lu, H., Wang, H., Ruan, X.: Amulet: aggregating multi-level convolutional features for salient object detection. In: Proceedings of the ICCV. IEEE (2017)

43. Zhang, P., Wang, D., Lu, H., Wang, H., Yin, B.: Learning uncertain convolutional features for accurate saliency detection. In: Proceedings of the ICCV, pp. 212–221. IEEE (2017)
44. Zheng, S., et al.: Conditional random fields as recurrent neural networks. In: Proceedings of the ICCV, pp. 1529–1537. IEEE (2015)

Dimensionality Reduction
for Visualization of Time Series
and Trajectories

Pattreeya Tanisaro[(✉)] and Gunther Heidemann

Institute of Cognitive Science, University of Osnabrück, Osnabrück, Germany
pattanisaro@uni-osnabrueck.de

Abstract. Visualization is essential for data analysis and it is particularly challenging for data in high-dimensional space, especially for temporal information. Many techniques have been employed in an attempt to transform multivariate time series data to one-dimensional data by reducing the number of features in order to visualize their time-dependent behaviors. However, the applicability of these approaches is restricted to a limited number of data instances that can be visualized simultaneously.

We present a technique to visualize time series and trajectories that overcomes these limitations by transforming these data into subspaces which allows data analysts to easily select the instance of interest from a bunch of data. The benefits of our proposed method are threefold: it provides (i) a visual representation of time-dependent data in a massive amount simultaneously, (ii) a very concise feature representation and (iii) an easy identification of anomalies. The results are demonstrated by employing this technique to various data traits from public archives, they are (i) univariate time series data from the UCR archive, (ii) multivariate time series data from several sources, and (iii) human motion trajectories from two motion capture (MoCap) datasets.

Keywords: Dimensionality reduction · Visualization · Time series

1 Introduction

Visualization techniques help us to understand data by observing its patterns. A common approach to meet this challenge is to transform the high-dimensional data representation into lower dimensions. High-dimensional datasets typically have certain traits that can be captured after a transformation to a different coordinate system, and become directly visible to the human eye when mapped to two or three-dimensional space. Although there are numerous dimensionality

Electronic supplementary material The online version of this chapter (https://doi.org/10.1007/978-3-030-20205-7_21) contains supplementary material, which is available to authorized users.

M. Felsberg et al. (Eds.): SCIA 2019, LNCS 11482, pp. 246–257, 2019.
https://doi.org/10.1007/978-3-030-20205-7_21

reduction techniques available; nevertheless, there are much fewer dimensionality reduction approaches that are practical enough for the general application of which take the temporal information into account. Some interesting techniques for visualization of time-dependent data, for example [4, 7, 9] are tied to a domain-specific application and their data are not publicly accessible; therefore, it raises a question of whether to adopt those techniques to a new domain application even though the data may be categorized in the same time characteristics.

Generally, a known method for visualizing time series data is by using a line graph which is widely used in the monitoring of vital signs in order to detect the abnormal exceeding of a specified threshold. However, the line graph does not work well for multivariate time series, and it is especially difficult to visualize a large collection of signals. On top of that, for the case of a multivariate time series where the interdependencies occur among many variables, detecting the outliers happens to be much more difficult and cannot be solved by visualizing each data feature on the timeline. A conventional approach to visualize high-dimensional time series data is to examine their distance matrices. One benefit of using a distance matrix such as Euclidean distance is that we can further analyze the matrix using a recurrence plot (RP) by applying a threshold distance and the Heaviside function. The RP is well-known for the visualization of time series because it allows any high-dimensional phase space trajectories to be visualized in subspaces through a two-dimensional representation of it recurrences.

Unlike other traditional dimensionality reduction approaches for temporal data which allow a user to analyze signals over time, **our technique allows the user to inspect the structure of a bunch of time series data or trajectories simultaneously and to detect the outliers**. Particularly for multivariate time series which have many practical usages in real-world applications, there is no general solution to compare a bunch of information at the same time. We demonstrate that it is possible to apply conventional dimensionality reduction approaches from a non-time-series to transform high-dimensional time series into low-dimensional subspaces **by neglecting time information in the display**. Although the dimensionality reduction techniques themselves are not new, to the best of our knowledge, such an attempt to visualize the time-dependent data by neglecting the time axis has never been investigated before. The advantages of our approach are threefold. They allow the data analyst: *(i) to visualize the large-scale time series data clusters simultaneously, (ii) to get a very concise feature representation of the time series regardless of its length and the number of features, and (iii) to detect an anomaly in the data.*

2   Data Transformation to Subspaces

Let p be the total number of instances in the dataset. For any given instance i, each individual instance is specified by $\{X^i\}$ where $i \in \{1, ..., p\}$. For any high-dimensional data sequence X^i with a fixed number of features m and arbitrary length T_i, we can be interpreted X^i as a real-valued matrix X with a dimension $m \times T_i$ as illustrated in Fig. 1a. Pick the number of selected components

c_n for any transformation F to the matrix X^i where n is the number of dimensionality reduction technique used. For the chosen first principal components c_1 at $n=1$, we obtain $F_1(X^i)$ as illustrated in Fig. 1b where $T_i \geq c_1$. Hence, to apply n-*times* of dimensionality reduction of F to X^i for c_n components, namely $F_n(F_{n-1}(...F_1(X^i)...))$ as shown in Fig. 1c, requires:

$$T_i \geq c_1 \quad \forall i \in \{1, \ldots, p\} \quad \text{and} \quad (m \cdot c_1) \geq c_2... \geq c_n \qquad (1)$$

Usually, the sequence length of any signal instance is much larger than the selected number of principal components, that is $T_i \gg c_1 \forall i \in \{1, \ldots, p\}$. Before applying the first order transformation, $n = 1$, we may build a feature vector by normalizing each $X^i_{j,k}$ where $j \in \{1, ..., m\}$ and $k \in \{1, ..., T_i\}$ as:

$$X^i_{j,k} \Leftarrow X^i_{j,k} - \bar{X}^i_j \qquad (2)$$

where $\bar{X}^i_j$ is the average over the sequence length T_i of feature j. Likewise, for the case of the trajectories of MoCap dataset, we first normalize the stick-figure's joint positions which were computed by the marker positions following [12] by subtracting the position of the center of the torso from each joint position. The normalization by subtracting the mean is optional but is proved to enhance the visualization in many cases. For the case of different scaling of features, the rescaling prior to applying the dimensionality reduction transformation can be beneficial. However, normalizing time series data by dividing it by its standard deviation does not improve our visualization in general. Similar evidence was reported in [11] for human motion classification. After applying the first transformation of F_1 on each normalized X^i, the data sequence X^i can be newly represented as $F_1(X^i) \in \mathbb{R}^{m \times c_1}$ as depicted in Fig. 1b. The time axis now has been replaced with the number of principal components of the first transformation. The feature vector for the second order transformation may be arranged using a concatenation of an average vector to $F_1(X^i)$ as $[\bar{X}^i_j; F_1(X^i)]$. After a second order transformation, $F_2(F_1(X^i))$, the new matrix can be shortly written as $F_2{}^i \in \mathbb{R}^{1 \times c_2}$ which is depicted in Fig. 1c.

3   Datasets

The datasets in this paper were selected by considering the number of data classes up to twelve classes which can be easily identified by different colors. There is no restriction on the number of features nor sequence lengths.

3.1   Univariate Time Series

The UCR archive [3] contains 85 datasets of univariate time series. It is target for benchmarking time series classification. Each dataset consists of a separate training and test set of a fixed sequence length which was already normalized to have zero mean and a standard deviation of one. We picked five datasets from this archive and merged the training and test data together because we only focus on the visualization of data and not on classification. These datasets are *Plane, ItalyPowerDemand, Wafer, CBF* and *ECG5000*.

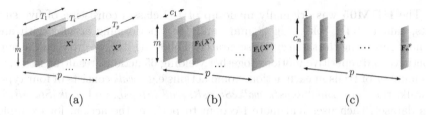

(a)   (b)   (c)

Fig. 1. Transformation of time-dependent data into subspaces. (a) p instances of time-dependent data of m features with arbitrary sequence lengths T_i. (b) Results after the first transformation of F_1. From this point onward, the arbitrary size of "time dimension" T_i has become all equal with the selected principal components c_1. (c) The data after an arbitrary n^{th} transformation giving each signal instance of size c_n which can portray a small feature representation of the data.

3.2 Multivariate Time Series

We selected three datasets which are frequently used in benchmarking classification tasks as found in [1,5,6]. These three datasets were: *Japanese Vowel*, *NetworkFlow* and *Wafer* (It has the same dataset name but different set from the UCR). The *Japanese Vowel* dataset was a collection of nine male speakers for a total of 640 sequences. Each utterance forms a sequence with lengths in the range of 7–29 and consists of 12 features each. The *Networkflow* dataset represents a network traffic protocol of a total of 1337 sequences with the sequence length of 50–997 where a series of network packets define a sequence. Each packet consists of four attributes which are used to identify the applications that generated the traffic flow. These attributes are a packet size, transfer direction, payload, and the duration. The *Wafer* stands for silicon wafer in semiconductor manufacture. The dataset contains 1194 sequences with the sequence length of 104–198. Each sequence consists of six measurement variables recorded during the etch process. Each wafer is marked as normal or defective.

3.3 Motion Capture

We chose two different MoCap datasets, the UTD-MHAD [2] and the HDM05 [8] to demonstrate the effectiveness of our proposed technique.

The **UTD-MHAD** consists of 27 different actions performed by eight subjects. Each action was recorded using 20 markers in 3D coordinates, resulting in the total number of 60 features. Each subject repeated the same actions four times (trials) for only one cycle, and each action trial has different sequence length. Hence, we have only 32 sequences for each action in total. This small amount of data is statistically not interesting. Based on the results of a quasi-view independent of human movement in 3D described in [12], an eigenvector of the largest eigenvalue still maintains its projection size even when a subject performs the same action facing in a different direction. Therefore, we rotated the actor's default view by 10, 20 and 30° in order to obtain more samples.

The **HDM05** was originally made up of 130 classes consisting of five subjects, called "bd", "bk", "dg", "mm" and "tr", performing actions with and without repeating the same cycles separately. Following [10], we grouped the non-repetitive and repetitive motions together yielding 65 actions, resulting in a various number of trials in each action. Some actions e.g., *walk* consists of four types of walk, they are *walk2StepsL*, *walk2StepsR*, *walk4StepsL*, and *walk4StepsR*. In this dataset, each user had more freedom to perform the action, for example, the numbers of repetitions and the directions of movement were not fixed.

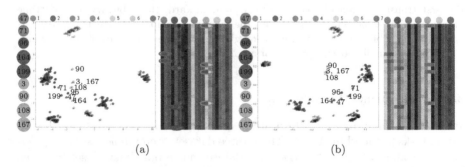

(a)   (b)

Fig. 2. Results of the dimensionality reduction of 210 sequences of "Plane" using (a) PCA and (b) Kernel PCA with RBF kernel. Nine outliers listed on the left side of each image (a) and (b) can be easily identified in the two-dimensional views (That is only the first two principal components are drawn). The right side of each image shows the feature representation map of the corresponding algorithm from three principal components of a matrix size $30 \times (3 \cdot 7)$, where 30 signals of each data class are in the rows and three components of seven classes are in the columns. The irregular patterns in each class found in the feature representation map highlighted in ellipses at (a)-right can be found in the same positions at the (b)-right. The feature vectors of the data class ● and ● as seen in the feature maps are very similar.

4   Visualization Results

In this section, we will examine the outputs from projecting data on 2D and 3D space after applying the transformations discussed in Sect. 2. Without prior knowledge of the characteristics of the data, the dimensionality reduction techniques were randomly chosen from two characteristics, linear projections i.e., PCA and nonlinear projections such as kernel PCA with nonlinear kernels and t-SNE. We selected some interesting outputs to be demonstrated here.

4.1   Visualization Results of the Univariate Time Series

The results of applying two dimensionality reduction techniques to *Plane* in the UCR archive are displayed in Fig. 2a and b. Not only do our outputs exhibit to

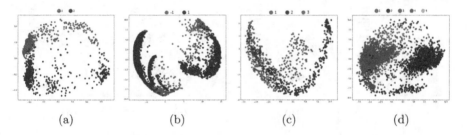

(a)   (b)   (c)   (d)

Fig. 3. Results of the dimensionality reduction of selected datasets in the UCR archive. (a) 1097 sequences of "ItalyPowerDemand" using Kernel PCA. (b) 7174 sequences of "Wafer" using PCA. (c) 930 sequences of "CBF" using PCA. (d) 5000 sequences of "ECG5000" using PCA. This dataset has much of unbalancing in the data in each class. The number of signals in each class are: (●) 2919, (●) 1767, (●) 96, (●) 194 and (●) 24.

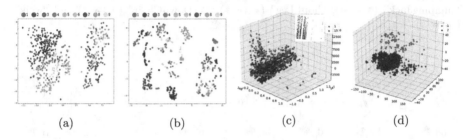

(a)   (b)   (c)   (d)

Fig. 4. Results of the dimensionality reduction of multivariate time series. (a) "JapaneseVowel" with PCA followed by t-SNE ($n = 2$, the perplexity of t-SNE 40). (b) "JapaneseVowel" with PCA followed by double t-SNE ($n = 3$, the perplexity of t-SNE 40 and 30, respectively). (c) "NetworkFlow" using PCA and t-SNE. (d) "Wafer" using PCA and t-SNE.

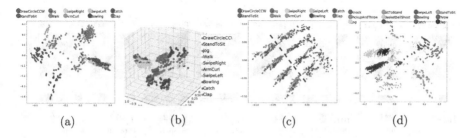

(a)   (b)   (c)   (d)

Fig. 5. Results of the dimensionality reduction of human movements in the UTD-MHAD. (a) Ten actions using PCA followed by Kernel PCA. (b) 3D projection of the same action set as (a) using Kernel PCA and PCA. (c) The same action set as (a) using Kernel PCA with two kernels, RBF and polynomial, accordingly. The dashed line was drawn to separate another view. (d) Twelve actions using PCA and Kernel PCA.

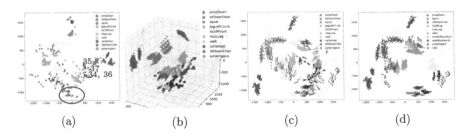

(a)   (b)   (c)   (d)

Fig. 6. Results of the dimensionality reduction of human movements in the HDM05. (a) 446 number of actions from a default view using Kernel PCA and PCA. Three movements of "jumpDown" (●) of user "dg" (34, 35, 36) and one movement of user "mm" (37) are laid far away from the others (in the brown ellipse). (b) Three-dimensional projection of 1784 trials from ten actions as (a) with additional movements of rotating subjects by 10, 20 and 30°. (c) Two-dimensional projection of (b). (d) A similar effect in a different subset of motions of four viewpoints comparing to (c) depicted in different colors from (d) → (c) as the following: "jumpDown" (●), "squat" (● → ●), "jumpingJack" (● → ●), "hopLLeg" (● → ●), "sitDownChair" (● → ●) and "walk" (● → ●).

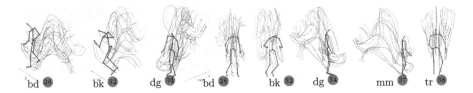

bd 28   bk 32   dg 34   bd 28   bk 32   dg 34   mm 37   tr 38

Fig. 7. Five subjects performs "JumpDown" (●) from the default view as seen in Fig. 6a. From left to right: the first three images are the 3D projection of three subjects. The next five images are the simplified 2D projections in which the trajectories are much easier to be observed. The subjects "dg" and "mm" face 90° opposing to the direction of "bd", "bk", and "tr" causing different patterns of the trajectories and are considered as another group as seen in Fig. 6a.

$T_{28} = 317$ $T_{34} = 341$ $T_{37} = 381$ $T_{216} = 158$ $T_{228} = 323$ $T_{252} = 145$ $T_{272} = 325$ $T_{290} = 258$

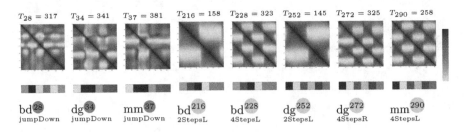

bd 28   dg 34   mm 37   bd 216   bd 228   dg 252   dg 272   mm 290
jumpDown   jumpDown   jumpDown   2StepsL   4StepsL   2StepsL   4StepsR   4StepsL

Fig. 8. A comparison of eight trials in the HDM05 between applying the unthresholded RP and our proposed algorithm with six principal components lying below each corresponding RP. The first three images on the left are from the action "jumpDown" (●) as depicted in Fig. 7. The next five images are obtained from four types of "walking" (●). Notice the time length (T_i) where the repetitions of the walking cycle occur.

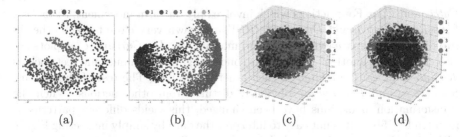

(a)   (b)   (c)   (d)

Fig. 9. Variations of transformation. (a) "CBF" using MDS. (b) "ECG5000" using Kernel PCA with polynomial kernel. (c) "TwoPatterns" in the UCR archive using PCA. (d) "TwoPatterns" using Kernel PCA with third-degree polynomial.

the viewer the intrinsic properties of each data cluster, but they also reveal the outliers that laid afar from their groups. It is obvious that using just three principal components as illustrated in Fig. 2a and b can make a time series much easier to interpret. Even employing different dimensionality reduction techniques, we can easily spot the same outliers from the feature representation maps on Fig. 2b-right (no highlight) at the same locations on Fig. 2a-right (highlighted with small ellipses). Furthermore, the outputs of four other datasets in the same archive, namely, *ItalyPowerDemand*, *Wafer*, *CBF* and *ECG5000* were illustrated in Fig. 3a–d. As the figures show, several thousands of time series can be displayed simultaneously in the same plane. The unbalanced data, the data clusters, and anomalies can be easily identified.

4.2   Visualization Results of the Multivariate Time Series

For multivariate time series, the result of applying PCA followed by t-SNE, namely using $n = 2$ to *JapaneseVowel* is displayed in Fig. 4a. Figure 4b is the output of adding a second t-SNE ($n = 3$) with smaller perplexity to Fig. 4a. Generally, applying just two appropriate transformations should be sufficient to capture an important structure of the data, however in this case we prefer to have more compact clusters. Figure 4c displays two patterns of traffic data flow from the *NetworkFlow*. An inset in the figure shows a two-dimensional projection. The characteristics of the data are very different in large scale, that is the direction of the traffic is just either 1 or 0, whereas the payload sizes are about a few thousand of units. Nevertheless, our approach allows a user to easily spot an outlier. An output of *Wafer* where the wafers were marked either defective (•) or not defect (•) from 1194 signals has been revealed in Fig. 4d.

4.3   Visualization Results of the Motion Capture

The UTD-MHAD Dataset. The outputs of applying the proposed method to the UTD-MHAD can be seen in Fig. 5a–d. Ten actions from Fig. 5a are *DrawCircleCCW, StandToSit, Jog, Walk, SwipeRight, ArmCurl, SwipeLeft, Bowling,*

Catch, and *Clap*. Four actions which involve only one arm movement, *SwipeLeft*, *SwipeRight*, *Catch*, and *DrawCircleCCW* are drawn very close to each other in two-dimensional space; while two-hand movements, *ArmCurl* and *Clap* plots are also close to one another. The actions concerning moving hands and feet such as *Jog* and *Walk* can be related to each other in the plot. The rest of the actions, *StandToSit* and *Bowling* are obviously distinct from other actions. When the transformation algorithms have been changed, this yields different patterns as found in Fig. 5b–c. It is not easy to interpret the data by simply inspecting Fig. 5c without understanding the underlying patterns. There are two viewpoints to be used to interpret this figure: (i) two groups of actions are separated by the dashed line and (ii) four groups of actions which are perpendicular to the dashed line. The first view divides actions into two groups, one group involving actions with just "hands" moving lies on the left side of the dashed line and another group on the right involves actions in which both, "hands" and "legs" move. From the second viewpoint, the data can be seen as four clusters, as data lies perpendicular to the dashed line which is the consequence of rotating subjects around an axis by viewing the same action from four angles (0, 10, 20, and 30°). As a result, these four groups look quite similar to each other but just shifted along the same axis. Moreover, the results of the transformation of twelve actions are displayed in Fig. 5d. We take out three actions, *DrawCircleCCW*, *SwipeRight* and *ArmCurl* and add five actions, *Knock*, *PickupAndThrow*, *SitToStand*, *BasketballShoot*, and *Throw* to the plot. The action *StandToSit* now gets closer to the new action *SitToStand*, whereas the actions about one arm movement *Knock*, *Throw*, *SwipeLeft* and *Catch* lie close to each other. Some data of *Jog* and *Walk* lay close to each other, and the rest of actions such as *BasketballShoot*, *Clap*, *Bowling*, *PickupAndThrow* are properly clustered.

The HDM05 Dataset. The results of applying similar techniques as to the UTD-MHAD to the **HDM05** can be found in Fig. 6a–d. Figure 6a shows 446 trials from ten actions using the default view (0°) of MoCap. The action *jumpDown* (●) has the minimum number of trials because it consists of only 13 trials, of which four trials are from the subject "bd", three trials from the subject "dg" and another three trials from the subject "tr", two trials from the subject "bk" and one trial from the subject "mm". Notice that four trials of the *jumpDown* from the subject "dg" and "mm", ㉞, ㉟, ㊱ and ㊲ lay far away from the others in the brown ellipse. When we looked closely to these particular sequences as depicted in Fig. 7, we found that the subjects "dg" and "mm" have completely different trajectories compared to the subjects "bd", "bk", and "tr". This is because these two subjects turn completely by 90° difference to the camera, or in perpendicular to the other three subjects "bd", "bk", and "tr". This is the reason why those four trials of *jumpDown* are laid afar from the group. Next, when we slightly rotated these five subjects in all trials by 10, 20, and 30°, the patterns of each action in these four viewpoints can be observed in Fig. 6b–d. Figure 6b shows the first three principal components of these four views from the rotations (0°, 10°, 20°, 30°). After exchanging four of ten actions, while six actions are kept as depicted in Fig. 6c and d, **the shapes and distributions**

of these actions still remain the same in the subspaces. Notice the distributions of *jumpDown*, *squat*, *jumpingJack*, *hopLLeg*, *sitDownChair* and *walk* in Fig. 6c comparing to Fig. 6d. Additionally, eight images in Fig. 8 show the comparison of the visualization of *jumpDown* and *walk* between the unthresholded RPs and our feature representations. The RPs are symmetric matrices of size $T_i \times T_i$ but we fit them to the same image size for a comparison. By comparing our extracted features with six components which are laid below each corresponding RP, we can easily spot two distinct groups of action *jumpDown* and *walk*. The RP of action *jumpDown* from the subject "dg" ③④ has a distinctive pattern other than the subject "mm" ③⑦, whereas the extracted features from our method for both actions show about the same features which are in accordance to the trajectories illustrated in Fig. 7. The action *walk* consists of four types of walking, "2StepsL", "2StepsR", "4StepsL", and "4StepsR". The number "2" and "4" indicate the walking steps, while the "L" and "R" indicate whether left or right leg starts. By comparing the RPs of *walk* in Fig. 8, the repetitive actions such as two steps (2Steps) or four steps (4Steps) by our method yield similar fixed small features. The "4Steps" *walk* in the RP reveals two harmonic oscillations or two complete cycles, while "2Steps" shows one cycle of action. Furthermore, an output from the subject "bk" have a distinct feature but quite close to "bd", while the features of "dg" and "mm" are about the same. These results comply with Figs. 6, 7 and 8. The trivial changes e.g., either left leg (L) or right leg (R) starting first have no significance considering from the involved markers on one leg versus the markers on the whole body. The concept of principal components makes the results robust to noise and the trivial changes.

5   Discussion

5.1   Stability and Robustness

The current trends of time series and trajectory classification are to use deep networks by fine-tuning millions of parameters to achieve the best output performance. However, it lacks an explanation of why a particular signal fails. Furthermore, some outliers may lead to overfitting of the training data. Yet, our approach can complement this deficiency by offering a concise feature representation which can give data analyst an understanding of the underlining patterns. By projecting the extracted features onto a two- or three-dimensional space, it provides a visual representation for a data analyst to have an overview of a bunch of data simultaneously. The results are robust to small changes as seen in Figs. 6c, d and Fig. 8. Five images in Fig. 8 show similar feature representations for different types of *walk* (and three images of *jumpDown*) from various subjects leading to the same direction. In addition, even though we employed different transformation techniques, we can still spot the same outliers in different visual representations as the results shown from "Plane" dataset.

5.2   Limitations and Variations of Transformation

Our proposed technique has a few limitations. First and foremost, the dimensionality reduction methods employed in our experiment were selected from several known techniques based on the assumption of linear subspace embedding and nonlinear manifold learning of the data. Therefore, we are not able to tell which technique is the best choice. For instance, the output of employing Multidimensional Scaling (MDS) on *CBF* (previously PCA was employed) now can be seen in Fig. 9a. This new figure shows better separation of three data clusters comparing to Fig. 3c. Changing the transformation of *ECG5000* from PCA (depicted in Fig. 3d) to Kernel PCA in Fig. 9b gives us an interesting alternative viewpoint. Nevertheless, we have had several cases of failure, for instance, *TwoPatterns* in the UCR archive which composes of 5000 sequences. The data clusters cannot be clustered in the way we had expected. The results are shown in Fig. 9c–d. Another failure was also found in case of visualizing the UTD-MHAD dataset when all the actions in a subset involved only hand gestures. This may be because the changes in the movement due to one arm gestures with three corresponding markers (of dimension 3×3) were considered insignificant when compared with the movement of a whole body consisting of 20 markers (of dimension 20×3). Considering PCA which we employed Singular Value Decomposition (SVD) for a matrix decomposition, for any given element i, X^i has an arbitrary size of $m \times T_i$. We may assume that the best rank r of the matrix X^i is the number of crucial time points c_1. The matrix X^i is just a product of two matrices U and V where U is an $m \times c_1$ matrix expressing the weighted factor, and V is a $c_1 \times T_i$ matrix. We keep the most highest weighted factors in U and repeat the process for n times. Hence, the principal components c_n are to be in the final results.

6   Conclusion

In this paper, we have presented a new approach for time series and trajectory visualization by employing existing well-known non-time-series dimensionality reduction techniques. Our proposed methodology does not seek to make an interpretation of an individual signal nor to inspect the changes of data over time. Nonetheless, we can reveal some meaningful information such as the overview of data clusters. Moreover, outliers of each data class can be easily identified. By integrating this technique into a visual analytic pipeline in visualization tools, it can take the load off a data analyst in order to investigate any anomalies presented in the large data size. The datasets applied in the experiments were selected from diverse sources to demonstrate and enforce the robustness of our proposed technique. This technique is not tailored to any particular data type, hence it can be integrated into any application domain. In addition, our approach is very simple to implement and lightweight as well as reproducible across different runs. Finally, it is to be noted that good clustering depends on the inter-relationship of the data structure and the correctly applied manifold learning method to achieve the optimum results.

References

1. Baydogan, M.G., Runger, G.: Time series representation and similarity based on local autopatterns. Data Min. Knowl. Discov. **30**(2), 476–509 (2016). https://doi.org/10.1007/s10618-015-0425-y
2. Chen, C., Jafari, R., Kehtarnavaz, N.: UTD-MHAD: a multimodal dataset for human action recognition utilizing a depth camera and a wearable inertial sensor, vol. 2015-December, pp. 168–172. IEEE Computer Society (2015). https://doi.org/10.1109/ICIP.2015.7350781. http://www.utdallas.edu/~kehtar/UTD-MHAD.html
3. Chen, Y., et al.: The UCR time series classification archive (2015). http://www.cs.ucr.edu/~eamonn/time_series_data/
4. Jäckle, D., Fischer, F., Schreck, T., Keim, D.A.: Temporal mds plots for analysis of multivariate data. IEEE Trans. Vis. Comput. Graph. **22**(1), 141–150 (2016). https://doi.org/10.1109/TVCG.2015.2467553
5. Karim, F., Majumdar, S., Darabi, H., Harford, S.: Multivariate LSTM-FCNs for time series classification (2018)
6. Luczak, M.: Combining raw and normalized data in multivariate time series classification with dynamic time warping. J. Intell. Fuzzy Syst. **34**(1), 373–380 (2018). https://doi.org/10.3233/JIFS-171393
7. Martin, S., Quach, T.-T.: Interactive visualization of multivariate time series data. In: Schmorrow, D.D.D., Fidopiastis, C.M.M. (eds.) AC 2016. LNCS (LNAI), vol. 9744, pp. 322–332. Springer, Cham (2016). https://doi.org/10.1007/978-3-319-39952-2_31
8. Müller, M., Röder, T., Clausen, M., Eberhardt, B., Krüger, B., Weber, A.: Documentation MoCap database HDM05. Technical report CG-2007-2, Universität Bonn, June 2007
9. Nguyen, M., Purushotham, S., To, H., Shahabi, C.: M-TSNE: a framework for visualizing high-dimensional multivariate time series. CoRR abs/1708.07942 (2017)
10. Tanisaro, P., Heidemann, G.: An empirical study on bidirectional recurrent neural networks for human motion recognition. In: The 25th International Symposium on Temporal Representation and Reasoning (TIME) (2018)
11. Tanisaro, P., Lehman, C., Sütfeld, L., Pipa, G., Heidemann, G.: Classifying bio-inspired model of point-light human motion using echo state networks. In: Lintas, A., Rovetta, S., Verschure, P.F.M.J., Villa, A.E.P. (eds.) ICANN 2017. LNCS, vol. 10613, pp. 84–91. Springer, Cham (2017). https://doi.org/10.1007/978-3-319-68600-4_11
12. Tanisaro, P., Mahner, F., Heidemann, G.: Quasi view-independent human motion recognition in subspaces. In: Proceedings of 9th International Conference on Machine Learning and Computing (ICMLC), Singapore, 24–26 February 2017 (2017)

Matching, Tracking and Geometry

Combining Depth Fusion and Photometric Stereo for Fine-Detailed 3D Models

Erik Bylow[1]([⊠])[iD], Robert Maier[2][iD], Fredrik Kahl[3][iD], and Carl Olsson[1,3][iD]

[1] Lund University, Lund, Sweden
erikb@maths.lth.se
[2] Technical University of Munich, Munich, Germany
robert.maier@in.tum.de
[3] Chalmers University of Technology, Gothenburg, Sweden
{fredik.kahl,caols}@chalmers.se

Abstract. In recent years, great progress has been made on the problem of 3D scene reconstruction using depth sensors. On a large scale, these reconstructions look impressive, but often many fine details are lacking due to limitations in the sensor resolution. In this paper we combine two well-known principles for recovery of 3D models, namely fusion of depth images with photometric stereo to enhance the details of the reconstructions. We derive a simple and transparent objective functional that takes both the observed intensity images and depth information into account. The experimental results show that many details are captured that are not present in the input depth images. Moreover, we provide a quantitative evaluation that confirms the improvement of the resulting 3D reconstruction using a 3D printed model.

1 Introduction

Three-dimensional object reconstruction is a classical problem in computer vision. It is still a highly active research area, and we have witnessed steady progress on recovering reliable and accurate representations of scene geometry. There is a wide range of applications where fine-detailed 3D reconstructions play a central role, including visualization, 3D printing, refurbishment and e-commerce.

Several different methods exist for recovering 3D scene geometry. Classical algorithms include Structure from Motion [1,2] which yields sparse point clouds and multiple-view stereo [3,4] which generates dense reconstructions. Since the advent of the Microsoft Kinect, a lot of effort has been put into developing methods that can create dense models directly from the depth images. Kinect-Fusion [5] and extensions like [6,7] can reliably compute high-quality 3D models. However, due to limitations in the resolution of the depth sensor, fine details are often missed in the reconstruction.

To obtain highly detailed 3D models, a common approach is to use photometric stereo [8,9], which can capture fine details under the assumption of

© Springer Nature Switzerland AG 2019
M. Felsberg et al. (Eds.): SCIA 2019, LNCS 11482, pp. 261–274, 2019.
https://doi.org/10.1007/978-3-030-20205-7_22

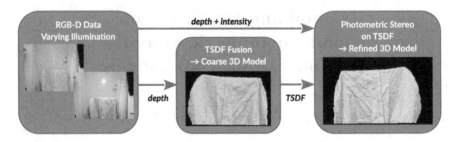

Fig. 1. Out method first fuses all depth images into a single coarse 3D reconstruction without details. This fused 3D model and the intensity images with varying illumination are used to compute a refined 3D model with fine-scale details.

a Lambertian surface [10, Chapter 2]. This technique originates from Shape-from-Shading [11] where surface normals are estimated from a single image. Shape-from-Shading is often considered to be an ill-posed problem. In contrast, photometric stereo uses several images with varying illumination of the same scene, which makes the problem of recovering surface normals well-posed with known lighting. Although some works that utilize multiple views exist, e.g. [12], many methods require that the images are captured from the same view point [9].

The advantages with our formulation are manifold. Many papers that combine depth images and shading only refine a single depth image [13–17]. How to fuse refined depth images from multiple views is not a trivial task. In contrast, we derive an energy functional on the surface using a Truncated Signed Distance Function (TSDF) [18]. This has the advantage that we can combine measurements from different views and refine the whole model at once. Another benefit is that the implicit representation makes it easy to estimate normals since these are directly obtained from the gradient of the TSDF.

Our main contribution is that we derive an objective functional using a TSDF [18] as a parametrization of the surface. This functional takes both intensity and depth information into account together with a varying light source and allows us to handle data captured from different viewpoints. Figure 1 shows a schematic overview of our method. We experimentally demonstrate on real imagery that this results in a system that can recover finer details than current state-of-the-art depth fusion methods. Both quantitative and qualitative evaluations are provided.

1.1 Related Work

Since the launch of the Kinect, several papers have tried to incorporate techniques like Shape-from-Shading [11] into the reconstruction process to enhance the quality of the depth images. For example, [13] improves the entire depth image by estimating the shading and reflectance from a single image. In [14–17], Shape-from-Shading techniques are applied in conjunction with RGB-D images. These approaches typically employ strong priors such as piece-wise constant albedo to constrain the optimization problem. The depth image is often used as a means to resolve the Bas-Relief ambiguity [19]. The idea is to separate albedo and shading to catch fine surface details that are not visible in the depth image. In [20] a fixed depth sensor captures multiple images under varying illumination. Super-resolution and photometric stereo are then combined in a variational framework to get a more detailed depth image. All papers above have in common that they try to obtain a high resolution depth image. In contrast, we work directly over the entire surface and take all views simultaneously into account.

The most closely related work to ours are [21] are [22], where the 3D model is encoded in a TSDF surface representation [18] and refined using Shape-from-Shading techniques. In [21] the fused color information and the fused depth information in the voxel grid are incorporated in a shading based energy functional. The resulting functional is optimized to get an improved reconstruction. Just recently, [22] extended and improved [21] by approximating multiple static light sources to better model the illumination. They additionally used the input intensity images instead of the fused color to measure the difference between rendered intensity gradient and observed intensity gradient. Both [21] and [22] regularize the surface with a Laplacian and the albedo by measuring chromaticity differences between neighboring voxels. Furthermore, [22] also regularizes the light sources with a Laplacian.

In this paper we investigate how one can benefit from the TSDF representation and the observed color and depth images by using ideas from photometric stereo. The main difference between [21,22] and our work is that we allow the light source to vary between the input RGB-D frames. The theoretical motivation to move both the light source as well as the camera is that varying the light source generates richer data, in contrast to keeping the light source fixed as in [21,22].

Furthermore, in addition to the intensity error measure, our energy only has two additional terms: an error penalty that measures deviations from the observed depth maps and an albedo regularizer that penalizes large albedo changes between neighboring voxels. In contrast, both [21] and [22] require smoothness priors on the surface. To the best of our knowledge, we are the first to combine photometric stereo with the TSDF parametrization of the surface. Our results show that by illuminating the object from different directions one can get both a smoother (where appropriate) and a more detailed reconstruction without any explicit smoothness prior. Our results are also compared to [22] and evaluated on a 3D printed model with ground truth data.

2   The Lambertian Surface Model

In this work we assume that the objects we are observing are diffuse. Under the Lambertian reflectance model, the image intensity at a projected point is given by

$$\mathcal{I}(\pi(\mathbf{x})) = \rho(\mathbf{x})\mathbf{s}^T\mathbf{n}(\mathbf{x}), \tag{1}$$

Fig. 2. Two images captured from almost identical viewpoints, but with different illumination. The wrinkles appear differently in the two images, with more prominent details on the right. This effect is caused by the varying light source and not by the surface.

where $\mathcal{I}$ is the observed grayscale image, $\pi(\mathbf{x})$ is the projection of the 3D point $\mathbf{x}$, $\rho(\mathbf{x})$ and $\mathbf{n}(\mathbf{x})$ are the per-voxel surface albedo and normal at $\mathbf{x}$ respectively, and $\mathbf{s}$ is the lighting direction. We assume a rigid scene, hence only the position of the light source and the camera are changing between consecutive input frames. Consequently, by illuminating the scene from varying directions, the observed intensity will be different as visualized in Fig. 2. We show that optimizing the illumination, the albedo and the surface normals to generate image projections that agree with the observed image results in a more detailed reconstruction.

To represent the surface and its albedo we use a TSDF [18], i.e. a voxel grid where each voxel V consists of 8 corners. A corner is denoted with v and contains the two values d_v and ρ_v representing the estimated distance from v to the surface and the albedo at v respectively. We use tri-linear interpolation between the voxel corners to compute distance and albedo estimates within a voxel. We let $g_V : \mathbb{R}^3 \times \mathbb{R}^8 \to \mathbb{R}$ be an interpolation function that takes a point $\mathbf{x}$ within the voxel and the 8 corner values, either $\boldsymbol{\rho}_V = (\rho_{v_1}, ..., \rho_{v_8})$ or $\mathbf{d}_V = (d_{v_1}, ..., d_{v_8})$, where $v_i \in V$, and computes the distance and albedo estimates $g_V(\mathbf{x}, \boldsymbol{\rho}_V)$ and $g_V(\mathbf{x}, \mathbf{d}_V)$ at $\mathbf{x}$.

The Lambertian model in Eq. (1) also requires surface normals in order to estimate image intensities. By normalizing the gradient we get the expression for the normal at a surface point $\mathbf{x} \in V$ by

$$\mathbf{n}(\mathbf{x}, \mathbf{d}_V) = \frac{\nabla g_V(\mathbf{x}, \mathbf{d}_V)}{\|\nabla g_V(\mathbf{x}, \mathbf{d}_V)\|}, \tag{2}$$

where ∇ is a spatial gradient with respect to $\mathbf{x}$.

It was shown in [9] that general lighting conditions can often be better estimated than Eq. (1) by employing low-order spherical harmonics. Their formulation essentially replaces $\mathbf{n}$ and $\mathbf{s}$ in Eq. (1) with 9-dimensional vectors $\tilde{\mathbf{n}}$ and $\tilde{\mathbf{s}}$, where the elements of $\tilde{\mathbf{n}}$ are quadratic expressions in the elements of $\mathbf{n}$. To compute $\tilde{\mathbf{n}}$ we thus first compute $\mathbf{n}$ via Eq. (2) and then use the quadratic functions from [9].

3   Objective Functional

In this section we derive our objective functional that consists of the three terms presented in the following sections.

3.1   Intensity Error Term

We first consider a term that takes the agreement between rendered intensity and the observed image into account. Let us now assume that we have captured a sequence of depth and intensity images $\mathcal{D}$ and $\mathcal{I}$, respectively. We denote the depth image at time step k by $\mathcal{D}^k$ and the corresponding gray-scale intensity image by $\mathcal{I}^k$.

We assume that we have a set $\mathcal{S}$ of surface points that we project into the images and a set of voxels $\mathcal{V}$ that contain the surface. In Sect. 3.2 we describe how these points are extracted from the TSDF. Projecting a surface point $\mathbf{x} \in \mathcal{S}$ contained in voxel V on image k, we can extract the observed intensity at $\mathcal{I}^k(\pi(\mathbf{x}))$. Through the Lambertian reflectance model, we should have

$$\mathcal{I}^k(\pi(\mathbf{x})) \approx \rho(\mathbf{x}, \boldsymbol{\rho}_V)\tilde{\mathbf{n}}(\mathbf{x}, \mathbf{d}_V)^T \tilde{\mathbf{s}}^k. \tag{3}$$

Our first term penalizes deviations from this assumption using

$$E_{\text{Lambert}}(\mathbf{d}, \boldsymbol{\rho}, \tilde{\mathbf{s}}^1, \dots, \tilde{\mathbf{s}}^K) = \sum_{k=1}^{K} \sum_{V \in \mathcal{V}^k} \sum_{\mathbf{x} \in V \cap \mathcal{S}} (\mathcal{I}^k(\pi(\mathbf{x})) - \rho(\mathbf{x}, \boldsymbol{\rho}_V)\tilde{\mathbf{n}}(\mathbf{x}, \mathbf{d}_V)^T \tilde{\mathbf{s}}^k)^2,$$

$$\tag{4}$$

where $\mathcal{V}^k$ is the set of voxels containing the surface observed in frame k, $\mathbf{d}_V$ and $\boldsymbol{\rho}_V$ are the distances and the albedo in the voxel corners of V and $\mathbf{x}$ is a detected surface point in voxel V. The set $\mathcal{V}^k$ is constructed by projecting all voxels in $\mathcal{V}$ into the depth image $\mathcal{D}^k$ and keeping those that are close to the observed surface. Note that each view has its own light source $\tilde{\mathbf{s}}^k$, allowing the lighting conditions to change between views. This error term permits the normals, albedo and the light source to change so that the observed intensities coincide with the rendered intensity. By varying the light source, the same surface point will have different intensities in the images; using that, we seek to improve the three-dimensional shape of the surface.

3.2   Sampling Surface Points

In order to evaluate Eq. (4), we need to compute a set of surface points. Recall that the surface is located in the zero crossing of the TSDF. Any voxel V that is intersected by the surface has both positive and negative values among the distances $\mathbf{d}_V = (d_{v_1}, \dots, d_{v_8})$ stored in the voxel corners $(\mathbf{x}_{v_1}, \dots, \mathbf{x}_{v_8})$. By randomly generating N points $\{\hat{\mathbf{x}}_n\}_{n=1}^N$ in the voxel and computing their interpolations $\hat{d}_n = g_V(\hat{\mathbf{x}}_n, \mathbf{d}_V)$, we get a set of points with signed distances $\{\hat{d}_n\}_{n=1}^N$ to the

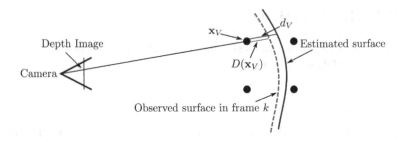

Fig. 3. To penalize large deviations from the observed depth images, we penalize the observed distance to the object surface. This is done for all frames and resolves the Generalized Bas-Relief ambiguity.

surface. If $\hat{d}_n$ is positive, we match it to one of the corner points with negative distances and vice versa. This gives a pair of points $(\mathbf{x}_{v_i}, \hat{\mathbf{x}}_n)$, where the surface lies somewhere on the line segment defined by these points. To find a surface point, we simply traverse the segment until we are sufficiently close to the zero crossing.

3.3 Depth Error Term

The Lambertian term (4) is by itself not sufficient for estimating the normals, albedo and light sources uniquely, due to the well known Generalized Bas-Relief ambiguity [19]. Additionally, while it gives good local normal estimates, computing the surface from local orientation estimates alone is a sensitive process. When normals are integrated, error buildup can cause large depth deviations if the surface depth is not sufficiently constrained. To ensure uniqueness and constrain the overall surface depth, we include information from the depth images.

We define the depth error term as

$$E_{\text{depth}}(\mathbf{d}) = \sum_{k=1}^{K} \sum_{v \in \mathcal{V}^k} (D^k(\mathbf{x}_v) - d_v)^2, \tag{5}$$

where d_v is the currently stored estimated distance to the surface for voxel corners v in $\mathcal{V}^k$ as in [23]. $D^k(\mathbf{x}_v)$ is the estimated distance between observed surface and the voxel in frame k, computed as in [23].

This error term penalizes solutions where the estimated distance is far from the observed depth image, which constrains the surface to resolve the Generalized Bas-Relief ambiguity. We illustrate the underlying idea behind this data term in Fig. 3.

3.4 Albedo Regularization

It is common to put some form of prior on the albedo, see [22] and [24], and we do the same to favor solutions where neighboring voxel corners have similar albedo. This helps to disambiguate between variations in the albedo and the surface geometry. Considered a voxel V with corners $(v_1, \ldots, v_8)$, we penalize the albedo differences between all its neighbouring corners. By summing over all voxels, we get:

$$E_{\text{albedo}}(\boldsymbol{\rho}) = \sum_{V \in \mathcal{V}} \sum_{v_i \neq v_j \in V} (\rho_{v_i} - \rho_{v_j})^2. \tag{6}$$

Note that the corners typically occur among several voxels.

4 Optimization

With the three different error terms defined in Eqs. (4), (5) and (6), we assemble our final objective functional as follows:

$$E(\mathbf{d}, \boldsymbol{\rho}, \tilde{\mathbf{s}}^1, \ldots, \tilde{\mathbf{s}}^K) = E_{\text{Lambert}}(\mathbf{d}, \boldsymbol{\rho}, \tilde{\mathbf{s}}^1, \ldots, \tilde{\mathbf{s}}^K) + \lambda E_{\text{depth}}(\mathbf{d}) + \mu E_{\text{albedo}}(\boldsymbol{\rho}), \tag{7}$$

where λ and μ are positive weights for the individual cost terms.

To optimize over the variables we perform alternating optimization:

1. Extract voxels $\mathcal{V}$ that contain the surface and create the sets $\mathcal{V}^1, \ldots, \mathcal{V}^K$ containing the voxels in $\mathcal{V}$ visible in frame k. Then find surface points in each voxel V.
2. Optimize the light sources $\tilde{\mathbf{s}}^1, \ldots, \tilde{\mathbf{s}}^K$:

$$(\tilde{\mathbf{s}}_{n+1}^1, \ldots, \tilde{\mathbf{s}}_{n+1}^K) = \arg\min_{\tilde{\mathbf{s}}^1, \ldots, \tilde{\mathbf{s}}^K} \sum_{k=1}^K \|A_{\tilde{s}_n}^l \tilde{\mathbf{s}}^k - \mathbf{b}_{\tilde{s}_n}^l\|^2. \tag{8}$$

3. Optimize the albedo values $\boldsymbol{\rho}$:

$$\boldsymbol{\delta}_{\boldsymbol{\rho}}^* = \arg\min_{\boldsymbol{\delta}_{\boldsymbol{\rho}}} \|A_{\rho_n}^l \boldsymbol{\delta}_{\boldsymbol{\rho}} - \mathbf{b}_{\rho_n}^l\|^2 + \mu\|A_{\rho_n}^\rho \boldsymbol{\delta}_{\boldsymbol{\rho}} - \mathbf{b}_{\rho_n}^\rho\|^2 + \gamma_\rho\|\boldsymbol{\delta}_{\boldsymbol{\rho}}\|^2 \tag{9}$$

$$\boldsymbol{\rho}_{n+1} = \boldsymbol{\rho}_n + \boldsymbol{\delta}_{\boldsymbol{\rho}}^*. \tag{10}$$

4. Optimize the distance values $\mathbf{d}$:

$$\boldsymbol{\delta}_{\mathbf{d}}^* = \arg\min_{\boldsymbol{\delta}^{\mathbf{d}}} \|A_{\mathbf{d}_n}^l \boldsymbol{\delta}_{\mathbf{d}} - \mathbf{b}_{\mathbf{d}_n}^l\|^2 + \lambda\|A_{\mathbf{d}_n}^d \boldsymbol{\delta}_{\mathbf{d}} - \mathbf{b}_{\mathbf{d}_n}^d\|^2 + \gamma_{\mathbf{d}}\|\boldsymbol{\delta}_{\mathbf{d}}\|^2 \tag{11}$$

$$\mathbf{d}_{n+1} = \mathbf{d}_n + \boldsymbol{\delta}_{\mathbf{d}}^*. \tag{12}$$

5. Update the TSDF with $\mathbf{d}_{n+1}$ and $\boldsymbol{\rho}_{n+1}$.

In Eq. (8) we optimize directly over the light sources, given the current estimates ρ_n and $\mathbf{d}_n$, which is a linear least-squares problem. To optimize over ρ_n in Eq. (9), we linearize $\rho(\mathbf{x}, \rho_V)$ for each voxel V and obtain the matrices $A^l_{\rho_n}$ and $\mathbf{b}^l_{\rho_n}$. We also put a damping on the step size of δ_ρ to prevent too rapid changes in the albedo. Similarly, for Eq. (11) we linearize $\tilde{\mathbf{n}}(\mathbf{x}_V, \mathbf{d}_V)$ with respect to $\mathbf{d}_V$ analytically and put a damping on the step size. This is crucial, since a too big step can alter the surface severely and ruin the optimization. Furthermore, we are doing local refinements of the surface, so we have a prior that the step size should be small. In fact, the voxel cube has a fixed side-length α, so the distance between the surface and a voxel in that cube cannot be greater than $\sqrt{3}\alpha$. Hence in each iteration we do not want the distance to change more than a fraction of the cube's side-length. Note that due to the use of tri-linear interpolation, all derivatives with respect to $\mathbf{d}_V$ and ρ_V can be computed analytically.

Surface Initialization via Depth Fusion. We essentially follow [5, 18, 23] to initialize the TSDF. Similarly, each voxel corner is assigned an initial albedo estimate ρ derived from the captured gray-scale images. This is used to estimate the appearance of the surface. The light sources are initialized randomly.

5   Experimental Results

To evaluate our method we perform a number of experiments. Note that the approaches [21, 22] do not vary the illumination between images, while other works either fix the light source or do not vary the camera position. The datasets from [21, 22] with fixed light sources are consequently not directly applicable for our approach. Instead, we collect our own data where we record the scene using a depth sensor and illuminate the object with a detached lamp from different directions. For the recordings, we put the camera on a tripod, illuminate the object with a lamp and capture one image at a time.

We also recorded some datasets with fixed light in order to enable a comparison with the approach in [22]. The recordings were taken from approximately the same distance and view point as our sequences. All the results from the algorithm in [22] in our paper were produced by the original implementation.

Furthermore, a sequence of a 3D printed object was acquired. The ground truth for the object is known, hence we can register the obtained reconstructions to the ground truth model and get a quantitative evaluation as well. All sequences were captured using an Asus Xtion Pro Live Sensor with a resolution of 640×480 for both color and depth.

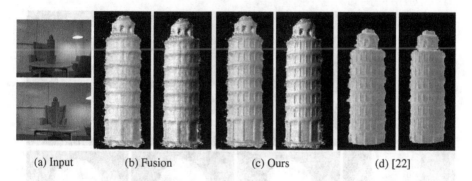

(a) Input   (b) Fusion   (c) Ours   (d) [22]

Fig. 4. (a) Two used input images from the *Tower* sequence. (b) Two shading images from the initial reconstruction using only the depth images. (c) Two shading images from our refined model. (d) Two resulting shadings from [22].

5.1   Qualitative Results

In this section we show results from several experiments on real data and compare our method with [22]. The first result in Fig. 4 is from the *Tower* sequence where we also show some of the input images. The models shown in all experiments are visualized by synthetically rendering the shading image from one of the estimated camera poses with optimized light source.

There is a clear difference between the shading from just fusing the depth and the refined shading using our proposed method, with significantly enhanced details. The presented result of [22] exhibits comparable quality. For this experiment we set $\lambda = 0.001$ and $\mu = 8.5$ and we used 15 images in both our sequence and the sequence for the algorithm in [22].

In the second experiment we scan a statue (Fig. 5) and a shirt with a lot of wrinkles (Fig. 2). The results are displayed in Figs. 5(b)–(d) and 6(b)–(d). The rendered shading images exhibit a significant refinement of the surface normals. In Fig. 5, the eyes and mouth of the statue are much more detailed and fine-scaled compared to the initial solution. The wrinkles in Fig. 6 are much sharper and more prominent in the refined shading image (d) compared to the initial fused shading image (c). In the top row of Fig. 6 the initial albedo (a) can be seen together with the optimized albedo (b). In the initial solution, most shading effects are present in the albedo estimation, in contrast to the optimized solution where most details are in the shading image and the estimated albedo is roughly constant.

The *Statue* experiment consists of 19 images and we set $\lambda = 0.05$ and $\mu = 12.5$, the *Shirt* sequence contains 9 images with the same set of parameters.

5.2   3D Renderings

For a qualitative evaluation, we also render the obtained surfaces with Phong-shading using Menderer [25] in order to visualize the reconstructed 3D model differences between our proposed method and the algorithm from [22]. The results

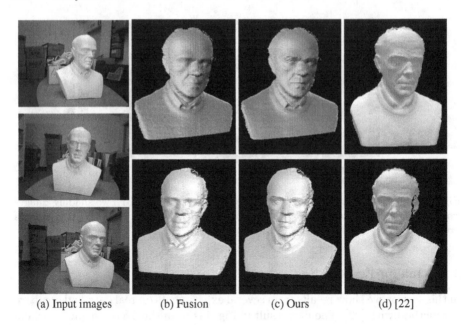

| | | | |
| (a) Input images | (b) Fusion | (c) Ours | (d) [22] |

Fig. 5. (a) Input images from the *Statue* sequence. Shading of initial TSDF (a) in comparison with our method (c) and with [22] (d). The optimized shadings are considerably improved, which is particularly visible at the eyes, mouth and sharper edges of the shirt.

of the *Statue* sequence in Fig. 7 suggest that our method better preserves details on the refined 3D model. Comparing Figs. 7a and b, it is clear that the details on the shirt are better preserved in Fig. 7a. For a better visualization, close-ups are provided in Fig. 7. We believe that the surface regularization in [22] is a reason to why these details are smoothed out. Please note that the holes in Fig. 7a are rendering artifacts due to inverted normals.

Implementation Details. All code is implemented in Matlab. The generally most runtime expensive part is the extraction of 3D points. For the *Shirt* experiment, which is the most time consuming dataset, our method required about 16 seconds per frame. Computing the matrices for optimization takes about 6 seconds per image on a desktop computer with 6 Intel i7-4930K cores and 48 GB of RAM. All experiments typically converged after about 50 iterations.

5.3   Quantitative Evaluation

In the following, we provide quantitative results on the *Tower* dataset, where we have the ground truth 3D model for the 3D printed object. We generated two point clouds, one from the initial model P_{init} and one from the optimized model P_{opt}. Moreover, we also rendered a point cloud from the ground truth data P_{gt}. To measure the quantitative difference between the reconstructions, we selected

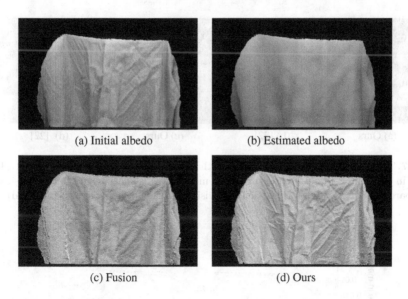

(a) Initial albedo	(b) Estimated albedo
(c) Fusion	(d) Ours

Fig. 6. *Shirt* sequence: (a) Input albedo to our framework. (b) Estimated albedo. (c) Shading from initial solution. (d) Shading from optimized model.

Table 1. RMSE in meters for the initial and the optimized models compared to ground truth. The RMSE for the optimized model is approximately 18% lower.

	Initial model	Optimized model
RMSE (m)	0.00128	0.00105

a part of the ground truth model with valid existing correspondences on the reconstructed model. Then we registered P_{init} and P_{gt}, matched each point in P_{gt} to a point in P_{init} and computed the Root Mean Square Error (RMSE). Similarly, we got the RMSE for P_{opt}.

The results are given in Table 1. The error is about 18% lower for the optimized model, which is a significant improvement. Hence, we obtain millimeter accuracy in the reconstruction. To visualize the quantitative difference, Fig. 8 provides a contour plot of the ground truth, the initial and the optimized models. Looking at the optimized green line and comparing that to the ground truth blue line, it is evident that we manage to get a more exact estimation of the surface. This demonstrates the advantages of (i) optimizing over rendered intensity and (ii) observing the surface from different views to reduce the impact of occlusions.

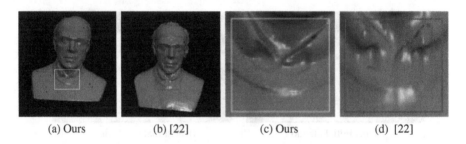

| (a) Ours | (b) [22] | (c) Ours | (d) [22] |

Fig. 7. Qualitative comparison of our method with [22] on the *Statue* dataset. The shirt in the Phong-shaded rendering of our method (a) is sharper and better preserved compared to [22] (b). This is particularly visible in the close-ups shown in (c)–(d).

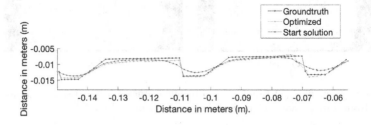

Fig. 8. Contour of the initial surface (red), the optimized surface (green) and the true surface (blue) in a slice through the reconstructed *Tower*. Note that the optimized model better captures the shape of the true surface. (Color figure online)

6   Conclusion and Future Work

In this paper we have successfully combined ideas from photometric stereo and volumetric depth fusion in order to refine a 3D model represented as a TSDF. The derived objective functional favors solutions where the distance values in the TSDF and the albedo make the rendered images consistent with the observations. By illuminating the object from different directions, it is possible to significantly improve the recovery of fine-scale details in the 3D models. The experimental evaluation demonstrates both quantitatively and qualitatively that we obtain accurate reconstruction results of high quality. Potential future work could be how to disambiguate shading from albedo without the L_2-norm.

Acknowledgements. This work was funded by The Swedish Research Council (grant no. 2018-05375), the Wallenberg AI, Autonomous Systems and Software Program (WASP) funded by the Knut and Alice Wallenberg Foundation.

References

1. Thormählen, T., Broszio, H., Weissenfeld, A.: Keyframe selection for camera motion and structure estimation from multiple views. In: Pajdla, T., Matas, J. (eds.) ECCV 2004. LNCS, vol. 3021, pp. 523–535. Springer, Heidelberg (2004). https://doi.org/10.1007/978-3-540-24670-1_40
2. Enqvist, O., Kahl, F., Olsson, C.: Non-sequential structure from motion. In: ICCV Workshops, pp. 264–271, November 2011
3. Newcombe, R.A., Lovegrove, S., Davison, A.J.: DTAM: dense tracking and mapping in real-time. In: ICCV, pp. 2320–2327 (2011)
4. Barnes, C., Shechtman, E., Finkelstein, A., Goldman, D.B.: Patchmatch: a randomized correspondence algorithm for structural image editing. ACM Trans. Graph. 28(3), 24:1–24:11 (2009)
5. Newcombe, R., et al.: Kinectfusion: real-time dense surface mapping and tracking. In: ISMAR, pp. 127–136 (2011)
6. Whelan, T., Leutenegger, S., Salas-Moreno, R.F., Glocker, B., Davison, A.J.: Elasticfusion: dense slam without a pose graph. In: RSS, Rome, Italy, pp. 1697–1716 (2015)
7. Steinbruecker, F., Kerl, C., Sturm, J., Cremers, D.: Large-scale multi-resolution surface reconstruction from RGB-D sequences. In: ICCV, Sydney, Australia (2013)
8. Woodham, R.J.: Photometric method for determining surface orientation from multiple images. Opt. Eng. 19(1), 191139 (1980)
9. Basri, R., Jacobs, D., Kemelmacher, I.: Photometric stereo with general, unknown lighting. IJCV 72(3), 239–257 (2007)
10. Szeliski, R.: Computer Vision: Algorithms and Applications. Springer, Heidelberg (2010). https://doi.org/10.1007/978-1-84882-935-0
11. Horn, B.K.: Shape from shading: a method for obtaining the shape of a smooth opaque object from one view. Technical report, Massachusetts Institute of Technology, Cambridge, MA, USA (1970)
12. Esteban, C.H., Vogiatzis, G., Cipolla, R.: Multiview photometric stereo. T-PAMI 30(3), 548–554 (2008)
13. Barron, J.T., Malik, J.: Intrinsic scene properties from a single RGB-D image. In: CVPR 2013, pp. 17–24 (2013)
14. Han, Y., Lee, J.Y., Kweon, I.S.: High quality shape from a single RGB-D image under uncalibrated natural illumination. In: ICCV, pp. 1617–1624, December 2013
15. Yu, L.F., Yeung, S.K., Tai, Y.W., Lin, S.: Shading-based shape refinement of RGB-D images. In: CVPR, pp. 1415–1422, June 2013
16. Kim, K., Torii, A., Okutomi, M.: Joint estimation of depth, reflectance and illumination for depth refinement. In: ICCV Workshops, pp. 199–207. IEEE Computer Society (2015)
17. Maurer, D., Ju, Y.C., Breuß, M., Bruhn, A.: Combining shape from shading and stereo: a variational approach for the joint estimation of depth, illumination and albedo. In: BMVC, pp. 76.1–76.14 (2016)
18. Curless, B., Levoy, M.: A volumetric method for building complex models from range images. In: Conference on Computer Graphics and Interactive Techniques, New York, USA, pp. 303–312 (1996)
19. Belhumeur, P., Kriegman, D., Yuille, A.: The bas-relief ambiguity. Int. J. Comput. Vis. 35(1), 33–44 (1999)
20. Peng, S., Haefner, B., Quèau, Y., Cremers, D.: Depth super-resolution meets uncalibrated photometric stereo. In: ICCV Workshops (2017)

21. Zollhöfer, M., et al.: Shading-based refinement on volumetric signed distance functions. ACM Trans. Graph. **34**(4), 96:1–96:14 (2015)
22. Maier, R., Kim, K., Cremers, D., Kautz, J., Nießner, M.: Intrinsic3D: high-quality 3D reconstruction by joint appearance and geometry optimization with spatially-varying lighting. In: ICCV, Venice, Italy, October 2017
23. Bylow, E., Sturm, J., Kerl, C., Kahl, F., Cremers, D.: Real-time camera tracking and 3D reconstruction using signed distance functions. In: RSS, Berlin, Germany, vol. 9 (2013)
24. Quéau, Y., Lauze, F., Durou, J.-D.: Solving the uncalibrated photometric stereo problem using total variation. In: Kuijper, A., Bredies, K., Pock, T., Bischof, H. (eds.) SSVM 2013. LNCS, vol. 7893, pp. 270–281. Springer, Heidelberg (2013). https://doi.org/10.1007/978-3-642-38267-3_23
25. Maier, R.: Menderer - batch mesh renderer (2019). https://github.com/robmaier/menderer

Camera Localization by Single View
Query Using One Circular Target

Damien Mariyanayagam$^{(\boxtimes)}$, Pierre Gurdjos, Sylvie Chambon,
and Vincent Charvillat

IRIT, Toulouse, France
damien.mariyanayagam@enseeiht.fr

Abstract. We are concerned with the problem of computing the pose of a (so-called query) camera, from the sole contour of a circular marker in a single view, assuming that we have at one's disposal a set of reference views seeing circular markers, from which the full camera pose and calibration have been precisely estimated. In the calibrated case, regarding the query image alone, there is also a twofold ambiguity in the pose as well as an unknown rotation in the supporting plane of the marker that cannot be fixed. The key idea of this paper is to show that with the additional information of one pair of matched points in both query and reference views, an exact solution for the query pose can be obtained. In order to answer the question whether a given reference view corresponds to the query view, another pair of matched points in both views is then necessary. With multiple matched point pairs, it is possible to deploy a RANSAC-based scheme to assess accurately the best configuration while maintaining robustness to mismatched point pairs. This method shows some promising results especially when the set of point correspondences contains a lot of outliers (erroneous matches).

1 Introduction

The problem of estimating the pose of a calibrated camera in a single view has been widely studied in the computer vision literature e.g., see in [1]. The general case consists in solving a so-called PnP (Perspective-n-Point) problem, using n correspondences of 2D-3D points. The "minimal" problem i.e., which requires the minimal amount of information, is known as P3P and consists in recovering the pose of a calibrated camera from $n = 3$ correspondences with up to 16 real solutions. On the other hand, when using a pair of views, the relative pose of one calibrated camera to another calibrated one can be recovered by using only 2D-2D correspondences. The problem is then that of estimating the essential matrix which has 10 exact solutions given 5 points [2], where the decomposition of such a matrix delivers the pose parameters up to an unknown scale factor. Recently, it is worth noting that a hybrid approach proposes to both use 2D-2D and 2D-3D correspondences to combine the strengths of each method [3].

© Springer Nature Switzerland AG 2019
M. Felsberg et al. (Eds.): SCIA 2019, LNCS 11482, pp. 275–286, 2019.
https://doi.org/10.1007/978-3-030-20205-7_23

In a controlled environment, artificial markers can be laid out into the scene to offer reliable features which are easier to detect and to be matched with others than natural scene features. The most popular artificial markers are probably planar markers [4]. The mapping between a planar marker and its image is a 2D projective transformation known as (world-to-image) homography and can be estimated from at least four world-to-image correspondences. The simplest planar marker is a square, and, consequently, square markers are commonly used [4,5]. Once the camera is calibrated, the decomposition of the homography matrix allows to recover the pose of the marker relative to the camera [6]. Other well-known artificial markers, recently investigated, consist of planar circles [7–10]. In the calibrated case, the image of only one circle suffices to recover the camera pose but there are two solutions for it. In [11], a theoretical framework has been proposed where the pose two-fold ambiguity was investigated. Moreover, the rotation around the normal to the circle (i.e., to its supporting plane) remains unknown. Additional features can be introduced on the circular marker to fix the rotation but it can be really tricky to detect them, in particular when the marker is far from the camera.

In this work, we are concerned with the problem of computing the pose of a circular marker, given a reference view when only its (elliptical) contour is detected in a so-called query view. To our knowledge, the issue of using multiple views of circles in combination with natural point 2D correspondences has been marginally studied. Kahl *et al.* proposed to estimate the fundamental matrix by using correspondences of 5 points and one conic, leading to 10 solutions [12]. Alvarez *et al.* studied the estimation of the world-to-image homography in sport scenarios by using only one circle with some additional information (e.g., like the central line and the central point or a touch line) [13]. Huang et al. proposed a general fusion frame of circles and points to estimate the pose. Starting from an initial guess computed from geometric constraints, they optimized the reprojection error by solving a non-linear least squares problem [14]. However in the case of only one circle in combination with only one additional point as initial guess, their proposed approach lacks of robustness by not considering outliers, which limits its practicability.

We state the problem in the following way. We assume to have at one's disposal a (reference) view of a circular marker from which the full camera pose and calibration could be precisely estimated. Given a second (query) calibrated view in which only the circle is seen, our contribution is to estimate the pose of the second camera w.r.t. the same 3D frame as the first by using additional 2D-2D matches of natural 3D points between the reference and query views. Hence, the 2D arbitrary rotation on the supporting plane can be fixed. First, the pose of the circle is estimated in both images with the previous method published in [11]. It is important to note that any additional point constrains the remaining unknown rotation angle. Consequently, the key idea is to use matched points in a RANSAC-based approach to fix the unknown 2D rotation and, so, the essential matrix. As only one point correspondence is required to compute the essential matrix, we show that our proposed method can be robust to an important number of outliers (erroneous matches) with very few inliers (correct matches).

In the Sect. 2, the problem and its formulation are introduced. Then, in the Sect. 3, the two proposed approaches for solving this problem are described. Finally, results using both synthetic and real data are presented in Sect. 4.

2   Problem Statement

2.1   Context

Suppose a scenario where a collection of circular markers has been placed in some environment, as seen in Fig. 1. Assume that a set of reference views of all these circular markers are given. Moreover, for each view, the local pose of the camera has been pre-computed, possibly using additional information. Indeed, a 3D frame can be attached to the target support plane such that this plane has equation $Z = 0$ and the circle of the target is centered at the origin with its radius equals 1.

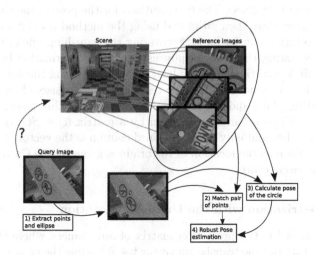

Fig. 1. Illustration of the pose estimation problem. The circle (in red) and points of interest (in green) are first detected and then matched with their counterparts in the reference views. These correspondences are exploited in the proposed approach for pose estimation. (Color figure online)

Given a new view, so-called query view, the aim is to locate the camera associated with the query view i.e. to determine the camera pose, by finding within the dataset the "best" view in which the same marker is seen at the same 3D position. It is already known that using only one image of a circle provides an infinity of solutions with only one degree of freedom for the (calibrated) camera poses. This is due to the ambiguity in rotation around the circle axis which prevents to set a local coordinate system on the marker's support plane. Moreover, each reference view is associated with a unique camera pose w.r.t. the marker's support plane. Consequently, given a reference view and a query view, we get a similar infinity of solutions for the epipolar geometry (in terms of the fundamental or essential matrices) of the view pair. The goal of this paper is to show that with the additional information of one pair of matched points in both views, an exact solution for the query pose (and so for the fundamental/essential matrix) can be obtained. In order to answer the question whether a given reference view corresponds to the query view, another pair of matched points in both views is then necessary. And, with multiple matched point pairs, it is possible to deploy a RANSAC-based scheme to assess accurately the best configuration while maintaining robustness to mismatched point pairs.

2.2   Formulation of the Problem

We consider a pinhole camera model whose intrinsic parameters are known, or, equivalently, without any loss of generality, whose calibration matrix [1] K satisfies $K = I$. For each query view, the ellipse, corresponding to the projection of the circle, is first detected. The two solutions for the pose of the circle relative to the query camera are then estimated using the method provided in [11]. The steps for one solution consist in: (i) recovering the vanishing line of the support plane; (ii) calculating the homography using a parameterization based on the image of the circle and the vanishing line; (iii) decomposing the homography to find the pose in the camera frame. The resulting pose consists of an orientation of the supporting plane and the location of the origin of this plane, fixed to be the circle center. The orientation is given by a matrix $R_q \in SO(3)$ whose first two columns can be randomly fixed and third column is the vector of the normal to this plane. Whereas the location of the origin is given by the Cartesian vector $t_q \in \mathbb{R}^3$ of the circle center.

2.3   Parametrization with the Unknown Rotation

Denote by $P = [R \mid t]$ the projection matrix of any camera where the rotation matrix $R \in SO(3)$ and the translation vector $t \in \mathbb{R}^3$ define the camera pose w.r.t. the object frame. On the one hand, the projection matrix of a reference camera $P_{ref} = [R_{ref} \mid t_{ref}]$ is completely known. On the other hand, the projection matrix of a query camera seeing a circle can be determined up to an unknown rotation around the circle axis. This projection writes $P_q = [R_q R(\theta) \mid t_q]$ where (R_q, t_q) has been computed from the image of a circle and the 2D rotation parameterized by an unknown angle θ:

$$R(\theta) = \begin{bmatrix} \cos\theta & -\sin\theta & 0 \\ \sin\theta & \cos\theta & 0 \\ 0 & 0 & 1 \end{bmatrix}$$

Suppose that a point is seen on both the reference image and the query image, with their respective augmented vectors $\mathbf{u}_1 = [u_1, v_1, 1]^\top$ and $\mathbf{u}_2 = [u_2, v_2, 1]^\top$. If we assume that these two image points are in correspondence i.e., they are the images of the same 3D point with augmented Cartesian vector $\mathbf{X} = [X, Y, Z, 1]^\top$, then the unknown rotation $R(\theta)$ can be solved using the system of two equations $\mathbf{u}_1 \sim [R_{\text{ref}} \mid \mathbf{t}_{\text{ref}}]\mathbf{X}$ and $\mathbf{u}_2 \sim [R_q R(\theta) \mid \mathbf{t}_q]\mathbf{X}$. To get rid of the 3D point $\mathbf{X}$, this hypothesis is used: the rotation $R(\theta)$ of the second camera (corresponding to query image) has to be estimated so that the back-projection rays (obtained by back-projecting the matched image points $\mathbf{u}_1$ and $\mathbf{u}_2$) intersect in 3D space. For a camera with projection matrix P, the 3D line corresponding to the back projection of an image point $\mathbf{u} = [u, v, 1]^\top$ can be expressed in matrix form using its Plücker representation as[1]:

$$L = P^\top [\mathbf{u}]_\times P \quad \text{and} \quad L = \begin{pmatrix} [\mathbf{m}]_\times & \mathbf{d} \\ -\mathbf{d}^\top & 0 \end{pmatrix} \tag{1}$$

with $\mathbf{d}, \mathbf{m} \in \mathbb{R}^3$ where $(\mathbf{d}, \mathbf{m})$ is the so-called Plücker coordinates of the line.

Call the reference camera the camera number 1: the Plücker coordinates $(\mathbf{d}_1, \mathbf{m}_1)$ of the line obtained by back-projecting a reference point $\mathbf{u}_1$ are

$$(\mathbf{d}_1, \mathbf{m}_1) = ((R_{\text{ref}})^\top \mathbf{u}_1, \mathbf{c}_1 \times \mathbf{d}_1)$$

where $\mathbf{c}_1 = -(R_{\text{ref}})^\top \mathbf{t}_{\text{ref}}$. Call the query camera the camera number 2: we have almost the same equation for the Plücker coordinates $(\mathbf{d}_2, \mathbf{m}_2)$ of the back-projection of a reference point $\mathbf{u}_2$ with the difference that there is an unknown rotation matrix $R(\theta)$

$$(\mathbf{d}_2, \mathbf{m}_2) = (R(\theta)^\top \mathbf{d}_2', R(\theta)^\top \mathbf{m}_2')$$

where $\mathbf{d}_2' = (R_q)^\top \mathbf{u}_2$, $\mathbf{m}_2' = \mathbf{c}_2' \times \mathbf{d}_2'$ and $\mathbf{c}_2' = -(R_q)^\top \mathbf{t}_q$.

Now, it is necessary to determine θ. We seek a value of θ such that the distances between the two 3D lines obtained by back-projections from the reference and query cameras is zero i.e., such that the two lines intersect. For that, the so-called reciprocal product of the Plücker coordinates [15] is introduced. Any two 3D lines have a common perpendicular which intersects both at right angles at two points (one on each line) called the feets of the common perpendicular. The distance between the two lines equals the distance between these two feets which are the closest points in space on the respective lines. Its expression involves the *reciprocal product* of the Plücker coordinates of the two lines which is defined as

$$(\mathbf{d_1}, \mathbf{m_1}) * (\mathbf{d_2}, \mathbf{m_2}) = \mathbf{d}_1 R(\theta)^\top \mathbf{m}'_2 + \mathbf{d}_2'^\top R(\theta) \mathbf{m}_1 \tag{2}$$

and equals zero when the two 3D lines intersect.

---

[1] $[\mathbf{a}]_\times = \begin{pmatrix} 0 & -a_3 & a_2 \\ a_3 & 0 & -a_1 \\ a_2 & a_1 & 0 \end{pmatrix}$ is the order-3 skew-symmetric matrix of $\mathbf{a} \in \mathbb{R}^3$ such that

$[\mathbf{a}]_\times \mathbf{b} = \mathbf{a} \times \mathbf{b}$, for all $\mathbf{b} \in \mathbb{R}^3$.

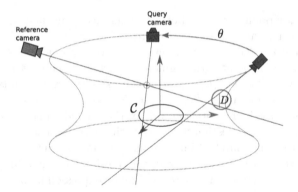

Fig. 2. Which angle θ makes the back-projection of a matched point from the query camera intercept that of the reference camera?

It is worth noting that, by varying θ, and thus rotating the back-projection ray of the second camera (query) around the axis defined by the normal of the circle $\mathcal{C}$ and its center, we generate a hyperboloid, see Fig. 2. As the problem becomes that of finding the intersection of the hyperboloid of one sheet with a line, there are exactly zero, one or two real solutions. The ambiguity cannot be solved directly without some other considerations. As an example, in some theoretical cases, the intersections of the hyperboloid with the back-projection ray are separated with the principal plane whereas, in practical cases, both solutions are in front of the camera and most of the time in a small sphere centered around the marker. The correct solutions can be identified only if several points are involved. In this context, we propose two methods to solve the problem. First, several points are used to obtain a linear system of equations in cosine and sinus with the circular constraint. Second, the minimal case with only one correspondence can be considered, the equation is directly solved (two exact solutions are estimated) and a consensus approach using all the other correspondences are then used.

3   Pose Estimation from One Circle and Several Correspondences

We explained previously that, to estimate the full pose of the query camera relative to the reference camera, we need to determine a 2D rotation in the supporting plane of the circle. To that end, each point correspondence brings a new equation, depending on the rotation angle θ, in which the reciprocal product (2) vanishes. In this section, we will explain how to calculate this angle in a robust way using several correspondences of points. Here, only one reference image is considered but this step must be carried out for every candidate reference image. The correct reference image can then be picked up as that of providing the greatest number of correspondences (inliers in robust case).

3.1   Linear Formulation with Quadratic Constrains

As already said, the revolution of a back-projection ray from a query point, around the axis defined by the normal of the circle and its center, forms a hyperboloid of one sheet in 3-space, see Fig. 2. Solving the rotation consists in finding its intersection with the back-projection ray of a corresponding reference point. Several cases are then possible, there are zero, one or two real solutions to this problem. It is easy to see that the equation obtained by vanishing (2) can be written as a linear combination of $x_1 = \cos\theta$ and $x_2 = \sin\theta$ with the constraint $x_1^2 + x_2^2 = 1$. In fact, it can be interpreted in 2D as the problem of intersecting a circle $(x_1^2 + x_2^2 = 1)$ with a line $(ax_1 + bx_2 + c = 0)$, where a, b, c are parameters only depending on the Plücker coordinates of the back-projection lines.

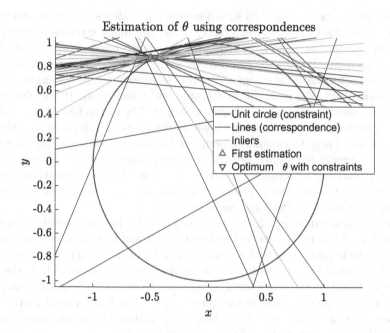

Fig. 3. Example of lines, solution of the Eq. 2 in x_1 and x_2. (Color figure online)

In this part, we want to study if several pairs of matched points can be used jointly to solve the problem of estimating the missing rotation. Instead of having one line to intersect a circle, we will have a bunch of lines intersecting each others and the circle, see Fig. 3. It can be interesting to normalize the equation vanishing (2) before using them with a solver. Indeed, if we normalize the Plücker coordinates of the 3D lines then the reciprocal product (2) corresponds to the moment between the lines. We can write [15]

$$\mathtt{d}_1 \mathtt{R}(\theta)^T \mathtt{m}_2' + \mathtt{d}_2' \mathtt{R}(\theta) \mathtt{m}_1 = D \sin\gamma \tag{3}$$

where γ is the angle between the two lines and D is their relative distance. Thus, minimizing the set of equations, with norm L_1 for robustness to erroneous data, is then minimizing the sum of the distances between the back-projection rays of image features.

First, the solution is initialized using a linear least squares solution without the circular constraint. We can see, in Fig. 3, that the linear least squares solution, represented by a red triangle point, does not lie necessary on the circle but tries to fit a maximum of lines. Then, we use a non linear squares solver ensuring the circular constraint, the blue triangle on Fig. 3 now corresponds to this solution.

3.2   Robust Solution Using Minimal Number of Correspondences

The first proposition implies to simultaneously use all the correspondences to calculate a solution. However, in practice there are many erroneous correspondences of points. We have seen that only one correspondence is sufficient to calculate an angle. Indeed, we can directly solve the cosine equation which can lead up to 2 solutions for the angle. We propose to use a random sample consensus approach, MSAC (M-estimator SAmple and Consensus) [16], to deal with cases where many points are incorrectly matched. The method consists in selecting the minimal number of correspondences (only one in our case) to estimate the angle and, then, to evaluate among all the other points, the inliers which fit the pose model (estimated with this correspondence). The process is then repeated iteratively to minimize a fitting function while ensuring that enough points are selected as inliers. The inlier points can then be used at the end of the process to estimate the angle more precisely.

The equation vanishing (2) can be solved directly but this direct estimation can lead from 0 to 2 real solutions for the angle. If there is at least one solution for the angle, the hypothesis is then evaluated with the others points. Once an angle has been estimated we can evaluate which points validate the model. As the real location of the 3D point is unknown, we propose to evaluate the distance in pixel of a point to its epipolar line in the query image. The fundamental matrix can be constructed as follows using the projection matrix of the reference camera P_{ref} and the projection matrix of the query camera P_q:

$$O_{ref} \sim P_q \left[t_{ref}\ 1 \right]^\top$$

$$F \sim [O_{ref}]_\times P_q P_{ref}^+$$

where P_{ref}^+ is the pseudo-inverse of the reference camera projection matrix (see [17, p. 244]). We can note that O_{ref} is the coordinates of the center of the reference camera in the query camera frame. Then, to calculate the distance of a point to the model, we first calculate its epipolar line in the query image, $l_{ref} \sim F u_1$ and calculate its distance to this line. Consequently, the greater the distance, the more likely it is that the point is an outlier. To distinguish outliers from inliers, we can apply a threshold to this distance[2].

---

[2] Experimentally, this threshold has been set to 5 pixels.

4   Results

We have evaluated our method on both synthetic and real images. We compute the accuracy of the relative pose of the camera related to the marker and assess the correctness of the reference image identification, i.e. how the approach is able to identify the corresponding reference image.

4.1   Test Description

Image Dataset. For the synthetic tests, we used the virtual office room from the ICL-NUIM dataset[3] to generate a virtual scene by adding circular markers on different elements of the scene, and also some synthetic images from different points of views using PovRay. More precisely, 8 circular markers have been projected on the scene, at different locations. We have first generated one reference image for each marker. Then, 25 new images have been generated from 25 different points of view, far enough from the marker so it can not be recognized by its code. These 25 views are used as query images, i.e. images where we want to recognize the marker, based on the detection of the contour of the ellipse of the marker and the points of interest detected around this marker.

For the real images we have placed 14 markers in an office room. Our "ground truth" for the camera poses has been computed using a chessboard around each marker. Finally, 44 images have been taken using a OnePlus 5 smartphone camera with at least 2 different views for each marker. Some examples of the synthetic and real images used in our test can be seen in Fig. 4.

Fig. 4. Samples of the images used in our test: real at left, synthetic at right

Points of Interest. They have been detected and matched for each pair of reference/query images by using the AliceVision[4] library which is based on SIFT for detection and for matching. We have limited the number of points to 1000 per image. This restriction assures that the best points are kept and that they cover an equally distributed grid on the image. Points have been matched and filtered with Lowe ratio criteria [18] set at 0.8. Ellipses in both synthetic and

---

[3] https://www.doc.ic.ac.uk/~ahanda/VaFRIC/iclnuim.html.

[4] https://alicevision.github.io/.

real images are detected by following these steps: first ellipse points are detected using a Sobel filter, second, these points are connected using propagation of an elliptical arc and then the parameters of the ellipse are estimated with [19].

Criteria. For each query image, using the proposed method, we compute the identification of the marker and the pose of the camera relative to the plane. Regarding the pose, what is evaluated is the angle, θ, which is the sole unknown dof of the 2D rotation in the support plane of the circle. Additionally, the errors on the relative orientation and the position of the camera have been computed. The first criterion evaluates how the addition of new point correspondences allows the calculation of the missing dof (rotation). The last criteria evaluate the global quality of the pose estimation given by both the circle image and points.

4.2 Results on the Pose Estimation

The Table 1 displays the results for the recognition rate of the marker and the Fig. 5 shows the error on the estimated pose. We distinguish the two proposed P1CnP (Perspective with 1 Circle and n Points) methods: "P1CnP least-square" refers to that described in Sect. 3.1 which solves the problem directly with all correspondences and "P1CnP MSAC" to that introduced in Sect. 3.2 which solves the problem using a RANSAC-based scheme.

Table 1. Percentage of recognition, we distinguish real and synthetic data.

Method	True positive	
	Real	Synthetic
P1CnP least-square	70.45%	88%
P1CnP MSAC	84.09%	84%

A first general comment is that the results on the synthetic images are worst that on real images. This can be explained because there are more untextured regions or repetitive textures in our synthetic images than in real images, so, we have obtained a lower number of correct matches and, therefore, the pose estimation contains more errors. On Fig. 5, we can see that the method using only 1 point with the random consensus is more accurate than the direct least-square method with the constraint. The first line of figures are the most interesting, we can see that additional correspondences of points give an accurate estimation of the rotation around the normal of the plane, the median is below 2° for real images. The other figures show the results on the complete method to estimate the pose: the orientation and the position. The results are quite good for the pose estimation for real images especially if we consider the apparent small size of the marker in comparison to the image as we can see in the image samples (the marker is at the center of the chessboard pattern). Moreover the markers are generally well identified using the reference images as seen in Table 1. However there are some cases on both synthetic and real images where the identification fails. The identification only relies on the number of inlier correspondences. So when some markers are close to each other and share common points of interest, the angle may not be discriminant enough to distinguish the correct reference. Additionally, we think that the initial pose obtained can be easily improved if we suppose that we can use this initial estimation in a further optimization process using the estimated coordinates of the inliers points. Concerning the execution time for the pose estimation, the MSAC algorithm converges rather quickly. For instance with a request image with 1000 correspondences to a reference image, the algorithm takes about 30 ms using Matlab and without any particular optimization.

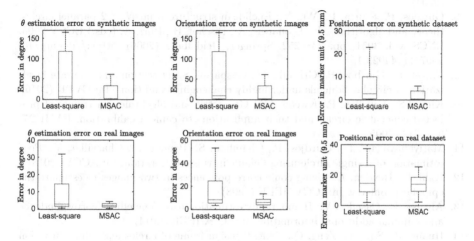

Fig. 5. Results on synthetic (top) and real (bottom) images: Error on the rotation $R(\theta)$ (left), orientation error (middle) and position error (right)

5   Conclusion

In this paper, using circular markers to estimate the pose, we have introduced a new method that is able to produce an accurate solution, assuming that only the contour of this marker can be reliably detected. The originality of the approach is to combine the detection of the contour of the marker with the use of several points of interest in correspondence. We have shown that this method can provide a good estimation even when there are many erroneous matches.

References

1. Szeliski, R.: Computer Vision: Algorithms and Applications. Springer, Heidelberg (2010). https://doi.org/10.1007/978-1-84882-935-0
2. Nistér, D.: An efficient solution to the five-point relative pose problem. PAMI **26**, 756–777 (2004)
3. Camposeco, F., Cohen, A., Pollefeys, M., Sattler, T.: Hybrid camera pose estimation. In: CVPR (2018)
4. Fiala, M.: Designing highly reliable fiducial markers. PAMI **32**, 1317–1324 (2010)
5. Wagner, D., Schmalstieg, D.: Artoolkitplus for pose tracking on mobile devices. In: Computer Vision Winter Workshop (2007)
6. Sturm, P.: Algorithms for plane-based pose estimation. In: CVPR, vol. 1. IEEE (2000)
7. Wu, H., Chen, Q., Wada, T.: Conic-based algorithm for visual line estimation from one image. In: Conference on Automatic Face and Gesture Recognition. IEEE (2004)
8. Gurdjos, P., Sturm, P., Wu, Y.: Euclidean structure from $N \geq 2$ parallel circles: theory and algorithms. In: Leonardis, A., Bischof, H., Pinz, A. (eds.) ECCV 2006. LNCS, vol. 3951, pp. 238–252. Springer, Heidelberg (2006). https://doi.org/10.1007/11744023_19
9. Calvet, L., Gurdjos, P., Griwodz, C., Gasparini, S.: Detection and accurate localization of circular fiducials under highly challenging conditions. In: CVPR (2016)
10. Kim, J.S., Gurdjos, P., Kweon, I.S.: Geometric and algebraic constraints of projected concentric circles and their applications to camera calibration. PAMI **27**, 637–642 (2005)
11. Mariyanayagam, D., Gurdjos, P., Chambon, S., Brunet, F., Charvillat, V.: Pose estimation of a single circle using default intrinsic calibration. In: ACCV (2018)
12. Kahl, F., Heyden, A.: Using conic correspondences in two images to estimate the epipolar geometry. In: ICCV. IEEE (1998)
13. Alvarez, L., Caselles, V.: Homography estimation using one ellipse correspondence and minimal additional information. In: ICIP. IEEE (2014)
14. Huang, B., Sun, Y., Zeng, Q.: General fusion frame of circles and points in vision pose estimation. Optik **154**, 47–57 (2018)
15. Mason, M.T.: Mechanics of Robotic Manipulation. MIT Press, Cambridge (2001)
16. Torr, P.H., Zisserman, A.: MLESAC: a new robust estimator with application to estimating image geometry. CVIU **78**, 138–156 (2000)
17. Hartley, R., Zisserman, A.: Multiple View Geometry in Computer Vision. Cambridge University Press, Cambridge (2003)
18. Lowe, D.G.: Distinctive image features from scale-invariant keypoints. IJCV **60**, 91–110 (2004)
19. Szpak, Z.L., Chojnacki, W., van den Hengel, A.: Guaranteed ellipse fitting with a confidence region and an uncertainty measure for centre, axes, and orientation. JMIV **52**, 173–199 (2015)

Global Trifocal Adjustment

Patrik Persson$^{(\boxtimes)}$ and Kalle Åström$^{(\boxtimes)}$

Centre for Mathematical Sciences, Lund University, Lund, Sweden
{patrik.persson,karl.astrom}@math.lth.se

Abstract. In this paper we introduce a fast and robust structure-less alternative to full bundle adjustment. The method is based on optimizing algebraic errors for trilinear constraints from triplets of views. It is shown that the error generated by a triplet of views can be described by a fixed triangular 27×27 matrix regardless of the number of feature correspondences between the views. The method has been evaluated on various real and synthetic datasets and shows good convergence properties with a large convergence basin and solutions that are close to the optimal solution. The method has been compared to Global Epipolar Adjustment, GEA, which is based on the bilinear constraint. It will be shown that the method can handle the degenerate configurations of GEA.

Keywords: Structure-less bundle adjustment · SFM · Optimization

1 Introduction

Structure from motion [10], is the problem of estimating the parameters of scene structure and of camera motion using image features. Assuming that feature position errors are zero-mean Gaussian, the maximum likelihood estimate is that of minimizing the sum of squares of the residuals. The theory and methods go back to the developments of Gauss and Legendre, cf. [8,15]. In the photogrammetry and computer vision literature this process is denoted bundle adjustment, where 'bundle' refers to the bundle of light rays connecting each camera with each 3D point. For an overview of the literature and theory see [25]. For examples of bundle adjustment in photogrammetry see [9].

Bundle adjustment is almost always used both as a final step for the estimation of the parameters, and as an intermediary steps e.g. during tracking, where it has been demonstrated to reduce failures, [6,14]. There are several software packages for bundle adjustment, e.g. SBA [18], Bundler [23,24], and general optimization packages such as Ceres [1]. Many of these take advantage of recent developments in making large scale bundle adjustment fast using e.g. the sparsity and the structure of the problem, [3,4]. This has made it possible to solve large scale bundle adjustment problems as shown in [2,5,20,23]. It has also been shown how bundle adjustment can be used in real-time as a component of SLAM systems using autonomous vehicles.

© Springer Nature Switzerland AG 2019
M. Felsberg et al. (Eds.): SCIA 2019, LNCS 11482, pp. 287–298, 2019.
https://doi.org/10.1007/978-3-030-20205-7_24

Despite these development, many of these algorithms still need to go through all data at each step. This limits how fast the bundle adjustment can be. As an alternative there are structure less approaches, which although approximate can give satisfactory results at a much increased speed. One example of this is the approach of Global Epipolar Adjustment [17,22], in which a simplified error metric based on the linear constraint on the epipolar constraints for each pair of images. Another is incremental light bundle adjustment, iBLA, [13] in which an error metric based on a combination of epipolar constraints and a variant of the trifocal constraint is used.

In this paper we introduce a method based on the trifocal constraint from each image triplet. One argument for this is the fact that bilinearities do not restrict the image correspondences fully as shown in [12], whereas trilinearities are sufficient. Another argument is that bilinearites does not restrict camera motions, e.g. if the camera motion is linear. As will be demonstrated in the paper it turns out that using trilinearities gives a larger basin of convergence as compared to using bilinearities. Contrary to iBLA, the proposed method can significantly reduce the number of residuals that need to be evaluated to a fix 27 residuals per triplet of views regardless of the number of feature correspondences. In iBLA each feature correspondence in three views would result in a residual. This makes the computational cost dependent on the number of correspondences which typically is in the order of hundreds.

2 The Bundle Adjustment Problem

A widely accepted model of image formation is the pinhole camera model

$$\lambda \mathbf{x} = \begin{bmatrix} \gamma f & s & x_0 \\ 0 & f & y_0 \\ 0 & 0 & 1 \end{bmatrix} \begin{bmatrix} R & -RT \end{bmatrix} \begin{bmatrix} X \\ Y \\ Z \\ 1 \end{bmatrix} \iff \qquad (1)$$

$$\lambda \mathbf{x} = K \begin{bmatrix} R & -RT \end{bmatrix} \mathbf{X} = P\mathbf{X}, \qquad (2)$$

where $\mathbf{X} = \begin{bmatrix} X\,Y\,Z\,1 \end{bmatrix}^T$ denotes homogeneous object coordinates, $\mathbf{x} = \begin{bmatrix} x\,y\,1 \end{bmatrix}^T$ homogeneous image coordinates, λ depth, rotation matrix R and translation vector T are the extrinsic parameters and K contains the intrinsic parameters.

Given an initial set of cameras P_i, object points $\mathbf{X}_p$ and observations of these $\mathbf{x}_{ip}$, bundle adjustment seeks to minimize the total re-projection error in all views

$$e = \sum_i \sum_p \| x_{ip} - \frac{1}{\lambda_{ip}} P_i \mathbf{X}_p \|^2 \qquad (3)$$

by optimizing over the cameras and object points. This error function can be minimized using iterative algorithms. Several fast algorithms exists that exploit the sparse structure of the problem.

Typically the number of object points greatly exceed the number of cameras. To avoid having to include all the object points in the bundle adjustment, the global epipolar adjustment method [17, 22], GEA, exploits the epipolar, also called bilinear, constraint between camera pairs. This constraint only depends on the camera parameters and the observed features and do not include object points. This allows the adjustment method to only optimize over the camera parameters allowing for structure-less bundle adjustment.

The epipolar constraint between view i and j is expressed as

$$x_{ip}^T E_{ij} x_{jp} = x_{ip}^T R_i \left[\frac{T_j - T_i}{\|T_j - T_i\|} \right]_\times R_j^T x_{jp} = 0, \tag{4}$$

where R_i, R_j represents the rotations and T_i, T_j the camera center of cameras i and j. Here x_{ip} and x_{jp} represents the observations of object point p in camera i and j. By collecting all the epipolar constraints between possible pairs of views

$$C_e = \sum_{i,j} \sum_p (x_{ip}^T E_{ij} x_{jp})^2 \tag{5}$$

the cost function used in GEA is found. This cost function can be rewritten as

$$C_e = \sum_{i \neq j} e_{ij}^T M_{ij}^T M_{ij} e_{ij}, \tag{6}$$

where e_{ij} is a vectorized column matrix of E_{ij} and M_{ij} is the Jacobian of the constraints between view i and j with respect to e_{ij}. The matrix M_{ij} is of size $n_{ij} \times 9$ where n_{ij} is the number of corresponding points between the views. The matrix can be reduced to an equivalent 9×9 matrix $\tilde{M}_{ij}$ in the sense that the error $e_{ij}^T M_{ij}^T M_{ij} e_{ij} = e_{ij}^T \tilde{M}_{ij}^T \tilde{M}_{ij} e_{ij}$ will be the same for all e_{ij}. $\tilde{M}$ can be calculated using QR factorization of M_{ij}. This greatly reduces the number of residuals that need to be evaluated at each iteration.

The matrices M_{ij} and $\tilde{M}_{ij}$ are independent of the camera parameters and can be computed once and then be reused in future iterations.

3   The Trifocal Tensor

While GEA uses the bilinear constraint to perform optimization, GTA uses the trilinear constraint involving three cameras instead of two. The constraint can be expressed as [11]

$$\frac{1}{2} \epsilon_{ii'i''} \epsilon_{jj'j''} \epsilon_{kk'k''} \det \begin{bmatrix} A^{i'} \\ A^{i''} \\ B^j \\ C^k \end{bmatrix} x_A^i x_B^{j'} x_C^{k'} = 0_{j''k''}, \tag{7}$$

where A, B and C denote the three camera matrices and x_A, x_B and x_C the observations of an object point. A^i corresponds to the i:th row of A and

$\mathbf{x}_A = \begin{bmatrix} x_A^1 & x_A^2 & x_A^3 \end{bmatrix}^T$. Here $\epsilon_{ii'i''}$ denotes the permutation symbol, j'' and k'' denotes free indices and can be selected from $\in [1, 2, 3]$. From these 9 constraints only 4 are linear independent.

Using the trifocal tensor

$$_I^{JK}T_i^{jk} = \frac{1}{2}\epsilon_{ii'i''} \det \begin{bmatrix} P_I^{i'} \\ P_I^{i''} \\ P_J^{j} \\ P_K^{k} \end{bmatrix} \tag{8}$$

the constraint can be expressed as

$$_I^{JK}T_i^{jk}\mathbf{x}_I^i\epsilon_{jj'j''}\mathbf{x}_J^{j'}\epsilon_{kk'k''}\mathbf{x}_K^{k'} = 0_{j''k''}. \tag{9}$$

This constraint is linear in the components of the trifocal tensor, which makes it possible to estimate it using linear methods. By vectorizing the tensor $_I^{JK}T_i^{jk}$ into a 27×1 column-vector $\mathbf{t}$ and forming the Jacobian matrix A of the trilinear constraints with respect to t, the equation system

$$A\mathbf{t} = 0 \tag{10}$$

can be formed. The tensor can now be found by solving this equation system. Next, the camera matrices can be extracted from the tensor. For a more comprehensive description of how to form A, see [21]. In the rest of the paper, A will be called cost matrix.

Besides the trilinear constraint on point correspondences, there exists constraints involving line correspondences and combinations of lines and points, see [11] and [21].

4   Global Trifocal Adjustment

One issue with using linear methods to solve for the trifocal tensor is, that due to noise in the feature correspondences, the solution may not result in a valid tensor. Instead of directly solving for the trifocal tensors and then extracting the camera matrices, we propose to parameterize the trifocal tensors with the rotation and translation of the cameras and solving the minimization problem

$$\Theta = \underset{(\theta_1,\cdots,\theta_n)}{\arg\min} \sum_{(i,j,k)\in Q} W_{ijk}^2\|A_{ijk}\mathbf{t}_{ijk}(\theta_i, \theta_j, \theta_k)\|^2, \tag{11}$$

$$W_{ijk} = \frac{1}{\|T_i - T_j\|} + \frac{1}{\|T_i - T_k\|} + \frac{1}{\|T_k - T_j\|} \tag{12}$$

using an iterative scheme such as Levenberg-Marquardt (LM) [16,19]. We use Q to denote the set of triplets of cameras, A_{ijk} is the cost matrix for the triplet and $\mathbf{t}_{ijk}$ is the vectorized trifocal tensor of the triplet. Here $\theta_i = (R_i, T_i)$ parameterize the rotation and camera center of camera i respectively. The first camera in the set of all the cameras defines the coordinate system and the distance to the second camera is constrained to one to fix the scale. Using this parameterization, we can ensure that all estimated trifocal tensors are valid at every iteration. W_{ijk} has been added to prevent the system form converging to the trivial solution where all camera centres coincide.

It is important to notice that several cameras are optimized jointly in (11) and Q is the set of triplets of these cameras, where one camera can belong to several triplets. The set Q can be formed in several ways, ranging from forming all possible triplets of the involved cameras to a minimum of connected triplets of cameras.

4.1   Reducing the Number of Residuals

Each cost matrix A_{ijk} is of size $N_{ijk} \times 27$. Here N_{ijk} depends on the number of corresponding features between the three views and the number of linear independent constraints that can be generated from each correspondence, e.g. for a point correspondence there exists 4 independent constraints. Similar to the procedure in GEA, the A_{ijk} matrix can be replaced by an equivalent reduced matrix $\tilde{A}_{ijk}$, this time of dimensions 27×27.

Considering the error of one triplet of cameras

$$e = \|A_{ijk}\mathbf{t}_{ijk}\|^2 \tag{13}$$

$$= \mathbf{t}_{ijk}^T A_{ijk}^T A_{ijk}\mathbf{t}_{ijk}, \tag{14}$$

QR decomposition of $A_{ijk} = QR$ can be performed. Substituting in the above expression we get

$$e = \mathbf{t}_{ijk}^T A_{ijk}^T A_{ijk}\mathbf{t}_{ijk} = \mathbf{t}_{ijk}^T R^T Q^T Q R \mathbf{t}_{ijk} \tag{15}$$

$$= \mathbf{t}_{ijk}^T R^T R \mathbf{t}_{ijk} = \mathbf{t}_{ijk}^T \begin{bmatrix} R_1^T & 0 \end{bmatrix} \begin{bmatrix} R_1 \\ 0 \end{bmatrix} \mathbf{t}_{ijk} \tag{16}$$

$$= \mathbf{t}_{ijk}^T R_1^T R_1 \mathbf{t}_{ijk}. \tag{17}$$

Here R_1 is of dimension 27×27. The reduced matrix can thus be selected as $\tilde{A}_{ijk} = R_1$. This matrix will be equivalent to A_{ijk} in the sense that they will generate the same error $\mathbf{t}_{ijk}^T A_{ijk}^T A_{ijk}\mathbf{t}_{ijk} = \mathbf{t}_{ijk}^T \tilde{A}_{ijk}^T \tilde{A}_{ijk}\mathbf{t}_{ijk}$ for all $\mathbf{t}_{ijk}$.

The large reduction in the dimensions of the cost matrix greatly reduces the amount of computations needed in each iteration. Since neither A_{ijk} nor $\tilde{A}_{ijk}$ depend on the parameters of the cameras i, j and k, they need only be evaluated once and can be reused in the next iterations. This is of benefit in incremental structure form motion, since only a handful of new cost matrices need to be calculated at the insert of a new keyframe. The rest can be reused.

5   Experimental Validation

The method has been evaluated using both real and synthetic datasets. Each dataset contains initial camera poses, object points and a ground "truth". For the synthetic datasets, the ground truths consist of the simulated tracks and for the real datasets, the ground truths are generated by bundle adjustment. The termination criterion used to determine convergence is the norm of the gradient and the norm of the delta update should be smaller than selected thresholds. The thresholds are the same for all of the methods.

Besides investigating and comparing GTA and GEA, a combination of the epipolar and trifocal constraints called Global Epipolar and Trifocal Adjustment (GETA) will also be investigated. In this version the cost-matrices in GEA and GTA are used simultaneously.

5.1   Real Datasets

The real datasets consist of the publicly available VGG datasets [26] *Corridor* and *Model House*, and a two new datasets *Long Corridor* and *Dining Hall*, illustrated in Fig. 1.

Fig. 1. Sample image from the four datasets: top-left *Corridor*, top-left *Model House*, bottom-left *Long Corridor*, bottom-right *Dining Hall*.

VGG Datasets *Corridor* and *Model House*. The VGG datasets provide point and line correspondences, initial camera matrices and 3d structure. However, only the point correspondences and the calibration matrices retrieved from the initial camera matrices are used.

Datasets *Long Corridor* and *Dining Hall*. Two longer datasets *Long Corridor* and *Dining Hall* were collected. The *Long Corridor* dataset captures motion along a long straight corridor, while *Dining Hall* captures a more general motion. The datasets were collected using a Samsung Galaxy s7 mobile phone camera with a resolution of 1512×2016 pixels and variable focus. A structure from motion system based on [7] was used to find the initial structure of the datasets.

The program assumes fixed calibration and to account for varying focal length, bundle adjustment was applied.

Constraint History. The average error of the solutions when varying the number of previous cameras a camera is allowed to form constraints with, is illustrated in Fig. 2. This will be called the constraint history. From the plot it can be seen that GEA requires a longer constraint history to achieve a low position error compared to GTA and GETA. The latter methods achieve a low error even for the shortest constraint history. Furthermore, a clear minimum error can be observed where additional constraints degrade the solution. The rotation error decreases for both of the methods as the constraints increase.

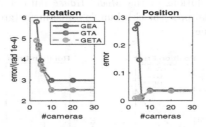

Fig. 2. The error on the *corridor* dataset relative to the optimal solution varying to the number of previous cameras a camera is allowed to form constraints with, starting at 3. The rotation error is small regardless of constraint history, while GTA and GETA both have much smaller position error compared to GEA for short histories.

Rotational and Positional Error. The position and rotation error of the methods relative to the bundle adjustment solution is displayed in Figs. 4. It can be seen that GTA and GETA has a lower position error compared to GEA in both datasets. Figure 3 illustrates how close GEA and GTA converges to the bundle adjustment solution in the *Model House* dataset. A significant overlap can be seen indicating close convergence to the bundle adjustment solution.

We studied the number of iterations needed for convergence and similar to the previous dataset, few iterations are required and the three methods worked equally well in this respect.

Sensitivity to Noise. The average error when increasing the observation noise is displayed in Fig. 5. It can be seen that the performance of GEA deteriorate significantly compared to GTA, even at low noise levels, when subject motion along a corridor.

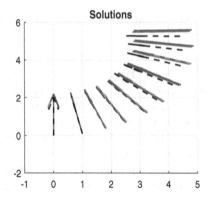

Fig. 3. Superimposed solutions of the *Model House* dataset using GEA, GTA and bundle adjustment. Initial pose (black), bundle adjustment (green), GEA (red), GTA (blue) (Color figure online)

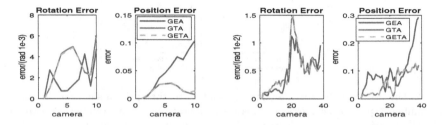

Fig. 4. Error relative to bundle adjustment solution in the *Model House* and *Dining Hall* datasets. GEA has a larger position error compared to the others.

Convergence Basin. If the initial guess is not very close to the optimum GEA has problems converging, which is illustrated in the convergence histograms in Fig. 6. The histograms shows the percentage of times GEA and GTA converged when initialized with various perturbation of the optimal solution. The convergence at each combination of rotation and translation perturbation is tested independently 10 times, such that spurious convergence and divergence can be seen.

From the histogram it can be seen that GEA quickly becomes unstable when the initial guess is perturbed from the optimal solution. In contrast, GTA has a much larger convergence region and does not suffer from the same instability issues on the dataset.

6   Synthetic Validation

To study the behavior of GEA and GTA in the case of collinear and near collinear movement, synthetic rooms and trajectories have been generated. The trajectory is generated by starting in one end of a room with a constant velocity and

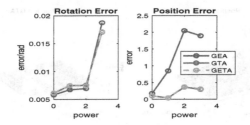

Fig. 5. The average error relative to the optimal solution at different noise level on the *Long Corridor* datasets. The resolution has been divided with 2^x. Highest resolution 1512×2016, lowest 189×252. Here it can be seen that the GEA solution quickly deteriorates when the noise increases, while GTA and GETA are largely unaffected.

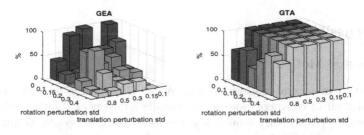

Fig. 6. A histogram over the number of times GEA (top) and GTA (bottom) converged when the solution is perturbed different amounts in rotation and translation from the ground truth for the *Long Corridor* dataset. It can be seen that GEA quickly fails when perturbed from the optimal solution, whereas GTA converges for a wider range of perturbations.

applying an constant acceleration acting perpendicular to the initial velocity direction. The amplitude of the acceleration is determined by a parameter called curvature. This generates curves similar to those in the *Corridor* and *Long Corridor* datasets, where a smaller value will generate a straighter trajectory while larger values generate a more curved trajectory. Several such datasets have been generated with varying curvature, observation noise and perturbations form the ground truth. GEA and GTA have then been applied to the datasets. The results can be seen in Fig. 7 where the median of the mean position error has been plotted as a function of the curvature and observation noise.

Here the position error for GEA grows large as the curvature decreases and the noise increases. For small curvatures the error grows significantly when the noise is increased. As the curvature grows larger the dependency on noise become less prominent. In contrast to GEA, the error of GTA is shows no large dependency of the curvature and depends only on the observation noise.

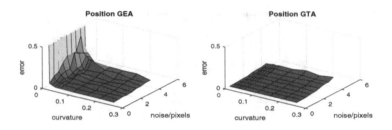

Fig. 7. The average error of GEA (left) and GTA (right) on the syntactic dataset with varying degrees of collinearity and observation noise. A large dependency on the curvature parameter can be seen for GEA, whereas GTA is largely independent of the curvature parameter.

7   Discussion

7.1   General Motion

In the setting of general motion, both GEA and GTA have a large convergence basin and tend to converge close to the bundle adjustment solution. Moreover the methods typically only require few iterations to convergence, despite poor initial guesses and large amounts of cameras. A pattern can be observed where GTA tends to have a lower position error compared to GEA.

7.2   Near Collinear Motion

GEA showed a significant performance decrease in the near collinear case. If the observation noise is sufficiently low, the constraint history is long enough and that the initial guess is very close to the optimal solution, GEA could converge. However, if these conditions are not met, the solution quickly deteriorates or diverge. This issue was described in [22] where isolated chains of cameras with collinear camera centers could gain additional degrees of freedom.

This is expected behavior since if only the bifocal constraint is used and the cameras have moved on a line, the camera translations can theoretically not be resolved [12]. In contrast, this is no restriction when using the trifocal constraint, which can resolve even collinear cameras. This explains why GTA performed better in the near collinear case compared to GEA.

7.3   Relation to Constraint History

Considering the relationship between the errors and the constraint history it can be seen that GEA consistently has a larger position error for short constraint histories compared to GTA, which is largely unaffected by the constraint history.

If the constraint history is restricted, the local camera configuration will become more collinear. If the constraint history is progressively restricted, the cameras may eventually become too collinear in relation to the noise for GEA to accurately estimate the translations. As stated before, GTA does not suffer from the collinearity problem and performs equally well in the exact collinear case as in the case of more general case. This explain why GTA is not affected as much by the constraint history.

8 Conclusions

In this paper a novel extension to the Global Epipolar Adjustment method has been presented called Global Trifocal Adjustment, which is based on the well known trifocal constraint. It has been shown that the method has a large convergence basin, can handle the degenerate configurations of GEA, is less sensitive to the constraint history compared to GEA and in general only require few iterations to converge close to the bundle adjustment solution. Furthermore GTA can, in addition to points, also use lines and combinations of linens and points to form the cost matrices, while GEA is restricted to using only points.

The method is completely structure-less leading to a vast reduction in the optimization parameters compared to bundle adjustment. Furthermore the number of residuals can be reduced to 27 residuals per trifocal constraint irrespective of the number of feature correspondences. The cost matrices are independent of the camera parameters and need only be evaluated once and can be reused in future computations. The combination of decreased number of parameters, the large reduction in residuals and the constant cost matrices, leads to a potentially fast method well suited to real-time slam systems.

Acknowledgements. This work was partially supported by the strategic research projects ELLIIT and eSSENCE, the Swedish Foundation for Strategic Research project, Semantic Mapping and Visual Navigation for Smart Robots (grant no. RIT15-0038), and Wallenberg AI, Autonomous Systems and Software Program (WASP) funded by Knut and Alice Wallenberg Foundation.

References

1. Agarwal, S., Mierle, K., et al.: Ceres solver. http://ceres-solver.org
2. Agarwal, S., Snavely, N., Simon, I., Seitz, S.M., Szeliski, R.: Building rome in a day. In: Proceedings 12th International Conference on Computer Vision, Kyoto, Japan (2009)
3. Byröd, M., Åström, K.: Efficient bundle adjustment using conjugate gradients with multiscale preconditioning. In: British Machine Vision Conference (2009)
4. Byröd, M., Åström, K.: Conjugate gradient bundle adjustment. In: Daniilidis, K., Maragos, P., Paragios, N. (eds.) ECCV 2010. LNCS, vol. 6312, pp. 114–127. Springer, Heidelberg (2010). https://doi.org/10.1007/978-3-642-15552-9_9
5. Cornelis, N., Leibe, B., Cornelis, K., Van Gool, L.: 3D urban scene modeling integrating recognition and reconstruction. Int. J. Comput. Vis. (IJCV) **78**(2–3), 121–141 (2008)
6. Engels, C., Stewenius, H., Nister, D.: Bundle adjustment rules. In: PCV 2006 (2006)
7. Enqvist, O., Kahl, F., Olsson, C.: Non-sequential structure from motion (2011)

8. Gauss, C.F.: Theoria Motus Corporum Coelestium in sectionibus conicis solem ambientium. Göttingen (1809)
9. Granshaw, S.I.: Bundle adjustment methods in engineering photogrammetry. Photogram. Rec. **10**(56), 181–207 (1980)
10. Hartley, R., Zisserman, A.: Multiple View Geometry in Computer Vision, Second Edn. Cambridge University Press, Cambridge (2004)
11. Heyden, A.: Tensorial properties of multiple view constraints. Math. Methods Appl. Sci. **23**(2), 169–202 (2000)
12. Heyden, A., Åström, K.: Algebraic properties of multilinear constraints. Math. Methods Appl. Sci. **20**(13), 1135–1162 (1997)
13. Indelman, V., Roberts, R., Beall, C., Dellaert, F.: Incremental light bundle adjustment, 01 2012
14. Klein, G., Murray, D.: Parallel tracking and mapping for small AR workspaces. In: 6th IEEE and ACM International Symposium on Mixed and Augmented Reality, ISMAR 2007, pp. 225–234. IEEE (2007)
15. Legendre, A.M.: Nouvelles méthodes pour la détermination des orbites des comètes. F. Didot (1805)
16. Levenberg, K.: A method for the solution of certain non-linear problems in least squares. Q. Appl. Math. **2**(2), 164–168 (1944)
17. Rodríguez López, A.L.: Algebraic epipolar constraints for efficient structureless multiview motion estimation. Ph.D. thesis, Universidad de Murcia. Facultad de Informática. Departamento de Ingeniería y Tecnología de Computadores (2013)
18. Lourakis, M.I.A., Argyros, A.A.: SBA: a software package for generic sparse bundle adjustment. ACM Trans. Math. Softw. **36**(1), 1–30 (2009)
19. Marquardt, D.W.: An algorithm for least-squares estimation of nonlinear parameters. J. Soc. Ind. Appl. Math. **11**(2), 431–441 (1963)
20. Akbarzadeh, A., Mordohai, P.: Towards urban 3D reconstruction from video (2006)
21. Ressl, C.: Geometry, constraints and computation of the trifocal tensor. Ph.D. thesis, Technische Universität Wien, Austria (2003)
22. Rodríguez, A.L., López-de Teruel, P.E., Ruiz, A.: Reduced epipolar cost for accelerated incremental SfM. In: 2011 IEEE Conference on Computer Vision and Pattern Recognition (CVPR), pp. 3097–3104. IEEE (2011)
23. Snavely, N., Seitz, S.M., Szeliski, R.: Modeling the world from internet photo collections. Int. J. Comput. Vis. **80**(2), 189–210 (2007)
24. Snavely, N., Seitz, S.M., Szeliski, R.: Photo tourism: exploring photo collections in 3D. In: ACM SIGGRAPH 2006 Papers, SIGGRAPH 2006, pp. 835–846. ACM, New York (2006)
25. Triggs, B., McLauchlan, P.F., Hartley, R.I., Fitzgibbon, A.W.: Bundle adjustment—a modern synthesis. In: Triggs, B., Zisserman, A., Szeliski, R. (eds.) IWVA 1999. LNCS, vol. 1883, pp. 298–372. Springer, Heidelberg (2000). https://doi.org/10.1007/3-540-44480-7_21
26. VGG: Visual geometry group - data (2004). http://www.robots.ox.ac.uk/~vgg/data/data-mview.html. Accessed 12 July 2018

A Robust Human Activity Recognition Approach Using OpenPose, Motion Features, and Deep Recurrent Neural Network

Farzan Majeed Noori[1]([✉]) [iD], Benedikte Wallace[1,2] [iD], Md. Zia Uddin[1] [iD],
and Jim Torresen[1,2] [iD]

[1] Department of Informatics, University of Oslo, Oslo, Norway
{farzanmn,benediwa,mdzu,jimtoer}@ifi.uio.no
[2] RITMO Centre for Interdisciplinary Studies in Rhythm, Time and Motion,
Oslo, Norway

Abstract. With the emerging advancements in computer vision and pattern recognition, methods for human activity recognition have become increasingly accessible. In this paper, we present a robust approach for human activity recognition which uses the open source library *Open-Pose* to extract anatomical key points from RGB images. We further use these key points to extract robust motion features considering their movements in consecutive frames'. Then, a Recurrent Neural Network (RNN) with Long Short-term Memory cells (LSTM) is used to recognize the activities associated with these features. To make the approach person-independent, different subjects from different camera angles are used. The proposed method shows promising performance, with the best result reaching an overall accuracy of 92.4% on a publicly available activity data set, which outperforms the conventional approaches (i.e. support vector machines, decision trees, and random forests) which achieve maximum accuracy of 78.5%. The proposed activity recognition system can contribute in prominent research fields such as image processing and computer vision with practical applications such as caregiving for older people to help them live more independently.

Keywords: Human activity recognition · LSTM · OpenPose · RNNs

1 Introduction

Nowadays, perceiving human activity is one of the vital areas of computer vision research. The goal of human activity recognition (HAR) is to distinguish and analyze activities based on data extracted from sensors such as wearables [17]

First and second authors contributed equally to this work. This work is partially supported by The Research Council of Norway (RCN) as a part of the Multimodal Elderly Care systems (MECS) project, under grant agreement 247697 and the RCN Centres of Excellence scheme, project number 262762.

© Springer Nature Switzerland AG 2019
M. Felsberg et al. (Eds.): SCIA 2019, LNCS 11482, pp. 299–310, 2019.
https://doi.org/10.1007/978-3-030-20205-7_25

or external sensing modalities. HAR can be used in smart-homes [18,22], sports [16], as well as in health monitoring [19], assistance for the elderly [13] and in mental health care [8].

Recently, there has been an increase in the popularity of external sensors such as Kinect and RGB sensors over wearable sensors as they can be seen as less intrusive. In various computer vision applications, depth images have been used widely among researches. In [24], temporal motion energies were extracted from human activity depth images and a Hidden Markov Model (HMM) was applied to model the activities using depth image features [14]. In computer vision, 2D pose estimation is widely used and several algorithms have been proposed to localize body joints. Fujimori et al. developed a wearable suit to capture body motion with tactile sensors, using motion sensors to estimate the user's orientation [10]. Liu et al. obtained static gestures from individual pictures by using skeletal tracking with a Kinect camera [15].

These conventional approaches of activity recognition, though suitable for a variety of tasks, are often slow and lack reliability and performance in complex environments. *OpenPose* [6,23], an open source library developed at Carnegie Mellon University in 2017 achieved significant interest among researchers due to its computational performance for extraction of body joints. OpenPose can operate in real-time detecting facial expressions, body and hand joints by feeding RGB images through deep convolutional neural networks (CNNs) [20,21].

In this work, we propose deep learning approach using *OpenPose* and recurrent neural nets (RNN) to facilitate activity recognition. The *OpenPose* library was used to detect 14 body joints. Using this data, we extract the changes in magnitude and angle between joints in consecutive frames. These robust features are then used as the input for a sequence classifier which uses an RNN with Long Short-term Memory cells (LSTM). As LSTMs have the ability to retain salient information over a sequence of time steps, it lends itself well to sequence classification tasks such as activity recognition. In this work, the LSTM is trained to recognize which activities are performed by learning the sequence of motion features associated with each activity. The main contributions of this work, therefore, are the extraction of robust motion features from the body joints acquired using *OpenPose*, combined with the use of LSTM-RNNs to recognize the activities and boost the performance compared to other conventional approaches such as SVM, Decision Trees, and Random Forests.

This paper is organized as follows: Sect. 2 describes our methodology, where we discuss the data set and the extraction of motion features, as well as give an overview of the LSTM architecture and the other classifiers compared with our experiments. Section 3 presents the experiments and results. The paper is concluded in Sect. 4 where we also discuss the limitations of our approach and possibilities for future work.

2   Methodology

In this section, we present the steps included in our proposed method of activity recognition. Specifically, Sect. 2.1 describes the extraction of key points using

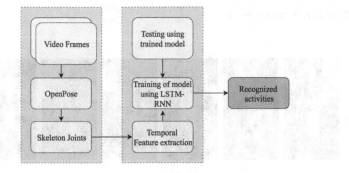

Fig. 1. Flow of work

OpenPose and Sect. 2.2 defines the motion features. The data set and classifiers are described in Sects. 2.3 and 2.4, respectively. Figure 1 gives an overview of the general flow of our process.

2.1 Extracting Joints

OpenPose takes RGB images as input and generates 2-dimensional anatomical key-points for individual bodies detected in the image. The first stage in two-branched CNN predicts confidence maps, and the second stage predicts part affinity fields - a 2D vector which encodes the position and orientation of each limb [5].

Furthermore, both the confidence maps and affinity fields are parsed by greedy inference to visualize the 2D key-points of all individuals in the image [7,23]. *OpenPose* generates the location of 18 body joints. These body joints can then be exported and used for applications such as gesture and activity recognition.

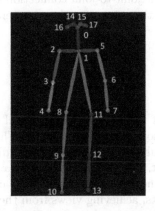

Fig. 2. OpenPose skeleton joints

2.2   Motion Features

Fig. 3. Extracted body joints from several frames while performing jumping jacks

In our work, we compute the two temporal features magnitude and angle from 14 body joints (L) between consecutive frames. Joints 14, 15, 16 and 17 pertain to the face and head as shown in Fig. 2. These key points are excluded from the data as they are not necessarily useful for activity recognition. Formally, we derive the magnitude M at a joint number N at time frame t as follows:

$$M_t^N = \sqrt{(L_{Nx(t+1)} - L_{Nx(t)})^2 + (L_{Ny(t+1)} - L_{Ny(t)})^2} \tag{1}$$

The angles of a body joint N for frame t^{th} are computed as follows:

$$A_{N(x,y)t} = tan^{-1}\left(\frac{L_{Ny(t+1)} - L_{Ny(t)}}{L_{Nx(t+1)} - L_{Nx(t)}}\right) \tag{2}$$

where L_{Nx} and L_{Ny} are the distances between the two-consecutive frames in x-axis and y-axis. For each example, we extract the body joints from a sequence of consecutive frames. Figure 3 shows the several frames of jumping jacks, while the dotted lines represent the joint-to-joint connection for motion features. Thus, the motion features (T) at time step t can be represented as:

$$T_t = [M_t^N, A_{N(x,y)t}] \tag{3}$$

2.3   Data Set

Our data set is a subset of the Berkeley Multimodal Human Action Database [1]. MHAD contains 11 actions, as listed in Table 1. These actions are performed by 7 male and 5 female subjects recorded using audio, video, accelerometers, motion capture, and kinect. For current work, we have chosen to use a subset containing the image sequences captured by 12 RGB cameras placed in clusters surrounding the participants, achieving views from the front and back as shown in Fig. 4. We use the images produced by the video recordings of all 12 subjects performing each action for approximately 5 s. The image sequences are captured by each of the four camera clusters as shown in Fig. 5. Cluster C1 and C2 contain

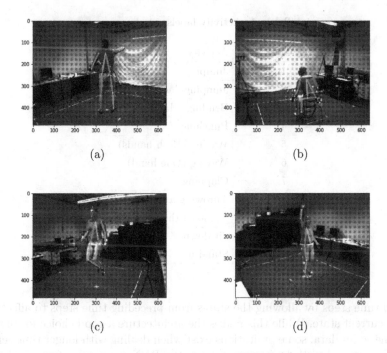

Fig. 4. Examples of images from the MHAD [1] database.

four cameras. The remaining two clusters, C3 and C4 contain two cameras each. We include the images from all four clusters in an effort to make our system view-invariant, as each camera captures the video at a different angle.

The number of images in each recording varies from around 40 (approx. 3 s of video at 22 Hz) to 130 frames (approx. 10 s of video). Activities which involved less complex movements, such as standing up or sitting down, consist of fewer than 40 frames. To mediate this difference in sequence lengths and ensure consistency in the data-set, the longer sequences were clipped after 85 frames and the shorter sequences were extended by stacking them. Each camera captures 132 sequences. This results in a data-set of 1584 sequences of 85 images each consisting of 12 participants performing 11 actions captured by 12 cameras. Each sequence of images thereby represents the view captured by a single camera in one of the clusters and a single data point in training and test data. Finally, z-score standardization was applied before applying the classifiers to the data.

2.4 Classification

Recurrent Neural Networks (RNN). An RNN with LSTM cells was implemented in order to tackle the long term dependencies found in our data. RNNs and LSTMs have previously been shown to be effective in modeling temporal sequences such as those found in speech [11] and handwriting recognition [12] and also in music [9]. This is due to their ability to retain 'memory' over

Table 1. Activity labels: 11 classes

Class label	Activity
1	Jumping
2	Jumping Jacks
3	Bending (Hands up)
4	Punching
5	Waving (Both hands)
6	Waving (One hand)
7	Clapping
8	Throwing a ball
9	Sit down then stand up
10	Sit down
11	Stand up

several time steps by allowing the states from preceding time steps to affect the RNNs current state. While this makes the architecture a good choice for modeling time series data, some limitations exist when dealing with longer time series. If the sequence length becomes too long, the RNN may suffer from vanishing or exploding gradients during back-propagation through time (BPTT). LSTMs mitigates this problem by adding multiple learnable parameters, or gates, which affect weight updates during BPTT enabling more control over what is retained in the internal state of the LSTM cell and what it 'forgets' at each time step. As illustrated in Fig. 6, the features which describe the variations of magnitude and angle of each joint between consecutive frames are fed to the network at each time step.

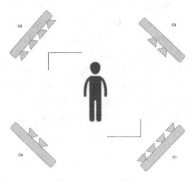

Fig. 5. Setup of cameras from Berkeley MHAD acquisition system [1]

The model used in this work consist of two layers containing 256 LSTM cells with hyperbolic tangent activation function. The output layer is a dense layer with softmax activation and 11 units representing the different activities. Categorical cross entropy is used as the loss function during batch gradient descent and RMSprop with a learning rate of 0.001, is used as the optimizer. The model is trained for 300 epochs with a batch size of 256 samples and a 0.4 dropout rate. These hyperparameters were chosen empirically according to which values yielded the best results for the task.

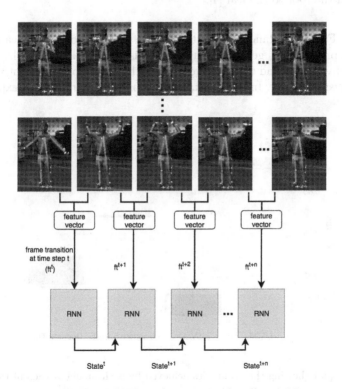

Fig. 6. LSTM-RNN implementation for all activities

Support Vector Machine (SVM). SVM has been widely used in HAR systems due to its high classification performance [2,3]. SVM creates hyper-planes that maximize the margins between several classes, which enables maximum classification accuracy. The vectors are used to represent hyper-planes are called support vectors. By minimizing the cost function, an optimal solution can be obtained i.e. maximize the distance between hyper-plane and the nearest training point. Herein, a non-linear multi-class SVM with *sigmoid* kernel was used.

Decision Trees. A decision support tool that utilizes a model of decisions or tree-like graph and their possible consequences including utility, and chance event outcomes, called a decision tree. A decision tree is a well-known classifier in machine learning. Its structure is similar to the flowchart in which each internal node represents a test on an attribute; for instance, whether it would be heads or tails by flipping a coin. Each branch is responsible for the test's outcome, and the class label would be represented by each leaf node. The decision would be taken after applying all features. The classification rules would be based on the paths from the root to the leaf [4].

Random Forests. Random Forests method used in both classification and regression problems. It generates multiple decision trees based on the random selection of variables and data, and recognizes the classes of dependent variables based on decision trees. In this work, 10 decision trees were used to explore the classes.

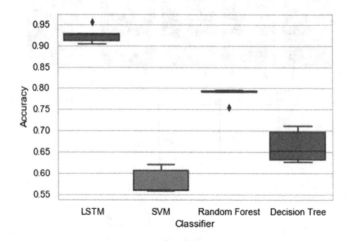

Fig. 7. Box plot showing the accuracies achieved by each model at each of the 5 folds

3   Experiments and Results

In this section, the experiments performed to validate the performance of the proposed method are explained. The accuracy of each classifier is evaluated by performing stratified 5-fold cross-validation. The average accuracy of each classifier is listed in Table 2. Figure 7 shows the distribution of the results achieved by the different classifiers. Figure 8 and Table 3 displays confusion matrices and the precision and recall values generated from the *predictions* of each classifier from a single fold of the data. Moreover, Fig. 9 shows the confusion matrices of the *number of samples* classified as belong to each class.

Table 2. Average accuracy from 5-fold cross validation of each classifier

Classifier	Accuracy (%)
SVM	58.1
Decision Trees	66.3
Random Forests	78.5
LSTM	**92.4**

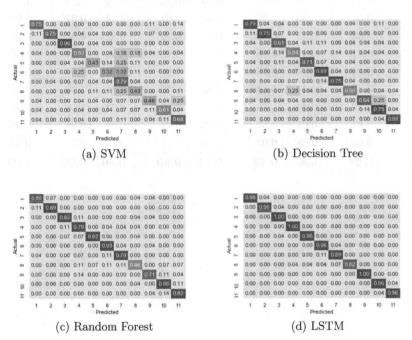

(a) SVM

(b) Decision Tree

(c) Random Forest

(d) LSTM

Fig. 8. Confusion matrices for (a) SVM, (b) Decision Trees, (c) Random Forests and (d) LSTM calculated on a test set of 308 sequences. These show the percentage of predictions for each class

As shown in Fig. 8(a), SVM was unable to distinguish the difference among waving one hand, waving both hands and clapping activities. Furthermore, Decision trees and Random forests showed better performance i.e. 0.66 and 0.78 as shown in Table 2. Moreover, both classifiers outperformed SVM in precision and recall, respectively. Still, both were lacking in their ability to differentiate all activities properly. The LSTM model outperformed the conventional approaches, achieving the highest average accuracy at 92,4%. Student's t-test was applied to validate the statistically discriminant. The p values obtained LSTM versus other approaches were less than 0.05, thus proofing the statistical significance of the LSTM approach. It can be seen clearly from the accuracy achieved at each fold shown in the box plot in Fig. 8 that LSTM showed superior results compared to the other approaches, with a higher median and higher accuracy for all folds.

Table 3. Precision and recall of Decision tree, SVM, Random Forest, and LSTM on a test set of 308 sequences

Activity	SVM		Decision Tree		Random Forest		LSTM	
	Precision	Recall	Precision	Recall	Precision	Recall	Precision	Recall
1	0.75	0.75	0.79	0.79	0.86	0.86	1.00	0.96
2	0.95	0.75	0.95	0.75	0.93	0.89	0.96	0.96
3	0.96	0.96	0.57	0.61	0.82	0.82	0.93	1.00
4	0.50	0.50	0.52	0.54	0.61	0.79	0.97	1.00
5	0.63	0.43	0.83	0.71	0.92	0.82	0.96	0.96
6	0.47	0.32	0.68	0.89	0.79	0.93	0.87	0.96
7	0.39	0.79	0.78	0.75	0.81	0.79	0.89	0.89
8	0.43	0.43	0.61	0.50	0.72	0.46	1.00	0.82
9	0.57	0.46	0.75	0.64	0.83	0.71	1.00	1.00
10	0.81	0.61	0.57	0.75	0.73	0.86	0.96	0.96
11	0.54	0.68	0.93	0.89	0.79	0.82	0.96	0.96
Avg	**0.64**	**0.61**	**0.72**	**0.71**	**0.80**	**0.80**	**0.96**	**0.95**

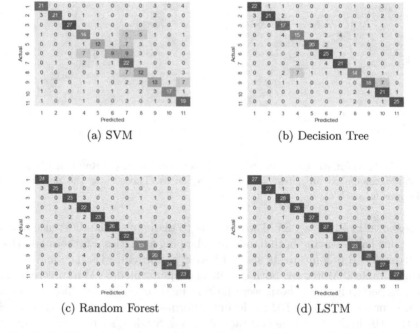

(a) SVM

(b) Decision Tree

(c) Random Forest

(d) LSTM

Fig. 9. Confusion matrices showing the number of samples classified as belonging to each class

4 Conclusions

In this work, person independent and view-invariant activity recognition approach has been proposed. The OpenPose library was used to detect anatomical key points in the image sequences collected from the MHAD database. Afterward, temporal motion features were extracted from consecutive frames in each sequence. Lastly, different classifiers were applied to detect human activities. The classification accuracy of these models was compared to the proposed approach of using an LSTM-RNN. Our approach shows improved results compared to the conventional approaches, it is able to correctly classify activities performed by several different subjects and from various camera angles. Although OpenPose is able to detect several persons in a frame, our work will not be able to correctly classify the activity of several people at once. In future work, the proposed network would be implemented in a real-time system to detect different activities and gestures.

References

1. Berkeley multimodal human action database. http://tele-immersion.citris-uc.org/berkeley_mhad
2. Abidine, B.M., Fergani, L., Fergani, B., Oussalah, M.: The joint use of sequence features combination and modified weighted SVM for improving daily activity recognition. Pattern Anal. Appl. **21**(1), 119–138 (2018)
3. Adama, D.A., Lotfi, A., Langensiepen, C., Lee, K., Trindade, P.: Human activity learning for assistive robotics using a classifier ensemble. Soft Comput. **22**(21), 7027–7039 (2018)
4. Altun, K., Barshan, B., Tunçel, O.: Comparative study on classifying human activities with miniature inertial and magnetic sensors. Pattern Recognit. **43**(10), 3605–3620 (2010)
5. Cao, Z., Hidalgo, G., Simon, T., Wei, S.-E., Sheikh, Y.: OpenPose: realtime multi-person 2D pose estimation using part affinity fields. arXiv preprint arXiv:1812.08008 (2018)
6. Cao, Z., Simon, T., Wei, S.-E., Sheikh, Y.: Realtime multi-person 2D pose estimation using part affinity fields. arXiv preprint arXiv:1611.08050 (2016)
7. Cao, Z., Simon, T., Wei, S.-E., Sheikh, Y.: Realtime multi-person 2D pose estimation using part affinity fields. In: CVPR (2017)
8. Ceron, J.D., Lopez, D.M., Ramirez, G.A.: A mobile system for sedentary behaviors classification based on accelerometer and location data. Comput. Ind. **92**, 25–31 (2017)
9. Eck, D., Schmidhuber, J.: Finding temporal structure in music: blues improvisation with LSTM recurrent networks. In: Proceedings of the 2002 12th IEEE Workshop on Neural Networks for Signal Processing, pp. 747–756. IEEE (2002)
10. Fujimori, Y., Ohmura, Y., Harada, T., Kuniyoshi, Y.: Wearable motion capture suit with full-body tactile sensors. In: IEEE International Conference on Robotics and Automation, ICRA 2009, pp. 3186–3193. IEEE (2009)
11. Graves, A., Jaitly, N.: Towards end-to-end speech recognition with recurrent neural networks. In: International Conference on Machine Learning, pp. 1764–1772 (2014)

12. Graves, A., Liwicki, M., Bunke, H., Schmidhuber, J., Fernández, S.: Unconstrained on-line handwriting recognition with recurrent neural networks. In: Advances in Neural Information Processing Systems, pp. 577–584 (2008)
13. Hassan, M.M., Huda, S., Uddin, M.Z., Almogren, A., Alrubaian, M.: Human activity recognition from body sensor data using deep learning. J. Med. Syst. **42**(6), 99 (2018)
14. Jalal, A., Uddin, M.Z., Kim, J.T., Kim, T.-S.: Recognition of human home activities via depth silhouettes and transformation for smart homes. Indoor Built Environ. **21**(1), 184–190 (2012)
15. Liu, L., Wu, X., Wu, L., Guo, T.: Static human gesture grading based on kinect. In: 2012 5th International Congress on Image and Signal Processing (CISP), pp. 1390–1393. IEEE (2012)
16. Margarito, J., Helaoui, R., Bianchi, A.M., Sartor, F., Bonomi, A.G., et al.: User-independent recognition of sports activities from a single wrist-worn accelerometer: a template-matching-based approach. IEEE Trans. Biomed. Eng. **63**(4), 788–796 (2016)
17. Noori, F.M., Garcia-Ceja, E., Uddin, M.Z., Riegler, M.: Fusion of multiple representations extracted from a single sensor's data for activity recognition using CNNs. In: International Joint Conference on Neural Networks (IJCNN). IEEE (2019)
18. Nweke, H.F., Teh, Y.W., Al-Garadi, M.A., Alo, U.R.: Deep learning algorithms for human activity recognition using mobile and wearable sensor networks: state of the art and research challenges. Expert Syst. Appl. **105**, 233–261 (2018)
19. Nweke, H.F., Teh, Y.W., Mujtaba, G., Al-garadi, M.A.: Data fusion and multiple classifier systems for human activity detection and health monitoring: review and open research directions. Inf. Fusion **46**, 147–170 (2019)
20. Qiao, S., Wang, Y., Li, J.: Real-time human gesture grading based on OpenPose. In: 2017 10th International Congress on Image and Signal Processing, BioMedical Engineering and Informatics (CISP-BMEI), pp. 1–6. IEEE (2017)
21. Simon, T., Joo, H., Matthews, I.A., Sheikh, Y.: Hand keypoint detection in single images using multiview bootstrapping. In: CVPR, vol. 1, p. 2 (2017)
22. Uddin, M.Z., Kim, D.-H., Kim, J.T., Kim, T.-S.: An indoor human activity recognition system for smart home using local binary pattern features with hidden markov models. Indoor Built Environ. **22**(1), 289–298 (2013)
23. Wei, S.-E., Ramakrishna, V., Kanade, T., Sheikh, Y.: Convolutional pose machines. In: CVPR (2016)
24. Yang, X., Zhang, C., Tian, Y.: Recognizing actions using depth motion maps-based histograms of oriented gradients. In: Proceedings of the 20th ACM International Conference on Multimedia, pp. 1057–1060. ACM (2012)

Video Frame Interpolation via Cyclic Fine-Tuning and Asymmetric Reverse Flow

Morten Hannemose[1]([✉]), Janus Nørtoft Jensen[1], Gudmundur Einarsson[1], Jakob Wilm[2], Anders Bjorholm Dahl[1], and Jeppe Revall Frisvad[1]

[1] DTU Compute, Technical University of Denmark, Kongens Lyngby, Denmark
{mohan,jnje,abda,jerf}@dtu.dk
[2] SDU Robotics, University of Southern Denmark, Odense, Denmark

Abstract. The objective in video frame interpolation is to predict additional in-between frames in a video while retaining natural motion and good visual quality. In this work, we use a convolutional neural network (CNN) that takes two frames as input and predicts two optical flows with pixelwise weights. The flows are from an unknown in-between frame to the input frames. The input frames are warped with the predicted flows, multiplied by the predicted weights, and added to form the in-between frame. We also propose a new strategy to improve the performance of video frame interpolation models: we reconstruct the original frames using the learned model by reusing the predicted frames as input for the model. This is used during inference to fine-tune the model so that it predicts the best possible frames. Our model outperforms the publicly available state-of-the-art methods on multiple datasets.

Keywords: Slow motion · Video frame interpolation ·
Convolutional neural networks

1 Introduction

Video frame interpolation, also known as inbetweening, is the process of generating intermediate frames between two consecutive frames in a video sequence. This is an important technique in computer animation [19], where artists draw keyframes and lets software interpolate between them. With the advent of high frame rate displays that need to display videos recorded at lower frame rates, inbetweening has become important in order to perform frame rate up-conversion [2]. Computer animation research [9,19] indicates that good inbetweening cannot be obtained based on linear motion, as objects often deform and follow nonlinear paths between frames. In an early paper, Catmull [3] interestingly argues that inbetweening is "akin to difficult artificial intelligence problems" in that it must be able understand the content of the images in order to accurately handle e.g. occlusions. Applying learning-based methods to the problem of inbetweening thus seems an interesting line of investigation.

© Springer Nature Switzerland AG 2019
M. Felsberg et al. (Eds.): SCIA 2019, LNCS 11482, pp. 311–323, 2019.
https://doi.org/10.1007/978-3-030-20205-7_26

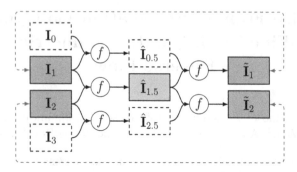

Fig. 1. Diagram illustrating the cyclic fine-tuning process when predicting frame $\hat{\mathbf{I}}_{1.5}$. The model is first applied in a pairwise manner on the four input frames $\mathbf{I}_0, \mathbf{I}_1, \mathbf{I}_2$, and $\mathbf{I}_3$, then on the results $\hat{\mathbf{I}}_{0.5}, \hat{\mathbf{I}}_{1.5}$, and $\hat{\mathbf{I}}_{2.5}$. The results of the second iteration, $\tilde{\mathbf{I}}_1$ and $\tilde{\mathbf{I}}_2$, are then compared with the input frames and the weights of the network are updated. This process optimizes our model specifically to be good at interpolating frame $\hat{\mathbf{I}}_{1.5}$.

Some of the first work on video frame interpolation using CNNs was presented by Niklaus et al. [17,18]. Their approach relies on estimating kernels to jointly represent motion and interpolate intermediate frames. Concurrently, Liu et al. [11] and Jiang et al. [6] used neural networks to predict optical flow and used it to warp the input images followed by a linear blending.

Our contribution is twofold. Firstly, we propose a CNN architecture that directly estimates asymmetric optical flows and weights from an unknown intermediate frame to two input frames. We use this to interpolate the frame in-between. Existing techniques either assume that this flow is symmetric or use a symmetric approximation followed by a refinement step [6,11,16]. For nonlinear motion, this assumption does not hold, and we document the effect of relaxing it. Secondly, we propose a new strategy for fine-tuning a network for each specific frame in a video. We rely on the fact that interpolated frames can be used to estimate the original frames by applying the method again with the in-between frames as input. The similarity of reconstructed and original frames can be considered a proxy for the quality of the interpolated frames. For each frame we predict, the model is fine-tuned in this manner using the surrounding frames in the video, see Fig. 1. This concept is not restricted to our method and could be applied to other methods as well.

2   Related Work

Video frame interpolation is usually done in two steps: motion estimation followed by frame synthesis. Motion estimation is often performed using optical flow [1,4,25], and optical flow algorithms have used interpolation error as an error metric [1,12,23]. Frame synthesis can then be done via e.g. bilinear interpolation and occlusion reasoning using simple hole filling. Other methods use phase decompositions of the input frames to predict the phase decomposition of the intermediate frame and invert this for frame generation [14,15], or they use local per pixel convolution kernels on the input frames to both represent motion and synthesize new frames [17,18]. Mahajan et al. [13] determine where each pixel in an intermediate frame comes from in the surrounding input frames by solving an expensive optimization problem. Our method is similar but replaces the optimization step with a learned neural network.

The advent of CNNs has prompted several new learning based approaches. Liu et al. [11] train a CNN to predict a symmetrical optical flow from the intermediate frame to the surrounding frames. They synthesize the target frame by interpolating the values in the input frames. Niklaus et al. [17] train a network to output local 38×38 convolution kernels for each pixel to be applied on the input images. In [18], they are able to improve this to 51×51 kernels. However, their representation is still limited to motions within this range. Jiang et al. [6] first predict bidirectional optical flows between two input frames. They combine these to get a symmetric approximation of the flows from an intermediate frame to the input frames, which is then refined in a separate step. Our method, in contrast, directly predicts the final flows to the input frames without the need for an intermediate step. Niklaus et al. [16] also initially predict bidirectional flows between the input frames and extract context maps for the images. They warp the input images and context maps to the intermediate time step using the predicted flows. Another network blends these to get the intermediate frame.

Liu et al. [10] propose a new loss term, which they call cycle consistency loss. This is a loss based on how well the output frames of a model can reconstruct the input frames. They retrain the model from [11] with this and show state-of-the-art results. We use this loss term and show how it can be used during inference to improve results. Meyer et al. [14] estimate the phase of an intermediate frame from the phases of two input frames represented by steerable pyramid filters. They invert the decomposition to reconstruct the image. This method alleviates some of the limitations of optical flow, which are also limitations of our method: sudden light changes, transparency and motion blur, for example. However, their results have a lower level of detail.

3   Method

Given a video containing the image sequence $I_0, I_1, \cdots, I_n$, we are interested in computing additional images that can be inserted in the original sequence to increase the frame rate, while keeping good visual quality in the video. Our method doubles the frame rate, which allows for the retrieval of approximately any in-between frame by recursive application of the method. This means that we need to compute estimates of $I_{0.5}, I_{1.5}, \cdots, I_{n-0.5}$, such that the final sequence would be:

$$I_0, I_{0.5}, I_1, \cdots, I_{n-0.5}, I_n.$$

We simplify the problem by only looking at interpolating a single frame I_1, that is located temporally between two neighboring frames I_0 and I_2. If we know the

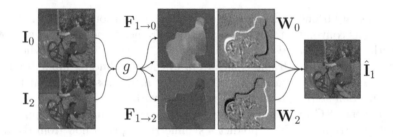

Fig. 2. Illustration of the frame interpolation process with g from Eq. (2). From left to right: Input frames, predicted flows, weights and final interpolated frame.

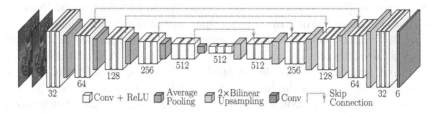

Fig. 3. The architecture of our network. Input is two color images $\mathbf{I}_0$ and $\mathbf{I}_2$ and output is optical flows $\mathbf{F}_{1\to0}, \mathbf{F}_{1\to2}$, and weights $\mathbf{W}_0, \mathbf{W}_2$. Convolutions are 3×3 and average pooling is 2×2 with a stride of 2. Skip connections are implemented by adding the output of the layer that arrows emerge from to the output of the layers they point to.

optical flows from the missing frame to each of these and denote them as $\mathbf{F}_{1\to0}$ and $\mathbf{F}_{1\to2}$, we can compute an estimate of the missing frame by

$$\hat{\mathbf{I}}_1 = \mathbf{W}_0 \mathcal{W}(\mathbf{F}_{1\to0}, \mathbf{I}_0) + \mathbf{W}_2 \mathcal{W}(\mathbf{F}_{1\to2}, \mathbf{I}_2), \tag{1}$$

where $\mathcal{W}(\cdot, \cdot)$ is the backward warping function that follows the vector to the input frame and samples a value with bilinear interpolation. $\mathbf{W}_0$ and $\mathbf{W}_2$ are weights for each pixel describing how much of each of the neighboring frames should contribute to the middle frame. The weights are used for handling occlusions. Examples of flows and weights can be seen in Fig. 2. We train a CNN g with a U-Net [20] style architecture, illustrated in Fig. 3. The network takes two images as input and predicts the flows and pixel-wise weights

$$g(\mathbf{I}_0, \mathbf{I}_2) \to \mathbf{F}_{1\to0}, \mathbf{F}_{1\to2}, \mathbf{W}_0, \mathbf{W}_2. \tag{2}$$

Our architecture uses five 2×2 average pooling layers with stride 2 for the encoding and five bilinear upsampling layers to upscale the layers with a factor 2 in the decoding. We use four skip connections (addition) between layers in the encoder and decoder. It should be noted that our network is fully convolutional, which implies that it works on images of any size, where both dimensions are a multiple of 32. If this is not the case, we pad the image with boundary reflections.

Our model for frame interpolation is obtained by combining Eqs. (1) and (2) into

$$f(\mathbf{I}_0, \mathbf{I}_2) = \hat{\mathbf{I}}_1, \tag{3}$$

where $\hat{\mathbf{I}}_1$ is the estimated image. The model is depicted in Fig. 2. All components of f are differentiable, which means that our model is end-to-end trainable. It is easy to get data in the form of triplets $(\mathbf{I}_0, \mathbf{I}_1, \mathbf{I}_2)$ by taking frames from videos that we use as training data for our model.

3.1   Loss-Functions

We employ a number of loss functions to train our network. All of our loss functions are given for a single triplet $(\mathbf{I}_0, \mathbf{I}_1, \mathbf{I}_2)$, and the loss for a minibatch of triplets is simply the mean of the loss for each triplet. In the following paragraphs, we define the different loss functions that we employ.

Reconstruction loss models how well the network has reconstructed the missing frame:

$$\mathcal{L}_1 = \left\lVert \mathbf{I}_1 - \hat{\mathbf{I}} \right\rVert_1. \tag{4}$$

Bidirectional reconstruction loss models how well each of our predicted optical flows is able to reconstruct the missing frame on its own:

$$\mathcal{L}_b = \lVert \mathbf{I}_1 - \mathcal{W}(\mathbf{F}_{1\to0}, \mathbf{I}_0) \rVert_1 + \lVert \mathbf{I}_1 - \mathcal{W}(\mathbf{F}_{1\to2}, \mathbf{I}_2) \rVert_1. \tag{5}$$

This has similarities to the work of Jiang et al. [6] but differs since the flow is estimated from the missing frame to the existing frames, and not between the existing frames.

Feature loss is introduced as an approximation of the perceptual similarity by comparing feature representation of the images from a pre-trained deep neural network [7]. Let ϕ be the output of `relu4_4` from VGG19 [21], then

$$\mathcal{L}_f = \left\lVert \phi(\mathbf{I}_1) - \phi(\hat{\mathbf{I}}_1) \right\rVert_2^2. \tag{6}$$

Smoothness loss is a penalty on the absolute difference between neighboring pixels in the flow field. This encourages a smoother optical flow [6,11]:

$$\mathcal{L}_s = \lVert \nabla \mathbf{F}_{1\to0} \rVert_1 + \lVert \nabla \mathbf{F}_{1\to2} \rVert_1, \tag{7}$$

where $\lVert \nabla \mathbf{F} \rVert_1$ is the sum of the anisotropic total variation for each (x, y) component in the optical flow $\mathbf{F}$. For ease of notation, we introduce a linear combination of Eqs. (4) to (7):

$$\mathcal{L}_r(\mathbf{I}_0, \mathbf{I}_1, \mathbf{I}_2) = \lambda_1 \mathcal{L}_1 + \lambda_b \mathcal{L}_b + \lambda_f \mathcal{L}_f + \lambda_s \mathcal{L}_s. \tag{8}$$

Note that we explicitly express this as a function of a triplet. When this triplet is the three input images, we define

$$\mathcal{L}_\alpha = \mathcal{L}_r(\mathbf{I}_0, \mathbf{I}_1, \mathbf{I}_2). \tag{9}$$

Similarly, for ease of notation, let the bidirectional loss from Eq. (5) be a function

$$\mathcal{L}_B(\mathbf{I}_0, \mathbf{I}_1, \mathbf{I}_2, \mathbf{F}_{1\to0}, \mathbf{F}_{1\to2}) = \mathcal{L}_b \qquad (10)$$

where, in this case, $\mathbf{F}_{1\to0}$ and $\mathbf{F}_{1\to2}$ are the flows predicted by the network.

Pyramid loss is a sum of bidirectional losses for downscaled versions of images and flow maps:

$$\mathcal{L}_p = \sum_{l=1}^{l=4} 4^l \mathcal{L}_B\Big(A_l(\mathbf{I}_0), A_l(\mathbf{I}_1), A_l(\mathbf{I}_2), A_l(\mathbf{F}_{1\to0}), A_l(\mathbf{F}_{1\to2})\Big), \qquad (11)$$

where A_l is the $2^l \times 2^l$ average pooling operator with stride 2^l.

Cyclic Loss Functions. We can apply our model recursively to get another estimate of $\mathbf{I}_1$, namely

$$\tilde{\mathbf{I}}_1 = f\left(\hat{\mathbf{I}}_{0.5}, \hat{\mathbf{I}}_{1.5}\right) = f\Big(f(\mathbf{I}_0, \mathbf{I}_1), f(\mathbf{I}_1, \mathbf{I}_2)\Big). \qquad (12)$$

Cyclic loss is introduced to ensure that outputs from the model work well as inputs to the model [10]. It is defined by

$$\mathcal{L}_c = \mathcal{L}_r\left(\hat{\mathbf{I}}_{0.5}, \mathbf{I}_1, \hat{\mathbf{I}}_{1.5}\right). \qquad (13)$$

Motion loss is introduced in order to get extra supervision on the optical flow and utilizes the recursive nature of our network.

$$\mathcal{L}_m = ||\mathbf{F}_{1\to0} - 2\mathbf{F}_{1\to0.5}||_2^2 + ||\mathbf{F}_{1\to2} - 2\mathbf{F}_{1\to1.5}||_2^2 \qquad (14)$$

This is introduced as self-supervision of the optical flow, under the assumption that the flow $\mathbf{F}_{1\to0}$ is approximately twice that of $\mathbf{F}_{1\to0.5}$ and similarly for $\mathbf{F}_{1\to2}$ and $\mathbf{F}_{1\to1.5}$, and assuming that the flow is easier to learn for shorter time steps.

3.2 Training

We train our network using the assembled loss function

$$\mathcal{L} = \mathcal{L}_\alpha + \mathcal{L}_c + \lambda_m \mathcal{L}_m, \qquad (15)$$

where $\mathcal{L}_\alpha$, $\mathcal{L}_c$ and $\mathcal{L}_m$ are as defined in Eqs. (9), (13) and (14) with $\lambda_r = 1$, $\lambda_b = 1$, $\lambda_f = 8/3$, $\lambda_s = 10/3$ and $\lambda_m = 1/192$. The values have been selected based on the performance on a validation set.

We train our network using the Adam optimizer [8] with default values $\beta_1 = 0.9$ and $\beta_2 = 0.999$ and with a minibatch size of 64.

Inspired by Liu et al. [10], we first train the network using only $\mathcal{L}_\alpha$. This is done on patches of size 128×128 for 150 epochs with a learning rate of 10^{-5}, followed by 50 epochs with a learning rate of 10^{-6}. We then train with the full loss function $\mathcal{L}$ on patches of size 256×256 for 35 epochs with a learning rate of 10^{-5} followed by 30 epochs with a learning rate of 10^{-6}. We did not use batch-normalization, as it decreased performance on our validation set. Due to the presence of the cyclic loss functions, four forward and backward passes are needed for each minibatch during the training with the full loss function.

Training Data. We train our network on triplets of patches extracted from consecutive video frames. For our training data, we downloaded 1500 videos in 4k from youtube.com/4k and resized them to 1920×1080. For every four frames in the video not containing a scene cut, we chose a random 320×320 patch and cropped it from the first three frames. If any of these patches were too similar or if the mean absolute differences from the middle patch to the previous and following patches were too big, or too dissimilar, they were discarded to avoid patches that either had little motion or did not include the same object. Our final training set consists of 476,160 triplets.

Data Augmentation. The data is augmented while we train the network by cropping a random patch from the 320×320 data with size as specified in the training details in Sect. 3.2. In this way, we use the training data more effectively. We also add a random translation to the flow between the patches, by offsetting the crop to the first and third patch while not moving the center patch [18]. This offset is ± 5 pixels in each direction. Furthermore, we also performed random horizontal flips and swapped the temporal order of the triplet.

3.3 Cyclic Fine-Tuning (CFT)

We introduce the concept of fine-tuning the model during inference for each frame that we want to interpolate and refer to this as cyclic fine-tuning (CFT). Recall that the cyclic loss $\mathcal{L}_c$ measures how well the predicted frames are able to reconstruct the original frames. This gives an indication of the quality of the interpolated frames. The idea of CFT is to exploit this property at inference time to improve interpolation quality. We do this by extending the cyclic loss to ± 2 frames around the desired frame and fine-tuning the network using these images only.

When interpolating frame $\mathbf{I}_{1.5}$, we would use surrounding frames $\mathbf{I}_0, \mathbf{I}_1, \mathbf{I}_2$, and $\mathbf{I}_3$ to compute $\hat{\mathbf{I}}_{0.5}, \hat{\mathbf{I}}_{1.5}$, and $\hat{\mathbf{I}}_{2.5}$, which are then used to compute $\tilde{\mathbf{I}}_1$ and $\tilde{\mathbf{I}}_2$ as illustrated in Fig. 1 on page 2. Note that the desired interpolated frame $\hat{\mathbf{I}}_{1.5}$ is used in the computation of both of the original frames. Therefore by fine-tuning of the network to improve the quality of the reconstructed original frames, we are improving the quality of the desired intermediate frame indirectly.

Specifically, we minimize the loss for each of the two triplets $(\hat{\mathbf{I}}_{0.5}, \mathbf{I}_1, \hat{\mathbf{I}}_{1.5})$ and $(\hat{\mathbf{I}}_{1.5}, \mathbf{I}_2, \hat{\mathbf{I}}_{2.5})$ with the loss for each triplet given by

$$\mathcal{L}_{CFT} = \mathcal{L}_c + \lambda_p \mathcal{L}_p, \tag{16}$$

where $\lambda_p = 10$, and $\mathcal{L}_p$ is the pyramid loss described in Sect. 3.1. In order for the model to be presented with slightly different samples, we only do this fine-tuning on patches of 256×256 with flow augmentation as described in the previous section. For computational efficiency, we only do this for 50 patch-triplets for each interpolated frame.

More than ± 2 frames can be applied for fine-tuning, however, we found that this did not increase performance. This fine-tuning process is not limited to our model and can be applied to any frame interpolation model taking two images as input and outputting one image.

Overlaid input frames   Ground truth   SepConv $\mathcal{L}_1$ [18]   CyclicGen [10]   Ours

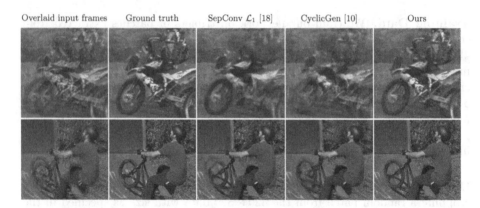

Fig. 4. Qualitative examples on the SlowFlow dataset. Images shown are representative crops taken from the full images. Note that our method performs much better for large motions. The motion of the dirt bike is approximately 53 pixels, and the bike tire has a motion of 34 pixels.

Table 1. Overview of the datasets we used for evaluation.

Dataset	Number of sequences	Resolution	Number of frames		Avg. sequence length
			Interpolated	Total	
SlowFlow [5]	34	$1280 \times \{1024, 720\}$	17,871	20,458	602
See You Again	117	1920×1080	2,503	5,355	46
UCF101 [22]	379	256×256	379	1,137	3

4   Experiments

We evaluate variations of our method on three diverse datasets: UCF101 [22], SlowFlow [5] and See You Again [18]. These have previously been used for frame interpolation [6,11,18]. UCF101 contains different image sequences of a variety of actions, and we evaluate our method on the same frames as Liu et al. [11], but did not use any motion masks as we are interested in performing equally well over the entire frame. SlowFlow is a high-fps dataset that we include to showcase our performance when predicting multiple in-between frames. For this dataset, we have only used every eighth frame as input and predicted the remaining seven in-between in a recursive manner. All frames in the dataset have been debayered, resized to 1280 pixels on the long edge and gamma corrected with a gamma value of 2.2. See You Again is a high-resolution music video, where we predict the even-numbered frames using the odd-numbered frames. Furthermore, we have divided it into sequences by removing scene changes. A summary of the datasets is shown in Table 1.

Table 2. Interpolation results on SlowFlow, See You Again and UCF101. PSNR, SSIM: higher is better. Our baseline is our model trained only with $\mathcal{L}_1 + \mathcal{L}_b + \mathcal{L}_s$ and constrained to symmetric flow. Elements are added to the model cumulatively. Larger patches means training on 256×256 patches. Bold numbers signify that a method performs significantly better than the rest on that task with $p < 0.02$.

Method	SlowFlow		See You Again		UCF101	
	PSNR	SSIM	PSNR	SSIM	PSNR	SSIM
DVF [11]	-	-	-	-	34.12	0.941
SuperSloMo [6]	-	-	-	-	34.75	0.947
SepConv $\mathcal{L}_1$ [18]	34.03	0.899	42.49	0.983	34.78	0.947
CyclicGen [10]	31.33	0.839	41.28	0.975	**35.11**	**0.949**
Our baseline	34.28	0.903	42.50	0.984	34.39	0.946
+ asymmetric flow	34.33	0.904	42.54	0.985	34.40	0.946
+ feature loss	34.29	0.901	42.62	0.984	34.60	0.948
+ cyclic loss	34.33	0.900	42.73	0.984	34.62	0.947
+ motion loss	34.31	0.900	42.74	0.984	34.61	0.948
+ larger patches	34.60	0.907	43.14	0.986	34.69	0.948
+ CFT	**34.91**	**0.912**	**43.21**	**0.986**	34.94	**0.949**

We have compared our method with multiple state-of-the-art methods [6, 10, 11, 18] which either have publicly available code and/or published their predicted frames. For the comparison with SepConv [18], we use the $\mathcal{L}_1$ version of their network for which they report their best quantitative results. For each evaluation, we report the Peak Signal to Noise Ratio (PSNR) and the Structural Similarity Index (SSIM) [24].

Comparison with State-of-the-Art. Table 2 shows that our best method, with or without CFT, clearly outperforms the other methods on SlowFlow and See you Again, which is also reflected in Fig. 4. On UCF101 our best method performs better than all other methods except CyclicGen, where our best method has the same SSIM but lower PSNR. We suspect this is partly due to the fact that our CFT does not have access to ± 2 frames in all sequences. For some of the sequences, we had to use $-1, +3$ as the intermediate frame was at the beginning of the sequence. Visually, our method produces better results as seen in Fig. 5. We note that CyclicGen is trained on UCF101, and their much worse performance on the two other datasets could indicate overfitting.

Effect of Various Model Configurations. Table 2 reveals that an asymmetric flow around the interpolated frame slightly improves performance on all three datasets as compared with enforcing a symmetric flow. There is no clear change in performance when we add feature loss, cyclic loss and motion loss.

Input frames   Ground truth   DVF [11]   SepConv $\mathcal{L}_1$ [18]   CyclicGen [10]   SuperSlomo [6]   Ours

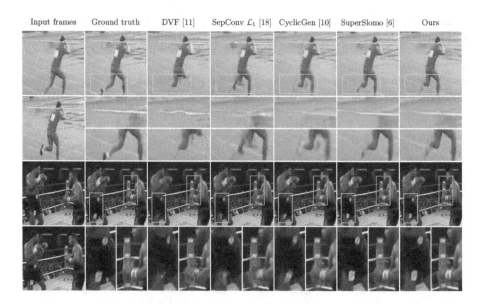

Fig. 5. Qualitative comparison for two sequences from UCF101. Top: our method produces the least distorted javelin and retains the detailed lines on the track. All methods perform inaccurately on the leg, however, SuperSlomo and our method are the most visually plausible. Bottom: our method and SuperSlomo create accurate white squares on the shorts (left box). Our method also produces the least distorted ropes and white squares on the corner post, while creating foreground similar to the ground truth (right box).

For all three datasets, performance improves when we train on larger image patches. Using larger patches allows for the network to learn larger flows and the performance improvement is correspondingly seen most clearly in SlowFlow and See You Again which, as compared with UCF101, have much larger images with larger motions. We see a big performance improvement when cyclic fine-tuning is added, which is also clearly visible in Fig. 6.

Discussion. Adding CFT to our model increases the run-time of our method by approximately 6.5 s per frame pair. This is not dependent on image size, as we only fine-tune on 256×256 patches for 50 iterations per frame pair. For reference, our method takes 0.08 s without CFT to interpolate a 1920×1080 image on an NVIDIA GTX 1080 TI. It should be noted that CFT is only necessary to do once per frame pair in the original video, and thus there is no extra overhead when computing multiple in-between frames.

Overlaid input frames   Ground truth   Ours without CFT   Ours

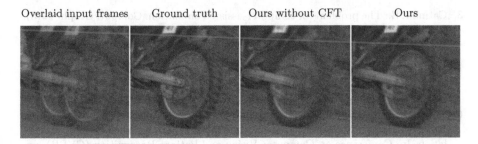

Fig. 6. Representative example of how the cyclic fine-tuning improves the interpolated frame. It can be seen that the small misalignment of the tire and the number "41" is corrected by the cyclic fine-tuning.

Training for more than 50 iterations does not necessarily ensure better results, as we can only optimize a proxy of the interpolation quality. The best number of iterations remains to be determined, but it is certainly dependent on the quality of the pre-training, the training parameters, and the specific video.

As of now, CFT should only be used if the target is purely interpolation quality. Improving the speed of CFT is a topic worthy of further investigation. Possible solutions of achieving similar results include training a network to learn the result of CFT, or training a network to predict the necessary weight changes.

5 Conclusion

We have proposed a CNN for video frame interpolation that predicts two optical flows with pixelwise weights from an unknown intermediate frame to the frames before and after. The flows are used to warp the input frames to the intermediate time step. These warped frames are then linearly combined using the weights to obtain the intermediate frame. We have trained our CNN using 1500 high-quality videos and shown that it performs better than or comparably to state-of-the-art methods across three different datasets. Furthermore, we have proposed a new strategy for fine-tuning frame interpolation methods for each specific frame at evaluation time. When used with our model, we have shown that it improves both the quantitative and visual results.

Acknowledgements. We would like to thank Joel Janai for providing us with the SlowFlow data [5].

References

1. Baker, S., Scharstein, D., Lewis, J.P., Roth, S., Black, M.J., Szeliski, R.: A database and evaluation methodology for optical flow. Int. J. Comput. Vis. **92**(1), 1–31 (2011)
2. Castagno, R., Haavisto, P., Ramponi, G.: A method for motion adaptive frame rate up-conversion. IEEE Trans. Circuits Syst. Video Technol. **6**(5), 436–446 (1996)

3. Catmull, E.: The problems of computer-assisted animation. Comput. Graph. **12**(3), 348–353 (1978). SIGGRAPH 1978
4. Herbst, E., Seitz, S., Baker, S.: Occlusion reasoning for temporal interpolation using optical flow. Technical report, Microsoft Research, August 2009
5. Janai, J., Güney, F., Wulff, J., Black, M., Geiger, A.: Slow flow: exploiting high-speed cameras for accurate and diverse optical flow reference data. In: IEEE Conference on Computer Vision and Pattern Recognition, pp. 1406–1416 (2017)
6. Jiang, H., Sun, D., Jampani, V., Yang, M.H., Learned-Miller, E., Kautz, J.: Super SloMo: high quality estimation of multiple intermediate frames for video interpolation. In: Conference on Computer Vision and Pattern Recognition (CVPR), pp. 9000–9008 (2018)
7. Johnson, J., Alahi, A., Fei-Fei, L.: Perceptual losses for real-time style transfer and super-resolution. In: Leibe, B., Matas, J., Sebe, N., Welling, M. (eds.) ECCV 2016. LNCS, vol. 9906, pp. 694–711. Springer, Cham (2016). https://doi.org/10.1007/978-3-319-46475-6_43
8. Kingma, D.P., Ba, J.: Adam: a method for stochastic optimization. CoRR abs/1412.6980 (2014)
9. Lasseter, J.: Principles of traditional animation applied to 3D computer animation. Comput. Graph. **21**(4), 35–44 (1987). SIGGRAPH 1987
10. Liu, Y.L., Liao, Y.T., Lin, Y.Y., Chuang, Y.Y.: Deep video frame interpolation using cyclic frame generation. In: AAAI Conference on Artificial Intelligence (2019)
11. Liu, Z., Yeh, R.A., Tang, X., Liu, Y., Agarwala, A.: Video frame synthesis using deep voxel flow. In: International Conference on Computer Vision, pp. 4463–4471 (2017)
12. Long, G., Kneip, L., Alvarez, J.M., Li, H., Zhang, X., Yu, Q.: Learning image matching by simply watching video. In: Leibe, B., Matas, J., Sebe, N., Welling, M. (eds.) ECCV 2016. LNCS, vol. 9910, pp. 434–450. Springer, Cham (2016). https://doi.org/10.1007/978-3-319-46466-4_26
13. Mahajan, D., Huang, F.C., Matusik, W., Ramamoorthi, R., Belhumeur, P.: Moving gradients: a path-based method for plausible image interpolation. ACM Trans. Graph. **28**(3), 42:1–42:11 (2009)
14. Meyer, S., Djelouah, A., McWilliams, B., Sorkine-Hornung, A., Gross, M., Schroers, C.: Phasenet for video frame interpolation. In: Conference on Computer Vision and Pattern Recognition (CVPR), pp. 498–507 (2018)
15. Meyer, S., Wang, O., Zimmer, H., Grosse, M., Sorkine-Hornung, A.: Phase-based frame interpolation for video. In: IEEE Conference on Computer Vision and Pattern Recognition (CVPR), pp. 1410–1418 (2015)
16. Niklaus, S., Liu, F.: Context-aware synthesis for video frame interpolation. In: Conference on Computer Vision and Pattern Recognition, pp. 1701–1710 (2018)
17. Niklaus, S., Mai, L., Liu, F.: Video frame interpolation via adaptive convolution. In: Conference on Computer Vision and Pattern Recognition, pp. 670–679 (2017)
18. Niklaus, S., Mai, L., Liu, F.: Video frame interpolation via adaptive separable convolution. In: International Conference on Computer Vision, pp. 261–270 (2017)
19. Reeves, W.T.: Inbetweening for computer animation utilizing moving point constraints. Comput. Graph. **15**(3), 263–269 (1981). (SIGGRAPH 1981)
20. Ronneberger, O., Fischer, P., Brox, T.: U-Net: convolutional networks for biomedical image segmentation. In: Navab, N., Hornegger, J., Wells, W.M., Frangi, A.F. (eds.) MICCAI 2015. LNCS, vol. 9351, pp. 234–241. Springer, Cham (2015). https://doi.org/10.1007/978-3-319-24574-4_28
21. Simonyan, K., Zisserman, A.: Very deep convolutional networks for large-scale image recognition. CoRR abs/1409.1556 (2014)

22. Soomro, K., Zamir, A.R., Shah, M., Soomro, K., Zamir, A.R., Shah, M.: UCF101: a dataset of 101 human actions classes from videos in the wild. CoRR abs/1212.0402 (2012)

23. Szeliski, R.: Prediction error as a quality metric for motion and stereo. In: IEEE International Conference on Computer Vision (ICCV), vol. 2, pp. 781–788 (1999)

24. Wang, Z., Bovik, A.C., Sheikh, H.R., Simoncelli, E.P.: Image quality assessment: from error visibility to structural similarity. IEEE Trans. Image Process. **13**(4), 600–612 (2004)

25. Werlberger, M., Pock, T., Unger, M., Bischof, H.: Optical flow guided TV-L^1 video interpolation and restoration. In: Boykov, Y., Kahl, F., Lempitsky, V., Schmidt, F.R. (eds.) EMMCVPR 2011. LNCS, vol. 6819, pp. 273–286. Springer, Heidelberg (2011). https://doi.org/10.1007/978-3-642-23094-3_20

Iris Identification in 3D

Fernand Cohen, Sowrirajan Sowmithran, and Chenxi Li[✉]

ECE Department, Drexel University, Philadelphia, PA 19104, USA
{fsc22,ss4537,cl982}@drexel.edu

Abstract. In the presence of eyelids and eyelashes movement, pupil dilation, poor lighting, blur due to movement during iris image acquisition, factors that collectively cause distortion in the iris image, 2D image-based iris identification techniques become limited and might lead to iris misclassification. To alleviate this problem, we introduce a novel 3D iris model and reader for iris identification. Using a set of at least two 2D images taken from different views, a small set of reliable and corresponding salient fiducial points (corner points taken from crypts, corona and serpentine rings of iris pattern) in the two images are extracted, from which a set of 3D iris salient points are constructed using triangulation. Corresponding salient points in the 2D images are found using the Random Sampling Consensus (RANSAC) algorithm, which is robust in identifying the inlier points that correspond to each other in the different views of the iris. From this small and reliable salient point set, a denser (high resolution) set of extra salient feature points is constructed at minimum cost using a loop subdivision method that yields corresponding extra salient points in the two images upon which a high-resolution 3D iris model is obtained. This 3D model construction method allows for a 3D distortion invariant classification of a test iris to one of many possible irises stored in the database.

Keywords: 3D iris identification · 3D iris reader · 3D high resolution iris

1 Introduction

There exist different forms of biometrics such as fingerprint, voiceprints, signature patterns, retinal scan, face recognition, etc. Iris recognition has been proven to be a most efficient and reliable biometric method. Since iris morphogenesis depends on the conditions of embryonic mesoderm, it cannot be affected by any external factors over time. Unlike fingerprint or any other signature, the phenotype expression of two irises (even if they are from twins) of any genotype gives uncorrelated minutiae. Not every iris will have the same number of ridges, rings, or folds. The iris features do not change over time/age with the only exception being certain surgeries that can change iris color. Irises are very hard to forge hence their attraction as a reliable biometric.

Most of the iris recognition methods at present focus on iris identification using 2D iris image taken from a test subject and classifying it across iris image-based information stored in a database in the form of iris binary codes. Considering how 2D

This chapter was not presented during the Scandinavian Conference on Image Analysis (SCIA) 2019. SCIA is embraced by IAPR and following the IAPR policy, only papers presented at the respective conference should be included in the proceedings. Thus, this chapter is not officially part of the SCIA conference proceedings. Unfortunately, at the time of production of LNCS 11482, this fact was not known and therefore the manuscript is erroneously available for download within the proceedings. The correction to this chapter is available at https://doi.org/10.1007/978-3-030-20205-7_41

© Springer Nature Switzerland AG 2019
M. Felsberg et al. (Eds.): SCIA 2019, LNCS 11482, pp. 324–335, 2019.
https://doi.org/10.1007/978-3-030-20205-7_27

images can be affected by occlusion caused by eyelids, eye lashes and pupil dilation, bad lighting, and blur, 2D image-based classification methods may lead to mismatch in the identification of the correct iris. These issues are overcome using a 3D based iris model, which is invariant and blind to these image-based distortions.

This paper deals with the problem of constructing a 3D textured model of an iris from images (at least two) of the irises by extracting corresponding salient points (corner points) on the 2D images. The salient points need to be intrinsic and invariant under the projection transformation, i.e. salient points appear as salient points after the transformation unless there is occlusion. Using RANSAC we find a coarse set of corresponding affine invariant salient tessellated to form a high-resolution triangular mesh using a loop subdivision process. Using at least two images, the iris 3D coordinates and appearance is reconstructed in accordance with the observed images. The 3D model reconstruction method allows for a 3D classification of a test iris to one of many possible irises stored in the database. The classification is based on a geometric 3D point cloud shape error.

The paper is organized as follows. In Sect. 2 we briefly cover related work, while in Sect. 3 we outline our approach and method. Method evaluation and conclusions are given in Sects. 4 and 5, respectively.

2 Related Work

At present, iris recognition is being preferred over other biometrics due to its reliability. It is being used in wide range of fields, ranging from airport security, to bank transactions, to laboratories, and even in smart phones for security locking purposes. Notwithstanding their success, current iris recognition systems do have shortcomings.

Many 2D iris recognition were inspired by the Daugman's model [1, 2] for iris recognition, with about every technique following by and large four steps with different methods proposed for each step. The pre-processing first step usually involves locating the iris from the input image, smoothing the image, and segmenting for iris localization. The iris image might be distorted due to gaze deviation, contact lenses, extreme Mydriasis (excessive pupil dilation), occlusion created by the eyelashes and eyelids and the pupil dilation, and non-ideal illumination (see Fig. 1).

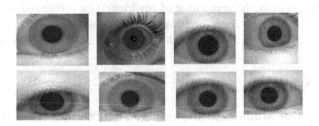

Fig. 1. Input eye images

In the second step, features are extracted from the pre-processed image and the information about the different irises is stored in a database for registration (third step) then classification/identification (fourth step) usually in a form of the iris code proposed by the Daugman's model [1, 2]. This method is highly accurate and is fast when the test iris image is taken under 'friendly' controlled conditions. The method proposed by Wildes [3] applies Laplacian of Gaussian filters to the image to get an isotropic bandpass decomposition. The proposed method in [4] employs a translation, scale, and rotation invariant technique based on zero crossings to identify the iris features. In general, these 2D methods lose their iris identification power when dealing with images taken under non-ideal conditions such as poor lighting and blurry conditions.

There is an abundance of work [5–7] for 3D scene recognition that are based on SIFT point features. The method proposed in [8] implements an iris 3D reconstruction from multiple 2D iris images taken by a customized hardware system that uses a Raspberry Pi v2.1 camera to acquire Near Infrared Region (NIR) images of the iris. Using a python's photogrammetry toolbox a 3D image is obtained. The work in [9] uses a novel approach of constructing a 3D model of buildings from just 2D images.

In our paper, we use corner points as our salient fiducial points (see Sect. 3.3). These are invariably present in corners of the iris patterns in the crypts, corona, and serpentine rings. Moreover, these are intrinsic points that are preserved under the projection model (affine transformation). A coarse set of corresponding corner points on the generic and the images are obtained using RANSAC algorithm [10]. Note that we have limited our transformation to affine since the transformation obtained from the camera model (perspective transformation) is well approximated locally by an affine transformation. This set is considered an intrinsic affine preserved set and go beyond the scale and rotation preserving property inherent in SIFTs.

There are various methods for 3D iris model reconstruction. The method in [11] uses a microplenoptic camera to capture the three-dimensional (3D) topography of the anterior iris surface. This method provides 3D resolution of about 10–80 μm capture of the ridges and folds of the iris. The second method in [8] uses multiple high resolution 2D NIR images taken under proper lighting conditions. The captured 2D images of the iris are then used to acquire the 3D structure by using the Python Photogrammetry toolbox [8]. In this paper, we adopt a third method that efficiently and easily finds a coarse set of corresponding salient fiducial iris points in the images (at least two images) that are intrinsic and invariant under the image projection, from which a dense high-resolution set of corresponding salient points are easily obtained resulting in the synthesis of the 3D iris structure using triangulation. The texture for the 3D model can be obtained by importing the appearance of any triangle (at low resolution converging to a point at high resolution) on the images to the corresponding triangle using ray tracing on the 3D structure. This approach was used for 3D Building synthesis in [9].

3   3D Iris Synthesis

3.1   Situating Our Synthesis Method Within the Different Classes of Iris Synthesis

In this section we situate our proposed method in relation to the iris reconstruction methods mentioned in Sect. 2. The first method is direct, but the use of the specially designed hardware and cost make it complicated. The second method suffers from the fact that the input NIR images are taken under strict environmental constraints, such as ideal lighting and still conditions resulting in no blur using special cameras. In addition, at least 6 images are required to get a proper 3D model of the iris. The third method, while inexpensive and portable, does not require any special cameras or specific lighting conditions, it requires the tracking of corresponding points on the images to be able to reconstruct the 3D cloud via triangulation of a dense set of corresponding points. The method in this paper belongs to the third class of methods. Figure 2 shows a set of input images and the 3D synthesized iris model obtained using this method. It is interesting to note how similar the 3D façade of the iris is to the iris appearance of the two images.

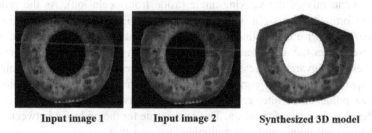

Input image 1   **Input image 2**   **Synthesized 3D model**

Fig. 2. Iris 3D construction process

3.2   Pre-processing

For this step, two input images of an iris are acquired from different views and pre-processed to remove the distortions present in the image of the eye in the form of blur, gaze deviation and extreme Mydriasis. Iris being a thin layer, it is very meticulous to cover its image from a higher angle, so a baseline distance of about 20 mm is considered to capture the effective features of the iris. The input images shown in Fig. 3, is first smoothed by a 5×5 Gaussian filter and the smoothed image is histogram equalized to facilitate the feature point detection process and make it easier. The iris is segmented from the pupil using the integral-differential operator [1, 2]. Both the centers and radii of the pupil and the iris are found, and the iris is segmented out from the input image leaving the sclera and the pupil as shown in Fig. 3(c) and (f). The two images are now ready for fiducial point extraction.

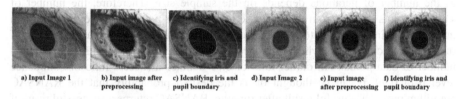

a) Input Image 1   b) Input image after preprocessing   c) Identifying iris and pupil boundary   d) Input Image 2   e) Input image after preprocessing   f) Identifying iris and pupil boundary

Fig. 3. Preprocessing of input image and segmentation

We only need to obtain a relatively small set of reliable corresponding salient points in contrast to most of 2D methods that require a dense set of fiducial points for recognition. A denser set of extra salient fiducial points is constructed at minimum cost using a loop sub-division method that yields corresponding extra salient points in the two images and a corresponding high-resolution 3D iris model.

3.3   Intrinsic and Invariant Salient Points

When viewing an iris from different points of view, salient points on the iris would appear in the images of that iris unless there is occlusion. This set of salient points are intrinsic and projective invariant. Namely, salient points that will appear as salient points independently of the viewing angle (aside from occlusion). As the projective image transformation for a pin hole camera is well approximated by an affine transformation or piecewise local affine transformations, it suffices to find salient points that are preserved under the affine transformation. One such set of salient points are corner points. These are invariably present in the set of different irises as the end points, the ridges, serpentine rings, and cornea. Under affine transformation, corner points map onto corner points since intersection points between two lines map into intersection points after the affine transformation. This is also true for the midpoint between the line joining two salient points and any midpoints between those.

3.4   Establishing Correspondences Between Salient Points in Two Images

To establish correspondences between the salient points obtained in the two images, we use RANSAC [10], which is a very efficient technique in solving the correspondence problem. In this paper, we choose a version of the RANSAC algorithm that allows the user to set a distance threshold for inliers. We elected not to use the 7-point algorithm as it returns 3 fundamental matrices, which makes the computation more tedious and non-unique.

The RANSAC algorithm consists of 4 steps to find the corresponding points. The first step involves sampling the number of data points required to fit the model. Secondly, the model parameters are computed using the sampled data points, which is based on the 8 corresponding sample points. Thirdly, a score is given for each trial based on the fraction of the inliers present within the preset threshold of the model. Finally, the first 3 steps are repeated until the best fit for the model is found.

Choosing the points for the sample step is the most important part of the algorithm as the number of iterations depends on the sample size. Therefore, the number of sampled points chosen from the larger set of consistent points must be the minimum number of points required to fit the model efficiently under affine map. A metric of outlier ratio is considered, which is defined as the ratio of number of outliers to the total number of data points. An outlier ratio of 0.01 denotes a success ratio or confidence level p of 0.99. p can be thought of as the desired probability that the RANSAC algorithm provides a useful result after running. RANSAC returns a successful result if in some iteration it selects only inliers (n of them) from the input data set from which the model parameters are estimated, with (1-p) being the probability that the algorithm never selects n points of inliers. An efficient way is choosing 8 samples and following an 8-point algorithm under an affine map. The corresponding points of the iris from the two images found through RANSAC serve as the basis for the loop subdivision resulting in a dense set of corresponding salient points.

3.5 Obtaining a High-Density Salient Point Set

A Delaunay triangulation is formed from the coarse set of salient points for the two images to tessellate the salient points in a triangular mesh. These salient meshes has correspondences between the two images at both the vertex-to-vertex and at triangle-to-triangle levels. To get a high-resolution 3D output, a dense set of salient points is required, so the Loop Subdivision routine in [9, 12, 13] is applied to each mesh. A midpoint is chosen for each side of a triangle in the mesh. The vertex-to-vertex correspondences are maintained since a midpoint on a line is affine preserved. This mesh loop subdivision is shown in Fig. 4 for the image of the iris shown in Fig. 3.

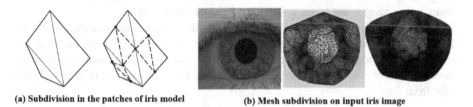

(a) Subdivision in the patches of iris model   (b) Mesh subdivision on input iris image

Fig. 4. Mesh loop subdivision

The salient points and the resulting new salient points after subdivision are also shown in Fig. 4(b). During the loop subdivision process, any three salient points that lie at the boundary of the pupil and form a triangle will generate midpoints that will fall inside the pupil. The pupil is never considered in the classification process due to the varying pupil dilations. So, the triangles that are formed inside the pupil region during the tessellation of the dense set of salient points are removed from the connectivity list. This is done by considering the boundary of the pupil and eliminating those vertices of the triangle that are formed inside the pupil's perimeter. A dense 3D cloud of the reconstructed model is attained using triangulation. Using ray tracing and triangulation of corresponding points in the high-resolution mesh in Fig. 4(b).

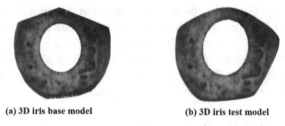

(a) 3D iris base model   (b) 3D iris test model

Fig. 5. Shows base model constructed from the first two images and the test model of the same iris constructed from the other two images of the same iris.

For every individual's eye we consider, a set of 4 images are taken. The first two images are taken under ideal lighting conditions, with no movement and are used to construct the 3D iris model (see Fig. 5(a)). This serves as the base model with its 3D points obtained from these two images. The other two images are used as the test images. These are taken under far from ideal conditions, with possible occlusion, blur, and poor lighting conditions. The test 3D iris model is synthesized as shown in Fig. 5 (b) for a given individual. The 3D high resolution synthesized model for iris 1 is shown in Fig. 5(b) and is almost identical to the base iris model (see Fig. 5(a)) constructed from the two images are taken under ideal lighting conditions.

To show how close the iris base and test 3D models are, we compute the point error distance between a point on the test iris model and its closest point on the base iris model. The error map distribution between test iris1 and base iris1 is close to zero (flat), whereas the error map distribution between base iris 1 and another test (e.g. test iris 93) is far from flat.

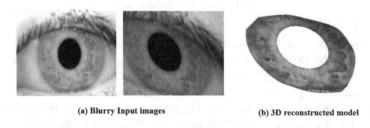

(a) Blurry Input images   (b) 3D reconstructed model

Fig. 6. 3D iris reconstruction for two input 2D iris images with noise.

We can add a textured appearance to the 3D iris model by importing the appearance of any triangle on the images to the corresponding triangle using ray tracing on the 3D structure. Unlike the 2D iris recognition, which is highly dependent on the image quality for recognition, a 3D based iris identification should in principle not be, as the 3D model is constructed from two input images even when blurry, affected by occlusion due to eyelids and pupil dilation, and/or not taken under different lighting conditions as each other or as the base images used in constructing the base model (see Fig. 6(a)). The constructed iris 3D model based on the images in Fig. 6(a) is shown in Fig. 6(b).

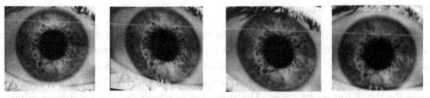

(a) Input images for base models under ideal conditions   (b) Input images for test models under unideal conditions

Fig. 7. Input images for base and test models.

Fig. 8. Comparison of common points of the base and test model of same iris in 4 different views.

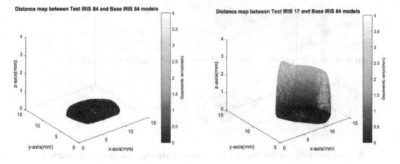

Fig. 9. Error cloud between base and test models of same iris under different image acquisition conditions compared to base and test models of different irises.

To show how well our 3D reconstruction technique fairs when the input test images are acquired under non ideal conditions as compared to base iris input images taken under ideal conditions as shown in Fig. 7(a). Test images for the same iris are taken under the non-ideal conditions are shown in Fig. 7(b). The resulting 3D model clouds obtained for input images in Fig. 7(a) and (b) are very close as shown in Fig. 8, which displays common points between the 3D constructed iris models under ideal and non-ideal conditions. As we can see the two 3D model cloud surfaces viewed here from 4 different 3D views are very close despite the blurring and occlusion involved. This is also reflected in the classification results in Sect. 4 shown in Table 1, as well as in Fig. 9, which shows the error cloud distance distribution between the 3D model constructed from the images in Fig. 7(a) to the one constructed from Fig. 7(b) contrasted to the error cloud distance distribution between the 3D model constructed from the images in Fig. 7(a) compared to a different iris base 3D model.

3.6   Failing 2D Iris Recognition

2D iris identification when the input iris test image is taken under non-ideal conditions or contains artifacts due to gaze deviation, blurring, or Mydriasis (extreme pupil dilation) is a difficult one. To illustrate that point, consider how well the famous Daugman's iris recognition model [14] implemented in [15, 16] performs on test images for the 3 following cases. The first case is where the test iris image is taken under ideal conditions and is compared to a base image also obtained under ideal conditions. As expected, the identification is successful as shown in Fig. 10(a), with the left iris image showing the base image and the right iris image is the test image, both acquired from the same individual. The second case is for two different iris images (corresponding to 2 different individuals) each taken under ideal conditions. The system once again correctly declares a mismatch between the iris images as shown in Fig. 10(b). In the third case, however, we consider an input image of an iris subjected to Mydriasis taken under ideal condition and compare it to a second image of the same iris where is blur due to motion during the image acquisition took place. This time 2D recognition system fails to identify the person as shown in Fig. 10(c).

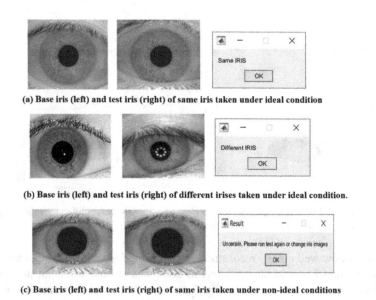

(a) Base iris (left) and test iris (right) of same iris taken under ideal condition

(b) Base iris (left) and test iris (right) of different irises taken under ideal condition.

(c) Base iris (left) and test iris (right) of same iris taken under non-ideal conditions

Fig. 10. 2D iris recognition method.

In contrast, the 3D iris identification for the same test case succeeds. The reconstructed 3D models overlaid over 4 different 3D views are shown in Fig. 11. It can be seen that, we are able to get a good 3D model. Thus, even in the presence of pupil dilation and blur, our 3D iris reconstruction is capable of correct iris identification when 2D based methods are not. As shown in Table 1 we can see that for iris 13 (Iris with Mydriasis) we get a good match with minimal geometric error.

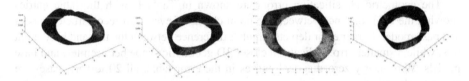

Fig. 11. Comparison of 3D common points of the Base and test models of same iris under mydriasis and mydriasis and blur.

Note that the work in [17] proposes reducing the effects of blur, occlusion due to eyelids, and pupil dilation (minimal dilation) present in the input iris image for 2D identification by using the multiple thresholding technique. In contrast, our 3D reconstruction algorithm proposed in this paper, does not require additional techniques for handling these distortions.

4 Evaluation

The performance of our 3D model-based method is tested on a data base consisting of 20 iris 3D base models (corresponding to 20 different individuals), which are constructed using for each base iris a set of two images acquired under ideal conditions. Using a set of two different (than the base) images acquired under non-ideal conditions, a test 3D model was constructed for every individual in the database, and hence a total of 20 test 3 iris models. A geometric error is obtained by calculating the mean square error (MSE) between one point in the test reconstructed model and its nearest neighbor point in the candidate base model. The geometric errors are calculated between reconstructed model (test model) and each possible base model (after centering to the same coordinate system). The entries in Table 1 shows the overall geometric error, which is the square root of the average of the squared of the individual errors over all points in the test model.

Table 1. Geometric error evaluation

Geometric error	Base Iris1	Base Iris2	Base Iris3	Base Iris4	Base Iris5	Base Iris6	Base Iris7	Base Iris8	Base Iris9	Base Iris10	Base Iris11	Base Iris12	Base Iris13	Base Iris14	Base Iris15	Base Iris16	Base Iris17	Base Iris18	Base Iris19	Base Iris20
Test Iris1	0.00	0.79	0.55	0.26	0.49	0.74	1.14	0.54	0.61	0.34	0.46	0.41	0.40	0.53	0.51	0.51	0.49	0.33	0.43	0.58
Test Iris2	0.13	0.00	0.30	0.24	0.35	0.30	0.24	0.19	0.40	0.30	0.24	0.25	0.12	0.16	0.51	0.21	0.26	0.16	0.11	0.25
Test Iris3	0.31	0.25	0.00	0.22	0.17	0.14	0.46	0.25	0.15	0.27	0.11	0.15	0.10	0.08	0.43	0.23	0.22	0.07	0.08	0.16
Test Iris4	0.16	0.70	0.37	0.03	0.21	0.42	0.93	0.58	0.44	0.08	0.45	0.19	0.42	0.41	0.71	0.26	0.23	0.20	0.29	0.53
Test Iris5	0.10	0.43	0.26	0.11	0.00	0.24	0.72	0.45	0.22	0.13	0.15	0.11	0.15	0.22	0.44	0.23	0.15	0.10	0.16	0.27
Test Iris6	0.08	0.25	0.09	0.14	0.18	0.00	0.47	0.18	0.18	0.19	0.08	0.15	0.07	0.09	0.43	0.14	0.14	0.02	0.05	0.17
Test Iris7	0.26	0.18	0.47	0.37	0.53	0.46	0.00	0.32	0.58	0.41	0.40	0.41	0.19	0.27	0.64	0.32	0.38	0.28	0.15	0.40
Test Iris8	0.09	0.16	0.13	0.14	0.18	0.15	0.33	0.00	0.23	0.19	0.11	0.14	0.05	0.04	0.41	0.14	0.15	0.04	0.05	0.14
Test Iris9	0.14	0.27	0.15	0.15	0.14	0.22	0.44	0.32	0.00	0.16	0.13	0.17	0.15	0.17	0.28	0.18	0.16	0.12	0.15	0.17
Test Iris10	0.16	0.64	0.29	0.07	0.29	0.52	0.38	0.58	0.63	0.00	0.32	0.28	0.32	0.28	0.58	0.23	0.20	0.15	0.19	0.41
Test Iris11	0.09	0.36	0.17	0.31	0.32	0.22	0.65	0.37	0.25	0.49	0.00	0.14	0.07	0.05	0.56	0.25	0.30	0.92	0.07	0.15
Test Iris12	0.21	0.69	0.39	0.29	0.31	0.35	0.92	0.50	0.46	0.57	0.47	0.00	0.44	0.41	0.85	0.36	0.35	0.24	0.30	0.56
Test Iris13	0.16	0.29	0.42	0.26	0.50	0.45	0.62	0.38	0.58	0.25	0.32	0.35	0.06	0.19	0.68	0.20	0.28	0.24	0.07	0.28
Test Iris14	0.11	0.33	0.19	0.19	0.31	0.24	0.61	0.33	0.34	0.34	0.15	0.22	0.08	0.06	0.50	0.17	0.17	0.12	0.06	0.20
Test Iris15	0.20	0.23	0.13	0.16	0.15	0.17	0.34	0.21	0.22	0.15	0.15	0.19	0.15	0.15	0.00	0.15	0.15	0.15	0.16	0.16
Test Iris16	0.11	0.33	0.18	0.07	0.25	0.25	0.56	0.29	0.33	0.09	0.23	0.18	0.17	0.11	0.44	0.00	0.10	0.09	0.09	0.24
Test Iris17	0.10	0.31	0.15	0.07	0.25	0.16	0.54	0.30	0.29	0.06	0.19	0.21	0.13	0.11	0.44	0.06	0.00	0.11	0.03	0.23
Test Iris18	0.10	0.46	0.17	0.12	0.12	0.31	0.69	0.40	0.24	0.15	0.13	0.19	0.14	0.12	0.42	0.19	0.16	0.09	0.09	0.24
Test Iris19	0.19	0.49	0.44	0.40	0.44	0.47	0.75	0.44	0.54	0.45	0.35	0.35	0.23	0.19	0.75	0.45	0.44	0.27	0.00	0.43
Test Iris20	0.10	0.21	0.13	0.14	0.20	0.14	0.48	0.25	0.24	0.20	0.07	0.16	0.06	0.06	0.40	0.11	0.13	0.06	0.07	0.00

The geometric classification errors are shown in Table 1, with the table entries showing the MSE distance between the point clouds of every test reconstructed model and base model. Larger error depicts a higher difference between the test and base point sets, while a smaller error indicates a closer 3D geometric shape between test and base models. With nearly zero diagonal entries in the error table, all 20 test iris cases are properly classified.

5 Conclusions

We constructed a 3D textured model of iris model from images of the iris by extracting corresponding intrinsic and invariant (under the projection transformation) salient fiducial points (corner points) on the 2D images. We construct the correspondences between 2 sets of salient points using RANSAC algorithm. These coarse corresponding feature points are tessellated to form a high-resolution triangular mesh using a loop subdivision process, where the midpoints of each edge of the triangles is itself a new salient point. The subdivision produces a dense set of corresponding landmarks on the images of the iris, and results in a high-resolution 3D iris model. Finally, the appearance of a triangular patch in the image is imported or rendered onto the personalized model. With multiple images, all coordinates and appearances are reconstructed in accordance with the observed images. Our 3D reconstruction iris model yields accurate iris identification even for cases where the test images are taken under non-ideal conditions or with artifacts due to gaze deviation, blurring, or Mydriasis. This is particularly useful when 2D image-based iris identification techniques become limited due to these distortions during the image acquisition.

References

1. Daugman, J.G.: High confidence visual recognition of persons by a test of statistical independence. IEEE Trans. Pattern Anal. Mach. Intell. **15**(11), 1148–1161 (1993)
2. Daugman, J.: The importance of being random: statistical principles of iris recognition. Pattern Recogn. **36**(2), 279–291 (2003)
3. Wildes, R.P.: Iris recognition: an emerging biometric technology. Proc. IEEE **85**(9), 1348–1363 (1997)
4. Boles, W.W., Boashash, B.: A human identification technique using images of the iris and wavelet transform. IEEE Trans. Signal Process. **46**(4), 1185–1188 (1998)
5. Wu, C., et al.: 3D model matching with viewpoint-invariant patches (VIP). In: 2018 IEEE Conference on Computer Vision and Pattern Recognition, pp. 1–8. IEEE, Anchorage (2008)
6. Lowe, D.G.: Distinctive image features from scale-invariant keypoints. Int. J. Comput. Vis. **60**(2), 91–110 (2004)
7. Fritz, G., Seifert, C., Kumar, M., Paletta, L.: Building detection from mobile imagery using informative SIFT descriptors. In: Kalviainen, H., Parkkinen, J., Kaarna, A. (eds.) SCIA. LNCS, vol. 3540, pp. 629–638. Springer, Berlin (2005). https://doi.org/10.1007/11499145_64
8. Bastias, D., et al.: A method for 3D iris reconstruction from multiple 2D near-infrared images. In: 2017 IEEE International Joint Conference on Biometrics (IJCB), pp. 503–509. IEEE, Denver (2017)

9. Cohen, F.S., Li, C.: 3D Building synthesis based on images and affine invariant salient features. In: Proceedings of the 2nd Mediterranean Conference on Pattern Recognition and Artificial Intelligence, pp. 44–51. ACM, Rabat (2018)

10. Fischler, M.A., Bolles, R.C.: Random sample consensus: a paradigm for model fitting with applications to image analysis and automated cartography. Commun. ACM **24**(6), 381–395 (1981)

11. Chen, H., et al.: Human iris three-dimensional imaging at micron resolution by a microplenoptic camera. Biomed. Opt. Express **8**(10), 4514–4522 (2017)

12. Liu, Z., Cohen, F.S.: 3D face reconstruction from image(s) based on gender and ethnicity models. In: IADIS International Conference Big Data Analytics, Data Mining and Computational Intelligence, pp. 79–86. IADIS, Lisbon (2017)

13. Zhang, C., Cohen, F.S.: 3-D face structure extraction and recognition from images using 3-D morphing and distance mapping. IEEE Trans. Image Process. **11**(11), 1249–1259 (2002)

14. Vatsa, M., Singh, R., Gupta, P.: Comparison of iris recognition algorithms. In: Proceedings of International Conference on Intelligent Sensing and Information Processing, pp. 354–358. Citeseer, Chennai (2004)

15. Loni, P.: Iris recognition system using 2D log-gabor filter. Int. J. Adv. Comput. Theory Eng. **1**(2), 59–62 (2002)

16. Matlab source code for a biometric identification system based on iris patterns. http://people. csse.uwa.edu.au/pk/studentprojects/libor/. Accessed 28 Jan 2019

17. Dehkordi, A.B., Abu-Bakar, S.A.: Noise reduction in iris recognition using multiple thresholding. In: 2013 IEEE International Conference on Signal and Image Processing Applications (ICSIPA), pp. 140–144. IEEE, Melaka (2013)

Parametric Model-Based 3D Human Shape and Pose Estimation from Multiple Views

Zhongguo Li$^{(\boxtimes)}$, Anders Heyden, and Magnus Oskarsson

Centre for Mathematical Sciences, Lund University, Lund, Sweden
{zhongguo.li,anders.heyden,magnus.oskarsson}@math.lth.se

Abstract. Human body pose and shape estimation is an important and challenging task in computer vision. This paper presents a novel method for estimating 3D human body pose and shape from several RGB images, using detected joint positions in the images and based on a parametric human body model. Firstly, the 2D joint points of the RGB images are estimated using a deep neural network, which provides a strong prior on the pose. Then, an energy function is constructed based on the 2D joint points in the RGB images and a parametric human body model. By minimizing the energy function, the pose, shape and camera parameters are obtained. The main contribution of the method over previous work, is that the optimization is based on several images simultaneously using only estimated joint positions in the images. We have performed experiments on both synthetic and real image data-sets, that demonstrate that our method can reconstruct 3D human bodies with better accuracy than previous single view methods.

Keywords: Human body · Parametric model · RGB images ·
Pose and shape estimation · Camera

1 Introduction

A 3D model of the human body is required in many applications, such as video games, e-commerce, virtual reality, biomedical research, etc. It is therefore important to have robust and accurate methods for recovering models of humans from one or several RGB-images. This is however a difficult problem, due to non-rigid motion, different clothing and complex articulation. This makes 3D body reconstruction a very challenging and interesting task in computer vision.

Aiming at effectively acquiring a realistic and personalized 3D human body, several methods have been proposed during the past decades, many using expensive active reconstruction equipment or improving the performance of reconstruction algorithms based on structure from motion methods. Using 3D scanners or multiple calibrated cameras in a controlled environment can obtain 3D models with very high accuracy [1]. The disadvantage of such methods is that these systems are very expensive and relatively complicated to build.

© Springer Nature Switzerland AG 2019
M. Felsberg et al. (Eds.): SCIA 2019, LNCS 11482, pp. 336–347, 2019.
https://doi.org/10.1007/978-3-030-20205-7_28

Besides these scanning systems, another line of research is to obtain 3D models from images acquired by ordinary cameras or depth sensors by stereo reconstruction algorithms or fusion algorithms [5–7]. These methods do not require expensive equipment or complicated set-ups, but are instead based on computationally expensive computer vision algorithms. Structure from motion (SfM) can reconstruct the 3D model of a person with static pose from a moving camera. Using depth sensors, for instance the Kinect, one can also obtain a 3D model through fusion of the geometries obtained from different view-points. These methods do not require any prior information, such as human shape.

Although these ideas have achieved a lot of progress on effectively obtaining 3D reconstructions, there is still a need for simpler methods to reconstruct 3D human body model. With the remarkable progress of human pose estimation based on deep neural networks (DNN), poses have been shown to provide useful information for the reconstruction. Therefore, other methods based on strong prior information are proposed to reconstruct 3D models and are shown to have good performance. These methods can estimate a 3D human body model from one monocular RGB image by fitting the statistical human body model to the human pose predicted by a DNN [22,23]. However, only one image is not sufficient in order to provide sufficient accurate 3D reconstruction in many cases, due to self-occlusion and complicated articulated motion.

In this paper we propose to use several (e.g. a sequence of) RGB images which are acquired from different viewpoints to reconstruct the 3D human body based on a skinned multi-person linear shape model (SMPL) [2]. We construct an energy function which measures the difference between the 2D joint points of the RGB images and the 2D joint points of the projected SMPL model. The 2D joint points of the RGB images are predicted by OpenPose [3]. The difference between our method and SfM-based methods is that we only use the estimated joint positions to reconstruct the 3D model. At the same time, the camera orientations are also regarded as parameters when the energy function is minimized. The advantage is that several images from different viewpoints can provide more accurate 3D information and the number of the images used in our method is in general fewer compared with SfM-based methods. Experiments on synthetic data and Human3.6M [4] show that our method obtains more accurate pose estimation and 3D shape, than similar methods based on a single image.

2   Related Work

As shown in [25], related work is basically divided into two categories: methods that do not use parametric models and methods based on parametric models.

Non-parametric model based methods typically reconstruct 3D models from images acquired by a camera from different viewpoints or from the fusion of depth sensors. The results of the methods can be obtained accurately without using any strong prior information. However, the person should stand still to capture the data and the computation is quite complex and time-consuming. The most well-known algorithm is KinectFusion [5] which creates 3D models in real time by incrementally fusing the partial scans from a moving RGB-D-sensor. It has good performance for rigid objects, but is not designed for articulated motion. Therefore, for the 3D reconstruction of a static person, some approaches [6,7] inspired by KinectFusion are proposed. These methods cannot achieve satisfying result for the dynamic person since the human body typically is moving non-rigidly between different views. DynamicFusion [8], which is the pioneering work for the reconstruction of non-rigid objects, can reconstruct the 3D geometry in real time for a slowly moving person. Other methods such as KillingFusion [9] and BodyFusion [12] are proposed to improve the results based on DynamicFusion. However, these approaches are only suitable for slow motion and have high computational complexity. In order to obtain more accurate results, multiple Kinect sensors or several calibrated cameras can be utilized to create 3D human body models. In [10], the authors propose to use eight Kinects to obtain the 3D model with high accuracy. Multiple cameras are also used in [1,11] to reconstruct the 3D human body. However, there are technical challenges and it is expensive to build a system with eight Kinects or to build the indoor environment like [1] for many practical applications.

Parametric model-based methods often rely on a template which provides strong prior information during the reconstruction. The template can be reconstructed from depth data or using a pre-computed human body model. In [13–15], a novel non-rigid registration algorithm is proposed to register a pre-scanned model to other partial depth data acquired by Kinect. In [14], a template is obtained through registering several high quality partial scans and then a personalized 3D model is reconstructed by fitting to the template. Some other algorithms [16,17] have similar ideas but they use more complicated information or hardware to improve the accuracy and efficiency. Besides pre-scanning the template, a number of statistical human body models have been proposed based on training of a human body set, such as SCAPE [18], SMPL [2] and so on [19]. In [20] the authors use the SCAPE model to fit the depth image to obtain a 3D model. The improved SCAPE model, Delta, is proposed in [21] and a detailed body reconstruction algorithm is presented in this paper. In [22], the authors propose to fit the SMPL model by using 2D joint points predicted by a DNN-based method. Huang et al. [23] use a similar idea but they focus on the video problem, using temporal information. In [24] an end-to-end adversarial learning method is used to estimate the human pose and shape parameters by fitting the SMPL model. Alldieck et al. [25] propose an algorithm to obtain the consensus shape and then use both pose and consensus shape to fit the SMPL model in order to obtain better result.

3   Method

Our aim is to obtain the 3D model of a human body from several RGB images taken from different view-points. Our approach is inspired by the work in [22] where the 3D human body model is estimated from only one RGB image. Although the method in [22] has achieved some accuracy, the error is still noticeable in many cases since one RGB image cannot supply enough information. As

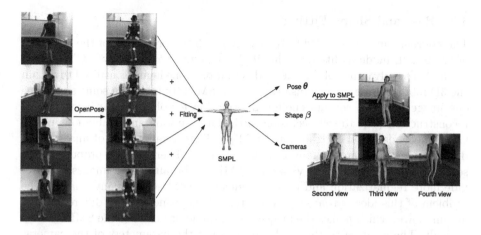

Fig. 1. The overview of our method.

an improvement, we propose to use several RGB images taken from different view-points to reconstruct the 3D model. This leads to a more challenging optimization problem, since the motion of the cameras is unknown, and we need to introduce the parameters of the cameras as variables to estimate. Firstly, we estimate the positions of the 2D joint points of the person in the images by using OpenPose. Then, the SMPL model is fitted to the pose of the person in different views by optimizing an energy function in which the camera parameters are included. Finally, the pose, shape and the camera parameters are estimated to obtain the 3D model of the human. The pipeline of our method is summarized in Fig. 1. In the following, we firstly introduce SMPL model, then the energy function and finally the optimization that gives the estimation of the camera parameters as well as the pose and shape parameters of the 3D human model.

3.1 SMPL Model

The SMPL model encodes both pose and shape parameters [22]. The pose is defined from the parameter θ, which represents the relative rotations of the 23 joint points with respect to the root joint. The shape is represented by the parameter β, which describes the strength of each mode in a shape space obtained from a principal component analysis (PCA) from a registered training set. The pose parameters are represented as a vector $\theta \in \mathbb{R}^{72}$ and the shape parameters as a vector $\beta \in \mathbb{R}^{10}$.

The output of the SMPL model after introducing pose and shape is a mesh with $N = 6890$ vertices and $F = 13776$ faces, $M(\theta, \beta) \in \mathbb{R}^{N \times 3}$. In this model, the 3D joints are obtained by linear regression from the surface mesh vertices, i.e., a function of the pose and shape coefficients. Therefore, the pose and shape parameters can be estimated by optimizing an energy function based on the joint points.

3.2   Pose and Shape Fitting

The approach in [22] is called SMPLify, in which the projection of the 3D joints of the SMPL model is fitted to the 2D joint points predicted by a CNN-based method. The advantage of this method is that only one image is utilized to obtain the 3D model. However, one disadvantage of SMPLify is that in some situations one image does not contain enough information for obtaining an accurate 3D reconstruction (due to self-occlusion, articulated motion and ambiguous pose). Other methods based on traditional SfM pipelines, require a lot of images from different views and are computationally intensive. Therefore, we propose to use several images from different views into SMPLify because more images will provide more regularization and it is convenient to not use too many images. The problem of this idea is that the parameters of the cameras from different views are unknown, which makes the projection of the joint points of the SMPL model difficult. The solution to this problem is to use the parameters of the cameras together with the pose and shape of the SMPL model as the variables of an energy function during the optimization. The advantage of this method is that we can obtain not only an estimate of the pose and shape but also an estimate of the cameras parameters (position and orientation).

The energy function contains three parts: the pose-fitting term, the shape parameter regularization term and the pose parameter regularization term. We define the energy function as:

$$E(\boldsymbol{\theta}, \boldsymbol{\beta}, R_i) = E_J(\boldsymbol{\theta}, \boldsymbol{\beta}, R_i) + \lambda_\theta E_\theta(\boldsymbol{\theta}) + \lambda_\beta E_\beta(\boldsymbol{\beta}), \tag{1}$$

where $E_J(\boldsymbol{\theta}, \boldsymbol{\beta}, R_i)$ is the pose fitting term, $E_\theta(\boldsymbol{\theta})$ is the pose parameters regularization term, $E_\beta(\boldsymbol{\beta})$ is the shape parameters regularization term and λ_θ and λ_β are weights. In the energy function, the pose $\boldsymbol{\theta}$, the shape $\boldsymbol{\beta}$ and the rotation of the camera R_i can be estimated through

$$\hat{\boldsymbol{\theta}}, \hat{\boldsymbol{\beta}}, \hat{R}_i = arg \min E(\boldsymbol{\theta}, \boldsymbol{\beta}, R_i). \tag{2}$$

The most important term is E_J in our method and it is defined as

$$E_J(\boldsymbol{\theta}, \boldsymbol{\beta}, R_i) = \sum_{i=1}^{N} \sum_{k=1}^{K} \rho(\Pi_i(J_{S,k}) - J_{2d,k}^{(i)}), \tag{3}$$

where N is the number of images, K is the number of joint points, $J_{S,k}$ is the k-th 3D joint points of the SMPL model, Π_i is the i-th camera, $J_{2d,k}^{(i)}$ is the k-th 2D joint points estimated by OpenPose for the i-th image and R_i is the rotation for i-th camera. The error ρ is measured by the Geman-McClure function [26] which gives robustness to large noise and outliers. This function is defined as

$$\rho(x) = \frac{x^2}{\sigma^2 + x^2}, \tag{4}$$

where x is the absolute errors of 2D joint points and σ is a constant. The projection of the 3D joint points of the SMPL model in the i-th camera is

$$\Pi_i(J_S) = R_i J_S + t_i,$$

where t_i is the translation of the i-th camera. The translation is calculated separately using the shoulders and hips, which implies that we can assume that the person is standing parallel to the image plane. Because the projection is linear, the derivatives of the error function can be computed easily during the optimization.

The pose regularization is needed for avoiding the knees and elbows bending unnaturally and it is defined as

$$E_\theta(\boldsymbol{\theta}) = \alpha \sum_i exp(\theta_i), \qquad (5)$$

where $\boldsymbol{\theta}_i$ denotes the pose of the joint points of elbows and knees and α is a constant that controls the penalization. The shape regularization term is defined as

$$E_\beta(\boldsymbol{\beta}) = \sum \beta_i, \qquad (6)$$

i.e. as the sum of the elements of $\boldsymbol{\beta}$.

3.3 Optimization

The optimization is performed in two steps. In the first step the camera translation is estimated. Here the focal length of the camera is assumed to be known. The camera translation can be estimated through fitting the shoulders and hips in the SMPL model and the predicted 2D pose.

In the second step the model is fitted through minimization of (3). The parameters λ_θ and λ_β are decreased gradually during the optimization. The minimization method is based on Powell's dogleg method, which is provided by the python module OpenDR [27] and Chumpy [28]. For four different views (image size 320×240), it takes about 2 min for the minimization on a desktop machine.

4 Experiment

In this section some experiments are presented to illustrate the performance of our method. In the first experiment, we generate a small synthetic dataset based on SURREAL [29] in which a large amount of synthetic human bodies with different poses and shapes are created based on the SMPL model. Since the SURREAL only provides videos from one view, we generate three more images from the other views. Then, for the real images, our method is evaluated on the Human3.6M which is for the evaluation of human pose estimation.

In our experiments, the parameters $(\lambda_\theta, \lambda_\beta)$ decrease as (404, 100), (404, 50), (58, 5), (4.78, 1). The σ is set to 100 and α is 10. The maximum number of iterations is 100 for every stage and the stopping criteria is that the error of the energy function is smaller than 10^{-3}. The experiments are implemented in Python and our desktop machine has a 4 core Intel i5-6500 CPU @ 3.20 GHz with 8 GB RAM.

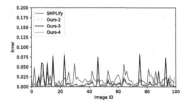 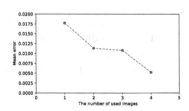

Fig. 2. The errors of the 100 samples and the mean error. Left shows the errors of the 100 samples. Right shows the mean error of the 100 samples of SMPLify and our method with two, three and four images.

Table 1. The mean errors of SMPLify compared with our method using respectively 2, 3 and 4 images.

	SMPLify	Ours-2	Ours-3	Ours-4
Mean error	0.0177	0.0113	0.0108	0.00525

4.1 Results on Synthetic Data

The synthetic images are generated based on SURREAL. We utilize 100 pose and shape parameters from the training information data of SURREAL into the SMPL model to generate 100 different 3D human bodies. Then, four images whose sizes are 320×240 are projected by cameras from different view-points for each human body model. At the same time, the joint points of the human body in each image are also computed. (We will provide this small dataset online). In our method the 3D models are estimated from two, three and four views respectively. As comparison, the 3D models obtained by SMPLify are also given. In order to quantitatively compare the results, the metric for evaluation is defined as:

$$Error = \frac{1}{N} \sum_{i=1}^{N} ||J_i^{gt} - J_i^{est}||_2, \tag{7}$$

where J_i^{gt} is the ground truth of the 3D joint points and J_i^{est} is the estimated 3D joint points. In this part, there are a total of 24 joint points for the SMPL model.

The errors for the 100 samples and the mean error using different number of images are given in Fig. 2. It is shown that the error is smaller when more images are used in the method for most samples. In some cases, the error of our method with two or three images is greater. This is because images from two different views may influence each others since the camera at the side position cannot capture all of the joint points. The mean error of the 100 samples is also given in Table 1. We can see that the mean error decreases when more images are utilized and that the performance of our method surmounts that of SMPLify, which shows that more images indeed can provide more useful information. In Fig. 3 some images are given as qualitative results. Each row corresponds to one

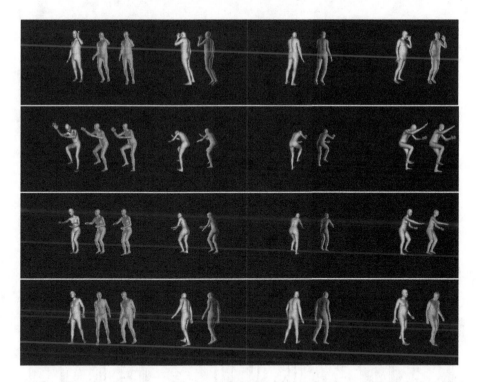

Fig. 3. The figure shows results on synthetic data. Each row corresponds to one person with some unknown shape and pose. For each row the left hand image in each column is the input image for frame one to four. The middle image in column one is the result from SMPLify using only the input image from frame one. The right hand image in each column is the result of our method using all four input frames.

person with some unknown shape and pose. For each row the left hand image in each column is the input image for frame one to four. The middle image in column one is the result from SMPLify using only the input image from frame one. The right hand image in each column is the result of our method using all four input frames. We can see from the first image that our method has better performance, especially the last one. The images from other views show that the estimation of the cameras by our method is very correct, which demonstrates the effectiveness of our method.

4.2   Results on Human3.6M

There are total of 11 subjects (6 males, 5 females) in Human3.6M and every person has 15 actions. In order to test our method sufficiently, we choose S1 which is a female and S6 which is a male to evaluate our method on 8 actions: Directions, Discussion, Eating, Greeting, Phoning, Posing, Purchasing and Sitting. For each action, we sample the video every five frames and take total of 100 frames. The

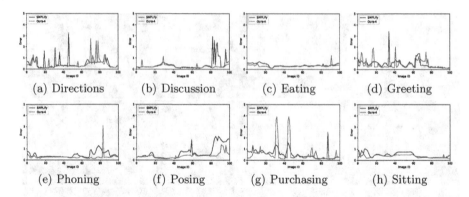

(a) Directions	(b) Discussion	(c) Eating	(d) Greeting
(e) Phoning	(f) Posing	(g) Purchasing	(h) Sitting

Fig. 4. The errors of every frame of the eight actions for S1.

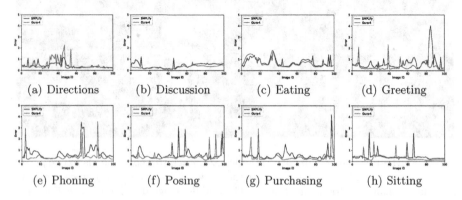

(a) Directions	(b) Discussion	(c) Eating	(d) Greeting
(e) Phoning	(f) Posing	(g) Purchasing	(h) Sitting

Fig. 5. The errors of every frame of the eight actions for S6.

results of SMPLify and our method with four images are compared. The metric for the comparison is also computed according to Eq. (7). In this part there are 16 joint points because the number of joints in Human3.6M is 16. Similarly, the errors of every frame in the different actions for S1 and S6 are shown in Figs. 4 and 5. The mean errors of the 100 frames in each action for S1 and S2 are shown in Tables 2 and 3. It is shown in these results that our method can obtain more accurate estimation in most cases.

In addition, some images from the dataset are shown in Fig. 6. We can see from Fig. 6 that SMPLify has obvious errors such as the occlusion of the arms and bodies. Our method sometimes also have unexpected errors because of having a side-view such as such as the fifth sample. The reason is that our method relies on all of the observed images. Therefore, if one camera translation is not estimated correctly, it will affect the images from other views and then the final results may be incorrect after the optimization. However, SMPLify only uses one image and if this image is not captured from the side view, the result is sometimes better than ours. In general, our method can achieve better estimation than SMPLify.

Table 2. The mean errors of the eight actions of S1.

	Directions	Discussion	Eating	Greeting	Phoning	Posing	Purchasing	Sitting
SMPLify	0.4866	0.4205	0.7401	0.6624	0.7270	0.6746	0.5410	0.4784
Ours-4	0.4281	0.3048	0.6952	0.3357	0.4144	0.3938	0.5471	0.3470

Table 3. The mean errors of the eight actions of S6.

	Directions	Discussion	Eating	Greeting	Phoning	Posing	Purchasing	Sitting
SMPLify	0.4880	0.3870	0.3597	0.4895	0.4543	0.5815	0.5530	0.4291
Ours-4	0.4280	0.2416	0.3114	0.4395	0.2711	0.4203	0.3372	0.2891

Fig. 6. Some samples from S1 and S6. The first images are given the results of SMPLify and our method from left to right.

5   Conclusion

We have proposed a method to reconstruction a 3D human body model from several RGB images taken from different view-points. Our approach starts by estimating the 2D joint points of the images by using a DNN-based method called OpenPose. Then, a statistical human body model, SMPL, is utilized to fit the predicted 2D joint points from the images by minimizing an energy function over all images simultaneously. Finally, our method estimates both the pose and shape parameters of the human body as well as the camera parameters. Experiments on synthetic and real data quantitatively and qualitatively demonstrate that the results of our method are better regarding the pose error compared to the previous method based on only one image.

Our method also has some limitation. If the images are captured from the side view, the joint points will be very close to each other or even at the same position, which makes our method unstable. Also, we mainly focus on the estimation of the pose and this implies that the shape of the reconstruction is less accurate. However, this is a fundamental limitation of all methods that only use the joint positions and disregard the contours of the body.

References

1. Joo, H., et al.: Panoptic studio: a massively multiview system for social interaction capture. IEEE Trans. Pattern Anal. Mach. Intell. **44**(1), 190–204 (2017)
2. Loper, M., Mahmood, N., Romero, J., Pons-Moll, G., Black, M.: SMPL: a skinned multi-person linear model. ACM Trans. Graph. **34**(6), 248:1–248:16 (2015)
3. Cao, Z., Simon, T., Wei, S., Sheikh, Y.: Realtime multi-person 2D pose estimation using part affinity fields. In: CVPR, pp. 1302–1310. IEEE, Honolulu (2017)
4. Ionescu, C., Papava, D., Olaru, V., Sminchisescu, C.: Human3.6M: large scale datasets and predictive methods for 3D human sensing in natural environments. IEEE Trans. Pattern Anal. Mach. Intell. **36**(7), 1325–1339 (2014)
5. Izadi, S., et al.: KinectFusion: real-time 3D reconstruction and interaction using a moving depth camera. In: 24th Annual ACM Symposium on User Interface Software and Technology, pp. 559–568. ACM, New York (2011)
6. Shapiro, A., et al.: Rapid avatar capture and simulation using commodity depth sensors. Comput. Animat. Virtual Worlds **25**(3–4), 201–211 (2014)
7. Cui, Y., Chang, W., Nöll, T., Stricker, D.: KinectAvatar: fully automatic body capture using a single kinect. In: Park, J.-I., Kim, J. (eds.) ACCV 2012. LNCS, vol. 7729, pp. 133–147. Springer, Heidelberg (2013). https://doi.org/10.1007/978-3-642-37484-5_12
8. Newcombe, R., Fox, D., Seitz, S.: DynamicFusion: reconstruction and tracking of non-rigid scenes in real-time. In: CVPR, pp. 343–352. IEEE, Boston (2015)
9. Slavcheva, M., Baust, M., Cremers, D., Ilic, S.: KillingFusion: non-rigid 3D reconstruction without correspondences. In: CVPR, pp. 5474–5483. IEEE, Honolulu (2017)
10. Dou, M., et al.: Fusion4D: real-time performance capture of challenging scenes. ACM Trans. Graph. **35**(4), 114:1–114:13 (2016)
11. Leroy, V., Franco, J., Boyer, E.: Multi-view dynamic shape refinement using local temporal integration. In: ICCV, pp. 3113–3122. IEEE, Venice (2017)

12. Yu, T., et al.: BodyFusion: real-time capture of human motion and surface geometry using a single depth camera. In: ICCV, pp. 910–919. IEEE, Venice (2017)
13. Li, H., Adams, B., Guibas, L.J., Pauly, M.: Robust single-view geometry and motion reconstruction. ACM Trans. Graph. **28**(5), 175:1–175:10 (2009)
14. Zhang, Q., Fu, B., Ye, M., Yang, R.: Quality dynamic human body modeling using a single low-cost depth camera. In: CVPR, pp. 676–683. IEEE, Columbus (2014)
15. Guo, K., Xu, F., Wang, Y., Liu, Y., Dai, Q.: Robust non-rigid motion tracking and surface reconstruction using L0 regularization. In: ICCV, pp. 3083–3091. IEEE, Santiago (2015)
16. Zollhofer, M., et al.: Real-time non-rigid reconstruction using an RGB-D camera. ACM Trans. Graph. **33**(4), 156:1–156:12 (2014)
17. Xu, W., et al.: MonoPerfCap: human performance capture from monocular video. ACM Trans. Graph. **37**(2), 27:1–27:15 (2018)
18. Anguelov, D., Srinivasan, P., Koller, D., Thrun, S., Rodgers, J., Davis, J.: SCAPE: shape completion and animation of people. ACM Trans. Graph. **24**(3), 408–416 (2005)
19. Pons-Moll, G., Romero, J., Mahmood, N., Black, M.J.: Dyna: a model of dynamic human shape in motion. ACM Trans. Graph. **34**(4), 120:1–120:14 (2015)
20. Weiss, A., Hirshberg, D., Black, M.J.: Home 3D body scans from noisy image and range data. In: ICCV, pp. 1951–1958. IEEE, Barcelona (2011)
21. Bogo, F., Black, M.J., Loper, M., Romero, J.: Detailed full-body reconstructions of moving people from monocular RGB-D sequences. In: ICCV, pp. 2300–2308. IEEE, Santiago (2015)
22. Bogo, F., Kanazawa, A., Lassner, C., Gehler, P., Romero, J., Black, M.J.: Keep it SMPL: automatic estimation of 3D human pose and shape from a single image. In: Leibe, B., Matas, J., Sebe, N., Welling, M. (eds.) ECCV 2016. LNCS, vol. 9909, pp. 561–578. Springer, Cham (2016). https://doi.org/10.1007/978-3-319-46454-1_34
23. Huang, Y., et al.: Towards accurate marker-less human shape and pose estimation over time. In: 3DV, pp. 421–430. IEEE, Qingdao (2017)
24. Kanazawa, A., Black, M., Jacobs, D., Malik, J.: End-to-end recovery of human shape and pose. In: CVPR. IEEE, Salt Lake City (2018)
25. Alldieck, T., Magnor, M., Xu, W., Theobalt, C., Pons-Moll, G.: Video based reconstruction of 3D people models. In: CVPR. IEEE, Salt Lake City (2018)
26. Geman, S., McClure, D.: Statistical methods for tomographic image reconstruction. Bull. Int. Stat. Inst. **52**, 5–21 (1987)
27. Loper, M.M., Black, M.J.: OpenDR: an approximate differentiable renderer. In: Fleet, D., Pajdla, T., Schiele, B., Tuytelaars, T. (eds.) ECCV 2014. LNCS, vol. 8695, pp. 154–169. Springer, Cham (2014). https://doi.org/10.1007/978-3-319-10584-0_11
28. Chumpy. http://chumpy.org
29. Varol, G., et al.: Learning from synthetic humans. In: CVPR, pp. 4627–4635. IEEE, Honolulu (2017)

Efficient Merging of Maps and Detection of Changes

Gabrielle Flood$^{(\boxtimes)}$ (iD), David Gillsjö(iD), Anders Heyden(iD), and Kalle Åström(iD)

Centre for Mathematical Sciences, Lund University, Lund, Sweden
{gabrielle,davidg,heyden,kalle}@maths.lth.se

Abstract. With the advent of cheap sensors and computing capabilities as well as better algorithms it is now possible to do structure from motion using crowd sourced data. Individual estimates of a map can be obtained using structure from motion (SfM) or simultaneous localization and mapping (SLAM) using e.g. images, sound or radio. However the problem of map merging as used for collaborative SLAM needs further attention. In this paper we study the basic principles behind map merging and collaborative SLAM. We develop a method for merging maps – based on a small memory footprint representation of individual maps – in a way that is computationally efficient. We also demonstrate how the same framework can be used to detect changes in the map. This makes it possible to remove inconsistent parts before merging the maps. The methods are tested on both simulated and real data, using both sensor data from radio sensors and from cameras.

Keywords: Map merging · Change detection · Collaborative SLAM · SfM

1 Introduction

Structure from motion [5], is the problem of estimating the parameters of a map and of sensor motion using only sensor data. The map is typically a set of 2D or 3D points each consisting of a position and a feature vector. Assuming that feature errors are zero-mean Gaussian, the maximum likelihood estimate is that of minimising the sum of squares of the residuals. Within the field of computer vision this process is denoted bundle adjustment, where *bundle* refers to the bundle of light rays connecting each camera with each 3D point. For an overview of the literature and theory, see [13].

These optimization techniques are applicable not only to vision, but also to other types of sensors, such as audio, [9,14] and radio [1]. With the advent of cheaper sensors and computing capabilities as well as better algorithms, it is now possible to gather and use much larger datasets. Instead of mapping a city every 5 years using special measurement cars or aerial photography, it is in principle possible for every car to add to the map of cities as they drive through them. Thus there is an additional need for research on map merging, including

© Springer Nature Switzerland AG 2019
M. Felsberg et al. (Eds.): SCIA 2019, LNCS 11482, pp. 348–360, 2019.
https://doi.org/10.1007/978-3-030-20205-7_29

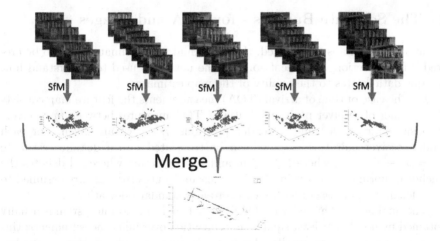

Fig. 1. Structure from motion (SfM) is used to estimate a 3D map of scene features using images (or other sensors). In this paper we study the problem of detecting changes and merging maps, given multiple maps estimated by SfM from datasets collected at different occasions.

the problem of determining what has changed in a map. In this paper we study the basic principles behind map merging and collaborative SLAM. A straight-forward method to merge several individual maps is to take all measurements into account simultaneously. However, non-linear optimization using all data can be prohibitively slow. We will study how a small memory footprint representation of a map can be generated and used to merge maps in a way that is computationally efficient, while still retaining most of the information from each individual bundle adjustment. We also demonstrate how the same framework can be used to detect changes in the map. This makes it possible to remove changing parts before merging the stationary parts of the map. The idea is demonstrated in Fig. 1.

The idea of approximating the result from parts of the data has previously been used in the rotation averaging literature, cf. [2]. These approximate methods can give satisfactory results at a much increased speed. Another example of this idea is the approach of Global Epipolar Adjustment [12], in which a simplified error metric is based on the linear epipolar constraints for image pairs. Another approach is incremental light bundle adjustment, iBLA, [6] in which an error metric based on a combination of epipolar constraints and a variant of the trifocal constraint is used.

The main contributions of this paper are a novel method for computationally efficiently merging of individual maps obtained from bundle adjustment, utilizing a compact representation of the Jacobian matrix, and a change detection method based on a statistical analysis of the residuals.

2   The Separate Bundles - for TOA and Images

Before different maps are merged, the individual map estimates have to be created. In this section we present some of the notations used to understand how the raw data relates to the quality of the map estimates.

For the case of time of arrival (TOA) measurements the feature map consists of a number of receiver positions. Initially, TOA measures between m receivers at positions $x_i \in \mathcal{R}^3$ and n sender positions $y_j \in \mathcal{R}^3$ are given. For each sender-receiver pair this measure can be translated into a distance estimate $d_{ij} = |x_i - y_j| + \varepsilon_{ij}$, where $1 \leq i \leq m$ and $1 \leq j \leq n$ and where $|\cdot|$ denotes the Euclidean norm of a vector in $\mathcal{R}^3$. The measurements errors ε_{ij} are assumed to be independent, Gaussian with mean zero and standard deviation σ.

The final map estimate for a TOA or structure from motion system is usually obtained by non-linear least squares minimization over inlier measurements; this process is referred to as bundle adjustment in computer vision. Here, a few key components from the optimization are presented.

For the TOA data, let $\mathbf{r}$ denote the measurements residuals,

$$\mathbf{r} = \begin{bmatrix} r_{11} \ldots r_{1n}\, r_{21} \ldots r_{2n}\, r_{m1} \ldots r_{mn} \end{bmatrix}^T, \qquad r_{ij} = d_{ij} - |x_i - y_j|, \quad (1)$$

and denote the parameters of interest, which are optimized, by $\mathbf{z}$. This would typically be the receiver and the sender positions,

$$\mathbf{z} = (x_1, x_2, \ldots x_m, y_1, \ldots y_n). \tag{2}$$

The computer vision case is analogous. Denoting the camera matrices P_i and the 3D points U_j, each image point u_{ij} gives a residual r_{ij}. The residual vector $\mathbf{r}$ is found by stacking all image feature residuals r_{ij} and the parameters are collected in a parameter vector

$$\mathbf{z} = (P_1, P_2, \ldots P_m, U_1, \ldots U_n). \tag{3}$$

The maximum likelihood estimate of $\mathbf{z}$ is found by minimizing the sum of the squares of the residuals, i.e.

$$\mathbf{z}^* = \mathrm{argmin}_{\mathbf{z}} \mathbf{r}^T \mathbf{r}, \tag{4}$$

which gives the optimal parameter update

$$\Delta \mathbf{z} = -(J^T J)^{-1} J^T \mathbf{r}. \tag{5}$$

For more details on the optimization, see [13]. For the analysis, the estimate of the matrix J (the Jacobian) is containing the derivatives of the residuals with respect to the parameters is of interest, i.e. $\mathbf{r}$ with respect to $\mathbf{z}$, further on denoted $\partial \mathbf{r}/\partial \mathbf{z}$.

The map points can only be estimated up to a choice of coordinate system. For simplicity we will in the TOA case normalize the coordinate system so that the first receiver is placed in the origin, the second along the x-axis, the third in the xy-plane and so forth. By removing this gauge freedom with dimension ϕ we see that the effective number of degrees of freedom in the problem is $d_{dof} = (m + n)\rho - \phi$, where ρ denotes the dimension. For TOA problems in 3D we have $\rho = 3$ and $\phi = 6$. The effective degrees of freedom for the computer vision case becomes $d_{dof} = (6m + 3n) - \phi$, with gauge freedom $\phi = 7$ since we are free to choose position, orientation and scale of the coordinate system.

3   Merging Separate Maps

Once the N separate maps are obtained they can be merged to get a single more accurate map. We have investigated three different ways to do this.

3.1   The Full Bundle

One way to add the maps is do one large bundle where all the individual measurements are used simultaneously. Merging all maps through a large bundle is a good way to get an accurate map. However, the method is time consuming and if a new measurement is made after the original merge, the whole map has to be re-bundled. In that sense, there is no way to *add* new information to the existing, which makes this method unsuitable for online applications.

3.2   The Kalman Filter

A traditional method designed to update parameters gradually is the Kalman filter [8]. The algorithm for the Kalman filter looks as follows:

Priori estimate update: Measurement update:

$$x_1 = A \cdot x_0 \tag{6}$$
$$K = P_1 \cdot H^T \cdot (H \cdot P_1 \cdot H^T + R)^{-1} \tag{8}$$
$$P_1 = A \cdot P_0 \cdot A^T + Q \tag{7}$$
$$x_2 = x_1 + K \cdot (u - H \cdot x_1) \tag{9}$$
$$P_2 = (I - K \cdot H) \cdot P_1. \tag{10}$$

Then, $H \cdot x_2$ is the new state prediction, and x_2 and P_2 are the new estimates replacing x_0 and P_0 for the next iteration. In our case x_0 will be the receivers from the first measurement occasion, $x_0 = q^{(1)}$ (superscript denoting measurement occasion), while the observation u will be the receiver values from the following $N - 1$ measurements s.t. $u_{k-1} = q^{(k)}$, $2 \le k \le N$. Both the update matrix and the observation matrix are identity matrices, $A = I$, $H = I$ and the covariance of the random excitation is set to $Q = 0.1 \cdot I$. Finally, P_0 and R are measurement uncertainties, $P_0 = C[\Delta q^{(1)}]$ and $R_{k-1} = C[\Delta q^{(k)}]$, $2 \le k \le N$. The covariance $C[\Delta q]$ can be extracted from the covariance of Δz from Eq. (5). This is given by

$$C[\Delta z] = (J^T J)^{-1} J^T \cdot E[r^T r] \cdot J(J^T J)^{-1} = \sigma^2 (J^T J)^{-1}. \tag{11}$$

The covariance of the map, $C[\Delta q]$, can be retrieved by picking the rows and columns in $C[\Delta z]$ that correspond to q and the variance of r can be approximated by [7, p. 148]

$$\sigma^2 \approx \frac{1}{m \cdot n - d_{dof}} \cdot r^T r = \frac{1}{m \cdot n - d_{dof}} \cdot \sum_{i=1}^{m \cdot n} r_i^2. \tag{12}$$

The Kalman filter is a computationally cheap method. However, it is not as accurate as the full bundle. Also, the parameters need to be tuned for the specific problem and it is not evident either how to detect and handle changes in the map.

3.3   The Linearized Method

The idea of this method is that the optimal residuals from the separate bundles can be linearized – such that all that needs to be saved is a small memory footprint representation – to avoid the large bundles. Having the optimal residuals $r^{(k)}$ and the optimal Jacobians $J^{(k)}$ from each run k, the residuals can be linearized using a first order Taylor approximation. A key idea here is to divide the unknown parameters in z into two parts q and s, where q are the parameters that exist in several SLAM sessions. The parameters s can be thought of as auxiliary paramters, e.g. those that are relevant only for one specific bundle session. In the time-of-arrival case, some of the 3D anchors might be constant over several SLAM sessions whereas the measurement points and some of the anchors might be different. For vision based structure from motion, some of the 3D points are the same (these go into q) whereas the rest of the points and camera matrices go into s.

The Compressed Residual. First, the Jacobian is divided into two blocks

$$J = \begin{bmatrix} J_a & J_b \end{bmatrix}, \tag{13}$$

where J_a contains the columns that correspond to the main parameters q and J_b contains the columns corresponding to the auxiliary parameters s. The squared Jacobian is

$$J^T J = \begin{bmatrix} J_a^T \\ J_b^T \end{bmatrix} \cdot \begin{bmatrix} J_a & J_b \end{bmatrix} = \begin{bmatrix} J_a^T J_a & J_a^T J_b \\ J_b^T J_a & J_b^T J_b \end{bmatrix} = \begin{bmatrix} U & W \\ W^T & V \end{bmatrix}. \tag{14}$$

Furthermore, if we insert this in the equation for the optimal update from (5) we get

$$\Delta z = \begin{bmatrix} \Delta q \\ \Delta s \end{bmatrix} = -(J^T J)^{-1} J^T r \qquad \Leftrightarrow \qquad \begin{bmatrix} U & W \\ W^T & V \end{bmatrix} \begin{bmatrix} \Delta q \\ \Delta s \end{bmatrix} = -J^T r. \tag{15}$$

The product $-J^T r$ is zero in an optimal point and so the second row provides a connection between q and s. This gives a linear constraint on how to adjust the auxiliary parameters $\mathbf{s}$ when the main parameters $\mathbf{q}$ change. Thus the partial derivatives of $\mathbf{s}$ with respect to $\mathbf{q}$ is

$$W^T \Delta \mathbf{q} + V \Delta \mathbf{s} = 0 \quad \Leftrightarrow \quad \Delta \mathbf{s} = -V^{-1} W^T \Delta \mathbf{q} \quad \Rightarrow \quad \frac{\partial \mathbf{s}}{\partial \mathbf{q}} = -V^{-1} W^T. \quad (16)$$

We can use this together with the definition $J = \partial \mathbf{r} / \partial \mathbf{z}$ to find how the residuals change if we change the receiver map

$$\Delta \mathbf{r} = \begin{bmatrix} J_a & J_b \end{bmatrix} \begin{bmatrix} \Delta \mathbf{q} \\ \Delta \mathbf{s} \end{bmatrix} = \left(J_a + J_b \cdot \frac{\partial \mathbf{s}}{\partial \mathbf{q}} \right) \Delta \mathbf{q}. \quad (17)$$

Thus, $J_a + J_b \frac{\partial \mathbf{s}}{\partial \mathbf{q}}$ will be the Jacobian for the map, further on denoted J_q.

Now, denote the residuals as a function of $\Delta \mathbf{q}$. A first order Taylor expansion gives

$$\mathbf{r}(\Delta \mathbf{q}) \approx \mathbf{r}|_o + \mathbf{r}'_{\Delta \mathbf{q}}|_o \Delta \mathbf{q} = \mathbf{r}|_o + J_q|_o \Delta \mathbf{q}. \quad (18)$$

Here o denotes an optimal point and $|_o$ denotes evaluating an expression at the point o. Then, the square of these residuals will be

$$\mathbf{r}^T \mathbf{r} \approx (\mathbf{r}|_o + J_q|_o \Delta \mathbf{q})^T (\mathbf{r}_o + J_q|_o \Delta \mathbf{q}) = \mathbf{r}|_o^T \mathbf{r}_o + 2\mathbf{r}|_o^T J_q|_o \Delta \mathbf{q} + \Delta \mathbf{q}^T J_q|_o^T J_q|_o \Delta \mathbf{q}. \quad (19)$$

In a minimum point $\mathbf{r}|_o^T J_q$ is zero. Furthermore, using the QR-decomposition of the Jacobian we get

$$\Delta \mathbf{q}^T J_q^T J_q \Delta \mathbf{q} = \Delta \mathbf{q}^T (QR)^T QR \Delta \mathbf{q} = \Delta \mathbf{q}^T R^T Q^T QR \Delta \mathbf{q} = \Delta \mathbf{q}^T R^T R \Delta \mathbf{q}. \quad (20)$$

Introducing the notation $a = (\mathbf{r}|_o^T \mathbf{r}|_o)^{1/2}$, the squared residuals from (19) can be written shorter as

$$\mathbf{r}^T \mathbf{r} \approx a + \Delta \mathbf{q}^T R^T R \Delta \mathbf{q}, \quad (21)$$

and this is our compressed expression for the residuals.

The Merge. Furthermore, this compressed expression can be used to add two separate maps. Assume that we have the residuals for the two maps,

$$\left(\mathbf{r}^{(i)} \right)^T \left(\mathbf{r}^{(i)} \right) = \left(a^{(i)} \right)^2 + \left(\Delta \mathbf{q}^{(i)} \right)^T \left(R^{(i)} \right)^T R^{(i)} \Delta \mathbf{q}^{(i)}, \qquad i = 1, 2. \quad (22)$$

Adding the two equations and writing $\Delta \mathbf{q}^{(i)} = \mathbf{q} - \mathbf{q}^{(i)}$ for an arbitrary $\mathbf{q}$ gives

$$\sum_{i=1}^{2} \left(\mathbf{r}^{(i)} \right)^T \left(\mathbf{r}^{(i)} \right) = \sum_{i=1}^{2} \left(a^{(i)} \right)^2 + \left(\Delta \mathbf{q}^{(i)} \right)^T \left(R^{(i)} \right)^T R^{(i)} \Delta \mathbf{q}^{(i)} = \left(a^{(1)} \right)^2 + \left(a^{(2)} \right)^2$$

$$+ \begin{bmatrix} R^{(1)} \left(\mathbf{q} - \mathbf{q}^{(1)} \right) \\ R^{(2)} \left(\mathbf{q} - \mathbf{q}^{(2)} \right) \end{bmatrix}^T \begin{bmatrix} R^{(1)} \left(\mathbf{q} - \mathbf{q}^{(1)} \right) \\ R^{(2)} \left(\mathbf{q} - \mathbf{q}^{(2)} \right) \end{bmatrix} = \left(a^{(1)} \right)^2 + \left(a^{(2)} \right)^2 + \hat{\mathbf{r}}^T \hat{\mathbf{r}}. \quad (23)$$

The terms $(a^{(1)})^2$ and $(a^{(2)})^2$ are fixed while the third term $\hat{\mathbf{r}}^T \hat{\mathbf{r}}$ can be minimized to minimize the sum of the residuals. Introducing new notations M and b, $\hat{\mathbf{r}}$ can be written

$$\hat{\mathbf{r}} = \begin{bmatrix} R^{(1)} \left(\mathbf{q} - \mathbf{q}^{(1)} \right) \\ R^{(2)} \left(\mathbf{q} - \mathbf{q}^{(2)} \right) \end{bmatrix} = \begin{bmatrix} R^{(1)} \\ R^{(2)} \end{bmatrix} \mathbf{q} - \begin{bmatrix} R^{(1)} \mathbf{q}^{(1)} \\ R^{(2)} \mathbf{q}^{(2)} \end{bmatrix} = M \mathbf{q} - b. \quad (24)$$

To minimize $\hat{\mathbf{r}}$ and thus $\hat{\mathbf{r}}^T\hat{\mathbf{r}}$ is a least squares problem which can be solved using the pseudo inverse. Denoting the merged map $\mathbf{q}^*$ gives

$$\mathbf{q}^{(*)} = (M^T M)^{-1} M^T b. \tag{25}$$

We can also compress the final result. Using that a general $\mathbf{q}$ can be written $\mathbf{q} = \Delta\mathbf{q}^{(*)} + \mathbf{q}^{(*)}$, the third term in (23) can be expressed

$$\begin{aligned}
\hat{\mathbf{r}}^T\hat{\mathbf{r}} &= (M\mathbf{q} - b)^T(M\mathbf{q} - b) = \left(M\mathbf{q}^{(*)} - b + M\Delta\mathbf{q}^{(*)}\right)^T\left(M\mathbf{q}^{(*)} - b + M\Delta\mathbf{q}^{(*)}\right) \\
&= \left(M\mathbf{q}^{(*)} - b\right)^T\left(M\mathbf{q}^{(*)} - b\right) + \left(\Delta\mathbf{q}^{(*)}\right)^T M^T M \Delta\mathbf{q}^{(*)},
\end{aligned} \tag{26}$$

where the linear term vanishes due to orthogonality. Using this in Eq. (23) gives

$$\left(\mathbf{r}^{(*)}\right)^T\mathbf{r}^{(*)} = \left(a^{(1)}\right)^2 + \left(a^{(2)}\right)^2 + \left(M\mathbf{q}^{(*)} - b\right)^T\left(M\mathbf{q}^{(*)} - b\right) + \left(\Delta\mathbf{q}^{(*)}\right)^T M^T M \Delta\mathbf{q}^{(*)}. \tag{27}$$

If M is QR-decomposed in a similar manner as J_q was in (20) this total result can be compressed as

$$\left(\mathbf{r}^{(*)}\right)^T\mathbf{r}^{(*)} = \left(a^{(*)}\right)^2 + \left(\Delta\mathbf{q}^{(*)}\right)^T\left(R^{(*)}\right)^T R^{(*)}\Delta\mathbf{q}^{(*)}, \tag{28}$$

with $R^{(*)}$ being the triangular matrix from the QR-decomposition of M and

$$a^{(*)} = \left(\left(a^{(1)}\right)^2 + \left(a^{(2)}\right)^2 + \left(M\mathbf{q}^{(*)} - b\right)^T\left(M\mathbf{q}^{(*)} - b\right)\right)^{\frac{1}{2}}. \tag{29}$$

By this, the representation of the final map is the same as in (21) and the merged map can be treated as one of the original. Furthermore, more maps can be added using the algorithm described above. Thus, to add maps, all we need to save from the separate bundles are the maps $\mathbf{q}^{(i)}$, the squared residuals $a^{(i)}$, and the triangular matrices $R^{(i)}$ from the QR-decompositions of the Jacobians.

In some cases the linearized method is similar to the Kalman filter. However, several maps can be added at once using the linearized model and it also allows for better control. We will also show that this method can be developed to detect map changes.

4   Detection of Changes

Once we know how to merge two or more maps we can also use this to detect whether the map has changed between the measurement occasions. For this, assume that we have two maps $\mathbf{q}^{(1)}$ and $\mathbf{q}^{(2)}$ and their merge $\mathbf{q}^{(*)}$. Furthermore, we have the norms of their residuals, $a^{(1)}$, $a^{(2)}$ and $a^{(*)}$. An approximation for the residual variance is derived in (12). This can be used to find the estimated value of how the squared residuals change when we add maps. Rearranging terms from (12), we get

$$\mathbf{E}\left[\left(a^{(i)}\right)^2\right] = \mathbf{E}\left[\left(\mathbf{r}^{(i)}\right)^T\left(\mathbf{r}^{(i)}\right)\right] = \sigma^2(mn - (n\rho + m\rho - \phi)), \qquad i = 1, 2 \tag{30}$$

$$\mathbf{E}\left[\left(a^{(*)}\right)^2\right] = \mathbf{E}\left[\left(\mathbf{r}^{(*)}\right)^T\left(\mathbf{r}^{(*)}\right)\right] = \sigma^2(mn - (Nn\rho + m\rho - \phi)), \tag{31}$$

and subtracting these – in this case with $N = 2$ maps – gives

$$\mathbf{E}\big[(a^{(*)})^2 - (a^{(1)})^2 - (a^{(2)})^2\big] = \sigma^2(N-1)(m\rho - \phi). \tag{32}$$

If we use real data, σ is unknown, but it can be estimated from the separate bundles using (12), s.t. $\hat{\sigma}^2 = ((\sigma^{(1)})^2 + (\sigma^{(2)})^2)/2$.

The values in (32) can be seen as a sum of $(N-1)(m\rho-\phi)$ Gaussian variables, and a sum of 2ν independent Gaussian distributed variables with mean zero and standard deviation σ_n has a Γ distribution with density [3, p. 47]

$$f_{\alpha,\nu}(x) = \frac{1}{\Gamma(v)}\alpha^\nu x^{\nu-1}e^{-\alpha x}, \tag{33}$$

with $\alpha = 1/(2\sigma_n^2)$ and Γ being the gamma function. This density will be denoted $\Gamma(\alpha, \nu)$ (two parameters). Furthermore, using $\tilde{a} = (a^{(1)})^2 + (a^{(2)})^2 - (a^{(*)})^2$ and $\gamma = (N-1)(m\rho - \phi)$ we get that $\tilde{a} \sim \Gamma(1/(2\sigma^2), \gamma/2)$. Thus, to know whether a map has changed we can compare the estimated $\tilde{a}$ to the distribution. A reasonable choice is that if the difference $\tilde{a}$ lies within the 99 percentile of $\Gamma(1/(2\sigma^2), \gamma/2)$ there has not been any change in the map, but if $\tilde{a}$ is higher than this limit, a change has probably occured.

If a change between two maps is discovered, we further investigate those maps. By comparing the positions for each map point, we say that if the distance between them is larger than $3\hat{\sigma}$ the map point has probably moved. This could also be used to decrease the variance even further for the receivers that have not changed, by using information from all maps for these receivers.

5   Experimental Validation

To validate the method suggested in this paper, experiments on simulated TOA data as well as real ultra-wideband (UWB) data have been performed. We have also developed the method to work for, and tried it on, 3D-reconstructions from image data.

5.1   Time of Arrival – Simulated Data

For each of the simulated experiments m receivers in 3D were generated from a uniform distribution, $\mathbf{q}^{(t)} \sim \mathcal{U}(0, 10)$, superscript (t) denoting the true value. We simulated N different measurement occasions with n sender positions $\mathbf{s}^{(t)} \sim \mathcal{U}(0, 10)$ each and calculated the mn sender-receiver distances. Gaussian noise with standard deviation σ was added to achieve distance measurements. For each measure we performed a separate bundle to get the N maps $\mathbf{q}^{(1)}, \ldots, \mathbf{q}^{(N)}$ and the compressed representation explained in Sect. 3.3 and more specifically in (21).

Test of Time and Accuracy. For the first experiment $m = 10$, $\sigma_n = 0.3$, $N = 2$ and no change occured in the true map. The experiments were run four times with $n = 10, 100, 1000, 4000$ respectively. For each case, the merge was computed using the three methods presented in this paper and the runtimes were measured. We computed the error norm $\sqrt{\sum_{i=1}^{m} |q_i^{(t)} - q_i|^2}$ and for the full bundle and the linearized method, we also computed the squared distance residuals per residual $\mathbf{r}^T \mathbf{r}/(mn) = a^2/(mn)$. The results can be seen in Table 1.

Table 1. The results from the experiment explained in Sect. 5.1. The values come from a merge of two maps between which no change has occured. These values are the mean of 10 similar runs.

	n	10	100	1000	4000
Runtime [s]	Full bundle	$2.3 \cdot 10^{-2}$	0.19	3.8	54.7
	Linearized	$1.9 \cdot 10^{-3}$	$3.2 \cdot 10^{-4}$	$4.7 \cdot 10^{-4}$	$3.3 \cdot 10^{-4}$
	Kalman	$2.4 \cdot 10^{-3}$	$2.1 \cdot 10^{-4}$	$2.2 \cdot 10^{-4}$	$2.1 \cdot 10^{-4}$
$\| \|\mathbf{q}^{(t)} - \mathbf{q}\| \|$	Full bundle	1.20	0.11	$1.6 \cdot 10^{-2}$	$3.0 \cdot 10^{-3}$
	Linearized	1.34	0.11	$1.6 \cdot 10^{-2}$	$3.0 \cdot 10^{-3}$
	Kalman	1.48	0.12	$2.2 \cdot 10^{-2}$	$5.8 \cdot 10^{-3}$
$\frac{\mathbf{r}^T \mathbf{r}}{mn} = \frac{a^2}{mn}$	Full bundle	0.11	0.12	0.13	0.13
	Linearized	0.11	0.12	0.13	0.13

Even if the runtime is highly dependent on the implementations, the table gives a valid comparison between the methods. The linearized method is almost as accurate as the full bundle. Moreover, when only the sender positions increase, and thus also the number of distances, the runtime for the linearized method and the Kalman filter does not increase notably, while the runtime for the full bundle does. Hence, the linearized method is faster than the full bundle and more accurate than the Kalman filter.

Validating the Detection Threshold. To validate the threshold for detection of changes described in Sect. 4, we tested the distribution of $\tilde{a}$ empirically. Using $m = 30, n = 200, N = 2$ and $\sigma_n = 0.5$ the distances were computed. The separate bundles as well as the merge using both the full bundle and the linearized method were then conducted. For all of the different maps we computed the compressed representations from (21). We then computed

$$\tilde{a}_{full} = \left(a^{(1)}\right)^2 + \left(a^{(2)}\right)^2 - \left(a_{full}^{(*)}\right)^2, \quad \text{and} \quad \tilde{a}_{lin} = \left(a^{(1)}\right)^2 + \left(a^{(2)}\right)^2 - \left(a_{lin}^{(*)}\right)^2, \tag{34}$$

where subscript index $full$ and lin denotes the full bundle and the linearized method respectively. This was re-made 2000 times with different noise. The total degrees of freedom were $\gamma = (N-1)(m \cdot \rho - \phi) = 30 \cdot 3 - 6 = 84$. The results of $\tilde{a}_{full}$ and $\tilde{a}_{lin}$ were then plotted in a histogram together with a $\Gamma(2, 42)$ distribution in Fig. 2. The histograms agree well with the gamma distribution in both cases; hence, this can be used to test the significance.

Detection of Changed Maps. Furthermore, we did an experiment where the map actually had changed. This time we used $m = 10, n = 30, N = 3$ and

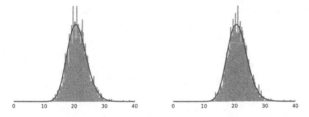

Fig. 2. The plots show histograms of the residuals $\tilde{a}_{full}$ (to the left) and $\tilde{a}_{lin}$ (to the right) computed using the full bundle and the linearized method respectively. The curve (–) shows the Γ distribution which we expect $\tilde{a}$ to belong to.

$\sigma_n = 0.5$. Four of the ten receivers moved before the last measurement. After running the separate bundles and merging the maps both using a full bundle and our linearized method we investigated the differences in the residuals. The system had $\gamma = 2 \cdot (10 \cdot 3 - 6) = 48$ degrees of freedom and thus $\tilde{a}$ should be such that it could come from a $\Gamma(1/(2\hat{\sigma}^2), 24)$ distribution if no changes has occured. Using the estimate $\hat{\sigma}^2$ the 99-percentile of this was $\tilde{a} = 17.7$. In this specific case, the results from the merge gave $\tilde{a}_{full} = 603$ and $\tilde{a}_{lin} = 749$ and this clearly showed that something had changed. The results from the unsuccessful merge can be seen to the left in Fig. 3. To the right in Fig. 3 are the results from the merge between the first and second map, after the system successfully had detected the change.

5.2   Time of Arrival – Real Data

To test our method $N = 9$ experiments were conducted using a Bitcraze Crazyflie quadcopter and their Loco-positioning system which consists of $m = 5$ anchors with UWB chips and a flying quadcopter with a mounted UWB chip, giving approximately $n = 600$ sender positions for each measurement. The five anchors were positioned around the room and one of them was moved before the last three runs. The experiment was conducted in a MOCAP studio to record the ground truth flightpath as well as the anchor positions. Distance measurements from the quadcopter (sender) to all the anchors (receivers) were measured at a frequency of 30 Hz.

The problem was solved as explained in previous sections, except that the threshold for $\tilde{a}$ now was 10 times the 99 percentile for the Γ distribution. This threshold was used for all real data experiments. In Fig. 4 the results from the Kalman filter and the linearized method are shown. While the dynamics of the Kalman filter makes the estimated receivers end up further away from the true positions – *on their way* to the correct position – for some of the measurements, the linearized method correctly detects when a change has occured. Thereafter, only the similar maps are merged.

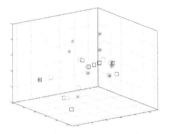
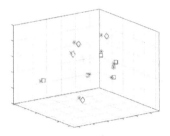

Fig. 3. An unsuccessful merge of map 1,2 and 3 (left) and a successful merge of map 1 and 2 (right). The stars (∗) show the true receiver positions, the squares the results from full bundle (□) and the linearized method ( ). In the right figure, the points for which a change has been detected are (correctly) marked by a diamond (◇,). (Color figure online)

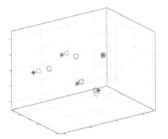
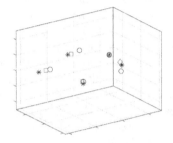

Fig. 4. Results from two of the maps from the experiments with UWB data. The stars (∗) show the true receiver positions, the circles (o) the results from the Kalman filter and the squares (□) from the linearized method. The change between the maps has been correctly detected by the linearized method and changed receivers are marked with a diamond (◇). (Color figure online)

5.3   Images – Real Data

In this experiment, $N = 5$ sets of images were taken of an indoor scene, a bookshelf with a number of toy models, as depicted in Fig. 1. In between set 2 and 3 an R2D2 model was moved, which we wanted to detect. As a first step we used a structure from motion pipeline [11] to obtain a 3D reconstruction for each set. The points in this reconstruction are the feature points in the map, corresponding to the receivers in the TOA experiments.

Unlike the TOA experiments, correspondence between 3D points in the different datasets are not given. Prior to merging, we performed data association by SIFT [10] feature matching and geometric alignment in a RANSAC [4] framework. After this the maps were also in the same coordinate system, which is required for the linearized method and speeds up the full bundling method.

Fig. 5. Changes detected in merge between dataset 2 and 3. Feature points are maked with blue dots and changed features are circled in cyan. (Color figure online)

Using the same method as in Sect. 5.2 – with detection based on a Γ distribution and the feature point distances – the algorithm detected change during the merge of dataset 2 and 3, which is correct. In Fig. 5 we see that the feature points on R2D2 are correctly detected as changed. Note that some features are not present in both datasets and therefore these features on the R2D2 are not marked as changed. Figure 6 shows the 3D reconstruction from above. Here we see that the merged points on R2D2 does not align with either dataset 2 or 3.

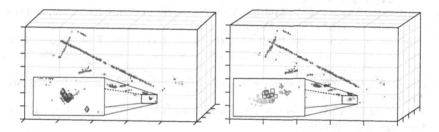

Fig. 6. To the left, the merge between dataset 1 and 2 where no change was detected. The separate maps are marked with dots (•,•) and the merge by diamonds (◇). To the right, the merge between dataset 2 and 3, where a change was detected. The points for which a change was detected are marked by squares (□). (Color figure online)

6   Conclusions

We have presented a novel and efficient method, with small memory footprint, for merging individual maps obtained from bundle adjustment optimization along with a statistically motivated method for detecting changes in the map. The method has been compared favorably to using full bundle adjustment and the Kalman filter and is shown to be a good compromise between performance and time efficiency. This makes the method suitable for online applications as well as the use of crowd sourced data. The performance has been confirmed on both TOA and vision problems for both simulated and real data. One limitation is that the map points used for the coordinate system normalization need to be consistent for all maps. However, if this problem is solved, we believe that the method could be further developed to a full collaborative SLAM system.

Acknowledgments. This work was partially supported by the strategic research projects ELLIIT and eSSENCE, the Swedish Foundation for Strategic Research project, Semantic Mapping and Visual Navigation for Smart Robots (grant no. RIT15-0038), and Wallenberg AI, Autonomous Systems and Software Program (WASP) funded by Knut and Alice Wallenberg Foundation.

References

1. Batstone, K., Oskarsson, M., Åström, K.: Robust time-of-arrival self calibration and indoor localization using Wi-Fi round-trip time measurements. In: Proceedings of International Conference on Communication (2016)
2. Enqvist, O., Olsson, C., Kahl, F.: Non-sequential structure from motion. In: Workshop on Omnidirectional Vision, Camera Networks and Non-Classical Cameras (OMNIVIS), Barcelona, Spain (2011)
3. Feller, W.: An Introduction to Probability Theory and Its Applications, vol. 2. Wiley, Hoboken (1968)
4. Fischler, M.A., Bolles, R.C.: Random sample consensus: a paradigm for model fitting with applications to image analysis and automated cartography. Commun. ACM **24**(6), 381–395 (1981)
5. Hartley, R., Zisserman, A.: Multiple View Geometry in Computer Vision, 2nd edn. Cambridge University Press, Cambridge (2004)
6. Indelman, V., Roberts, R., Beall, C., Dellaert, F.: Incremental light bundle adjustment. In: 2012 Electronic Proceedings of the British Machine Vision Conference, BMVC 2012, January 2012
7. Jakobsson, A.: An Introduction to Time Series Modeling, 1st edn. Studentlitteratur AB, Lund (2013)
8. Kalman, R.E.: A new approach to linear filtering and prediction problems. J. Basic Eng. **82**(1), 35–45 (1960)
9. Kuang, Y., Burgess, S., Torstensson, A., Åström, K.: A complete characterization and solution to the microphone position self-calibration problem. In: ICASSP (2013)
10. Lowe, D.G.: Distinctive image features from scale-invariant keypoints. Int. J. Comput. Vis. **60**(2), 91–110 (2004)
11. Olsson, C., Enqvist, O.: Stable structure from motion for unordered image collections. In: Heyden, A., Kahl, F. (eds.) SCIA 2011. LNCS, vol. 6688, pp. 524–535. Springer, Heidelberg (2011). https://doi.org/10.1007/978-3-642-21227-7_49
12. Rodríguez, A.L., López-de Teruel, P.E., Ruiz, A.: Reduced epipolar cost for accelerated incremental SfM. In: 2011 IEEE Conference on Computer Vision and Pattern Recognition (CVPR), pp. 3097–3104. IEEE (2011)
13. Triggs, B., McLauchlan, P.F., Hartley, R.I., Fitzgibbon, A.W.: Bundle adjustment—a modern synthesis. In: Triggs, B., Zisserman, A., Szeliski, R. (eds.) IWVA 1999. LNCS, vol. 1883, pp. 298–372. Springer, Heidelberg (2000). https://doi.org/10.1007/3-540-44480-7_21
14. Zhayida, S., Andersson, F., Kuang, Y., Åström, K.: An automatic system for microphone self-localization using ambient sound. In: 22nd European Signal Processing Conference (2014)

Alignment of Building Footprints Using Quasi-Nadir Aerial Photography

Dimitri Bulatov[1,2](✉)

[1] Department Scene Analysis, Fraunhofer IOSB,
Gutleuthausstr. 1, 76275 Ettlingen, Germany
dimitri.bulatov@iosb.fraunhofer.de
[2] Department of Spatial Sciences, Curtin University of Technology,
Perth, WA 6102, Australia
http://www.iosb.fraunhofer.de

Abstract. In this paper, we consider the alignment problem of building outlines, provided by openly available sources, and high resolution aerial images. This problem can be transferred to that of matching images with different modalities. After studying related works, we propose to minimize a cost function penalizing both color and gradient discrepancies. Semantic context is extensively taken into account, and additional information, such as classification result, can be integrated. Pyramid-based coarse registration and median-filtering-based outlier suppression were implemented as pre- and post-processing modules, respectively. We performed extensive tests with three very different datasets and achieved encouraging results, which were very stable once application of pre- and post-processing took place.

Keywords: Alignment · Building outlines · GIS ·
Multimodal registration · Optimization

1 Introduction and Previous Research

Motivation. Buildings represent essential part of urban infrastructure and their correct geo-localization is important for many applications, such as city planning, civil security, and disaster management. In this last application, up-to-date information about building footprints are needed both by emergency services for setting up rescue missions, and insurance companies, who in a shortest possible time must assess the damage and restitute to the policyholder the relevant amount of money. The company usually sends a so-called loss adjuster to assess the damage of each building in the company's portfolio. To spare this loss adjuster the tedious process of roof-climbing, close-range quasi-nadir aerial or UAV images with a very high resolution are increasingly being applied to assess the roof damages. Automatic evaluation of damage by means of image processing methods, such as those described by [9] and [15], is another quite efficient concept of saving costs for the insurer. A very important detail about

© Springer Nature Switzerland AG 2019
M. Felsberg et al. (Eds.): SCIA 2019, LNCS 11482, pp. 361–373, 2019.
https://doi.org/10.1007/978-3-030-20205-7_30

both contributions is that damage assessment is carried out not building-wise but region-wise, which allows to assess whether tiles were blown away by the wind, damaged by heavy trees, or whether the roof was entirely collapsed. From this information, the damage degree and thus the compensation amount can be calculated. However, the necessary assumption for this is a correct delineation of buildings in the portfolio. Bearing this application in mind, the task covered in this paper will be alignment of building footprints provided by GIS data with the relevant image data. As [4,16] have pointed out, the deviations between the GIS database and the image can be quite high (≈ 8 m) and the main reasons for this are: the three-dimensional character of buildings, occasional discrepancy between roof polygons and ground plans, as well as changes with respect to out-to-date database. We wish to exclude these coarse systematic errors and accomplish the alignment task with the high-resolution image data and available geographical data only, keeping in mind that time is a critical factor and that training examples are hardly available or useful because some buildings may be damaged or destroyed. In what follows, we will briefly review the existing approaches, explain their insufficiencies, and outline our contributions.

Previous Works. We start with the interactive approach [2], where images were segmented with a commercial software, after which segments were processed manually. Since for large scenes, interactive processing is cumbersome and since we wish to make use of available outlines, we turned our attention towards automatic methods. Active contour models [10,11], such as snakes, are helpful for evolution of already available approximate values, but are often an overkill if alignment transformations can be described by a few parameters, to the same extent as methods based on fitting preferably rectangular primitives, as do [1] by means of Marked Point Processes. For rigid alignment transformation, matching key-points, such as [8], and model instantiation using RANSAC is probably the fastest strategy. Here two main challenges are incorporating the context information (typical properties of buildings) and matching key-points in extremely different images. Furthermore, there exist change detection methods, such as [3], where a subdivision into new, modified, remaining, and not-anymore-existing building was presented. Particularly interesting is their suggestion to take local maximums of gradient maps as seed points for building outlines. However, 3D data must be acquired from the satellite images. As for purely image-based methods, convolutional neural networks (CNNs) are increasingly being applied for outlining [10,13] and aligning [14,16] buildings. The latter contribution establishes analogy with the traditional gradient descent method while the conventional matching based on pyramids inspired the design of their neural network architecture (encoder-decoder like ones or with U-connections as in [12]). The big advantage of a CNN-based approach is that it can easily be generalized to other problem settings, such as medical image registration, however, we find it a pity that the well-known properties of buildings were sacrificed in favor of dozens of training examples. Finally, [14] propose a rather flat architecture that allows them to obtain a *heatmap* (of inverse likelihood) as data cost term.

Optimization runs over all offsets, as random variables on a Markov Random Field, using this data term as well as the usual smoothness assumption that neighboring buildings must have similar offsets. In our work, we will avoid computing heatmaps since for high-resolution data (building masks having 40000 and more pixels as well as 60 pixels offset), this could be costly. Thus, the aforementioned non-local energy minimization is simplified to a procedure reminding median filtering.

Most interesting to the authors are procedures operating without training data and possibly independent on resolution. Variational approaches are excellent examples for this. In [5], intensity values are interpreted as samples of two random processes and are linked by a probability density function (such as Mutual Information). The transformation is computed pixelwise and a regularization term is added to penalize transformations of neighboring pixels. What we consider as a bottleneck is the gradient-based energy minimization scheme because, especially for destroyed buildings, outliers must be treated with care. At cost of computation time, we will minimize a median-based energy function by means of the downhill simplex algorithm.

Contributions. We interpreted the alignment problem between the rasterized building outline and the image fragment as registration of two multimodal images and implemented a robust and fast approach for obtaining the unknown registration parameters. Technically, an energy function consisting of a color consistency and a gradient consistency terms is minimized. These terms are specific for the current building, but they are weighted by factors taking general building properties into account. In spite of an occasional presence of destroyed buildings, neither training data is required nor retrieving pixelwise cost functions (heatmaps). Even though it does not fully apply to the pre- and post-processing modules, the core part of the approach shows a very similar behavior for datasets having a different resolution. Finally, a classification result can be easily considered yielding better results and making dispensable the gradient-based term.

2   Methodology

The main part of our work is organized as follows. The most common variable names and basic definitions will be provided in Sect. 2.1, after which we give the cost function and details on its minimization (Sect. 2.2) concluded by the pre- and post-processing modules (Sect. 2.3).

2.1   Preliminaries

For a large amount of cities, there exist GIS data for building footprints ($\mathcal{P}$) that we wish to align with the actual image data. Let $\mathcal{I}$ denote a region of interest in a geo-referenced airborne image with three or more channels, containing a building with some surrounding area and let $\mathcal{M}$ be the mask obtained by rasterization of the corresponding footprint $\mathcal{P}$. That is, for points inside of the polygon, the value of $\mathcal{M}$ is 1 and outside it is zero (see Fig. 2 of [16]). A special value (2) is given to pixels at the border of the rasterization. We are looking for a transformation φ to align $\mathcal{M}$ with the roof of the building that way that the corresponding edges of the transformed outline $\mathcal{P}(\varphi)$ coincide with the roof silhouettes in $\mathcal{I}$. For φ, we consider a two-dimensional translation within a known range (search range), but if necessary, our approach can be generalized for a four- or even six-dimensional vector representing an Euclidean or affine transformation, respectively.

2.2   Minimization of Energy Function

In the case that freely available building outlines and roofs fit quite well, there is a sufficient overlap between the building footprint and the requested roof area to guarantee good starting values for our target function. Consequently, a modification of the mutual information can be applied, taking into account the homogeneity of the dominant color $\mathbf{f} \in \mathbb{R}^3$ sampled from a 3D histogram over the color values of all pixels $\mathbf{p}$ in $\mathcal{I}$ labeled as *inside* of $\mathcal{M}$. The number b of the histogram bins was 16; that is, color resolution of 16 for an 8-bit image. Sometimes, a building roof contains more than one dominant color, which is mostly true if the building is destroyed. Additionally, there may be some considerable fair or dark spots, like dormers, chimneys, or their shadows. To cope with this, the penalization between $\mathcal{I}$ and the dominant color $\mathbf{f}$ over the channels of and later over pixels is carried out using the L_1-norm which is more robust to such outliers. We denote this penalization (our *first* energy term) by $\|\mathcal{I}_{\mathbf{f}}(\mathbf{p})\|$. An additional weighting $w_{\mathbf{f}}$ can be applied according to how likely a pixel is supposed to belong to a building. Ideally, this should reflect the likelihood for the building class in the classification result $\mathcal{C}(p)$. In order not to lose too many resources for classification, we consider merely the pixelwise NDVI (Normalized Difference Vegetation Index) measure rescaled between 0 and 1. This measure is very popular in Remote Sensing if it comes to separate buildings from vegetation. We applied the term $\mathcal{C} = (1 + \mathcal{R}/\mathcal{N})^{-1}$, which is close to 0 if the near infra-red channel $\mathcal{N}$ is negligible compared to the red channel $\mathcal{R}$ while in the opposite case, it is 1.

As our *second* energy term, we wish to enforce the norm of the image gradient to be significantly higher at *border* pixels than *inside* $\mathcal{P}(\varphi)$. Analogously to $w_{\mathbf{f}}$, the weighting w_{∇} takes on the minimum value on the border, a small positive value inside and, as an option, a smoothly decreasing function outside the mask, since around buildings, high texture variations (gardens, roads, cars) are often present. The overall cost function is thus

$$E(\varphi) = \sum_{\mathbf{p} \in \mathcal{M}(\varphi)} \left\{ \alpha w_{\mathbf{f}}(\mathbf{p}) \|\mathcal{I}_{\mathbf{f}}(\mathbf{p})\| + (1 - \alpha)\tilde{w}_{\nabla}(\mathbf{p}) \|\nabla \mathcal{I}(\mathbf{p})\| \right\}, \qquad (1)$$

where

$$w_{\mathbf{f}}(\mathbf{p}) = \begin{cases} \mathcal{C}(\mathbf{p}) \text{ OR } 1 & \text{if } m > 0, \\ 0 & \text{if } m = 0 \end{cases}, \quad w_{\nabla}(\mathbf{p}) = \begin{cases} -1 & \text{if } m = 2, \\ 0.01 & \text{if } m = 1 \\ -e^{\frac{-d(\mathbf{p})}{\sigma}} \text{ OR } 0 & \text{if } m = 0 \end{cases}, \quad (2)$$

and $m = \mathcal{M}(\mathbf{p})$. Furthermore, d is the distance from $\mathbf{p}$ to where $\mathcal{M}$ is 1 (to be computed as a morphological operation at the binary image patch), σ is a constant around 0.5, α is a balance parameter to be explored in the experiments section together with both OR options in (2), and $\tilde{}$ denotes Gaussian smoothing. Note that while both w.-terms in (1) are supposed to fit the outline $\mathcal{P}$ to *a* building, both terms involving $\| \cdot \|$ pull $\mathcal{P}$ to *the* relevant building.

To minimize (1), we used the gradient-free Nelder-Mead method implemented by [7]. Its big disadvantage is to get occasionally stuck in a local minimum. However, it is several orders of magnitude faster than simulated annealing. Out of this reason, the Nelder-Mead method has been run for several starting values of φ after which the value yielding the minimum energy is chosen. At a lower resolution, an alternative to this method is to perform the exhaustive search for every single integer offset. Even though it is neither feasible for high resolution images nor for higher-dimensional search space, computation of cost function can be performed as a sliding window approach, with a sequence of convolutional operators (similar to CNNs), thus allowing to obtain a heatmap $\mathcal{H}(\varphi)$, see Fig. 1.

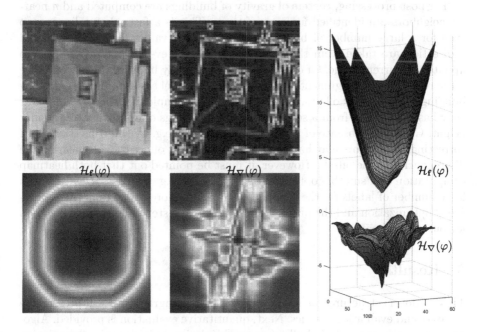

Fig. 1. Visualization of input data and cost function: top left and middle: $\mathcal{I}$ and $\nabla \mathcal{I}$. Bottom left and middle: Heatmaps $\mathcal{H}$ induced by both terms in (1), whereby blue means low energy/high likelihood. Right: heatmaps $\mathcal{H}$ represented as 3D surfaces. Note the numerous side minima for the gradient-based heatmap $\mathcal{H}_\nabla$. (Color figure online)

2.3   Modification and Post-processing

Similar to [16], an approach based on image pyramids has been implemented. In order to keep the results section concise, we restrict ourselves to only one downsampling step p, 2 to 8. The searching range is, logically, diminished by the factor $1/p$ which allows to perform a coarse registration in around $1/p^2$ of time. The subsequent fine registration uses the original resolution and the searching step has now the order of magnitude of the pyramid size. Note that doing so, a failed coarse registration cannot be corrected during fine registration. To cope with this, we firstly wish to avoid getting stuck in a local minimum by performing exhaustive search as described above; moreover, we choose quite neutral parameter values, such as $\alpha = 0.5$ in (1) and $w_\nabla = 0$ outside in (2). The fine registration takes place using Nelder-Mead method with varying parameters, whereby the starting value at original resolution is computed via nearest neighbor interpolation; that is, in our case $p \arg \min_{\phi'}(\mathcal{H}(\phi'))$. Secondly, we hope that a gross misalignment will only happen to a few isolated buildings such that the upcoming post-processing step will correct these outliers.

For post-processing, centers of gravity of buildings are computed and n nearest neighbors are identified for each of them. This is a fast, almost linear step even for a large number of buildings. Now, median values for offsets in x and y direction are taken from the set of neighbors for every building in order to update the current value. Of course, this step will only improve the performance if the reason for misalignment is justified by our model assumption that close-by buildings have similar offsets. This happens, for example, if a slightly non-nadir view has been taken from a scene containing buildings of approximately similar height. Clearly, in absence of the heatmap proposed e.g. by [14], this strategy of correcting gross errors may have a negative side effect of occasional smearing the discrepancies in the offsets. However, it must be pointed out that both heatmap computation and suitable optimization framework, e.g. by [6], especially with a large number of labels for the random variable, are more costly than the Nelder-Mead optimization and the proposed post-processing step. The value of n chosen for our experiments is 4.

3   Results

This section is structured as follows: In the first paragraph, we will present the datasets and evaluation metrics. Next, quantitative evaluation is provided. Algorithm parameters are varied allowing graphical visualization and interpretation of the results. Also, comparison with previous approaches [14] and [10] is carried out. The last two paragraphs of this section are dedicated to qualitative results and remarks on computation time.

In order to demonstrate the universality of our pipeline, we wish to consider several datasets having completely different properties. Firstly, the settlement called Marco Island, Florida, USA, represents a post-event high resolution data, captured from the air after the Irma hurricane in 2017. The thus captured images were mosaicked without consideration of the non-nadir perspective. Because of the high resolution (5 cm), the roof structures appear quite inhomogeneous; moreover, there are several damaged or destroyed buildings. The offsets are quite high, up to 60 pixels or 3 m. In total, there were 13 tiles from which we considered two and used 103 and 156 buildings, respectively, which are alignable by a pure translation. We refer to these datasets as D1 and D2. The third dataset, recorded at a much coarser resolution 0.5 m, is a densely built region in Perth (Australia), called City of Melville. The shapefile, which contains some 1500 buildings, is quite obsolete; hence, 154 buildings were selected for evaluation. The offsets are between −5 and 8 pixels whereby a moderate bias was kept intentionally. This dataset is denoted as D3. In all datasets, the offsets were measured manually. To measure the accuracy of our algorithm, we compared the ground truth offsets with the manually measured ones recording the widely used root mean square (rms) error. That is, L_2 norms of deviations were computed, averaged and shown in Fig. 2 as variable δ for each set of parameters. Additionally, in datasets D1 and D2, we differentiated between damaged and non-damaged buildings. As for the parameters, we varied α between 0 (only gradient-based) and 1 (only color-based) as well as w_∇ and w_f in dataset D3 (since infrared channel was available) according to the choices from (2).

The first observation one can immediately derive from the graphs in Fig. 2, top, is that for good parameter sets, the errors in relative deviations can be reduced below 6 pixels in dataset D1 and even below 4 pixels in D2, corresponding to 0.3 or 0.2 m, respectively. What is not recorded in the graphs is that the *distribution* of errors (medians of deviations below 1 pixel) indicates that there are some outliers degrading the performance. Unfortunately, these outliers are often those buildings with damaged roofs as we indicated by circles: the larger the radius, the larger the ratio between average inaccuracies over all damaged and all non-damaged buildings. The most dramatic ratios of almost 2.0 tend to be obtained for the choices of $w_\nabla(\mathbf{p}) \neq 0$ outside of the building mask without pyramids (red curves) while for green curves, the changes between accuracy over damaged or non-damaged buildings are more or less statistical (0.7 to 1.1 with pyramids for D2). The reason is that occasional gradient discontinuities within the roofs of destroyed buildings lead to confusion with usual texture elements outside. Even though the best results were obtained without pyramids, the strategy of applying the Nelder-Mead method on high resolution data seems to be a risky business because the balance parameter α must be chosen with care. For the strategy based on pyramids, the course of the graphs is much more flat. This means that the job of coarse registration has mostly been done well. Notably, the dashed green curve lies below the red one for D1 and above for D2.

Turning our attention to dataset D3 and Fig. 2, bottom, we can see that the rms errors can be reduced to values between 1.5 and 1 pixels and that there are basically two ways to achieve it. First, we could proceed similarly to D1 and D2 by choosing a reasonable α in (1). Alternatively, we could consider the classification result by $C(m)$ in (2) and here it is recommendable to *omit* the gradient-based term. Similarly to D1 and D2, the red and orange curves show

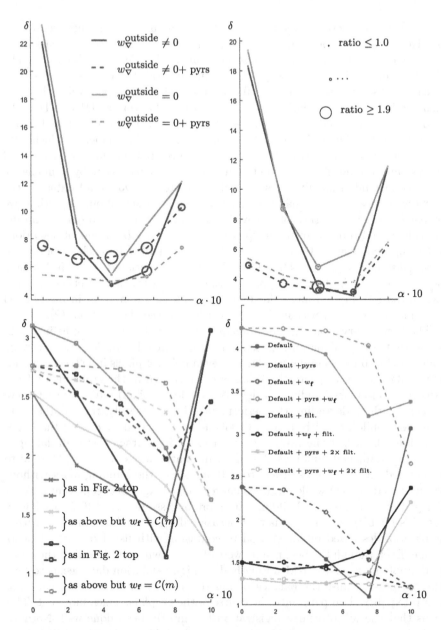

Fig. 2. Top row: results for datasets D1 (left) and D2 (right) depending on the parameter choice. For convenience, α in (1) was multiplied by 10. By circles we indicate to what extent the performance on damaged roofs was worse than for those with non-damaged roofs. Bottom row: results for dataset D3 depending on the parameter choice. Please note that red and orange solid curves in the left image coarsely correspond to red curves on the right while red and orange dashed curves in the left image coarsely correspond to orange curves on the right. See legend for more details. (Color figure online)

a sharper minimum (or a higher sensitivity to the balance parameter α) than the green and cyan ones. Differently to the datasets taken at a finer resolution, all configurations perform *worse* if pyramids are applied which gives us a hint that a resolution of 1 meter and coarser could be critical for our method. With respect to the post-processing, we took the red and orange curves in Fig. 2, left, with a little different value of σ, performed registration for *all* $\approx$1500 buildings, and, after applying filtering, recorded the results only for the selected ones. Two reasons to consider the red and orange curves are that they are most promising and, at the same time, they exhibit a sharper minimum with respect to α, which we hope to smooth during post-processing (blue curves). Moreover, if we use pyramids and post-process twice (once after the coarse and once after fine registration), we obtain cyan curves. We see that the range of acceptable values of parameters becomes more stable and that for almost all configurations, blue and cyan curves are lying below their respective red and orange counterparts. The last observation, not recorded in Fig. 2, concerns application of (1) without term $\|\mathcal{I}_\mathbf{f}\|$. The results become worse especially for quite large and small α, which means that outlines occasionally jumps to a neighboring building. In other words, the classification result alone could be insufficient.

To compare our approach with other state-of-the-art procedures, e.g. [14] and [10], we should first mention that they worked with different (to each other and to us) and geographically hardly comparable datasets, had different problem settings and evaluation metrics. The precision and recall of [14] were 80% and 64% respectively. However, since our final offsets are given in pixels, we must take into account the average building size and make some simplification assumptions. Assuming that the area of a roof is $12 \times 12 = 144\,\mathrm{m}^2$ and that the offsets in both x and y are $0.5/\sqrt{2} \approx 0.35\,\mathrm{m}$ (to yield a not unrealistic result of $0.5\,\mathrm{m}$ rms), both precision and recall in our approach would be approximately $(1 - 2 \cdot 0.35/12)^2 \approx 0.88$ in the worst case. This is slightly better than their values and at each case can be considered as a good result since some buildings are destroyed and the running time is less than half. The intersection over union, used by [10], ranges between 0.65 and 0.84 while ours would be 0.79 in this worst case.

For qualitative results, we refer to Fig. 3, where the overall good performance and, at the same time, some few shortcomings of the proposed method can be observed. In Fig. 3, top left, we see why post-processing is not recommendable for D1 and D2: Sometimes, the composition of tiles in the orthophoto is not accurate, but there seem to be other error sources. For example, two neighboring utmost-left buildings are similar in their roof shape, but the offset between the input shape (red) and the manually clicked ground truth (green) differ dramatically. Out of nine building in this fragment, seven were registered successfully. In the top right image, the building marked by 1 exemplifies how the gradient-based term in (1) was deceived by the footpath which has a similar color to the roof. The building was aligned to the border between this path and grass area. Moreover, the image shows a successful registration of a widely non-damaged (2) and severely damaged building roof (3). For dataset D3, in Fig. 3, bottom, we see how buildings 1 and 2 could be correctly aligned after taking into account

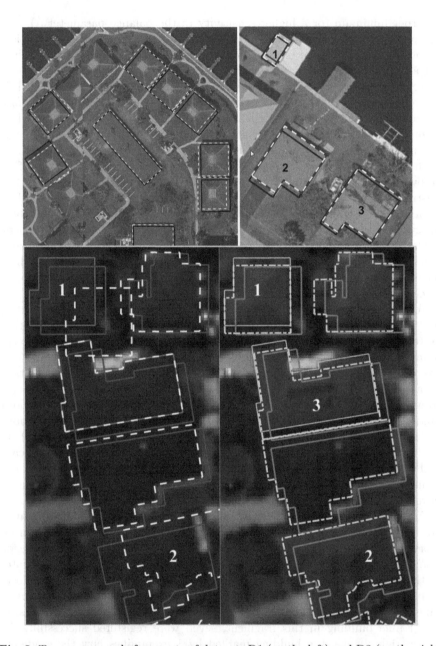

Fig. 3. Top row: example fragments of datasets D1 (on the left) and D2 (on the right, as gray image). Manually measured ground truth, input outlines, and results of our algorithm are specified by green, red, and dashed yellow lines, respectively. Bottom row: example fragment of dataset D3. Here, results of our algorithm before and after post-processing are specified by dashed yellow lines on the left, respectively, dashed blue lines on the right. For more details (numbers), see text. (Color figure online)

the offsets of the surrounding buildings in the post-processing step. At the same time, the result for building 3 on the right became slightly degraded.

From the point of view of computing time, for datasets D1 and D2, averagely 5.25 and 9 s are needed per building, whereby the approach was run on a standard PC with default parameters and without pyramids. If pyramids are used, the computation times for coarse and fine registration are 2.75 s resp. 4.25 s for D1 and 3.2 s and 7.7 s for D2. Clearly, the lions' share for the computation time is made up by the repeated evaluation of our cost function for energy minimization. This explains why the optimization using pyramids does *not* run in a lower time: this number of evaluations does not grow with the resolution since the method is not pixelwise. Only because of better initial values, less internal iterations are needed. As for the exhaustive approach, we noted that while the convolutional operators work efficiently until a certain matrix size (2.75 s per building for the pyramid step $p = 8$), the computation cost already explodes for the next level, $p = 4$, to 170 s per building. The computing type for D3 measures less than 1.5 s per building and the time spent on the post-processing step was negligible. It remains to say that the current MATLAB code was only optimized algorithmically, but not computationally.

4   Conclusions

We presented an approach for adjustment of building outlines stemming from the GIS data with quasi-nadir aerial images. This approach was developed and successfully tested for a real-case application, namely, roof damage assessment after a severe disaster. Its core procedure is based on minimization of an energy function consisting of two terms linked by balance parameter. In all datasets, reasonable values of α allow to achieve best results, which were around 0.2 m and almost 0.5 m for datasets having a finer and coarser resolution, respectively. Another valid conclusion is that depending on how to penalize the gradient outside the building area, more or less stable the curves are with changing balance parameter α. One may think that the algorithm has quite many parameters: b (number of color histogram bins), α in (1), choices of w_f, and w_{∇}, σ in (2), number of searching locations for energy minimization and that of surrounding buildings (n) in Sect. 2.3. However, our modules for pre-processing (coarse registration at a lower scale) and post-processing (outlier suppression using a median-filter-based approach) allowed to keep the results stable for a wide ranges of these parameters, as dashed curves in Fig. 2, top and bottom left, as well as blue and cyan curves in Fig. 2, bottom right, show.

We could see that even a quite basic classification result based on NDVI not only strongly improves the results but also the makes gradient-based term widely unnecessary. This is an important conclusion: nowadays context-free CNN approaches based on nested gradient computation are very popular. However, just a little of context helps to obtain good results without training data at all. Therefore, more effort must be put in the future to improve the classification. Here, CNNs will show themselves more than helpful.

For the dataset at a coarse resolution, the pyramid-based approach has turned out to be less successful. It would be, however, interesting to explore how the heatmap can be exploited: either upsampled to a finer resolution using a higher degree polynomial, instead of the currently used Nearest Neighbor Interpolation, or considered it as a data term in non-local energy minimization framework.

Acknowledgment. We thank to City of Melville and, in particular, Dr. Petra Helmholz from Curtin University, for providing the dataset D3.

References

1. Benedek, C., Descombes, X., Zerubia, J.: Building detection in a single remotely sensed image with a point process of rectangles. In: Proceedings of International Conference on Pattern Recognition (ICPR), pp. 1417–1420. IEEE (2010)
2. Brooks, R., Nelson, T., Amolins, K., Hall, G.B.: Semi-automated building footprint extraction from orthophotos. Geomatica **69**(2), 231–244 (2015)
3. Champion, N., Stamon, G., Deseilligny, M.P.: Automatic GIS updating from high resolution satellite images. In: International Conference on Machine Vision Applications (MVA), pp. 374–377. Citeseer (2009)
4. Haklay, M.: How good is volunteered geographical information? A comparative study of OpenStreetMap and Ordnance Survey datasets. Environ. Plann. B Plann. Des. **37**(4), 682–703 (2010)
5. Hermosillo, G., Chefd'Hotel, C., Faugeras, O.: Variational methods for multimodal image matching. Int. J. Comput. Vis. **50**(3), 329–343 (2002)
6. Hirschmüller, H.: Stereo processing by semi-global matching and mutual information. Trans. Pattern Anal. Mach. Intell. **30**(2), 328–341 (2008)
7. Lagarias, J.C., Reeds, J.A., Wright, M.H., Wright, P.E.: Convergence properties of the Nelder-Mead simplex method in low dimensions. SIAM J. Optim. **9**(1), 112–147 (1998)
8. Lowe, D.G.: Distinctive image features from scale-invariant keypoints. Int. J. Comput. Vis. **60**(2), 91–110 (2004)
9. Lucks, L., Pohl, M., Bulatov, D., Thönessen, U.: Superpixel-wise assessment of building damage from aerial images. In: International Conference on Computer Vision Theory and Applications (VISAPP), pp. 211–220 (2019)
10. Marcos, D., et al.: Learning deep structured active contours end-to-end. In: Conference on Computer Vision and Pattern Recognition (CVPR), pp. 8877–8885. IEEE (2018)
11. Peng, J., Zhang, D., Liu, Y.: An improved snake model for building detection from urban aerial images. Pattern Recogn. Lett. **26**(5), 587–595 (2005)
12. Ronneberger, O., Fischer, P., Brox, T.: U-Net: convolutional networks for biomedical image segmentation. In: Navab, N., Hornegger, J., Wells, W.M., Frangi, A.F. (eds.) MICCAI 2015. LNCS, vol. 9351, pp. 234–241. Springer, Cham (2015). https://doi.org/10.1007/978-3-319-24574-4_28
13. Tasar, O., Maggiori, E., Alliez, P., Tarabalka, Y.: Polygonization of binary classification maps using mesh approximation with right angle regularity. In: International Geoscience and Remote Sensing Symposium (IGARSS). IEEE (2018)
14. Vargas-Muñoz, J., Marcos, D., Lobry, S., Dos Santos, J.A., Falcão, A.X., Tuia, D.: Correcting misaligned rural building annotations in open street map using convolutional neural networks evidence. In: International Geoscience and Remote Sensing Symposium (IGARSS), pp. 1284–1287. IEEE (2018)

15. Vetrivel, A., Gerke, M., Kerle, N., Nex, F., Vosselman, G.: Disaster damage detection through synergistic use of deep learning and 3D point cloud features derived from very high resolution oblique aerial images, and multiple-kernel-learning. ISPRS J. Photogramm. Remote Sens. **140**, 45–59 (2018)
16. Zampieri, A., Charpiat, G., Girard, N., Tarabalka, Y.: Multimodal image alignment through a multiscale chain of neural networks with application to remote sensing. In: European Conference on Computer Vision (ECCV) (2018)

Evaluation of Feature Detectors, Descriptors and Match Filtering Approaches for Historic Repeat Photography

Ann-Katrin Becker$^{(\boxtimes)}$ and Oliver Vornberger

Media Computer Science Group, Osnabrueck University,
Wachsbleiche 27, 49069 Osnabrueck, Germany
`ann_katrin.becker@uos.de`

Abstract. This work analyzes the suitability of classic feature detectors and descriptors as well as different match filters for matching historical to modern images. A variety of prominent detector and descriptor combinations are evaluated on a new dataset, that is composed of repeat photographs of various scenes exposed to tremendous change across years. Results show that a dense keypoint sampling is more effective than classic feature detection, while several descriptors achieve comparable performances. Yet, more important is an adequate match filtering approach that identifies correct correspondences despite their large descriptor distances. We show that the standard ratio test is unsuitable for matching historic to modern image pairs, while other filters based on keypoint geometry boost performance. Finally, we establish a complete pipeline including detectors, descriptors and match filtering methods. Our pipeline shows high performance on challenging image pairs beyond repeat photography, as our tests on another dataset show.

Keywords: Matching · Historic repeat photography · Benchmark

1 Introduction

Repeat photography, or rephotography, is the process of retaking an old photograph from the same viewpoint. The resulting picture pair provides a compelling visualization of the respective location's change throughout the years. In ecology repeat photography is used to document vegetation and climate change [9, 20], glacier melting [12] and geological erosion [13], while sociologists use it to study urban development and social change [31]. However, even for experienced rephotographers recapturing the original view "by eye" is often tedious and time consuming. In practice there are two approaches to support this process. The first is to match the original and its approximate rephotograph via postprocessing, while the second supports the process of recovering the original viewpoint

© Springer Nature Switzerland AG 2019
M. Felsberg et al. (Eds.): SCIA 2019, LNCS 11482, pp. 374–386, 2019.
https://doi.org/10.1007/978-3-030-20205-7_31

[5]. The full automation of both processes requires the solution to a single under-lying challenge. This is the automatic identification of similarities between the original typically historic image and the modern scene. Due to dramatic varia-tions in lightning and weather, high occlusion and different acquisition devices, this is a challenging problem. Examples are shown in Fig. 1.

Fig. 1. Rephotographies from our dataset, including a view of a single building, a street corner lined with houses and a park. All image pairs feature high occlusion due to scene changes, show variations in lightning, and have been acquired by different cameras.

Feature matching is widely used for image alignment as well as 3D recon-struction. However, diverse opinions exist whether classic feature detectors such as SIFT [18] are suitable in the context of historical repeat photography. Bae et al. [5] and Schindler and Dellaert [25] agree that SIFT fails to match historic and modern images. Ali and Whitehead [2] instead, claim high performance on historical and modern image matching for at least some classic detector and descriptor combinations. Datasets from other studies do not adequately repli-cate the conditions present in historic repeat photography [14,27]. Overall no detailed study exists that allows a conclusion whether classic feature detectors and descriptors are suitable for historic to modern image matching.

This paper presents such a detailed study. First of all we present a new dataset composed of publicly available rephotographs of Manhattan. This does not only contain images of single buildings, but also whole streets lined with houses that are subject to great change across the years. Secondly we analyze the suitability of a variety of feature detector and descriptor combinations. Afterwards the top performing detector and descriptor pairs are analyzed in more detail and their parameters are varied to optimize performance. Furthermore we apply different match filtering approaches to improve the low precision values faced with most detector and descriptor combinations.

From our detailed analysis, we draw the following conclusions: (1) We agree with Fernando et al. [10] and Stylianou et al. [27] and propose a dense sampling of keypoints instead of the application of classic detectors. (2) RootSIFT and SURF but also binary descriptors such as BRIEF [8] and LATCH [16] are suitable for matching historic and modern images. For the latter we recommend increasing descriptive power by extending descriptor length. (3) Due to high descriptor distances of correct matches, classic filtering approaches such as the ratio test

[18] fail in the context of historic repeat photography. Instead the application of other filtering approaches based on keypoint geometry boosts performance.

Finally we successfully apply our established feature detection, description and match filtering pipeline to the dataset of Hauagge and Snavely [14]. Thus the approach we present in this paper is applicable to challenging image pairs beyond rephotography, including day and night shots and images of varying rendering style.

2   Related Work

Few research concerned with matching historical to modern images has been presented in the literature. Closely related to this work is the evaluation of Gat et al. [11] who compared a set of classic feature detectors on repeat photographs of various mountain landscapes. Unfortunately, no different feature descriptors are assessed, though other works have shown that often specific detector and descriptor combinations outperform others [10, 14, 27]. Ali and Whitehead [2] on the other hand evaluate various detector and descriptor combinations on their own dataset, including images of popular sights across different time periods. Their results depict that even the most successful ORB/SURF combination often fails for matching historic and modern images separated by large time spans.

Bae et al. [5], who present a software prototype that supports recapturing of photograph, state that SIFT fails to identify similarities between historic and modern image pairs and allocate this task to the user. A similar statement is made by Schindler and Dellaert [25], who sort a collection of historic images with the help of manual user interaction.

Stylianou et al. [27] analyse feature matching performance over time periods of five years. They show that the influence of structural changes on matching is tiny compared to changes in weather and lightning. Yet, five years are a rather short time span in historic repeat photography. Similarly Valgren and Lilienthal [30] study the impact of seasonal changes upon localization in outdoor environments over a period of nine months. Other works [6, 14] propose entirely new features for challenging image pairs, including historic repeat photographs, as well as day and night images and images of different rendering styles.

In image retrieval further works on matching disparate images, including historic ones, exist. Shrivastava et al. [26] developed a method for cross domain image matching based on densely sampled HOG features with learned weights. Similarly Aubry et al. [4] use the HOG descriptor to align images from multiple domains to a 3D model. Fernando et al. [10] aim at recognizing the location of an old photograph given modern labeled images from the Internet. Torii et al. [28] address the challenge of large-scale place recognition on day and night images from modern day Tokyo, Both [10, 28] propose a combination of dense sampling and RootSIFT for feature detection and description. Anyhow, it remains unknown whether image representation and classifier training on large datasets compensate for poor actual descriptor performance.

3   Evaluation

In this paper we analyze the suitability of classic detectors and descriptors for matching historic and modern image pairs as they arise during historic repeat photography. A majority of previous studies revealed that such pairs pose a challenge to classic detectors and descriptors. Hence, our evaluation not only tests general performance but also analyses measures to improve it. These include varying detector and descriptor parameters as well as applying different match filtering techniques. To compare these measures for a large set of detector and descriptor combinations we use a two step approach. At first we perform an initial evaluation applying a large amount of detector and descriptor combinations to our new dataset using default parameters. Afterwards a detailed evaluation follows, where we improve matching performance for the top detector and descriptor pairs. In the following we provide an overview of our dataset, the evaluation criteria, tested detectors and descriptors and match filters.

3.1   Dataset

Since the datasets used in related studies do not meet the conditions of this work [14], are not publicly available [11], or both [2], we constructed our own dataset for this study, which is available online[1]. This contains 52 rephotographies of Manhattan from a collection created by Paul Sahner[2]. The modern photographs were taken between 2009 and 2013, while the originals span the whole 20th century. The collection contains a variety of scenes including single buildings, as well as views of park areas or whole streets lined with houses. For some examples refer to Fig. 1. Furthermore the scenes are exposed to different amounts of structural change across the years. Additional variations between image pairs are caused by changes in lightning and weather as well as different acquisition devices or rendering styles.

As taken by a professional rephotographer most of the image pairs of the collection are already well aligned. Yet for further improvement we additionally computed a homography between all image pairs based on manual selection.

3.2   Evaluation Criteria

Related studies use *repeatability, precision, recall* [14] and *pass rate* [11] to evaluate detector and descriptor performance.

Repeatability assesses feature detector performance. For each detected keypoint the ground truth homography is used to measure whether a corresponding keypoint at the same location and of similar size exists [21]. In the context of rephotography often structures disappear and thus their features can no longer be repeated in the modern image. Instead accidental correspondences arise, since new structures feature new keypoints. Thus standard repeatability measures

---

[1] https://github.com/AnnKatrinBecker/nyc-grid-dataset.
[2] http://www.paulsahner.com, http://www.nyc-grid.com.

many more keypoint correspondences than can actually be returned during the descriptor based matching process. So that reachable recall rates (number of correct matches devided by the number of repeated keypoints) drop far below 100%. To establish a reliable ground truth for repeatability in the context of historic and modern images requires to annotate each region suffering from occlusion manually. Thus we refrain from using repeatability and recall in our evaluation.

Precision depicts the ratio of inliers among all corresponding keypoints returned by the matching process. Compared to repeatability this inlier rate suffers from very few false positives since it is reliant on descriptor distance. *Average precision* depicts the average precision value among the whole dataset. Unfortunately this value does not provide any information on the precision distribution.

Pass rate [11] instead, is calculated on the entire dataset and requires minimum thresholds for precision and the number of correct matches. Then pass rate is the percentage of image pairs from the dataset that exceed the appointed thresholds. Especially if few images show a high number of correct correspondences, while others hardly contain any, pass rate is more meaningful than average precision. Thus we prefer pass rate in our evaluation.

3.3   Detectors and Descriptors

We aimed at including all detectors and descriptors in our test set that showed good performance in related studies, including dense sampling [10,14,28], Root-SIFT [10,28] and the combinations of SURF/U-SURF [30], SIFT/SIFT [14] and ORB/SURF [2]. Afterwards we extended it with prominent detectors such as MSER and FAST as well as features only recently proposed (e.g. LATCH, AKAZE). Furthermore our test set includes fast binary as well as more computational expensive floating point descriptors.

In summary the detectors compared in this paper include dense sampling, MSER [19] and FAST [22]. Tested descriptors are U-SURF [7], RootSIFT [3], BRIEF [8] and LATCH [16]. Moreover the following features are used as detectors and descriptors: SIFT [18], SURF [7], ORB [24], BRISK [15], AKAZE [1]. We use the OpenCV implementation of all these features, including their respective default parameters. Only for ORB we limit the maximum number of keypoints to 10000 instead of 500.

3.4   Match Filtering Approaches

For match filtering we use classic approaches such as the ratio test [18] and maximal descriptor distance. However, as correct matches feature large descriptor distances in the context of historic and modern image pairs, descriptor distance is not a well distinguishing feature. Thus we additionally evaluate filtering approaches beyond descriptor distance. This includes the disparity gradient filter (DGF) proposed by Roth and Whitehead [23], exclusively based on the geometry of keypoints, as well as K-VLD [17], that evaluates both geometric as well as photometric consistency in the local neighborhood of a keypoint pair.

Disparity Gradient Filter. Given an image pair the disparity gradient measures the geometric compatibility of two of its correspondences [29]. Let P_1 and P_2 be keypoints in the first image and $f(P_1)$ and $f(P_2)$ be their correspondences in the second image, than their disparity gradient

$$d = \frac{|(P_1 - P_2) - [f(P_1) - f(P_2)]|}{\frac{1}{2}|(P_1 - P_2) + [f(P_1) - f(P_2)]|} \tag{1}$$

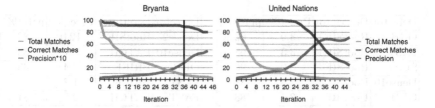

Fig. 2. Detailed course of applying the disparity gradient filter to individual image pairs. Both graphs illustrate the severe drop in total matches, while only few correct matches are discarded. This boosts precision. Beyond our point of termination (vertical line), precision values increase, but the loss of correct matches becomes more significant.

In case two correspondences conform well their disparity gradient is small. For general image registration Roth and Whitehead [23] sum up the disparity gradient for each correspondence with respect to each other correspondence. Afterwards correspondences with a high DGS are removed. Both steps are performed iteratively until the $max\ DGS$ is less than twice the $min\ DGS$.

In general we follow the approach of Roth and Whitehead [23], while we apply a softer termination criterion and discard false matches by the following rule. During each iteration we determine the $median\ DGS$ and discard all correspondences featuring a DGS greater than the median times a certain factor. Initially this factor is set to $1\frac{1}{2}$. Afterwards it decreases to $1\frac{1}{4}$, $1\frac{1}{8}$ and so on if

$$factor * median \geq max\ DGS \tag{2}$$

Furthermore we decrease the factor if less than 1% of correspondences were eliminated during the last iteration. During initial testing we also realized that the termination criterion of $min\ DGS * 2 > max\ DGS$ is to tight for our image pairs. Thus after analyzing initial results, see Fig. 2 we changed it to

$$min\ DGS * 3 > max\ DGS \tag{3}$$

4   Results

4.1   Initial Evaluation

In the initial evaluation we assess the performance of diverse feature detectors and descriptors on historic and modern image pairs. We apply all possible combinations of the feature detectors and descriptors listed in Sect. 3.3 to our new dataset. In the case of dense sampling, we apply two variants named Dense10 (dense sampling with a step size and a keypoint radius of 10) and Dense25 (step size and radius equal 25 as proposed in [14]). For matching keypoints nearest neighbor search is performed using the hamming distance or L2 norm, depending on the descriptor used.

Table 1. Set of top ten detector and descriptor combinations after the initial evaluation. All combinations are ranked by pass rate 16 (last column).

Detector	Descriptor	Prec.(%)	pr16(%)	Detector	Descriptor	Prec.(%)	pr16(%)
ORB	RootSIFT	3.9	96	Dense25	RootSIFT	12.0	83
FAST	RootSIFT	3.3	92	Dense10	LATCH	2.7	83
SURF	RootSIFT	3.9	90	ORB	BRIEF	2.4	83
Dense10	RootSIFT	3.8	88	FAST	BRIEF	1.7	83
ORB	U-SURF	3.1	88	FAST	LATCH	2.5	81

Previous studies report that it is critical to find enough correct matches at all for rephotographic image pairs [25]. Thus, initially we refrain from applying any filters, since these also eliminate correct matches. Of course this leads to poor precision values. Consequently in the initial evaluation we only use the number of correct matches to compare feature detectors and descriptors with each other, while we expect to improve precision during the detailed evaluation.

Therefore, we compute pass rates requiring a minimum number of 16 correct correspondences, while imposing no threshold on precision. We choose 16 as minimum value, since it is the required minimum number of correct correspondences in [25]. Table 1 depicts the top ten detector and descriptor combinations sorted by pass rate 16. Note that RootSIFT showed higher or similar performance as SIFT for all relevant combinations, thus we omit displaying the results of SIFT. Our further detailed evaluation tried to optimize the performance of these top combinations.

4.2   Varying Detector and Descriptor Parameters

At first we vary the parameters of dense sampling. Initially we keep the spacing of 10 pixels and sample dense keypoints with radii of 25, 35 and 50 pixels. While increasing the keypoint radius to 25 has a positive effect on pass rate, further increasing the radius to 35 or 50 does not improve but rather diminishes pass rate. Secondly we decrease keypoint spacing to only 5 pixels so that the total number of keypoints sampled is increased. Especially in combination with LATCH this shows a positive impact on pass rate as well, while there is no significant negative effect on precision.

Thus we decided to consider DENSE5:25/RootSIFT and DENSE5:25/ LATCH in our further evaluation. However, we note that dense sampling requires image pairs of similar scale and ideal keypoint scale is related to image resolution. Hence, if image resolution varies from our dataset (around 800 × 600 pixel) other radii may show better performances.

In the case of dense sampling raising the number of keypoints increased performance. Thus, we also analyze the effects of varying keypoint number for other detectors among the top ten. For ORB we evaluate a restriction of keypoints to 10000, 15000 and 20000, while for SURF we vary the Hessian Threshold from 100 to 50 and 25. In general an increase in the number of sampled keypoints results in an increase in pass rate, while precision values are hardly effected. Only for the combination ORB/BRIEF sampling 20000 keypoints diminishes performance. We attribute this effect towards the lower descriptive power of BRIEF as a binary descriptor compared to its floating point counter parts RootSIFT and U-SURF. Furthermore in the case of SURF detector a Hessian threshold of 50 depicts the best performance. Thus we use ORB20k/RootSIFT, ORB20k/U-SURF, ORB15k/BRIEF and SURF/RootSIFT with a hessian threshold of 50 for our further evaluation. Since FAST already samples around 15000 keypoints on each image, we did not change its parameters further.

At last we vary descriptor length to enhance discriminative power, especially for binary descriptors. For BRIEF and LATCH we compare descriptor lengths of 16, 32 and 64 bytes, while for U-SURF we compare a descriptor lengths of 64 and 128 floating point numbers. As expected for binary descriptors increasing descriptor length shows positive effects on pass rate and precision. For U-SURF instead changing descriptor length has hardly any effect.

In summary, we remain with the following nine detector and descriptor combinations for our further evaluation: Dense5:25/RootSIFT, Dense5:25/LATCH64, ORB20k/RootSIFT, ORB20k/U-SURF, FAST/RootSIFT, SURF/RootSIFT, FAST/BRIEF64, ORB15k/BRIEF64, FAST/LATCH64.

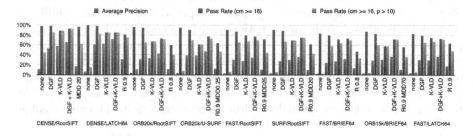

Fig. 3. Illustration of the performance of different match filtering approaches. In detail for each detector and descriptor combination results of applying no filter, DGF, K-VLD, the combination of both and the top performing standard filter (ratio test, maximal descriptor distance, or their combination) are displayed. For most detector and descriptor combinations pure K-VLD performs a little poorer than DGF in terms of pass rate, while similar average precision values are reached. Overall applying DGF followed by K-VLD, shows the best performance for most combinations.

4.3   Match Filtering

At first we applied the standard ratio test, with thresholds of 0.9, 0.8 [18] and 0.6 [25] for match filtering. However, only a weak threshold of 0.9 leads to slight performance increase in terms of precision and pass rate. For stricter values there still is an increase in precision, but this is accompanied by a reduction of correct correspondences below 16 for a significant number of image pairs.

Secondly, we evaluated the effects of applying a maximal descriptor distance threshold. Results are similar to those of applying the ratio test. Only very soft thresholds lead to slight increases in pass rate, while tighter ones diminish too many correct matches. Also a combination of both, ratio test and maximal descriptor distance threshold, does not result in promising increases in pass rate if a precision above 10% is required. Exemplary results are illustrated in the last column of Fig. 3.

Thirdly we applied the disparity gradient filter (DGF) [23] with our previously described iteration method and termination criterion. Our evaluation shows that DGF hardly discards any correct matches while lots of false correspondences are eliminated. Hence, DGF is able to boost precision by factors of 10 to 30, even for extremely low initial precision values beyond 1%, see also Fig. 2. The number of correct matches on the other hand does not diminish significantly upon DGF application.

At last we evaluated the performance of K-VLD [17] as a match filter for historic and modern image pairs. Overall K-VLD performs a little poorer then DGF in terms of pass rate, even though average precision is similar or slightly higher than for DGF. For a direct comparison please refer to Fig. 3. For individual images K-VLD leads to a greater boost in precision, but it also discards more correct matches. Hence for some image pairs its application results in a drop of correct matches below 16.

Due to the individual shortcomings of DGF (low precision) and K-VLD (few correct matches) for individual image pairs, we propose to combine both filters. At first DGF is used to discard a majority of false correspondences and reach precision values above 1% or 2%. Afterwards K-VLD is applied to achieve a further boost in performance. The results of applying this filter combination to our dataset are displayed in the fourth column of Fig. 3. Compared to single DGF application a clear performance increase in average precision is visible, while such is not accompanied by a drop in pass rate as in the case of single K-VLD use.

In summary the generally low performance of standard filters, such as the ratio test and maximal descriptor distance, can be ascribed to their dependence on descriptor distance. This is, since for image pairs featuring major appearance changes, even correct matches feature high descriptor distances. Thus descriptor distance is not a distinctive feature between correct and false correspondences of modern and historic image pairs. Instead, measures such as DGF, exclusively based on keypoint geometry, and K-VLD, based on photometric as well as geometric measures, are much more effective for filtering correspondences.

4.4   Application Beyond Rephotography

Finally we verify the applicability of our established pipeline to other challenging image pairs beyond rephotography and our own dataset. To do so we apply our top nine detector and descriptor combinations together with our proposed filtering mechanisms to the dataset of Hauagge and Snavely [14]. This is composed of various challenging image pairs, including day and night images and images of different rendering styles.

Table 2. Comparison with the results of Hauagge and Snavely [14]

(a) Mean average precision of [14].

	GRID	SIFT	SYM-I	SYM-G
Self-Sim.	0.29	0.14	0.12	0.16
SIFT	0.49	0.21	0.28	0.25
SYMD	0.41	0.22	0.20	0.25
SIFT-SYMD	0.58	0.28	0.35	0.36

(b) Average precision of our pipeline.

	none	DGF	K-VLD	both
Dense5:25/RootSIFT	0.24	0.69	0.79	0.84
Dense5:25/LATCH64	0.13	0.71	0.77	0.85
ORB20k/RootSIFT	0.11	0.56	0.58	0.71
ORB20k/U-SURF	0.10	0.64	0.65	0.74

Table 2 depicts the average precision of our top four combinations, without match filtering, after applying DGF or K-VLD and the combination of both. Overall the average precision values reached on the dataset of Hauagge and Snavely [14] are higher than those achieved for our own dataset reported in Fig. 3. Hence as expected, our dataset is more challenging due to the presence of major structural changes.

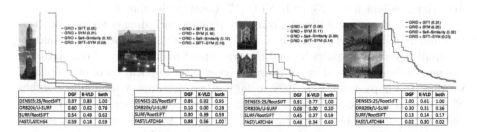

Fig. 4. Comparison of results for individual image pairs from [14]. At the top the image pairs and their respective recall and precision curves for dense sampling as reported by [14] are displayed. At the bottom the precision values of a variety of our detector and descriptor combination reached after match filtering are shown. For the majority of image pairs our proposed pipeline reaches high precision values

The mean average precision values reached by [14] are repeated in Table 2. Unfortunately, their mean average precision values are not directly comparable to our average precision reached after filtering, since they applied a variety of ratio thresholds for filtering and report mean average precision of all these tests.

Anyhow, there is a distance of more than 0.25 between their mean average precision values for dense sampling (GRID) and the average precision values after DGF and K-VLD application for our top two combinations using dense sampling. This suggests that our proposed pipeline outperforms the approach of [14] in matching image pairs containing high appearance variations. To confirm this we also compared the performance of both approaches on individual image pairs, which have shown to be extremely challenging based on the results of [14]. A subset of these image pairs is displayed in Fig. 4. These examples show that for a majority of image pairs, that feature rather low precision and recall curves in [14], our pipeline is able to generate high precision values after match filter application.

5   Conclusion

In this work we analyzed the suitability of classic feature detectors and descriptors for matching historical and modern image pairs. In this context we created a new challenging publicly available dataset, composed of rephotographies of a variety of scenes exposed to moderate up to tremendous change across years. Our evaluation results show that selective feature detection is not suitable if image pairs contain great variations. More effective is a dense sampling of keypoints. As descriptors overall RootSIFT and SURF but also the binary descriptors BRIEF and LATCH show the highest feature matching performance. Furthermore we discovered that a suitable match filtering approach is much more important than the individual classic detector and descriptor combination used. In detail filters based on descriptor distance are not suitable in the presence of great appearance changes. Instead the application of filters based on geometry such as the disparity gradient filter [23] or K-VLD [17] boost performance.

In summary, we established a complete pipeline including detectors, descriptors and matching filtering methods. This also shows high performance in matching challenging image pairs beyond historic repeat photography as our comparison on another dataset showed. However, even after application of our pipeline, we only reach pass rates of 70% to 90% if we presume a minimum number of 16 correct matches and precision values above 10%, remember Fig. 3. Given these requirements, between 10% to 30% of image pairs of our dataset remain unmatchable. Consequently further research and possibly completely new feature matching approaches are required to match even the most challenging historic repeat photographs. Further more the performance of feature detectors and descriptors in more natural non urban environments still needs to be assessed.

References

1. Alcantarilla, P.F., Solutions, T.: Fast explicit diffusion for accelerated features in nonlinear scale spaces. TPAMI **34**(7), 1281–1298 (2011)
2. Ali, H.K., Whitehead, A.: Feature matching for aligning historical and modern images. Int. J. Comput. Appl. **21**(3), 188–201 (2014)

3. Arandjelović, R., Zisserman, A.: Three things everyone should know to improve object retrieval. In: CVPR, pp. 2911–2918 (2012)
4. Aubry, M., Russell, B.C., Sivic, J.: Painting-to-3D model alignment via discriminative visual elements. TOG **33**(2), 14 (2014)
5. Bae, S., Agarwala, A., Durand, F.: Computational rephotography. ACM Trans. Graph. **29**(3), 1–15 (2010)
6. Bansal, M., Daniilidis, K.: Joint spectral correspondence for disparate image matching. In: CVPR, pp. 2802–2809 (2013)
7. Bay, H., Tuytelaars, T., Van Gool, L.: SURF: speeded up robust features. In: Leonardis, A., Bischof, H., Pinz, A. (eds.) ECCV 2006. LNCS, vol. 3951, pp. 404–417. Springer, Heidelberg (2006). https://doi.org/10.1007/11744023_32
8. Calonder, M., Lepetit, V., Strecha, C., Fua, P.: BRIEF: binary robust independent elementary features. In: Daniilidis, K., Maragos, P., Paragios, N. (eds.) ECCV 2010. LNCS, vol. 6314, pp. 778–792. Springer, Heidelberg (2010). https://doi.org/10.1007/978-3-642-15561-1_56
9. Clements, F.E.: Research methods in ecology. The University Publishing Company, Lincoln (1905)
10. Fernando, B., Tommasi, T., Tytelaars, T.: Location recognition over large time lags. Comput. Vis. Image Underst. **139**, 21–28 (2015)
11. Gat, C., Albu, A.B., German, D., Higgs, E.: A comparative evaluation of feature detectors on historic repeat photography. In: Bebis, G., et al. (eds.) ISVC 2011. LNCS, vol. 6939, pp. 701–714. Springer, Heidelberg (2011). https://doi.org/10.1007/978-3-642-24031-7_70
12. Gore, A.: An Inconvenient Truth: The Planetary Emergency of Global Warming and What We Can Do About It. Rodale, Emmaus (2006)
13. Hall, F.C.: Photo point monitoring handbook: part a-field procedures. Technical report, PNW: USDA Forest Service (2002)
14. Hauagge, D.C., Snavely, N.: Image matching using local symmetry features. In: CVPR, pp. 206–213 (2012)
15. Leutenegger, S., Chli, M., Siegwart, R.Y.: Brisk: binary robust invariant scalable keypoints. In: ICCV, pp. 2548–2555 (2011)
16. Levi, G., Hassner, T.: LATCH: learned arrangements of three patch codes. In: WACV, pp. 1–9 (2016)
17. Liu, Z., Marlet, R.: Virtual line descriptor and semi-local matching method for reliable feature correspondence. In: BMVC, p. 16-1 (2012)
18. Lowe, D.G.: Distinctive image features from scale-invariant keypoints. Int. J. Comput. Vis. **60**(2), 91–110 (2004)
19. Mata, J., Chum, O., Urban, M., Pajdla, T.: Robust wide-baseline stereo from maximally stable extremal regions. Image Vis. Comput. **22**(10), 761–767 (2004)
20. Meyer, J.L., Youngs, Y.: Historical landscape change in yellowstone national park. Geogr. Rev. **108**(3), 387–409 (2018)
21. Mikolajczyk, K., et al.: A comparison of affine region detectors. Int. J. Comput. Vis. **65**(1–2), 43–72 (2005)
22. Rosten, E., Drummond, T.: Machine learning for high-speed corner detection. In: Leonardis, A., Bischof, H., Pinz, A. (eds.) ECCV 2006. LNCS, vol. 3951, pp. 430–443. Springer, Heidelberg (2006). https://doi.org/10.1007/11744023_34
23. Roth, G., Whitehead, A.: Using projective vision to find camera positions in an image sequence. In: Conference on Vision Interface 2000, Canada, pp. 87–94 (2000)
24. Rublee, E., Rabaud, V., Konolige, K., Bradski, G.: ORB: An efficient alternative to SIFT and SURF. In: ICCV, pp. 2564–2571 (2011)

25. Schindler, G., Dellaert, F.: 4D cities: analyzing, visualizing, and interacting with historical urban photo collections. J. Multimedia **7**(2), 124–131 (2012)
26. Shrivastava, A., Malisiewicz, T., Gupta, A., Efros, A.A.: Data-driven visual similarity for cross-domain image matching. TOG **30**(6), 154 (2011)
27. Stylianou, A., Abrams, A., Pless, R.: Characterizing feature matching performance over long time periods. In: WACV, pp. 892–898 (2015)
28. Torii, A., Arandjelović, R., Sivic, J., Okutomi, M., Pajdla, T.: 24/7 place recognition by view synthesis. In: CVPR, pp. 1808–1817 (2015)
29. Trivedi, H.P., Lloyd, S.A.: The role of disparity gradient in stereo vision. Perception **14**(6), 685–690 (1985)
30. Valgren, C., Lilienthal, A.J.: SIFT, SURF & seasons: appearance-based long-term localization in outdoor environments. Robot. Auton. Syst. **58**(2), 149–156 (2010)
31. Walker, J., Leib, J.: Revisiting the Topia road: walking in the footsteps of West and Parsons. Geogr. Rev. **92**(4), 555–581 (2002)

An RNN-Based IMM Filter Surrogate

Stefan Becker[✉][ID], Ronny Hug[ID], Wolfgang Hübner[ID], and Michael Arens[ID]

Fraunhofer Institute for Optronics, System Technologies, and Image Exploitation
(IOSB), Gutleuthausstr. 1, 76275 Ettlingen, Germany
stefan.becker@iosb.fraunhofer.de

Abstract. The problem of varying dynamics of tracked objects, such as pedestrians, is traditionally tackled with approaches like the Interacting Multiple Model (IMM) filter using a Bayesian formulation. By following the current trend towards using deep neural networks, in this paper an RNN-based IMM filter surrogate is presented. Similar to an IMM filter solution, the presented RNN-based model assigns a probability value to a performed dynamic and, based on them, puts out a multi-modal distribution over future pedestrian trajectories. The evaluation is done on synthetic data, reflecting prototypical pedestrian maneuvers.

Keywords: Trajectory forecasting · Path prediction · IMM filter · Multiple model filter

1 Introduction

The applications of pedestrian trajectory prediction cover a broad range from autonomous driving, robot navigation, smart video surveillance to object tracking. Traditionally, the task of object motion prediction is done by using a Bayesian formulation in approaches such as the Kalman filter [17], or non-parametric methods, such as particle filters [4]. Driven by the success of recurrent neural networks (RNNs) in modeling temporal dependencies in a variety of sequence processing tasks, such as speech recognition [10,13] and caption generation [12,27], RNNs are increasingly utilized for object motion prediction [2,3,7,15,16]. When relying on traditional approaches, the challenge of varying dynamics over time is commonly addressed with the Interacting Multiple Model (IMM) filter [9]. The IMM filter is a well established approach to elegantly combine a set of candidate models into a single context by weighting each individual model. Each model corresponds to a specific motion pattern and contributes to the final state estimation depending on its current weight. According to the IMM filter solution, in this paper an RNN-based IMM filter surrogate is presented. On the one hand, the presented RNN-based model is able to also provide a confidence value for the performed dynamic and on the other hand can overcome some limitations of the classic IMM filter. The suggested RNN-encoder-decoder model generates the probability distribution over future pedestrian paths conditioned on a dynamic class. The model is based on the work of Deo and Trivedi [11]. For

© Springer Nature Switzerland AG 2019
M. Felsberg et al. (Eds.): SCIA 2019, LNCS 11482, pp. 387–398, 2019.
https://doi.org/10.1007/978-3-030-20205-7_32

the case study of freeway traffic, they used an two branch RNN-encoder-decoder network for vehicle maneuver and trajectory prediction. Since for vehicle applications an on-board lane estimation algorithm is mostly available, a stationary frame of reference, with the origin fixed at the vehicle being predicted, is used in their work. Although this makes the model independent of road curvature and independent of how vehicle tracks are obtained, it can not be applied without adjustments for pedestrian motion prediction. Thus, our RNN-based model infers like classical filters the current position and uses only a single RNN branch for encoding the maneuver class, the filtered position and the trajectory information. In the context of vehicle motion prediction, maneuver or rather dynamic classes can be better defined than for pedestrians. For example by changing or keeping the lane. Due to the dynamic behavior of pedestrians, the maneuver classes are here defined based on the deviation from a straight walking pedestrian. The presented network also extends the maneuver network of Deo and Trivedi [11] with insights from the work of Becker et al. [7] to better adapt to pedestrian motions.

Moreover, this paper aims to highlight some relations between traditional multiple model approaches such as the IMM filter and the suggested RNN-based IMM filter surrogate. By combining the different views on maneuver predictions, this work contributes to an exploration of the connections between both problem formulations. The decoder uses the de-noised position estimate and a context vector, encoding the dynamic classes, to predict future positions. The analysis is done on synthetic data reflecting prototypical scenarios capturing pedestrians maneuvers.

In the following, a brief formalization of the problem and a description of the RNN-based model are provided. The achieved results are presented in Sect. 3. Finally, a conclusion is given in Sect. 4.

2   RNN-Based IMM Filter Surrogate

The goal is to devise a model that can successfully predict future paths of pedestrians and represent alternating pedestrian dynamics, e.g. dynamics that can transition from a straight walking to a turning maneuver or stopping. Here, trajectory prediction is formally stated as the problem of predicting the future trajectories of a pedestrian, conditioned on its track history. Given an input sequence $\mathcal{Z} = \{(x^t, y^t) \in \mathbb{R}^2 | t = 1, \ldots, t_{obs}\}$ of T_{obs} consecutive observed pedestrian positions $\boldsymbol{z}^t = (x^t, y^t)$ at time t along a trajectory, the task is to generate a multi-modal prediction for the next T_{pred} positions $\{\boldsymbol{x}^{t+1}, \boldsymbol{x}^{t+2}, \ldots, \boldsymbol{x}^{t+T_{pred}}\}$ and to filter the current position $\boldsymbol{x}^t = (x^t, y^t)$. One insight from the work Becker et al. [7] is that motion continuity is easier to express in offsets or velocities, because it takes considerably more modeling effort to represent all possible conditioning positions. In order to exploit scene-specific knowledge for trajectory prediction, additional use of the position information is required. When sufficient training samples from a particular scene are available, Hug et al. [15] showed that RNN-based trajectory prediction models are able to capture spatially dependent behavior changes only from motion data. However, here the offsets are additionally used for conditioning the network $\mathcal{Z} = \{(x^t, y^t, \delta_x^t, \delta_y^t) \in \mathbb{R}^4 | t = 2, \ldots, t_{obs}\}$. Apart from the smaller modeling effort to represent conditioned offsets, the shift to offsets helps to prevent undefined states due to a limited data range [7] and it is easier to make better generalizations across datasets. Since, we analyze the model capabilities on synthetic data reflecting prototypical pedestrian maneuvers for a fixed scenario, the amount of training samples is not restricted. Thus, in order to localize in the reference system position information is used to estimate the true position. The future trajectory is denoted with $\mathcal{Y} = \{(x^t, y^t) \in \mathbb{R}^2 | t = t_{obs} + 1, \ldots, t_{pred}\}$. The model estimates the conditional distribution $P(\mathcal{Y}, x^t | \mathcal{Z})$. In order to identify specific dynamics under M desired maneuver classes (e.g. turning maneuvers, stopping and straight walking), this term can be given by:

$$P(\mathcal{Y}, x^t | \mathcal{Z}) = \sum_{i=1}^{M} P_\Theta(\mathcal{Y}, x^t | m_i, \mathcal{Z}) P(m_i | \mathcal{Z}) \tag{1}$$

Here, $\Theta = \{\Theta^{t_{obs}+1}, \ldots, \Theta^{t_{pred}}\}$ are the parameters of a L component Gaussian mixture model $\Theta^t = (\mu_l^t, \Sigma_l^t, w_l^t)_{l=1,\ldots,L}$. By adding the maneuver context in form of the posterior mode probability, $P(m_i | \mathcal{Z}) \stackrel{\wedge}{=} \alpha_i$ the analogy to the classic IMM filter becomes apparent. For an IMM filter, the mode probability is used to calculate the mixing probabilities to combine the set of chosen candidate models into a merged estimate. The time behavior of the basic filter set is modeled as a homogeneous (time invariant) Markov chain with a fixed transition probability matrix (TPM) $m_{ij} \stackrel{\wedge}{=} P(m_i^t | m_j^{t-1})$. Under the assumption that M models describe the variation of the dynamics, the posterior density of the IMM filter can be written as follows:

$$P(x^t | \mathcal{Z}) = \sum_{i=1}^{M} P_{\Theta_{IMM}}(x^t | m_i, \mathcal{Z}) P(m_i | \mathcal{Z}) \tag{2}$$

Here, $P_{\Theta_{IMM}}(x^t | m_i, \mathcal{Z})$ is in the context of an IMM filter a Gaussian distribution and $P(m_i | \mathcal{Z}) \stackrel{\wedge}{=} \alpha_i$ is the posterior mode probability for the IMM filter. As mentioned above, the transition between different dynamics is modeled as a first order Markov chain for an IMM filter. The law of total probability allows to compute new mode probabilities based on the transition probabilities. Given the current mode probabilities and transition probabilities, the mixing probabilities $\alpha_{i|j}$ for the mixing step of the IMM filter can be calculated. For each model M_i and M_j, they are calculated as $\alpha_{i|j}^{t-1} = \frac{1}{\bar{c}_j} m_{ij} \alpha_i^{t-1}$ with a normalization factor $\bar{c}_j = \sum_{i=1}^{M} m_{ij} \alpha_i^{t-1}$. Then, in the prediction stage, each filter is applied independently using the calculated mixed initial condition. Subsequently, the model probabilities are adapted according to the likelihood of each filter.

RNN-IMM: Whereas an explicit modeling of the switching behavior and the object dynamics of the IMM filter stands in contrast to an implicit dynamic encoding of an RNN-based approach. In order to provide an IMM filter surrogate, the proposed model also estimates mode probabilities and filters or rather de-noises the current position based on noisy observations $\mathcal{Z}$. By writing the conditional distribution $P(\mathcal{Y}, \boldsymbol{x}|\mathcal{Z})$ of the RNN-based approach in form of Eq. 1, the desired estimates can be inferred from the hidden states of the RNN $\boldsymbol{h}$. This formulations does not require to set the parameters of the TPM matrix manually, which is commonly done based on the mean sojourn time (the mean time an object stays in a motion type [5,24]) or as stated in the work of Bar-Shalom [5], an ad-hoc approach to fill the diagonals with values close to one. For the proposed RNN-based IMM filter surrogate (RNN-IMM), the basic architecture is a recurrent encoder-decoder model. The encoder takes the frame by frame input sequence $\mathcal{Z}$. The hidden state vector of the encoder is updated at each time step based on the previous hidden state and the current observation. The generated internal representation is used to predict mode probabilities $\boldsymbol{\alpha}^t$ at the current time step and $\boldsymbol{x}^t$. With embedding of the current observations, the encoder can be defined as follows:

$$e^t_{encoder} = \text{EMB}(\boldsymbol{z}^t; W_{ee})$$
$$h^t_{encoder} = \text{RNN}(h^{t-1}_{encoder}, e^t_{encoder}; W_{encoder})$$
$$\hat{\boldsymbol{x}}^t, \boldsymbol{\alpha}^t_{logits} = \text{MLP}(h^t_{encoder}; W_{en})$$
$$\hat{\boldsymbol{\alpha}}^t = \frac{\exp{(\boldsymbol{\alpha}^t_{logits})}}{\sum_{j=1}^{M} \exp{(\alpha^t_{logits,j})}}$$

Here, RNN($\cdot$) is the recurrent network, $\boldsymbol{h}$ the hidden state of the RNN, MLP($\cdot$) the multilayer perceptron, and EMB($\cdot$) an embedding layer. W represents the weights and biases of the MLP, EMB or respectively RNN. The final state of the encoder can be expected to encode information about the track histories. For generating a trajectory distribution over dynamic modes, the encoder hidden state is appended to a one-hot encoded vector corresponding to specific maneuvers and the filtered current position. Instead of only filtering the position, the encoder could also be used to parametrize a mixture density output layer (MDL). The decoder of the model can be defined as follows:

$$h^t_{decoder} = \text{RNN}(h^{t-1}_{decoder}[h^t_{encoder}], \hat{\boldsymbol{x}}^t, \boldsymbol{\alpha}^t; W_{decoder})$$
$$\hat{\mathcal{Y}} = \{(\hat{\boldsymbol{\mu}}^t_l + \hat{\boldsymbol{x}}^{t_{obs}}, \hat{\Sigma}^t_l, \hat{w}^t_l)|t = t_{obs} + 1, \ldots, t_{pred}\} = \text{MLP}(h^t_{decoder}; W_{de})$$

The decoder is used to parametrize a mixture density output layer (MDL) or rather Θ directly for several positions in the future (one distribution for every time step). Nevertheless, the overall RNN-IMM uses the trajectory prediction and dynamic classification jointly, the loss function for training is split into three parts.

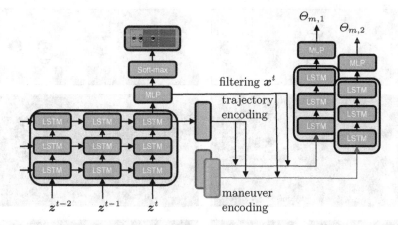

Fig. 1. Visualization of the RNN-based IMM filter surrogate (RNN-encoder-decoder network) for jointly predicting specific dynamic probabilities and corresponding future distributions of trajectory positions. The encoder predicts the dynamic probabilities and the filtered position for the current time step. The decoder uses the context vector and the position estimate to predict future pedestrian locations.

Dynamic classification is trained to mimimize the sum of cross-entropy losses of the different M motion model classes:

$$\mathcal{L}(\mathcal{Z})_{maneuver} = -\sum_{j=1}^{M} \alpha_{j,GT}^t \log(\hat{\alpha}_j^t) \qquad (3)$$

Additionally, the encoder is trained by minimizing the filtering loss $\mathcal{L}(\mathcal{Z})_{filter}$ in form of the mean squared error to the ground truth current pedestrian locations. In case the encoder should generate the parameter of a mixture of Gaussian or single Gaussian distribution, the negative log likelihood for the ground truth pedestrian locations can be minimized. Finally, the complete encoder-decoder is trained by minimizing the negative log likelihood for the ground truth future pedestrian locations conditioned under the performed maneuver class. The context vector is appended with the ground truth values of the dynamic model or maneuver classes for each training trajectory. This results in the following loss function:

$$\mathcal{L}(\mathcal{Z})_{pred} = -\log(P_\Theta(\hat{\mathcal{Y}}|m_{GT}, \mathcal{Z})P(m_{GT}|\mathcal{Z}))$$

$$\mathcal{L}(\mathcal{Z})_{pred} = \sum_{t=t_{obs}+1}^{t_{pred}} -\log(\sum_{l=1}^{L} \hat{w}_l^t \mathcal{N}(\boldsymbol{x}^t|\hat{\boldsymbol{\mu}}_l^t + \boldsymbol{x}^{t_{obs}}, \hat{\Sigma}_l^t; m_{GT})) \qquad (4)$$

The overall architecture is visualized in Fig. 1. The context vector combines the encoding of the track history with the encoding of the alternating dynamic classes. Together with the filtered position, it is used as input for the decoder.

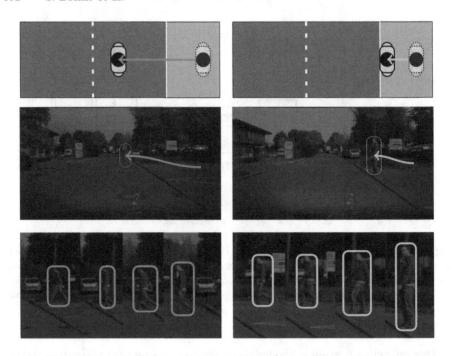

Fig. 2. Illustration of typical pedestrian motions. The above images depict the two chosen maneuver classes of straight walking or rather crossing and stopping. The images on the left show a person crossing the street. The images on the right show a person changing from walking to standing at the curbside of the street. In particular changing from straight walking to stopping [24].

3   Data Generation and Evaluation

This section consists of a brief evaluation of the proposed RNN-IMM. The evaluation is concerned with verifying the overall viability of the approach in maneuver situations. For initial results, a synthetic test condition is used in order to gain insight into the model behavior in different typical pedestrian motion types. A prototypical maneuver performed by a pedestrian, which has important implications for the field of intelligent vehicles and video surveillance is a stopping or deceleration maneuver.

Data Generation and Reference Methods: For the first mentioned context of intelligent vehicles, Schneider et al. [24] performed a comparative study on recursive Bayesian filters for pedestrian path prediction at short time horizons (below 2 s). They applied different filters on typical pedestrian motion types. Although, the comparison was done on the Daimler path prediction dataset, we evaluate on synthetic data but make use of the provided real data to capture a similar condition. Firstly, the Daimler path prediction dataset provides only a maximum amount of 23 sequences for single motion types. As mentioned before, in order to avoid problems such as a limited number of training samples and to gain some insights into a controlled setup, synthetic data is used. Secondly, the location information is biased in the dataset. Since recursive Bayesian filters make in their standard formulation no use of the spatial context of a scene, this does not harm their mutual comparison. However, RNN-based prediction networks are able to capture spatially dependent behavior changes [15], thus a fair comparison is difficult to achieve. The evaluation on the Daimler dataset is done in an ego-motion compensated reference system. The frame rate of the camera system inside the recording vehicle is 16 fps and it is taken over accordingly for our experiments. The pedestrians change their behavior abruptly. Therefore, the sensible time horizons are short. Here, 8 (0.5 s) consecutive positions are observed, before predicting the next 8 (0.5 s), 12 (0.75 s) and 16 (1 s).

For generating synthetic trajectories of a basic maneuvering pedestrian, random agents are sampled from a Gaussian distribution according to a preferred pedestrian walking speed [26] ($\mathcal{N}(1, 38\,\text{m}, 0.37\,\text{m})$) from the distribution of starting positions of the corresponding Daimler dataset sequences. During a single trajectory simulation the agents can perform a stopping maneuver or cross the street. Figure 2 illustrates such maneuvers with example images from the Daimler dataset [24]. For mapping the pedestrian detections to a vehicle-motion compensated ground plane, Schneider et al. used on-board sensors for velocity and yaw rate and a stereo camera system to compute the median disparity. Due to the non-linear observation model based on a perceptive camera model, an inevitable linearized extension for the Kalman and IMM filter observation models are required. Here, the observation uncertainty of the position sensor is assumed to be Gaussian distributed $r^t \sim \mathcal{N}(0, 0.01\,\text{m})$ in the compensated reference system. Thus, the standard formulation of the Bayesian filters are well suited for this task. For the stopping maneuver or rather the event of deceleration till standing, a mean sojourn time of 1 s with a standard deviation of 0.1 s is used. As long as a person moves in a straight line at a reasonably constant speed, their dynamics can be captured with a Kalman filter using a constant velocity model. During the maneuver, the relation to one fixed process model describing the dynamics fails due to an additional deceleration. Similar to Schneider et al. [24] or Kooij et al. [21], the reference IMM filter is set up by combining two basic models, in particular, the constant velocity (CV) and the constant acceleration (CA) model. For avoiding side effects due to independent motions in different directions, see for example [6], only the crossing direction, from the vehicle perspective, the lateral motion is considered. Following the aforementioned explanations, the IMM-RNN is compared to an IMM filter with two motion models (CV, CA), a Kalman filter with a single CV model, a Kalman filter with a single CA model, and as baseline to a linear interpolation. Also correspondingly to Schneider et al., the process noise q is determined by $Q(t) = Q_0(t)q$, where $q \in \{\sigma_{CV}, \sigma_{CA}\}$ are spectral densities (continuous time variances) of the process noise, describing the changes in velocity or respectively in acceleration over a sampling period Δt (CV: $\sqrt{Q_{22}} = \sqrt{\Delta t \cdot q}$; CA: $\sqrt{Q_{33}} = \sqrt{\Delta t \cdot q}$, see for example [23]). Based on this process noise model, the optimal process noise parameters for the different chosen filters (IMM filter (CV, CA), Kalman filter CV, CA) on the Daimler dataset are for the two IMM filter models $\sigma_{IMM,CV} = 0.70, \sigma_{IMM,CA} = 0.80$ and for the single Kalman filters $\sigma_{CV} = 0.77$ and $\sigma_{CA} = 0.44$ [24]. These parameters are consistent with the suggested practical setting in Bar-Shalom [5] and the chosen sojourn time for the simulation.

As mentioned above, a definition of maneuver classes for pedestrians is harder to establish than for vehicles. Hence, the main interest is here to detect the deviation from a standard behavior, and whether the pedestrian is in a *normal* mode. A set of deviation in velocity, deceleration, along with the tangential ground truth trajectory is used to assign a maneuver label to a time step of a single trajectory. Thus, the RNN-IMM and IMM filter have a similar basic dynamic model set description. As the distribution over the trajectories for the RNN-IMM is captured with a Gaussian mixture model, the maneuver description for a single model can still be multi-modal. Since the IMM filter predicts a multi-modal distribution in form of a combination of the uni-modal model specific prediction, in the presented results the RNN-IMM is set to also only predict conditioned on a single maneuver class a uni-modal Gaussian distribution.

Implementation Details: The model has been implemented using *Tensorflow* [1] and is trained for 2000 epochs using ADAM optimizer [19] with a decreasing learning rate, starting from 0.01 with a learning rate decay of 0.95 and a delay factor of 1/10. During the learning rate adaption, the number of epochs is multiplied by the delay factor. For the experiments, the RNN variant Long Short-Term Memory (LSTM) [14] is used.

Results and Analysis: In Fig. 3, predictions for two different preformed motion types are depicted for 8 future positions weighted by the predicted maneuver probability. In the shown images the positions are normalized to start at the origin. The resulting multi-modal prediction is visualized as a heatmap. On the left, it can be seen that for a crossing sequence with straight walking the RNN-IMM mainly uses the corresponding straight walking model. On the right, where the deceleration started, the straight walking probability is visibly lower and the predicted distribution maximum is very close to the last observation. For the quantitative evaluation, 1000 noisy trajectories have been synthetically generated, where 80% are used for training and 20% for the comparison to the recursive Bayesian filters. The results are summarized in Table 1.

The performance is compared with the final displacement error (FDE) (see for example [22]) of the lateral motion (from the vehicle perspective) for three different time horizons, in particular 8 steps (0.5 s), 12 steps (0.75 s) and 16 steps (1 s). These results show that the presented RNN-IMM is able to faster capture the change in dynamic for the synthetically generated data. In terms of the single motion models (CV vs. CA), one can observe the benefits for the CA in capturing the deceleration. The IMM filter combines both and shows an improvement. Hence, the aim of this paper is more on highlighting the relation between traditional multiple model approaches and the suggested RNN-based

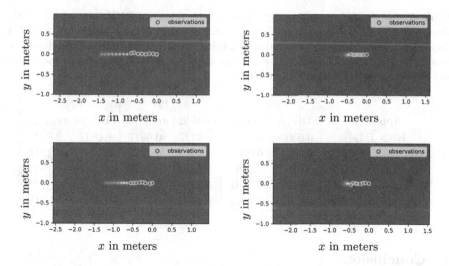

Fig. 3. Visualization of the predicted multi-modal distributions of future position as heatmap. (Left) Density plots for crossing or rather straight walking examples. (Right) Density plots for stopping examples in which the maximum of the predicted distribution is visible close to the last observation.

IMM filter surrogate, it should be mentioned that RNN-based approaches are designed to receive input data for every time step, whereas Bayesian filters are well suited for handling missing observations. Especially with such a short initialization time, this can be crucial. One argument towards a learning based RNN-IMM is that we only choose the maneuver definition based on deviation of standard straight walking. The engineering task of finding the best model set up for IMM filters and their extensions can lead to an improved behavior (see for example Keller et al. [18]) in specific maneuver situations, but is also very tedious to find a good setting. It should also be mentioned that recent work like the approaches of Kooij et al. [20] show options how to further improve the prediction performance by including scene context and using more cues than pedestrian point kinematics (e.g. head orientation, gaze, body tilt, articulated body information).

In summary, the presented RNN-IMM is able to also provide a confidence value $P(m_i|\mathcal{Z}) \stackrel{\wedge}{=} \alpha_i$ for the performed dynamic, but avoids modeling the dynamic transitions with a fixed transition probability matrix $P(m_i^t|m_j^{t-1})$. Similar to the provided mode probabilities of IMM filters, this can be used for further processing steps or rather applications (see for example [8,25]). Further, instead of choosing the basic filter set, the prediction model is learned. In case there exists some well known model for describing the standard dynamic of the desired target, only deviations from the known dynamic can be used to define additional maneuver classes. This study on synthetically generated data shows, that by exploiting the connections between different views on maneuver prediction some perspectives on overcoming respective limitations can be gained.

Table 1. Results for the comparison between the proposed RNN-IMM and an IMM filter with two motion models (CV, CA), a Kalman filter with a single CV model, a Kalman filter with a single CA model, and using linear interpolation on the simulated maneuver situations. The prediction is done for 8, 12, and 16 time steps conditioned on 8 observations for a frame rate of 16 fps.

	8/8		8/12		8/16	
Approach	FDE [m]	σ_{FDE} [m]	FDE [m]	σ_{FDE} [m]	FDE [m]	σ_{FDE} [m]
RNN-IMM	0.0309	0.0404	0.0427	0.0817	0.0517	0.0941
IMM filter (CV,CA)	0.0674	0.0602	0.1188	0.1255	0.1862	0.1915
Kalman filter (CA)	0.0796	0.0638	0.1575	0.1137	0.2386	0.1696
Kalman filter (CV)	0.1578	0.1601	0.2890	0.2965	0.4701	0.4700
Linear interpolation	0.1587	0.1610	0.2903	0.2978	0.4724	0.4718

4 Conclusion

In this paper, an RNN-encoder-decoder model, which can be interpreted as an IMM filter surrogate, has been presented. The RNN-IMM is able to jointly predict specific motion probabilities and corresponding distributions of future pedestrian trajectory. The model capabilities were shown on synthetic data that were reflecting typical pedestrian maneuvers. By conditioning on specific dynamic models or rather deviation from standard behavior, the model makes it possible to generate additional information in terms of an assigned maneuver probability similar to an IMM filter, but reduces the amount of explicit modeling of filter parameters (e.g. the dynamic transitions matrix). Thus, the presented RNN-IMM helps to reduce the amount of hard-coded engineering of traditional multiple model filter such as the IMM filter.

References

1. Abadi, M., et al.: TensorFlow: large-scale machine learning on heterogeneous systems (2015). Software: https://www.tensorflow.org/
2. Alahi, A., Goel, K., Ramanathan, V., Robicquet, A., Fei-Fei, L., Savarese, S.: Social LSTM: human trajectory prediction in crowded spaces. In: Conference on Computer Vision and Pattern Recognition (CVPR), pp. 961–971. IEEE (2016)
3. Alahi, A., et al.: Learning to predict human behaviour in crowded scenes. In: Group and Crowd Behavior for Computer Vision. Elsevier (2017)
4. Arulampalam, M., Maskell, S., Gordon, N., Clapp, T.: A tutorial on particle filters for online nonlinear/non-Gaussian Bayesian tracking. Trans. Sig. Process. **50**(2), 174–188 (2002). https://doi.org/10.1109/78.978374
5. Bar-Shalom, Y., Kirubarajan, T., Li, X.R.: Estimation with Applications to Tracking and Navigation. Wiley, New York (2002)
6. Becker, S., Hübner, W., Arens, M.: State estimation for tracking in imagespace with a de- and re-coupled IMM filter. Multimedia Tools Appl. **77**(15), 20207–20226 (2018). https://doi.org/10.1007/s11042-017-5324-3

7. Becker, S., Hug, R., Hübner, W., Arens, M.: RED: a simple but effective baseline predictor for the *TrajNet* benchmark. In: Leal-Taixé, L., Roth, S. (eds.) ECCV 2018. LNCS, vol. 11131, pp. 138–153. Springer, Cham (2019). https://doi.org/10.1007/978-3-030-11015-4_13

8. Becker, S., Münch, D., Kieritz, H., Hübner, W., Arens, M.: Detecting abandoned objects using interacting multiple models. In: Proceedings of SPIE, Optics and Photonics for Counterterrorism, Crime Fighting, and Defence, vol. 9652 (2015)

9. Blom, H., Bar-Shalom, Y.: The interacting multiple model algorithm for systems with Markovian switching coefficients. Trans. Autom. Control **33**(8), 780–783 (1988). https://doi.org/10.1109/9.1299

10. Chung, J., Kastner, K., Dinh, L., Goel, K., Courville, A., Bengio, Y.: A recurrent latent variable model for sequential data. In: Advances in Neural Information Processing Systems (NIPS) (2015)

11. Deo, N., Trivedi, M.M.: Multi-modal trajectory prediction of surrounding vehicles with maneuver based LSTMs. In: Intelligent Vehicles Symposium (IV), pp. 1179–1184. IEEE (2018). https://doi.org/10.1109/IVS.2018.8500493

12. Donahue, J., et al.: Long-term recurrent convolutional networks for visual recognition and description. In: Conference on Computer Vision and Pattern Recognition (CVPR). IEEE (2015)

13. Graves, A., Mohamed, A., Hinton, G.: Speech recognition with deep recurrent neural networks. In: International Conference on Acoustics, Speech and Signal Processing, pp. 6645–6649 (2013). https://doi.org/10.1109/ICASSP.2013.6638947

14. Hochreiter, S., Schmidhuber, J.: Long short-term memory. Neural Comput. **9**(8), 1735–1780 (1997). https://doi.org/10.1162/neco.1997.9.8.1735

15. Hug, R., Becker, S., Hübner, W., Arens, M.: On the reliability of LSTM-MDL models for pedestrian trajectory prediction. In: International Workshop on Representations, Analysis and Recognition of Shape and Motion from Imaging Data (RFMI), Savoie, France (2017)

16. Hug, R., Becker, S., Hübner, W., Arens, M.: Particle-based pedestrian path prediction using LSTM-MDL models. In: International Conference on Intelligent Transportation Systems (ITSC), pp. 2684–2691 (2018). https://doi.org/10.1109/ITSC.2018.8569478

17. Kalman, R.E.: A new approach to linear filtering and prediction problems. ASME J. Basic Eng. **82**, 35–45 (1960)

18. Keller, C.G., Hermes, C., Gavrila, D.M.: Will the pedestrian cross? Probabilistic path prediction based on learned motion features. In: Mester, R., Felsberg, M. (eds.) Pattern Recogn., pp. 386–395. Springer, Berlin Heidelberg (2011). https://doi.org/10.1007/978-3-642-23123-0_39

19. Kingma, D.P., Ba, J.: Adam: a method for stochastic optimization. In: International Conference for Learning Representations (ICLR) (2015)

20. Kooij, J.F.P., Flohr, F., Pool, E.A.I., Gavrila, D.M.: Context-based path prediction for targets with switching dynamics. Int. J. Comput. Vis. (2018). https://doi.org/10.1007/s11263-018-1104-4

21. Kooij, J.F.P., Schneider, N., Flohr, F., Gavrila, D.M.: Context-based pedestrian path prediction. In: Fleet, D., Pajdla, T., Schiele, B., Tuytelaars, T. (eds.) ECCV 2014. LNCS, vol. 8694, pp. 618–633. Springer, Cham (2014). https://doi.org/10.1007/978-3-319-10599-4_40

22. Pellegrini, S., Ess, A., Schindler, K., van Gool, L.: You'll never walk alone: Modeling social behavior for multi-target tracking. In: International Conference on Computer Vision (ICCV). pp. 261–268. IEEE (2009). https://doi.org/10.1109/ICCV.2009.5459260

23. Särkkä, S.: Bayesian Filtering and Smoothing. Institute of Mathematical Statistics Textbooks, Cambridge University Press, Cambridge (2013). https://doi.org/10.1017/CBO9781139344203

24. Schneider, N., Gavrila, D.M.: Pedestrian path prediction with recursive Bayesian filters: a comparative study. In: Weickert, J., Hein, M., Schiele, B. (eds.) GCPR 2013. LNCS, vol. 8142, pp. 174–183. Springer, Heidelberg (2013). https://doi.org/10.1007/978-3-642-40602-7_18

25. Stierlin, S., Dietmayer, K.: Scale change and TTC filter for longitudinal vehicle control based on monocular video. In: International Conference on Intelligent Transportation Systems (ITSC), pp. 528–533 (2012). https://doi.org/10.1109/ITSC.2012.6338681

26. Teknom, K.: Microscopic pedestrian flow characteristics: development of an image processing data collection and simulation model. Ph.D. thesis, Tohoku University (2002)

27. Xu, K., et al.: Show, attend and tell: neural image caption generation with visual attention. In: International Conference on Machine Learning (ICML), vol. 37, pp. 2048–2057. PMLR, Lille (2015)

Real-Time Tracking-by-Detection in Broadcast Sports Videos

Sigurdur Sverrisson[✉], Volodya Grancharov, and Harald Pobloth

Ericsson Research, Ericsson AB, 164 80 Stockholm, Sweden
sigurdur.sverrisson@ericsson.com

Abstract. This paper presents a novel algorithm for real-time tracking-by-detection of players in sports videos. The solution consists of a Convolutional Neural Network with optimized architecture and a new type of Inter Frame Connection logic for data association and tracklet handling. The proposed data association connects region proposals in the current frame with detected objects in the previous frames. The association is established before thresholding the region proposals and used to stabilize the detection performance. The proposed solution demonstrates superior performance over the existing pre-trained detection models and tracking concepts.

Keywords: Convolutional Neural Networks · Tracking-by-detection · Data association · Sports videos

1 Introduction

The ability to automatically detect and track multiple objects across a scene has been a long standing challenge within the Computer Vision community. Detection and tracking of players in broadcast sports videos is a particularly difficult task due to the complex motion pattern and severe occlusion between the objects of interest.

In early years sport graphics systems were dominated by background subtraction and template matching concepts. The pioneering work [14] deals with the problem of tracking players in American football. Two years later the problem of detecting and tracking players in a soccer game captured from a broadcasted TV signal is addressed in [7]. One of the key studies dealing with the problem of multiple players tracking in sports videos is presented in [19]. It builds on a track graph approach with similarity measurements between the tracks being calculated to infer the optimal configuration of paths for all targets.

In the last 15 years, the tracking-by-detection approach has attracted a lot of attention in the research community. Tracking-by-detection involves continuous application of a detection algorithm in individual frames and the association of detections across frames. Work on detecting and tracking hockey players was presented in [20], where detections based on Viola-Jones framework [26] were

© Springer Nature Switzerland AG 2019
M. Felsberg et al. (Eds.): SCIA 2019, LNCS 11482, pp. 399–411, 2019.
https://doi.org/10.1007/978-3-030-20205-7_33

used to guide the particle filter. The approach in [6] uses a graded observation model, based on monitoring the detection confidence. The authors examine both HOG [8] and ISM [16] based detectors, and used particle filters based tracking under the assumption of a constant velocity motion model. The strategy to first detect players and then link detections into tracks was also exploited in [18]. In this work the player detector was based on the Deformable Part Model [11] and Kalman filtering was used to predict the bounding boxes from the tracks. Euclidean distance was used to associate predicted boxes with bounding boxes generated by the detector.

With the emergence of Convolutional Neural Networks (CNNs) more powerful visual object detectors were engaged in the player's tracking-by-detection task. Experiments with Faster R-CNN [23] can be found in [5]. This work uses an off-the-shelf detector, but focuses on handling of the frame-to-frame associations, which results in the Simple Online and Realtime Tracking (SORT) algorithm. The inter-frame displacements of each object are approximated with a linear constant velocity model. Further experiments with SORT were presented in [4], with an object detector based on the YOLO framework [21].

The tracking-by-detection algorithm presented in this paper is related to [5] and [4] in the sense that it uses a CNN based detector, followed by tracklet handling logic. The main novelty in the introduced CNN with Inter Frame Connection (CNN-IFC) is that the data association logic connects region proposals in the current frame with detected objects in the previous frame. This is used to adapt the detection probabilities in the current frame before final thresholding, which allows objects from stable tracklets to stay above the decision threshold. Further, a domain specific optimization of data association logic and CNN architecture is introduced. This allows the proposed CNN-IFC to outperform in terms of detection and tracking accuracy the existing off-the-shelf models, only at a fraction of their processing time.

The proposed tracking-by-detection system was built for Piero 3D sports graphics [1] with the purpose of producing real-time bounding box level detections of all players and officials in a broadcast sports video. Piero is a system designed to enhance the coverage of sports on TV. Its early versions were developed at BBC Research [2] and the system was further extended at Red Bee Media [1]. The presented tracking-by-detection module is a small part of such system and has to operate under the severe requirements of less than 8 ms processing time for a single video frame, and less than 1 GB of the available GPU memory.

2   Visual Object Detector with Inter Frame Connection

In this section we present the proposed CNN-IFC tracking-by-detection algorithm. It is a fully automated, real-time system that detects and tracks players in broadcast sports videos. Both the visual object detector and the tracklet handling logic are applied on every single video frame to output position of all players and unique identifiers (IDs) of the corresponding tracklets. The Piero

3D sports graphics system covers all popular sports. In this paper we present, in detail, the tracking-by-detecting solution in the context of a soccer game (court view, single pan-tilt-zoom camera).

2.1 Core Detector

A highly-accurate, lightweight detector is realized through the CNN architecture presented in Table 1. It is based on the concept presented in [21], but customized to the specific sports videos scenario. Input dimension (640×368) of the network is selected to better reflect the aspect ratio of input broadcast videos and at the same time be divisible by 2^M, where M is number of max-pooling layers. Output resolution is set to (40×23), to handle a large number of closely located objects, which is a scenario that occurs frequently in team sports. Depth of the network is optimized to achieve the desired accuracy with the lowest number of parameters. With its 4M parameters the proposed CNN architecture is significantly smaller than the commonly used off-the-shelf models. For comparison, the two models discussed further in this paper, Tiny-YOLO-v2 [3] and VGG-16 [25], consist of 16M and 138M parameters, respectively. The detection model is optimized on soccer video data provided by the Piero team [1]. The training set consists of 116,000 labelled bounding boxes across 9,000 frames. Labelling is done with a single class *player*, which is used to capture players from both teams, as well as officials present in the field. The training of the CNN uses transfer learning. The first 8 layers of the CNN, see Table 1, are populated with the weights from Tiny-YOLO-v2, which is trained on the PASCAL VOC [10] dataset. The weights in the remaining layers are randomized and the entire network is trained on the new dataset with the procedure specified in [3].

Table 1. Architecture CNN-IFC's detection module.

#	Layer	Filters	Size/stride	Input	Output
0	conv	16	$3 \times 3/1$	$640 \times 368 \times 3$	$640 \times 368 \times 16$
1	max		$2 \times 2/2$	$640 \times 368 \times 16$	$320 \times 184 \times 16$
2	conv	32	$3 \times 3/1$	$320 \times 184 \times 16$	$320 \times 184 \times 32$
3	max		$2 \times 2/2$	$320 \times 184 \times 32$	$160 \times 92 \times 32$
4	conv	64	$3 \times 3/1$	$160 \times 92 \times 32$	$160 \times 92 \times 64$
5	max		$2 \times 2/2$	$160 \times 92 \times 64$	$80 \times 46 \times 64$
6	conv	128	$3 \times 3/1$	$80 \times 46 \times 64$	$80 \times 46 \times 128$
7	max		$2 \times 2/2$	$80 \times 46 \times 128$	$40 \times 23 \times 128$
8	conv	256	$3 \times 3/1$	$40 \times 23 \times 128$	$40 \times 23 \times 256$
9	conv	512	$3 \times 3/1$	$40 \times 23 \times 256$	$40 \times 23 \times 512$
10	conv	512	$3 \times 3/1$	$40 \times 23 \times 512$	$40 \times 23 \times 512$
11	conv	5	$1 \times 1/1$	$40 \times 23 \times 512$	$40 \times 23 \times 5$

For a given input video frame I^n (RGB, 640×368) the CNN outputs 920 (40× 23) region proposals, which are further reduced by a non-maximum suppression (NMS) [24] algorithm to J_{NMS} region proposals

$$I^n \xrightarrow{\text{CNN}} \{(\mathbf{X}_k^n, P_k^n)\}_{k=1}^{920} \xrightarrow{\text{NMS}} \{(\mathbf{X}_j^n, P_j^n)\}_{j=1}^{J_{NMS}} \tag{1}$$

Here $\mathbf{X} = [x, y, \omega, h]$ is 4-dimensional vector that consists of normalized bounding box coordinates (center of the bounding box $[x, y]$, as well as the width ω and height h of the bounding box, all normalized with width and height of the image). P is the detection probability associated with a particular region proposal.

The conventional approach in detection would be to threshold the set of region proposals by detection probability P and determine the set of detected objects in the current frame n as $\{(\mathbf{X}_j^n, P_j^n)\}_{P_j^n \geq \Theta}$, where Θ is a pre-determined detection threshold. We do not perform thresholding at this stage, but only after data association followed by a probability adaptation, which are described next.

2.2   Post Processing

Let us first introduce some notation, required to describe the post-processing operations. Let the set Ψ^n consist of current frame's region proposals (after NMS), as well as the corresponding color histograms $\mathbf{C}$ from the image area under each bounding box

$$\Psi^n = \{(\mathbf{X}_j^n, \mathbf{C}_j^n, P_j^n)\}_{j=1}^{J_{NMS}}. \tag{2}$$

The exact definition and reasons for including color histogram in this set will become evident soon. Region proposals of Ψ^n are visualized in Fig. 2. Let us also introduce, the set Φ^{n-1}, which consists of previous frame's detected objects, their corresponding color histograms, and the associated track IDs

$$\Phi^{n-1} = \{(\mathbf{X}_i^{n-1}, \mathbf{C}_i^{n-1}, P_i^{n-1}, ID_i^{n-1})\}_{i=1}^{J_O}, \tag{3}$$

where J_O is the number of detected objects in frame $n - 1$. The position of detected objects from Φ^{n-1} together with the track IDs are visualized in Fig. 1. To increase the readability in the rest of the presentation, the superscripts n and $n - 1$ will be often omitted, but in such cases indices i and j will uniquely identify a variable with past or current frame, respectively.

The aim of the post processing logic is to obtain a set Φ^n, based on the available region proposals from the current frame Ψ^n and the set of detections from the previous frame Φ^{n-1}, i.e., $\{\Psi^n, \Phi^{n-1}\} \xrightarrow{\text{Post Proc}} \Phi^n$. This task is achieved in a three step procedure, outlined below.

Data Association Algorithm. The first step in the post processing algorithm is to match detections from previous frame Φ^{n-1} to the predictions Ψ^n from the current frame, schematically illustrated in Fig. 3. This concept differs from the popular approach in the research community which is to associate bounding

Fig. 1. Visualization of the $J_O = 17$ detections in frame $n-1$. The number of detected objects in Φ^{n-1} varies, but $J_O \leq 25$ for the court view soccer recordings, which is significantly lower than the number of region proposals in Ψ^n. This figure also illustrates the identity tracking concept, addressed in this paper - each object on the pitch has its own ID (white number in the top-left corner of the bounding box), that should be preserved throughout the video shot.

Fig. 2. Region proposals in frame n, visualized by means of the corresponding bounding boxes. For this particular frame the variable number of region proposals in Ψ^n is $J_{NMS} = 865$. For better visibility the probabilities associated to each region are not presented. The conventional detection approach to directly threshold this set of region proposals ignores any information related to objects location and is very sensitive to fluctuation in estimated detection probabilities.

boxes generated by the visual object detector with predicted boxes (e.g., from Kalman or particle filtering). Our motivation for looking into an alternative data association method is based on the observation that players in sports videos have complicated, unpredictable motions with frequent complex interactions. In most of the cases a constant velocity model is a poor predictor of the true dynamics of players. Instead, the proposed algorithm is an attempt to improve the stability of the tracklets, by using an improved matching logic across the video sequence.

The data association algorithm first calculates a matching score matrix D for each pair of past detections and current region proposals:

$$\text{for } i \in \Phi^{n-1}$$
$$\text{for } j \in \Psi^n \tag{4}$$
$$D_{ij} = \alpha \|\mathbf{X}_i - \mathbf{X}_j\| + \beta \|\mathbf{C}_i - \mathbf{C}_j\| + \gamma |P_i - P_j|.$$

The first term in (4) guarantees that the objects connected across frames will be spatially close and of similar size. The second term guarantees that these object will have similar visual appearance. For the particular application we found that it is sufficient to build marginal color histograms $\mathbf{C}$ directly on RGB color spaces with 16 bins per channel. The third term in (4) reflects the fact that we want to establish connection between accepted objects from frame $n - 1$, which by definition have P_i above a threshold, and region proposals from frame n with P_j in the same range. Note that most of the probabilities in Ψ^n are close to zero, as they correspond to the pitch and surrounding background. Weights (α, β, γ) are experimentally found. For the case of soccer game, matching the visual object appearance was found to be very important and the weights were set to $(0.25, 0.50, 0.25)$.

Given the score matrix D, the object matching is typically achieved with the Hungarian (Kuhn-Munkres) algorithm [15] or sequential data association algorithms such as Joint Probabilistic Data Association (JPDA) [12] or Multiple Hypothesis Tracking (MHT) [22]. To keep the algorithmic complexity under control we used a greedy approach, which was found to be sufficient also in [27] and [6]. In this approach the pair with lowest score in D is iteratively selected:

$$(i, j) = \underset{i^* \in \Phi, j^* \in \Psi}{\arg \min} \ D_{i^* j^*} \tag{5}$$

the set of connected pairs is updated $\Upsilon = \Upsilon \cup (i, j)$ and the corresponding row and column are removed from further search, i.e., $\Phi = \Phi \backslash \{i\}$ and $\Psi = \Psi \backslash \{j\}$. This is repeated until all previously accepted objects from frame $n - 1$ are connected to a region proposal from frame n. Special treatment is need for the case when object from Φ^{n-1}, is completely occluded or has left the visual scene in frame n. As this will create an invalid mapping, the set Υ is checked against a criteria for rejection, and the final set of accepted mappings Ω is created:

Initialize: $\Omega = \{\}$

for $(i,j) \in \Upsilon$

$$\text{if } \left(|x_i - x_j| + |y_i - y_j| \right) \leq \frac{1}{2} \left(\frac{\omega_i + \omega_j}{2} + \frac{h_i + h_j}{2} \right) \tag{6}$$

$$\Omega = \Omega \cup (i,j)$$

The idea of the criteria, described in (6), is for a given mapping (matched objects across frames) to compare distance between centres of the corresponding bounding boxes with the half of the averaged width/height. Based on that criteria, certain pairs of matched bounding boxes are considered spatially separated, and the corresponding mappings are not accepted.

Probability Adaptation Algorithm. In the second step of the post processing algorithm the pairs of matched objects are used to adapt the detection probability of the region proposal in the current frame, see Fig. 4. The adaptation is performed in a single loop over the set of accepted mappings Ω:

$$\text{for } (i,j) \in \Omega^{n,n-1}$$
$$\text{if } \left(P_i^{n-1} > P_j^n \right) \& \left(P_j^n > \Theta_{min} \right) \tag{7}$$
$$P_j^n = (1 - \lambda) P_j^n + \lambda P_i^{n-1}$$

The probability adaptation stabilizes existing tracklets by preventing sudden loss of an object if the detection probability of the corresponding region proposal P_j^n drops below a pre-determined detection threshold Θ (set to 0.5 for the particular application). Adaptation only takes place if connected object from the previous frame has higher detection probability, and the detection probability of the region proposal in the current frame is above a threshold Θ_{min}. The value of Θ_{min} is set to 80% or 40% of the detection threshold Θ, based on the closeness of the visual appearances of the connected objects (measured as a distance between their color distributions). Lowest level of $\Theta_{min} = 0.2$ is set for $\|C_i - C_j\| \leq 0.1$, otherwise $\Theta_{min} = 0.4$. With a forgetting factor $\lambda = 0.98$, the probability adaptation logic will effectively keep objects, connected to a stable tracklet, above the decision threshold, even if the detector produces erroneous scores (temporary drop in P_j^n).

Object Acceptance and Tracklet Handling Logic. The logic of region proposals thresholding in frame n as well as *ID* handling is presented in (8):

Initialize: $\Phi^n = \{\}$

for $j \in \Psi^n$

   if $P_j \geq \Theta$

      if $(i,j) \in \Omega^{n,n-1}$ (8)

         $\Phi^n = \Phi^n \cup \{(\mathbf{X}_j, \mathbf{C}_j, P_j, ID_i)\}$

      otherwise

         $\Phi^n = \Phi^n \cup \{(\mathbf{X}_j, \mathbf{C}_j, P_j, \max(ID) + 1)\}.$

The desired set of accepted detections Φ^n consists of all region proposals with detection probability equal or larger than Θ. Every entry in this set has a track ID, which is either transferred from the paired object from frame $n - 1$ or created by incrementing the largest track ID number. In the proposed tracklet handling logic, a new tracklet is initiated when a detected object in frame n is left unpaired (there is no corresponding detection in frame $n - 1$), see Fig. 5. A track is terminated if it is left without detection in the current frame. After collecting the final output of the tracking-by-detection system at frame n (position of detected objects and their IDs), the entire set Φ^n is propagated to the next frame $n - 1$.

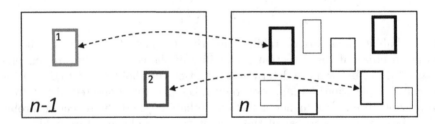

Fig. 3. Data association step: detected object in frame $n - 1$ are connected to the best matching region proposals in frame n. For the sake of visualization, thickness of the bounding boxes is made proportional to the detection probability associated to a particular region, and unique colors are associated with the individual tracklets IDs.

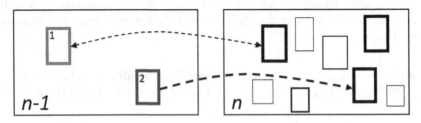

Fig. 4. Probability adaptation step: before the thresholding of the candidate objects in frame n, adaptation of detection probability is performed. In this example, detection probability of the region proposal in frame n, associated with the track $ID = 2$ (*red* track) is increased. (Color figure online)

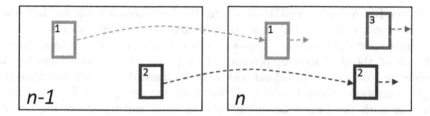

Fig. 5. Tracklet handling step: after the thresholding the accepted detections in frame n either receive the track ID of the associated object from frame $n-1$ or a new track is initiated for objects without association. In this example, for the new object (in *blue*) entering the visual scene, a new track with $ID = 3$ is created. (Color figure online)

3 Evaluation

As a part of the Piero system, the proposed tracking-by-detection algorithm has undergone significant visual inspection and optimization. In this section we present results from additional objective evaluation on three types of representative recordings from the Piero dataset. All recordings consist of several hundred frames court view video shots of soccer game, with the ground truth created by manually labelling all players and officials present in the visual scene. REC A consists of high quality 1080p video. REC B is 720p intermediate quality video with some coding artefacts. REC C is 720p low quality video with significant amount of blur. None of these recordings were present at the stage of training and optimizing the core detector or tracklet handling logic.

3.1 Detection Performance

First, we present comparison of the detection accuracy of CNN-IFC vs Faster R-CNN with VGG16 (for that system we use only the class *person* from the detector's output). In this section we do not report result from simulations with Tiny-YOLO-v2 model, which has similar size as CNN-IFC, and also allows for real-time detections. The reason is that Faster R-CNN with VGG16 significantly outperforms Tiny-YOLO-v2 for the particular scenario, and therefore Faster R-CNN was selected as benchmark system for these experiments. Evaluations are based on PASCAL VOC definition of Mean Average Precision (mAP). Results from simulations, presented in Table 2, clearly demonstrate the superior performance of the customized model of CNN-IFC over one of the best publicly available benchmarks.

Table 2. Evaluation of detection performance in terms of mAP per recording type.

System	mAP (%)		
	REC A	REC B	REC C
Faster R-CNN	60.80	60.37	18.80
CNN-IFC	**87.43**	**86.50**	**85.35**

Faster R-CNN with VGG16 is among the best known bounding box level generic object detectors, but it is not optimized for the particular scenario of broadcast sports videos. The purpose of this experiment is to evaluate the gap between off-the-shelf models, pre-trained on public benchmarks datasets and models customized on broadcast video. It is interesting to observe that the largest performance gap between systems is on the low quality REC C, which coincides with the largest deviation between train and test condition for the selected benchmark system.

3.2 Tracking Performance

To evaluate the effectiveness of the proposed tracking scheme, we created a benchmark system (CNN-SORT) which consists of the core detector, presented in Sect. 2.1, but tracking is handled by the SORT algorithm [5]. Since both CNN-SORT and CNN-IFC use the same core detector, any difference in their performance is due to the tracklet handling module. Two types of evaluation metrics are used to compare stability of created tracklets. The first metric is F1 (the harmonic mean of precision and recall), $F1 = 2 \times \frac{Recall \times Precision}{Recall + Precision}$. Both Recall and Precision are calculated under the assumption of correct object identification when Intersection over Union (IoU) between predicted and ground truth bounding boxes is larger than 0.5, as defined in [10]. Results, reported in Table 3, suggest that the post processing algorithm, presented in Sect. 2.2, produces more stable tracklets. This is mainly a result of the bias introduced in the detection probability (7), which prevents objects, associated to tracks, to be abruptly lost if detection probability erroneously drops below the threshold for a few frames.

Table 3. F1, averaged over all tracklets and frames in a particular video recording.

System	F1		
	REC A	REC B	REC C
CNN-SORT	0.87	0.93	0.89
CNN-IFC	**0.90**	**0.94**	**0.92**

The second metric used to evaluate the tracking performance is the Identity Tracking Performance (ITP), introduced in [17] for evaluation of sports graphics systems. This measure calculates the number of correct *ID* associations with respect to the ground truth. The average results, presented in Table 4, indicate that the proposed post processing has small but consistent advantage over the benchmark system. Close inspection of *ID* swapping cases indicates that using object's visual appearance (modelled by means of color histograms) in the data association process, is the main factor that contributes to the more stable *ID* association in crowded scenes.

Table 4. Average ITP per system and video recording.

System	ITP (%)		
	REC A	REC B	REC C
CNN-SORT	98.61	99.20	97.57
CNN-IFC	**99.21**	**99.47**	**98.00**

4 Conclusions

Detection and tracking of players in sports such as soccer is a long standing and difficult task due to large number of occlusions and erratic movements of the players. The tracking-by-detection approach, presented in this paper, is an example of a system, optimized for this particular scenario, under severe performance requirements. In that sense, the paper provides a recipe for customization of a tracking-by-detection system. Furthermore, the performed experiments give insights with implications beyond the particular application. The main observations of this research can be summarized as follows:

First, a customization of the visual object detector model for a particular scenario leads to clearly superior results against one of the best general purpose detectors. The optimized architecture allows the visual object detector to process a video frame in less than 8 ms on a PC with an inexpensive mid-range NVIDIA GTX card, while producing highly-accurate detections. In addition to pre-training on data with relevant statics, important part of model customization is selecting the appropriate input and output resolution of the neural network. The input CNN resolution has to reflect the aspect ratio of the test images/videos, while output resolution has to reflect number and distribution of objects location.

Second, in scenarios with complex motion patterns, there are alternatives to tracking under the assumption of linear constant velocity model. Connecting past object detections with region proposals from the current frame not only allows for a simple tracklet handling logic, but opens the possibility for adaptation of detection probability. Which in turn allows the detector to exploit the fact that it is applied on a video sequence and there is shared information between the consecutive frames. The post processing logic, presented in this paper, is generic and can be used with different types of detectors. As long as the detection is performed on consecutive video frames, the presented data association followed by probability adaptation step can improve detection accuracy in a large number of applications.

Third, using object's visual appearance in the data association logic significantly improves the accuracy of the mapping. Incorporating model of visual object appearance in data association step is a logical way to stabilize tracklets and prevent ID swaps between closely located objects. The particular way to model visual object appearance is application dependent. Since sports videos typically have constraints in the color space, e.g, players uniforms and the colour of the playing field, a good model could be based on color histograms. In the general scenario, the choice of visual cues could be based on the models used by the state-of-the-art visual tracking algorithms, e.g., [9,13].

Acknowledgments. The authors would like to thank the Piero team at Red Bee Media for the fruitful collaboration.

References

1. Piero at Red Bee Media. www.redbeemedia.com/portfolio/piero-sports-graphics/
2. Piero at BBC R&D. www.bbc.co.uk/rd/projects/piero/
3. YOLO. https://pjreddie.com/darknet/yolov2/
4. Acuna, D.: Towards real-time detection and tracking of basketball players using deep neural networks. In: Proceedings of NIPS (2017)
5. Bewley, A., Ge, Z., Ott, L., Ramos, F., Upcroft, B.: Simple online and realtime tracking. arXiv:1602.00763v2 (2017)
6. Breitenstein, M., Reichlin, F., Leibe, B., Koller-Meier, E., Van Gool, L.: Online multiperson tracking-by-detection from a single, uncalibrated camera. TPAMI **33**, 1820–1833 (2011)
7. Choi, S., Seo, Y., Kim, H., Hong, K.S.: Where are the ball and players?: Soccer game analysis with color-based tracking and image mosaick. In: Proceedings of ICIAP (1997)
8. Dalal, N., Triggs, B.: Histograms of oriented gradients for human detection. In: Proceedings of ICCV (2005)
9. Danelljan, M., Bhat, G., Khan, F., Felsberg, M.: ECO: efficient convolution operators for tracking. In: Proceedings of CVPR (2017)
10. Everingham, M., Gool, L., Williams, C., Winn, J., Zisserman, A.: The Pascal visual object classes (VOC) challenge. J. Comput. Vis. **88**, 303–338 (2010)
11. Felzenszwalb, P., Girshick, R., McAllester, D., Ramanan, D.: Object detection with discriminatively trained part based models. TPAMI **32**, 1627–1645 (2010)
12. Fortmann, T., Shalom, Y.B., Scheffe, M.: Sonar tracking of multiple targets using joint probabilistic data association. J. Oceanic Eng. **8**, 173–184 (1983)
13. Henriques, J., Caseiro, R., Martins, P., Batista, J.: High-speed tracking with kernelized correlation filters. TPAMI **37**, 583–596 (2015)
14. Intille, S., Bobick, A.: Closed-world tracking. In: Proceedings of ICCV (1995)
15. Kuhn, H.: The Hungarian method for the assignment problem. Naval Res. Log. Q. **2**, 83–97 (1955)
16. Leibe, B., Leonardis, A., Schiele, B.: Robust object detection with interleaved categorization and segmentation. J. Comput. Vis. **77**, 259–289 (2008)
17. Li, Y., Dore, A., Orwell, J.: Evaluating the performance of systems for tracking football players and ball. In: Proceedings of AVSS (2005)
18. Lu, W., Ting, J., Little, J., Murphy, K.: Learning to track and identify players from broadcast sports videos. TPAMI **35**, 1704–1716 (2013)
19. Nillius, P., Sullivan, J., Carlsson, S.: Multi-target tracking-linking identities using Bayesian network inference. In: Proceedings of CVPR (2006)
20. Okuma, K., Taleghani, A., de Freitas, N., Little, J.J., Lowe, D.G.: A boosted particle filter: multitarget detection and tracking. In: Pajdla, T., Matas, J. (eds.) ECCV 2004. LNCS, vol. 3021, pp. 28–39. Springer, Heidelberg (2004). https://doi.org/10.1007/978-3-540-24670-1_3

21. Redmon, J., Farhadi, A.: YOLO9000: better, faster, stronger. In: Proceedings of CVPR (2017)

22. Reid, D.: An algorithm for tracking multiple targets. TACON **24**, 843 (1979)

23. Ren, S., He, K., Girshick, R., Sun, J.: Faster R-CNN: towards real-time object detection with region proposal networks. TPAMI **39**(6), 1137–1149 (2017)

24. Rothe, R., Guillaumin, M., Van Gool, L.: Non-maximum suppression for object detection by passing messages between windows. In: Cremers, D., Reid, I., Saito, H., Yang, M.-H. (eds.) ACCV 2014. LNCS, vol. 9003, pp. 290–306. Springer, Cham (2015). https://doi.org/10.1007/978-3-319-16865-4_19

25. Simonyan, K., Zisserman, A.: Very deep convolutional networks for large-scale image recognition. In: Proceedings of ICLR (2014)

26. Viola, P., Jones, M.: Rapid object detection using a boosted cascade of simple features. In: Proceedings of CVPR (2001)

27. Wu, B., Nevatia, R.: Detection and tracking of multiple, partially occluded humans by Bayesian combination of edgelet based part detectors. J. Comput. Vis. **75**, 247–266 (2007)

Medical and Biomedical Image Analysis

Fast Cross Correlation for Limited Angle Tomographic Data

Ricardo M. Sánchez[1,2]([✉]), Rudolf Mester[3,4], and Mikhail Kudryashev[1,2]

[1] Max Planck Institute for Biophysics, Frankfurt am Main, Germany
{ricardo.sanchez,misha.kudryashev}@biophys.mpg.de
[2] Buchmann Institute for Molecular Life Sciences, Goethe University,
Frankfurt, Germany
[3] Visual Sensorics and Inf. Proc. Lab, Goethe University, Frankfurt/Main, Germany
mester@vsi.cs.uni-frankfurt.de
[4] Norwegian Open AI Lab, CS Department (IDI), NTNU, Trondheim, Norway

Abstract. The cross-correlation is a fundamental operation in signal processing, as it is a measure of similarity and a tool to find translations between signals. Its implementation in Fourier space is used for large datasets, as it is faster than the one in real space, however, it does not consider any special properties which signals may have, as is the case of Limited Angle Tomography. The Fourier space of limited angle tomograms, which are reconstructed from a reduced number of projections, has a large number of empty values. As a consequence, most operations needed to calculate the cross-correlation are executed on empty data. To address this issue, we propose the *projected Cross Correlation (pCC)* method, which calculates the cross-correlation between a reference and a limited angle tomogram more efficiently. To reduce the number of operations, *pCC* follows a *project, cross-correlate, reconstruct* process, instead of the typical *reconstruct, cross-correlate* process. Both methods are equivalent, but the proposed one has lower computational complexity and provides significant speedup for larger tomograms, as we confirm with our experiments. Additionally, we propose the usage of a l_1 penalty on the cross-correlation to improve its sensitivity and its robustness to noise. Our experimental results show that the improvements are achieved with no significant additional computational cost.

Keywords: Limited angle tomography · Template matching · Volume Alignment · Cryo electron tomography

1 Introduction

Cross-correlation is a fundamental and widely used operation in signal processing. It can be used as a measure of similarity between signals [14], and for estimation of the translation between them. Due to computational efficiency it is calculated in Fourier space, and, as a general method, it does not take into consideration any special property the signals may have. This is the case, for example, of limited angle tomographic data, where the Fourier space is sparse.

© Springer Nature Switzerland AG 2019
M. Felsberg et al. (Eds.): SCIA 2019, LNCS 11482, pp. 415–426, 2019.
https://doi.org/10.1007/978-3-030-20205-7_34

Limited angle tomography is encountered when the data acquisition is restricted to a reduced number of views. For example, in cryo-electron tomography (cryoET) for structural biology [6] the samples are very sensitive to radiation damage. This limits the acquisition to only 41 projections with very low SNR, filling, in some cases, 20% of the Fourier space or less. This field is the inspiration for the present work, as a typical workflow in cryoET includes the registration of 1000 to 50000 tomograms to one or several references by cross-correlation. This alignment process takes multiple days on modern hardware.

In this paper we propose a new method to calculate the cross-correlation between a reference and a set of projections, which reduces the number of operations by using the sparsity of the Fourier space of limited angle tomograms (Fig. 1). The method, called *projected Cross Correlation (pCC)*, has lower computational complexity and provides significant speedup for larger tomograms. Furthermore, we use the l_1 penalty function to the cross-correlation to improve its robustness to noise. The lower complexity of the proposed method and its improved robustness makes it potentially useful for cryoET data processing.

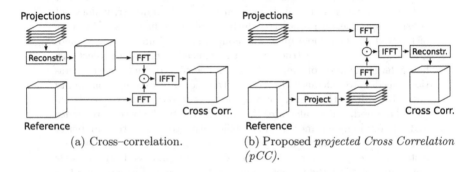

(a) Cross–correlation.   (b) Proposed *projected Cross Correlation (pCC)*.

Fig. 1. Scheme of the computation of 3D cross correlation between a set of 2D projections and a 3D reference. (a) The typical computation follows a *reconstruct* then *cross-correlate* process. (b) The proposed *projected Cross Correlation (pCC)* follows a *project, cross-correlate* and *reconstruct* process

1.1 Related Work

The main proposals to speed up the computation of the cross-correlation are the precalculation of look-up tables [9] and split the calculations into blocks [11]. These approaches work for any kind of signals and do not take into account any type of property those signals may have.

Similar to our approach, the Projection-based Volume Alignment (PBVA) [15] method uses the *project, cross-correlate* approach, but it estimates the peak of cross-correlation instead of calculating it. PBVA has similar computational complexity to *pCC*, and it can be seen as a special case of it: it approximates the peak value instead of reconstructing the cross-correlation. It is a faster procedure, but it is more sensitive to noise and it does not find the translation between signals.

2   Theoretical Context

The Fourier central slice theorem is the mathematical foundation for transmission tomography. It defines a relationship between a N^m-dimensional signal and a N^{m-1}-dimensional projection of it.

2.1   Fourier Central Slice Theorem

Let s and S be a signal and its Fourier transform, and $\mathbf{F}$, the discrete Fourier transform matrix, such that $S = \mathbf{F}s$ and $s = \mathbf{F}^{-1}S$. Then, given the matrix $\mathbf{E}_{\theta_i}$, that extracts a slice crossing the center of coordinates in the angle θ_i, the projection p_{θ_i} is defined as [7]:

$$p_{\theta_i} = \mathbf{F}^{-1}\mathbf{E}_{\theta_i}\mathbf{F}s. \tag{1}$$

Equation (1) can be interpreted as: *The projection p_{θ_i} of s in the direction θ_i is the inverse Fourier transform of the slice through S in the corresponding direction*

To recover s we have to write $\mathbf{E}_{\theta_i}$ as the product of the rotation $\mathbf{R}_{\theta_i}$ and the binary mask $\mathbf{M}_{\theta_i}$. Then, by using the element-wise multiplication operator $\odot$, Eq. (1) takes the following form:

$$p_{\theta_i} = \mathbf{F}^{-1}\mathbf{R}_{\theta_i}\mathbf{M}_{\theta_i} \odot (S). \tag{2}$$

We must note that the rotation matrix $\mathbf{R}_{\theta_i}$ is invertible while the mask matrix $\mathbf{M}_{\theta_i}$ is not. Then, by using $P_{\theta_i} = \mathbf{F}p_{\theta_i}$ we have:

$$\mathbf{R}_{\theta_i}^{-1}P_{\theta_i} = \mathbf{M}_{\theta_i} \odot (S). \tag{3}$$

This last equation defines an insertion-like operation, as the projection P_{θ_i} *fills* the slice of S defined by the matrix $\mathbf{M}_{\theta_i}$. To recover S we need multiple projections in different orientations such that $\mathbf{M}_{\theta_i} \neq 0$ can be inverted [3].

2.2   Analytic Tomogram Reconstruction

Let $\tilde{S}$ be the reconstruction of S from a given set of projections p_{θ_i}, and let $\mathbf{W}_\Theta$ be an unknown weighting matrix. Then, $\tilde{S}$ can be calculated using the following equation:

$$\tilde{S} = \mathbf{W}_\Theta \odot \left(\sum_i \mathbf{R}_{\theta_i}^{-1}P_{\theta_i} \right) \tag{4}$$

Using Eq. (3) and by defining $\mathbf{M}_\Theta = \sum_i \mathbf{M}_{\theta_i}$, we can rewrite the last equation as $\tilde{S} = \mathbf{W}_\Theta \odot (\mathbf{M}_\Theta \odot S)$. Finally, to obtain the proper reconstruction $\tilde{S} = S$, the matrix $\mathbf{W}_\Theta$ must be:

$$\mathbf{W}_\Theta = \mathbf{M}_\Theta^{-1}. \tag{5}$$

If the Fourier space of S is fully and uniformly sampled, matrix $\mathbf{W}_\Theta$ takes the form $\mathbf{W}_\Theta = 1/|w|$. This form is called *radial filter* and it is used in the

Weighted Back Projection reconstruction algorithm [12]. If the Fourier space is fully but non-uniformly sampled, we can use Eq. (5) to find $\mathbf{W}_\Theta$ [13].

If the Fourier space is not fully sampled some values of $\mathbf{M}_\Theta$ will be 0, making the reconstruction an ill-posed inverse problem, as $\mathbf{M}_\Theta$ is non-invertible matrix. This is the case of limited angled tomography, where we have few projections of the signal we want to reconstruct and, therefore, a sparse Fourier transform of the reconstructed tomogram (Fig. 2). The approaches to address this issue use *a priori* information of the signal, and solve the ill-posed system by imposing a regularization factor [1,4,5,8,10]

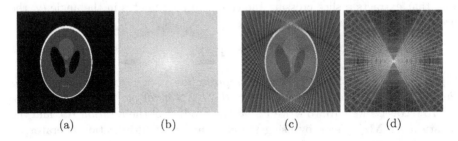

(a)   (b)   (c)   (d)

Fig. 2. (a), (b) Shepp–Logan phantom and its power spectrum. (b), (c) limited angle tomogram from 25 projections (from $-60°$ to $60°$, $5°$ step), and its power spectrum.

In our case we do not need the reconstruction of the limited angle tomogram to calculate its cross-correlation against a reference: the proposed *projected Cross Correlation* method calculates it directly. Nevertheless, a reconstruction algorithm is used in the final stage of the *pCC* and it can use *a priori* information to improve its results. If two signals are similar, the cross-correlation ressembles a *delta dirac function*, which is sparse in real space. In the following section we describe the *pCC* method and how to use the l_1 regularization to add the real space sparsity constrain to the cross-correlation.

3   Fast Correlation for Limited Angle Tomography

In this section we find a relationship between the cross-correlation of a reference signal s and a set of projections p_{θ_i}. We start by stating the definition of cross-correlation φ: let $\overline{\mathbf{F}s}$ be the complex conjugate of $\mathbf{F}s$, and given two signals s and g, then:

$$\varphi_{sg} = \mathbf{F}^{-1}\left(\mathbf{F}s \odot \overline{\mathbf{F}g}\right). \tag{6}$$

The relationship we describe in this section can be applied, in a similar way, to the normalized cross-correlation (NCC), zero-normalized cross-correlation (ZNCC) and the phase correlation. But, for the sake of simplicity, and without losing generality, we use this Eq. (6) to represent all the family of cross-correlation functions.

3.1   Cross Correlation for Limited Angle Tomograms

Given s, a signal used as reference, and $\tilde{p}$, a signal reconstructed from the set of projections p_{θ_i}, we use Eq. (6) to calculate the cross-correlation between them:

$$\varphi_{\tilde{p}s} = \mathbf{F}^{-1}\left(\mathbf{F}\tilde{p} \odot \overline{\mathbf{F}s}\right). \tag{7}$$

The projection $\varphi_{\tilde{p}s}^{(\theta_i)}$ is found using Eq. (2):

$$\varphi_{\tilde{p}s}^{(\theta_i)} = \mathbf{F}^{-1}\mathbf{R}_{\theta_i}\mathbf{M}_{\theta_i} \odot \left(\mathbf{F}\tilde{p} \odot \overline{\mathbf{F}s}\right). \tag{8}$$

As the binary mask M_{θ_i} is idempotent, we expand the last equation into:

$$\varphi_{\tilde{p}s}^{(\theta_i)} = \mathbf{F}^{-1}\mathbf{R}_{\theta_i}\left(\mathbf{M}_{\theta_i} \odot \mathbf{M}_{\theta_i}\right) \odot \left(\mathbf{F}\tilde{p} \odot \overline{\mathbf{F}s}\right), \tag{9}$$

and by rearranging the element-wise multiplications and by using Eq. (3):

$$\varphi_{\tilde{p}s}^{(\theta_i)} = \mathbf{F}^{-1}\mathbf{R}_{\theta_i}(\underbrace{(\mathbf{M}_{\theta_i} \odot \mathbf{F}\tilde{p})}_{\mathbf{R}_{\theta_i}^{-1}\mathbf{F}p_{\theta_i}} \odot \underbrace{(\mathbf{M}_{\theta_i} \odot \overline{\mathbf{F}s})}_{\mathbf{R}_{\theta_i}^{-1}\overline{\mathbf{F}s_{\theta_i}}}). \tag{10}$$

Finally, we factorize $\mathbf{R}_{\theta_i}^{-1}$:

$$\varphi_{\tilde{p}s}^{(\theta_i)} = \mathbf{F}^{-1}\mathbf{R}_{\theta_i}(\mathbf{R}_{\theta_i}^{-1}(\mathbf{F}p_{\theta_i} \odot \overline{\mathbf{F}s_{\theta_i}})), \tag{11}$$

and use the definition of cross-correlation to obtain:

$$\varphi_{\tilde{p}s}^{(\theta_i)} = \underbrace{\mathbf{F}^{-1}\left(\mathbf{F}p_{\theta_i} \odot \overline{\mathbf{F}s_{\theta_i}}\right)}_{\varphi_{p_{\theta_i}s_{\theta_i}}}. \tag{12}$$

This results in the intuitive property: *A projection of the cross-correlation of two signals is the cross-correlation of the projection of those signals in the same slice.* Furthermore, we can calculate the cross-correlation of two signals from their projections by reconstructing the cross-correlation of those projections:

$$\mathbf{F}\varphi_{\tilde{p}s} = \mathbf{W}_\Theta \odot \left(\sum_i \mathbf{R}_{\theta_i}^{-1}\left(P_{\theta_i} \odot \overline{E_{\theta_i}S}\right)\right). \tag{13}$$

This equation is the core of the *projected Cross Correlation (pCC)* method, which calculates the cross-correlation between a reference and a set of projections (Fig. 1) and it is described in Algorithm 1. We must note here that we reconstruct a cross-correlation function instead of a signal, allowing us to impose constrains to the reconstruction process, like sparsity in real space.

Algorithm 1. projected Cross-Correlation (pCC)

Input : p_{θ_i}, a set of K projections; θ_i, a set of K angles; s, a reference signal
Output: $cc = \varphi_{\tilde{p}s}$
$S \leftarrow \overline{\mathbf{F}s}$;
/* Cross-correlation of projections   */
for $i \leftarrow 1$ **to** K **do**
  $S_{\theta_i} \leftarrow \text{Extract}(S, \theta_i)$;
  $cc_{\theta_i} \leftarrow \mathbf{F}^{-1}\left(S_{\theta_i} \odot \mathbf{F}p_{\theta_i}\right)$;
/* Reconstruct cross-correlation   */
$cc \leftarrow \text{Reconstruct}(cc_{\Theta}, \Theta)$;

Computational Complexity. Given s, a signal with N^m elements, and a set of k projections p_{θ_i}, with N^{m-1} elements each, the computational cost of calculating the cross-correlation using Eq. (6) is:

$$N_{op}(\varphi_{\tilde{p}s}) = \underbrace{O(kN^m)}_{reconstruction} + \underbrace{3O(N^m logN)}_{FFTs} + \underbrace{O(N^m)}_{\odot}. \tag{14}$$

In the other hand, the computational cost of calculating the cross-correlation using Eq. (13) is:

$$N_{op}(pCC(p_{\theta_i}, s)) = \underbrace{3O(kN^{m-1}logN)}_{FFTs} + \underbrace{O(kN^{m-1})}_{\odot} + \underbrace{O(kN^m)}_{reconstruction}. \tag{15}$$

If $k < N$, then $N_{op}(\varphi_{\tilde{p}s}) < N_{op}(pCC(p_{\theta_i}, s))$: for limited angle tomography the calculation of pCC is faster than the calculation of $\varphi_{\tilde{p}s}$.

3.2   Fast Implementations

The computational performance of the implementation of Algorithm 1 is dominated by the reconstruction algorithm used. We can improve this performance by using an approximation of Eq. (13) or by reducing the size of the reconstruction. The first approach is called Projection-Based Volume Alignment (PBVA) and it will be used as a reference algorithm. We call the second one *pCC on a Region Of Interest (pCC_ROI)*, and we add the sparsity constrain to the *pCC_ROI* to obtain the *Regularizated pCC on a ROI (pCC_ROI_Reg)*. These three algorithm will be explained next.

Projection-Based Volume Alignment (PBVA). The cross-correlation is used to assess the similarity between two signals by finding its maximum value. We can reduce the number of operations if we focus on finding the peak of cross-correlation instead of calculating the whole cross-correlation function. If we explore Eq. (13), and by noting that $0 \leq \mathbf{W}_{\Theta} \leq 1$:

$$\mathbf{F}\varphi_{\tilde{p}s} = \mathbf{W}_{\Theta} \odot \left(\sum_i \mathbf{R}_{\theta_i}^{-1}(P_{\theta_i} \odot \overline{\mathbf{E}_{\theta_i}S})\right) \leq \sum_i \mathbf{R}_{\theta_i}^{-1}(P_{\theta_i} \odot \overline{\mathbf{E}_{\theta_i}S}). \tag{16}$$

This equation defines an upper bound for the cross-correlation, and it is used in the PBVA method [15] as a fast estimator of $max(\varphi_{\tilde{p}s})$:

$$\tilde{m}_\varphi = \max(\varphi_{\tilde{p}s}) \le PVBA(\tilde{p}, s) = \sum_i max\left(\varphi_{p_{\theta_i} s_{\theta_i}}\right). \tag{17}$$

Calculation of $PVBA(\tilde{p}, s)$ is fast, as it does not need the final reconstruction, but it is not as robust as the cross-correlation, and it cannot calculate the translation between the signals. $PBVA$ is described in Algorithm 2.

Algorithm 2. PBVA [15]

Input : p_{θ_i}, a set of K projections; θ_i, a set of K angles; s, a reference signal
Output: $\tilde{m}_\varphi = PVBA(p_{\theta_i}, s)$
$S \leftarrow \mathbf{F}s$;
$\tilde{m}_\varphi \leftarrow 0$;
/* Cross-correlation of projections and average their maximums   */
for $i \leftarrow 1$ **to** K **do**
    $S_{\theta_i} \leftarrow$ Extract(S, θ_i);
    $cc_{\theta_i} \leftarrow \mathbf{F}^{-1}\left(S_{\theta_i} \odot \mathbf{F}p_{\theta_i}\right)$;
    $\tilde{m}_\varphi \leftarrow \tilde{m}_\varphi +$ Max$(cc_{\theta_i})/K$;

3.3 Localized Reconstruction

The cross-correlation is used to find a spatio-temporal translation between two signals, which is done by finding t_φ, the position of the peak of cross-correlation. Typically, the maximum translation is constrained to a known area. Let M_L be a matrix with L non-zero elements that defines the area of search for the peak of cross-correlation. We can find t_φ by solving:

$$t_\varphi = \operatorname{argmax}\{M_L \odot (\varphi_{sg})\}. \tag{18}$$

From this result, we can devise an algorithm that only reconstructs the cross-correlation in the area defined by M_L. The number of operations and memory requirements are reduced, as we only need to find $m_\varphi = \max(\varphi_{\tilde{p}s})$ and t_φ. To achieve this, we propose pCC_ROI (Algorithm 3), which reconstructs the cross-correlation on a Region of Interest (ROI) and returns m_φ and t_φ.

Each element of the cross-correlation can be calculated independently, making this algorithm suitable for implementations on GPUs. The computational complexity of the pCC_ROI is:

$$N_{op}(pCC\_ROI(p_{\theta_i}, s)) = \underbrace{3O(kN^{m-1}logN)}_{FFTs} + \underbrace{O(kN^{m-1})}_{\odot} + \underbrace{O(kL)}_{reconstruction}. \tag{19}$$

3.4 Localized Reconstruction with Regularization

As we mentioned before, the cross-correlation between similar signals ressembles a delta dirac function, which has the property of being sparse in real space.

Algorithm 3. pCC on a Region Of Interest (pCC_ROI)

Input : p_Θ, a set of K projections; Θ, a set of K angles; s, a reference signal,
c_L, a set of L coordinates where $M_L > 0$ (ROI)
Output: $m_\varphi = \max\{\varphi_{p_{\theta_i}} s\}$; $t_\varphi = \mathrm{argmax}\{\varphi_{p_{\theta_i}} s\}$

$m_\varphi \leftarrow 0; rec_\varphi \leftarrow 0;$
$W \leftarrow \texttt{CreateRadialWeight}();$
/* Cross-correlation of projections   */
$S_\Theta \leftarrow \texttt{Extract}(\mathbf{F}s, \Theta);$
$cc_\Theta \leftarrow \mathbf{F}^{-1}(W \odot (S_\Theta \odot \mathbf{F}p_\Theta));$
/* Reconstruct on a ROI   */
foreach c in c_L **do**
    for $i \leftarrow 1$ **to** K **do**
        $rec_\varphi[c] \leftarrow rec_\varphi[c] + cc_{\theta_i}[\texttt{Project}(c, \theta_i)];$

/* Peak values   */
$m_\varphi = \texttt{Max}(rec_\varphi);$
$t_\varphi = \texttt{ArgMax}(rec_\varphi);$

We use said property to improve the cross-correlation peak and to make it more robust to noise. The sparsity condition is imposed in the following optimization problem: Let φ_Θ be a collection of projections $\varphi^{(\theta_i)}$, then the estimated $\tilde{\varphi}$ is obtained by: $\mathrm{argmin}_{\tilde{\varphi}} ||Proj(\tilde{\varphi}, \Theta) - \varphi_\Theta||_2^2 + \lambda||\tilde{\varphi}||_1$. Solving this requires the reconstruction of $\tilde{\varphi}$ multiple times. To save computation time we work with the reconstructed cross-correlation φ, and impose the sparse condition to it. The new optimization problem to solve is:

$$\mathrm{argmin}_{\tilde{\varphi}} ||\tilde{\varphi} - \varphi||_2^2 + \lambda||\tilde{\varphi}||_1, \tag{20}$$

and we use the Alternating Direction Method of Multipliers (ADMM) algorithm to solve it [2]. Let $\mathcal{S}_\lambda()$ be the *shrinkage* function, λ be the regularization parameter, and ρ be the fidelity coefficient; then the formulas for the j-th ADMM iteration are:

$$x^{j+1} = \frac{\varphi + \rho(z^j - u^j)}{1 + \rho}, \tag{21}$$

$$z^{j+1} = \mathcal{S}_\lambda(x^{j+1} + u^j) = \begin{cases} (x^{j+1} + u^j) - \lambda & , (x^{j+1} + u^j) > \lambda \\ 0 & , |x^{j+1} + u^j| \leq \lambda \\ (x^{j+1} + u^j) + \lambda & , (x^{j+1} + u^j) < \lambda, \end{cases} \tag{22}$$

$$u^{j+1} = u^j + x^{j+1} - z^{j+1}. \tag{23}$$

Finally, we devise the *Regularized pCC_ROI* algorithm (Algorithm 4).

As in the previous algorithm, the reconstruction and also the ADMM iteration can be implemented independently for each value of the cross-correlation, making it also suitable for implementations on GPUs. The computational complexity is also similar to the previous one, with the only addition of the J iterations of the ADMM algorithm:

$$N_{op}(pCC\_ROI\_reg(p_{\theta_i}, s)) = N_{op}(pCC\_ROI(p_{\theta_i}, s)) + \underbrace{O(JL)}_{ADMM}$$

Algorithm 4. Regularizated pCC on a ROI (pCC_ROI_Reg)

Input : p_Θ, a set of K projections; Θ, a set of K angles; s, a reference signal,
c_L, a set of L coordinates where $M_L > 0$ (ROI),
J, λ, ρ, the parameters for the ADMM procedure
Output: $m_\varphi = \max\{\varphi_{p_{\theta_i}s}\}$, $t_\varphi = \text{argmax}\{\varphi_{p_{\theta_i}s}\}$

$rec_\varphi \leftarrow 0$; $x \leftarrow 0$; $u \leftarrow 0$; $z \leftarrow 0$;
$W \leftarrow$ CreateRadialWeight();
/* Cross-correlation of projections   */
$S_\Theta \leftarrow$ Extract($\overline{\mathbf{F}s}, \Theta$);
$cc_\Theta \leftarrow \mathbf{F}^{-1}\left(W \odot (S_\Theta \odot \mathbf{F}p_\Theta)\right)$;
/* Reconstruct on a ROI   */
$rec_\varphi \leftarrow$ ReconstructROI(cc_Θ, Θ, c_L);
/* ADMM   */
for $j \leftarrow 1$ **to** J **do**
$\quad x = \dfrac{rec_\varphi + \rho(z-u)}{1+\rho}$;
$\quad z = $ Shrink($x + u$); $u = u + x - z$;

/* Peak values   */
$m_\varphi = $ Max(rec_φ); $t_\varphi = $ ArgMax(rec_φ);

---

4 Experimental Results

We performed three computational experiments to test the performance of the proposed algorithms in terms of correctness, robustness against noise, and execution time. We used the Shepp–Logan phantom of various sizes as the test image, and we projected it using three schemes that are similar to the ones used in cryoET: 41 projections, from $-60°$ to $60°$ with $3°$ step; 25 projections, from $-60°$ to $60°$ with $5°$ step; and 17 projections, from $-64°$ to $64°$ with $8°$ step.

The algorithms were implemented in Matlab and in C++, in the form of MEX files, and executed on an Intel Core i7-8550U CPU (8 cores, 1.8 GHz), with Linux as operative system and 16 GB of RAM memory.

4.1 Cross Correlation and Noise

For this experiment we used a 256×256 pixels Shepp–Logan phantom and we generate two sets of projections from it. The first one adds a shift to the reference image (Fig. 3(A)), and the second one adds an extra rotation (Fig. 3(B)). Both sets were projected using the scheme with $5°$ step ($K = 25$), and, we added gaussian noise to both sets (Fig. 3(C) and 3(D)). Equation 6 was used to calculate the cross-correlation between the reference and the transformed images, and between the reference and the reconstructions. Algorithms 1, 3, and 4 were used to calculate the cross-correlation between the reference and the projections sets. We do not include PBVA in this test as it does not calculate the cross-correlation.

The results show that the cross-correlations calculated using the pCC and the pCC_ROI algorithms are similar to the ones obtained using Eq. 6 for all the projections sets. For the aligned ones, the pCC_ROI_REG algorithm gives a well defined peak. When the projections are not aligned, pCC_ROI_REG scales the intensity of the cross-correlation only. This is an expected behavior, as the cross-correlation of different signals is no longer sparse. Nevertheless, the maximum value of cross-correlation of the not aligned data is always lower than the aligned one, as we will show in the next test.

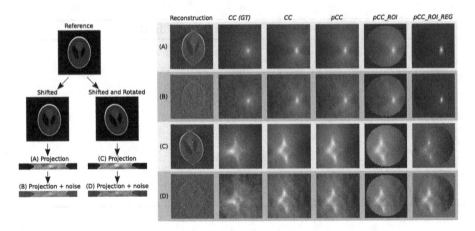

Fig. 3. On the left: setup of the experiment, showing the projections sets used (A,B,C and D). On the right: reconstructed images, and the cross-correlation of the reference against the transformed images (CC (GT)), against the reconstructions (CC), and between the reference and the projections (using Algorithms 1, 3, and 4).

4.2   Alignment

In this experiment we find the rotation angle between the reference and a set of projections [6]. The reference is rotated multiple times and cross-correlated with the projections, we pick the angle that gives the highest peak of cross-correlation. For the *projected Cross Correlation*-based algorithms the rotation is embedded into the *Extraction* part of the algorithms. We also add two levels of noise, and set the ADMM parameters for the *pCC_ROI_REG* algorithm to $\rho = 0.02$, $\lambda = 0.05$, and $J = 20$. And additional test with $\lambda = 0.1$ was performed.

The result (Fig. 4) shows that most algorithms find the angles correctly, as PBVA fails to do it when the noise level is high. The cross-correlation values found using *CC*, *pCC* and *pCC_ROI*, are almost identical, showing that the algorithms are equivalent. PBVA behaves as an upper bound with no sharp peaks where it reaches its maximum value. In contrast, the regularization used in *pCC_ROI_Reg* makes sharper peaks of cross-correlation, but this depends on the level of noise and the value of λ.

4.3   Running Time

To measure the running time, we tested different sizes for the reference, from 100×100 pixels to 800×800 pixels, with increments of 100 pixels. The ROI for the reconstructions were circles with radius of 10, and 20 pixels.

The results shows a clear quadratic behavior for the traditional cross correlation calculation (Eq. 6), and also the *pCC*, while the other algorithms behave in an almost linear manner (Fig. 5). We can also note that there is almost no difference in running time between *pCC_ROI* and *pCC_ROI_Reg*. This is because the

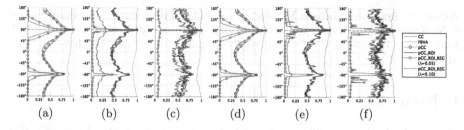

Fig. 4. Angular search: cross-orrelation values for different angles between a reference and a set of rojections. (a), (b), and (c) uses a 41 projections scheme, while (d), (e) and (f), uses 17 projections. The SNR, in dB, of the projections are $-35.39, -54.15, -60.15, -29.80, -50.75$ and -56.36, for (a) to (f) respectively.

ADMM iterations are fast and simple, making the use of the regularized version of the cross-correlation negligibly fast. Finally, we can see a difference between *PBVA* and *pCC_ROI*. This difference is due to the reconstruction step, and it was expected from the computational complexity analysis of the algorithms.

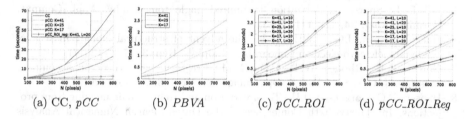

(a) CC, *pCC* (b) *PBVA* (c) *pCC_ROI* (d) *pCC_ROI_Reg*

Fig. 5. Comparison of the running time of alignment of projections against a template. Eq. (6) and the full *pCC* behave quadratically while the other algorithms, linearly.

5 Conclusions

In the present document we propose a method that exploits the sparsity inherent to the limited angle tomography to calculate the cross-correlation with lower computational complexity. For images, the initial quadratic complexity is reduced to almost a linear one; and for volumes, the cubic complexity could be reduced to a quadratic one. This is achieved by using a localized reconstruction algorithm to reduce the number of operations. Additionally, we added a regularization constrain to the calculation of the cross-correlation at almost no computational cost, which enhances its robustness to noise.

The proposed algorithms could be used to speed up computationally demanding tasks that involves the usage of cross correlation. This tasks can be image or volume alignment, classification or segmentation, and it can be used in areas like cryo-electron tomography (cryoET) or computed tomography (CT).

Acknowledgments. Ricardo M. Sánchez and Mikhail Kudryashev are funded by the Sofja Kovalevskaja Award from the Alexander von Humboldt Foundation to Mikhail Kudryashev. Ricardo M. Sánchez is partially supported by the starter Fellowship from SFB807.

References

1. Aniridh, R., Kim, H., Thiagarajan, J.J., Mohan, K.A., Champley, K., Bremer, T.: Lose the views: limited angle CT reconstruction via implicit sinogram completion. In: Computer Vision and Pattern Recognition (2017)
2. Boyd, S., Parikh, N., Chu, E., Peleato, B., Eckstein, J.: Distributed optimization and statistical learning via the alternating direction method of multipliers. Found. Trends Mach. Learn. **3**, 1–122 (2011)
3. Crowther, R.A., DeRosier, D.J., Klug, A.: The reconstruction of a three dimensional structure from projections and its application to electron microscopy. In: Proceedings of the Royal Society A: Mathematical, Physical and Engineering Sciences (1970)
4. Dong-Jiang, J., Wen-Zhang, H., Xiao-Bing, Z.: TV OS-SART with fractional order integral filtering. In: Eighth International Conference on Computational Intelligence and Security (2012)
5. Frikel, J.: Sparse regularization in limited angle tomography. Appl. Comput. Harminic Anal. **24**, 117–141 (2013)
6. Galaz-Montoya, J.G., Ludtke, S.J.: The advent of structural biology in situ by single particle cryo-electron tomography. Biophys. Rep. **3**, 17–35 (2017)
7. Garces, D.H., Rhodes, W.T., Peña, N.M.: Projection-slice theorem: a compact notation. J. Opt. Soc. Am. A, Opt. Image Sci. Vis. **28**, 766–769 (2011)
8. Hansen, P.C., Jørgensen, J.H.: Total variation and tomographic imaging from projections. In: Thirty-Sixth Conference of the Dutch-Flemish Numerical Analysis Communities (2011)
9. Hii, A.J.H., Hann, C., Chase, J.G., Houten, E.E.E.W.V.: Fast normalized cross correlation for motion tracking using basis functions. Comput. Methods Programs Biomed. **82**, 144–156 (2006)
10. Lu, X., Sun, Y., Yuan, Y.: Optimization for limited angle tomography in medical image processing. Pattern Recogn. **44**, 2427–2435 (2011)
11. Mori, M., Kashino, K.: Fast template matching based on normalized cross correlation using adaptive block partitioning and initial threshold estimation. In: IEEE International Symposium on Multimedia (2010)
12. Penczek, P.A.: Fundamentals of three-dimensional reconstruction from projections. In: Methods in Enzymology (2010)
13. Pipe, J.G., Menon, P.: Sampling density compensation in MRI: rationale and an iterative numerical solution. Magn. Reson. Med. **41**, 179–186 (1999)
14. Rickgauer, J.P., Grigorieff, N., Denk, W.: Single-protein detection in crowded molecular environments in cryo-EM images. eLife **6**, e25648 (2017)
15. Yu, L., Snapp, R.R., Ruiz, T., Radermacher, M.: Projection-based volume alignment. J. Struct. Biol. **182**, 93–105 (2013)

Sulcal and Cortical Features for Classification of Alzheimer's Disease and Mild Cognitive Impairment

Maciej Plocharski$^{(\boxtimes)}$ ⓘ, Lasse Riis Østergaard ⓘ,
and the Alzheimer's Disease Neuroimaging Initiative

Department of Health Science and Technology,
Aalborg University, Aalborg, Denmark
mpl@hst.aau.dk

Abstract. Prominent changes in sulcal morphology and cortical thickness characterize the neurodegeneration in Alzheimer's disease (AD). A combination of these measures has a potential of predicting AD and distinguishing it from mild cognitive impairment (MCI) and cognitively normal control subjects (CN). The purpose of this study was to propose a machine learning and pattern recognition approach of combining sulcal morphology features and cortical thickness measures as biomarkers for AD. Sulcal features (depth, length, mean and Gaussian curvature, surface area) and cortical thickness measures were extracted from 241 T1 MRI scans from ADNI database (81 AD, 75 MCI, 85 CN). SVM classifiers provided the highest accuracy of 95.0%, 93.0% sensitivity, and 97.0% specificity (AUC of 0.95) when classifying CN and AD. The majority of the features were located in the left hemisphere, which in AD is reported to be more severely affected by atrophy, and to lose gray matter faster than the right. Results indicate that a combination of sulcal and cortical features provides high classification results, which are competitive with the state-of-the-art techniques.

Keywords: Pattern recognition · Alzheimer's disease · SVM · Morphology · Feature extraction

1 Introduction

Computer-assisted diagnosis and prognosis for brain disorders has always been of great interest in Alzheimer's disease (AD) [1]. AD, a progressive, neurodegenerative disorder, is characterized by structural brain changes, leading to a

Data used in preparation of this article were obtained from the Alzheimer's Disease Neuroimaging Initiative (ADNI) database (adni.loni.usc.edu). As such, the investigators within the ADNI contributed to the design and implementation of ADNI and/or provided data but did not participate in analysis or writing of this report. A complete listing of ADNI investigators can be found at: http://adni.loni.usc.edu/wp-content/uploads/how_to_apply/ADNI_Acknowledgement_List.pdf.

M. Felsberg et al. (Eds.): SCIA 2019, LNCS 11482, pp. 427–438, 2019.
https://doi.org/10.1007/978-3-030-20205-7_35

gradual loss of cognitive functions [2]. Mild cognitive impairment (MCI) is an intermediate condition between normal ageing and dementia, distinguished by a cognitive decline greater than expected for a patient's age and level of education, but which does not interfere with the patient's daily life activities [3]. Some MCI patients do not convert to AD, and some even return to normal over time, but there is always a significant risk of AD conversion. In fact, more than half of MCI individuals do convert within 5 years [3]. MCI is therefore considered a substantial risk factor for AD.

Distinguishing MCI and cognitively normal (CN) controls from AD with intent to predict its onset or conversion has in recent years received a great amount of interest [4–9]. Multiple structural biomarkers, derived from magnetic resonance imaging (MRI), such as decreases in cortical thickness, in gray and white matter or subcortical volumes, have been extensively investigated for that purpose [10–12]. Multimodal studies involving various biomarkers, such as MRI or positron emission tomography (PET), resulted in high results for distinguishing between AD, MCI, and controls [10,13]. Recent studies using deep learning approaches to brain imaging analysis have also obtained promising results within brain disorder diagnosis and prognosis [9,13,14].

The neuroanatomical abnormalities in AD have also been demonstrated to be reflected in the morphology of cortical sulci (Fig. 2a). They are considered as boundaries between various functional areas of the brain and are therefore related to its functional organization. Sulcal morphology is a promising neurological biomarker in AD and MCI [16–19]. Increase in sulcal widths [15–17] and reductions in depth [16,19] have been observed in AD as a result of gray matter atrophy, when compared to normal ageing.

In this paper we postulated that a machine learning and pattern recognition approach involving a combination of sulcal and cortical features would result in higher AD classification results than if these features were used separately from each other. We hypothesized that these measures would be discriminative in classifying early MCI and AD, and that they would differ in their sensitivity in detecting the varying levels of brain atrophy in the elderly control subjects, in the early MCI subjects, and in advanced AD. Finally, we demonstrate the results of using either sulcal morphology or cortical thickness individually to distinguish between MCI, AD, and CN.

2   Methods

Sulcal and cortical features were extracted from T1-weighted MRI scans and used for classification of AD subjects from CN and MCI subjects, in a process illustrated on Fig. 1, using linear and Gaussian support vector machines (SVM). Additionally, we individually tested the classification performances of only sulcal features, as well as only cortical thickness features.

2.1 Data

Data used in the preparation of this article were obtained from the Alzheimer's Disease Neuroimaging Initiative (ADNI) database (adni.loni.usc.edu). The ADNI was launched in 2003 as a public-private partnership, led by Principal Investigator Michael W. Weiner, MD. The primary goal of ADNI has been to test whether serial magnetic resonance imaging (MRI), positron emission tomography (PET), other biological markers, and clinical and neuropsychological assessment can be combined to measure the progression of mild cognitive impairment (MCI) and early Alzheimer's disease (AD).

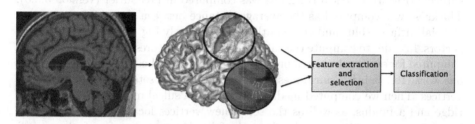

Fig. 1. Classification workflow: cortical sulci and cortical thickness measures were extracted from T1-weighted MR images to compute and select the most discriminating features for classification of AD and early MCI from CN.

241 1.5T pre-processed T1-weighted magnetization-prepared rapid gradient echo (MP-RAGE) MRI scans of 85 CN, 75 MCI, and 81 AD subjects were acquired from the database. The demographics distribution for the three subject groups is presented in Table 1. The general inclusion/exclusion criteria were as follows: *CN*: Mini-Mental State Exam (MMSE) score between 24 and 30 (inclusive), Clinical Dementia Rating (CDR) of 0, non-depressed, non-demented, with no MCI. *MCI*: MMSE between 24 and 30 (inclusive), CDR of 0.5, general cognition and functional performance sufficiently preserved, negative AD diagnosis. *AD*: MMSE score between 20 and 26 (inclusive), CDR of 0.5 or 1.0; NINCDS/ADRDA criteria for probable AD.

Table 1. Demographic characteristics of CN, MCI, and AD subjects. The age, MMSE, and CDR scores are represented as mean and standard deviations.

	CN	MCI	AD
Number	85	75	81
Male/Female	47/38	38/37	40/41
Average age (years)	76.1 ± 5.0	76.5 ± 6.8	77.8 ± 7.5
MMSE (score)	29.0 ± 1.1	26.5 ± 1.6	19.3 ± 5.3
CDR	0.0 ± 0.0	0.5 ± 0.0	1.3 ± 0.6

2.2   Sulcal and Cortical Feature Extraction

The T1-weighted MR images were first normalized and resampled to $1\,\text{mm}^3$ voxels in SPM12 (Statistical Parametric Mapping software package for analysis of brain imaging data sequences). Then, cerebral sulci were extracted from the images using Morphologist 2013 pipeline included in the BrainVISA 4.4.0 software platform [20]. BrainVISA is a fully automatic anatomical segmentation pipeline, which produces a triangular mesh of the inner cortical surface of each brain hemisphere. Sulcal features were computed and extracted from 24 sulci in MATLAB R2018b, both the left and the right hemisphere from each of the 241 subjects (Fig. 3). Cortical thickness was computed in FreeSurfer (version 5.3.0). Thickness was computed as the average distance between the white matter and the pial surfaces (blue and green outlines, respectively Fig. 2b), along the normal vectors. In order to compute the sulcal morphology features, a medial surface was computed for every sulcus, in a process previously described in detail in our previous work [19]. In brief, sulcal meshes were computed as sets of three-dimensional vertices. Then we computed medial surfaces from sulcal meshes, consisting of a ridge and a fundus, as well as the set of new vertices located between the two faces of a sulcal mesh. For each sulcus, the following medial surface features were computed: length, mean depth, mean curvature, mean Gaussian curvature, and surface area. Fig. 4 illustrates the process of extracting the sulcal meshes, and computing the medial surfaces for subsequent feature extractions.

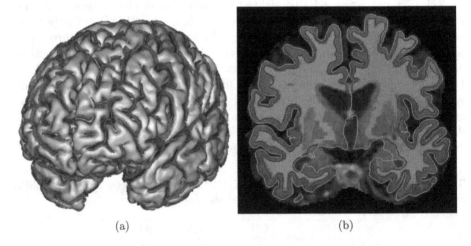

(a)   (b)

Fig. 2. (a) 3D view of the brain of a CN subject and the cortical sulci (blue). (b) the coronal view of the output volumes produced by FreeSurfer. The pial surface is shown as a green outline encapsulating the cortex, and the white matter is shown as the blue outline. (Color figure online)

2.3   Feature Selection and Classification

In total, 310 features were computed for every subject: 70 cortical thickness features (34 from each hemisphere, one average thickness per hemisphere), and 240 sulcal features (mean depth, length, mean curvature, mean Gaussian curvature, medial surface area). Next, a feature selection process was applied in order to reduce their dimensionality, and select a feature combination that yielded the best classification results. Feature normalization was applied to standardize the features by rescaling them to the $[0, 1]$ range (Eq. 1):

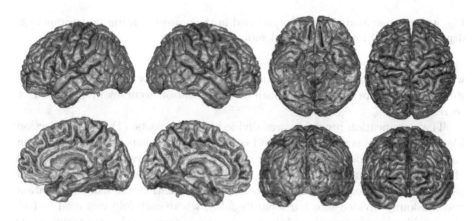

Fig. 3. The 24 cortical sulci extracted from each of the 241 subjects.

$$X_{scaled} = \frac{X - \min(X)}{\max(X) - \min(X)} \tag{1}$$

where X was the original feature value, and X_{scaled} was the normalized one. Forward feature selection was performed, where each iteration of adding one feature to the SVM classifier was evaluated on the classification accuracy and a balance index B, defined in Eq. 2 (Garde et al. [21]), which permitted the extraction of features that maximized the classification accuracy, and at the same time provided a low difference between the true positives and negatives.

$$B = \frac{|(1 - \text{Specificity}) - (1 - \text{Sensitivity})|}{[(1 - \text{Specificity}) + (1 - \text{Sensitivity})]} \tag{2}$$

SVM classifiers with a linear kernel and a Gaussian radial basis function kernel were used, with standardized predictor matrices, uniform prior probabilities for two classes, and a default value for the C parameter ($C = 1$). We selected a feature subset based on the SVM classifiers' accuracy using 10-fold cross-validation from the set of 310 features. The best feature was added to the feature set, provided that this feature increased the accuracy, while simultaneously maintaining the balance index value under 0.4 [21]. All the other remaining features

Fig. 4. Representation of the steps included in the process of feature extraction (e.g. depth and length) from sulcal medial surfaces.

were individually tested in conjunction with the previously selected feature. This iterative procedure was repeated until the classification accuracy would no longer increase.

The classification procedure was divided into two parts: (1) feature selection identified a combination of sulcal and cortical features that distinguish between CN and AD in order to classify CN vs. MCI, and MCI vs. AD; (2) individual classifications using only sulcal and only cortical features. We performed ten realizations of 10-fold cross-validations. In each realization, the study population was randomly divided into ten separate folds, where each fold was used to test the classifiers' performance, and the remaining folds were used as the training set. This procedure was independently repeated ten times, so that any bias possibly introduced by randomly partitioning the dataset in the cross-validation would be avoided.

3   Results

The cortical regions in which the atrophic changes were the most sensitive to classification between CN and AD are shown in Table 2. Six regions were identified in the left hemisphere, and two in the right. The left hemisphere has been reported in AD to be more severely affected by atrophy, and to lose gray matter faster than right, although a faster gray matter loss also occurs in age-matched healthy controls [2]. The selected features provided the highest CN vs. AD classification accuracy obtained with a linear SVM classifier (95.0% ± 0.92 accuracy, 93.0% ± 1.00 sensitivity, and 97.0% ± 1.30 specificity, 0.95 AUC). The Gaussian kernel provided a higher AUC, but lower accuracy and specificity (Table 3).

This feature combination was then applied to both the CN vs. MCI and the MCI vs. AD classifications. We achieved the highest average accuracy of 74.0% when classifying CN vs. MCI using a linear SVM kernel (67.0% using Gaussian kernel), and a similar result for the MCI vs. AD classification, also with a linear SVM (Table 3). The Receiver Operating Characteristic (ROC) curves for the three classifications using two SVM kernels are shown of Fig. 5: CN vs. AD on the left, CN vs. MCI in the middle, and MCI vs. AD on the right.

3.1 Classification with Either Sulcal or Cortical Features

Following the same feature selection procedure, we have identified two additional sets of features for CN vs. AD, CN vs. MCI, and MCI vs. AD classifications, in which only sulcal features and only cortical thickness features were used for classification. Table 4 shows the results using the linear and Gaussian radial basis function kernels, and the number of selected features. When used separately, cortical thickness features provided higher classification results than sulcal features for CN vs. AD, while sulcal features were more discriminating MCI from both CN and AD. However, the combination of both sulcal and cortical thickness yielded higher values of accuracy, sensitivity, specificity, and AUC for all three classification scenarios, than if these measures were used separately. The linear kernel SVM classifier provided higher classification results.

Table 2. Cortical regions providing the highest distinction between the CN and AD groups using a linear SVM classifier. The CN, MCI, and AD values are represented as mean feature values and their standard deviations.

Hemisphere	Region	Feature	CN	MCI	AD
Left	Entorhinal cortex	Cortical thickness	3.29 (0.32)	2.91 (0.48)	2.43 (0.51)
	Posterior occipito-temp. lateral sulcus	Sulcal curvature	0.03 (0.01)	0.04 (0.01)	0.05 (0.02)
	Olfactory sulcus	Sulcal curvature	−0.033 (0.01)	−0.030 (0.01)	−0.030 (0.01)
	Polar temporal sulcus	Sulcal depth	11.12 (1.61)	9.98 (1.44)	9.98 (1.66)
	Rostral anterior cingulate cortex	Cortical thickness	2.79 (0.25)	2.76 (0.28)	2.60 (0.28)
	Marginal frontal sulcus	Sulcal Gaussian curvature	−0.016 (0.01)	−0.02 (0.01)	−0.022 (0.02)
Right	Medial orbitofrontal cortex	Cortical thickness	2.30 (0.18)	2.20 (0.16)	2.09 (0.22)
	Central sulcus	Sulcal length	113.00 (6.50)	112.86 (5.55)	112.35 (6.03)

Table 3. Classification results for CN, MCI, and AD subjects obtained with the two types of SVM kernels using ten realizations of 10-fold cross-validations. Results are shown as means and standard deviations.

Classification	SVM	Accuracy (%)	Sensitivity (%)	Specificity (%)	AUC
CN vs. AD	Linear	95.0 ± 0.92	93.0 ± 1.00	97.0 ± 1.30	0.95 ± 0.00
	Gaussian	91.2 ± 1.03	93.0 ± 0.93	89.3 ± 1.40	0.96 ± 0.01
CN vs. MCI	Linear	74.0 ± 2.04	70.3 ± 2.40	77.4 ± 2.45	0.79 ± 0.02
	Gaussian	67.0 ± 0.83	70.0 ± 1.70	64.0 ± 1.78	0.71 ± 0.01
MCI vs. AD	Linear	74.2 ± 1.38	77.2 ± 2.25	71.0 ± 0.87	0.80 ± 0.01
	Gaussian	72.4 ± 0.82	74.0 ± 0.90	71.0 ± 1.94	0.77 ± 0.01

4   Discussion

In this paper we propose a machine learning and pattern recognition approach of integrating sulcal morphology and cortical thickness measurements for classification of AD and MCI. Linear and Gaussian SVM classifiers were trained with a selection of sulcal and cortical thickness features to classify CN vs. AD, CN vs. MCI, and MCI vs. AD. Additionally, separate sulcal and cortical features were individually tested for classification performance in these three classification scenarios.

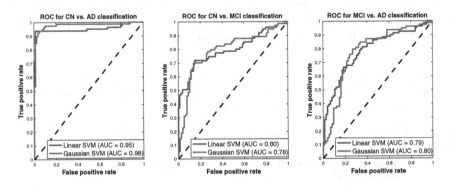

Fig. 5. ROC curves for the CN vs. AD (left), CN vs. MCI (middle) and MCI vs. AD (right) classifications. Dashed lines represent random classification, blue curves represent the linear kernel SVM, and red curves illustrate the performance of the Gaussian kernel SVM. (Color figure online)

SVMs with different kernels were chosen due to their high performances in high dimensional feature spaces [8,22–24]. Cali et al. [23] reported no statistically significant differences between early-stage AD classification using Naïve Bayes, Logistic Regression and SVMs, but the SVMs outperformed the other classifiers with a combination of sulcal measures, cortical thickness, cortical volume, subcortical volumes and the MMSE score. Similarly, we obtained the highest classification results with linear SVM. Daliri [22] obtained a superior classification rate when using linear over Gaussian kernel SVM. Polynomial and sigmoid kernels provided even lower AD-classification rates, and thus were not implemented in our study. To evaluate the classifiers, we used 10-fold cross-validation, a statistical method for validating a predictive model by partitioning the original data into a training set, and a test set to evaluate its classification performance by averaging over ten iterations.

Our results confirmed that the combination of the sulcal and cortical measures were highly discriminative between CN and early MCI and AD subjects. The CN vs. AD classification yielded the 10-fold cross-validated, averaged accuracy of 95.0%, sensitivity of 93.0%, and specificity of 97.0% (0.95 AUC) with a linear SVM classifier. Suk et al. [9] used a deep ensemble learning of sparse

Table 4. Comparison between the classification results obtained with only sulcal features, only with cortical thickness measurements, and the combination of sulcal features and cortical thickness measurements.

Classification	Results	Sulcal		Cortical		Both	
		Linear SVM	Gaussian SVM	Linear SVM	Gaussian SVM	Linear SVM	Gaussian SVM
CN vs. AD	Number of features	8		8		9	
	Accuracy	86.2%	76.0%	91.7%	88.5%	96.4%	92.3%
	Sensitivity	82.8%	69.0%	88.9%	87.6%	94.0%	91.3%
	Specificity	89.6%	82.4%	94.2%	90.5%	99.0%	92.8%
	AUC	0.87	0.82	0.94	0.94	0.95	0.98
CN vs. MCI	Number of features	13		7		11	
	Accuracy	87.0%	82.1%	79.3%	73.7%	89.4%	84.4%
	Sensitivity	86.3%	85.0%	70.4%	72.0%	89.1%	82.3%
	Specificity	87.1%	79.0%	86.9%	76.0%	89.4%	86.0%
	AUC	0.85	0.85	0.79	0.78	0.89	0.84
MCI vs. AD	Number of features	9		6		8	
	Accuracy	80.1%	75.0%	79.4%	68.5%	86.0%	81.5%
	Sensitivity	82.8%	74.2%	80.1%	72.0%	85.3%	81.7%
	Specificity	76.8%	75.3%	78.9%	64.3%	87.1%	81.3%
	AUC	0.78	0.76	0.81	0.74	0.83	0.83

regression models and obtained a maximum accuracy of 91.02% for CN vs. AD and 73% for CN vs. MCI classifications, using 10-fold cross-validation. Choi et al. [13] studied the brain metabolism using amyloid PET imaging and achieved an 86.6% accuracy with an SVM, and a 96.0% accuracy using a deep convolutional neural network, when classifying AD from controls. Beheshti et al. [25] used an approach for feature selection based on the t-test and a Fisher Criterion, using a voxel-based morphometry technique to compare the global and local gray matter differences in AD subjects and healthy controls using SVM. They reported a 96.32% accuracy using a 10-fold cross validation.

Furthermore, our results show that the features discriminating between CN and advanced AD provide relatively low accuracies when distinguishing early MCI from CN (77.2% accuracy with linear kernel), or advanced AD (73.3% accuracy with Gaussian kernel SVM). These inferior results may be due to the fact that the spread of atrophy in AD is hypothesized to be a non-linear process, and thus the structural cortical changes that distinguish AD from controls may be less sensitive to separate the controls from early MCI. Classification results reported in Table 3 suggest that the features characterizing an advanced atrophy of an AD patient are not as sensitive at detecting the differences between the brain of an early MCI subject and a control. They appear to be even less sensitive in distinguishing between early MCI and advanced AD.

Biomarker studies aiming at distinguishing between AD and normal controls often use either sulcal [15–17] or cortical features [11,12]. However, the novelty of study is in combining these MRI-derived features, but also at analyzing them separately on the same data set, even though we acknowledge that some studies [13, 25] outperform our classification results. In our previous work [6] we aimed to identify the sulcal and cortical features to distinguish between stable MCI subjects and those converting to AD in order to identify features predicting AD-conversion. The separate feature selection process employed in this study revealed that sulcal features alone were superior to the cortical thickness at distinguishing early MCI from both AD and CN. This is likely due to the structural brain changes and regional volume losses being a natural part of normal ageing, occurring both in the cognitively normal elderly, and in AD patients. Therefore, cortical thickness alone may not be a sufficient biomarker, since a certain level of atrophy was already present in these two groups. In advanced AD, brain atrophy is highly pronounced, thus making cortical thickness a more sensitive biomarker (91.7% vs. 86.2%). However, sulcal features were the most sensitive for classifying early MCI from AD and CN. This indicates that sulcal morphology could be a potentially powerful biomarker in conjunction with cortical thickness for early-stage detection of neurodegenerative disorders.

5   Conclusion

The main contribution of this machine learning and pattern recognition study is a finding that a combination of sulcal morphology and cortical thickness measurements provides high classification results in discriminating between AD, MCI, and elderly control subjects. These results are competitive with the state-of-the-art techniques. Moreover, sulcal features were observed to be more sensitive at distinguishing MCI from AD and CN than cortical thickness, suggesting their potential as a structural biomarker for early detection of AD.

Acknowledgements. Support for this research was provided by The Lundbeck Foundation.

Data Availibility Statement. Data collection and sharing for this project was funded by the Alzheimer's Disease Neuroimaging Initiative (ADNI) (National Institutes of Health Grant U01 AG024904) and DOD ADNI (Department of Defense award number W81XWH-12-2-0012). ADNI is funded by the National Institute on Aging, the National Institute of Biomedical Imaging and Bioengineering, and through generous contributions from the following: AbbVie, Alzheimer's Association; Alzheimer's Drug Discovery Foundation; Araclon Biotech; BioClinica, Inc.; Biogen; Bristol-Myers Squibb Company; CereSpir, Inc.; Eisai Inc.; Elan Pharmaceuticals, Inc.; Eli Lilly and Company; EuroImmun; F. Hoffmann-La Roche Ltd and its affiliated company Genentech, Inc.; Fujirebio; GE Healthcare; IXICO Ltd.; Janssen Alzheimer Immunotherapy Research & Development, LLC.; Johnson & Johnson Pharmaceutical Research & Development LLC.; Lumosity; Lundbeck; Merck & Co., Inc.; Meso Scale Diagnostics, LLC.; NeuroRx Research; Neurotrack Technologies; Novartis Pharmaceuticals Corporation; Pfizer Inc.; Piramal Imaging; Servier; Takeda Pharmaceutical Company; and Transition Therapeutics. The Canadian Institutes of Health Research is providing funds to support ADNI clinical sites in Canada. Private sector contributions are facilitated by the Foundation for the National Institutes of Health (www.fnih.org). The grantee organization is the Northern California Institute for Research and Education, and the study is coordinated by the Alzheimer's Disease Cooperative Study at the University of California, San Diego. ADNI data are disseminated by the Laboratory for Neuro Imaging at the University of Southern California.

Conflicts of Interest. None.

References

1. Cuingnet, R., et al.: Automatic classification of patients with Alzheimer's disease from structural MRI: a comparison of ten methods using the ADNI database. Neuroimage **56**(2), 766–781 (2011)
2. Thompson, P.M., et al.: Dynamics of gray matter loss in Alzheimer's disease. J. Neurosci. **23**(3), 994–1005 (2003)
3. Gauthier, S., et al.: Mild cognitive impairment. Lancet **367**(9518), 1262–1270 (2006)
4. de Vos, F., et al.: Combining multiple anatomical MRI measures improves Alzheimer's disease classification. Hum. Brain Map. **37**(5), 1920–1929 (2016)
5. Altaf, T., Anwar, S.M., Gul, N., Majeed, M.N., Majid, M.: Multi-class Alzheimer's disease classification using image and clinical features. Biomed. Sig. Process. Control **43**, 64–74 (2018)
6. Plocharski, M., Østergaard, L.R.: Prediction of Alzheimer's disease in mild cognitive impairment using sulcal morphology and cortical thickness. In: Lhotska, L., Sukupova, L., Lacković, I., Ibbott, G.S. (eds.) World Congress on Medical Physics and Biomedical Engineering 2018. IP, vol. 68/1, pp. 69–74. Springer, Singapore (2019). https://doi.org/10.1007/978-981-10-9035-6_13
7. Basaia, S., et al.: Automated classification of Alzheimer's disease and mild cognitive impairment using a single MRI and deep neural networks. NeuroImage: Clin. **21**, 101645 (2018)
8. Rathore, S., Habes, M., Iftikhar, M.A., Shacklett, A., Davatzikos, C.: A review on neuroimaging-based classification studies and associated feature extraction methods for Alzheimer's disease and its prodromal stages. NeuroImage **155**, 530–548 (2017)
9. Suk, H.I., Lee, S.W., Shen, D., Alzheimer's Disease Neuroimaging Initiative: Deep ensemble learning of sparse regression models for brain disease diagnosis. Medical image analysis **37**, 101–113 (2017)
10. Westman, E., Muehlboeck, J.S., Simmons, A.: Combining MRI and CSF measures for classification of Alzheimer's disease and prediction of mild cognitive impairment conversion. Neuroimage **62**(1), 229–238 (2012)
11. Eskildsen, S.F., Coupé, P., Fonov, V.S., Pruessner, J.C., Collins, D.L., Alzheimer's Disease Neuroimaging Initiative: Structural imaging biomarkers of Alzheimer's disease: predicting disease progression. Neurobiol. Aging **36**, S23–S31 (2015)
12. Zheng, W., Yao, Z., Hu, B., Gao, X., Cai, H., Moore, P.: Novel cortical thickness pattern for accurate detection of Alzheimer's disease. J. Alzheimer's Disease **48**(4), 995–1008 (2015)
13. Choi, H., Jin, K.H., Alzheimer's Disease Neuroimaging Initiative: Predicting cognitive decline with deep learning of brain metabolism and amyloid imaging. Behav. Brain Res. **344**, 103–109 (2018)

14. Suk, H.I., Lee, S.W., Shen, D., Alzheimer's Disease Neuroimaging Initiative: Latent feature representation with stacked auto-encoder for AD/MCI diagnosis. Brain Struct. Funct. **220**(2), 841–859 (2015)
15. Liu, T., et al.: Longitudinal changes in sulcal morphology associated with late-life aging and MCI. Neuroimage **74**, 337–342 (2013)
16. Im, K., Lee, J.M., Seo, S.W., Kim, S.H., Kim, S.I., Na, D.L.: Sulcal morphology changes and their relationship with cortical thickness and gyral white matter volume in mild cognitive impairment and Alzheimer's disease. Neuroimage **43**(1), 103–113 (2008)
17. Hamelin, L., et al.: Sulcal morphology as a new imaging marker for the diagnosis of early onset Alzheimer's disease. Neurobiol. Aging **36**(11), 2932–2939 (2015)
18. Andersen, S.K., Jakobsen, C.E., Pedersen, C.H., Rasmussen, A.M., Plocharski, M., Østergaard, L.R.: Classification of Alzheimer's disease from MRI using sulcal morphology. In: Paulsen, R.R., Pedersen, K.S. (eds.) SCIA 2015. LNCS, vol. 9127, pp. 103–113. Springer, Cham (2015). https://doi.org/10.1007/978-3-319-19665-7_9
19. Plocharski, M., Østergaard, L.R., Alzheimer's Disease Neuroimaging Initiative: Extraction of sulcal medial surface and classification of Alzheimer's disease using sulcal features. Comput. Methods Programs Biomed. **133**, 35–44 (2016)
20. Rivière, D., Geffroy, D., Denghien, I., Souedet, N., Cointepas, Y.: BrainVISA: an extensible software environment for sharing multimodal neuroimaging data and processing tools. Neuroimage **47**, S163 (2009)
21. Garde, A., Voss, A., Caminal, P., Benito, S., Giraldo, B.F.: SVM-based feature selection to optimize sensitivity-specificity balance applied to weaning. Comput. Biol. Med. **43**(5), 533–540 (2013)
22. Daliri, M.R.: Automated diagnosis of Alzheimer disease using the scale-invariant feature transforms in magnetic resonance images. J. Med. Syst. **36**(2), 995–1000 (2012)
23. Cai, K., et al.: Identification of early-stage Alzheimer's disease using sulcal morphology and other common neuroimaging indices. PloS ONE **12**(1), e0170875 (2017)
24. Previtali, F., Bertolazzi, P., Felici, G., Weitschek, E.: A novel method and software for automatically classifying Alzheimer's disease patients by magnetic resonance imaging analysis. Comput. Methods Programs Biomed. **143**, 89–95 (2017)
25. Beheshti, I., Demirel, H., Alzheimer's Disease Neuroimaging Initiative: Feature-ranking-based Alzheimer's disease classification from structural MRI. Magn. Reson. Imaging **34**(3), 252–263 (2016)

On the Effectiveness of Generative Adversarial Networks as HEp-2 Image Augmentation Tool

Tomáš Majtner[1]($\boxtimes$), Buda Bajić[2], Joakim Lindblad[3,4], Nataša Sladoje[3,4], Victoria Blanes-Vidal[1], and Esmaeil S. Nadimi[1]

[1] Group of Machine Learning and AI, The Maersk Mc-Kinney Moller Institute, University of Southern Denmark, Odense, Denmark
tomaj@mmmi.sdu.dk
[2] Faculty of Technical Sciences, University of Novi Sad, Novi Sad, Serbia
[3] Centre for Image Analysis, Department of Information Technology, Uppsala University, Uppsala, Sweden
[4] Mathematical Institute of the Serbian Academy of Sciences and Arts, Belgrade, Serbia

Abstract. One of the big challenges in the recognition of biomedical samples is the lack of large annotated datasets. Their relatively small size, when compared to datasets like ImageNet, typically leads to problems with efficient training of current machine learning algorithms. However, the recent development of generative adversarial networks (GANs) appears to be a step towards addressing this issue. In this study, we focus on one instance of GANs, which is known as deep convolutio nal generative adversarial network (DCGAN). It gained a lot of attention recently because of its stability in generating realistic artificial images. Our article explores the possibilities of using DCGANs for generating HEp-2 images. We trained multiple DCGANs and generated several datasets of HEp-2 images. Subsequently, we combined them with traditional augmentation and evaluated over three different deep learning configurations. Our article demonstrates high visual quality of generated images, which is also supported by state-of-the-art classification results.

Keywords: Deep learning · Image recognition · HEp-2 image classification · GAN · CNN · GoogLeNet · VGG-16 · Inception-v3 · Transfer learning

1 Introduction

Human Epithelial (HEp-2) cells are commonly used in the Indirect Immunofluorescence (IIF) tests to detect autoimmune diseases. Nowadays, the evaluation of IIF test is done mostly by humans and therefore it is a subjective method too dependent on the experience of the physician. Usually, two or three specialists need to analyze patients' specimen images via fluorescence microscopes and

© Springer Nature Switzerland AG 2019
M. Felsberg et al. (Eds.): SCIA 2019, LNCS 11482, pp. 439–451, 2019.
https://doi.org/10.1007/978-3-030-20205-7_36

vote to decide the staining patterns. Thus, computer-aided systems aim to assist doctors with the diagnosis by automatic classification of HEp-2 images.

A number of automated methods addressing the problem of cell staining pattern recognition have been proposed in the literature. Many of them are the result of the HEp-2 cell classification contests [7,12,13], where datasets of samples were made publicly available for method evaluation. While most of the research groups at the time of these competitions still approached the problem by using methods based on extracting so-called *hand-crafted features* for pattern discrimination, nowadays the deep convolutional neural networks (also known as CNNs) are used almost exclusively [2,9,16,21].

To train a successful deep neural network, a large amount of training images is required. It is typically very difficult to collect and label biomedical images due to the lack of experts' time and the cost of imaging devices. It is therefore common to increase the number of training samples by various methods of image augmentation. For HEp-2 images, the flipping operation and the rotation around the central image point are the most common approaches [2,9,16,21].

Our paper investigates an alternative method for data augmentation by utilizing Generative Adversarial Network (GAN). This method has been demonstrated to be a powerful technique to perform an unsupervised generation of new synthetic images with the visual appearance of the real ones. We have employed deep convolutional GAN (DCGAN) [19] for this particular purpose. Our motivation is supported with the fact that the original DCGAN architecture was demonstrated to be stable for images of size 64×64, which is very close to the average size of HEp-2 cells images. The comparison of different augmentation techniques is done using the transfer learning framework. We compare the performances of fine-tuned GoogLeNet, VGG-16, and Inception-v3 with augmented data obtained by traditional methods and by utilization of DCGAN.

The next section of the article presents the current state-of-the-art in HEp-2 image recognition and development of GANs. Subsequently, we describe the dataset used in this article and our methods of preprocessing and augmentation of the images. The last sections are dedicated to evaluation together with presentation and discussion of experiments and results, where we demonstrate the effectiveness of our solution.

2   Related Work

The recent progress of pattern recognition techniques for IIF image analysis has been covered by a special issue of Pattern Recognition Letters [11]. Novel techniques, including those examining the role of Gaussian Scale Space theory as a pre-processing approach [18], a superpixel based classification method calculating the sparse codes of image patches [6], a multi-process system based on ensemble of 15 support vector machines [4], and many others, were introduced.

Even more recently, Gao et al. [9] analyzed the impact of hyper-parameter settings of proposed fully-connected CNN on the classification accuracy. The influence of several preprocessing techniques on HEp-2 image classification has been studied by Bayramoglu et al. [2]. Shen et al. were focusing on a very deep residual network for HEp-2 pattern classification [21] and some authors tried simultaneous cell segmentation and classification by utilizing proposed residual network [16]. All of these papers are focusing on very specific problems but none of them deals with comparison of various augmentation methods, which is the main focus of our paper.

GANs, a class of neural networks, were introduced in 2014 [10]. They typically consist of two CNNs - the generator and the discriminator, which compete with each other in a zero-sum game. The role of the generator is to produce random samples that look like real images, while the role of the discriminator is to correctly classify and recognize these generated images. GANs have been successfully used for biomedical imaging tasks including the image synthesis and classification [25], and also for medical segmentation [3].

In the context of automated analysis of HEp-2 images, GANs were used only for segmentation task [15], while for the HEp-2 images classification there are no peer-reviewed publications focusing on exploring the possibilities. Our article aims at filling this gap with an extensive comparison over three different network configurations.

3   Dataset

In this article, we are using publicly available dataset of HEp-2 images, which was also previously used for benchmarking [13]. The entire dataset contains 13,596 pre-segmented and annotated cell images with their ground truth classes. It utilizes 419 unique positive sera extracted from 419 randomly selected patients. The specimens, one for each patient serum, were automatically photographed using a monochrome high dynamic range cooled microscopy camera. The image dataset is divided into six categories: Centromere (Ce), Golgi (Go), Homogeneous (Ho), Nucleolar (Nu), Nuclear Membrane (Nm), and Speckled (Sp). See the top most part of Fig. 1 for illustration.

Since there are no official independent publicly available test samples, some researchers opt for N-fold cross-validation over the all available images to evaluate the performance of their algorithms. However, this approach is criticized from statistical point of view [1] and it leads to biased results, where the performance tends to drop significantly when the algorithm is applied on new, previously unseen data. Therefore, we use a holdout validation approach on the available part of the dataset. We randomly partitioned the dataset into 70% for training, 10% for validation, and 20% for testing. The validation part is used to evaluate the performance during the training of deep learning, whereas independent testing part is used at the very end to report the final performance. The total number of images in each class, before any form of augmentation, is summarized in Table 1.

4   Proposed Method

When we look at the entire dataset, the average size of an image is 68.75 × 68.73 pixels with a standard deviation of 6.32 and 6.19 pixels, respectively. For comparison purposes, all images were resized to the same size of 64 × 64 pixels using bicubic interpolation. Since the brightness and contrast of the images vary a lot, we employed normalization of image intensities. The intensity adjustment was performed by linear stretching, where 1% of the pixels are saturated at low and at high end of the intensity range in order to maximize the contrast. The following two subsections describe the two forms of augmentation employed for the training images in this study. The version of training dataset without any form of augmentation is further referred to as *original*.

Table 1. The division of images before augmentation of the training part of the dataset.

	Ce	Go	Ho	Nu	Nm	Sp	Total
Training	1,918	506	1,745	1,819	1,546	1,981	9,515
Validation	274	72	249	259	220	283	1,357
Testing	549	146	500	520	442	567	2,724
Total	2,741	724	2,494	2,598	2,208	2,831	13,596

4.1   Augmentation by Rotation and Flipping

There are multiple different forms of augmentation, where their usability is typically subject to the nature of the data. Since we are working with pre-segmented cell images that were acquired using the same microscope settings, the samples are centered and have the same resolution. Therefore, augmentation by shifting or zooming is not appropriate here. On the other hand, the most common and natural technique to augment these biomedical datasets is to use image rotation around the image center. We rotated each image by 90°, 180°, and 270°, which, together with the flipping operation, results in seven unique images generated out of each original input.

The original dataset is unbalanced, with one class (Golgi) having 3–4× lower number of images than the remaining five classes (see Table 1). We therefore additionally rotated each Golgi image by angles of size $23° \times i$, where $i \in \{1, 2, 3\}$. After adding three more rotations, Golgi class reached similar number of images (4×506) as the remaining classes. In this augmentation step, rotated images are first cropped to the size of the largest rectangle within the input image and later resized back to the size of 64 × 64. The bicubic interpolation is used in both cases. The training part of the dataset derived by this sequence of steps is further referred to as *rotated*. The problem of unbalanced classes is addressed in literature by different approaches, e.g., by using RUSBoost [20] approach to alleviating class imbalance. These methods, however, usually follow the strategy of under-sampling the majority class or classes, which is not optimal in this study, where we have one minority class.

In addition, we also wanted to examine the effect of even stronger augmentation by adding more image rotations. Therefore, we created another version of training dataset, where each image from the *rotated* dataset is further rotated by 45°. This leads to doubling the number of training samples. Also here, the images are cropped and resized in the same fashion as previously described for Golgi class. This version of training dataset is further referred to as *rotated*$_{+45°}$. The exact sizes of both *rotated* and *rotated*$_{+45°}$ datasets are specified in Table 3.

4.2 Augmentation by Generative Adversarial Networks

As aforementioned, we use the DCGAN [19] to generate more HEp-2 samples for increasing the size of the training dataset. The authors of DCGAN introduced several techniques for successful learning: converting the max-pooling layers to convolution layers, converting the fully connected layers to global average pooling layers in the discriminator, using batch normalization layers in the generator and the discriminator, and using leaky ReLU activation functions in the discriminator. In their configuration, a 100 dimensional uniform distribution is projected to a small spatial extent convolutional representation. Subsequently, the series of four fractionally-strided convolutions convert the representation into a 64×64 pixel image. For more details about the network configuration, we refer the reader to the original paper introducing DCGAN [19].

For application of this approach to the HEp-2 images, we train individual DCGAN for each of the six classes. In total, two different training scenarios are followed. In the first one, we use the *original* dataset to train the DCGANs, while in the second one, we use the *rotated* dataset. To distinguish between images generated from GANs trained on *original* dataset and those generated from GANs trained on *rotated* dataset, we use the subscript *rot* for the latter version, i.e., we refer to these datasets as *generated* and *generated*$_{rot}$, respectively. The motivation is to test the influence of larger and already pre-augmented dataset by rotation and flipping on the quality of generated images via DCGANs. All our models are trained with mini-batch stochastic gradient descent with a mini-batch size of 128. All weights are initialized from a zero-centered normal distribution with standard deviation 0.02. The learning rate is set to 0.0002 and we train all models for 300 epochs. Figure 1 illustrates both versions of generated datasets.

Since there is no limit in the number of derived images using DCGANs, we use this fact to create also the perfectly balanced classes. In this scenario, we start from the *rotated* set, however, we did not use the additional rotation of Golgi class, where bicubic interpolation and resizing was needed. Therefore, each image from *original* set is only rotated by 90°, 180°, and 270° and flipped, which leads to higher unbalance between classes than in previous scenarios. We subsequently use generated images to fill up those classes having lower number of samples than the most populated class, the Speckled class. The new datasets created using this approach are further referred to as *balanced* and *balanced*$_{rot}$.

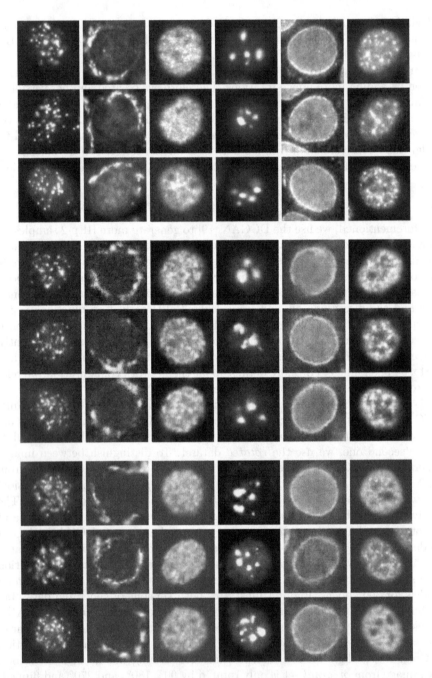

Fig. 1. Examples of *original* HEp-2 images (first three rows), images **generated by DCGAN** from *original* dataset (three middle rows), and images **generated by DCGAN** from *rotated* dataset (last three rows). Each column represents a different image class, in order: Ce, Go, Ho, Nu, Nm, Sp.

Lastly, we create two more datasets that match the number of images in $rotated_{+45°}$. We start with $rotated$ dataset here and instead of employing additional rotations that were used to create $rotated_{+45°}$ set, we utilize images generated from GANs to match the number of samples in $rotated_{+45°}$. These new datasets are referred as $rotated\&generated$ and $rotated\&generated_{rot}$, depending on the type of images used to train GANs. The overview of all created training datasets is in Table 2 and the summary of their exact size is in Table 3.

Table 2. The brief overview of all created training datasets. In $balanced$ and $balanced_{rot}$ datasets, we eliminated the additional rotation of Golgi class.

	Description
$original$	original data, no augmentation
$rotated$	each image flipped and rotated, additional rotation for Golgi class
$generated$	GANs trained on $original$, equal output size as $rotated$
$generated_{rot}$	GANs trained on $rotated$, equal output size as $rotated$
$balanced$	$rotated$ dataset perfectly balanced using GANs trained on $original$
$balanced_{rot}$	$rotated$ dataset perfectly balanced using GANs trained on $rotated$
$rotated_{+45°}$	$rotated$ dataset plus additional rotation by $45°$
$rotated\&generated$	$rotated$ dataset plus $generated$ dataset
$rotated\&generated_{rot}$	$rotated$ dataset plus $generated_{rot}$ dataset

Table 3. The total number of images in different versions of the training dataset after various forms of augmentation. In $balanced$ and $balanced_{rot}$ datasets, we eliminated the additional rotation of Golgi class. Therefore, balanced classes have lower number of samples than the maximum of $rotated$ dataset.

	Ce	Go	Ho	Nu	Nm	Sp
$original$	1,918	506	1,745	1,819	1,546	1,981
$rotated$, $generated$, $generated_{rot}$	15,344	16,192	13,960	14,552	12,368	15,848
$balanced$, $balanced_{rot}$	15,848	15,848	15,848	15,848	15,848	15,848
$rotated_{+45°}$, $rotated\&generated$, $rotated\&generated_{rot}$	30,688	32,384	27,920	29,104	24,726	31,696

5   Evaluation

In the experimental part, we are using three different pretrained convolutional neural networks, namely GoogLeNet [23], VGG-16 [22], and Inception-v3 [24]. All three networks were pretrained on ImageNet [5]; we perform fine-tuning, also known as the transfer learning [26], to adjust them for HEp-2 image recognition.

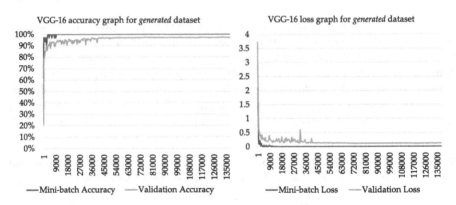

Fig. 2. Accuracy (left) and loss (right) for VGG-16 network during its training on *generated* dataset. The number of iterations is displayed on the x-axis.

This implies that, for all three networks, we replace their last three layers with a fully-connected layer, a softmax layer, and a classification layer, which classifies images directly to the six categories of HEp-2 images.

For this fine-tuning, we utilize stochastic gradient descent with momentum optimizer, initial learning rate of 0.001, and a mini-batch size of 32 images. All the networks are trained for 50 epochs, to be sure that the training is stabilized (see the stable curves in Fig. 2 with almost no fluctuations at the end). Images are resized to appropriate input size for each network separately. All tests are performed using MATLAB R2018b. During the training, we validate the performance using an independent validation dataset and at the end, the final version of each model is evaluated using the test dataset. For illustration of the development of training process, Fig. 2 depicts accuracy and loss for VGG-16 network trained on *generated* dataset.

Evaluation of classification performance is performed using two different metrics. The first one is the overall accuracy (OA), defined as the overall correct classification rate of all images. In some previous works on HEp-2 image recognition, this metric is also known as the average classification accuracy (ACA). The second one, the mean class accuracy (MCA), is defined as

$$MCA = \frac{1}{K} \sum_{k=1}^{K} CCR_k \tag{1}$$

where CCR_k is the classification accuracy of a particular cell class k and K is the number of cell classes.

6   Results and Discussion

The comparison of all tested variants is summarized in Table 4 and the overall accuracy is also plotted in Fig. 3. From the results we can see that already the performance on the *original* dataset is relatively high, which confirms the quality of our preprocessing and the appropriate choices of deep learning techniques. The performance on the *generated* and *generated_rot* datasets is lower, when compared to corresponding *rotated* dataset (see also Table 5 for confusion matrices of *generated* and *rotated* versions). Despite of the very good visual appearance of generated images (see Fig. 1), their standalone classification performance is not as convincing.

Table 4. The comparison of performances of all three network configurations on all derived training datasets for both tested metrics. In the table, G-net stands for GoogLeNet, V-net stands for VGG-16, and I-net stands for Inception-v3. Presented values are in %.

	OA			MCA		
	G-net	V-net	I-net	G-net	V-net	I-net
original	96.84	96.26	95.99	97.10	96.45	96.04
generated	95.96	96.33	96.48	95.94	96.49	96.39
generated_rot	96.33	96.62	96.26	96.40	96.68	96.07
balanced	97.98	98.13	98.20	98.17	98.31	98.17
balanced_rot	98.31	98.24	98.49	98.44	98.22	98.53
rotated&generated	98.27	97.91	98.38	98.41	97.94	98.36
rotated&generated_rot	98.35	**98.27**	**98.60**	98.47	**98.34**	98.55
rotated_+45°	**98.60**	97.72	98.42	98.61	97.76	98.38
rotated	**98.60**	98.13	98.49	**98.71**	98.30	**98.62**

Table 5. GoogLeNet confusion matrices for *generated* and *rotated* versions of training dataset. Presented values are in %.

Generated version

	Ce	Go	Ho	Nu	Nm	Sp
Ce	98.00	0.36	0.00	0.36	0.18	1.10
Go	0.00	95.22	0.68	2.74	0.68	0.68
Ho	0.60	0.60	95.00	0.20	0.60	3.00
Nu	0.96	0.96	0.77	95.58	0.38	1.35
Nm	0.00	0.68	0.68	0.23	98.18	0.23
Sp	2.65	0.18	2.12	1.05	0.35	93.65

Rotated version

	Ce	Go	Ho	Nu	Nm	Sp
Ce	98.89	0.19	0.00	0.73	0.00	0.19
Go	0.00	99.32	0.00	0.68	0.00	0.00
Ho	0.20	0.20	98.80	0.40	0.00	0.40
Nu	0.38	0.58	0.19	97.89	0.38	0.58
Nm	0.00	0.00	0.23	0.45	99.32	0.00
Sp	0.00	0.00	0.53	0.88	0.53	98.06

This result confirms the observation made by Perez and Wang [17] for real-world images. They also concluded that GANs do not perform better than traditional augmentations. However, there is still a potential in combining them

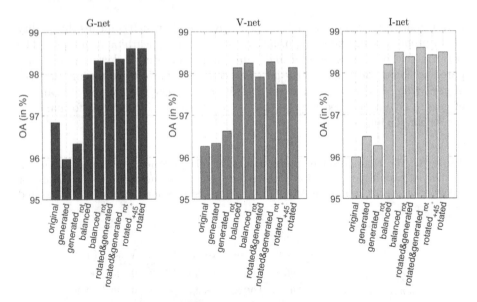

Fig. 3. The overall accuracy (OA) graphs for GoogLeNet (G-net), VGG-16 (V-net), and Inception-v3 (I-net).

together, as was shown by Frid-Adar et al. [8] for liver lesion classification, where inclusion of the GAN-based augmentation does help. Our results for VGG-16 and also for Inception-v3 support this conclusion also for HEp-2 images, since we observe a slight increase in accuracy achieved by combining rotated and generated images during the training.

Table 6. Comparison with other approaches on the same dataset and with the same division of publicly available part of HEp-2 images. Presented values are in %.

	OA	MCA
Kastaniotis et al. [14]	–	93.6
Gao et al. [9]	97.24	96.76
Shen et al. [21]	**98.82**	98.62
Our top performing method	98.60	**98.71**

We also observe that the versions with the subscript *rot* have generally slightly higher performance than their corresponding variants without this subscript. This indicates importance of the amount and variability of training samples for performance of DCGANs, as well as an effect that the quality of training data has on the resulting quality of generated images. Finally, both balanced datasets exhibit slightly lower performance. However we note that the original dataset is relatively balanced, with only one class with lower number of training samples, which is primarily compensated by additional rotations. As a result, the effect of perfect class balancing does not turn out to be important.

To provide a look at the HEp-2 image classification from a broader perspective, we present the comparison of our top performing approach with the methods from the literature in Table 6. To enable a fair comparison, we include only the methods using the same, or almost the same, split technique for training and test datasets as we did. Table 6 suggests that we share the top position together with the Shen et al. [21], depending on the choice of metric used for evaluation. Shen et al. [21] proposed a deep cross residual network (DCRNet) for HEp-2 cell classification and their method is the winner of the most recent HEp-2 image recognition contest, with achieved accuracy which exceeds all of the top performers in the previous contests. Our solution is based on transfer learning and we used slightly less images for training (70% vs. 80%), when compared to their presented solution.

7   Conclusion

In this article, we compare and discuss augmentation techniques for HEp-2 images for their classification. We evaluate the usage of the recently proposed DCGAN and we observe that these type of networks are capable of producing very realistically looking images of HEp-2 cells. However, application of DCGAN for classification purposes does not lead to convincing results, in particular when the generated images are used independently, without the combination with original ones. This result is not surprising and it supports the conclusions from the similar comparison performed in a different image domain [17]. The potential of combining generated and rotated images is, however, still interesting, as is also demonstrated by our results, especially for the VGG-16 and Inception-v3 network configurations.

For future work, we would like to focus on further improvement of the quality of the generated dataset by an external measure. There is a possible problem of large intra-class variance, which was not discussed and covered in this work and which could lead to the low quality of synthetic images. Despite some of the weak performances presented here, we still see a potential of GANs in biomedical and medical domain for helping to address the problem of small annotated datasets.

Acknowledgement. This research was supported by a research grant from the University of Southern Denmark, Odense University Hospital, Danish Cancer Society, and Region of Southern Denmark through the Project EFFICACY and by Swedish Research Council through Projects 2015-05878 and 2017-04385, Sweden's Innovation Agency VINNOVA through Project 2017-02447, and Ministry of Education, Science and Technological Development of the Republic of Serbia through Projects ON174008 and III44006.

References

1. Babyak, M.: What you see may not be what you get: a brief, nontechnical introduction to overfitting in regression-type models. Psychosom. Med. **66**(3), 411–421 (2004)
2. Bayramoglu, N., Kannala, J., Heikkilä, J.: Human epithelial type 2 cell classification with convolutional neural networks. In: 15th International Conference on Bioinformatics and Bioengineering, pp. 1–6. IEEE (2015)
3. Bowles, C., et al.: GAN augmentation: augmenting training data using generative adversarial networks. arXiv preprint arXiv:1810.10863 (2018)
4. Cascio, D., Taormina, V., Cipolla, M., Bruno, S., Fauci, F., Raso, G.: A multi-process system for HEp-2 cells classification based on SVM. Pattern Recogn. Lett. **82**, 56–63 (2016)
5. Deng, J., Dong, W., Socher, R., Li, L.J., Li, K., Fei-Fei, L.: ImageNet: a large-scale hierarchical image database. In: IEEE Conference on Computer Vision and Pattern Recognition, pp. 248–255. IEEE (2009)
6. Ensafi, S., Lu, S., Kassim, A.A., Tan, C.: Accurate HEp-2 cell classification based on sparse coding of superpixels. Pattern Recogn. Lett. **82**, 64–71 (2016)
7. Foggia, P., Percannella, G., Soda, P., Vento, M.: Benchmarking HEp-2 cells classification methods. IEEE Trans. Med. Imaging **32**(10), 1878–1889 (2013)
8. Frid-Adar, M., Diamant, I., Klang, E., Amitai, M., Goldberger, J., Greenspan, H.: GAN-based synthetic medical image augmentation for increased CNN performance in liver lesion classification. arXiv preprint arXiv:1803.01229 (2018)
9. Gao, Z., Wang, L., Zhou, L., Zhang, J.: HEp-2 cell image classification with deep convolutional neural networks. IEEE J. Biomed. Health Inform. **21**(2), 416–428 (2017)
10. Goodfellow, I., et al.: Generative adversarial nets. In: Advances in Neural Information Processing Systems, pp. 2672–2680 (2014)
11. Harandi, M., Lovell, B., Percannella, G., Saggese, A., Vento, M., Wiliem, A.: Executable thematic special issue on pattern recognition techniques for indirect immunofluorescence images analysis. Pattern Recogn. Lett. **82**, 1–2 (2016)
12. Hobson, P., Lovell, B., Percannella, G., Saggese, A., Vento, M., Wiliem, A.: HEp-2 staining pattern recognition at cell and specimen levels: datasets, algorithms and results. Pattern Recogn. Lett. **82**, 12–22 (2016)
13. Hobson, P., Lovell, B., Percannella, G., Vento, M., Wiliem, A.: Benchmarking human epithelial type 2 interphase cells classification methods on a very large dataset. Artif. Intell. Med. **65**(3), 239–250 (2015)
14. Kastaniotis, D., Fotopoulou, F., Theodorakopoulos, I., Economou, G., Fotopoulos, S.: HEp-2 cell classification with vector of hierarchically aggregated residuals. Pattern Recogn. **65**, 47–57 (2017)
15. Li, Y., Shen, L.: cC-GAN: a robust transfer-learning framework for HEp-2 specimen image segmentation. IEEE Access **6**, 14048–14058 (2018)
16. Li, Y., Shen, L., Yu, S.: HEp-2 specimen image segmentation and classification using very deep fully convolutional network. IEEE Trans. Med. Imaging **36**(7), 1561–1572 (2017)
17. Perez, L., Wang, J.: The effectiveness of data augmentation in image classification using deep learning. arXiv preprint arXiv:1712.04621 (2017)
18. Qi, X., Zhao, G., Chen, J., Pietikäinen, M.: HEp-2 cell classification: the role of gaussian scale space theory as a pre-processing approach. Pattern Recogn. Lett. **82**, 36–43 (2016)

19. Radford, A., Metz, L., Chintala, S.: Unsupervised representation learning with deep convolutional generative adversarial networks. arXiv preprint arXiv:1511.06434 (2015)
20. Seiffert, C., Khoshgoftaar, T., Van Hulse, J., Napolitano, A.: RUSBoost: a hybrid approach to alleviating class imbalance. IEEE Trans. Systems Man Cybern. Part A: Syst. Hum. **40**(1), 185–197 (2010)
21. Shen, L., Jia, X., Li, Y.: Deep cross residual network for HEp-2 cell staining pattern classification. Pattern Recogn. **82**, 68–78 (2018)
22. Simonyan, K., Zisserman, A.: Very deep convolutional networks for large-scale image recognition. arXiv preprint arXiv:1409.1556 (2014)
23. Szegedy, C., et al.: Going deeper with convolutions. In: Proceedings of the IEEE Conference on Computer Vision and Pattern Recognition, pp. 1–9 (2015)
24. Szegedy, C., Vanhoucke, V., Ioffe, S., Shlens, J., Wojna, Z.: Rethinking the inception architecture for computer vision. In: Proceedings of the IEEE Conference on Computer Vision and Pattern Recognition, pp. 2818–2826 (2016)
25. Yi, X., Walia, E., Babyn, P.: Generative adversarial network in medical imaging: a review. arXiv preprint arXiv:1809.07294 (2018)
26. Yosinski, J., Clune, J., Bengio, Y., Lipson, H.: How transferable are features in deep neural networks? In: Advances in Neural Information Processing Systems, pp. 3320–3328 (2014)

Parameter Selection for Regularized Electron Tomography Without a Reference Image

Yan Guo[✉] and Bernd Rieger

Department of Imaging Physics, Delft University of Technology,
Lorentzweg 1, 2628 CJ Delft, The Netherlands
{y.guo-3,b.rieger}@tudelft.nl

Abstract. Regularization has been introduced to electron tomography for enhancing the reconstruction quality. Since over-regularization smears out sharp edges and under-regularization leaves the image too noisy, finding the optimal regularization strength is crucial. To this end, one can either manually tune regularization parameters by trial and error, or compute reconstructions for a large set of candidate values and compare them to a reference image. Both are cumbersome in practice. In this paper, we propose an image quality metric Q to quantify the reconstruction quality for automatically determining the optimal regularization parameter λ without a reference image. Specifically, we use the oriented structure strength described by the highest two responses in orientation space to simultaneously measure the sharpness and noisiness of reconstruction images. We demonstrate the usefulness of Q on a recently introduced total nuclear variation regularized reconstruction technique using simulated and experimental datasets of core-shell nanoparticles. Results show that it can replace the full-reference correlation coefficient to find the optimal λ. Moreover, observing that the curve of Q versus λ has a distinct maximum attained for the best quality, we adopt the golden section search for the optimum to effectively reduce the computational time by 85%.

Keywords: Image quality assessment · Electron tomography ·
X-ray spectroscopy · Image reconstruction

1 Introduction

Electron tomography enables materials scientists to characterize nanoparticles in three dimensions (3D) [12]. Scanning transmission electron microscopy (STEM) has many imaging modes such as high-angle annular dark-field (HAADF) [12], in

This work is partially supported by the Dutch Technology Foundation STW, which is part of the Netherlands Organization for Scientific Research, and partially by the Ministry of Economic Affairs, Agriculture and Innovation under project number 13314.

M. Felsberg et al. (Eds.): SCIA 2019, LNCS 11482, pp. 452–464, 2019.
https://doi.org/10.1007/978-3-030-20205-7_37

which the sample under study is exposed to a focused electron beam and tilted to obtain two-dimensional (2D) projections at different angles. In tomography, the collection of projections is called a tilt-series, from which we can reconstruct a 3D image that represents the sample. Although HAADF tomography can clearly reveal the inner structure of the sample, it cannot explicitly provide its compositional information. To better understand samples with more complex chemical compositions, spectral imaging techniques like energy dispersive X-ray spectroscopy (EDS) [19] must be pursued. EDS tomography, however, is currently hampered by slow data acquisition, resulting in a limited number of elemental maps with low signal-to-noise ratio (SNR) [19].

Electron tomography is an ill-posed inverse problem whose solution is not stable and unique. Therefore, l_1 regularizations (e.g., total variation (TV) [8] and higher order total variation (HOTV) [16,17]) have been introduced to enhance the reconstruction quality. However, regularizations, especially the common TV, inevitably aggravate jaggy edges and staircase artifacts when being applied to the (noisy) EDS datasets. To alleviate such artifacts yet still benefiting from regularization, Zhong et al. incorporated the HAADF-STEM projections with high SNR into EDS maps using total nuclear variation (TNV) to enforce anti-/parallel gradients and common edges in joint reconstructions [21]. Like other regularization-based approaches, TNV also requires a fine-tuning parameter λ to determine the strength of regularization. The "best" λ is now chosen by computing reconstructions for a large set of candidate values and comparing them to a reference image with the correlation coefficient [21]. Since this is infeasible if the reference is unavailable, we need to automatically measure the reconstruction quality for determining the optimal λ.

So far, many no-reference quality assessment algorithms have been proposed to set appropriate parameters for inverse problems. For instance, Zhu and Milanfar developed a structure tensor based image content index to optimize denoising algorithms [22]. Since this index is easy to compute, it has also been adopted to determine the optimal regularization parameter for the TV reconstruction technique [11]. Applications dedicated to electron tomography also exist [9,13]. For example, Okariz et al. derived the optimal number of iterations for simultaneous iterative reconstruction technique (SIRT) by statistically analyzing the edge profile of reconstructions [13]. Furthermore, we recently proposed a non-distortion-specific image quality metric to quantify the cross-atomic contamination and noise so as to select the optimal weighting factor for bimodal tomography [9]. However, automatically selecting parameters for regularized electron tomography has still not been widely investigated to the best of our knowledge.

In this paper, we aim to automatically find the optimal regularization parameter λ for TNV in the absence of a reference image. Specifically, we extend the concept of image content index [22] to orientation space (OS) [5], in which we develop a metric Q to assess the reconstruction quality regarding the sharpness and noisiness. We demonstrate our Q on simulated and experimental datasets of core-shell nanoparticles containing gold and silver. Results show that this OS-based Q is more robust to noise than the original tensor-based version. Moreover, it can replace the full-reference correlation coefficient used in [21] to determine the optimal λ. In Sect. 2, we introduce the TNV-regularized reconstruction technique and its relations to TV. Section 3 elaborates the orientation space as prior work, followed by our quality assessment framework for parameter determination. We present the experiments and results in Sect. 4, and summarize our work in Sect. 5.

2   TNV Regularized Electron Tomography

Originally proposed for color images [10], total nuclear variation (TNV) has later been applied to multi-channel spectral CT data for encouraging common edge locations and a shared gradient direction among the different channels [15]. Let us assume that an arbitrary 3D image $\mathbf{A}$ has a number of L channels, in which $\mathbf{A}_n = [A_n^{(1)}, \cdots, A_n^{(L)}]^T \in \mathbb{R}^{L \times 1}$ is the intensity value tuple of its n-th voxel. Denote the Jacobian matrix of $\mathbf{A}$ as $\mathbf{J}_n \mathbf{A}$ [21], then TNV of $\mathbf{A}$ is

$$\text{TNV}(\mathbf{A}) = \sum_n \|\mathbf{J}_n \mathbf{A}\|_\star \tag{1}$$

where $\|\mathbf{J}_n \mathbf{A}\|_\star$, the nuclear norm of $\mathbf{J}_n \mathbf{A}$, is the sum of its singular values [15]. When $L = 1$, TNV reduces to the isotropic (l_2-norm) TV [21].

We consider a specimen with a number of E different chemical elements. Each element $e = 1, \cdots, E$ has its EDS map $\mathbf{p}^{(e)} \in \mathbb{R}^{M^e \times 1}$, and is associated with one unknown reconstruction volume $\mathbf{x}^{(e)} \in \mathbb{R}^{N \times 1}$. M^e is the number of pixels in the map and N the number of discretized voxels to be reconstructed. Similarly, let $\mathbf{p}^h \in \mathbb{R}^{M^h \times 1}$ and $\mathbf{x}^h \in \mathbb{R}^{N \times 1}$ be the projection and volumetric reconstruction of HAADF, respectively. Note that M^h, the number of pixels in the HAADF projection, is not equal to M^e if the HAADF tilt-series has more acquisition angles than the EDS.

Given $\mathbf{A}_n$ as a two-channel image $\mathbf{A}_n = [x_n^{(e)}, x_n^h]^T$, i.e., one element of interest plus HAADF, the TNV-regularized EDS and HAADF joint tomography is [21]

$$\mathbf{x}^{(e)*}, \mathbf{x}^{h*} = \underset{\mathbf{x}^{(e)}, \mathbf{x}^h}{\arg\min} \left\| \mathbf{p}^{(e)} - \mathbf{W}^{(e)} \mathbf{x}^{(e)} \right\|_2^2 + \left\| \mathbf{p}^h - \mathbf{W}^h \mathbf{x}^h \right\|_2^2 + \lambda \text{TNV}(\mathbf{x}^{(e)}, \mathbf{x}^h). \tag{2}$$

Extending $\mathbf{A}_n$ to multiple channels with more than one element is also possible, as long as they share common edges [21]. In Eq. (2), $\mathbf{W}^{(e)} \in \mathbb{R}^{M^e \times N}$ and $\mathbf{W}^h \in \mathbb{R}^{M^h \times N}$ are the projection matrices of the EDS and HAADF, respectively, whose entries $w_{mn}^{(e)}$ and w_{mn}^h are determined by the intersected area between the m-th ray integral and n-th voxel. When the HAADF term is removed and $A_n = x_n^{(e)}$, Eq. (2) reduces to the TV-regularized EDS tomography [8].

The parameter λ in Eq. (2) determines the strength of TNV regularization. A large λ may blur sharp edges and produce an over-smoothed reconstruction, whereas a small one may make the regularization ineffective. To choose this crucial parameter, Zhong et al. computed the reconstructions $\mathbf{x}^{(e)*}$ for a large set of λ (e.g., 100 values uniformly sampled from 10^{-3} to 10^1 on the logarithmic scale) and compared them to a noise-free image using the correlation coefficient [21]. Since this is infeasible in industry, we need a no-reference quality metric to quantify the reconstruction quality so as to (blindly) determine the optimal λ.

3   No-Reference Regularization Parameter Determination

Considering that the effect of regularization varies spatially, we propose to use the local oriented structure strength (OSS) to measure the image quality; it has large values for well structured patches containing lines and edges and small values for blurry/noisy ones. In this section, we first introduce the concept of orientation space [5], from which we then present our OSS-based quality assessment framework.

3.1   Orientation Space

The linear orientation space of a 3D input image $I(\mathbf{x})$ can be constructed as

$$I_h(\mathbf{x}, \phi, \theta) = I(\mathbf{x}) * h(\mathbf{x}; \phi, \theta) \tag{3}$$

where $\mathbf{x}$ is the Cartesian coordinate tuple containing x, y and z. Operator $*$ denotes convolution. $h(\mathbf{x}; \phi, \theta)$ is obtained by rotating an elongated template filter $h(\mathbf{x})$ over angles ϕ and θ in a unit sphere. $\phi \in [0, 2\pi)$ is the counterclockwise angle measured from the positive x-axis in the xy-plane; $\theta \in [0, \pi)$ is the angular distance from the positive z-axis [5]. One promising candidate for $h(\mathbf{x})$ is a Gabor filter [4]; however, it cannot produce a zero response to a constant signal. Therefore, we use a similar filter which is zero for a constant signal [5].

According to van Ginkel et al., the choice of the template filter $h(\cdot)$ is largely free, as long as the scale and orientation can be dealt with separately [7]. To this end, Faas and van Vliet constrained the Fourier transform of $h(\mathbf{x})$ to have separable radial and angular parts, that is, $\mathcal{F}\{h(\mathbf{x})\} = H(\mathbf{f}) = H_{\mathrm{rad}}(f)H_{\mathrm{ang}}(\phi, \theta)$ where $\mathbf{f}$ is the polar coordinate tuple containing f, ϕ and θ in the Fourier domain [5]. The radial component $H_{\mathrm{rad}}(f; f_c, b_f)$ is a Gaussian-like bandpass filter where f_c and b_f are the central frequency and bandwidth of the Gaussian profile, respectively. It reaches its maximum for $f = f_c$ and goes to zero for $f = 0$. The angular component $H_{\mathrm{ang}}(\phi, \theta; N)$ relies on a parameter N to control the orientation selectivity, which is the number of orientations in the upper half of the unit sphere formed by ϕ and θ. For details of mathematical expressions see [5]. When θ is removed, $H(\mathbf{f})$ becomes the 2D filterbank presented in [7].

$I_h(\mathbf{x}, \phi, \theta)$ has a number of peaks: the amplitude of the strongest peak $A_1(\mathbf{x}) = \max_{\phi, \theta} |I_h(\mathbf{x}, \phi, \theta)|$ captures highly regular regions with one single orientation; the amplitude of the second strongest peak $A_2(\mathbf{x})$ highlights special patterns such as deformation and bifurcation; the remaining peaks and noise are described by a residue term $R(\mathbf{x}, \phi, \theta)$ which reflects chaotic regions [7]. Intuitively, a large A_1 and a small A_2 indicate a prominent elongated structure.

3.2   Reconstruction Quality Assessment Using Orientation Space

Our patch-based quality assessment algorithm consists of three steps: (i) construct an orientation space; (ii) compute the local and (iii) global quality metrics, see Fig. 1. Note that this method is currently implemented and discussed here in 2D in a first result.

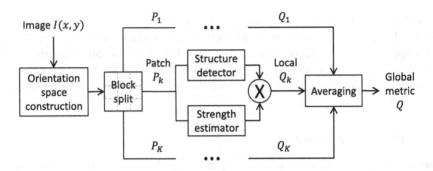

Fig. 1. Framework for reconstruction quality assessment. Details in Sect. 3.2.

Construct Orientation Space. For each reconstruction slice $I(x, y)$, we first construct its orientation space $I_h(x, y, \phi)$ using Eq. (3). Then, we extract the amplitudes of the two strongest peaks $A_1(x, y)$ and $A_2(x, y)$. Throughout this paper, $I_h(x, y, \phi)$, $A_1(x, y)$ and $A_2(x, y)$ are computed with the open source DIPimage toolbox [1]. Moreover, we set $f_c = 0.25$, $b_f = 0.8 f_c$ and $N = 8$, so that the template filter $h(x, y; f_c, b_f, N)$ behaves as a line/edge detector [7].

Compute Local Metric. Divide $I(x, y)$ into a number of K non-overlapped rectangular patches P_k, $k = 1, \cdots, K$; each goes through two modules: structure detector and strength estimator. The *structure detector* determines whether P_k contains any prominent structure (e.g., edges) by measuring its contrast. To eliminate outliers such as noise, we define the contrast of P_k as the interquartile range (75 percentile minus 25 percentile) rather than the full range (maximum minus minimum) of its pixel intensities. We set is_stru$_k = 1$ if the contrast of P_k is larger than the average intensity of $I(x, y)$, and is_stru$_k = 0$ otherwise. The *strength estimator* quantifies the saliency of patch P_k, for which the gradient structure tensor has been considered earlier. For instance, Zhu and Milanfar proposed the image content index [22]

$$q = s_1 \frac{s_1 - s_2}{s_1 + s_2} \tag{4}$$

where s_1 and s_2 are the singular values of the 2×2 tensor matrix. In this paper, we replace s_1 and s_2 by the amplitudes A_1 and A_2, because the latter two are more sensitive to fine structures under noise [6]. Consequently, the oriented structure strength of P_k is given by

$$\text{OSS}_k = 1 - \frac{\text{geomean}\{q_i\}}{\text{mean}\{q_i\}}, \quad q_i = A_{1,i}\frac{A_{1,i} - A_{2,i}}{A_{1,i} + A_{2,i}}, \quad i \in P_k, \quad (5)$$

in which geomean$\{\cdot\}$ and mean$\{\cdot\}$ represent the geometric- and arithmetic mean, respectively. The underlying rationale is that the more "spiky" q is, the stronger the oriented structure in P_k. Moreover, if P_k is constant or exactly at the boundary between two orientation fields (i.e., $A_{1,i} = A_{2,i} = 0$, or $A_{1,i} = A_{2,i}, \forall i \in P_k$ [7]), we set $\text{OSS}_k = 0$. Finally, we compute the local quality metric by multiplying the outputs of the two independent modules: $Q_k = \text{is\_stru}_k \times \text{OSS}_k$.

Compute Global Metric. We define the global quality metric Q as the geometric mean of all nonzero Q_k, that is, $Q = \text{geomean}\{Q_k\}$, $Q_k \neq 0$, $k = 1, \cdots, K$. We do not consider the arithmetic mean because it (unwanted) gives higher weight to Q_k with larger numeric range.

4   Experiments and Results

In this section, we demonstrate that our quality metric Q can select a close-to-optimal λ for the TNV-regularized reconstruction technique. Hereinafter, we consider simulated and experimental datasets of core-shell nanoparticles containing gold (Au) in the core and silver (Ag) in the shell. These two chemical elements have distinct atomic numbers ($Z_{\text{Au}} = 79$, $Z_{\text{Ag}} = 47$), and hence can produce high Z-contrast HAADF-STEM projections for the TNV to augment EDS maps. Moreover, the TNV-regularized tomography was realized by Douglas-Rachford primal-dual splitting algorithm with the operator discretization library [2]. We set 400 iterations to guarantee convergence, and sampled 100 points for λ which were uniformly distributed between 0.001 and 1.0 on the logarithmic scale.

4.1   Simulated Dataset

To begin with, we simulated a noise-free multislice dataset using a AuAg nanoparticle in a box with a size of 40 nm × 40 nm × 40 nm, see Fig. 2(a). For details of simulation see [3]. HAADF-STEM projections and EDS maps with a size of 128 pixel × 128 pixel ($\approx$4Å/pixel) were simulated in every 2.5° over [0°, 180°). We used a focused electron beam normalized to an intensity of 1, a convergence angle of 10 mrad, and a detector with an inner angle of 90 mrad and outer 230 mrad. Since we did not include any (spherical) aberration, we set the accelerating voltage to 120 kV rather than 200 kV [19] for a broader beam.

Then, we introduced several post-processing steps to make this noiseless dataset more realistic. HAADF-STEM projections were blurred by Gaussian smoothing ($\sigma = 1.0$ pixel), and corrupted by Poisson noise with a mean of the number of electron counts (up to 10^5 per pixel) and Gaussian noise with a standard deviation of 0.2. Projections suffering from the channelling effect were removed [18]. For EDS maps, we set the maximum X-ray count per pixel to 4 for Au and 3 for Ag, so that the total number of X-ray counts per angle were comparable to real experimental data [19]. Since EDS maps were much noisier, we employed a Gaussian filter ($\sigma = 1.0$ pixel) for denoising. Finally, we subsampled the EDS tilt-series by a factor of 2, as in practice the number of EDS maps is typically smaller than HAADF projections due to acquisition time. The resulting HAADF-STEM and EDS data are shown in Fig. 2.

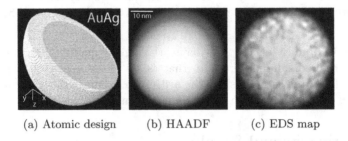

(a) Atomic design   (b) HAADF   (c) EDS map

Fig. 2. (a) Atomic design of a core-shell nanoparticle consisting of gold (Au, yellow) and silver (Ag, white). (b) Simulated HAADF-STEM projection and (c) superposed EDS map at 7.5°. (Color figure online)

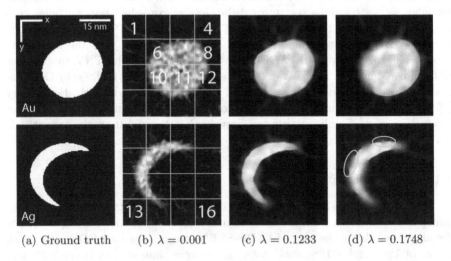

(a) Ground truth   (b) $\lambda = 0.001$ (c) $\lambda = 0.1233$ (d) $\lambda = 0.1748$

Fig. 3. Au (upper) and Ag (lower) xy-slices for the simulated dataset at $z = 24$. (a) Ground truth, hand-segmented from SIRT reconstructions with 100 iterations using 72 elemental maps between $[0, 180°)$; (b)–(d) TNV reconstructions with regularization parameter $\lambda \in \{0.001, 0.1233, 0.1748\}$. The size of the reconstruction volume is $128 \times 128 \times 128$ pixels. (Color figure online)

Figure 3 illustrates the xy-slices of Au and Ag at $z = 24$, which are reconstructed with TNV using different λ. Two binary images in Fig. 3(a) are the ground truth segmented from SIRT reconstructions with 100 iterations given the full-view noiseless EDS maps. Figure 3(b) shows 16 patches with four different types of structures: foreground (P_{11}), background (P_4, P_{16}), background with streak artifacts (P_1, P_{13}), and edge (P_6, P_8, P_{10}, P_{12}). For $\lambda = 0.001$, a weak regularization leads to an overall noisy reconstruction. However, when λ is increased up to a certain level (e.g., $\lambda = 0.1748$), strong regularization starts to nonuniformly degrade the sharp edges, see yellow circles in Fig. 3(d).

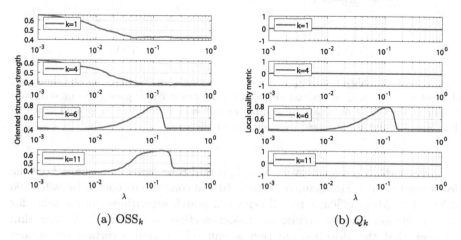

(a) OSS_k \qquad\qquad (b) Q_k

Fig. 4. Oriented structure strength OSS_k and local quality metric Q_k versus λ for four patches P_k in Fig. 3. P_1: background with streak artifacts; P_4: background; P_6: edge; P_{11}: foreground. Results are averaged over ten noise realizations.

Figure 4(a) plots the oriented structure strength (OSS) as a function of λ for four patches selected from Fig. 3. OSS curves of the background patches P_1 and P_4 (w/ and w/o perceptible streak artifacts) are decreasing when λ is increasing, because stronger regularization can more effectively suppress the noise. In addition, OSS curves of the edge (P_6) and foreground (P_{11}) patches are similar, whereas the former has a clearer unique maximum. Figure 4(b) shows the corresponding local quality metrics, in which only Q_6 with is_stru$_6 = 1$ is nonzero.

Figure 5 depicts our main result, in which we plot the global quality metric Q and correlation coefficient (CC) as a function of λ. Q is derived either from our orientation space (OS) or from the structure tensor (ST) [22]; CC is calculated by comparing reconstructions to the binary segmentation of the noiseless SIRT reconstruction. It can be observed that our OS-based Q has a very good agreement with CC for the optimal λ, i.e., λ values around the maxima of OS-based Q and CC are almost the same. Moreover, our OS-based Q has a higher dynamic range than the ST-based version especially for Ag, see Fig. 5(b). As a result, it would be more robust to small fluctuations such as noise in practice.

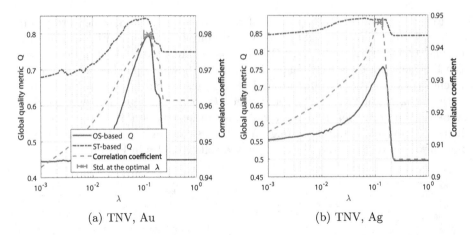

(a) TNV, Au   (b) TNV, Ag

Fig. 5. Global quality metric Q and correlation coefficient versus λ for the simulated dataset at $z = 24$. Q is derived either from the orientation space (OS) or structure tensor (ST); CC is obtained by comparing reconstructions to the ground truth in Fig. 3(a). Results are averaged over ten noise realizations.

Note that TNV is an iterative technique that takes significant amount of time for reconstruction. For example, it took 10 h to compute reconstructions for 100 different λ. Many efficient one-dimensional search algorithms are available for time reduction, and we choose the golden section search [14]. This algorithm assumes that the objective function is unimodal within a certain range, and evaluates it at triples of points whose values form the golden ratio [14]. Since the golden section search can narrow the original 100 values of λ down to no more than 15, it would effectively reduce the total computational time by approximately 85%.

4.2   Experimental Dataset

Our experimental AuAg core-shell nanoparticle was scanned in a FEI Tecnai Osiris microscope which was operated with an accelerating voltage of 120 kV and equipped with four Super-X energy dispersive silicon drift detectors [20]. HAADF-STEM projections with a size of 300 pixels × 300 pixels were acquired at 31 tilt angles, ranging from $-75°$ to $+75°$ with an increment of $5°$. In addition, one X-ray spectral image has also been recorded at each angle for 300 seconds. The raw dataset was then processed before reconstruction. The HAADF-STEM tilt-series was aligned using cross-correlation; X-ray spectral images were denoised by principal component analysis and deconvolved into two equi-sized elemental maps, one for Au and the other for Ag [20]. Figure 6 gives an example of the post-processed experimental dataset, for which we hand-segmented the HAADF reconstruction to obtain the ground truth of EDS.

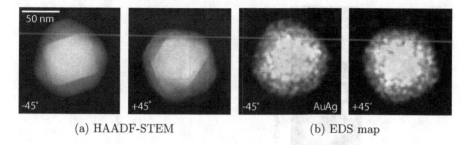

(a) HAADF-STEM   (b) EDS map

Fig. 6. Experimental (a) HAADF-STEM projections and (b) superposed EDS maps of a Au-Ag core-shell nanoparticle at $-45°$ and $+45°$.

Figure 7 shows the variation of the optimal λ w.r.t. different slices. λ values found by our no-reference metric Q and the full-reference metric CC are comparable, considering that the search space spans over 3 orders of magnitude. Moreover, golden section search and exhaustive search lead to the same λ most of the time, though the former may terminate at the local maximum before reaching the global one (e.g., slice number 81 in Fig. 7(a)). Note that Fig. 7(b) has two "outliers", and we show the details of slice number 91 in Fig. 8. It is obvious that the Ag reconstruction computed from Q maintains finer structure than the one from CC, especially at the edges of the outer ring. From Fig. 8(d) we can see that the curve of CC strangely "jumps" after a certain λ, even though the underlying structures have already been smeared out. This shows that even using CC as a metric to choose the optimal λ for the TNV-regularized electron tomography is not always reliable.

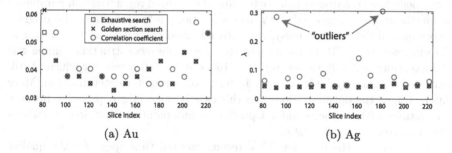

(a) Au   (b) Ag

Fig. 7. Optimal regularization parameter λ versus slice index for the experimental dataset. The size of the reconstruction volume is $300 \times 300 \times 300$ pixels.

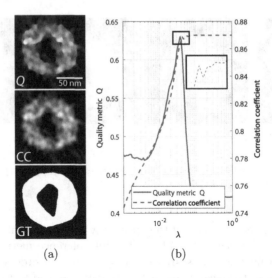

(a)   (b)

Fig. 8. (a) Ag TNV reconstructions at $z = 91$ with λ found by quality metric Q and correlation coefficient (CC), compared to the hand-segmented ground truth (GT). The corresponding curves of Q and CC versus λ are shown in (b).

5   Discussion and Conclusion

In this paper, we developed a no-reference quality metric Q to score the oriented structure strength of reconstruction images for detecting over- and under-regularization. Based on simulated and experimental datasets of AuAg core-shell nanoparticles, we demonstrated that our Q can replace the full-reference correlation coefficient to automatically determine the optimal regularization parameter λ for the recently proposed TNV reconstruction technique. Since the original experimental dataset was noisy, we further binned the tilt-series by a factor of 3 to increase the SNR. Consequently, the size of the reconstruction volume was reduced from $300 \times 300 \times 300$ pixels to $100 \times 100 \times 100$ pixels, for which Q still achieved a relatively high accuracy in terms of parameter determination. More interestingly, the optimal λ found in this case became larger, probably because the dataset with less noise did not produce severe paintbrush/staircase artifacts under a stronger regularization.

Compared to the iterative TNV reconstruction, time spent for the quality assessment is minor, e.g., 10 h versus 5 min for 100 different λ on a desktop equipped with eight Intel Xeon X5550 CPU cores (24 GB memory) and one NVIDIA GeForce GTX670 GPU (4 GB memory). Considering that the curve of reconstruction quality versus λ is unimodal with a distinct maximum, we adopted the golden section search to "predict" the optimal λ, which effectively reduced the total computational time (reconstruction plus assessment) by 85%.

As for future work, we consider testing the applicability of our quality metric to other iterative reconstruction techniques with (e.g., TV and HOTV) and/or without (e.g., SIRT) regularizations. Moreover, we will also extend the current framework to 3D.

References

1. DIPlib & DIPimage. http://www.diplib.org. Accessed 16 Dec 2018
2. Adler, J., Kohr, H., Öktem, O.: Operator discretization library (ODL) (2017). https://github.com/odlgroup/odl
3. Aveyard, R., Rieger, B.: Tilt series STEM simulation of a $25 \times 25 \times 25$ nm semiconductor with characteristic X-ray emission. Ultramicroscopy **171**, 96–103 (2016)
4. Chen, J., Sato, Y., Tamura, S.: Orientation space filtering for multiple orientation line segmentation. IEEE Trans. Pattern Anal. Mach. Intell. **22**, 417–430 (2000)
5. Faas, F.G.A., van Vliet, L.J.: 3D-orientation space; filters and sampling. In: Proceedings of the 13th Scandinavian Conference on Image Analysis, pp. 36–42 (2003)
6. van Ginkel, M.: Image analysis using orientation space based on steerable filters. Ph.D. thesis, Delft University of Technology, Delft, The Netherlands (2002)
7. van Ginkel, M., van Vliet, L.J., Verbeek, P.W.: Applications of image analysis in orientation space. In: Fourth Quinquennial Review 1996–2001 Dutch Society for Pattern Recognition and Image Processing, pp. 355–370 (2001)
8. Goris, B., et al.: Electron tomography based on a total variation minimization reconstruction technique. Ultramicroscopy **113**, 120–130 (2012)
9. Guo, Y., Rieger, B.: No-reference weighting factor selection for bimodal tomography. In: IEEE International Conference on Acoustics, Speech and Signal Processing, Calgary, Canada (2018)
10. Holt, K.M.: Total nuclear variation and Jacobian extensions of total variation for vector fields. IEEE Trans. Image Process. **23**, 3975–3989 (2014)
11. Liang, H., Weller, D.S.: Regularization parameter trimming for iterative image reconstruction. In: 49th Asilomar Conference on Signals, Systems and Computers, pp. 755–759 (2015)
12. Midgley, P.A., Weyland, M.: 3D electron microscopy in the physical sciences: the development of Z-contrast and EFTEM tomography. Ultramicroscopy **96**, 413–431 (2003)
13. Okariz, A., Guraya, T., Iturrondobeitia, M., Ibarretxe, J.: A methodology for finding the optimal iteration number of the SIRT algorithm for quantitative electron tomography. Ultramicroscopy **173**, 36–46 (2017)
14. Press, W.H., et al.: Numerical Recipes: The Art of Scientific Computing, 3rd edn. Cambridge University Press, Cambridge (2007)
15. Rigie, D.S., Riviére, P.J.L.: Joint reconstruction of multi-channel, spectral CT data via constrained total nuclear variation minimization. Phys. Med. Biol. **60**, 1741–1771 (2015)
16. Sanders, T., Gelb, A., Platte, R.B., Arslan, I., Landskron, K.: Recovering fine details from under-resolved electron tomography data using higher order total variation l_1 regularization. Ultramicroscopy **174**, 97–105 (2017)
17. Sanders, T., Platte, R.B.: Multiscale higher order TV operators for l_1 regularization. Adv. Struct. Chem. Imaging **4**, 12–29 (2018)
18. Scott, M.C., et al.: Electron tomography at 2.4-ångström resolution. Nature **483**, 444–447 (2012)
19. Slater, T.J.A., et al.: STEM-EDX tomography of bimetallic nanoparticles: a methodological investigation. Ultramicroscopy **162**, 61–73 (2016)
20. Zhong, Z., Goris, B., Schoenmakers, R., Bals, S., Batenburg, K.J.: A bimodal tomographic reconstruction technique combining EDS-STEM and HAADF-STEM. Ultramicroscopy **174**, 35–45 (2017)

21. Zhong, Z., Palenstijn, W.J., Adler, J., Batenburg, K.J.: EDS tomographic reconstruction regularized by total nuclear variation joined with HAADF-STEM tomography. Ultramicroscopy **191**, 34–43 (2018)
22. Zhu, X., Milanfar, P.: Automatic parameter selection for denoising algorithms using a no-reference measure of image content. IEEE Trans. Image Process. **19**, 3116–3132 (2010)

Can SPHARM-Based Features from Automated or Manually Segmented Hippocampi Distinguish Between MCI and TLE?

Michael Liedlgruber[1], Kevin Butz[2,3], Yvonne Höller[2], Georgi Kuchukhidze[2],
Alexandra Taylor[2], Aljoscha Thomschevski[2,3], Ottavio Tomasi[4],
Eugen Trinka[2,3], and Andreas Uhl[1(✉)]

[1] Department of Computer Sciences, University of Salzburg, Salzburg, Austria
uhl@cosy.sbg.ac.at
[2] Department of Neurology,
Christian Doppler Medical Centre and Centre for Cognitive Neuroscience,
Paracelsus Medical University, Salzburg, Austria
[3] Spinal Cord Injury and Tissue Regeneration Center Salzburg, Salzburg, Austria
[4] Department of Neurosurgery, Paracelsus Medical University, Salzburg, Austria

Abstract. Spherical Harmonics (SPHARM), when computed from hippocampus segmentations, have been shown to be useful features for discriminating patients with mild cognitive impairment (MCI) from healthy controls. In this paper we use this approach to discriminate patients with temporal lobe epilepsy (TLE) from healthy controls and for the first time, we aim to discriminate TLE patients from MCI ones. When doing so, we assess the impact of (i) using three different automated hippocampus segmentation techniques and (ii) three human raters with different qualification providing manual segmentation labels. We find that (only a fusion of) the considered automated segmentation tools deliver segmentation data which can finally be used to discriminate TLE from MCI, but for discriminating TLE from healthy controls automated techniques do not help. Further, the qualification of human segmenters has a decisive impact on the outcome of subsequent SPHARM-based classification, especially for distinguishing TLE from healthy controls (which is obviously the more difficult task).

Keywords: TLE · MCI · Spherical Harmonics ·
Hippocampus segmentation

1 Introduction

Mild cognitive impairment (MCI) is a condition of cognitive deterioration that is difficult to classify as normal aging or as a prodromal stage to dementia. Neuropsychological tests alone are highly valuable but not sufficient to determine MCI or early stages thereof, since they are not sensitive enough for patients with subjective complaints and no significant and clinically detectable deficits [33].

© Springer Nature Switzerland AG 2019
M. Felsberg et al. (Eds.): SCIA 2019, LNCS 11482, pp. 465–476, 2019.
https://doi.org/10.1007/978-3-030-20205-7_38

Further, the diagnosis of temporal lobe epilepsy (TLE) was, and still currently is, based on clinical assessment and electro-encephalographic (EEG) examination, which is sometimes inconclusive [31].

However, both diseases, i.e., MCI as well as TLE, need to be treated and handled adequately, in order to prevent massive memory decline or risks due to seizures [7]. MCI and TLE occur also as a co-morbid disease, when patients with MCI encounter seizures; moreover, the presentation of cognitive disorders in the elderly warrants a differential diagnosis of MCI or TLE, since seizures can mimic confusional episodes of MCI or Alzheimer's Disease without visible seizure activity with scalp electroencephalography [23]. Treating these seizures can restore cognitive functioning of these patients. However, diagnostics based on invasive electroencephalography bear significant risk and costs.

From a structural point of view, the hippocampus is an area of the brain that links MCI and TLE as it has been found that both diseases affect the hippocampal structure in some way [14]. It is therefore worth evaluating techniques for the diagnosis of these conditions that are based on distinctive features of this brain structure. Segmentation of the hippocampi is, of course, a prerequisite for such approaches. The hippocampus is atrophic in mild cognitive impairment and dementia [11], and it is sclerotic in specific subtypes of epilepsy [28], specifically in TLE. Thus volumetry alone is not sufficient for a discrimination which calls for shape-based features to be investigated.

For structural characterisation, the amount of time it takes an expert to segment the hippocampus is a significant obstacle. In a high-resolution magnetic resonance image, a specialist has to trace the contour of the formation in each slice and review the result in several dimensions. Even after a certain training, this might still take about up to one hour per hippocampus - i.e. two hours per patient. This motivates the use of automated segmentation techniques. A large variety of techniques and algorithms for automated hippocampus segmentation have been published over the last years, some of them targeted to specific disease or deformation classes (see e.g. [2,10,17,20,29,30,34,35,39,40]). The classical state-of-the-art algorithms for automated hippocampus segmentation [5,24] are based on multi-atlas segmentation (MAS [15]), with recent upcoming deep learning-based techniques (e.g. [36] – see also [1] for a review on deep learning-based brain MRI segmentation techniques).

Interestingly, in a recent large-scale study on algorithms for computer-aided diagnosis of dementia based on structural MRI [4], 6 out of 15 considered techniques (including the best performing algorithms) still relied on FreeSurfer segmentations (see Sect. 3) which is the majority of algorithms based on segmentation in this comparison. This massive employment of FreeSurfer in large-scale studies, although not any more being considered as state-of-the-art, underpins the need for publicly available and easy-to-use segmentation tools. This also holds true for the upcoming deep learning-based tools. Recent work [26] also demonstrates that employing publicly available and cost free segmentation tools were not able to reproduce MCI vs. control group classification results relying on a custom (private) hippocampus segmentation tool [13].

In this paper, we closely follow a shape-based approach originally used to distinguish hippocampi affected by MCI from those of a healthy control group by employing spherical harmonics coefficients (SPHARM) as potentially discriminating features [13,26,32]. However, as major original contribution, we investigate if this approach is suited to differentiate hippocampi affected by TLE from (i) those affected by MCI (which has never been investigated at all with any technique) and from (ii) those of a healthy control group, respectively (which has been done relying on manual segmentations only [9,18,19,21]). In this context, we investigate the impact of using different hippocampus segmentation approaches: Three cost-free and pre-compiled out-of-the-box hippocampus segmentation software packages as well as three segmentations independently conducted by human raters with different qualifications (the availability of which can be considered an extremely rare asset). This work discriminates itself from our earlier work [27] by not relying on the two hippocampi separately, thus not looking into lateralisation effects, leading to larger datasets and thus increased statistical result significance.

Section 2 briefly explains how we obtain SPHARM coefficients used to compose feature vectors subject to subsequent classification. In Sect. 3, we first explain the experimental setup in detail, specifically including the hippocampus segmentation variants and SPHARM coefficient selection strategy employed. Subsequently, classification results are shown and described. Section 4 concludes the paper by discussing the observed results.

2 Spherical Harmonics Descriptors in Structural MCI Characterisation

The features used for classification are based on Spherical Harmonics (SPHARM). These are a series of functions which are used to represent functions defined on the surface of a sphere. Once a 3D object has been mapped onto a unit sphere, it is also possible to describe that object in terms of coefficients for the basis function of SPHARM. In other words, the SPHARM coefficients can be used a shape descriptors. In this work we follow the approach described in [3] in order to obtain coefficients for the hippocampi voxel volumes.

Once a voxel volume for a hippocampus has been obtained, either by automatic or manual segmentation, we first fix the topology of the voxel objects. This is necessary since, in order to map a 3D object to a sphere, the respective voxel object must exhibit a spherical topology. Moreover, the voxel dimensions are adjusted to obtain isotropic voxel. Since the voxel volumes resulting from MRI scans yield voxels with a size depending on the scan parameters (i.e. often non-isotropic), we resample the data such that we end up with voxel cubes each having a side length of 1 mm. Sometimes the segmented data consists of one large, and two or more disconnected smaller voxel compounds, respectively. In such a case we determine all voxel compounds and remove all but the largest one. This step removes small spurious voxel masses which occur quite frequently especially in manual segmentation and hinder a mapping of the voxel object to a sphere.

Based on the resampled and fixed voxel volumes, we generate 3D objects. While other implementations create objects based on triangular faces, we decided to use quadriliterals since these more naturally correspond to voxels (see Fig. 1(a)). The 3D objects are then mapped onto a unit sphere during the initial parameterisation, which is followed by a constrained optimisation (described in more detail in [3]). The optimised parameterisation is then used to compute the SPHARM coefficients (see Fig. 1(b) and (c)).

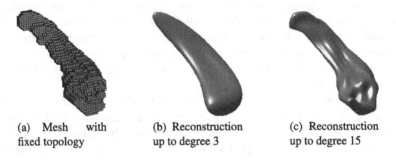

(a) Mesh with fixed topology

(b) Reconstruction up to degree 3

(c) Reconstruction up to degree 15

Fig. 1. Basic principle visualised.

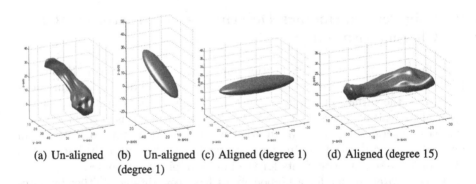

(a) Un-aligned

(b) Un-aligned (degree 1)

(c) Aligned (degree 1)

(d) Aligned (degree 15)

Fig. 2. The process of re-aligning the hippocampus. (a) original orientation (SPHARM reconstruction up to degree 15), (b) the same reconstruction but only to degree 1, (c) same as (b) but re-aligned to axes, and (d) the final object, same as (a) but re-aligned to axes.

We are mainly interested in shape differences and thus we want to ignore orientation differences which are found e.g. in malrotated hippocampi. Instead of using e.g. rotation invariant SPHARM representations [16] we resort to a classical alignment procedure, as invariant representation sometimes suffer from a lower extent of discriminativeness. For alignment, we compute a reconstruction of the hippocampus object up to SPHARM degree 1 (based on a triangulated sphere).

This results in an ellipsoid which is aligned with the main orientation of the 3D object. Using PCA we determine the principal axes of the ellipsoid and rotate the object such that all hippocampal volumes are always in the coordinate system of the principal axes (i.e. co-aligned). After the re-alignment we recompute the SPHARM coefficients up to degree 15 for each re-aligned object and use them for the subsequent classification process. Figure 2 shows the process of re-aligning a hippocampal 3D object.

Computing SPHARM coefficients up to degree J, we obtain a total of N complex coefficients per hippocampus, where N is computed as

$$N = 3 * (J + 1)^2. \tag{1}$$

Extracting SPHARM coefficients up to degree 15 we end up with 768 coefficients per hippocampus. We have used a custom MATLAB implementation following the *SPHARM-PDM* code (https://www.nitrc.org/projects/spharm-pdm).

The final feature vectors F_i available for the feature selection process are composed of the absolute coefficient values for the left and right hippocampi:

$$F_i = (|C_{i,1}^l|, \ldots, |C_{i,N}^l|, |C_{i,1}^r|, \ldots, |C_{i,N}^r|), \tag{2}$$

where $C_{i,n}^l$ and $C_{i,n}^r$ denote the n-th coefficient for the left and right hippocampus of subject i, respectively. These feature vectors contain 1536 coefficients in total out of which subsets can be selected for actual classification.

3 Experiments

3.1 Experimental Settings

Data. In this work we use 58 T1-weighted MRI volumes, a data set that has been acquired at the Department of Neurology, Paracelsus Medical University Salzburg, including patients with mild cognitive impairment (MCI, 20 subjects), temporal lobe epilepsy (TLE, 17 subjects), and a healthy control group (CG, 21 subjects). These data are a subset of a larger study [25]. We defined patients with amnestic MCI according to level three of the global deterioration scale for aging and dementia described by [12]. Diagnosis/ground truth w.r.t. MCI and TLE was based on multimodal neurological assessment, including imaging (high resolution 3 T magnetic resonance tomography, and single photon emission computed tomography with Hexamethylpropylenaminooxim), electroencephalography, and neuropsychological testing.

Hippocampus Segmentations. Manual segmentations have been performed by 3 experienced raters (one senior neurosurgeon – Rater1 – and two junior neuroscientists supervised by a senior neuroradiologist – Rater2 & Rater3) on a Wacom Cintiq 22HD graphic tablet device (resolution 1920 × 1200) using a DTK-2200 pen and employing the 32-bit 3DSlicer software for Windows (v. 4.2.2-1 r21513) to delineate hippocampus voxels for each slice separately. The raters independently used consensus on anatomical landmarks/boarders of the hippocampus based on Henry Duvemoy's hippocampal anatomy [22]. The procedure used was to depict the hippocampal outline in the view of all planes in the following order: sagittal – coronal – axial with subsequent cross line control through all planes.

For automated hippocampus segmentation, in contrast to most of the algorithms presented in literature, e.g. [40], all three employed hippocampus segmentation software packages are already pre-compiled and available for free [25]:

$FreeSurfer(FS)$[1] is a popular set of tools which allow an automated labelling of subcortical structures in the brain [10]. Such a subcortical labelling is obtained by using the volume-based stream which consists of five stages [10]. The result is a label volume, containing labels for various different subcortical structures (e.g. hippocampus, amygdala, and cerebellum). FreeSurfer is a highly popular tool in hippocampal analysis to assess clinical hypotheses [6,17,20,35,38] or to compare to newly proposed segmentation techniques (e.g. [29,30,40]). The winning algorithm in a recent large-scale study on algorithms for computer-aided diagnosis of dementia based on structural MRI [4] was based on FS segmentation, as well as 5 other out of 15 considered techniques in this work.

$AHEAD$ (Automatic Hippocampal Estimator using Atlas-based Delineation[2]) is specifically targeted at an automated segmentation of hippocampi [34] and employs multiple atlases and statistical learning method. After an initial rigid registration step, a deformable registration is carried out using the Symmetric Normalisation algorithm. From the result of these steps, the volume is normalised to the atlas. The hippocampus segmentation from the atlas is then warped back to the input volume. Based on multiple atlases and a statistical learning method, the final segmentation is obtained.

Although $BrainParser(BP)$[3] is usually able to label various different subcortical structures, we use a version of BrainParser which is specifically tailored to hippocampus segmentation. After re-orienting the input volume to the coordinate system of the included, pre-trained atlas, skull stripping is performed. This is followed by computing an affine transform between the input volume and the reference brain volume. Then a deformable registration between the input and the reference volume is carried out. Then, according to the trained atlas, the input volume is labelled.

We also fuse the segmentation results using voxel-based majority voting (abbreviated M.V. in the results – a voxel is active in the fused volume if at least two raters or segmentation tools marked that voxel as belonging to a hippocampus) and STAPLE [37] (abbreviated as STA). Since for human raters there is hardly a difference between majority voting and STAPLE, the latter results are not shown.

---

[1] v. 51.0, available at http://surfer.nmr.mgh.harvard.edu.

[2] v. 1.0, available at http://www.nitrc.org/projects/.

[3] available at http://www.nitrc.org/projects/.

Feature Selection, Classification, and Evaluation Protocol. Features used for actual classification are selected from the feature vectors F_i according to the degree J of their coefficients. The strategy "Cumula$J$" selects all coefficients with degree $\leq J$. Thus, for example, according to Eq. 1 for $J = 5$, Cumula5 employs 108 coefficients of degrees $J = 1 \ldots 5$.

For the classification of the features we use the Support Vector Machines (SVM) classifier [8] with a linear kernel. The choice for this classifier has been made since the classifier is known to be able to cope very well with high-dimensional features. However, this classifier does not guarantee that a large feature set containing a smaller one exhibits better classification when trained with the larger feature set compared to the smaller one.

To come up with classification accuracy estimation, we apply leave-one-out-cross-validation (LOOVC) for the feature vectors.

3.2 Experimental Results

Tables 1 and 2 display the overall classification accuracy in percent for our test data set. Results are shown up to $J = 7$. Depending on the underlying segmentations, for higher values of J, classification accuracy either decreases (for the automated techniques and low quality human segmentations) or does not increase any more (for high quality human segmentations).

The first impression of the results to discriminate TLE from CG (Table 1) is that there are no bold numbers in the left half of the table, i.e. the employment of automated segmentation tools does not lead to any decent classification results using the considered SPHARM approach and most results are hardly superior to random guessing.

Table 1. Classification results: temporal lobe epilepsy (TLE) vs. healthy control group (CG) (overall accuracy $\geq 75\%$ in bold).

	Automated segmentation					Human segmentation			
	STA	M.V	AHEAD	BP	FS	M.V	Rater1	Rater2	Rater3
Cumula1	55.6	55.3	67.5	56.4	56.4	53.9	66.7	43.6	51.3
Cumula2	50.0	31.6	47.5	56.4	43.6	59.0	**79.5**	66.7	64.1
Cumula3	50.0	52.6	52.5	46.2	38.5	64.1	**76.9**	61.5	66.7
Cumula4	47.2	36.8	62.5	66.7	41.0	66.7	**79.5**	46.2	51.3
Cumula5	50.0	42.1	42.5	64.1	48.7	64.1	**79.5**	64.1	53.9
Cumula6	61.1	60.5	42.5	69.2	43.6	74.4	**79.5**	43.6	**76.9**
Cumula7	47.2	57.9	47.5	71.8	43.6	69.2	**82.1**	53.9	74.4

Looking at the results of applying individual automated segmentation tools, BP is clearly the best technique with increasing classification rates for increasing J (which indicates that also coefficients representing finer detail are still useful), while FS and AHEAD based results are on a comparable level and worse than BP. Applying Majority Voting (M.V.) or STAPLE (STA) to the individual segmentations does not really help, indicating that these are too different to benefit from fusion strategies.

The situation is different for the results when basing SPHARM classification on human rater segmentations. There is a clear trend that Rater1, being the most qualified human rater, provides segmentations that lead to sensible classification results (increasing up to 82% for $J = 7$). Rater3 achieves some useful results as well, but lower ($\leq 77\%$) and for $J = 6, 7$ only, while Rater2 stays below 67%. Overall, the differences among the human raters in terms of achieved classification accuracy are considerable and applying fusion techniques does not lead to useful results (i.e. better than Rater2 and Rater3 in most settings, but clearly inferior to the Rater1 results).

Table 2. Classification results: temporal lobe epilepsy (TLE) vs. mild cognitive impairment (MCI) (overall accuracy $\geq 75\%$ in bold).

	Automated segmentation					Human segmentation			
	STA	M.V	AHEAD	BP	FS	M.V	Rater1	Rater2	Rater3
Cumula1	**80.6**	**84.2**	73.7	57.9	52.6	**75.7**	56.8	70.3	62.2
Cumula2	**75.0**	71.1	68.4	63.2	65.8	67.6	**81.1**	70.3	**81.1**
Cumula3	**75.0**	60.5	71.1	42.1	60.5	56.8	**81.1**	**81.1**	73.0
Cumula4	72.2	**79.0**	65.8	50.0	60.5	59.5	**83.8**	70.3	67.6
Cumula5	63.9	57.9	73.7	47.4	65.8	62.2	**81.1**	**75.7**	62.2
Cumula6	55.6	68.4	68.4	42.1	65.8	62.2	**86.5**	**81.1**	62.2
Cumula7	52.8	65.8	71.1	44.7	63.2	56.8	**83.8**	**78.4**	70.3

Considering the results to discriminate TLE affected hippocampi from those affected by MCI (see Table 2), we see a different picture. Automated segmentation tools at least deliver useful segmentations for classification when fusion techniques are applied (for small values of J only, again indicating that only coarser details contribute useful information for classification). Also the relation among the individual tools is different, with the clear ranking as AHEAD best, followed by FS, and BP worst (note that this is almost inverse to the classification task before).

Concerning manual segmentations, we notice a somewhat similar behaviour as before. Again, Rater1 (with the highest qualification) is the best, while for this classification task, segmentations of Rater2 also lead to quite decent classification results for higher values of J. Except for $J = 2$, Rater3 segmentations are the worst. Again, fusion of human segmentation results does not reach the classification results of the individual segmentations, except for $J = 1$ (but on a moderate level).

4 Discussion and Conclusion

The obtained results indicate that discriminating TLE patients from healthy controls is far more difficult that discriminating TLE patients from MCI patients. In the former case, only human segmentation (and only that provided by the most qualified human rater) leads to SPHARM coefficients that can be used to discriminate the two classes with reasonable accuracy. In this case, contrasting to the case of discriminating MCI affected patients from healthy controls [26], also applying fusion among the human segmentations does not work properly (obviously the segmentations are too different to benefit from fusion [25]). For discriminating TLE patients from healthy controls, the considered automated segmentation tools do not lead to sensible classification results under the employed SPHARM-methodology, neither applied individually, nor under fusion techniques (which might also explain the non-existence of corresponding publications).

The situation is different for the second case (i.e. discriminating TLE patients from MCI patients). While employing individual automated tools does not work, fusing the corresponding segmentations and using the lower order SPHARM coefficient for classification is successful. Obviously, the shape difference is so fundamental, that it is reflected in the coarse grain SPHARM details of the automated tools segmentations' in some complementary manner. The best qualified human rater's segmentations again lead to best classification results, but also the two other human raters achieve useful accuracy for some settings. Thus, the fundamental differences are also grasped by the less qualified human raters segmentations. As in the first case, human segmentations seem to be too different to provide useful results under fusion (see also [25] for corresponding segmentation result analysis confirming this assumption).

Acknowledgments. This work has been partially funded by the Austrian Science Fund (FWF) under Project No. KLI12-B00.

References

1. Akkus, Z., Galimzianova, A., Hoogi, A., Rubin, D., Erickson, B.: Deep learning for brain MRI segmentation: state of the art and future directions. J. Digit. Imaging **30**(4), 449–459 (2017)
2. Babakchanian, S., Chew, N., Green, A., et al.: Automated and manual hippocampal segmentation techniques: a comparison of results and reproducibility. Neorology **80**, P06.053 (2013)
3. Brechühler, C., Gerig, G., Kübler, O.: Parametrization of closed surfaces for 3-D shape description. Comput. Vis. Image Underst. **61**(2), 154–170 (1995)
4. Bron, E., et al.: Standardized evaluation of algorithms for computer-aided diagnosis of dementia based on structural MRI: the CADDementia challenge. NeuroImage **111**, 562–579 (2015)

5. Cardoso, J., Leung, K., et al.: STEPS: similarity and truth estimation for propagated segmentations and its application to hippocampal segmentation and brain parcelation. Med. Image Anal. **17**(6), 671–684 (2013)

6. Cherbuin, N., Anstey, K.J., Réglade-Meslin, C., Sachdev, P.S.: In vivo hippocampal measurement and memory: a comparison of manual tracing and automated segmentation in a large community-based sample. PLoS ONE **4**, 1–10 (2009)

7. Dodrill, C.: Neuropsychological effects of seizures. Epilepsy Behav. **5**(Suppl. 1), 22–24 (2004)

8. Duda, R.O., Hart, P.E., Stork, D.G.: Pattern Classification, 2nd edn. Wiley, Hoboken (2000)

9. Esmaeilzadeh, M., Soltanian-Zadeh, H., Jafari-Khouzani, K.: Mesial temporal lobe epilepsy lateralization using SPHARM-based features of hippocampus and SVM. In: Proceedings of Medical Image 2012, SPIE Proceedings, vol. 8314 (2012)

10. Fischl, B., et al.: Automatically parcellating the human cerebral cortex. Cereb. Cortex **14**(1), 11–22 (2004)

11. Fotuhi, M., Do, D., Jack, C.: Modifiable factors that alter the size of the hippocampus with ageing. Nat. Rev. Neurol. **8**, 189–202 (2012)

12. Gauthier, S., et al.: Mild cognitive impairment. Lancet **367**(9518), 1262–1270 (2006)

13. Geradin, E., Chetelat, G., et al.: Multidimensional classification of hippocampal shape features discriminates Alzheimer's disease and mild cognitive impairment from normal aging. Neuroimage **47**(4), 1476–1486 (2009)

14. Höller, Y., Trinka, E.: What do temporal lobe epilepsy and progressive mild cognitive impairment have in common? Front. Syst. Neurosci. **8**, 58 (2014)

15. Iglesias, J., Sabancu, M.: Multi-atlas segmentation of biomedical images: a survey. Med. Image Anal. **24**, 205–219 (2015)

16. Kazhdan, M., Funkhouser, T., Rusinkiewicz, S.: Rotation invariant spherical harmonic representation of 3D shape descriptors. In: Eurographics/ACM SIGGRAPH Symposium on Geometry Processing, pp. 156–164, June 2003

17. Kim, H., Chupin, M., Colliot, O., et al.: Automatic hippocampal segmentation in temporal lobe epilepsy: impact of developmental abnormalities. Neoroimage **59**, 3178–3186 (2012)

18. Kim, H., Bernhardt, B.C., Kulaga-Yoskovitz, J., Caldairou, B., Bernasconi, A., Bernasconi, N.: Multivariate hippocampal subfield analysis of local MRI intensity and volume: application to temporal lobe epilepsy. In: Golland, P., Hata, N., Barillot, C., Hornegger, J., Howe, R. (eds.) MICCAI 2014. LNCS, vol. 8674, pp. 170–178. Springer, Cham (2014). https://doi.org/10.1007/978-3-319-10470-6_22

19. Kim, H., Mansi, T., Bernasconi, N.: Disentangling hippocampal shape anomalies in epilepsy. Front. Neurol. **4**, 131 (2013)

20. Kim, J., Choi, D., et al.: Evaluation of hippocampal volume based on various inversion time in normal adults by manual tracing and automated segmentation methods. Investig. Magn. Reson. Imaging **19**(2), 67–75 (2015)

21. Kohan, Z., Azami, R.: Hippocampus shape analysis for temporal lobe epilepsy detection in magnetic resonance imaging. In: Proceedings of Medical Image 2016, SPIE Proceedings, vol. 9788, p. 97882T (2016)

22. Kuzniecky, R., Jackson, G.: Magnetic Resonance in Epilepsy. Raven Press, New York (1995)

23. Lam, A.D., Deck, G., et al.: Silent hippocampal seizures and spikes identified by foramen ovale electrodes in Alzheimer's disease. Nat. Med. **23**(6), 678–680 (2017)

24. Leung, K., Barnes, J., et al.: Automated cross-sectional and longitudinal hippocampal volume measurement in mild cognitive impairment and Alzheimer's disease. NeuroImage **51**(4), 1345–1359 (2013)

25. Liedlgruber, M., et al.: Pathology-related automated hippocampus segmentation accuracy. In: Maier-Hein, F.K., Deserno, L.T., Handels, H., Tolxdorff, T. (eds.) Bildverarbeitung für die Medizin 2017. I, pp. 128–133. Springer, Heidelberg (2017). https://doi.org/10.1007/978-3-662-54345-0_31

26. Uhl, A., et al.: Hippocampus segmentation and SPHARM coefficient selection are decisive for MCI detection. In: Maier, A., Deserno, L.T., Handels, H., Maier-Hein, F.K., Palm, C., Tolxdorff, T. (eds.) Bildverarbeitung für die Medizin 2018. I, pp. 239–244. Springer, Heidelberg (2018). https://doi.org/10.1007/978-3-662-56537-7_65

27. Liedlgruber, M., et al.: Lateralisation matters: discrimination of TLE and MCI based on SPHARM description of hippocampal shape. In: Proceedings of the 31st IEEE International Symposium on Computer-Based Medical Systems (CBMS 2018), pp. 129–134, June 2018

28. Malmgren, K., Thom, M.: Hippocampal sclerosis - origins and imaging. Epilepsia **53**, 19–33 (2012)

29. Morey, R., Petty, C., et al.: A comparison of automated segmentation and manual tracing for quantifying hippocampal and amygdala volumes. Neoroimage **45**(3), 855–866 (2009)

30. Pardoe, H., Pell, G., Abbott, D., Jackson, G.: Hippocampal volume assessment in temporal lobe epilepsy: how good is automated segmentation? Epilepsia **50**(12), 2586–2592 (2009)

31. Renzel, R., Baumann, C., Poryazova, R.: EEG after sleep deprivation is a sensitive tool in the first diagnosis of idiopathic generalized but not focal epilepsy. Clin. Neurophysiol. **127**(1), 38 (2016)

32. Shen, L., Saykin, A.J., Chung, M.K., Huang, H.: Morphometric analysis of hippocampal shape in mild cognitive impairment: An imaging genetics study. In: Proceedings of the 7th IEEE International Conference on Bioinformatics and Bioengineering (2007)

33. Stewart, R.: Mild cognitive impairment-the continuing challenge of its "real-world" detection and diagnosis. Arch. Med. Res. **43**, 609–14 (2012)

34. Suh, J.W., Wang, H., Das, S., Avants, B., Yushkevich, P.A.: Automatic segmentation of the hippocampus in T1-weighted MRI with multi-atlas label fusion using open source software: evaluation in 1.5 and 3.0T ADNI MRI. In: Proceedings of the International Society for Magnetic Resonance in Medicine Conference (ISMRM 2011) (2011)

35. Tae, W.S., Kim, S.S., Lee, K.U., Nam, E.C., Kim, K.W.: Validation of hippocampal volumes measured using a manual method and two automated methods (FreeSurfer and IBASPM) in chronic major depressive disorder. Neuroradiology **50**, 569–581 (2009)

36. Thyreau, B., Sato, K., Fukuda, H., Taki, Y.: Segmentation of the hippocampus by transferring algorithmic knowledge for large cohort processing. Med. Image Anal. **43**, 214–228 (2018)

37. Warfield, S., Zou, K., Wells, W.: Simulataneous truth and performance level estimation (STAPLE): an algortihm for the validation of image segmentation. IEEE Trans. Med. Imaging **23**(7), 903–921 (2004)

38. Wenger, E., Martensson, J., Hoack, H., et al.: Comparing manual and automatic segmentation of hippocampal volumes: reliability and validity issues in younger and older brains. Epilepsia **35**(8), 4236–4248 (2014)
39. Winston, G., Cardoso, M., et al.: Automated hippocampal segmentation in patients with epilepsy: available free online. Epilepsia **54**(12), 2166–2173 (2013)
40. Zarpalas, D., Gkontra, P., Daras, P., Maglaveras, N.: Accurate and fully automatic hippocampus segmentation using subject-specific 3D optimal local maps into a hybrid active contour model. IEEE J. Transl. Eng. Health Med. **2**, 1–16 (2014)

Color Normalization of Blood Cell Images

Emmy Sjöstrand, Jesper Jönsson[(✉)], Adam Morell, and Kent Stråhlén

CellaVision AB, Mobilvägen 12, 223 62 Lund, Sweden
jejo@cellavision.se
http://www.cellavision.com

Abstract. Traditional microscopes have been used a long time in hematology for blood analysis, but during the last decade many laboratories have started to replace them with digital microscope systems. The appearance of blood cells in the digital images is very important to the end user, ideally they should be identical to how they would look in a traditional microscope. There are several digital microscope systems on the market today with various optics and illumination, which means that images from different systems do not look the same. This is a cumbersome problem in many ways. For example this means cell classification networks need to be trained for every single system. In this paper we investigate the possibility of using deep learning to transform images between digital systems. The main focus is on a cyclic network setup where it is possible to transform the images between two systems. We present two different networks, a cyclic network with a perceptual loss based on the VGG-16 network and a conditional version of a cyclic generative adversarial network (GAN). With these networks we obtain very good results that are better than previous methods for transforming blood cell images.

Keywords: Deep learning · GAN · Color normalization ·
Blood cell images

1 Introduction

Modern health care is rapidly changing due to advances in artificial intelligence, and hematology is no exception. Blood analysis is a common tool when screening for different diseases and confirming diagnoses. The conventional way to analyze blood is to run it through a so called cell counter and based on the results, if needed, perform an in-depth analysis of the sample using a traditional microscope. This is time consuming and requires a large number of highly trained laboratory technicians. A more efficient way to analyze blood is to use a digital microscope system. For the end user it is very important that digital images of blood cells look like they would have in a traditional microscope. Digital images that have not been processed in any way are called raw images, and depending

Supported by CellaVision AB.

on which system the image was captured with they can look quite different. Two digital systems from CellaVision are used in this paper, the DM1200 from their third generation of systems and the DM96 from their second generation of systems. One of the major differences between them is the optics and the illumination. The DM1200 has an LED lamp and the DM96 has a halogen lamp. From now on the DM1200 will be called system X and the DM96 will be called system Y. Figure 1 shows a raw image from system X and a raw image from system Y.

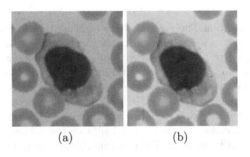

(a)   (b)

Fig. 1. Raw images from (a) system X and (b) system Y.

A raw image is not very similar to a microscope image. The process that makes the raw image resemble the microscope image is called normalization. In Fig. 2 a comparison between a raw image and a normalized image is shown. The normalization algorithm first finds a representative background color and uses an affine transform on the entire image to set this background to a predefined value. The dynamic of the image is also changed, for example by increasing sharpness and contrast in the image, especially in the nucleus of the cell, where also some hue adjustments are made. Using this kind of normalization algorithm it is clear that images from different systems cannot be normalized the same way because we want the result to look the same. One solution is to tweak the normalization algorithms so that each system has its own normalization process. It is however very hard to obtain results that are similar enough. Today an algorithm called Hedlund-Morell normalization (below called HM normalization) is used. The main idea of HM normalization is to segment the image and apply different transformations to different parts, see [4]. This works fairly well, but the result is not entirely satisfactory. One problem with the HM normalization is that it does not perform very well on certain cell types, especially those with red colors. A better solution would be to transform images from one system to look like they were captured with another system. Then it would be possible to use the same normalization algorithm for all systems. Unfortunately the transformation is not very simple and a global transformation does not work. The main reason for the complexity of the problem is the different illumination in the systems. An LED and a halogen lamp have different spectral characteristics which can lead to metameric failure [5]. Experts are often used to working with halogen images and think they look better than LED images.

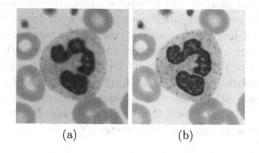

(a)   (b)

Fig. 2. (a) Raw image. (b) Normalized image.

Digital systems often come with analyzing software that uses artificial intelligence to perform different types of analyses. A differential count of white blood cells (WBCs) is a common analysis. A differential count means counting a predefined number of cells, classifying them into their cell type and the result is the proportions of each cell type. One way to do the classification of the WBCs is to use a neural network. Since training neural networks is time consuming and requires large sets of data labeled by experts it is desirable to be able to use the same network for images from several systems.

The aim of this paper is to develop a transformation, a color normalization, between system X and system Y. This should not be confused with the normalization process that makes a raw image look like it would in a microscope. Our color transformation will be a neural network. The goal is that transformed images from system X should be visually indistinguishable from images that were captured with system Y. A secondary goal is that a cell classification network should classify the transformed cell images the same way as their original counterpart, thus eliminating the need to retrain the classification network. This paper is based on a Master's thesis [13].

2   Generative Adversarial Networks (GANs)

In 2014 Goodfellow et al. presented their article "Generative Adversarial Nets" [2] where they introduce a framework consisting of two networks. One of the networks is called the discriminator and is used to define a loss function. The other network is called the generator and this is the network that produces the results. During training the two networks will compete against each other, hence the name "adversarial nets". This paper deals with image transformation so from now on it is assumed that the generator outputs an image. Given a set of images the generator's task is to produce images resembling these images. The discriminator's task is to decide if an image is from the real set of images or if it is a generated image. The discriminator is shown labeled examples of the real images as well as images from the generator in order to learn the difference. Then the generator tries to fool the discriminator by generating images which are similar to the real images. The generator's loss function is defined using the discriminator, if the generated image is assigned a high probability of being real then the generator's loss is low and vice versa. The two networks are trained alternately, competing against each other, forcing both networks to become better and better. Figure 3 illustrates the GAN framework, the generator is called G and the discriminator is called D. A simple application of a GAN would be to use the well known MNIST dataset to generate images of handwritten digits. For the case with blood cell images we want the generator to produce images that looks like they were captured with system Y.

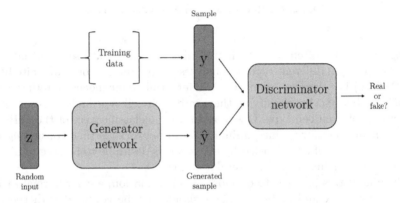

Fig. 3. Illustration of the GAN framework. It consists of two networks, the generator and the discriminator. The input to the generator is a sample from some noise prior. The output of the generator is passed along to the discriminator. The discriminator is trained to separate fake samples from real samples and the generator is trained to fool the discriminator.

For GANs the loss functions of the networks will not only depend on its own parameters. Let x_i and y_i be samples from system X and Y respectively. The discriminator will try to minimize

$$\mathcal{L}_{disc} = -\frac{1}{2N} \sum_i^N \log\left(D(y_i)\right) - \frac{1}{2N} \sum_i^N \log\left(1 - D(G(x_i))\right), \qquad (1)$$

but can only do so by manipulating its own weights, not the generator's weights. Similarly, the generator will try to minimize

$$\mathcal{L}_{gen} = -\frac{1}{N} \sum_i^N \log\left(D(G(x_i))\right), \qquad (2)$$

but can only do so by manipulating its own weights. This means training the networks will be more like a game than a traditional optimization problem. The solution will be a Nash equilibrium which is a local minimum of $\mathcal{L}_{disc}$ with respect to the weights of the discriminator and a local minimum of $\mathcal{L}_{gen}$ with respect to the weights of the generator [3].

The original GAN gives no control over what type of image is being generated, it just generates an image that looks like it came from the real set of images. In our case we want to transform the content of an image from system X so that it looks like it was captured with system Y, but the generator would just generate an image that looks like it came from system Y with no regards of the content. To be able to condition the generator on some information Mirza et al. created the conditional GAN in 2014 [9]. In the MNIST case this additional information could simply be what digit the generator should produce. In the case of cell images the generator is conditioned on the image from system X. The generator is not allowed to change the shape or structure of the cell in the image, so we do not send any noise which gives us a deterministic transformation from system X to system Y.

3 Cyclic GANs

A cyclic version of the GAN called cycleGAN is original work by Zhu et al. [15]. In 2017 they proposed a new type of framework which goal was to transform images between two different domains, without the need of paired data. Figure 4 illustrates the framework. It consists of two generators, G and F, and two discriminators, D_x and D_y. Generator G is a mapping from domain X to Y and generator F is a mapping from domain Y to X. Discriminator D_x is trained to separate true images from domain X from fake ones i.e. images transformed by generator F from domain Y. D_y is trained in a similar fashion but on images in domain Y. By sending an image through both generators it is possible to explore a loss based on the difference of the input and the output of the full cycle. Figure 5 illustrates the idea. The networks are trained to minimize this loss, called $\mathcal{L}_{cycle}$ defined in (3). This loss combined with the discriminators is the backbone of this framework. The authors do however experiment with using this loss in combination with another loss function, called $\mathcal{L}_{identity}$. It is defined as (4) and ensures the generators manage to perform identity mappings. If G is given an image from domain Y it should preferably output the same image that was given as input. Same argument with generator F if given input from domain X. By introducing this loss they could improve the colors of the transformed images.

$$\mathcal{L}_{cycle} = \|y - G(F(y))\|_1 + \|x - F(G(x))\|_1 \qquad (3)$$

$$\mathcal{L}_{identity} = \|y - G(y)\|_1 + \|x - F(x)\|_1 \qquad (4)$$

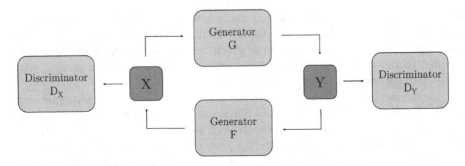

Fig. 4. Overview of the cycleGAN framework.

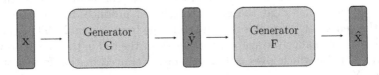

Fig. 5. Image describing the idea of a forward cycle loss. A sample from domain X is sent through both generators and is then evaluated how much in l^1-norm it differs from the input.

4   Perceptual Losses

Imagine an image where every other column is black and the other columns are white, like a zebra pattern. Suppose this is the target image for the generator. If the generator would produce an image that has the same zebra pattern as the target image, but shifted one column, then it has clearly captured the content of the image. Assuming the application is not very sensitive to shifts then this is a very good result, and the loss function should reflect that. In this case loss functions like the l^1-loss, which is the l^1-norm of the difference of the images, are bad choices since they do not capture perceptual differences between images. The l^1-loss between the target image and the generated image would be the highest possible value, despite the fact that the generator actually has captured the stylistic features of the image.

A perceptual loss function can be defined by using a pre-trained classification network. These kinds of losses have been used in many different applications, for example removing visual signs of rain and snow [14], generating an image with higher resolution than the original image [8] and to combine the content of one image with the style of another [7]. All of these applications have a loss function that uses the output from an intermediate layer of a pre-trained classification network. It is a type of loss function which has proven to give high quality images. Figure 6 shows an illustration of this loss with the VGG network [12] as the pre-trained network. The idea is to send the generated image as well as the target image through the classification network and compare higher level features. Some intermediate layer ϕ_j is chosen as the output layer. This drives the generator towards producing images with similar feature representation as the target images [14]. One way to define the actual loss is to take some norm of the difference between the feature representations. In [7] they make use of the Gram matrix to define a perceptual loss that captures stylistic features of the image.

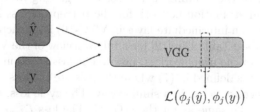

Fig. 6. Illustration of the idea of having a perceptual loss function based on a pre-trained network, in this case VGG.

5   Methodology

5.1   Pre-processing of Data

Data was augmented by rotating some of the images $90°$, $180°$ and $270°$. The rotated images look exactly like real data since there is no specific way a cell is positioned on a slide. Our data consists of 9810 cells that were captured with both system X and system Y and then paired and cropped in order to match as closely as possible pixel-wise. The number of each cell type in our data is approximately the same. The data was split into a training set (80%), a validation set (10%) and a test set (10%).

5.2   Conditional CycleGAN (ccGAN)

We have tried a conditional version of the cycleGAN which we call ccGAN (short for conditional cycleGAN). The difference from the original cycleGAN is that we define a loss function (5) that uses paired data. The complete loss function (6) for one generator in ccGAN consists of a loss coming from the discriminator (2), the cycle loss (3), the identity loss (4) and the paired loss (5), where the λ_i's are the weights of the loss functions. In our training we used $\lambda_1 = 1$ and $\lambda_i = 10$ for $i = 2, 3, 4$. The choice of λ's was based on experiments where we got better results when focusing less on the loss coming from the discriminator.

$$\mathcal{L}_{paired}(x_p, y_p) = \|y_p - G(x_p)\|_1 + \|x_p - F(y_p)\|_1 \qquad (5)$$

$$\mathcal{L}_{tot} = \lambda_1 \mathcal{L}_{gen} + \lambda_2 \mathcal{L}_{cycle} + \lambda_3 \mathcal{L}_{identity} + \lambda_4 \mathcal{L}_{paired} \qquad (6)$$

5.3   Perceptual Cycle Network (pcNet)

We have defined a new framework called a perceptual cycle network (pcNet) and
it is based on the cyclic idea from the cycleGAN and a perceptual loss based
on the VGG network. We only keep the cyclic part from the cycleGAN, i.e. two
generators but no discriminators. The pre-trained VGG-16 network is also used,
but it is not part of the training in the sense of getting its weights updated,
it only serves as an evaluation network for the perceptual loss function. In this
implementation ϕ_j (an intermediate layer in VGG-16) is extracted after the fifth
max-pooling layer, see Table 1 in [12] for a full overview of the VGG-16 network.
In Fig. 7 the setup of the framework is shown. The loss function which generator
F is trained against is defined in (7) where the λ_i's are the loss weights. The loss
for generator G is constructed in a similar way. The cycle loss, identity loss and
the paired loss are the same as for the ccGAN. The loss $\mathcal{L}_{feat}$ defined in (8) is
the feature reconstruction loss using the Gram matrix from [7]. For this network
we used the same loss weights for all losses, $\lambda_i = 10$ for $i = 1, 2, 3, 4$.

$$\mathcal{L}_{tot} = \lambda_1 \mathcal{L}_{cycle} + \lambda_2 \mathcal{L}_{identity} + \lambda_3 \mathcal{L}_{paired} + \lambda_4 \mathcal{L}_{feat} \tag{7}$$

$$\mathcal{L}_{feat}(x_p, y_p) = \|G_j^\phi\big(F(y_p)\big) - G_j^\phi(x_p)\|_F^2 \tag{8}$$

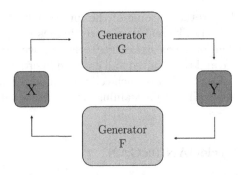

Fig. 7. Cyclic network with two generators and no discriminators.

5.4   Network Architectures

Generator. The architecture of all generators are the same, it is inspired by the
Pix2Pix paper [6] where they use a network based on the U-Net [11]. Figure 8
shows an overview of the architecture. The skip connections make it possible
to share information between layers which is very common in image mapping
when the input image shares structure with the target image. The generator
consists of encoding blocks and decoding blocks. An encoding block consists of
a convolution followed by a batch normalization and a Leaky ReLU activation
function. The size of the convolution kernel is 5×5 and the stride is 2. A decoding

block starts with upsampling, then a transposed convolution, a batch normalization followed by a ReLU activation function. A disadvantage of transposed convolutions is that artifacts such as checkerboard patterns can appear when the kernel size and stride do not match [10]. In our generator we have separated the transposed convolution with stride 2 into an upsampling process followed by a transposed convolution with stride 1. Our generator has approximately 20 million parameters which is almost twice the size of our discriminator.

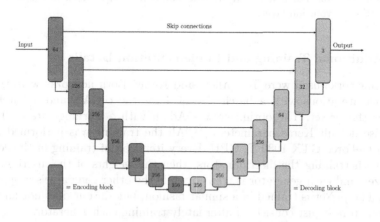

Fig. 8. Illustration of the generator architecture. The number in each block is the number of filters in the convolution layer.

Discriminator. The generators in the ccGAN are never trained solely against the discriminators, the total loss function is a combination of norm-based losses between two images and the loss given by the discriminator. The losses based on norms are good at capturing low frequency data, but might have problems with more general stylistic features of an image. The idea is that the discriminator will encourage the generation of high frequency information in the images by penalizing lack of high frequency data. A discriminator called "PatchGAN" was proposed in [6] and it has a receptive field of 70 × 70 pixels, small "patches". Each patch should capture the local style of the image. The output from the discriminator is the average of the result of the evaluation of each patch being real or fake. Our patch discriminator has about 11 million parameters and consists of 5 blocks that start with a convolutional layer, then a batch normalization followed by a Leaky ReLU activation. The convolutions have kernel size 4 × 4 and the stride is 2 for the first 3 blocks and 1 for the last 2 blocks. There is no batch normalization for the first and last block. The final activation function before the mean layer is a sigmoid instead of a Leaky ReLU. Figure 9 shows a simple illustration of our discriminator.

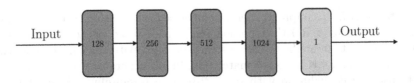

Fig. 9. Illustration of the discriminator architecture. The first blocks are regular convolution - batch normalization - Leaky ReLU blocks. The last block has a sigmoid activation function and a mean layer. The number in each block is the number of filters in the convolution layer.

5.5   Additional Training and Implementation Details

The frameworks used were Tensorflow and Keras. Both networks were trained for 50000 iterations with a batch size of 4 for the ccGAN and a batch size of 2 for the pcNet. The optimizer was Adam with a learning rate of 0.0002, otherwise default Keras parameters [1]. All the training was performed on an NVidia GeForce GTX 1080 Ti GPU. Every iteration of training of the ccGAN starts with training the discriminators, then the weights of the discriminators are frozen and each generator is trained while the other generator's weights are frozen. The pcNet is trained in a similar fashion, but since it does not have any discriminators it just consists of alternately training each generator.

6   Results and Conclusions

The results obtained in this paper are satisfactory and better than previous methods. It is very hard for a person to see any differences between a transformed image and its original counterpart. It is even harder to decide if an image is real or transformed when shown a single image. One problem with human evaluation is that it is subjective, but it is hard to come up with a metric that measures the important characteristics of this type of image. Popular metrics like PSNR (peak signal-to-noise ratio) and SSIM (structural similarity) do not seem to correlate with how good a person thinks the images are. The goal is however that the user should not be able to distinguish between transformed and real images and we think we have achieved that. Figure 10 shows a comparison of the two different networks. Experts think that pcNet is slightly better than ccGAN, but both are better than the current method.

The current method used is the HM normalization. Since the HM normalization does not only transform the image, it also normalizes it, we had to normalize our transformed images to be able to compare. Figure 11 shows the same images as Fig. 10 but normalized. The structure of the HM normalized cells are very good, but the colors could be better, especially for the cell type eosinophils (the cell type in the first row). Our transformation takes approximately 300 ms on a CPU (Intel Core i7-7700 at 3.60 GHz) and 10–20 ms on a GPU (NVidia GeForce GTX 1080 Ti). The advantage of the HM normalization compared to

system X   ccGAN   pcNet   system Y

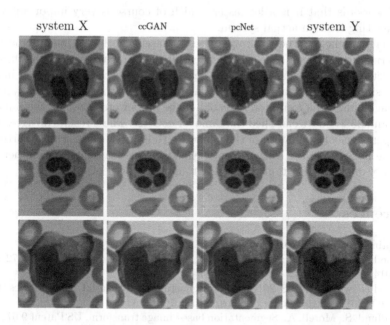

Fig. 10. Comparison of all networks with different raw cell images from the test set.

HM   ccGAN   pcNet   system Y

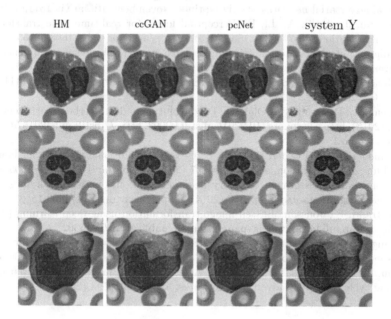

Fig. 11. Comparison of all networks with different normalized cell images from the test set.

our networks is that it is a lot faster, which of course is very important when implementing it in an actual system.

A cell classification network was used to classify both real images and their transformed counterpart. We do not necessarily care whether the classification is correct or not, the goal is that the real images and the transformed images are classified as the same cell type. This evaluation was performed by using 981 image pairs. The results were 88.6% of the pairs were classified the same for pcNet and 85.2% were classified the same for ccGAN. These results do agree with the experts visual evaluation of the network. To improve classification further it could be possible to use a layer from CellaVisions actual classification network instead of or in combination with VGG to define a perceptual loss.

References

1. Optimizers, 1 April 2019. https://keras.io/optimizers/
2. Goodfellow, I.J., et al.: Generative adversarial networks. In: NIPS, pp. 2672–2680 (2014)
3. Goodfellow, I.J.: NIPS 2016 tutorial: generative adversarial networks abs/1701. 00160 (2017). http://arxiv.org/abs/1701.00160
4. Hedlund, S., Morell, A.: Segmentation based image transform. US Patent 9,672,447, 14 May 2014. http://www.google.it/patents/US9672447B2
5. Hunt, R.: Measuring Color, 3 edn, p. 114. Fountain Press, Chichester (1998)
6. Isola, P., Zhu, J.Y., Zhou, T., Efros, A.A.: Image-to-image translation with conditional adversarial networks. ArXiv e-prints, November 2016. arXiv:1611.07004
7. Johnson, J., Alahi, A., Li, F.: Perceptual losses for real-time style transfer and super-resolution. abs/1603.08155 (2016). http://arxiv.org/abs/1603.08155
8. Ledig, C., et al.: Photo-realistic single image super-resolution using a generative adversarial network. arXiv preprint (2016)
9. Mirza, M., Osindero, S.: Conditional generative adversarial nets. arXiv:1411.1784 [cs.LG] (2014)
10. Odena, A., Dumoulin, V., Olah, C.: Deconvolution and checkerboard artifacts. Distill (2016). https://doi.org/10.23915/distill.00003. http://distill.pub/2016/deconv-checkerboard
11. Ronneberger, O., Fischer, P., Brox, T.: U-Net: convolutional networks for biomedical image segmentation. abs/1505.04597 (2015). http://arxiv.org/abs/1505.04597
12. Simonyan, K., Zisserman, A.: Very deep convolutional networks for large-scale image recognition. abs/1409.1556 (2014). http://arxiv.org/abs/1409.1556
13. Sjöstrand, E., Jönsson, J.: Cell image transformation using deep learning (2018). https://lup.lub.lu.se/student-papers/search/publication/8945302
14. Wang, C., Xu, C., Wang, C., Tao, D.: Perceptual adversarial networks for image-to-image transformation. abs/1706.09138 (2017). http://arxiv.org/abs/1706.09138
15. Zhu, J.Y., Park, T., Isola, P., Efros, A.A.: Unpaired image-to-image translation using cycle-consistent adversarial networks. abs/1703.10593 (2017)

Generating Diffusion MRI Scalar Maps from T1 Weighted Images Using Generative Adversarial Networks

Xuan Gu[1,2(✉)], Hans Knutsson[1,2], Markus Nilsson[4], and Anders Eklund[1,2,3]

[1] Division of Medical Informatics, Department of Biomedical Engineering,
Linköping University, Linköping, Sweden
xuan.gu@liu.se
[2] Center for Medical Image Science and Visualization (CMIV),
Linköping University, Linköping, Sweden
[3] Division of Statistics and Machine learning,
Department of Computer and Information Science,
Linköping University, Linköping, Sweden
[4] Department of Clinical Sciences, Radiology, Lund University, Lund, Sweden

Abstract. Diffusion magnetic resonance imaging (diffusion MRI) is a non-invasive microstructure assessment technique. Scalar measures, such as FA (fractional anisotropy) and MD (mean diffusivity), quantifying micro-structural tissue properties can be obtained using diffusion models and data processing pipelines. However, it is costly and time consuming to collect high quality diffusion data. Here, we therefore demonstrate how Generative Adversarial Networks (GANs) can be used to generate synthetic diffusion scalar measures from structural T1-weighted images in a single optimized step. Specifically, we train the popular CycleGAN model to learn to map a T1 image to FA or MD, and vice versa. As an application, we show that synthetic FA images can be used as a target for non-linear registration, to correct for geometric distortions common in diffusion MRI.

Keywords: Diffusion MRI · Generative Adversarial Networks · CycleGAN · Distortion correction

1 Introduction

Diffusion MRI is a non-invasive technique used for studying brain tissue microstructures. Diffusion-derived scalar maps provide rich information about microstructural characterization, but there are two major bottlenecks in obtaining these scalar maps. First, it is expensive and time consuming to acquire high quality diffusion data. Second, the accuracy of the diffusion-derived scalar

ⓒ Springer Nature Switzerland AG 2019
M. Felsberg et al. (Eds.): SCIA 2019, LNCS 11482, pp. 489–498, 2019.
https://doi.org/10.1007/978-3-030-20205-7_40

maps relies on elaborate diffusion data processing pipelines, including preprocessing (head motion, eddy current distortion and susceptibility-induced distortion corrections), diffusion model fitting and diffusion scalar calculation. Small errors occurring at any of these steps can contribute to the bias of the diffusion-derived scalars. For some advanced diffusion models e.g. mean apparent propagator (MAP) MRI [10], processing of a single slice of the brain can take hours to finish.

Generative Adversarial Networks (GANs) is one of the most important ideas in machine learning in the last 20 years [6]. GANs have already been widely used for medical image processing applications, such as denoising, reconstruction, segmentation, detection, classification and image synthesis. However, GANs for medical image translation are still rather unexplored, especially for cross-modality translation of MR images [7].

Implementations of CycleGAN and unsupervised image-to-image translation (UNIT) for 2D T1-T2 translation were reported in [13], and results showed that visually realistic synthetic T1 and T2 images can be generated from the other modality, proven via a perceptual study. In [2] a conditional GAN was proposed to do the translation between T1 and T2 images, in which a probabilistic GAN (PGAN) and a CycleGAN were trained for paired and unpaired source-target images, respectively. The proposed GAN demonstrated visually and quantitatively accurate translations for both healthy subjects and glioma patients. A patch-based conditional GAN [9] was proposed to generate magnetic resonance angiography (MRA) images from T1 and T2 images jointly. Steerable filter responses were incorporated in the loss function to extract directional features of the vessel structure. MR image translation based on downsampled images was investigated in [3], to reduce scan time. Three different types of input were fed to the GANs: downsampled target images, downsampled source images, and downsampled target and source images jointly. It was demonstrated that the GAN with the combination of downsampled target and source images as the input outperformed its two competitors in reconstructing higher resolution images, which resulted in a reduction of the scan time up to a factor of 50. A 3D conditional GAN [15] was applied to synthesize FLAIR images from T1, and the synthetic FLAIR images improved brain tumor segmentation, compared with using only T1 images.

In this work, we explored the possibility to generate diffusion scalar maps from structural MR images. We propose a new application of CycleGAN [16]; to translate T1 images to diffusion-derived scalar maps. To the best of our knowledge, this is the first study of GAN-based MR image translation between structural space and diffusion space. Both qualitative and quantitative evaluations of generated images were carried out in order to assess effectiveness of the method. We also show how synthetic FA images can be used as a target for non-linear registration, to correct for geometric distortions common in diffusion MRI.

2   Theory

2.1   Diffusion Tensor Model

In a diffusion experiment, the diffusion-weighted signal S_i of the ith measurement for one voxel is modeled by

$$S_i = S_0 \exp(-b\mathbf{g}_i^T \mathbf{D}\mathbf{g}_i), \quad \text{for} \quad i = 1, 2, \cdots, T, \tag{1}$$

where S_0 is the signal without diffusion weighting, b is the diffusion weighting factor, $\mathbf{D} = \begin{bmatrix} D_{xx} & D_{xy} & D_{xz} \\ D_{xy} & D_{yy} & D_{yz} \\ D_{xz} & D_{yz} & D_{zz} \end{bmatrix}$ is the diffusion tensor in the form of a 3×3 positive definite matrix, $\mathbf{g}_i$ is a 3×1 unit vector of the gradient direction, and T is the total number of measurements. Mean diffusivity (MD) and fractional anisotropy (FA) can be calculated from the estimated tensor, according to

$$MD = (\lambda_1 + \lambda_2 + \lambda_3)/3, \tag{2}$$

$$FA = \sqrt{\frac{(\lambda_1 - \lambda_2)^2 + (\lambda_2 - \lambda_3)^2 + (\lambda_3 - \lambda_1)^2}{2(\lambda_1^2 + \lambda_2^2 + \lambda_3^2)}}, \tag{3}$$

where λ_1, λ_2 and λ_3 are the three eigenvalues of the diffusion tensor $\mathbf{D}$. In our case weighted least squares was used to estimate the diffusion tensor.

2.2   CycleGAN

A CycleGAN [16] can be trained using two unpaired groups of images, to translate images between domain A and domain B. A CycleGAN consists of four main components, two generators (G_{A2B} and G_{B2A}) and two discriminators (D_A and D_B). The two generators synthesize domain A/B images based on domain B/A. The two discriminators are making the judgement if the input images belong to domain A/B. The translation between the two image domains is guaranteed by

$$G_{B2A}(G_{A2B}(I_A)) \approx I_A \tag{4}$$

$$G_{A2B}(G_{B2A}(I_B)) \approx I_B \tag{5}$$

where I_A and I_B are two images of domain A and B. The loss function contains two terms: adversarial loss and cycle loss, and can be written as [16]

$$L_{adv} = E_{a \in A}[(D_A(a) - 1)^2] + E_{b \in B}[(D_B(b) - 1)^2] \tag{6}$$

$$+ E_{a \in A}[D_B(G_{A2B}(a))^2] + E_{b \in B}[D_A(G_{B2A}(b))^2] \tag{7}$$

$$+ E_{a \in A}[(D_B(G_{A2B}(a)) - 1)^2] + E_{b \in B}[(D_A(G_{B2A}(b)) - 1)^2], \tag{8}$$

$$L_{cyc} = E_{a \in A}[|G_{B2A}(G_{A2B}(a)) - a|] + E_{b \in B}[|G_{A2B}(G_{B2A}(b)) - b|]. \tag{9}$$

The adversarial loss encourages the discriminators to approve the images of the corresponding groups, and reject the images that are generated by the corresponding generators. The generators are also encouraged to generate images that can fool the corresponding discriminators. The cycle loss guarantees that the image can be reconstructed from the other domain, as stated in Eq. 5. The total loss is the sum of the adversarial loss and the cycle loss, i.e.

$$L_{total} = L_{adv} + L_{cyc}. \tag{10}$$

2.3   Similarity Measure

The widely used structural similarity (SSIM) measure [4,14] was used to quantify the accuracy of the image translations. SSIM can measure local structural similarity between two images. The SSIM quantifies the degree of similarity of two images based on the impact of three characteristics: luminance, contrast and structure. The SSIM of pixel (x, y) in images A and B can be calculated as [12]

$$SSIM(x, y) = \frac{(2\mu_{w_A}\mu_{w_B} + c_1)(2\sigma_{w_A w_B} + c_2)}{(\mu_{w_A}^2 + \mu_{w_B}^2 + c1)(\sigma_{w_A}^2 + \sigma_{w_B}^2 + c_2)}, \tag{11}$$

where w_A and w_B are local neighborhoods centered at (x, y) in images A and B, μ_{w_A} and μ_{w_B} are the local means, σ_{w_A} and σ_{w_B} are the local standard deviations, $\sigma_{w_A w_B}$ is the covariance, c_1 and c_2 are two variables to stabilize the division. The mean SSIM ($MSSIM = SSIM/N_{voxel}$) within the brain area can be used as a global measure of the similarity between the synthetic image and the ground truth.

3   Data

We used diffusion and T1 images from the Human Connectome Project (HCP)[1] [5,11] for 1065 healthy subjects. The data were collected using a customized Siemens 3T Connectome scanner. The diffusion data were acquired with 3 different b-values (1000, 2000, and 3000 s/mm^2) and have already been pre-processed for gradient nonlinearity correction, motion correction and eddy current correction. The diffusion data consist of 18 non-diffusion weighted volumes (b = 0) and 90 volumes for each b-value, which yields 288 volumes of $145 \times 174 \times 145$ voxels with an 1.25 mm isotropic voxel size. The T1 data was acquired with a 320×320 matrix size and $0.7 \times 0.7 \times 0.7$ mm isotropic voxel size, and then downsampled by us to the same resolution as the diffusion data.

---

[1] Data collection and sharing for this project was provided by the Human Connectome Project (U01-MH93765) (HCP; Principal Investigators: Bruce Rosen, M.D., Ph.D., Arthur W. Toga, Ph.D., Van J.Weeden, MD). HCP funding was provided by the National Institute of Dental and Craniofacial Research (NIDCR), the National Institute of Mental Health (NIMH), and the National Institute of Neurological Disorders and Stroke (NINDS). HCP data are disseminated by the Laboratory of Neuro Imaging at the University of Southern California.

4   Methods

Diffusion tensor fitting and MAP-MRI fitting were implemented using C++ and the code is available on Github[2]. We used a Keras implementation of 2D CycleGAN, originating from the work by [13], which is also available on Github[3]. The statistics analysis was performed in MATLAB (R2018a, The MathWorks, Inc., Natick, Massachusetts, United States).

We followed the network architecture design given in the original CyceGAN paper [16]. We used 2 feature extraction convolutional layers, 9 residual blocks and 3 deconvolutional layers for the generators. For the discriminators we used 4 feature extraction convolutional layers and a final layer to produce a one-dimensional output. We trained the network with a learning rate of 0.0004. We kept the same learning rate for the first half of the training, and linearly decayed the learning rate to zero over the second half. A total of 1000 subjects were used for training, and 65 subjects were used for testing. An Nvidia Titan X Pascal graphics card was used to train the network. The experiment protocols and training times are summarized in Table 1.

Table 1. Experiment protocols used to train and evaluate the CycleGAN

	Training data	Test data	Training time (h)
Experiment 1	1000 subjects 1 slice per subject	65 subjects 1 slice per subject	6
Experiment 2	1000 subjects 1 slice per subject	65 subjects 17 slices per subject	6
Experiment 3	1000 subjects 17 slices per subject	65 subjects 17 slices per subject	107

5   Results

5.1   Synthetic FA and MD

Figure 1(a) shows the qualitative results of T1-to-FA image translation for 4 test subjects. The results show a good match between the synthetic FA images and their ground truth, for both texture of white matter tracts and global content. However, when compared with the ground truth, it is observed that the synthetic FA images have a reduced level of details on white matter tracts. The difference image shows the absolute error between synthetic and real FA images. Results of T1-to-MD image translation are shown in Fig. 1(b). The synthetic MD images demonstrate great visual similarity to the ground truth. The CSF region and its boundaries are accurately synthesized.

---

[2] https://github.com/xuagu37/dtb.
[3] https://github.com/xuagu37/CycleGAN.

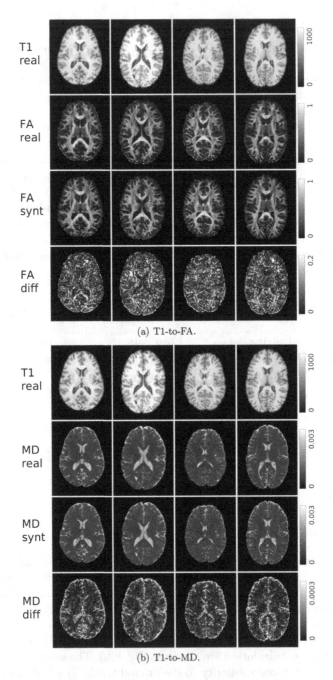

(a) T1-to-FA.

(b) T1-to-MD.

Fig. 1. T1-to-FA/MD image translation results for 4 subjects. First row: True T1 images, second row: true FA images, third row: synthetic FA images, fourth row: Difference of true and synthetic FA.

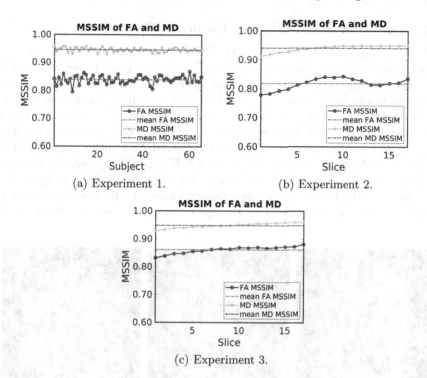

Fig. 2. MSSIM results of FA and MD for Experiment 1, 2 and 3. Experiment 1: training on 1000 subjects, 1 slice per subject, and test on 65 subjects, 1 slice per subject. The mean MSSIM of synthetic FA and MD across subjects are 0.839 and 0.937, respectively. Experiment 2: training on 1000 subjects, 1 slice per subject, and test on 65 subjects, 17 slices per subject. The mean MSSIM of synthetic FA and MD across slices are 0.818 and 0.940, respectively. Experiment 3: training on 1000 subjects, 17 slices per subject, and test on 65 subjects, 17 slices per subject. The mean MSSIM of synthetic FA and MD across slices are 0.861 and 0.948, respectively. Plots show that synthetic MD images demonstrate higher accuracy compared to synthetic FA, and that using a higher number of training slices mostly helps FA synthesis.

Figure 2(a) shows the MSSIM of synthetic FA and MD images for the 65 test subjects. MSSIM values showed high consistency among the different test subjects. The mean±std intervals of the MSSIM are 0.839 ± 0.014 and 0.937 ± 0.008 for synthetic FA and MD images, respectively. The MSSIM results for synthetic MD are higher compared to synthetic FA. This may be partly due to that FA images contain richer structure information, thus it is more difficult to synthesize (since FA is more non-linear than MD). Figure 2(b) and (c) show the MSSIM of synthetic FA and MD images for the 17 slices. It can been that the MSSIM result is sensitive to the slice position, and that a higher number of training slices leads to higher MSSIM results for the synthetic FA and MD maps.

5.2   Non-linear Registration for Distortion Correction

EPI distortions can be corrected by the FSL function topup, for data acquired with at least two phase encoding directions. However, it is hard to correct for EPI distortions for data acquired with a single phase encoding direction. A potential approach would be to generate a synthetic FA map from the undistorted T1 image, and then (non-linearly) register the distorted FA map to the undistorted synthetic one. This transform can then be applied to all other diffusion scalar maps. The FA map from EPI distortion corrected data (using topup) can be regarded as the gold standard. We used FNIRT in FSL to perform the non-linear registration. Figure 3 shows various FA maps for one test subject. The FA map from the proposed approach provides a result which is very similar to the gold standard. The benefit of our approach is that the scan time can be

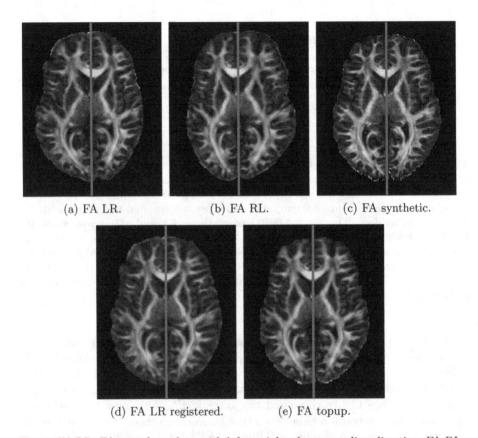

(a) FA LR.   (b) FA RL.   (c) FA synthetic.

(d) FA LR registered.   (e) FA topup.

Fig. 3. FA LR: FA map from data with left to right phase encoding direction. FA RL: FA map from data with right to left phase encoding direction. FA synthetic: FA map from CycleGAN. FA LR registered: FA LR non-linearly registered to synthetic FA. FA topup: FA map from EPI distortion corrected data (seen as gold standard). The benefit of using non-linear registration for distortion correction, instead of topup, is that the scan time is reduced by a factor 2.

reduced a factor 2, by acquiring data using a single phase encoding direction. It is of course theoretically possible to register the distorted FA image directly to the undistorted T1 image, but non-linear registration of images with different intensity can be rather challenging.

6   Discussion

Translation between structural and diffusion images has been shown using Cycle-GAN. The synthetic FA and MD images are remarkably similar to their ground truth. Quantitative evaluation using MSSIM of 65 test subjects shows that the trained CycleGAN works well for all test subjects, and that training using a larger number of slices improves the results.

While the synthetic FA images appear realistic, the training of the GAN will depend on the training data used. For example, if the GAN is trained using data from healthy controls it is likely that the GAN will be biased for brain tumor patients, and for example remove existing tumors [1].

Future research may focus on creating other diffusion-derived scalar maps from more advanced diffusion models, such as mean apparent propagator (MAP) MRI. In this work, we have only used 2D CycleGAN, but it has been reported that 3D GANs using spatial information [8] across slices yield better mappings between two domains (at the cost of a higher memory consumption and a higher computational cost). A comparison study of image translation using 2D and 3D GANs is thus worth looking into.

Acknowledgements. This study was supported by Swedish research council grants 2015-05356 and 2017-04889. Funding was also provided by the Center for Industrial Information Technology (CENIIT) at Linköping University, the Knut and Alice Wallenberg foundation project "Seeing organ function", Analytic Imaging Diagnostics Arena (AIDA) and the ITEA3/VINNOVA funded project "Intelligence based iMprovement of Personalized treatment And Clinical workflow supporT" (IMPACT). The Nvidia Corporation, who donated the Nvidia Titan X Pascal graphics card used to train the GANs, is also acknowledged.

References

1. Cohen, J.P., Luck, M., Honari, S.: Distribution matching losses can hallucinate features in medical image translation. arXiv preprint arXiv:1805.08841v3 (2018)
2. Dar, S.U.H., Yurt, M., Karacan, L., Erdem, A., Erdem, E., Çukur, T.: Image synthesis in multi-contrast MRI with conditional generative adversarial networks. arXiv preprint arXiv:1802.01221 (2018)
3. Dar, S.U.H., Yurt, M., Shahdloo, M., Ildız, M.E., Çukur, T.: Synergistic reconstruction and synthesis via generative adversarial networks for accelerated multi-contrast MRI. arXiv preprint arXiv:1805.10704 (2018)
4. Emami, H., Dong, M., Nejad-Davarani, S.P., Glide-Hurst, C.: Generating synthetic CTs from magnetic resonance images using generative adversarial networks. Med. Phys. **45**, 3627–3636 (2018)

5. Glasser, M.F., et al.: The minimal preprocessing pipelines for the human connectome project. Neuroimage **80**, 105–124 (2013)
6. Goodfellow, I., et al.: Generative adversarial nets. In: Advances in Neural Information Processing Systems, pp. 2672–2680 (2014)
7. Kazeminia, S., et al.: GANs for medical image analysis. arXiv preprint arXiv:1809.06222 (2018)
8. Nie, D., et al.: Medical image synthesis with context-aware generative adversarial networks. In: International Conference on Medical Image Computing and Computer-Assisted Intervention, pp. 417–425 (2017)
9. Olut, S., Sahin, Y.H., Demir, U., Unal, G.: Generative adversarial training for MRA image synthesis using multi-contrast MRI. In: International Conference on Medical Image Computing and Computer-Assisted Intervention, pp. 147–154 (2018)
10. Özarslan, E., et al.: Mean apparent propagator (MAP) MRI: a novel diffusion imaging method for mapping tissue microstructure. NeuroImage **78**, 16–32 (2013)
11. Van Essen, D.C., et al.: The WU-Minn human connectome project: an overview. Neuroimage **80**, 62–79 (2013)
12. Wang, Z., Bovik, A.C., Sheikh, H.R., Simoncelli, E.P.: Image quality assessment: from error visibility to structural similarity. IEEE Trans. Image Process. **13**(4), 600–612 (2004)
13. Welander, P., Karlsson, S., Eklund, A.: Generative adversarial networks for image-to-image translation on multi-contrast MR images-a comparison of CycleGAN and UNIT. arXiv preprint arXiv:1806.07777 (2018)
14. Wolterink, J.M., Dinkla, A.M., Savenije, M.H., Seevinck, P.R., van den Berg, C.A., Išgum, I.: Deep MR to CT synthesis using unpaired data. In: International Workshop on Simulation and Synthesis in Medical Imaging, pp. 14–23 (2017)
15. Yu, B., Zhou, L., Wang, L., Fripp, J., Bourgeat, P.: 3D cGAN based cross-modality MR image synthesis for brain tumor segmentation. In: IEEE 15th International Symposium on Biomedical Imaging, pp. 626–630 (2018)
16. Zhu, J.Y., Park, T., Isola, P., Efros, A.A.: Unpaired image-to-image translation using cycle-consistent adversarial networks. arXiv preprint arXiv:1703.10593v5 (2017)

Correction to: Iris Identification in 3D

Fernand Cohen, Sowrirajan Sowmithran, and Chenxi Li

Correction to:
Chapter "Iris Identification in 3D"
in: M. Felsberg et al. (Eds.): *Image Analysis*, LNCS 11482,
https://doi.org/10.1007/978-3-030-20205-7_27

The chapter "Iris Identification in 3D" by Fernand Cohen, Sowrirajan Sowmithran, and Chenxi Li (pp. 324–335) was not presented during the Scandinavian Conference on Image Analysis (SCIA) 2019. SCIA is embraced by IAPR and following the IAPR policy, only papers presented at the respective conference should be included in the proceedings. Thus, the chapter by Cohen et al. is not officially part of the SCIA conference proceedings LNCS 11482. Unfortunately, at the time of production of LNCS 11482, this fact was not known and therefore the manuscript is erroneously available for download within the proceedings.

The updated version of this chapter can be found at
https://doi.org/10.1007/978-3-030-20205-7_27

Author Index

Aanæs, Henrik 184
Abbott, A. Lynn 101
Aly, Sherin F. 101
Arens, Michael 387
Åström, Kalle 287, 348

Bajić, Buda 439
Bartoli, Adrien 3, 90
Becker, Ann-Katrin 374
Becker, Stefan 387
Bergström, David 115
Blanes-Vidal, Victoria 439
Brännlund, Carl 115
Brorsson, Andreas 115
Bulatov, Dimitri 361
Butz, Kevin 465
Bylow, Erik 261

Chambon, Sylvie 275
Charvillat, Vincent 275
Cohen, Fernand 324

Dahl, Anders Bjorholm 128, 152, 184, 311
Dahl, Vedrana A. 128
Dovletov, Gurbandurdy 78
Dueholm, Jacob V. 221

Eerola, Tuomas 67
Egiazarian, Karen 173
Ehsan, Shoaib 90
Einarsson, Gudmundur 311
Eklund, Anders 489
El Amine Seddik, Mohamed 3

Fagertun, Jens 221
Ferrarini, Bruno 90
Flood, Gabrielle 348
Flusser, Jan 140
Frisvad, Jeppe Revall 152, 184, 311

Gillsjö, David 348
Grancharov, Volodya 399
Gu, Xuan 489

Guo, Yan 452
Gurdjos, Pierre 275
Gustafsson, David 115

Haario, Heikki 67
Häikiö, Markus 28
Hannemose, Morten 311
Hegemann, Tobias 78
Heidemann, Gunther 246
Heikkilä, Janne 16, 41
Heyden, Anders 336, 348
Höller, Yvonne 465
Hong, Xiaopeng 233
Hou, Yuxin 54
Hübner, Wolfgang 387
Hug, Ronny 387
Huynh, Lam 16

Jakobsen, Ida Marie Groth 209
Jensen, Janus Nørtoft 311
Jensen, Patrick M. 128
Jönsson, Jesper 477
Jørgensen, Anders 221

Kahl, Fredrik 261
Kalervo, Ahti 28
Kälviäinen, Heikki 67
Kannala, Juho 28, 54
Karhu, Antti 28
Knutsson, Hans 489
Kostková, Jitka 140
Kuchukhidze, Georgi 465
Kudryashev, Mikhail 415

Lébl, Matěj 140
Lensu, Lasse 67
Leonardis, Aleš 90
Li, Chenxi 324
Li, Zhongguo 336
Liedlgruber, Michael 465
Lin, John 3
Lindblad, Joakim 439
Lyngby, Rasmus Ahrenkiel 152, 184

Maier, Robert   261
Majtner, Tomáš   439
Mariyanayagam, Damien   275
Matthiassen, Jannik Boll   184
McDonald-Maier, Klaus D.   90
Mester, Rudolf   415
Moeslund, Thomas B.   221
Morell, Adam   477

Nadimi, Esmaeil S.   439
Nguyen-Ha, Phong   16
Nilsson, Markus   489
Noori, Farzan Majeed   299

Olsson, Carl   261
Oskarsson, Magnus   336
Østergaard, Lasse Riis   427
Ostermayer, Gerald   164

Pauli, Josef   78
Pedone, Matteo   140
Persson, Patrik   287
Plattner, Michael   164
Plocharski, Maciej   209, 427
Pobloth, Harald   399
Ponomarenko, Mykola   173

Rahtu, Esa   16
Rieger, Bernd   452

Sánchez, Ricardo M.   415
Sharma, Puneet   197
Shustrov, Dmitrii   67

Sjöstrand, Emmy   477
Sladoje, Nataša   439
Solin, Arno   54
Sowmithran, Sowrirajan   324
Stets, Jonathan Dyssel   152
Stråhlén, Kent   477
Sverrisson, Sigurdur   399

Tamaazousti, Mohamed   3
Tamaazousti, Youssef   3
Tanisaro, Pattreeya   246
Taylor, Alexandra   465
Thomschevski, Aljoscha   465
Tomasi, Ottavio   465
Torresen, Jim   299
Trinderup, Camilla H.   128
Trinka, Eugen   465
Trosten, Daniel J.   197
Türkmen, Sercan   41

Uddin, Md. Zia   299
Uhl, Andreas   465

Vornberger, Oliver   374

Wallace, Benedikte   299
Wilm, Jakob   311

Xu, Yingyue   233

Ylioinas, Juha   28

Zhao, Guoying   233

Printed in the United States
By Bookmasters